# Data Analysis Using SQL and Excel®

# Data Analysis Using SQL and Excel®

Gordon S. Linoff

Wiley Publishing, Inc.

**Data Analysis Using SQL and Excel®**

Published by
Wiley Publishing, Inc.
10475 Crosspoint Boulevard
Indianapolis, IN 46256
www.wiley.com

ISBN: 978-0-470-09951-3

Manufactured in the United States of America

10 9 8 7 6 5 4 3 2 1

For general information on our other products and services or to obtain technical support, please contact our Customer Care Department within the U.S. at (800) 762-2974, outside the U.S. at (317) 572-3993, or fax (317) 572-4002.

Library of Congress Cataloging-in-Publication Data:

Linoff, Gordon.

 Data analysis using SQL and Excel / Gordon S. Linoff.

    p. cm.

 Includes index.

 ISBN 978-0-470-09951-3 (paper/website)

 1.  SQL (Computer program language) 2.  Querying (Computer science) 3.  Data mining. 4.  Microsoft Excel (Computer file)  I. Title.

 QA76.73.S67L56 2007

 005.75'85--dc22

                        2007026313

*To Giuseppe for sixteen years, five books, and counting . . .*

# About the Author

Gordon Linoff (gordon@data-miners.com) is a recognized expert in the field of data mining. He has more than twenty-five years of experience working with companies large and small to analyze customer data and to help design data warehouses. His passion for SQL and relational databases dates to the early 1990s, when he was building a relational database engine designed for large corporate data warehouses at the now-defunct Thinking Machines Corporation. Since then, he has had the opportunity to work with all the leading database vendors, including Microsoft, Oracle, and IBM.

With his colleague Michael Berry, Gordon has written three of the most popular books on data mining, starting with *Data Mining Techniques for Marketing, Sales, and Customer Support.* In addition to writing books on data mining, he also teaches courses on data mining, and has taught thousands of students on four continents.

Gordon is currently a principal at Data Miners, a consulting company he and Michael Berry founded in 1998. Data Miners is devoted to doing and teaching data mining and customer-centric data analysis.

# Credits

**Acquisitions Editor**
Robert Elliott

**Development Editor**
Ed Connor

**Technical Editor**
Michael J. A. Berry

**Production Editor**
William A. Barton

**Copy Editor**
Kim Cofer

**Editorial Manager**
Mary Beth Wakefield

**Production Manager**
Tim Tate

**Vice President and Executive Group Publisher**
Richard Swadley

**Vice President and Executive Publisher**
Joseph B. Wikert

**Project Coordinator, Cover**
Lynsey Osborn

**Graphics and Production Specialists**
Craig Woods, Happenstance Type-O-Rama
Oso Rey, Happenstance Type-O-Rama

**Proofreading**
Ian Golder, Word One

**Indexing**
Johnna VanHoose Dinse

**Anniversary Logo Design**
Richard Pacifico

# Contents

# Foreword

Gordon Linoff and I have written three and a half books together. (Four, if we get to count the second edition of *Data Mining Techniques* as a whole new book; it didn't feel like any less work.) Neither of us has written a book without the other before, so I must admit to a tiny twinge of regret upon first seeing the cover of this one without my name on it next to Gordon's. The feeling passed very quickly as recollections of the authorial life came flooding back — vacations spent at the keyboard instead of in or on the lake, opportunities missed, relationships strained. More importantly, this is a book that only Gordon Linoff could have written. His unique combination of talents and experiences informs every chapter.

I first met Gordon at Thinking Machines Corporation, a now long-defunct manufacturer of parallel supercomputers where we both worked in the late eighties and early nineties. Among other roles, Gordon managed the implementation of a parallel relational database designed to support complex analytical queries on very large databases. The design point for this database was radically different from other relational database systems available at the time in that no trade-offs were made to support transaction processing. The requirements for a system designed to quickly retrieve or update a single record are quite different from the requirements for a system to scan and join huge tables. Jettisoning the requirement to support transaction processing made for a cleaner, more efficient database for analytical processing. This part of Gordon's background means he understands SQL for data analysis literally from the inside out.

Just as a database designed to answer big important questions has a different structure from one designed to process many individual transactions, a *book* about using databases to answer big important questions requires a different approach to SQL. Many books on SQL are written for database administrators. Others are written for users wishing to prepare simple reports. Still others attempt to introduce some particular dialect of SQL in every detail. This one is written for data analysts, data miners, and anyone who wants to extract maximum information value from large corporate databases. Jettisoning the requirement to address all the disparate types of database user makes this a better, more focused book for the intended audience. In short, this is a book about how to use databases the way we ourselves use them.

Even more important than Gordon's database technology background, is his many years as a data mining consultant. This has given him a deep understanding of the kinds of questions businesses need to ask and of the data they are likely to have available to answer them. Years spent exploring corporate databases has given Gordon an intuitive feel for how to approach the kinds of problems that crop up time and again across many different business domains:

- **How to take advantage of geographic data.** A zip code field looks much richer when you realize that from zip code you can get to latitude and longitude and from latitude and longitude you can get to distance. It looks richer still when your realize that you can use it to join in census bureau data to get at important attributes such as population density, median income, percentage of people on public assistance, and the like.

- **How to take advantage of dates.** Order dates, ship dates, enrollment dates, birth dates. Corporate data is full of dates. These fields look richer when you understand how to turn dates into tenures, analyze purchases by day of week, and track trends in fulfillment time. They look richer still when you know how to use this data to analyze time-to-event problems such as time to next purchase or expected remaining lifetime of a customer relationship.

- **How to build data mining models directly in SQL.** This book shows you how to do things in SQL that you probably never imagined possible, including generating association rules for market basket analysis, building regression models, and implementing naïve Bayesian models and scorecards.

- **How to prepare data for use with data mining tools.** Although more than most people realize can be done using just SQL and Excel, eventually you will want to use more specialized data mining tools. These tools need data in a specific format known as a *customer signature*. This book shows you how to create these data mining extracts.

The book is rich in examples and they all use real data. This point is worth saying more about. Unrealistic datasets lead to unrealistic results. This is frustrating to the student. In real life, the more you know about the business context, the better your data mining results will be. Subject matter expertise gives you a head start. You know what variables ought to be predictive and have good ideas about new ones to derive. Fake data does not reward these good ideas because patterns that should be in the data are missing and patterns that shouldn't be there have been introduced inadvertently. Real data is hard to come by, not least because real data may reveal more than its owners are willing to share about their business operations. As a result, many books and courses make do with artificially constructed datasets. Best of all, the datasets used in the book are all available for download at the companion web site and from www.data-miners.com.

I reviewed the chapters of this book as they were written. This process was very beneficial to my own use of SQL and Excel. The exercise of thinking about the fairly complex queries used in the examples greatly increased my understanding of how SQL actually works. As a result, I have lost my fear of nested queries, multi-way joins, giant case statements, and other formerly daunting aspects of the language. In well over a decade of collaboration, I have always turned to Gordon for help using SQL and Excel to best advantage. Now, I can turn to this book. And you can too.

— *Michael J. A. Berry*

# Acknowledgments

Although this book has only one name on the cover, there are many people over a long period of time who have helped me both specifically on this book and more generally in understanding data, analysis, and presentation.

Michael Berry, my business partner and colleague since 1998 at Data Miners, has been tremendously helpful on all fronts. He reviewed the chapters, tested the SQL code in the examples, and helped anonymize the data. His insights have been helpful and his debugging skills have made the examples much more accurate. His wife, Stephanie Jack, also deserves special praise for her patience and willingness to share Michael's time.

Bob Elliott, my editor at Wiley, and the Wiley team not only accepted my original idea for this book, but have exhibited patience and understanding as I refined the ideas and layout.

Matt Keiser, President of Datran Marketing, and Howard Lehrman (formerly of Datran) were kind enough to provide computing power for testing many of the examples. Nick Drake, also of Datran, inspired the book, by asking for a SQL reference focused on data analysis.

Throughout the chapters, the understanding of data processing is based on dataflows, which Craig Stanfill of Ab Initio Corporation first introduced me to, once upon a time when we worked together at Thinking Machines Corporation.

Stuart Ward and Zaiying Huang (from the New York Times) have spent countless hours over the past several years explaining statistical concepts to me. Harrison Sohmer, also of the New York Times, taught me many Excel tricks, some of which I've been able to include in the book.

Anne Milley of SAS Institute originally suggested that I learn survival analysis. Will Potts, now at CapitalOne, taught me much of what I know about the subject, including helping to develop two of the earliest survival analysis–based forecasts (and finally convincing me that hazard probabilities really can't be negative). Brij Masand, a colleague at Data Miners, helped extend this knowledge to practical forecasting applications.

Jamie MacLennan and the SQL Server team at Microsoft have been helpful in answering my questions about the product.

There are a handful of people whom I've never met in person who have helped in various ways. Richard Stallman invented emacs and the Free Software Foundation; emacs provided the basis for the calendar table. Rob Bovey of Applications Professional, Inc. created the X-Y chart labeler used in several chapters. Robert Clair at the Census Bureau answered some questions via email. Juice Analytics inspired the example for Worksheet bar charts in Chapter 5 (and thanks to Alex Wimbush who pointed me in their direction). Edwin Straver of Frontline Systems answered several questions about Solver, introduced in Chapter 11.

Over the years, many colleagues, friends, and students have provided inspiration, questions, and answers. There are too many to list all of them, but I want to particularly thank Eran Abikhzer, Michael Benigno, Emily Cohen, Carol D'Andrea, Sonia Dubin, Lounette Dyer, Josh Goff, Richard Greenburg, Gregory Lampshire, Fiona McNeill, Karen Kennedy McConlogue, Alan Parker, Ashit Patel, Ronnie Rowton, Adam Schwebber, John Trustman, John Wallace, Kathleen Wright, and Zhilang Zhao. I would also like to thank the folks in the SAS Institute Training group who have organized, reviewed, and sponsored our data mining classes for many years, giving me the opportunity to meet many interesting and diverse people involved with data mining.

I also thank all those friends and family I've visited while writing this book and who (for the most part) allowed me the space and time to work — my mother, my father, my sister Debbie, my brother Joe, my in-laws Raimonda Scalia, Ugo Scalia, and Terry Sparacio, and my friends Jon Mosley, Paul Houlihan, Joe Hughes, and Maciej Zworski.

Finally, acknowledgments would be incomplete without thanking my life partner, Giuseppe Scalia, who has managed to maintain our sanity for the past year while I wrote this book.

Thank you everyone.

# Introduction

Data. Analysis. Presentation. These three key capabilities are needed for effectively transforming data into information. And yet, these three topics are rarely treated together. Other books focus on one or the other — on the details of relational databases, or on applying statistics to business problems, or on using Excel. This book approaches the challenges of data analysis from a more holistic perspective, and with the aim of explaining the relevant ideas both to people responsible for analyzing data and to people who want to use such information, responsibly.

The motivation for this approach came from a colleague, Nick Drake, who is a statistician by training. Once upon a time, he was looking for a book that would explain how to use SQL for the complex queries needed for data analysis. There are many books on SQL, few focused on using the language for queries, and none that come strictly from a perspective of analyzing data. Similarly, there are many books on statistics, none of which address the simple fact that most of the data being used resides in relational databases. This book is intended to fill that gap.

There are many approaches to data analysis. My earlier books, written with Michael Berry, focus on the more advanced algorithms and case studies usually falling under the heading "data mining." By contrast, this book focuses on the "how-to." It starts by describing data stored in databases and continues through preparing and producing results. Interspersed are stories based on my experience in the field, explaining how results might be applied and why some things work and other things do not. The examples are so practical that the data used for them is available on the companion web site and at www.data-miners.com.

One of the truisms about data warehouses and analysis databases in general is that they don't actually *do* anything. Yes, they store data. Yes, they bring together data from different sources, cleansing and clarifying along the way. Yes, they define business dimensions, store transactions about customers, and, perhaps, summarize important data. (And, yes, all these are very important!) However, data in a database resides on so many spinning disks and in complex data structures in a computer's memory. So much data. So little information.

Oil deposits and diamonds hidden in rich seams beneath the surface of the earth are worth much less than gasoline at the pump or Tiffany diamond rings. Prospectors can make a quick buck on such deposits. On the other hand, the companies willing to invest the dollars to transform and process the raw materials into marketable goods are the ones that uncover the long-term riches.

This book is about the basic tools needed for exploiting data, particularly data that describes customers. There are many fancy algorithms for statistical modeling and data mining. However, "garbage-in, garbage-out." The results of even the most sophisticated techniques are only as good as the data being used. Data is central to the task of understanding customers, understanding products, and understanding markets.

The chapters in this book discuss different aspects of data and several different analytic techniques. The analytic techniques range from exploratory data analysis to survival analysis, from market basket analysis to naïve Bayesian models, from simple animations to regression. Of course, the potential range of possible techniques is much larger than can be presented in one book. The methods have proven useful over time and are applicable in many different areas.

And finally, data and analysis are not enough. Data must be analyzed, and the results must be presented to the right audience. To fully exploit its value, we must transform data into stories and scenarios, charts and metrics, and insights.

## Overview of the Book and Technology

This book focuses on three key technological areas used for transforming data into actionable information:

- Relational databases store the data. The basic language for retrieving data is SQL.
- Excel spreadsheets are the most popular tool for presenting data. Perhaps the most powerful feature of Excel is the charting capability, which turns columns of numbers into pictures.
- Statistics is the foundation of data analysis.

These three technologies are presented together, because they are all interrelated. SQL answers the question "how do we pull data from a database?" Statistics answers the question "how is it relevant"? And Excel makes it possible to convince other people of the veracity of what we find.

The description of data processing is organized around the SQL language. Although there are extensions of SQL and other very powerful data manipulation languages, SQL is common to most databases. And, databases such as Oracle, IBM's DB2, and Microsoft SQL Server are common in the business world, storing the vast majority of business data transactions. Other databases such as mysql are available at no cost and easily downloaded. The good news is that all relational databases support SQL as a query language. However, just as England and the United States have been described as "two countries separated by a common language," each database supports a slightly different dialect of SQL. The Appendix contains a list of commonly used functions and how they are represented in various different dialects.

Similarly, there are beautiful presentation tools and professional graphics packages. However, very rare and exceptional is the workplace computer that does not have Excel (or an equivalent spreadsheet).

Statistics and data mining techniques do not always require advanced tools. Some very important techniques are readily available using the combination of SQL and Excel, including survival analysis, naïve Bayesian models, and association rules. In fact, the methods in this book are often more powerful than the methods available in many statistics and data mining tools, precisely because they are close to the data and customizable for specific applications. The explanation of the techniques covers both the basic ideas and the extensions that may not be available in other tools.

The chapters describing the various techniques provide a solid introduction to modeling and data exploration, in the context of familiar tools and data. They also highlight when the more advanced tools are useful, because there is not a simpler solution using more readily available tools.

In the interests of full disclosure, I should admit that in the early 1990s I worked on a package called Darwin at a company called Thinking Machines. In the intervening years, this package has become much more powerful and user-friendly, and has now grown into Oracle Data Mining. In addition to Oracle, SQL Server offers data mining extensions within the tool — an exciting development that brings advanced data analysis even closer to the data.

This book does not discuss such functionality at all. The methods in the chapters have been chosen for their general applicability to data stored in relational databases. The explicit purpose is not to focus on a particular relational database engine. In many ways, the methods discussed here complement such extensions.

# How This Book Is Organized

The twelve chapters in this book fall roughly into three parts. The first three introduce key concepts of SQL, Excel, and statistics. The six middle chapters discuss various methods of exploring data, and techniques specifically suited to SQL and Excel. The last three focus on the idea of modeling, in the sense of statistics and data mining.

Each chapter explains some aspect of data analysis using SQL and Excel from several different perspectives, including:

- Business examples for using the analysis;
- Questions the analysis answers;
- How the analytic techniques work;
- The SQL syntax for implementing the techniques; and,
- The results (as tables or charts), and how they are created in Excel.

Examples in the chapters are generally available in Excel at `www.data-miners.com`.

SQL is a concise language that is sometimes difficult to follow. Dataflows, graphical representations of data processing that explain data manipulations, are used to illustrate how the SQL works.

Results are presented in charts and tables, sprinkled throughout the book. In addition, important features of Excel are highlighted, and interesting uses of Excel graphics are explained. Each chapter has a couple of technical asides, typically explaining some aspect of a technique or an interesting bit of history associated with the methods described in the chapter.

## Introductory Chapters

The first chapter, "A Data Miner Looks at SQL," introduces SQL from the perspective of data analysis. This is the querying part of the SQL language, where data stored in databases is extracted using SQL queries.

Ultimately, data about customers and about the business is stored in SQL databases. This chapter introduces entity-relationship diagrams to describe the structure of the data — the tables and columns and how they relate to each other. It also introduces dataflows to describe the processing of queries; dataflows provide a graphical explanation of how data is processed.

The first chapter also describes the datasets used for examples throughout the book (and which are also available on the companion web site). This data includes tables describing retail purchases, tables describing mobile telephone customers, and reference tables that describe zip codes and the calendar.

The second chapter, "What's In a Table? Getting Started with Data Exploration," introduces Excel for exploratory data analysis and presentation. Of many useful capabilities in Excel, perhaps the most useful are charts. As the ancient Chinese saying goes, "a picture paints a thousand words," and Excel makes it possible to paint pictures using data. Such charts are not only useful aesthetically, but more practically for Word documents, PowerPoint, email, the Web, and so on.

Charts are not a means unto themselves. This chapter starts down the road of exploratory data analysis, using charts to convey interesting summaries of data. In addition, this chapter discusses summarizing columns in a table, as well as the interesting idea of using SQL to generate SQL queries.

Chapter 3, "How Different Is Different?", explains some key concepts of descriptive statistics, such as averages, p-values, and the chi-square test. The purpose of this chapter is to show how to use such statistics on data residing in tables. The particular statistics and statistical tests are chosen for their practicality, and the chapter focuses on applying the methods, not explaining the underlying theory. Conveniently, most of the statistical tests that we want to do are feasible in Excel and even in SQL.

## SQL Techniques

Several techniques are suited very well for the combination of SQL and Excel.

Chapter 4, "Where Is It All Happening? Location, Location, Location," explains geography and how to incorporate geographic information into data analysis. Geography starts with locations, described by latitude and longitude. There are then various levels of geography, such as census blocks, zip code tabulation areas, and the more familiar counties and states, all of which have information available from the Census Bureau. This chapter also discusses various methods for comparing results at different levels of geography. And, finally, no discussion of geography would be complete without maps. Using Excel, it is possible to build very rudimentary maps.

Chapter 5, "It's a Matter of Time," discusses another key attribute of customer behavior, when things occur. This chapter describes how to access features of dates and times in databases, and then how to use this information to understand customers.

The chapter includes examples for accurately making year-over-year comparisons, for summarizing by day of the week, for measuring durations in days, weeks, and months, and for calculating the number of active customers by day, historically. The chapter ends with a simple animation in Excel.

Chapters 6 and 7, "How Long Will Customers Last? Survival Analysis to Understand Customers and Their Value" and "Factors Affecting Survival: The What and Why of Customer Tenure," explain one of the most important analytic techniques for understanding customers over time. Survival analysis has its roots in traditional statistics. However, it is very well suited to problems related to customers.

Chapter 6 introduces the basic ideas of hazard probabilities and survival, explaining how to calculate them easily using the combination of SQL and Excel. Perhaps surprisingly, sophisticated statistical tools are not needed to get started using survival analysis. Chapter 6 then explains how important ideas in survival analysis, such as average customer lifetime, can be used in a business context. It continues by explaining how to put these pieces together into a forecast.

Chapter 7 extends the discussion in three different areas. First, it addresses a key problem in many customer-oriented databases, called left truncation. Second, it explains a very interesting idea in survival analysis called competing risks. This idea incorporates the fact that customers leave for different reasons. The third idea is to use survival analysis for before-and-after analysis. That is, how can we quantify what happens to customers when something happens during their lifetime — such as quantifying the effect of enrollment in a loyalty program or of a major billing fiasco.

Chapters 8 and 9, "Customer Purchases and Other Repeated Events" and "What's in a Shopping Cart? Market Basket Analysis and Association Rules," explain how to understand what customers are purchasing using SQL and Excel. Chapter 8 covers everything about the purchase — when it occurs, where it occurs, how often — except for the particular items being purchased. Purchases contain a lot of information, even before we dive into the details of the items.

Chapter 9 explains association rules, which are combinations of products purchased at the same time or in sequence. Building association rules in SQL is rather sophisticated, usually requiring intermediate tables. The methods in this chapter extend traditional association rule analysis, introducing alternative measures that make them more useful, and show how to produce combinations of different things, such as clicks that result in a purchase (to use an example from the web).

Chapters 8 and 9 also introduce SQL window functions (called "analytic functions" in Oracle). These are very powerful functions that should be part of the repertoire of all analysts using SQL.

## Modeling Techniques

The last three chapters discuss statistical and data mining modeling techniques and methods.

Chapter 10, "Data Mining Models in SQL," introduces the idea of data mining modeling and the terminology associated with building such models. It also discusses some important types of models that are well-suited to business problems and the SQL environment. Look-alike models find things similar to a given example. Lookup models use a lookup table to find model scores.

This chapter also discusses a more sophisticated modeling technique called naïve Bayesian models. This technique combines information along various business dimensions to estimate an unknown quantity.

Chapter 11, "The Best Fit Line: Linear Regression Models," covers a more traditional statistical technique, linear regression. Several variants of linear regression are introduced, including polynomial regression, weighted regression, multiple regression, and exponential regression. These are explained graphically, using Excel charts, along with the $R^2$ value that measures how well the model fits the data.

Regression is explained using both Excel and SQL. Although Excel has several built-in functions for regression, there is an additional method using Solver, which is more powerful than the built-in functions. This chapter introduces Solver (which is free and bundled with Excel) in the context of linear regression.

The final chapter, "Building Customer Signatures for Further Analysis," introduces the customer signature. This is a data structure that summarizes what a customer looks like at a particular point in time. Customer signatures are very powerful for modeling.

This chapter recognizes that although SQL and Excel are quite powerful, more sophisticated tools are sometimes necessary. The customer signature is the right way to summarize customer information, under many circumstances. And, SQL is a very powerful tool for this summarization.

## Who Should Read this Book

This book is designed for several audiences, with varying degrees of technical skills.

On the less technical side are managers, particularly those with a quantitative bent who are responsible for understanding customers or a business unit. Such people are often quite proficient in Excel, but, alas, much of the data they need resides in relational databases. To help them, this book provides examples of business scenarios where analysis provides useful results. These scenarios are detailed, showing not only the business problem, but the technical approach and the results.

Another part of the audience consists of people whose job is to understand data and customers, often having a job title including the word "analyst." These individuals typically use Excel and other tools, sometimes having direct access to the data warehouse or to some customer-centric database. This book can help by improving SQL querying skills, showing good examples of charts, and introducing survival analysis and association rules for understanding customers and the business.

At the most technical end are statisticians, who typically use special-purpose tools such as SAS, SPSS, and S-plus. However, the data resides in databases. This book can help the very technical with their SQL skills, and also provide examples of using analysis to solve particular business problems.

In addition, database administrators, database designers, and information architects may find this book interesting. The queries shown in the various chapters illustrate what people really want to do with the data, and should encourage database administrators and designers to create efficient databases that support these needs.

I encourage all readers, even the technically proficient, to read (or at least skim) the first three chapters. These chapters introduce SQL, Excel, and statistics all from the perspective of analyzing large quantities of data. This perspective is different from how these subjects are usually introduced. Certain ideas in these chapters, such as the example data, dataflows, SQL syntax, and good chart design, are used throughout the book.

## Tools You Will Need

This book is designed to be stand-alone. That is, readers should be able to learn the ideas and gain understanding directly from the text.

All the SQL in the book has been tested (in Microsoft SQL Server). The datasets and results are available on the companion web sites and at www.data-miners.com. Readers who want hands-on experience are encouraged to download the data and run the examples in the book.

Most examples in the book are vendor-neutral, so they should run with only minor modification on almost any fully functional relational database (I do not recommend Microsoft Access for this purpose). If you do not have a database, there are various software packages available for downloading — database vendors often have stand-alone versions of their software available at no cost. A trial version of SQL Server is available at http://www.microsoft.com/sql/ default.mspx. A trial version of Oracle 10*g* is available at http://www.oracle .com/technology/software/products/database/oracle10g/index.html. In addition, free database software is available, in the form of mysql and other databases.

Some examples in the book use SQL window functions, which are currently available only in Microsoft SQL and Oracle SQL. I do hope that these functions — which are part of the SQL standard — are adopted by more database vendors in the future because they are tremendously useful for data analysis and data mining.

## What's on the Web Site

The companion web site at Wiley and at `www.data-miners.com` contains the datasets used in the book. These datasets contain the following information:

- Reference tables. There are three reference tables, two containing census information (from the 2000 Census) and one containing calendar information about dates.
- Subscribers dataset. This is data describing a subset of customers in a mobile telephone company.
- Purchases dataset. This is data describing customer purchase patterns.

This data is available for download, along with instructions for loading it into SQL Server.

In addition, the companion web site has pages with additional information, such as spreadsheets containing the SQL queries and answers for all examples in the book and a discussion forum.

## Summary

The idea for this book originated with a colleague's question about a reference book for SQL for data analysis queries. However, another reference book on SQL is not needed, even one focused on the practical aspects of using the language for querying purposes.

For analyzing data, SQL cannot be learned in a vacuum. A SQL query, no matter how deftly crafted, is usually not the entire solution to a business problem. The business problem needs to be transformed into a question, which can be answered via a query. The results then need to be presented, often as tables or Excel charts.

I would extend this further. In the real world, statistics also cannot be learned in a vacuum. Once upon a time, collecting data was a time-consuming and difficult process. Now, there are web sites devoted to storing data sets and making them available to anyone who wants them. The companion web site for this book, for example, puts dozens of megabytes of data just a few clicks away. The problem of analyzing data now extends beyond the realm of a few statistical methods to the processes for managing and extracting data as well.

This book combines three key ideas into a single thread of solving problems. I hope this book helps readers with technical skills. Throughout my work as a data miner, I have found SQL, Excel, and statistics to be critical tools for analyzing data. More important than the specific technical skills, though, I hope this book helps readers improve their technical skills and gives them ideas so they can better understand their customers and their businesses.

# A Data Miner Looks at SQL

Everywhere data is being collected, every transaction, every web page visit, every payment — all these and much, much more are filling relational databases with raw data. Computing power and storage have been growing more cost effective over the past decades, a trend destined to continue in the future. Databases are no longer merely a platform for storing data. They are increasingly becoming powerful engines for transforming data into information, useful information about customers and products and business practices.

The focus on data mining has historically been on complex algorithms developed by statisticians and machine learning specialists. Not too long ago, data mining required downloading source code from a research lab or university, compiling the code to get it to run, sometimes even debugging it. By the time the data and software were ready, the business problem had lost urgency.

This book takes a different approach because it starts with the data. The billions of transactions that occur every day — credit cards swipes, web page visits, telephone calls, and so on — are now almost always stored in relational databases. This technology, which was only invented in the 1970s, is now the storehouse of the mountains of data available to businesses. Relational database engines count among the most powerful and sophisticated software products in the business world, so they are well suited for the task of extracting useful information.

The focus of this book is more on data and what to do with data and less on theory and proofs. Instead of trying to squeeze every last iota of information from a small sample — the goal of much statistical analysis — the goal is to find something useful in the gigabytes and terabytes of data stored by many businesses.

This book strives to assist anyone facing the problem of analyzing large databases, by describing the power of data analysis using SQL and Excel. SQL, which stands for Structured Query Language, is a language used to extract information from relational databases. Excel is a popular and useful tool for analyzing smaller amounts of data and presenting results. Its historical limit of 65,536 rows is even an advantage. If the source data fits easily in Excel, then Excel is probably powerful enough for analyzing it. Large databases start where Excel leaves off, and 65,536 rows is as good a definition of a large database as any.

The various chapters of this book are intended to build skill in and enthusiasm for SQL queries and the graphical presentation of results. Throughout the book, the SQL queries are used for more and more sophisticated types of analyses, starting with basic summaries of tables, and moving to data exploration. The chapters continue with methods for understanding time-to-event problems, such as when customers stop, and market basket analysis for understanding what customers are purchasing. The chapters continue with various techniques for building models. The final chapter, which introduces customer signatures, is about putting data into the format that works best for many traditional statistical and data mining tools.

This chapter introduces SQL for data analysis and data mining. Admittedly, this introduction is heavily biased, because the purpose is to explain SQL for the purpose of querying databases rather than building and managing them. SQL is presented from three different perspectives, some of which may resonate more strongly with different groups of readers. The first perspective is the structure of the data, with a particular emphasis on entity-relationship diagrams. The second is the processing of data using dataflows, which happen to be what is "under the hood" of most relational database engines. The third, and strongest thread through subsequent chapters, is the syntax of SQL itself. Although data is well described by entities and relationships, and processing by dataflows, ultimately the goal is to express the transformations in SQL and present the results through Excel.

## Picturing the Structure of the Data

In the beginning, there is data. Although data may seem to be without form and chaotic, there is an organization to it, an organization based on tables and columns and relationships between and among them.

This section describes databases by the data they contain. It introduces *entity-relationship diagrams*, in the context of the datasets (and associated data models) used with this book. These datasets are not intended to represent all the myriad different ways that data might be stored in databases; instead, they are intended as practice data for the ideas in the book. They are available on the companion web site, along with all the examples in the book.

## What Is a Data Model?

The definition of the tables, the columns, and the relationships among them constitute the *data model* for the database. A well-designed database actually has two data models. The *logical data model* explains the database in terms that business users understand. The logical data model is very important for communicating the contents of the database because it defines many business terms and how they are stored in the database.

The *physical data model* explains how the database is actually implemented. In many cases, the physical data model is identical to or very similar to the logical data model. That is, every entity in the logical data model corresponds to a table in the database; every attribute corresponds to a column. This is true for the datasets used in this book.

On the other hand, the logical and physical data models can differ. This is particularly true for larger and more complicated databases, because certain performance issues drive physical database design. A single entity might have rows split into several tables to improve performance, enhance security, enable backup-restore functionality, or facilitate dabase replication. Multiple similar entities might be combined into a single table, especially when they have many attributes in common. Or, a single entity could have different columns in different tables, with the most commonly used columns in one table and less commonly used ones in another table (this is called *vertical partitioning*, and is one method for improving query performance). Often these differences are masked through the use of *views* and other database constructs.

The logical model is quite important for analytic purposes, because it provides an understanding of the data from the business perspective. However, queries actually run on the database represented by the physical model, so it is convenient that the logical and physical structures are often quite similar.

## What Is a Table?

A table is a set of rows and columns that describe multiple instances of something — such as purchases customers have made, or visits to a web page, or zip codes with demographic details. Each row is an instance and each column contains one attribute, one item of information about the instance.

Any given column contains the same genre of information for all rows. So a zip code column should not be the "sent-to" zip code in one row and the "billed-to" zip code in another. Although these are both zip codes, they represent two different uses of the zip code, so they belong in two separate columns.

Some columns are permitted to take on the value NULL meaning that the value in a given row is not available or appropriate for a given instance. For instance, a row describing customers might contain a column for birthdate. This column would take on the value of NULL for all rows where the birthdate is not known.

A table can have as many columns as needed to describe an instance, although for practical purposes tables with more than a few hundred columns are rare. A table can have as many rows as needed; here the numbers easily rise to the millions and even billions, because these often represent customers or customer transactions.

As an example, Table 1-1 shows a few rows and columns from the Zipcensus table (which is available on the companion web site). This table shows that each zip code is in a particular state, which is the abbreviation in the STATE column. There is also a STATE2 column because some zip codes have parts in several states. For instance, 10004 is a zip code in New York City that covers Ellis Island. In 1998, the Supreme Court split jurisdiction of the island between New York and New Jersey, but the Post Office did not change the zip code. So, 10004 has a portion in New York and a smaller, unpopulated portion in New Jersey.

**Table 1-1:** Some Rows and Columns from Zipcensus

| ZIPCODE | STATE | STATE2 | POPULATION | LAND AREA MILES |
|---------|-------|--------|------------|-----------------|
| 10004 | NY | NJ | 1,225 | 0.6156 |
| 33156 | FL | <NULL> | 31,450 | 14.0901 |
| 48706 | MI | <NULL> | 40,647 | 69.7815 |
| 55403 | MN | <NULL> | 14,873 | 1.3903 |
| 73501 | OK | <NULL> | 22,230 | 345.7548 |
| 92264 | CA | <NULL> | 18,869 | 45.9745 |

Each zip code also has an area, which is measured in square miles and recorded in the LANDAREAMILES column. This column simply contains a number, and the database does not know what this number means. It could be area in acres, or square kilometers, or square inches, or pyongs (a Korean unit for area). What the number really means depends on information not stored in the tables. *Metadata* describes what the values in columns mean.

Databases typically do store some information about each column. Conveniently, there is often a label or description (and it is a good idea to fill this in when creating a table). More importantly, there is the data type of the column and whether NULL values are allowed. The next two sections discuss these two topics, because they are quite important for analyzing data.

### Allowing NULL Values

*Nullability* is whether or not a column may contain the NULL value. By default in SQL, a column in any row can contain a special value that says that the value is empty. Although this seems quite useful, NULLs have some unusual side effects. Almost every comparison and function returns NULL if any argument is NULL. So, the following simple query looks like it counts all the rows in the Zipcensus table where the STATE2 column is NULL. However, this query always returns zero:

```
SELECT COUNT(*)
FROM zipcensus zc
WHERE zc.state <> NULL
```

All comparisons return FALSE when either argument is NULL, so no rows are ever selected. The count is zero even though STATE has many non-NULL values. Of course, determining which rows have NULL values is quite useful, so SQL provides the special operators IS NULL and IS NOT NULL to make the comparison. These behave as expected, with the preceding query returning 32,038 instead of 0.

The problem is more insidious when comparing column values, either within a single table or between tables. For instance, the column STATE contains the primary state of a zip code and STATE2 contains the second state, if any. The following query counts the number of zip codes in total and the number where these two state columns have different values:

```
SELECT COUNT(*),
       SUM(CASE WHEN state <> state2 THEN 1 ELSE 0 END) as numsame
FROM zipcensus zc
```

Or does it? The columns STATE and STATE2 should always have different values, so the two counts should be the same. In reality, the query returns the values 32,038 and 42. Once again, the problem is NULL values. When STATE2 is NULL, the test always fails.

When a table is created, there is the option to allow NULL values on each row in the table. This is a relatively minor decision when creating the table. However, making mistakes on columns where NULL values are present is easy.

**WARNING** Designing databases is different from analyzing the data inside them. For example, NULL columns can cause unexpected — and inaccurate — results when analyzing data and make reading queries difficult. Be very careful when using columns that allow them.

### Column Types

The second important attribute of a column is its type, which tells the database exactly how to store values. A well-designed database usually has parsimonious columns, so if two characters suffice for a code, there is no reason to store eight. From the perspective of data analysis, the myriad of available column types is more detail than needed. However, there are a few important aspects of column types and the roles that columns play.

*Primary key* columns uniquely identify each row in the table. That is, no two rows have the same value for the primary key. Databases guarantee that primary keys are unique by refusing to insert rows with duplicate primary keys. Chapter 2 shows techniques to determine whether this condition holds for any given column.

*Numeric values* are values that support arithmetic and other mathematical operations. In SQL, these can be stored in different ways, such as floating-point numbers, integers, decimals, and long integers. The details of how these formats differ is much less important than what can be done with numeric data types.

Within the category of numeric types, one big difference is between integers, which have no fractional part, and real numbers, which do. When doing arithmetic on integers, the result might be an integer or it might be a real number, depending on the database. So 5/2 might evaluate to 2 rather than 2.5, and the average of 1 and 2 might turn out to be 1 instead of 1.5. To avoid this problem, examples in this book multiply integer values by 1.0 to convert them to decimal values as necessary.

Of course, just because it walks like a duck and talks like a duck does not mean that it is a duck. *False numeric values* are values that look like numbers, but really are not. Zip codes (in the United States) are a good example, as are primary key columns stored as numbers. What is the sum of two zip codes? What does it mean to multiply a primary key value by 2? These questions yield nonsense results (although the values can be calculated). Zip codes and primary keys just happen to look like numbers, but really are not.

In the datasets used in this book, zip codes are stored as character strings, but various primary keys are numbers. Often when writing false numerics, this book left pads the numbers with 0s so they have a constant length. After all, the zip code for Harvard Square in Cambridge, MA, is 02138, not 2,138.

*Dates* and *date-times* are exactly what their names imply. There are many things we want to do with them, such as determining the number of days between two dates, extracting the year and month, and comparing two times. There are functions that do all of these things. Unfortunately, most are not part of the SQL standard, so they often differ between databases. The Appendix provides a list of equivalent functions in different databases for functions used in this book, including date and time functions.

Another type of data is character string data. These are commonly codes, such as the state abbreviation in the zip code table, or a description of something, such as a product name or the full state name. SQL has some very rudimentary functions for handling character strings, which in turn support rudimentary text processing. Spaces at the end of a character string are ignored, so the condition "NY" = "NY " evaluates to TRUE. However, spaces at the beginning of a character string are counted, so "NY" = " NY" evaluates to FALSE. When working with data in character columns, it might be worth checking out whether there are spaces at the beginning (which is an example in Chapter 2).

## What Is an Entity-Relationship Diagram?

The "relational" in the name "relational databases" refers to the fact that different tables relate to each other via keys, and to the fact that columns in a given row relate to the values for that column. For instance, a zip code column in any table can link (that is "relate") to the zip code table. The key makes it possible to look up information available in the zip code table. For instance, Figure 1-1 shows the relationships between tables in the purchases dataset.

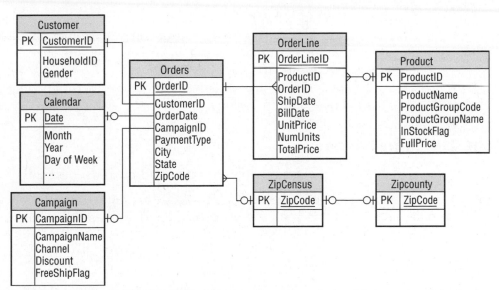

**Figure 1-1:** This entity-relationship diagram shows the relationship among entities in the purchase dataset. Each entity corresponds to one table.

These relationships have a characteristic called *cardinality*, which is the number of items related on each side. For instance, the relationship between Orders and Zipcensus is a zero/one-to-many relationship. This specifies that for every row in Orders there is at most one zip code. And, every zip code has zero, one, or more orders. Typically, this relationship is implemented by having a column in the first table contain the zip code, which is called a *foreign key*. A foreign key is just a column whose contents are the primary key of another table (ZIPCODE in Orders is a foreign key; ZIPCODE in Zipcensus is a primary key). To indicate that there is no match, the foreign key column could be nullable or contain a default missing value (such as "00000" which would indicate an invalid zip code).

There are some other interesting relationships between entities. The zero/one-to-one relationship says that there is at most one match between two tables. This is often a subsetting relationship. For instance, a database might contain sessions of web visits, some of which result in a purchase. Any given session would have zero or one purchases. Any given purchase would have exactly one session.

Another relationship is a many-to-many relationship. A customer might purchase many different products and any given product might be purchased by many different customers. In fact, the purchase dataset does have a many-to-many relationship between Orders and Products; this relationship is represented by the Orderline entity, which has a zero/one-to-many relationship with each of those.

Another type of relationship is the one-at-a-time relationship. At any given time, a customer resides in a particular zip code. However, the customer might move over time. Or, at any given time, a customer might have a particular handset or billing plan, but these can change over time.

With this brief introduction to entity-relationship diagrams, the following sections describe the datasets used in this book.

## The Zip Code Tables

The Zipcensus table consists of more than one hundred columns describing each zip code, or, strictly speaking, each zip code tabulation area (ZCTA) defined by the Census Bureau for the 2000 Census. This information was gathered from the census web site. Zipcensus derives information from 16 census tables, each of which has information about a particular aspect of the zip code. These 16 tables are a small subset of the hundreds of tables available from the Census Bureau.

The first few columns consist of overview information about each zip code, such as the state, the second state, population, latitude, and longitude. In addition to population, there are four more counts: the number of households, the number of families, the number of housing units, and the number of occupied housing units. Each of these has information associated with them.

The following information is available for the general population:

- Proportion of population in various racial categories.
- Proportion of population with various levels of education (among adults 25 years and older).

The following information is available for households:

- Proportion of population in various household configurations, such as the household size, gender of head of household, and presence of children.
- Proportion of households with social security income.
- Proportion of households on public assistance.
- Median household income.

The following information is available for families:

- Proportion of families with 1999 income in various groups.

The following information is available for housing units:

- Proportion with complete and lacking plumbing facilities.

The following information is available for occupied housing units:

- Proportion that are owned and rented.
- Proportion that are occupied by 1, 2, 3, 4, 5, 6, and 7 or more people.
- Proportion that use various types of heating fuel.
- Proportion with various combinations of unmarried couples.

Information on the columns and exact definitions of terms such as ZCTA are available at www.census.gov.

The second zip code table is Zipcounty, a companion table that maps zip codes to counties. It contains information such as the following:

- County name;
- Post office name;
- Population of county;
- Number of households in county; and,
- County land area.

This table has one row for each zip code, so it can be joined to Zipcensus and to other tables using the ZIPCODE column.

## Subscription Dataset

The subscription data is a simple example of an entity-relationship diagram, because it consists of only two entities, shown in Figure 1-2. This dataset paints a picture of a subscriber at a given point in time (the date when the snapshot was created).

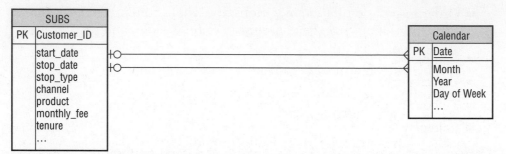

**Figure 1-2:** An entity-relationship diagram with only two entities describes the data in the customer snapshot dataset.

The Subs table describes customers in a subscription business. It is an example of a snapshot table that shows what customers (and former customers) look like as of a particular date. The columns in this table describe customers as they start and as they stop. This particular snapshot table does not have any intermediate behavior information.

The Calendar table is a general-purpose table that has information about dates, including:

- Year;
- Month number;
- Month name;
- Day of month;
- Day of week;
- Day of year; and,
- Holiday information.

This table has the date as a primary key, and covers dates from 1950 through 2050.

## Purchases Dataset

The purchases dataset contains entities typical of retail purchases; the entities in this dataset and their relationships are shown in Figure 1-1:

- Customer;
- Orders;
- Orderline;
- Product;
- Campaign;
- Zipcensus;
- Zipcounty; and,
- Calendar.

The data in the purchases dataset captures the important entities associated with retail purchases. The most detailed information is in the Orderline table, which describes each of the items in an order. To understand the terminology, think of a receipt. Each line on the receipt represents a different item in the purchase. In addition, the line has other information such as the product number, the price, and the number of items, which are all in this table. To tie all the items in a single purchase together, each row of Orderline has an ORDERID.

Each ORDERID, in turn, represents one row in the Orders table. This has information such as the date and time of the purchase, where the order was shipped to, and the type of payment. It also contains the total dollar amount of the purchase, summed up from the individual items. Because all order lines are in exactly one order and each order can have multiple order lines, there is a one-to-many relationship between these tables.

By the way, it is generally good practice to name entities in the singular, so Order would be preferred to Orders. However, ORDER is a keyword in SQL, so it is simpler to use the plural in this particular case.

Just as the ORDERID ties multiple order lines into an order, the CUSTOMERID assigns orders made at different points in time to the same customer. The existence of the CUSTOMERID prompts the question of how it is created. In one sense, it makes no difference how it is created; the CUSTOMERID is simply a given, defining the customer in the database. On the other hand, on occasion, it might be worth asking whether it is doing a good job — are a single customer's purchases being tied together most of the time? The aside "The Customer ID: Identifying Customers Over Time" discusses the creation of customer IDs.

---

**THE CUSTOMER ID: IDENTIFYING CUSTOMERS OVER TIME**

The CUSTOMERID column combines transactions over time into a single grouping, the customer (or household or similar entity). How is this accomplished? It all depends on the business and the business processes. Here are some ways:

- The purchases might contain name and address information. So, purchases with matching names and addresses would have the same customer ID.

- The purchases might all have telephone numbers, so the telephone number could provide the customer ID.

- Customers may have loyalty cards, and the loyalty number might provide the customer ID.

- The purchases might be on the web, so browser cookies could identify customers over time.

- The purchases might all be by credit card, so purchases with the same credit card number would have the same customer ID.

- And, of course, any combination of these or other methods might be used.

There are many ways to identify the same customer over time.

And all of these have their challenges. What happens when a customer purchases a new computer (and the web cookie changes) or deletes her web cookies? Or when customers forget their loyalty cards (so the loyalty numbers are not attached to the purchases)? Or move? Or change phone numbers? Or change their names? Keeping track of customers over time can be challenging.

---

The Product table provides information about products, such as the product group name and the full price. The table does not contain detailed product names. These were removed as part of the effort to anonymize the data.

The data model contains the Calendar table, which provides lookup information for dates. The final two tables in Figure 1-1 are Zipcensus and Zipcounty. These are the tables that provide information about zip codes and the lookup for county names.

## Picturing Data Analysis Using Dataflows

Tables store data, but tables do not actually do anything. Tables are nouns; queries are verbs. This book mates SQL and Excel for data manipulation, transformation, and presentation. However, these two tools are very different from each other. The differences are exacerbated because they often support the same operations, although in very different ways. For instance, SQL uses the GROUP BY clause to summarize data in groups. An Excel user, on the other hand, might use pivot tables, use the subtotal wizard, or manually do calculations using functions such as SUMIF(); however, nothing in Excel is called "group by."

Because this book intends to combine the two technologies, it is useful to have a common way of expressing data manipulations and data transformations, a common language independent of the tools being used. Dataflows provide this common language by showing the transformation operations fitting together like an architecture blueprint for data processing, a blueprint that describes what needs to be done, without saying which tool is going to do the work. This makes dataflows a powerful mechanism for thinking about data transformations.

## What Is a Dataflow?

A dataflow is a graphical way of visualizing data transformations. Dataflows have two important elements. The *nodes* in a dataflow diagram perform transformations on data, taking zero or more inputs and producing output. The *edges* in a dataflow diagram are pipes connecting the nodes. Think of the data flowing through the pipes and getting banged and pushed and pulled and flattened into shape by the nodes. In the end, the data has been transformed into information.

Figure 1-3 shows a simple dataflow that adds a new column, called SCF for Sectional Center Facility (something the U.S. Post Office uses to route mail). This column is the first three digits of a zip code. The output is each zip code with its SCF. The dataflow has four nodes, connected by three edges. The first, shaped like a cylinder, represents a database table or file and is the source of the data. The edge leaving this node shows some of the records being passed from it, records from the Zipcensus table.

The second node appends the new column to the table, which is also visible along the edge leading out from the node. The third selects two columns for output — in this case, ZIPCODE and SCF. And the final node simply represents the output. On the dataflow diagram, imagine a magnifying glass that makes it possible to see the data moving through the flow. Seeing the data move from node to node makes it easier to understand what is happening in the flow.

The actual processing could be implemented in either SQL or Excel. The SQL code corresponding to this dataflow is:

```
SELECT zc.zipcode, SUBSTRING(zc.zipcode, 1, 3) as scf
 FROM zipcensus zc
```

Alternatively, if the data in Zipcensus were in an Excel worksheet with the zip codes in column A, the following formula would extract the SCF:

```
=MID(A1, 1, 3)
```

Of course, the formula would have to be copied down the column.

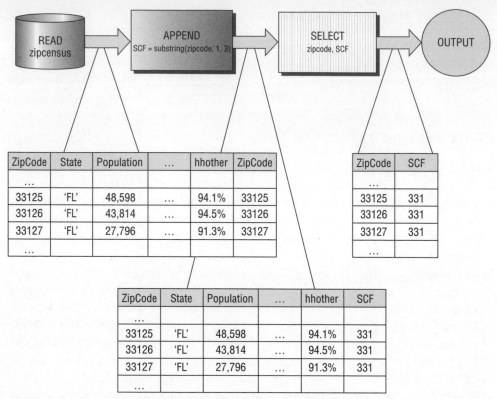

**Figure 1-3:** A simple dataflow reads the ZIPCODE, calculates and appends a new field called SCF, and outputs the SCF and ZIPCODE.

Excel, SQL, and dataflows are three different ways of expressing similar transformations. The advantage of dataflows is that they provide an intuitive way of expressing data manipulations, independent of the tool used for the processing. Dataflows facilitate understanding, but in the end, the work described in this book will be in SQL or Excel.

**TIP** When column A has a column of data and we want to copy a formula down column B, the following is a handy method based on keyboard shortcuts:

1. Type the formula in the first cell in column B where there is data in column A.

2. Move the cursor to column A.

3. Hit `<control>-<down arrow>` to go to the end of the data in column A.

4. Hit `<right arrow>` to move to column B.

5. Hit `<control>-<shift>-<up arrow>` to highlight all of column B.

6. Hit `<control>-D` to copy the formula down the column.

Voila! The formula gets copied without a lot of fiddling with the mouse and with menus.

## Dataflow Nodes (Operators)

Dataflows are a good way to think about the data transformations that SQL can accomplish. These, in turn, depend on a few basic types of nodes, which are explained in this section. Later in this chapter are several examples of dataflows along with the SQL used to produce them.

### READ: Reading a Database Table

The READ operator reads all the columns of data from a database table or file. In SQL, this operation is implicit when tables are included in the FROM clause of a query. The READ operator does not accept any input dataflows, but has an output. Generally, if a table is needed more than once in a dataflow, there is a separate READ for each occurrence.

### OUTPUT: Outputting a Table (or Chart)

The OUTPUT operator creates desired output, such as a table in a row-column format or some sort of chart based on the data. The OUTPUT operator does not have any outputs, but accepts inputs. It also accepts parameters describing the type of output.

### SELECT: Selecting Various Columns in the Table

The SELECT operator chooses one or more columns from the input and passes them to the output. It might reorder columns and/or choose a subset of them. The SELECT operator has one input and one output. It accepts parameters describing the columns to keep and their order.

### FILTER: Filtering Rows Based on a Condition

The FILTER operator chooses rows based on a TRUE or FALSE condition. Only rows that satisfy the condition are passed through, so it is possible that no rows ever make it through the node. The FILTER operator has one input and one output. It accepts parameters describing the condition used for filtering.

### APPEND: Appending New Calculated Columns

The APPEND operator appends new columns, which are calculated from existing columns and functions. The APPEND operator has one input and one output. It accepts parameters describing the new columns.

### UNION: Combining Multiple Datasets into One

The UNION operator takes two or more datasets as inputs and creates a single output that combines all rows from both of them. The input datasets need to have exactly the same columns. The UNION operator has two or more inputs and one output.

### AGGREGATE: Aggregating Values

The AGGREGATE operator groups its input based on zero or more aggregate key columns. All the rows with the same key values are summarized, and the output contains the aggregate key columns and the summaries. The AGGREGATE operator takes one input and produces one output. It also takes parameters describing the aggregate keys and the summaries to produce.

### LOOKUP: Looking Up Values in One Table in Another

The LOOKUP operator takes two inputs, a base table and a reference table, which have a key in common. The reference table should have at most one row for each key value. The LOOKUP operator appends one or more columns in the reference table to the base table, based on matching key values. The LOOKUP operator assumes that all keys in the base table are in the reference table. It takes two parameters. The first describes the key and the second describes which columns to append. Although this can also be accomplished with a JOIN, the LOOKUP is intended to be simpler and more readable.

### CROSSJOIN: General Join of Two Tables

The CROSSJOIN operator takes two inputs and combines them in a very specific way. It produces a wider table that contains all the columns in the two inputs. Every row in the output corresponds to a pair of rows, one from each input. For instance, if the first table has four rows, A, B, C, and D, and the second has three rows, X, Y, and Z, then the output consists of all twelve combinations of these: AX, AY, AZ, BX, BY, BZ, CX, CY, CZ, DX, DY, and DZ. This is the general join operation.

### JOIN: Join Two Tables Together Using a Key Column

The JOIN operator takes two inputs and a join condition, and produces an output that has all the columns in the two tables. The join condition specifies that at least one column in one table is equal to one column in the other. This common type of join, called an equijoin, is important for performance reasons when optimizing queries.

With an equijoin, it is possible to "lose" rows in one or both of the inputs. This occurs when there is no matching row in the other table. Because it is sometimes desirable to ensure that all rows in one or the other table are represented in the output, there is a slight variation called an outer join. Specifically, the LEFT OUTER JOIN keeps all rows in the first input table and the RIGHT OUTER JOIN keeps all rows in the second. Although it might seem desirable, a FULL OUTER JOIN is not available in standard SQL, so is not included here as an option.

### SORT: Ordering the Results of a Dataset

The SORT operator orders its input dataset based on one or more sort keys. It takes a parameter describing the sort keys and the sort order (ascending or descending).

## Dataflows, SQL, and Relational Algebra

Beneath the skin of many relational databases is an engine that is essentially a dataflow engine. Because dataflows focus on data and because SQL focuses on data, they are natural allies.

Historically, though, SQL has a slightly different theoretical foundation based on mathematical set theory. This foundation is called *relational algebra*, an area in mathematics that defines operations on unordered sets of *tuples*. A tuple is a lot like a row, consisting of attribute-value pairs. Although there are some small theoretical differences, an attribute-value pair is essentially the same as a column in a given row with its value. Relational algebra then includes a bunch of operations on sets of tuples, operations such as union and intersection, joins and projections, which are similar to the dataflow constructs just described.

The notion of using relational algebra to access data is credited to E. F. Codd who, while a researcher at IBM in 1970, wrote a paper called "A Relational Model of Data for Large Shared Data Banks." This paper became the basis of using relational algebra for accessing data, eventually leading to the development of SQL and modern relational databases.

A set of tuples is a lot like a table, but not quite. There are some theoretical differences between the two, such as the fact that a table can contain duplicate rows but a set of tuples cannot have duplicates. One difference, however, stands out: sets of tuples have no ordering, so there is no concept of the first, second, and third tuple in a set of them. To most people (or at least most people who are not immersed in set theory), tables have a natural order, defined perhaps by a primary key or perhaps by the sequence that rows were originally loaded into the table.

As a legacy of the history of relational algebra, standard SQL provides no construct for extracting the first row, or the first ten rows, from a table. Because databases live in the real world, most databases provide some mechanism for this functionality, as shown in Appendix A. Relational algebra is an elegant theory that inspired the creation of modern databases; dataflows, on the other hand, are probably more intuitive to most people and come closer to explaining how databases and data processing actually work.

## SQL Queries

This section provides the third perspective on SQL, an introduction to the SQL querying language. In one way, this introduction is only the tip of the iceberg of the SQL language, because it focuses on one aspect: extracting information from the database using queries. The querying part of SQL is the visible portion of an iceberg whose bulky mass is hidden from view. The hidden portion is the data management side of the language — the definitions of tables and views, inserting rows, updating rows, defining triggers, stored procedures, and so on. As data miners and analysts, our goal is to exploit the visible part of the iceberg, by extracting useful information from the database.

SQL queries answer specific questions. Whether the question being asked is actually the question being answered is a big issue for database users. The examples throughout this book include both the question and the SQL that answers it. Sometimes, small changes in the question or the SQL produce very different results.

### What to Do, Not How to Do It

An important characteristic of SQL, as a language, is its non-procedural nature. That is, SQL explains what needs to be done to data, but not how this is accomplished. This approach has several advantages. A query is isolated from the hardware and operating system where it is running. The same query should return equivalent results in two very different environments.

Being non-procedural means that SQL needs to be compiled into computer code on any given computer. This provides an opportunity to optimize it to run as fast as possible for the given data on a given computer. There are generally many different algorithms lurking inside a database engine, ready to be used under just the right circumstances. The specific optimizations, though, might be quite different in different environments.

Another advantage of being non-procedural is that SQL can take advantage of parallel processing. The language itself was devised in a world where computers were very expensive, had a single processor, limited memory, and one disk. The fact that SQL has adapted to modern system architectures where CPUs, memory, and disks are plentiful is a testament to the power and scalability of the ideas underlying relational database paradigm. When Codd wrote his paper suggesting relational algebra for "large data banks," he was probably thinking of a few megabytes of data, an amount of data that now easily fits in an Excel spreadsheet and pales in comparison to the terabytes of data found in corporate repositories.

## A Basic SQL Query

A good place to start with SQL is with the simplest type of query, one that selects a column from a table. Consider, once again, the query that returned zip codes along with the SCF:

```
SELECT zc.zipcode, SUBSTRING(zc.zipcode, 1, 3) as scf
FROM zipcensus zc
```

This query returns a table with two columns, one for the zip code and one for the scf. The rows might be returned in any order. In most databases, the rows are returned in the order that they are placed in the table, but you should never depend on this fact.

If you want the rows in a particular order, add an explicit ORDER BY clause to the query:

```
SELECT zc.zipcode, SUBSTRING(zc.zipcode, 1, 3) as scf
FROM zipcensus zc
ORDER BY zc.zipcode
```

**TIP** If you want the result from a query to be in a particular order, add an ORDER BY **clause. Without one, never assume that the result of a query will be in a particular order.**

Although this is a simple query, it already shows some of the structure of the SQL language. All queries begin with the SELECT clause that lists the columns being returned. The tables being acted upon come from the FROM clause, which follows the SELECT statement. And, the ORDER BY is the last clause in the query.

This example uses only one table, Zipcensus. In the query, this table has a *table alias*, or abbreviation, called zc. Throughout the query, "zc" refers to this table. So, the first part of the SELECT statement is taking the ZIPCODE column from zc. Although table aliases are optional in SQL, as a rule this book usually uses them, because aliases clarify where columns are coming from.

The second column returned by the query is calculated from the zip code itself, using the SUBSTRING() function, which in this case extracts the first three characters from the zip code. SUBSTRING() is just one of dozens of functions provided by SQL, and specific databases generally provide the ability for users to define functions. The second column has a *column alias*. That is, the column is named "SCF," which is the header of the column in the output.

The following query is a simple modification that returns the zip codes and SCFs only in Minnesota:

```
SELECT zc.zipcode, SUBSTRING(zc.zipcode, 1, 3) as scf
FROM zipcensus zc
WHERE state = 'MN'
ORDER BY 1
```

The query has an additional clause, the WHERE clause, which, if present, always follows the FROM clause. The WHERE clause specifies a condition; in this case, that only rows where the STATE column is equal to "MN" are included by the query. The ORDER BY clause then sorts the rows by the first column; the "1" is a reference to the first column, in this case, ZC.ZIPCODE. Alternatively, the column name could be used in the ORDER BY clause.

The dataflow corresponding to this modified query is in Figure 1-4. In this dataflow, the WHERE clause has turned into a filter after the data source, and the ORDER BY clause has turned into a SORT operator just before the output. Also notice that the dataflow contains several operators, even for a simple SQL query. SQL is a parsimonious language; some complex operations can be specified quite simply.

> **TIP** When a column value is NULL, any comparison in a WHERE clause — with the important exception of "IS NULL" — always returns FALSE. So, the clause "WHERE state <> 'MN'" really means "WHERE state IS NOT NULL AND state <> 'MN'".

## A Basic Summary SQL Query

A very powerful component of SQL is the ability to summarize data in a table. For instance, the following SQL counts the number of zip codes in the Zipcensus table:

```
SELECT COUNT(*) as numzip
FROM zipcensus zc
```

This query returns the number of rows in the table, and its form is very similar to the basic select query. The function COUNT(*), not surprisingly, counts the number of rows. The "*" means that all rows are being counted. It is also possible to count a column, such as COUNT(ZIPCODE), which counts the number of rows that do not have a NULL zip code.

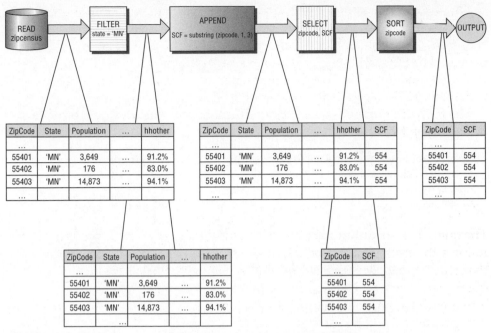

**Figure 1-4:** A WHERE clause in a query adds a filter node to the dataflow.

The preceding query is an aggregation query that treats the entire table as a single group. Within this group, the query counts the number of rows — which is the number of rows in the table. A very similar query returns the number of zip codes in each state:

```
SELECT state, COUNT(*) as numzip
FROM zipcensus zc
GROUP BY state
ORDER BY 2 DESC
```

Conceptually, this query is quite similar to the previous one. The GROUP BY clause says to treat the table as consisting of several groups defined by the different values in the column STATE. The result is then sorted in reverse order of the count (DESC stands for "descending"), so the state with the most zip codes (Texas) is first. Figure 1-5 shows the dataflow diagram for this query.

In addition to COUNT(), standard SQL offers three other useful aggregation functions. The SUM() and AVG() functions compute, respectively, the sum and average of numeric values. COUNT(DISTINCT) returns the number of distinct values. An example of using it is to answer the following question: *How many SCFs are in each state?*

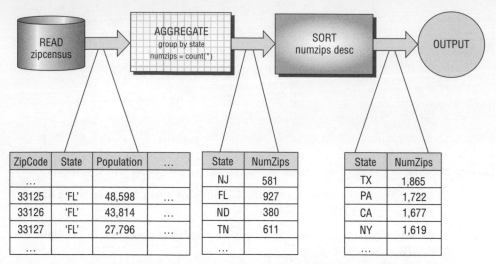

**Figure 1-5:** This dataflow diagram describes a basic aggregation query.

The following query answers this question:

```
SELECT zc.state, COUNT(DISTINCT SUBSTRING(zc.zipcode, 1, 3)) as numscf
FROM zipcensus zc
GROUP BY zc.state
ORDER BY zc.state
```

This query also shows that functions, such as SUBSTRING(), can be nested in the aggregation functions. SQL allows arbitrarily complicated expressions. Chapter 2 has other ways to answer this question using subqueries.

## What it Means to Join Tables

Because they bring together information from two tables, joins are perhaps the most powerful feature of SQL. SQL is non-procedural, so the database engine can figure out the most effective way to execute the join — and there are often dozens of algorithms and variants for the database engine to choose from. A lot of programming and algorithms are hidden beneath this simple construct.

As with anything powerful, joins need to be used carefully — not sparingly, but carefully. It is very easy to make mistakes using joins, especially the following two:

- ▪ "Mistakenly" losing rows in the result set, and
- ▪ "Mistakenly" adding unexpected additional rows.

Whenever joining tables, it is worth asking whether either of these could be happening. These are subtle questions, because the answer depends on the data being processed, not by the syntax of the expression itself. There are examples of both problems throughout the book.

The discussion of joins is about what joins do to data and how to use them rather than on the multitude of algorithms for implementing them (although the algorithms are quite interesting — to some people — they don't help us understand customers and data). The most general type of join is the cross-join. The discussion then explains the more common variants: look up joins, equijoins, nonequijoins, and outer joins.

> **TIP** Whenever joining two tables, ask yourself the following two questions:
>
> 1. **Could one of the tables accidentally be losing rows, because there are no matches in the other table?**
>
> 2. **Could the result set unexpectedly have duplicate rows due to multiple matches between the tables?**
>
> **The answers require understanding the underlying data.**

## Cross-Joins: The Most General Joins

The most general form of joining two tables is called the *cross-join* or, for the more mathematically inclined, the *Cartesian product* of the two tables. As discussed earlier in the section on dataflows, a cross-join on two tables results in an output consisting of all columns from both tables and every combination of rows from one table with rows from the other. The number of rows in the output grows quickly as the two tables become bigger. If the first table has four rows and two columns, and the second has three rows and two columns, then the resulting output has twelve rows and four columns. This is easy enough to visualize in Figure 1-6.

Because the number of rows in the output is the number of rows in each table multiplied together, the output size grows quickly. If one table has 3,000 rows and the other 4,000 rows, the result has 12,000,000 rows — which is a bit too big to illustrate here. The number of columns is the sum of the number of columns in each input table.

Tables in the business world often have thousands, or millions, or even more rows, so a cross-join quickly gets out of hand, with even the fastest computers. If this is the case, why are joins so useful, important, and practical?

The reason is that the general form of the join is not the form that gets used very often, unless one of the tables is known to have only one row. By imposing some restrictions — say by imposing a relationship between columns in the two tables — the result becomes more tractable. However, even though more specialized joins are more commonly used, the cross-join is still the foundation that explains what they are doing.

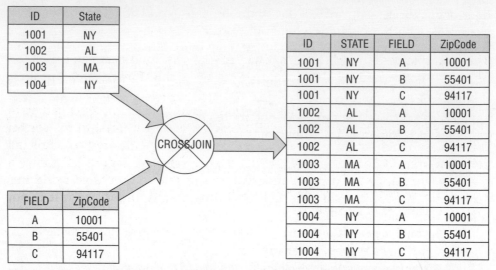

**Figure 1-6:** A cross-join on two tables, one with four rows and one with three rows, results in a new table that has twelve rows and all columns from both tables.

## Lookup: A Useful Join

Zipcensus is an example of a reference table that contains data derived from the 2000 census summarized at the zip code level. Each row describes a zip code and any given zip code appears exactly once in the table. As a consequence, the zip code column is called the *primary key*, making it possible to look up census information at the zip code level using a zip code column in another table. Intuitively, this is one of the most natural join operations, using a *foreign key* in one table to look up values in a reference table.

A lookup join makes the following two assumptions about the base and reference tables:

- All values of the key in the base table are in the reference table (missing join keys lose rows unexpectedly).

- The lookup key is the primary key in the reference table (duplicate join keys cause unexpected rows).

Unfortunately, SQL does not provide direct support for lookups because there is no simple check that these two conditions are true. However, the join mechanism does make it possible to do lookups, and this works smoothly when the two preceding conditions are true.

Consider the SQL query that appends the zip code population to each row of the Orders table, as an example of a lookup:

```
SELECT o.orderid, o.zipcode, zc.population
FROM orders o JOIN
```

```
        zipcensus zc
        ON o.zipcode = zc.zipcode
```

This example uses the ON clause to establish the condition between the tables. There is no requirement that the condition be equality in general, but for a lookup it is.

From the dataflow perspective, the lookup could be implemented with CROSSJOIN. The output from the CROSSJOIN is first filtered to the correct rows (those where the two zip codes are equal) and the desired columns (all columns from Orders plus POPULATION) are selected. Figure 1-7 shows a dataflow that appends a population column to the Orders table using this approach. Of course, using the LOOKUP operator is simpler, but it is not directly implemented in SQL.

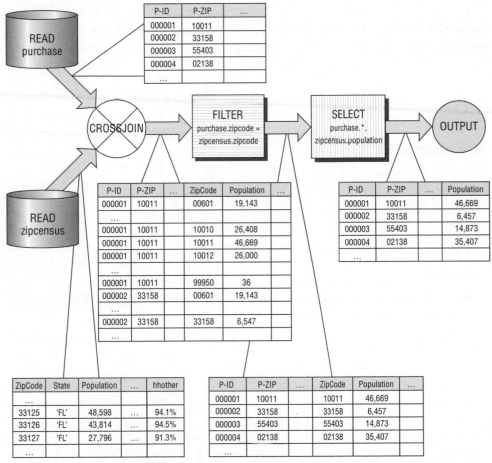

**Figure 1-7:** In SQL, looking up a value in one table is theoretically equivalent to creating the cross-join of the two tables and then restricting the values.

Unlike the dataflow diagram, the SQL query describes that a join needs to take place, but does not explain how this is done. The cross-join is one method, although it would be quite inefficient in practice. Databases are practical, so database writers have invented many different ways to speed up this type of operation. And, there are better ways to do a lookup. The details of such performance enhancements are beyond the scope of this book, and often proprietary to each database. It is worth remembering that databases are practical, not theoretical, and the database engine is usually trying to optimize the runtime performance of queries.

Although the preceding query does implement the look up, it does not guarantee the two conditions mentioned earlier. If there were multiple rows in Zipcensus for a given zip code, there would be extra rows in the output (because any matching row would appear more than once). If there were key values in Orders but not in Zipcensus, rows would unexpectedly disappear. This, in fact, is the case and the output has fewer rows than the original Orders table.

Having multiple rows in Zipcensus for a given zip code is not an outlandish idea. For instance, Zipcensus could also include rows for the 1990 and 2010 censuses, which would make it possible to see changes in zip codes over time. One way to do this would be to have another column, say, CENSUSYEAR to specify the year of the census. Now the primary key would be a compound key composed of ZIPCODE and CENSUSYEAR together. A join on the table using just zip code would result in multiple columns, one for each census year.

### Equijoins

An equijoin is a join that has at least one restriction between the two tables being joined, and this restriction asserts that two columns in the tables have equal values. In SQL, the restrictions are the conditions on the ON clause following the join statement. Note that these restrictions should always be connected by ANDs, not by ORs (unless you have a very good reason).

Lookups are a good example of an equijoin, because the join asserts that a foreign key in one table equals a primary key in a reference table. Lookups are a special case though, where the number of rows output is exactly the number of rows in the table with the foreign key.

An equijoin can return extra rows the same way that a cross-join can. If a column value in the first table is repeated three times, and the same value occurs in the second table four times, the equijoin between the two tables produces twelve rows of output for that column. In this example, the two columns are clearly not primary keys on their respective tables, because the same value appears on multiple rows. This is similar to the situation as depicted in Figure 1-6 that illustrates the cross-join. Using an equijoin, it is possible to add many rows to output that are not intended, especially when the equijoin is on non-key columns.

Although joins on primary keys are more common, there are some cases where such a many-to-many equijoin is desired. The following question about the Zipcensus table does require a many-to-many equijoin to be answered in SQL: *For each zip code, how many zip codes in the same state have a larger population?*

The following query answers this using a *self-join*, which simply means that two copies of the `zipcensus` table are joined together. In this case, the equijoin uses the state column as a key, rather than the zip code column.

```
SELECT zc1.zipcode,
       SUM(CASE WHEN zc1.population < zc2.population THEN 1
                ELSE 0 END)as numzip
FROM zipcensus zc1 JOIN
     zipcensus zc2
     ON zc1.state = zc2.state
GROUP BY zc1.zipcode
```

Notice that the Zipcensus table is mentioned twice in the FROM clause, in order to express the self-join.

The dataflow for this query is shown in Figure 1-8. This dataflow reads the Zipcensus table twice, with the two going into the JOIN operator. The JOIN in the dataflow is an equijoin, because the self-join is on the STATE column. The results from the join are then aggregated. Chapter 8 introduces a special class of functions called window functions that simplify this type of query.

## Nonequijoins

A nonequijoin is a join where none of the restrictions include an equality restriction between two columns. Nonequijoins are quite rare. This is fortunate because there are many fewer performance tricks available to make them run quickly. Often, a nonequijoin is actually a mistake and indicates an error.

Note that when any of the restrictions are equality, the join is an equijoin. Consider the following question about the Orders table: *How many orders are greater than the median rent where the customer resides?*

The following query answers this question:

```
SELECT zc.state, COUNT(*) as numrows
FROM orders o JOIN
     zipcensus zc
     ON o.zipcode = zc.zipcode AND
        o.totalprice > zc.hhumediancashrent
GROUP BY zc
```

The JOIN in this query has two conditions, one specifies that the zip codes are equal and the other specifies that the total amount of the order is greater than the median rent in the zip code. This is still an example of an equijoin, because of the condition on zip code.

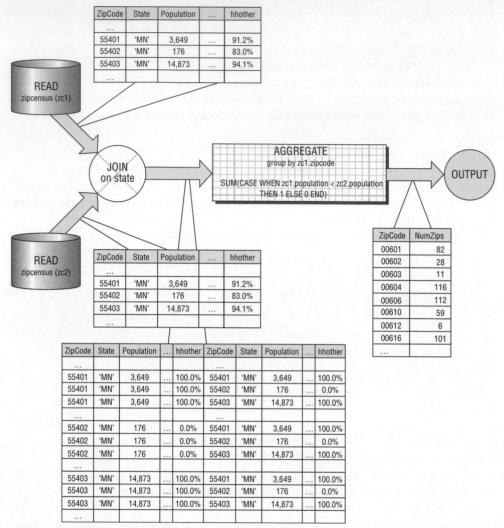

**Figure 1-8:** This dataflow illustrates a self-join and an equijoin on a non-key column.

## Outer Joins

The final type of join is the outer join, which guarantees that all rows from one of the tables remain in the result set, even if there are no matching rows in the other table. All the previous joins have been *inner joins*, meaning that only rows that match are included. For a cross-join, this does not make a difference, because there are many copies of rows from both tables in the result. However, for other types of joins, losing rows in one or the other table may not be desirable; hence the need for the outer join.

Outer joins comes in two flavors: the LEFT OUTER JOIN ensures that all rows from the first table remain in the result set and the RIGHT OUTER JOIN ensures that all rows from the second table remain. The FULL OUTER JOIN ensures that all rows from both tables are kept, although this functionality is not available in all databases.

What does this mean? Consider the Orders table, which has some zip codes that are not in the Zipcensus table. This could occur for several reasons. The Zipcensus table contains a snapshot of zip codes as of the year 2000, and new zip codes have appeared since then. Also, the Census Bureau is not interested in all zip codes, so they exclude some zip codes where no one lives. Or, perhaps the problem might lie in the Orders table. There could be mistakes in the ZIPCODE column. Or, as is the case, the Orders table might include orders from outside the United States.

Whatever the reason, any query using the inner join eliminates all rows where the zip code in the Orders table does not appear in Zipcensus. Losing such rows could be a problem, which the outer join fixes. The only change to the query is replacing the word JOIN with the phrase LEFT OUTER JOIN:

```
SELECT zc.state, COUNT(*) as numrows
FROM orders o LEFT OUTER JOIN
     zipcensus zc
     ON o.zipcode = zc.zipcode AND
        o.totalprice > zc.hhumediancashrent
GROUP BY zc.state
```

The results from this query are not particularly interesting. The results are the same as the previous query with one additional large group for NULL. This is because when there is no matching row in Zipcensus, ZC.ZIPCODE is NULL. On the other hand, if the SELECT and GROUP BY used O.ZIPCODE instead, the orders with non-matching zip codes would be spread through all the states.

Left outer joins are very practical. They are particularly important when there is one table that contains information about customers and we want to append more and more columns to create a customer signature. Chapter 12 is about creating customer signatures and uses them extensively.

## Other Important Capabilities in SQL

SQL has some other features that are used throughout the book. The goal here is not to explain every nuance of the language, because reference manuals and database documentation do a good job there. The goal here is to give a feel for the important capabilities of SQL needed for data analysis.

## UNION ALL

UNION ALL is a set operation that combines all rows in two tables, by just creating a new table with all the rows from each input table. There is no cross-product as there is with the join operator, so the number of columns must be the same in each of the input tables. Unlike the join operations, all input tables must have the same columns in them. In practice, this means that UNION ALL is almost always operating on subqueries, because it is unusual for two tables to have exactly the same columns.

SQL has other set operations, such as UNION and INTERSECTION. The UNION operation combines the rows in two tables together, and then removes duplicates. This means that UNION is much less efficient than UNION ALL, so it is worth avoiding. INTERSECTION takes the overlap of two tables — rows that are in both. However, it is often more interesting to understand the relationship between two tables — how many items are in both and how many are in each one but not the other. Solving this problem is discussed in Chapter 2.

## CASE

The CASE statement makes it possible to transform data conditionally. It has the general form:

```
CASE WHEN <condition-1> THEN <value-1>
   . . .
    WHEN <condition-n THEN <value-n>
    ELSE <default-value> END
```

The <condition> clauses look like conditions in a WHERE clause; they can be arbitrarily complicated. The <value> clauses are values returned by the statement, and these should all be the same type. The <condition> clauses are evaluated in the order they are written. When no <else> condition is present, the CASE statement returns NULL when previous clauses do not match.

One common use of the CASE statement is to create indicator variables. Consider the following question: *How many zip codes in each state have a population of more than 10,000 and what is the total population of these?* The following SQL statement is, perhaps, the most natural way of answering this question:

```
SELECT zc.state, COUNT(*) as numbigzip, SUM(population) as popbigzip
FROM zipcensus zc
WHERE population > 10000
GROUP BY zc.state
```

This query uses a WHERE clause to choose the appropriate set of zip codes.

Now consider the related question: *How many zip codes in each state have a population of more than 10,000, how many have a population of more than 1,000, and what is the total population of each of these sets?*

Unfortunately, the WHERE clause solution no longer works, because two overlapping sets of zip codes are needed. One solution would be to run two queries. This gets messy, though, especially because combining the results into a single query is easy:

```
SELECT zc.state,
       SUM(CASE WHEN population > 10000 THEN 1 ELSE 0 END) as num_10000,
       SUM(CASE WHEN population > 1000  THEN 1 ELSE 0 END) as num_1000,
       SUM(CASE WHEN population > 10000 THEN population ELSE 0 END
           ) as num_10000,
       SUM(CASE WHEN population > 1000  THEN population ELSE 0 END
           ) as num_1000
FROM zipcensus zc
GROUP BY zc.state
```

Notice that in this version, the SUM() function is being used to count the zip codes that meet the appropriate condition. COUNT() is not the right function, because it would count the number of non-NULL values.

**TIP** When a CASE statement is nested in an aggregation function, the appropriate function is usually SUM(), sometimes AVG(), and very rarely COUNT(). Check to be sure that you are using SUM() even when "counting" things up.

It is worth making a few comments about these queries. The following two statements are very close to being the same, but the second lacks the ELSE clause:

```
       SUM(CASE WHEN population > 10000 THEN 1 ELSE 0 END) as num_10000,
       SUM(CASE WHEN population > 10000 THEN 1 END) as num_10000,
```

Both of these count the number of zip codes where population is greater than 10,000. The difference is what happens when there are no zip codes with such a large population. The first returns the number 0. The second returns NULL. Usually when counting things, it is preferable to have the value be a number rather than NULL, so the first form is generally preferred.

The CASE statement can be much more readable than the WHERE clause because the CASE statement has the condition in the SELECT, rather than much further down in the query. On the other hand, the WHERE clause provides more opportunities for optimization, so in some cases it could run faster.

## IN

The IN statement is used in a WHERE clause to choose items from a set. The following WHERE clause chooses zip codes in New England states:

```
WHERE state IN ('VT', 'NH', 'ME', 'MA', 'CT', 'RI')
```

This use is equivalent to the following:

```
WHERE (state = 'VT' OR
       state = 'NH' OR
       state = 'ME' OR
       state = 'MA' OR
       state = 'CT' OR
       state = 'RI')
```

The IN statement is easier to read and easier to modify.

Similarly, the following NOT IN statement would choose zip codes that are not in New England:

```
WHERE state NOT IN ('VT', 'NH', 'ME', 'MA', 'CT', 'RI')
```

This use of the IN statement is simply a convenient shorthand for what would otherwise be complicated WHERE clauses. The next section on subqueries explores another use of IN.

## Subqueries Are Our Friend

Subqueries are exactly what their name implies, queries within queries. They make it possible to do complex data manipulation within a single SQL statement, exactly the types of manipulation needed for data analysis and data mining.

In one sense, subqueries are not needed. All the manipulations could be accomplished by creating intermediate tables, and combining them. The resulting SQL would be a series of CREATE TABLE statements and INSERT statements (or possibly CREATE VIEW), with simpler queries. Although such an approach is sometimes useful, especially when the intermediate tables are used multiple times, it suffers from several problems.

First, instead of thinking about solving a particular problem, the analyst ends up thinking about the data processing, the naming of intermediate tables, determining the types of columns, remembering to remove tables when they are no longer needed, deciding whether to build indexes, and so on. All the additional bookkeeping activity distracts from solving business problems.

Second, SQL optimizers can often find better approaches to running a complicated query than people can. So, writing multiple SQL statements impedes the optimizer from doing its job.

Third, maintaining a complicated chain of queries connected by tables can be quite cumbersome. For instance, adding a new column might require adding new columns in all sorts of places.

Fourth, the read-only SQL queries that predominate in this book can be run with a minimum of permissions for the user — simply the permissions to run queries. Running complicated scripts requires create and modify permissions on at least part of the database. These permissions are dangerous, because an analyst might inadvertently damage the database. Without these permissions, it is impossible to cause such damage.

Subqueries can appear in many different parts of the query, in the SELECT clause, in the FROM clause, and in the WHERE clause. However, this section approaches subqueries by why we want to use them rather than where they appear syntactically.

## Subqueries for Naming Variables

When it comes to naming variables, SQL has a shortcoming. The following is not syntactically correct in most SQL dialects:

```
SELECT population as pop, pop + 1
```

That is, the SELECT statement names columns for the output of the query, but these column names cannot be used in the same clause. Because queries should be at least somewhat understandable to humans, as well as database engines, this is a real shortcoming. Complicated expressions should have names.

Fortunately, subqueries provide a solution. The earlier query that summarized zip codes by population greater than 10,000 and greater than 1,000 could instead use a subquery that is clearer about what is happening:

```
SELECT zc.state,
       SUM(is_pop_10000) as num_10000,
       SUM(is_pop_1000) as num_1000,
       SUM(is_pop_10000*population) as pop_10000,
       SUM(is_pop_1000*population) as pop_1000
FROM (SELECT zc.*,
             (CASE WHEN population > 10000 THEN 1 ELSE 0 END
             ) as is_pop_10000,
             (CASE WHEN population > 1000 THEN 1 ELSE 0 END
             ) as is_pop_1000
      FROM zipcensus zc
     ) zc
GROUP BY zc.state
```

This version of the query uses two indicator variables, IS_POP_10000 and IS_POP_1000. These take on the value of 0 or 1, depending on whether or not the population is greater than 10,000 or 1,000. The query then sums the indicators to get the counts, and sums the product of the indicator and the population to get the population count. Figure 1-9 illustrates this process as a dataflow.

**TIP** Subqueries with indicator variables, such as IS_POP_1000, are a powerful and flexible way to build queries.

The dataflow does not include a "subquery." SQL needs the subquery because the aggregation functions are using the indicator variables.

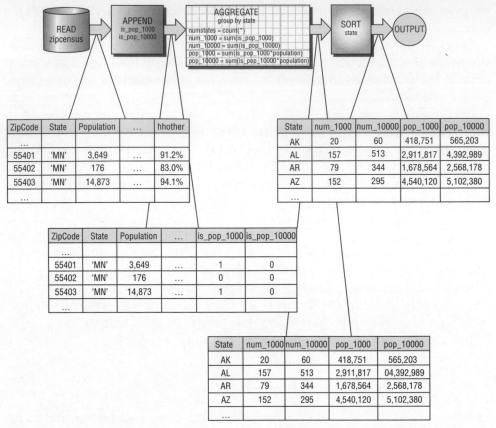

**Figure 1-9:** This dataflow illustrates the process of using indicator variables to obtain information about zip codes.

One advantage of using indicator variables is that they are easy to change. For instance, changing the limit of 1000 to 500 only requires changing the indicator variable, rather than making multiple changes in several places that might (or might not) be consistent.

Indicator variables are only one example of using subqueries to name variables. Throughout the book, there are many other examples. The purpose is to make the queries understandable to humans, relatively easy to modify, and might, with luck, help us remember what a query written six months ago is really doing.

## Subqueries for Handling Summaries

By far the most typical place for a subquery is as a replacement for a table in the FROM clause. After all, the source is a table and a query returns a table, so it makes a lot of sense to combine queries in this way. From the dataflow perspective, this use of subqueries is simply to replace one of the sources with a series of dataflow nodes.

Consider the question: *How many zip codes in each state have a population density greater than the average zip code population density in the state?* The population density is the population divided by the land area, which is in the column LANDAREAMILES.

Addressing this requires thinking about the different data elements needed to answer the question. The comparison is to the average zip code population density within a state. Obtaining the average zip code population density uses a subquery, which calculates the value for all zip codes in the state. The answer combines this information with the original zip code information, as in the following query:

```
SELECT zc.state, COUNT(*) as numzips,
       SUM(CASE WHEN zc.popdensity > zcsum.avgpopdensity
                THEN 1 ELSE 0 END) as numdenser
FROM (SELECT zc.*,
             population / landareamiles as popdensity
      FROM zipcensus zc
     ) zc JOIN
     (SELECT zc.state, AVG(population / landareamiles) as avgpopdensity
      FROM zipcensus zc
      GROUP BY zc.state) zcsum
    ON zc.state = zcsum.state
GROUP BY zc.state
```

The dataflow diagram for this query follows the same logic and is shown in Figure 1-10.

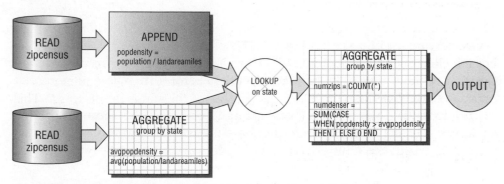

**Figure 1-10:** This dataflow diagram compares the zip code population density to the average zip code population density in a state.

There are a few things to note about this query. First, the population density of each state is not the same as the average of the population density within each zip code. That is, the preceding question is different from: *How many zip codes in each state have a population density greater than its state's population density?* The state's population density would be calculated in zcsum as:

```
SUM(population) / SUM(landareamiles) as statepopdensity
```

There is a relationship between these two densities. The zip code average gives each zip code a weight of 1, no matter how big in area or population. The state average is the weighted average of the zip codes by the land area of the zip codes.

The proportion of zip codes that are denser than the average zip code varies from about 4% of the zip codes in North Dakota to about 35% in Florida. Never are half the zip codes denser than the average. The density where half the zip codes are denser and half less dense is the median density rather than the average or average of averages. Averages, average of averages, and medians are all different.

## Subqueries and IN

The IN and NOT IN operators were introduced earlier as convenient shorthand for complicated WHERE clauses. There is another version where the "in" set is specified by a subquery, rather than by a fixed list. For example, the following query gets the list of all zip codes in states with fewer than 100 zip codes:

```
SELECT zc.*
FROM zipcensus zc
WHERE zc.state IN (SELECT state
                   FROM zipcensus
                   GROUP BY state
                   HAVING COUNT(*) < 100)
```

The subquery creates a set of all states in the Zipcensus table where the number of zip codes in the state is less than 100 (that is, DC, DE, HI, and RI). The HAVING clause sets this limit. HAVING is very similar to WHERE, except it is used for filtering rows after aggregating, rather than before. Then, the outer SELECT chooses zip codes when the state matches one of the states in the IN set. This process actually takes place as a join operation, as shown in Figure 1-11.

### Rewriting the "IN" as a JOIN

Strictly speaking, the IN operator is not necessary, because queries with INs and subqueries can be rewritten as joins. For example, the previous query could instead be written as:

```
SELECT zc.*
FROM zipcensus zc JOIN
     (SELECT state, COUNT(*) as numstates
      FROM zipcensus
      GROUP BY state
```

```
) zipstates
ON zc.state = zipstates.state AND
    zipstates.numstates < 100
```

Note that in the rewritten query, the Zipstates subquery has two columns instead of one. The second column contains the count of zip codes in each state, and could be added to the first SELECT clause. Using the IN statement with a subquery, it is not possible to get this information.

On the other hand, the IN does have a small advantage, because it guarantees that there are no duplicate rows in the output, even when the "in" set has duplicates. To guarantee this using the JOIN, aggregate the subquery by the key used to join the tables. In this case, the subquery is doing aggregation anyway to find the states that have fewer than one hundred zip codes. This aggregation has the additional effect of guaranteeing that there are no duplicate states in the subquery.

### Correlated Subqueries

A correlated subquery occurs when the subquery in the IN clause includes a reference to the outer query. An example shows this best. Consider the following question: *Which zip code in each state has the maximum population and what is the population?*

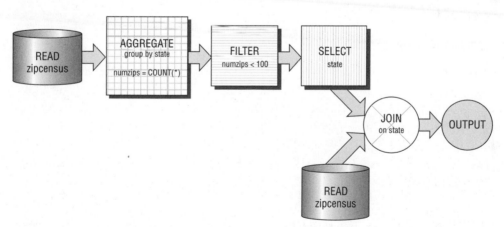

**Figure 1-11:** The processing for an IN with a subquery really uses a join operation.

There are two different ways to approach this problem. The first is to use a correlated subquery. The second is using a standard join, because all correlated subqueries can be rewritten as joins. The correlated subquery looks like:

```
SELECT zc.state, zc.zipcode, zc.population
FROM zipcensus zc
```

```
WHERE zc.population IN (SELECT MAX(zcinner.population)
                        FROM zipcensus zcinner
                        WHERE zcinner.state = zc.state
                        GROUP BY zcinner.state)
ORDER BY zc.state
```

The "correlated" part of the subquery is the WHERE clause, which specifies that the states in the inner table match the states in the outer table. Conceptually, this query reads one row from Zc (the table referenced in the outer query). Then, the subquery finds all rows in Zcinner that match this state and finds the maximum population. If the original row matches this maximum, it is selected. The outer query then moves on to the next row.

Correlated subqueries are generally cumbersome to understand. To make matters perhaps more confusing, the GROUP BY statement is strictly optional. Without the GROUP BY, the aggregation functions are present with no explicit aggregation. Although complicated, correlated subqueries are not a new way of processing the data; they are just another example of joins. The following query does exactly the same thing:

```
SELECT zc.state, zc.zipcode, zc.population
FROM zipcensus zc JOIN
     (SELECT zc.state, MAX(population) as maxpop
      FROM zipcensus zc
      GROUP BY zc.state) zcsum
     ON zc.state = zcsum.state AND
        zc.population = zcsum.maxpop
ORDER BY zc.state
```

This query makes it clear that there is a summary of Zipcensus by STATE and that this summary chooses the maximum population. The JOIN then finds the zip code (or possibly zip codes) that match the maximum population, returning information about them. In addition, this method makes it possible to include another piece of information, the number of zip codes where the maximum population is achieved. This is simply another variable in Zcsum, calculated using COUNT(*).

The examples throughout the book do not use correlated subqueries for SELECT queries, because they are more directly represented using joins, and these joins provide more flexibility for processing and analyzing data. They are, however, occasionally necessary when updating data.

### The NOT IN Operator

The NOT IN operator can also use subqueries and correlated subqueries. Consider answering the following question: *What zip codes in the Orders table are not in the Zipcensus table?* Once again, there are two ways to answer this question.

The second method is preferable (using joins). The first uses the NOT IN operator:

```
SELECT zipcode, COUNT(*)
FROM orders o
WHERE zipcode NOT IN (SELECT zipcode
                      FROM zipcensus zc)
 GROUP BY zipcode
```

This query is straightforward as written, choosing the zip codes in Orders with no matching zip code in Zipcensus, then grouping them and returning the number of purchases in each. One possible concern is performance. Many databases do a poor job of optimizing the NOT IN operator, perhaps because it is seldom used.

Fortunately, there is a readily available alternative, which uses the LEFT OUTER JOIN operator. Because the LEFT OUTER JOIN keeps all zip codes in the Orders table — even those that don't match — a filter afterwards can choose the non-matching set. This is how the following query is expressed:

```
SELECT o.zipcode, COUNT(*) as numorders
FROM orders o LEFT OUTER JOIN
     zipcensus zc
     ON o.zipcode = zc.zipcode
WHERE zc.zipcode IS NULL
GROUP BY o.zipcode
ORDER BY 2 DESC
```

This query joins the two tables using a LEFT OUTER JOIN and only keeps the results where there are no matching rows (because of the WHERE clause). This is equivalent to using NOT IN; however, many database engines optimize this version better than the NOT IN version.

Figure 1-12 shows the dataflow associated with this query. As with the correlated subqueries, the examples in this book use the LEFT OUTER JOIN instead of the NOT IN with a subquery.

## Subqueries for UNION ALL

The UNION ALL operator almost demands subqueries, because it requires that the columns be the same for all tables involved in the union. As a trivial example, consider the following query that returns all the values for latitude and longitude in a single column:

```
SELECT u.longlatval
FROM ((SELECT latitude as longlatval
       FROM zipcensus zc
      )
      UNION ALL
```

```
     (SELECT longitude as longlatval
      FROM zipcensus zc
     )
    ) u
```

This example uses subqueries to be sure that each part of the UNION ALL has the same columns.

## Lessons Learned

This chapter introduces SQL and relational databases from several different perspectives that are important for data mining and data analysis. The focus is exclusively on using databases to extract information from data, rather than on the mechanics of building databases, the myriad of options available in designing them, or the sophisticated algorithms implemented by database engines.

One very important perspective is the data perspective — the tables themselves and the relationships between them. Entity-relationship diagrams are a good way of visualizing the structure of data in the database and the relationships among tables. Along with introducing entity-relationship diagrams, the chapter also explained the various datasets used throughout this book.

Of course, tables and databases store data, but they don't actually do anything. Queries extract information, transforming data into information. The basic processing steps are better explained using dataflow diagrams rather than complex SQL statements. These diagrams show how various operators transform data. About one dozen operators suffice for the rich set of processing available in SQL. Dataflows are not only useful for explaining how SQL processes data; database engines generally use a form of dataflows for running SQL queries.

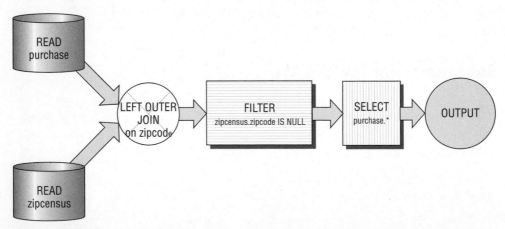

**Figure 1-12:** This dataflow shows the LEFT OUTER JOIN version of a query using NOT IN.

In the end, though, transforming data into information requires SQL queries, whether simple or complex. The focus in this chapter, and throughout the book, is on SQL for querying. This chapter introduced the important functionality of SQL and how it is expressed, with particular emphasis on JOINS, GROUP BYS, and subqueries, because these play an important role in data analysis.

The next chapter starts the path toward using SQL for data analysis by exploring data in a single table.

# What's In a Table? Getting Started with Data Exploration

The previous chapter introduced the SQL language from the perspective of data analysis. This chapter demonstrates the use of SQL for exploring data, the first step in any analysis project. The emphasis shifts from databases in general to data; understanding data — and the underlying customers — is a theme common to this chapter and the rest of the book.

The most common data analysis tool, by far, is the spreadsheet, particularly Microsoft Excel. Spreadsheets show users data in a tabular format. More importantly, spreadsheets give users power over their data, with the ability to add columns and rows, to apply functions, create charts, make pivot tables, and color and highlight and change fonts to get just the right look. This functionality and the what-you-see-is-what-you-get interface make spreadsheets a natural choice for analysis and presentation. Spreadsheets, however, are inherently less powerful than databases because they run on a single user's machine. Even without the historical limits in Excel on the number of rows (a maximum of 65,535 rows) and the number of columns (a maximum of 255 columns), the power of users' local machines limits the performance of spreadsheet applications.

This book assumes a basic understanding of Excel, particularly familiarity with the row-column-worksheet format used for laying out data. There are many examples of using Excel for basic calculations and charting. Because charts are so important for communicating results, the chapter starts by explaining some of the charting tools in Excel, providing tips for creating good charts.

The chapter continues with exploring data in a single table, column by column. Such exploration depends on the types of data in the column, so there are separate sections for numeric columns and categorical columns. Although dates and times are touched upon here, they are so important that Chapter 4 is devoted to them. The chapter ends with a method for automating some descriptive statistics for columns in general. Throughout the chapter, most of the examples use the purchases dataset, which describes retail purchases.

## What Is Data Exploration?

Data is stored in databases as bits and bytes, spread through tables and columns. The data lands there through various business processes. Operational databases capture the data as it is collected from customers — as they make airplane reservations, or complete telephone calls, or click on the web, or as their bills are generated. The databases used for data analysis are usually decision support databases and data warehouses where the data has been restructured and cleansed to conform to some view of the business.

Data exploration is the process of characterizing the data that is actually present in a database and understanding the relationships between various columns and entities. Data exploration is a hands-on effort. Often, data is described through the use of metadata or by documentation that explains what *should* be there. Data exploration is about understanding what is actually there, and, if possible, understanding how and why it got there. Data exploration is about answering questions about the data, such as:

- What are the values in each column?
- What unexpected values are in each column?
- Are there any data format irregularities, such as time stamps missing hours and minutes or names being both upper- and lowercase?
- What relationships are there between columns?
- What are frequencies of values in columns and do these frequencies make sense?

**TIP** Documentation tells us what should be in the data; data exploration finds what is actually there.

Almost anyone who has worked with data has stories about data quality or about discovering something very unexpected inside a database. At one telecommunications company, the billing system maintained customers' telephone numbers as an important field inside the data. Not only was this column stored as character strings rather than numbers, but several thousand telephone numbers actually contained letters intermixed with numbers. Clearly, the column called telephone number was not always a telephone number. And, in fact, after much investigation, it turned out that under some circumstances involving calls billed to third parties, the column could contain values other than telephone numbers.

Even when you are familiar with the data, it is still worthwhile to look at the data to see what is inside it. There are many different approaches for this. The simplest is to just look at rows and sample values in tables. This chapter talks about other methods as well. Seeing values is an important part of the endeavor. Much of this is possible by looking at summary tables. However, using charts is also important, because a good chart can convey much more information than a table of numbers. Before continuing with data exploration, the next section focuses on some important facets of charting in Excel.

## Excel for Charting

Excel's charting capability gives users much control over the visual presentation of data. A good presentation of results, however, is more than just clicking an icon and inserting a chart. Charts need to be accurate and informative, as well as visually elegant and convincing. Edward Tufte's books, starting with *The Visual Display of Quantitative Information*, are classics in how to display and convey information.

This section discusses charting in Excel, including various common chart types and good practices when using them. The discussion is necessarily specific, so some parts explain explicitly, click-by-click, what to do. The section starts with a basic example and then progresses to recommended formatting options. The intention is to motivate good practices by explaining the reasons, not to be a comprehensive resource explaining, click-by-click, what to do in Excel.

### A Basic Chart: Column Charts

The first example, in Figure 2-1, uses a simple aggregation query, the number of orders for each payment type. The chart format used is a column chart, which shows a value for each column. In common language, these are also called bar charts, but in Excel, bar charts have horizontal bars whereas column charts have vertical columns.

The query that pulls the data is:

```
SELECT paymenttype, COUNT(*) as cnt
FROM orders o
GROUP BY paymenttype
ORDER BY 1
```

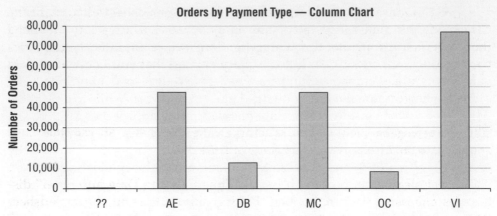

**Figure 2-1:** A basic column chart shows the number of orders for each payment type code.

This chart shows some good practices:

- The chart has a title;
- Appropriate axes have labels (none is needed for the horizontal axis because its meaning is clear from the title);
- Numbers larger than one thousand have commas, because people are going to read the values;
- Gridlines are very light so they do not overpower the data; and,
- Extraneous elements are kept to a minimum. For instance, there is no need for a legend (because there is only one series) and no need for vertical grid lines (because the columns serve the same purpose).

For the most part, charts throughout the book adhere to these conventions, with the exception of the title. Figures in a book have captions making titles unnecessary. This rest of this section explains how to create the chart with these elements.

### Inserting the Data

Creating the chart starts with running the query and copying the data into an Excel spreadsheet. The data is assumed to be generated by a database access tool, which can export data into Excel such as by using cut-and-paste (`<control>-C` and `<control>-V`, if the tool conforms to Windows standards). The basic query produces two columns of data, in the spreadsheet. It is also possible to run SQL directly from Excel; this requires setting various configuration options that are outside the scope of this book.

A good practice is to include the query in the spreadsheet along with the data itself. This makes it possible to remember exactly which query produced the results, something that becomes particularly important as analysis queries become more complex. Including the query ensures that you know what data is actually in the spreadsheet, even when you return to it hours, days, or months after running the query.

**TIP** Keeping the query with the results is always a good idea. So, copy the query into the Excel spreadsheets along with the data.

The technical aside "Common Issues When Copying Data into Excel" discusses some issues that occur when copying data. In the end, the spreadsheet looks something like Figure 2-2. Notice that this data includes the query used to generate the data.

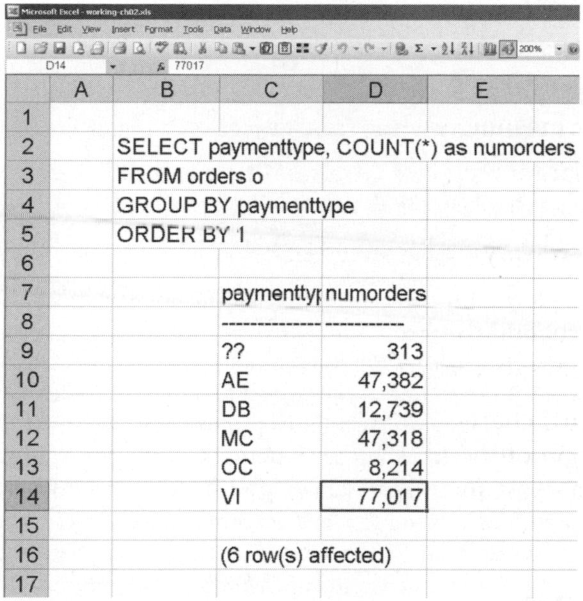

**Figure 2-2:** This spreadsheet contains the column data for payment types and orders.

## Creating the Column Chart

Creating a column chart — or any other type of chart — has just two steps. The first is inserting the chart; the second is customizing it to be clean and informative.

**COMMON ISSUES WHEN COPYING DATA INTO EXCEL**

Each database access tool may have its own peculiarities when copying data into Excel. One method is to export the data as a file and import the file into Excel. When copying the data directly through the clipboard, there are some common issues. The first is the data landing in a single column. The second is a lack of headers in the data. A third issue is the formatting of the columns themselves.

Under some circumstances, Excel places copied data in a single column rather than in multiple columns. This problem, which occurs because Excel recognizes the values as text rather than as columns, is easily solved by converting the text to columns using the following steps:

1. Highlight the inserted data that you want converted to columns. Use either the mouse or keystrokes. For keystrokes, go to the first cell and type `<shift><control><down arrow>`.

2. Bring up the "Text to Columns" wizard. Using the mouse, choose the menu item Data ⇨ Text to Columns. The keystrokes `<alt>-D <alt>-E` do the same thing.

3. Choose the appropriate options. The data may be delimited by tabs or commas, or the data may be fixed format. Buttons at the top of the wizard let you choose the appropriate format.

4. Finish the wizard. Usually the remaining choices are not important.

5. When finished, the data is transformed into columns, filling the columns to the right of the original data.

The second problem is a lack of headers. This occurs, for instance, when using SQL Server and copying the data from the grid. To get the column headers in SQL Server, output the data as text rather than in a grid. The alternative is to manually type in the names of the columns in the spreadsheet.

The third issue is the formatting of columns. Column formats are important; people read cell contents and formats help us understand the values.

By default, large numbers do not have commas. One way to insert commas is to highlight the column and change the format by using the format wizard launched from Format ⇨ Cells. Go to the "Number" tab, choose "Number," set "0" decimal places, and click the "Use 1000 Separator" box. Date fields usually need to have their format changed. For them, go to the "Custom" option and type in the string "yyyy-mm-dd". This sets the date format to a standard format. To set dollar amounts, choose the "Currency" option, with "2" as the decimal places and "$" as the symbol.

The simplest way to create the chart is with the following steps:

1. Highlight the data that goes into the chart. In this case, the query results have two columns and both columns, the payment type code and the count (along with their headers), go into the chart. If there is a non-data line between the header and the data, delete it (or copy the

headers into the cells just above the data). To use keystrokes instead of the mouse to highlight the data, go to the first cell and type `<shift><control><down arrow>`.

2. Bring up the Chart wizard. Using the mouse, choose the menu item Insert ⇨ Chart. The keystrokes `<alt>-I <alt>-H` do the same thing.

3. The default option for the sub-type of column chart is the one we want — the first sub-type under the column chart.

4. Click "Next" and be sure that the "Columns" button is checked rather than rows.

5. Click "Next" and add a title and axis labels. For this example, the title is "Number of Orders by Payment Type," and the Y-axis is "Num Orders."

6. Click "Finish." Further formatting can be done after the chart has been inserted.

7. Resize the chart to an appropriate size, if you like.

A chart, formatted with the default options, now appears in the spreadsheet. This chart can be copied and pasted into other applications, such as Power-Point, Word, and email applications. When pasting the chart into other applications, it can be convenient to paste the chart as a picture rather than as a live Excel chart. To do this, use the File ⇨ Paste Special (`<alt>-E <alt>-S`) menu option and choose the picture option.

## Formatting the Column Chart

The following are the formatting conventions to apply to the column chart:

- Resize the chart in the chart window;
- Format the legend;
- Change the fonts;
- Change chart colors; and,
- Adjust the horizontal scale.

For reference, Figure 2-3 shows the names of various components of a chart, such as the *chart area, plot area, horizontal gridlines, chart title, X-axis label, Y-axis label, X-axis title,* and *Y-axis title.*

### Resize the Chart in the Chart Window

By default, the chart does not take up quite all the space in the chart window. Why waste space? Click the gray area to select the plot area. Then make it bigger, keeping in mind that you usually don't want to cover the chart title and axis labels.

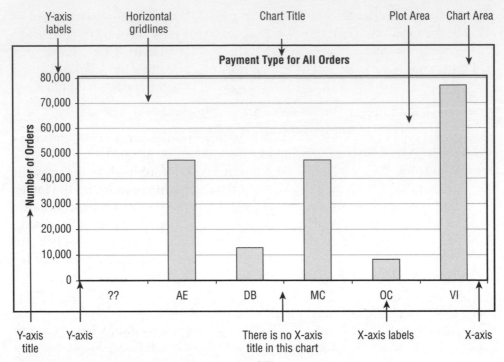

**Figure 2-3:** An Excel chart consists of many different parts.

### Format the Legend

By default, Excel adds a legend, containing the name of each series in the chart. Having a legend is a good thing. By default, though, the legend is placed next to the chart, taking up a lot of real estate and shrinking the plot area. In most cases, it is better to have the legend overlap the plot area. To do this, click the plot area (the actual graphic in the chart window) and expand to fill the chart area. Then, click the legend and move it to the appropriate place, somewhere where it does not cover data values.

When there is only one series, a legend is unnecessary. To remove it, just click the legend box and hit the <delete> key.

### Change the Fonts

The default fonts in the chart are variable sized. So, if the chart is made smaller, the fonts become almost invisible. If the chart is enlarged, the text dominates it.

To change all the fonts in the chart at once, double-click the white area to select options for the entire chart window. On the "Font" tab, deselect "Auto scale" on the lower left. Sizes and choices of fonts are definitely a matter of preference, but 8-point Arial is a reasonable choice.

This change affects all fonts in the window. The chart title should be larger and darker (such as Arial 12-point Bold), and the axis titles a bit larger and darker (such as Arial 10-point Bold). The "Format Chart Title" dialog box makes it possible to change the font. Access the dialog box by double-clicking the text boxes themselves or right-clicking and choosing the format option.

### Change Chart Colors

The default chart colors include a gray background. A white background is often preferable, because it highlights the colors and is more similar to the printed graphic. To change the background color, double-click the gray. In the "Format Plot Area" dialog box, click the little white square on the lower right to set the color. At the same time, eliminate the border on the chart area by changing the border from "Custom" to "None" on the right of the dialog box. To remove the outer border on the entire plot area, double-click the white space around the outside of the chart area and change the border option to "None."

### Adjust the Grid Lines

Grid lines should be visible to make chart values more readable. However, the grid lines are merely sideshows on the chart; they should be faint, so they do not interfere with or dominate the data points. On column charts, only horizontal grid lines are needed; these make it possible to easily match the vertical scale to the data points. On other charts, both horizontal and vertical grid lines are recommended.

By default, Excel includes the horizontal grid lines but not the vertical ones. To choose zero, one, or both sets of grid lines, right-click in the chart area, choose "Chart Options," and go to the "Gridlines" tab. Click the "Major Gridlines" boxes for both the X and Y axes, and then click "OK". The "Minor Gridlines" are rarely needed.

To adjust the color of the grids, double-click the grid lines themselves. The horizontal grid lines are present but not visible when they are the same shade as the background. If this is the case, double-click where they should be to bring up the "Format Gridlines" dialog box. A good choice of colors is the lightest shade of gray, just above the white.

### Adjust the Horizontal Scale

For a column chart, every category should be visible. By default, Excel might only show some of the category names. To change this, double-click the horizontal axis to bring up the "Format Axis" dialog box, and go to the "Scale" tab. Set the second and third numbers, "Number of Categories between tick-mark labels" and "Number of categories between tick-marks" both to 1. This controls the spacing of the marks on the axis and of the labels.

> **TIP** To include text in a chart that is connected to a cell (and whose value changes when the cell value changes), click the whole chart and type "=" and click the cell. A text box appears with the text; this can be formatted and moved however you choose. The same technique works for other text boxes, such as titles; click the title box, type "=", and click the cell.

## Useful Variations on the Column Chart

This simple column chart illustrates many of the basic principles of using charts in Excel. There are some useful variations on the column chart. To illustrate them, a somewhat richer set of data is needed, which is provided by a new query.

### A New Query

A richer set of data provides more information about the payment types, information such as:

- Number of orders with each code;
- Number of orders whose price is in the range $0–$10, $10–$100, $100–$1,000, and over $1,000; and,
- Total revenue for each code.

The following query produces this data:

```
SELECT paymenttype,
       SUM(CASE WHEN 0 <= totalprice AND totalprice < 10
               THEN 1 ELSE 0 END) as cnt_0_10,
       SUM(CASE WHEN 10 <= totalprice AND totalprice < 100
               THEN 1 ELSE 0 END) as cnt_10_100,
       SUM(CASE WHEN 100 <= totalprice AND totalprice < 1000
               THEN 1 ELSE 0 END) as cnt_100_1000,
       SUM(CASE WHEN totalprice >= 1000 THEN 1 ELSE 0 END) as cnt_1000,
       COUNT(*) as cnt, SUM(totalprice) as revenue
FROM orders
GROUP BY paymenttype
ORDER BY 1
```

The data divides the orders into four groups, based on the size of the orders. It is a good set of data for showing different ways to compare values using column charts.

### Side-by-Side Columns

Side-by-side columns, as shown in Figure 2-4, are the first method for comparing order sizes among different payment types. This chart shows the actual value of the number of orders for different groups. Some combinations are so small that the column is not even visible.

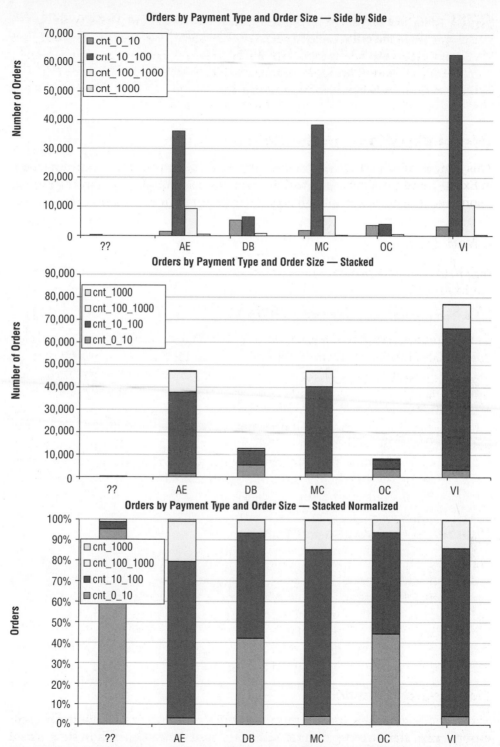

**Figure 2-4:** Three different charts using the same data emphasize different types of information, even though they contain the same raw data.

This chart makes it clear that three payment methods predominate: AE (American Express), MC (MasterCard), and VI (Visa). It also makes it clear that orders in the range of $10 to $100 predominate.

To create such a side-by-side chart, highlight the first five columns of the data, and then follow the chart wizard as described earlier. The side-by-side chart is the default when more than one data column is selected.

### Stacked Columns

The middle figure in Figure 2-4 shows stacked columns. This communicates the total number of orders for each payment type, making it possible to find out, for instance, where the most popular payment mechanisms are. Stacked columns maintain the actual values; however, they do a poor job of communicating proportions, particularly for smaller groups.

To create stacked columns, choose the second option under the column charts, to the right of the basic chart.

### Stacked and Normalized Columns

Stacked and normalized columns provide the ability to see proportions across different groups, as shown in the bottom chart in Figure 2-4. Their drawback is that small numbers — in this case, very rare payment types — have as much weight visually as the more common ones. These outliers can dominate the chart.

One solution is to include payment type codes that have only some minimum number of orders. Filtering the data, using the Data ⇨ Filter ⇨ Autofilter functionality, is one way to do this. Another is by sorting the data in descending order by the total count, and then choosing the top rows to include in the chart.

To create the chart, choose the third "Column Chart" option in the chart wizard. This is on the upper-right side.

### Number of Orders and Revenue

Figure 2-5 shows another variation, where one column has the number of orders, and the other has the total revenue. The number of orders varies up to several tens of thousands. The revenue varies up to several millions of dollars. On a chart with both series, the number of orders would disappear, because the numbers are so much smaller.

The trick is to plot the two series of data using different scales, which means plotting them on different axes: the number of orders on the left and the total revenue on the right. Set the colors of the axes and axis labels to match the colors of the columns.

Using a second axis for column charts creates overlapping columns. To get around this, the number of orders is wide and the revenue is narrow. Also, either chart can be modified to be of a different type, making it possible to create many different effects.

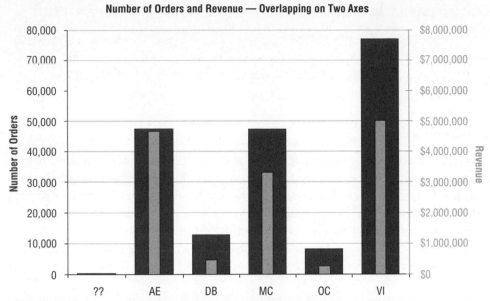

**Figure 2-5:** Showing the number of orders and revenue requires using two axes.

The first step is to include the revenue and number of orders data in the chart. One way to do this is to choose all the columns in the data. After creating the chart, right-click, choose "Source data," and go to the "Series" tab. One by one, remove the series that should not be part of the chart, in this case, all the counts of orders of particular size. An alternative method would be to add each series, one by one.

Second, the revenue series needs to move to the secondary axis. To do this, right-click the revenue columns. Choose "Format data series" and go to the "Axis" tab. There, click the "Secondary axis."

Third, add a title to the secondary axis by right-clicking the chart and choosing "Chart Options." The bottom choice is "Second value (y) axis." After adding the title, change the colors of the two axes to match the series; this makes it possible to eliminate the legend, reducing clutter on the chart.

When creating charts with two Y-axes, the grid lines should align to the tick marks on both axes. This requires some adjustment. In this case, set the scale on the right-hand axis so the maximum is $8,000,000, instead of the default $6,000,000. To do this, double-click the axis, go to the "Scale" tab, and change the "Maximum" value. The grid lines match the scales on both sides.

The final step is to get the effect of the fat and skinny columns. To create the fat column, double-click the number of orders data columns. Then go to the last tab, "Options," and set the "Overlap" to 0 and the "Gap Width" to 50. To get the skinny columns, double-click the revenue data series. Set the "Overlap" to 100 and the "Gap Width" to 400.

## Other Types of Charts

A few other types of charts are used throughout the book. This section is intended as an introduction to these charts. Many of the options are similar to the options for the column charts, so the specific details do not need to be repeated.

### Line Charts

The data in the column charts can all be represented as line charts, such as in Figure 2-6. Line charts are particularly useful when the horizontal axis represents a time dimension, because they naturally show changes over time. Line charts can also be stacked the same way as column charts, as well as normalized and stacked.

Line charts have some interesting variations that are used in later chapters. The simplest is deciding whether the line should have icons showing each point, or simply the line that connects them. This is controlled by choosing the sub-type of chart.

Other capabilities with line charts are the ability to add a trend line and error bars, which are introduced in later chapters as needed.

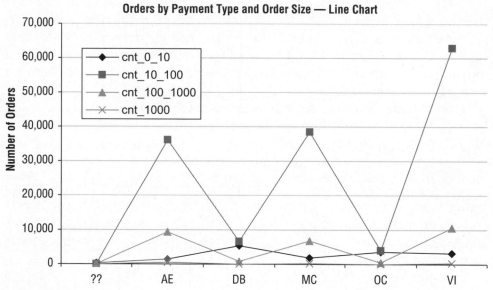

**Figure 2-6:** The line chart is an alternative to a column chart. Line charts can make it easier to spot certain types of trends.

## Area Charts

Area charts show data as a shaded region. They are similar to column charts, but instead of columns, there is only the colored region with no spaces between data points. They should be used sparingly, because they fill the plot area with color that does not convey much information. Their primary use is to convey information on the secondary axis using lighter, background colors.

Figure 2-7 shows the total orders as columns (with no fill on the columns) and the total revenue presented as an area chart on the secondary Y-axis. This chart emphasizes that there are three main payment types, AE, MC, and VI, which are responsible for most orders and most revenue. Notice, though, that AE and MC have about the same number of orders, but AE has much more revenue. This means that the average revenue for customers who pay by American Express is larger than the average revenue for customers who pay by MasterCard.

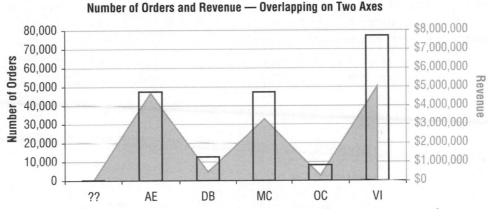

**Figure 2-7:** This example shows the revenue on the secondary axis as an area chart.

To create this chart, follow the same steps as used for Figure 2-5. Click once on the number of orders series to choose it. Then right-click and choose "Chart type." Under chart type, select "Area." The default sub-type is the correct one. To change the colors, double-click the colored area and choose appropriate borders and colors for the region.

To change the column fill to transparent, double-click the number of orders series. Under "Area" on the left, choose the button by "None."

## X-Y Charts (Scatter Plots)

Scatter plots are very powerful and are used for many examples. Figure 2-8 has a simple scatter plot that shows the number of orders and revenue for each payment type. This example has both horizontal and vertical gridlines, which is a good idea for scatter plots.

Unfortunately, in Excel, it is not possible to label the points on the scatter plot with codes or other information. You have to go back to the original data to see what the points refer to. The point above the trend line is for American Express. Orders paid for by American Express have more revenue than the trend line suggests.

In this example, there is an obvious relationship between the two variables — payment types with more orders have more revenue. According to the equation for the trend line, each additional order brings in about $75 additional revenue. To see the relationship, add a trend line (which is discussed in more detail in Chapter 11). Click the series to choose it, then right-click and choose "Add Trendline." On the "Options" tab, you can choose to see the equation by clicking the button next to the "Display equation on Chart." Click "OK" and the trend line appears. It is a good idea to make the trend line a similar color to the original data, but lighter, perhaps using a dashed line. Double-clicking the line brings up a dialog box with these options.

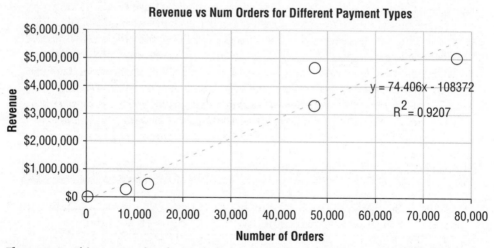

**Figure 2-8:** This scatter plot shows the relationship between the number of orders and revenue for various payment types.

This section has discussed credit card types without any discussion of how to determine the type. The aside "Credit Card Numbers" discusses the relationship between credit card numbers and credit card types.

# What Values Are in the Columns?

The basic charting mechanisms are a good way to see the data, but what do we want to see? The rest of this chapter discusses things of interest when exploring a single table. Although this discussion is in terms of a single table, remember that SQL makes it quite easy to join tables together to make them look like a single table — and the methods apply equally well in this case.

## CREDIT CARD NUMBERS

This section used payment types as the example, skipping how credit card types are extracted from credit card numbers. Credit card numbers have some structure:

- The first six digits are the Bank Identification Number (BIN). These are a special case of Issuer Identification Numbers defined by an international standard called ISO 7812.
- An account number follows, controlled by whoever issues the credit card.
- A checksum is at the end to verify the card number is valid.

Credit card numbers themselves are interesting, but don't use them! Storing credit card numbers, unencrypted in a database, poses privacy and security risks. However, there are two items of interest in the numbers: the credit card type and whether the same credit card is used on different transactions.

Extracting the credit card type, such as Visa, MasterCard, or American Express, from the credit card number is only challenging because the folks who issue the BINs are quite secretive about who issues which number. However, over the years, the most common credit card types have become known (Wikipedia is a good source of information). The BINs for the most common credit card types are in the following table:

| PREFIX | CC TYPE |
| --- | --- |
| 4 | VISA |
| 6011 | DISCOVER |
| 2014, 2149 | enRoute |
| 300–305, 36, 38, 55 | DINERS CLUB |
| 34, 37 | AMEX |
| 35, 2131, 1800 | JCB |
| 51–55 | MASTERCARD |
| 560, 561 | DEBIT |

*Continued on next page*

**CREDIT CARD NUMBERS** *(CONTINUED)*

The length of the prefix varies from 1 number to 4 numbers, which makes it a bit difficult to do a lookup in Excel. The following CASE statement shows how to assign credit card types in SQL:

```
SELECT (CASE WHEN LEFT(ccn, 2) IN ('51', '52', '53', '54', '55')
             THEN 'MASTERCARD'
             WHEN LEFT(ccn, 1) IN ('4') THEN 'VISA'
             WHEN LEFT(ccn, 2) IN ('34', '37') THEN 'AMERICAN EXPRESS'
             WHEN LEFT(ccn, 3) IN ('300', '301', '302', '303', '304',
                                   '305') OR
                  LEFT(ccn, 2) IN ('36', '38', '55')
             THEN 'DINERS CLUB'
             WHEN LEFT(ccn, 4) IN ('6011') THEN 'DISCOVER'
             WHEN LEFT(ccn, 4) IN ('2014', '2149') THEN 'ENROUTE'
             WHEN LEFT(ccn, 2) IN ('35') OR
                  LEFT(ccn, 4) IN ('2131', '1800')
             THEN 'JCB'
             WHEN LEFT(ccn, 3) IN ('560', '561') THEN 'DEBIT'
             ELSE 'OTHER' END) as cctypedesc
```

Recognizing when the same credit card number is used multiple times is both easy and challenging. The simple solution is to store the credit card number in the decision support database. However, this is not a good idea, for security reasons. A better approach is to transform the number into something else that doesn't look like a credit card number. One possibility is to encrypt the number (if your database supports this). Another mechanism is to maintain a lookup table for credit card numbers that does not allow duplicates. The row number in this table is then a good proxy for the credit card number. Using the row number instead makes it possible to identify the same credit card over time, without storing the credit card number explicitly.

The section starts by looking at frequencies of values, using histograms, for both categorical and numeric values. It then continues to discuss interesting measures (statistics) on columns. Finally, it shows how to gather all these statistics in one rather complex query.

## Histograms

A histogram is a basic chart that shows the distribution of values that a column contains. For instance, the following query creates a table with the number of orders in each state and the population of each state, answering the question: *What is the distribution of orders by state and how is this related to the state's population?*

```
SELECT state, SUM(numorders) as numorders, SUM(pop) as pop
FROM ((SELECT o.state, COUNT(*) as numorders, 0 as pop
       FROM orders o
```

```
        GROUP BY o.state
     )
     UNION ALL
     (SELECT state, 0 as numorders, SUM(pop) as pop
      FROM zipcensus
      GROUP BY state)) summary
GROUP BY state
ORDER BY 2 DESC
```

This query combines information from the Zipcensus and Orders tables. The first subquery counts the number of orders and the second calculates the population. These are combined using UNION ALL, to ensure that all states that occur in either database are included in the final result. Alternatively, there could be two queries producing two result tables that are then combined in Excel.

Figure 2-9 shows the results. Notice that in this chart, the population is shown as a lighter shaded area on the secondary axis and the number of orders as a column chart. These are ordered by the number of orders.

The chart shows several things. For instance, California, which has the largest population, is third in number of orders. Perhaps this is an opportunity for more marketing in California. At the very least, it suggests that marketing efforts are focused on the northeast, because New York and New Jersey have larger numbers of orders. This chart also suggests a measure of penetration in the state, the number of orders divided by the population.

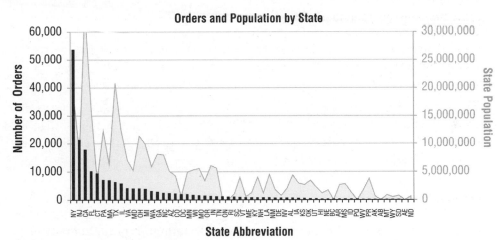

**Figure 2-9:** This example shows the states with the number of orders in columns and the population as an area.

The resulting chart is a bit difficult to read, because there are too many state abbreviations to show on the horizontal axis. In this case, it is possible to expand the horizontal axis and make the font small enough so all the abbreviations fit, just barely. This works for state abbreviations; for other variables it might be impractical, particularly if there are more than a few dozen values.

One way to make the results more intelligible is to place the data into groups. That is, take the states with few orders and collect them together into one "OTHER" category; states with many orders are kept individually. For this purpose, let's say that states with fewer than 100 orders are placed in the "OTHER" category. The following query answers the question: *What is the distribution of orders among states that have 100 or more orders?*

```
SELECT (CASE WHEN cnt >= 100 THEN state ELSE 'OTHER' END) as state,
       SUM(cnt) as cnt
FROM (SELECT o.state, COUNT(*) as cnt
      FROM orders o
      GROUP BY o.state
     ) a
GROUP BY (CASE WHEN cnt >= 100 THEN state ELSE 'OTHER' END)
ORDER BY 2 desc
```

This query puts the data in the same two-column format used previously for making a histogram.

This approach has one drawback, which is the requirement for a fixed value in the query — the "100" in the comparison. One possible modification is to ask a slightly different question: *What is the distribution of orders by state, for states that have more than 2% of the orders?*

```
SELECT (CASE WHEN bystate.cnt >= 0.02*total.cnt
             THEN state ELSE 'OTHER' END) as state,
       SUM(bystate.cnt) as cnt
FROM (SELECT o.state, COUNT(*) as cnt
      FROM orders o
      GROUP BY o.state
     ) bystate CROSS JOIN
     (SELECT COUNT(*) as cnt FROM orders) total
GROUP BY (CASE WHEN bystate.cnt >= 0.02*total.cnt
          THEN state ELSE 'OTHER' END)
ORDER BY 2 desc
```

The first subquery calculates the total orders in each state. The second calculates the total orders. Because the total orders has only one row, the query uses a CROSS JOIN. The aggregation then uses a CASE statement that chooses states that have at least 2% of all orders.

Actually, this query answers the question and goes one step beyond. It does not filter out the states with fewer than 2% of the orders. Instead, it groups them together into the "OTHER" group. This is preferable, because it ensures that no orders are filtered out, which helps prevent mistakes in understanding the data.

**TIP** When writing exploration queries that analyze data, keeping all the data is usually a better approach than filtering rows. In such a case, a special group can be made to keep track of what would have been filtered.

Another alternative is to have some number of states, such as the top 20 states, with everything else placed in the other category, answering the question: *What is the distribution of the number of orders in the 20 states that have the largest number of orders?* Unfortunately, such a query is quite complex. The easiest approach requires a row number calculation, which is non-standard across SQL dialects:

```
SELECT (CASE WHEN rank < 20 THEN state ELSE 'OTHER' END) as state,
       SUM(numorders) as numorders
FROM (SELECT o.state, COUNT(*) as numorders, <rownumber> as rank
      FROM orders o
      GROUP BY o.state
      ORDER BY COUNT(*) DESC
      ) bystate
GROUP BY (CASE WHEN rank < 20 THEN state ELSE 'OTHER' END)
ORDER BY 2 DESC
```

This query could also be accomplished in Microsoft SQL using the TOP option and a subquery with an ORDER BY clause (both of these are SQL extensions):

```
SELECT state, numorders
FROM (SELECT TOP 20 o.state, COUNT(*) as numorders
      FROM orders o
      GROUP BY o.state
      ORDER BY COUNT(*) DESC
      ) bystate
ORDER BY numorders desc
```

In this version, the subquery sorts the data by the number of orders in descending order. The TOP option then chooses the first twenty rows and returns only these. This method does not make it possible to create the "OTHER" category, so the results do not include data for all states.

The following version groups the other states into an "OTHER" category:

```
SELECT (CASE WHEN rank < 20 THEN state ELSE 'OTHER' END) as state,
       SUM(numorders) as numorders
FROM (SELECT bystate.*,
             ROW_NUMBER() OVER (ORDER BY numorders DESC) as rank
      FROM (SELECT o.state, COUNT(*) as numorders
            FROM orders o
            GROUP BY o.state
            ) bystate
      ) a
GROUP BY (CASE WHEN rank < 20 THEN state ELSE 'OTHER' END)
ORDER BY 2 DESC
```

This query uses the ROW_NUMBER() window function to define the ranking. A second layer of subqueries is needed because the window functions cannot be combined with aggregations. The ranking window functions are discussed in more detail in Chapter 8.

An interesting variation on histograms is the cumulative histogram, which makes it possible to determine, for instance, how many states account for half the orders. To create one of these, order the results by the number of orders in descending order (so the biggest states are at the top). Then, in Excel, add a cumulative column.

To do this, let's assume that the number of orders is in column B and the data starts in cell B2. The easiest way to calculate the cumulative total is type the formula "=C1+B2" in cell C2 and then copy this down the column. An alternative formula that does not reference the previous cell is "=SUM($B$2:$B2)." If desired, the cumulative number can be divided by the total orders to get a percentage, as shown in Figure 2-10.

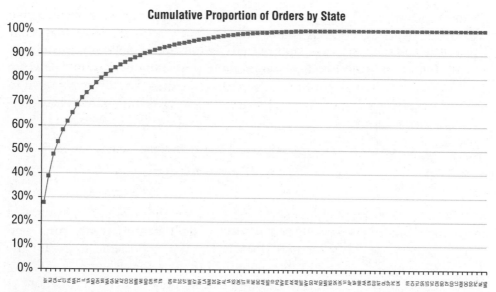

**Figure 2-10:** The cumulative histogram shows that four states account for more than half of all orders.

## Histograms of Counts

The number of states is relatively well-known. We learn that there are fifty states in the United States, although the Post Office recognizes 59 — because places such as Puerto Rico (PR), the District of Columbia (DC), Guam (GM), and the Virgin Islands (VI) are treated as states — plus two more abbreviations for "states" used for military post offices. Corporate databases might have even more, sometimes giving equal treatment to Canadian provinces and

American states, and even intermingling foreign country or province codes with state abbreviations.

Still, there are a relatively small number of states. By contrast, there are thousands of zip codes. More than fit in a single histogram. Where to start with such columns? A good question to ask is the histogram of counts question: *What is the number of zip codes that have a given number of orders?* The following query answers this:

```
SELECT numzips, COUNT(*) as numorders, MIN(zipcode), MAX(zipcode)
FROM (SELECT o.zipcode, COUNT(*) as numzips
      FROM orders o
      GROUP BY o.zipcode
     ) bystate
GROUP BY numzips
ORDER BY 1
```

The subquery calculates the histogram. The outer SELECT counts how often each count occurs in the histogram.

The result set says how many values occur exactly one time, exactly two times, and so on. For instance, in this data, there are 5,954 zip codes that occur exactly once. The query also returns the minimum and maximum values, which provide examples of such zip codes. Because the two examples in the first row are not valid zip codes, some or all of the one-time zip codes seem to be errors in the data. Note that for a primary key, all the values should be unique, so the histogram of counts shows all values as being one-time.

**TIP** The histogram of counts for a primary key always has exactly one row, where CNT is 1.

Another example comes from the Orderline table. The question is: *What is the number of order lines where the product occurs once (overall), twice, and so on?* The query that answers this is quite similar to the preceding query:

```
SELECT numol, COUNT(*) as numprods, MIN(productid), MAX(productid)
FROM (SELECT productid, COUNT(*) as numol
      FROM orderline
      GROUP BY productid
     ) a
GROUP BY numol
ORDER BY 1
```

The subquery counts the number of order lines where each product appears. The outer query then creates a histogram of this number.

This query returns 385 rows; the first few rows and last row are in Table 2-1. The last row of the table has the most common product, whose ID is 12820 and appears in 18,648 order lines. The least common products are in the first row; there are 933 that occur only once — about 23.1% of all products. However, these rare products occur in only 933/286,017 orders, about 0.02% of orders.

**Table 2-1:** Histogram of Counts of Products in Orderlines Table

| NUMBER OF ORDERS | NUMBER OF PRODUCTS | MINIMUM PURCHASEID | MAXIMUM PURCHASEID |
|---|---|---|---|
| 1 | 933 | 10017 | 14040 |
| 2 | 679 | 10028 | 14036 |
| 3 | 401 | 10020 | 14013 |
| 4 | 279 | 10025 | 14021 |
| 5 | 201 | 10045 | 13998 |
| 6 | 132 | 10014 | 13994 |
| 7 | 111 | 10019 | 13982 |
| 8 | 84 | 10011 | 13952 |
| . . . | | | |
| 18,648 | 1 | 12820 | 12820 |

How many different values of PRODUCTID are there? This is the sum of the second column in the table, which is 4,040. How many order lines? This is the sum of the product of the first two columns, which is 286,017. The ratio of these two numbers is the average number of order lines per product, 70.8; that is, a given product occurs in 70.8 order lines, on average. Calculating the number of order lines uses the Excel function SUMPRODUCT(), which takes two columns, multiplies them together cell by cell, and then adds the results together. The specific formula is "=SUMPRODUCT(C13:C397, D13:D397)."

## Cumulative Histograms of Counts

An interesting question is: *What is the proportion of products that account for half of all order lines?* Answering this question requires two cumulative columns, the cumulative number of order lines and the cumulative number of products, as shown in Table 2-2:

This table shows that products with 6 or fewer order lines account for 65.0% of all products. However, they appear in only 2.2% of order lines. We have to go to row 332 (out of 385) to find the middle value. In this row, the product appears in 1,190 order lines and the cumulative proportion of order lines crosses the halfway point. This middle value — called the *median* — shows that 98.7% of all products account for half the order lines, so 1.3% account for the other half. In other words, the common products are much more common than the rare ones. This is an example of the long tail that occurs when working with thousands or millions of products.

**Table 2-2:** Histrogram of Counts of Products in Orde Lines Table with Cumulative Order Lines and Products

| NUMBER | | CUMULATIVE | | CUMULATIVE % | |
| --- | --- | --- | --- | --- | --- |
| ORDER LINES | PRODUCTS | ORDER LINES | PRODUCTS | ORDER LINES | PRODUCTS |
| 1 | 933 | 933 | 933 | 0.3% | 23.1% |
| 2 | 679 | 2,291 | 1,612 | 0.8% | 39.9% |
| 3 | 401 | 3,494 | 2,013 | 1.2% | 49.8% |
| 4 | 279 | 4,610 | 2,292 | 1.6% | 56.7% |
| 5 | 201 | 5,615 | 2,493 | 2.0% | 61.7% |
| 6 | 132 | 6,407 | 2,625 | 2.2% | 65.0% |
| ... | | | | | |
| 1,190 | 1 | 143,664 | 3,987 | 50.2% | 98.7% |
| ... | | | | | |
| 18,648 | 1 | 286,017 | 4,040 | 100.0% | 100.0% |

The cumulative number of products is the sum of all values in NUMPRODS up to a given row. A simple way to calculate this is =SUM($D$284:$D284). When this formula is copied down the column, the first half of the range stays constant (that is, remains $D$284) and the second half increments (becoming $D284 then $D285 and so on). This form of the cumulative sum is preferable to the =H283+D284 form, because cell H283 contains a column title, which is not a number, causing problems in the first sum. (One way around this is to use: =IF(ISNUMBER(H283), H283, 0) + D284.)

The cumulative number of order lines is the sum of the product of the NUMOL and NUMPRODS values (columns C and D) up to that point. The formula is:

```
=SUMPRODUCT($C$284:$C284, $D$284:$D284)
```

The ratios are the value in each cell divided by the last value in the column.

## Histograms (Frequencies) for Numeric Values

Histograms work for numeric values as well as categorical ones. For instance, the NUMUNITS column contains the number of different units of a product included in an order and it takes on just a handful of values. How do we know this? The following query answers the question: *How many different values does NUMUNITS take on?*

```
SELECT COUNT(*) as numol, COUNT(DISTINCT numunits) as numvalues
FROM orderline
```

It only takes on 158 values. On the other hand, the column TOTALPRICE in the same table takes on over 4,000 values, which is a bit cumbersome for a histogram, although the cumulative histogram is still quite useful. A natural way to look at numeric values is by grouping them into ranges. The next section explains several methods for doing this.

### Ranges Based on the Number of Digits, Using Numeric Techniques

Counting the number of important digits — those to the left of the decimal point — is a good way to group numeric values into ranges. For instance, a value such as "123.45" has three digits to the left of the decimal point. For numbers greater than one, the number of digits is one plus the log in base 10 of the number, rounded down to the nearest integer:

```
SELECT FLOOR(1+ LOG(val) / LOG(10)) as numdigits
```

However, not all values are known to be greater than 1. For values between –1 and 1, the number of digits is zero, and for negative values, we might as well identify them with a negative sign. The following expression handles these cases:

```
SELECT (CASE WHEN val >= 1 THEN FLOOR(1+ LOG(val) / LOG(10))
             WHEN -1 < val AND val < 1 THEN 0
             ELSE - FLOOR(1+ LOG(-val) / LOG(10)) END) as numdigits
```

Used in a query for TOTALPRICE in Orders, this turns into:

```
SELECT numdigits, COUNT(*) as numorders, MIN(totalprice), MAX(totalprice)
FROM (SELECT (CASE WHEN totalprice >= 1
                   THEN FLOOR(1+ LOG(totalprice) / LOG(10))
                   WHEN -1 < totalprice AND totalprice < 1 THEN 0
                   ELSE - FLOOR(1+ LOG(-totalprice) / LOG(10)) END
             ) as numdigits, totalprice
      FROM orders
     ) a
GROUP BY numdigits
ORDER BY 1
```

In this case, the number of digits is a small number between 0 and 4, because TOTALPRICE is never negative and always under $10,000.

The following expression turns the number of digits into a lower and upper bounds, assuming that the underlying value is never negative:

```
SELECT SIGN(numdigits)*POWER(10, numdigits-1) as lowerbound,
       POWER(10, numdigits) as upperbound
```

This expression uses the SIGN() function, which returns –1, 0, or 1 depending on whether the argument is less than zero, equal to zero, or greater than zero. A similar expression can be used in Excel. Table 2-3 shows the results from the query.

**Table 2-3:** Ranges of Values for TOTALPRICE in Orders Table

| # DIGITS | LOWER BOUND | UPPER BOUND | # ORDERS | MINIMUM | MAXIMUM |
|---|---|---|---|---|---|
| 0 | $0 | $1 | 9,130 | $0.00 | $0.64 |
| 1 | $1 | $10 | 6,718 | $1.75 | $9.99 |
| 2 | $10 | $100 | 148,121 | $10.00 | $99.99 |
| 3 | $100 | $1,000 | 28,055 | $100.00 | $1,000.00 |
| 4 | $1,000 | $10,000 | 959 | $1,001.25 | $9,848.96 |

## Ranges Based on the Number of Digits, Using String Techniques

There is a small error in the table. The number "1000" is calculated to have three digits rather than four. The discrepancy is due to a rounding error in the calculation. An alternative, more exact method is to use string functions.

This calculates the length of the string representing the number, using only digits to the left of the decimal place. The SQL expression for this is:

```
SELECT LEN(CAST(FLOOR(ABS(val)) as INT))*SIGN(FLOOR(val)) as numdigits
```

This expression uses the non-standard LEN() function and assumes that the integer is converted to a character value. See Appendix A for equivalent statements in other databases.

## More Refined Ranges: First Digit Plus Number of Digits

Table 2-4 shows the breakdown of values of TOTALPRICE in Orders by more refined ranges based on the first digit and the number of digits. Assuming that values are always non-negative (and most numeric values in databases are non-negative), the expression for the upper and lower bound is:

```
SELECT lowerbound, upperbound, COUNT(*) as numorders, MIN(val), MAX(val)
FROM (SELECT FLOOR(val / POWER(10.0, SIGN(numdigits)*(numdigits - 1)))*
             POWER(10.0, SIGN(numdigits)*(numdigits-1)) as lowerbound,
             FLOOR(1+ (val / POWER(10.0, SIGN(numdigits)*(numdigits - 1))))*
             POWER(10.0, SIGN(numdigits)*(numdigits-1)) as upperbound, a.*
      FROM (SELECT (LEN(CAST(FLOOR(ABS(totalprice)) as INT)) *
                   SIGN(FLOOR(totalprice))) as numdigits,
                   totalprice as val
            FROM orders
           ) a
     ) b
GROUP BY lowerbound, upperbound
ORDER BY 1
```

This query uses two subqueries. The innermost calculates NUMDIGITS and the middle calculates LOWERBOUND and UPPERBOUND. In the complicated expressions for the bounds, the SIGN() function is used to handle the case when the number of digits is zero.

**Table 2-4:** Ranges of Values for TOTALPRICE in Orders Table by First Digit and Number of Digits

| LOWER-BOUND | UPPER-BOUND | NUMBER OF ORDERS | MINIMUM TOTALPRICE | MAXIMUM TOTALPRICE |
|---|---|---|---|---|
| $0 | $1 | 9,130 | $0.00 | $0.64 |
| $1 | $2 | 4 | $1.75 | $1.95 |
| $2 | $3 | 344 | $2.00 | $2.95 |
| $3 | $4 | 2 | $3.50 | $3.75 |
| $4 | $5 | 13 | $4.00 | $4.95 |
| $5 | $6 | 152 | $5.00 | $5.97 |
| $6 | $7 | 1,591 | $6.00 | $6.99 |
| $7 | $8 | 2,015 | $7.00 | $7.99 |
| $8 | $9 | 1,002 | $8.00 | $8.99 |
| $9 | $10 | 1,595 | $9.00 | $9.99 |
| $10 | $20 | 54,382 | $10.00 | $19.99 |
| $20 | $30 | 46,434 | $20.00 | $29.99 |
| $30 | $40 | 20,997 | $30.00 | $39.99 |
| $40 | $50 | 9,378 | $40.00 | $49.98 |
| $50 | $60 | 6,366 | $50.00 | $59.99 |
| $60 | $70 | 3,629 | $60.00 | $69.99 |
| $70 | $80 | 2,017 | $70.00 | $79.99 |
| $80 | $90 | 3,257 | $80.00 | $89.99 |
| $90 | $100 | 1,661 | $90.00 | $99.99 |
| $100 | $200 | 16,590 | $100.00 | $199.98 |
| $200 | $300 | 1,272 | $200.00 | $299.97 |
| $300 | $400 | 6,083 | $300.00 | $399.95 |
| $400 | $500 | 1,327 | $400.00 | $499.50 |
| $500 | $600 | 1,012 | $500.00 | $599.95 |

**Table 2-4**   *(continued)*

| LOWER-BOUND | UPPER-BOUND | NUMBER OF ORDERS | MINIMUM TOTALPRICE | MAXIMUM TOTALPRICE |
|---|---|---|---|---|
| $600 | $700 | 670 | $600.00 | $697.66 |
| $700 | $800 | 393 | $700.00 | $799.90 |
| $800 | $900 | 320 | $800.00 | $895.00 |
| $900 | $1,000 | 361 | $900.00 | $999.00 |
| $1,000 | $2,000 | 731 | $1,000.00 | $1,994.00 |
| $2,000 | $3,000 | 155 | $2,000.00 | $2,995.00 |
| $3,000 | $4,000 | 54 | $3,000.00 | $3,960.00 |
| $4,000 | $5,000 | 20 | $4,009.50 | $4,950.00 |
| $5,000 | $6,000 | 10 | $5,044.44 | $5,960.00 |
| $6,000 | $7,000 | 12 | $6,060.00 | $6,920.32 |
| $8,000 | $9,000 | 1 | $8,830.00 | $8,830.00 |
| $9,000 | $10,000 | 3 | $9,137.09 | $9,848.96 |

## Breaking Numerics into Equal-Sized Groups

Equal-sized ranges are perhaps the most useful type of ranges. For instance, the middle value in a list (the median) splits a list of values into two equal-sized groups. Which value is in the middle? Unfortunately, SQL does not provide native support for finding median values.

With a bit of cleverness — and useful SQL extensions — it is possible to find medians in most dialects of SQL. All that is needed is the ability to enumerate rows. If there are nine rows of data and with ranks one through nine, the median value is the value on the fifth row.

Finding quintiles and deciles is the same process as finding the median. Quintiles break numeric ranges into five equal-sized groups; four breakpoints are needed to do this — the first for the first 20% of the rows; the second for the next 20%, and so on. Creating deciles is the same process but with nine breakpoints instead.

The following query provides the framework for finding quintiles, using the ranking window function ROW_NUMBER():

```
SELECT MAX(CASE WHEN rownum <= totalrows * 0.2 THEN <val> END) as break1,
       MAX(CASE WHEN rownum <= totalrows * 0.4 THEN <val> END) as break2,
       MAX(CASE WHEN rownum <= totalrows * 0.6 THEN <val> END) as break3,
```

*(continued)*

```
           MAX(CASE WHEN rownum <= totalrows * 0.8 THEN <val> END) as break4
FROM (SELECT ROW_NUMBER() OVER (ORDER BY <val>) as rownum,
             (SELECT COUNT(*) FROM <table>) as totalrows,
             <val>
      FROM <table>)
```

It works by enumerating the rows in order by the desired column, and comparing the resulting row number with the total number of rows. This technique actually works for any type of columns. For instance, it can break up date ranges into equal-sized groups.

## More Values to Explore — Min, Max, and Mode

Apart from breaking values into ranges, there are other interesting characteristics of columns. This section discusses extreme values and the most common value.

### Minimum and Maximum Values

SQL makes it quite easy to find the minimum and maximum values in a table for any data type. By default, the minimum and maximum values for strings are based on the alphabetic ordering of the values. The query is simply:

```
SELECT MIN(<col>), MAX(<col>)
FROM <tab>
```

A related question is the frequency of maximum and minimum values in a particular column. Answering this question uses a subquery in the SELECT clause of the query. The general form is:

```
SELECT SUM(CASE WHEN <col> = minv THEN 1 ELSE 0 END) as freqminval,
       SUM(CASE WHEN <col> = maxv THEN 1 ELSE 0 END) as freqmaxval
FROM <tab> t CROSS JOIN
     (SELECT MIN(<col>) as minv, MAX(<col>) as maxv
      FROM <tab>) vals
```

This query uses the previous query as a subquery to calculate the minimum and maximum values. Because there is only one row, the CROSS JOIN operator is used for the join. This technique can be extended. For instance, it might be interesting to count the number of values within 10% of the maximum or minimum value for a numeric value. This calculation is as simple as multiplying MAX(<col>) by 0.9 and MIN(<col>) by 1.1 and replacing the "=" with ">=" and "<=" respectively.

## The Most Common Value (Mode)

The most common value is called the *mode*. The mode differs from other measures that we've looked at so far. There is only one maximum, minimum, median, and average. However, there can be many modes. A common, but not particularly interesting, example is the primary key of a table, which is never repeated. The only frequency is one, so all values are the mode.

It is possible to calculate the mode in standard SQL. However, the process is a bit cumbersome, and there are some alternative methods as well. The next three sections show three different approaches to the calculation.

### Calculating Mode Using Standard SQL

Calculating the mode starts with calculating the frequency of values in a column:

```
SELECT <col>, COUNT(*) as freq
FROM <tab>
GROUP BY <col>
ORDER BY 2
```

The mode is the last row (or the first row if the list is sorted in descending order). Unfortunately, there is no way to get the last row in standard SQL.

Instead, let's ask the question: *What column values have the same frequency as the maximum column frequency?*

```
SELECT <col>, COUNT(*) as freq
FROM <tab>
GROUP BY <col>
HAVING COUNT(*) = (SELECT MAX(freq)
                     FROM (SELECT <col>, COUNT(*) as freq
                           FROM <tab> GROUP BY <col>) b)
```

In this query, the HAVING clause is doing almost all the work. It selects the groups (column values) whose frequency is the same as the largest frequency. What is the largest frequency? The innermost subquery calculates all the frequencies, the level above that takes the maximum of these values. And the overall query returns all values whose frequency matches the maximum. The result is a list of the values whose frequencies match the maximum frequency, a list of the modes.

Because there could be more than one, the following variation returns the first mode:

```
SELECT MIN(<col>) as minmode
FROM (SELECT <col>, COUNT(*) as freq
      FROM <tab>
      GROUP BY <col>
      HAVING COUNT(*) = (SELECT MAX(freq)
```

*(continued)*

```
                         FROM (SELECT <col>, COUNT(*) as freq
                               FROM <tab> GROUP BY <col>) b)
     ) a
```

This variation simply uses the previous query as a subquery.

If, instead, we were interested in the values with the smallest frequency, the "MAX(freq)" expression would be changed to "MIN(freq)." Such values could be considered the antimode values.

These queries accomplish the task at hand. However, they are rather complex, with multiple levels of subqueries and two references to the table. It is easy to make mistakes when writing such queries, and complex queries are harder to optimize for performance. The next two sections look at alternatives that produce simpler queries, using SQL extensions.

## Calculating Mode Using SQL Extensions

Different dialects of SQL have extensions that do one of the following:

- Enumerate rows in a subquery; or,
- Return the first row from a subquery.

Microsoft SQL happens to support both.

The following query uses enumeration to find the mode:

```
SELECT *
FROM (SELECT a.*,
             ROW_NUMBER() OVER (ORDER BY cnt DESC) as rownum
      FROM (SELECT <col>, COUNT(*) as freq
            FROM <tab>
            GROUP BY <col>) a
     ) b
WHERE rownum = 1
```

The innermost query produces the list of frequencies for values. The next level adds the row counter. Unfortunately, Microsoft SQL does not allow ROW_NUMBER() in the WHERE clause, which would eliminate the need for one of the subqueries. So, the value is assigned to a column, which is then referenced in the outermost query.

An alternative approach is to return the first row from the frequencies subquery:

```
SELECT TOP 1 <col>, COUNT(*) as freq
FROM <tab>
GROUP BY <col>
ORDER BY COUNT(*) DESC
```

In many ways, this approach is the simplest and clearest about what is happening.

### Calculating Mode Using String Operations

The final method for calculating the mode looks at the problem in a different way. Instead of sorting the list and taking the maximum value, why can't we just request the value of `<col>` where the `<freq>` is maximized? The construct might look like "`SELECT MAX(<col> WHERE <freq> is MAX)`." However, SQL does not support such a statement.

There is a way to accomplish basically the same thing. Figure 2-11 shows the dataflow. The `freq` value is converted into a string representation, padded out with 0s. The `<col>` value is appended onto the string. The max of the result is the maximum frequency, with the associated `<col>` value appended. The SUB-STRING() function extracts the string at the end. Voila, the mode!

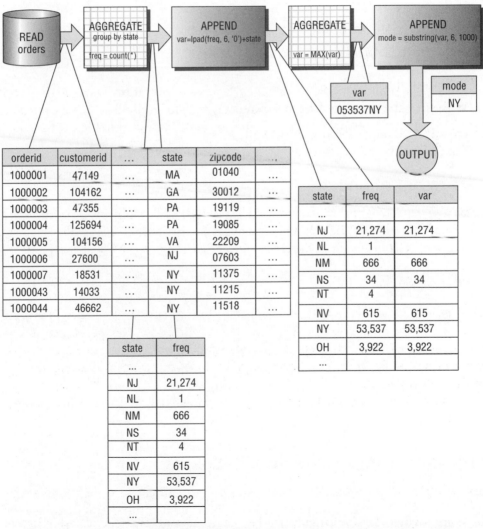

**Figure 2-11:** This dataflow shows how to calculate the mode using string operations.

The following SQL finds the mode of STATE in the Orders table:

```
SELECT SUBSTRING(MAX(RIGHT(REPLICATE('0', 6) + CAST(freq as VARCHAR), 6) +
                     CAST(state as VARCHAR)), 7, 1000)
FROM (SELECT state, COUNT(*) as freq
      FROM orders
      GROUP BY state) a
```

Most of this expression is converting the frequency into a zero-padded 6-digit number. The zero padding is needed because string values are ordered alphabetically for the MAX() function. With alphabetic ordering, "100000" comes before "9." Zero padding fixes this, so "100000" comes after "000009" alphabetically. STATE is then appended to the value, and the result is the maximum frequency with the state at the end. The SUBSTRING() function then extracts the most common value.

# Exploring String Values

String values pose particular challenges for data exploration, because they can take on almost any value. This is particularly true for free-form strings, such as addresses and names, which may not be cleaned. This section looks at exploring the length and characters in strings.

## Histogram of Length

A simple way to get familiar with string values is to do a histogram of the length of the values. The following answers the question: *What is the length of values in the CITY column in the Orders table?*

```
SELECT LEN(city) as length, COUNT(*) as numorders, MIN(city), MAX(city)
FROM orders
GROUP BY LEN(city)
ORDER BY 1
```

The name of the LEN() function may differ among databases.

This query provides not only a histogram of the lengths, but also examples of two values — the minimum and maximum values for each length. For the CITY column, there are lengths from 0 to 20, which is the maximum length the column stores.

## Strings Starting or Ending with Spaces

Spaces at the beginning or end of string values can cause unexpected problems. The value " NY" is not the same as "NY", so a comparison operation or join might fail — even though the values look the same to humans. It depends on the database whether "NY " and "NY" are the same.

The following query answers the question: *How many times do the values in the column have spaces at the beginning or end of the value?*

```
SELECT COUNT(*) as numorders
FROM orders
WHERE city IS NOT NULL AND LEN(city) <> LEN(LTRIM(RTRIM(city)))
```

This query works by stripping spaces from the beginning and end of the column, and then comparing the lengths of the stripped and unstripped values. The datasets provided with this book do not have this problem.

## Handling Upper- and Lowercase

Databases can be either case sensitive or case insensitive. Case sensitive means that upper- and lowercase characters are considered different; case insensitive means they are the same. Don't be confused by case sensitivity in strings versus case sensitivity in syntax. SQL keywords can be in any case ("SELECT," "select," "Select"). This discussion only refers to how values in columns are treated.

For instance, in a case-insensitive database, the following values would all be equal to each other:

- FRED;
- Fred; and,
- fRed.

By default, most databases are case insensitive. However, this can usually be changed by setting a global option or by passing hints to a particular query (such as using the COLLATE keyword in SQL Server).

In a case-sensitive database, the following query answers the question: *How often are the values uppercase, lowercase, or mixed case?*

```
SELECT SUM(CASE WHEN city = UPPER(city) THEN 1 ELSE 0 END) as uppers,
       SUM(CASE WHEN city = LOWER(city) THEN 1 ELSE 0 END) as lowers,
       SUM(CASE WHEN city NOT IN (LOWER(city), UPPER(city))
               THEN 1 ELSE 0 END) as mixed
FROM orders
```

In a case-insensitive database, the first two values are the same and the third is zero. In a case-sensitive database, the three add up to the total number of rows.

## What Characters Are in a String?

Sometimes, it is interesting to know exactly which characters are in strings. For instance, do email addresses provided by customers contain characters that they shouldn't? Such a question naturally leads to which characters are actually in the values. SQL is not designed to answer this question, at least in a simple way. Fortunately, it is still possible to make an attempt. The answer starts with a simpler question, answered by the following query: *What characters are in the first position of the string?*

```
SELECT SUBSTRING(city, 1, 1) as onechar,
       ASCII(SUBSTRING(city, 1, 1)) as asciival,
       COUNT(*) as numorders
FROM orders
GROUP BY SUBSTRING(city, 1, 1)
ORDER BY 1
```

The returned data has three columns: the character, the number that represents the character (called the ASCII value), and the number of times that the character occurs as the first character in the CITY column. The ASCII value is useful for distinguishing among characters that might look the same, such as a space and a tab.

**TIP** When looking at individual characters, unprintable characters and space characters (space and tabs) look the same. To see what character is really there, use the `ASCII()` function.

The following query extends this example to look at the first two characters in the CITY column:

```
SELECT onechar, ASCII(onechar) as asciival, COUNT(*) as cnt
FROM ((SELECT SUBSTRING(city, 1, 1) as onechar
       FROM orders WHERE LEN(city) >= 1)
      UNION ALL
      (SELECT SUBSTRING(city, 2, 1) as onechar
       FROM orders WHERE LEN(city) >= 2)
     ) a
GROUP BY onechar
ORDER BY 1
```

This query combines all the first characters and all the second characters together, using UNION ALL in the subquery. It then groups this collection of characters together, returning the final result. Extending this query to all twenty characters in the city is a simple matter of adding more clauses to the UNION ALL subquery.

There is a variation of this query, which might be more efficient under some circumstances. This variation pre-aggregates each of the subqueries. Rather than just putting all the characters together and then aggregating, it calculates the frequencies for the first position and then the second position, and then combines the results:

```
SELECT onechar, ASCII(onechar) as asciival, SUM(cnt) as cnt
FROM ((SELECT SUBSTRING(city, 1, 1) as onechar, COUNT(*) as cnt
       FROM orders WHERE LEN(city) >= 1
```

```
            GROUP BY SUBSTRING(city, 1, 1) )
        UNION ALL
        (SELECT SUBSTRING(city, 2, 1) as onechar, COUNT(*) as cnt
         FROM orders WHERE LEN(city) >= 2
         GROUP BY SUBSTRING(city, 2, 1) )
     ) a
GROUP BY onechar
ORDER BY 1
```

The choice between the two forms is a matter of convenience and efficiency, both in writing the query and in running it.

What if the original question were: *How often does a character occur in the first position versus the second position of a string?* This is quite similar to the original question, and the answer is to modify the original query with information about the position of the string:

```
SELECT onechar, ASCII(onechar) as asciival, COUNT(*) as cnt,
        SUM(CASE WHEN pos = 1 THEN 1 ELSE 0 END) as pos_1,
        SUM(CASE WHEN pos = 2 THEN 1 ELSE 0 END) as pos_2
FROM ((SELECT SUBSTRING(city, 1, 1) as onechar, 1 as pos
        FROM orders WHERE LEN(city) >= 1 )
      UNION ALL
      (SELECT SUBSTRING(city, 2, 1) as onechar, 2 as pos
       FROM orders WHERE LEN(city) >= 2)
     ) a
GROUP BY onechar
ORDER BY 1
```

This variation also works using the pre-aggregated subqueries.

# Exploring Values in Two Columns

Comparing values in more than one column is an important part of data exploration and data analysis. There are two components to this. This section focuses on the first component, describing the comparison. Do two states differ by sales? Do customers who purchase more often have larger average purchases? The second component is whether the comparison is statistically significant, a topic covered in the next chapter.

## What Are Average Sales By State?

The following two questions are good examples of comparing a numeric value within a categorical value:

- What is the average order totalprice by state?
- What is the average zip code population in a state?

SQL is particularly adept at answering questions such as these, using aggregations.

The following query provides the average sales by state:

```
SELECT state, AVG(totalprice) as avgtotalprice
FROM orders
GROUP BY state
ORDER BY 2 DESC
```

This example uses the aggregation function AVG() to calculate the average. The following expression could also have been used:

```
SELECT state, SUM(totalprice)/COUNT(*) as avgtotalprice
```

Although the two methods seem to do the same thing, there is a subtle difference between them, because they handle NULL values differently. In the first example, NULL values are ignored. In the second, NULL values contribute to the COUNT(*), but not to the SUM(). The expression COUNT(totalprice) fixes this, by returning the number of values that are not NULL.

**WARNING** Two ways of calculating an average look similar and often return the same result. However, AVG(<col>) and SUM(<col>)/COUNT(*) treat NULL values differently.

## How Often Are Products Repeated within a Single Order?

A reasonable assumption is that when a given product occurs multiple times in an order, there is only one order line for that product; the multiple instances are represented by the column NUMUNITS rather than by separate rows in Orderlines. It is always worthwhile to validate such assumptions. There are several different approaches.

### Direct Counting Approach

The first approach directly answers the question: *How many different order lines within an order contain the same product?* This is a simple counting query, using two different columns instead of one:

```
SELECT cnt, COUNT(*) as numorders, MIN(orderid), MAX(orderid)
FROM (SELECT orderid, productid, COUNT(*) as cnt
      FROM orderline ol
      GROUP BY orderid, productid
     ) a
GROUP BY cnt
ORDER BY 1
```

Here, CNT is the number of times that a given ORDERID and PRODUCTID appear in the Orderline table.

The results show that some products are repeated within the same order, up to a maximum of forty times. This leads to more questions. What are some examples of orders where duplicate products occur? For this, the minimum and maximum ORDERID provide examples. Another question might be: *Which products are more likely to occur multiple times within an order?*

A result table with the following information would help in answering this question:

- PRODUCTID, to identify the product;
- Number of orders containing the product any number of times; and,
- Number of orders containing the product more than once.

These second and third columns compare the occurrence of the given product overall with the multiple occurrence of the product within an order.

The following query calculates these columns:

```
SELECT productid, COUNT(*) as numorders,
       SUM(CASE WHEN cnt > 1 THEN 1 ELSE 0 END) as nummultiorders
FROM (SELECT orderid, productid, COUNT(*) as cnt
      FROM orderline ol
      GROUP BY orderid, productid
     ) a
GROUP BY productid
ORDER BY 2 desc
```

The results (which have thousands of rows) indicate that some products are, indeed, more likely to occur multiple times within an order than other products. However, many products occur multiple times, so the problem is not caused by one or a handful of products.

## Comparison of Distinct Counts to Overall Counts

Another approach to answering the question *"How often are products repeated in an order?"* is to consider the number of order lines in an order compared to the number of different products in the same order. That is, calculate two values for each order — the number of order lines and the number of distinct product IDs; these numbers are the same when order lines within an order all have different products.

One way of doing the calculation is using the COUNT(DISTINCT) function. The following query returns orders that have more order lines than products:

```
SELECT orderid, COUNT(*) as numlines,
       COUNT(DISTINCT productid) as numproducts
FROM orderline
```

```
GROUP BY orderid
HAVING COUNT(*) > COUNT(DISTINCT productid)
```

The `HAVING` clause chooses only orders that have at least one product on multiple order lines.

Another approach to use a subquery:

```
SELECT orderid, SUM(numproductlines) as numlines,
       COUNT(*) as numproducts
FROM (SELECT orderid, productid, COUNT(*) as numproductlines
      FROM orderline
      GROUP BY orderid, productid) op
GROUP BY orderid
HAVING SUM(numproductlines) > COUNT(*)
```

The subquery aggregates the order lines by ORDERID and PRODUCTID. This makes it possible to count both the number of products and the number of order lines. In general, a query using `COUNT(DISTINCT)` (or the much less frequently used `AVG(DISTINCT)` and `SUM(DISTINCT)`) can also be rewritten to use a subquery.

This results show that there are 4,878 orders that have more order lines than products, indicating that at least one product occurs on multiple lines in the order. However, the query does not give an idea of what might be causing this.

The following query calculates the number of orders that have more than one product broken out by the number of lines in the order:

```
SELECT numlines, COUNT(*) as numorders,
       SUM(CASE WHEN numproducts < numlines THEN 1 ELSE 0 END
           ) as nummultiorders,
       AVG(CASE WHEN numproducts < numlines THEN 1.0 ELSE 0 END
           ) as ratiomultiorders,
       MIN(orderid), MAX(orderid)
FROM (SELECT orderid, COUNT(*) as numproducts,
             SUM(numproductlines) as numlines
      FROM (SELECT orderid, productid, COUNT(*) as numproductlines
            FROM orderline
            GROUP BY orderid, productid) a
      GROUP BY orderid
     ) op
GROUP BY numlines
ORDER BY 1
```

This query uses the subquery approach to calculate the number of products and order lines within a query.

Table 2-5 shows the first few rows of the results. The proportion of multi-orders increases as the size of the order increases. However, for all order sizes, many orders still have distinct products. Based on this information, it seems that having multiple lines for a single product is a function of having larger orders, rather than being related to the particular products in the order.

**Table 2-5:** Number of Products Per Order by Number of Lines in Order (First Ten Rows)

| LINES IN ORDER | NUMBER OF ORDERS | ORDERS WITH MORE LINES THAN PRODUCTS | |
| --- | --- | --- | --- |
| | | NUMBER | % |
| 1 | 139,561 | 0 | 0.0% |
| 2 | 32,758 | 977 | 3.0% |
| 3 | 12,794 | 1,407 | 11.0% |
| 4 | 3,888 | 894 | 23.0% |
| 5 | 1,735 | 532 | 30.7% |
| 6 | 963 | 395 | 41.0% |
| 7 | 477 | 223 | 46.8% |
| 8 | 266 | 124 | 46.6% |
| 9 | 175 | 93 | 53.1% |
| 10 | 110 | 65 | 59.1% |

## Which State Has the Most American Express Users?

Overall, about 24.6% of the orders are paid by American Express (payment type AE). *Does this proportion vary much by state?* The following query answers this question:

```
SELECT state, COUNT(*) as numorders,
       SUM(CASE WHEN paymenttype = 'AE' THEN 1 ELSE 0 END) as numae,
       AVG(CASE WHEN paymenttype = 'AE' THEN 1.0 ELSE 0 END) as avgae
FROM orders
GROUP BY state
HAVING COUNT(*) >= 100
ORDER BY 4 DESC
```

This query calculates the number and percentage of orders paid by American Express, and then returns them with the highest proportion at the top. Notice that the query only chooses states that have at least 100 orders, in order to eliminate specious state codes. Table 2-6 shows the top ten states by this proportion.

**Table 2-6:** Percent of American Express Payment for Top Ten States with Greater Than 100 Orders

| STATE | # ORDERS | # AE | % AE |
| --- | --- | --- | --- |
| GA | 2,865 | 1,141 | 39.8% |
| PR | 168 | 61 | 36.3% |
| LA | 733 | 233 | 31.8% |
| FL | 10,185 | 3,178 | 31.2% |
| NY | 53,537 | 16,331 | 30.5% |
| DC | 1,969 | 586 | 29.8% |
| NJ | 21,274 | 6,321 | 29.7% |
| MS | 215 | 63 | 29.3% |
| MT | 111 | 29 | 26.1% |
| UT | 361 | 94 | 26.0% |

# From Summarizing One Column to Summarizing All Columns

So far, the exploratory data analysis has focused on different aspects of summarizing values in a single column. This section combines the various results into a single summary for a column. It then extends this summary from a single column to all columns in a table. In the process, we use SQL (or alternatively Excel) to generate a SQL query, which we then run to get the summaries.

## Good Summary for One Column

For exploring data, the following information is a good summary for a single column:

- The number of distinct values in the column;
- Minimum and maximum values;
- An example of the most common value (called the *mode* in statistics);
- An example of the least common value (called the *antimode*);
- Frequency of the minimum and maximum values;
- Frequency of the mode and antimode;

- Number of values that occur only one time;
- Number of modes (because the most common value is not necessarily unique); and,
- Number of antimodes.

These summary statistics are defined for all data types. Additional information might be of interest for other data types, such as the minimum and maximum length of strings, the average value of a numeric, and the number of times when a date has no time component.

The following query calculates these values for STATE in Orders:

```
SELECT COUNT(*) as numvalues,
       MAX(freqnull) as freqnull,
       MIN(minval) as minval,
       SUM(CASE WHEN state = minval THEN freq ELSE 0 END) as numminvals,
       MAX(maxval) as maxval,
       SUM(CASE WHEN state = maxval THEN freq ELSE 0 END) as nummaxvals,
       MIN(CASE WHEN freq = maxfreq THEN state END) as mode,
       SUM(CASE WHEN freq = maxfreq THEN 1 ELSE 0 END) as nummodes,
       MAX(maxfreq) as modefreq,
       MIN(CASE WHEN freq = minfreq THEN state END) as antimode,
       SUM(CASE WHEN freq = minfreq THEN 1 ELSE 0 END) as numantimodes,
       MAX(minfreq) as antimodefreq,
       SUM(CASE WHEN freq = 1 THEN freq ELSE 0 END) as numuniques
FROM (SELECT state, COUNT(*) as freq
      FROM orders
      GROUP BY state) osum CROSS JOIN
     (SELECT MIN(freq) as minfreq, MAX(freq) as maxfreq,
             MIN(state) as minval, MAX(state) as maxval,
             SUM(CASE WHEN state IS NULL THEN freq ELSE 0 END) as freqnull
      FROM (SELECT state, COUNT(*) as freq
            FROM orders
            GROUP BY state) osum) summary
```

This query follows a simple logic. There are two subqueries. The first summarizes the STATE column, calculating the frequency for it. The second summarizes the summary, producing values for:

- Minimum and maximum frequency;
- Minimum and maximum values; and
- Number of NULL values.

The results combine these two queries, making judicious use of the CASE statement.

The results for STATE are as follows:

- Number of values:              92
- Minimum value:                 ""

- Maximum value:              YU
- Mode:                       NY
- Antimode:                   BD
- Frequency of Nulls:          0
- Frequency of Min:        1,119
- Frequency of Max:            2
- Frequency of Mode:      53,537
- Frequency of Antimode:       1
- Number of Unique Values:    14
- Number of Modes:             1
- Number of Antimodes:        14

As mentioned earlier, this summary works for all data types. So, the same query using the TOTALPRICE column results in the following information:

- Number of values:        7,653
- Minimum value:           $0.00
- Maximum value:       $9,848.96
- Mode:                    $0.00
- Antimode:                $0.20
- Frequency of Nulls:          0
- Frequency of Min:        9,128
- Frequency of Max:            1
- Frequency of Mode:       9,128
- Frequency of Antimode:       1
- Number of Unique Values:  4,115
- Number of Modes:             1
- Number of Antimodes:     4,115

The most common value of TOTALPRICE is $0. One reason for this is that all other values have both dollars and cents in their values. The proportion of orders with $0 value is small. This suggests doing the same analysis but using only the dollar amount of TOTALPRICE. This is accomplished by replacing the table name with a subquery such as "(SELECT FLOOR(totalprice) as dollars FROM orders)".

The next two sections approach the question of how to generate this information for all columns in a table. The strategy is to query the database for all columns in a table and then use SQL or Excel to write the query.

## Query to Get All Columns in a Table

SQL does not have a standard mechanism for returning the names of all the columns in a table. However, databases are quite good at storing information. So, most databases store information about their columns and tables in special system tables. For instance, the following query returns the table name and column names of all the columns in the Orders table, using a syntax common to Microsoft SQL and mysql:

```
SELECT table_schema+'.'+table_name as table_name, column_name,
       ordinal_position
FROM information_schema.columns
WHERE table_name = 'orders'
```

See the Appendix for mechanisms in other databases.

The results are in Table 2-7, which is simply the table name and list of columns in the table. The information_schema.columns table also contains information that we are not using, such as whether the column allows NULL values and the type of the column.

**Table 2-7:** Column Names in Orders

| TABLE_NAME | COLUMN_NAME | ORDINAL_POSITION |
| --- | --- | --- |
| Orders | ORDERID | 1 |
| Orders | CUSTOMERID | 2 |
| Orders | CAMPAIGNID | 3 |
| Orders | ORDERDATE | 4 |
| Orders | CITY | 5 |
| Orders | STATE | 6 |
| Orders | ZIPCODE | 7 |
| Orders | PAYMENTTYPE | 8 |
| Orders | TOTALPRICE | 9 |
| Orders | NUMORDERLINES | 10 |
| Orders | NUMUNITS | 11 |

## Using SQL to Generate Summary Code

The goal is to summarize all the columns in a table, using an information summary subquery for each column. Such a query has the following pattern for Orders:

```
(INFORMATION SUBQUERY for orderid)
UNION ALL (INFORMATION SUBQUERY for customerid)
UNION ALL (INFROMATION SUBQUERY for campaignid)
UNION ALL (INFROMATION SUBQUERY for orderdate)
UNION ALL (INFROMATION SUBQUERY for city)
UNION ALL (INFROMATION SUBQUERY for state)
UNION ALL (INFROMATION SUBQUERY for zipcode)
UNION ALL (INFROMATION SUBQUERY for paymenttype)
UNION ALL (INFORMATION SUBQUERY for totalprice)
UNION ALL (INFORMATION SUBQUERY for numorderlines)
UNION ALL (INFORMATION SUBQUERY for numunits)
```

The information subquery is similar to the earlier version, with the mode and antimode values removed (just to simplify the query for explanation).

There are three other modifications to the query. The first is to include a placeholder called <start> at the beginning. The second is to include the column name and the third is to convert the minimum and maximum values to strings, because all values in a given column need to be of the same type for the UNION ALL. The resulting query has the general form:

```
<start> SELECT '<col>' as colname, COUNT(*) as numvalues,
       MAX(freqnull) as freqnull,
       CAST(MIN(minval) as VARCHAR) as minval,
       SUM(CASE WHEN <col> = minval THEN freq ELSE 0 END) as numminvals,
       CAST(MAX(maxval) as VARCHAR) as maxval,
       SUM(CASE WHEN <col> = maxval THEN freq ELSE 0 END) as nummaxvals,
       SUM(CASE WHEN freq = 1 THEN freq ELSE 0 END) as numuniques
FROM (SELECT totalprice, COUNT(*) as freq
      FROM <tab>
      GROUP BY <col>) osum CROSS JOIN
     (SELECT MIN(<col>) as minval, MAX(<col>) as maxval,
            SUM(CASE WHEN <col> IS NULL THEN 1 ELSE 0 END) as freqnull
      FROM (SELECT <col>
            FROM <tab>) osum) summary
```

The preceding query has been placed in a single line for generality, because some databases support strings that span multiple lines, and some do not. The resulting query is rather ugly:

```
SELECT REPLACE(REPLACE(REPLACE('<start> SELECT ''<col>'' as colname,
COUNT(*) as numvalues, MAX(freqnull) as freqnull, CAST(MIN(minval) as
VARCHAR) as minval, SUM(CASE WHEN <col> = minval THEN freq ELSE 0 END)
as numminvals, CAST(MAX(maxval) as VARCHAR) as maxval, SUM(CASE WHEN
```

```
<col> = maxval THEN freq ELSE 0 END) as nummaxvals, SUM(CASE WHEN freq =
1 THEN 1 ELSE 0 END) as numuniques FROM (SELECT <col>, COUNT(*) as freq
FROM <tab> GROUP BY <col>) osum CROSS JOIN (SELECT MIN(<col>) as minval,
MAX(<col>) as maxval, SUM(CASE WHEN <col> IS NULL THEN 1 ELSE 0 END) as
freqnull FROM (SELECT <col> FROM <tab>) osum) summary',
                          '<col>', column_name),
                '<tab>', table_name),
          '<start>',
            (CASE WHEN ordinal_position = 1 THEN ''
                ELSE 'UNION ALL' END))
FROM (SELECT table_name, column_name, ordinal_position
     FROM information_schema.columns
     WHERE table_name = 'orders') a
```

This query replaces three placeholders in the query string with appropriate values. The "<col>" string gets replaced with the column name, which comes from the information_schema.columns table. The "<tab>" string gets replaced with the table name. And, the "<starting>" string gets "UNION ALL" for all but the first row.

Table 2-8 shows the results from running the resulting query. This logic can also be accomplished in Excel, by copying the template query and using Excel's SUBSTITUTE() function.

**Table 2-8:** Information about the Columns in Orders Table

| COLNAME | # VALUES | # NULL | # MINIMUM VALUE | # MAXIMUM VALUE | # UNIQUE |
|---|---|---|---|---|---|
| orderid | 192,983 | 0 | 1 | 1 | 192,983 |
| customerid | 189,560 | 0 | 3,424 | 1 | 189,559 |
| campaignid | 239 | 0 | 5 | 4 | 24 |
| orderdate | 2,541 | 0 | 181 | 2 | 0 |
| city | 12,825 | 0 | 17 | 5 | 6,318 |
| state | 92 | 0 | 1,119 | 2 | 14 |
| zipcode | 15,579 | 0 | 144 | 1 | 5,954 |
| paymenttype | 6 | 0 | 313 | 77,017 | 0 |
| totalprice | 7,653 | 0 | 9,128 | 1 | 4,115 |
| numorderlines | 41 | 0 | 139,561 | 1 | 14 |
| numunits | 142 | 0 | 127,914 | 1 | 55 |

## Lessons Learned

Databases are well suited to data exploration because databases are close to the data. In fact, because they are inherently parallel — that is, they can take advantage of multiple processors and multiple disks — a database is often the best choice in terms of performance as well. Excel charting is a powerful companion, because it is familiar to end users and charts are a powerful way to communicate results. This chapter introduces several types of charts including column charts, line charts, and scatter plots.

Data exploration starts by investigating the values that are stored in various columns in the data. Histograms are a good way to see distributions of values in particular columns, although numeric values often need to be grouped to see their distributions. There are various ways of grouping numeric values into ranges, including "tiling" — creating equal-sized groups such as quintiles and deciles.

Various other things are of interest in columns. The most common value is called the mode, and there are several ways to calculate the mode using SQL. The standard mechanism is a bit cumbersome and often performs inefficiently. The alternatives are easier to understand, but require SQL extensions.

Ultimately, though, it is more efficient to investigate all columns at once rather than each column one at a time. The chapter ends with a mechanism for creating a single query to summarize all columns at the same time. This method uses SQL to create a complex query, which is then run to get summaries for all the columns in a table.

The next chapter moves from just looking at the data to determining whether patterns in the data are statistically significant.

# How Different Is Different?

The previous two chapters show how to do various calculations and visualizations using SQL and Excel. This chapter moves from calculating results to understanding the significance of the resulting measurements. When are two values so close that they are essentially the same? When are two values far enough apart that we are confident in their being different?

The study of measurements and how to interpret them falls under the applied science of statistics. Although theoretical aspects of statistics can be daunting, the focus here is on applying the results, using tools borrowed from statistics to learn about customers through data. As long as we follow common sense and a few rules, the results can be applied without diving into theoretical mathematics or arcane jargon.

The word "statistics" itself is often misunderstood. It is the plural of "statistic," and a statistic is just a measurement, such as the averages, medians, and modes calculated in the previous chapter. A big challenge in statistics is generalizing from results on a small group to a larger group. For instance, when a poll reports that 50% of likely voters support a particular political candidate, the pollsters typically also report a margin of error, such as 2.5%. This margin of error, called the *sampling margin of error*, means that the poll asked a certain number of people (the sample) a question and the goal is to generalize the results from the sample to the entire population. If another candidate has 48% support, then the two candidates are within the margin of error, and the poll does not show definitive support for either one.

In business, the preferences or behaviors of one group of customers might be similar to or different from another group; the measures are calculated from databases rather than from samples. Of course, any calculation on any two groups of customers is going to be different, if only in the fifth or sixth decimal place. But does the difference matter? Do the measurements suggest that the groups are equivalent? Or do the measurements provide evidence that the groups differ? These are the types of questions that statistics can help answer.

This chapter introduces the statistics used for addressing the question "how different is different," with an emphasis on the application of the ideas rather than their theoretical derivation. Throughout, examples use Excel and SQL to illustrate the concepts. The chapter starts with a discussion of key statistical concepts, such as confidence and the normal distribution, and how these are applied to the most common statistic of all, the average value.

Two other statistical techniques are also introduced. One is the difference of proportions, which is often used for comparing the response rates between groups of customers. The other is the chi-square test, which is also used to compare results among different groups of customers and determine whether the groups are essentially the same or fundamentally different. Throughout the chapter there are simple examples with small amounts of data to illustrate the ideas. There are also larger examples using the purchase and subscriptions databases to illustrate how to apply the ideas on real datasets stored in databases.

## Basic Statistical Concepts

Over the past two centuries, statistics has delved into the mathematics of understanding measurements and their interpretation. Although the theoretical aspects of the subject are beyond the range of this book, there are some basic concepts that are very useful for our analyses. In fact, not using the foundation of statistics would be negligent, because so many brilliant minds have already answered questions quite similar to the ones being asked. Of course, the great minds of statistics who were developing these techniques a century ago did not have access to modern computing and data access, much less to the vast volumes of data available today. Many of their methods, however, have withstood the test of time.

This section discusses the some important concepts in statistics, in the spirit of introducing useful ideas and terminology. These concepts are:

- The Null Hypothesis;
- Confidence (versus probability); and,
- Normal Distribution.

The later sections in this chapter build on these ideas, applying the results to real-world data.

## The Null Hypothesis

Statisticians are naturally skeptical, and that is a good thing. When looking at data, their default assumption is that nothing out-of-the-ordinary is going on. This, in turn, implies that any observed differences among groups are just due to chance. So, if one candidate is polling 50% and the other 45%, statisticians start with the assumption that there is no difference in support for the candidates. Others may be astounded by such an assumption, because 50% seems quite different from 45%. The statistician starts by assuming that the different polling numbers are just a matter of chance, probably due to the particular people who were included in the poll.

**TIP** Perhaps the most important lesson from statistics is skepticism and the willingness to ask questions. The default assumption should be that differences are due to chance; data analysis has to demonstrate that this assumption is highly unlikely.

The assumption that nothing extraordinary is occurring has a name, the *Null Hypothesis*. A vocabulary note: "Null" here is a statistical term and has nothing to do with the database use of the term. To avoid ambiguity, "Null Hypothesis" is a statistical phrase and any other use of "NULL" refers to the SQL keyword.

The Null Hypothesis is the hallmark of skepticism, and also the beginning of a conversation. The skepticism leads to the question: *How confident are we that the Null Hypothesis is true?* This question is equivalent to: *How confident are we that the observed difference is due just to chance?* And these questions have an answer. The *p-value* is an estimate of how often the Null Hypothesis is true. When the p-value is very small, such as 0.1%, the statement "I have very little confidence that the observed difference is due just to chance" is quite reasonable. This, in turn, implies that the observed difference is due to something other than chance. In the polling example, a low p-value suggests the following: "The poll shows that there is a significant difference in support for the two candidates."

Statistical significance is equivalent to saying that the p-value is less than some low number, often 5% or 10%. When the p-value is larger, the Null Hypothesis has pretty good standing. The right way to think about this is "There is no strong evidence that something occurred, so I'll assume that the difference was due to chance." In the polling example, we might say "The polling shows no definitive difference in support for the two candidates." One candidate might have slightly higher polling numbers than the other in the small number of people polled. Alas, the difference is not large enough for us to have confidence that one candidate has larger support than the other in the much larger general (or voting) population.

Imagine running a bunch of different polls at the same time, with the same questions and the same methodology. The only difference among these polls is the people who are contacted; each is a different random sample from the overall population. The p-value says what proportion of all these polls would have a difference at least as great as what the first poll finds, assuming that each question has equal support for both sides.

Sometimes, just formulating the Null Hypothesis is valuable, because it articulates a business problem in a measurable and testable way. This chapter includes various Null Hypotheses, such as:

- The average order amount in New York is the same as the average in California.

- A committee with five members was chosen without taking gender into account.

- The stop rate for customers who started on 28 Dec 2005 is the same, regardless of the market where they started.

- There is no affinity between the products that customers buy and the states where customers live. That is, all customers are as likely to purchase a particular product, regardless of where they live.

These hypotheses are stated in clear business terms. They can be validated, using available data. The answers, however, are not simply "true" or "false." The answers are a confidence that the statement is true. Very low p-values (confidence values) imply a very low confidence that the statement is true, which in turn implies that the observed difference is significant.

## Confidence and Probability

The idea of confidence is central to the notion of measuring whether two things are the same or different. Statisticians do not ask "are these different?" Instead, they ask the question "how confident are we that these are the same?" When this confidence is very low, it is reasonable to assume that the two measurements are indeed different.

Confidence and probability often look the same, because both are measured in the same units, a value between zero and one that is often written as a percentage. Unlike probabilities, confidence includes the subjective opinion of the observer. Probability is inherent in whatever is happening. There is a certain probability of rain today. There is a certain probability that heads will appear on a coin toss, or that a contestant will win the jackpot on a game show, or that a particular atom of uranium will decay radioactively in the next minute. These are examples where there is a process, and the opinions of the observer do not matter.

On the other hand, after an election has occurred and before the votes are counted, one might be *confident* in the outcome of the election. The votes have already been cast, so there is a result. Both candidates in the election might be confident, believing they are going to win. However, each candidate being 90% confident in his or her odds of winning does not imply an overall confidence of 180%! Although it looks like a probability, this is confidence, because it is based on subjective opinion.

There is a tendency to think of confidence as a probability. This is not quite correct because a probability is exact, with the uncertainty in the measurement. A confidence may look exact, but the uncertainty is, at least partially, in the opinion of the observer. The Monty Hall Paradox, explained in the aside, is a simple "probability" paradox that illustrates the difference between the two.

The inverse notion of "how different is different" is "when are two things the same." One way of expressing this is by asking how confident we are that the difference is or is not zero. In the polling example, where one candidate has 50% support and the other 45%, the Null Hypothesis on the difference is: "The difference in support between the two candidates is zero," meaning the two candidates actually have the same support in the overall population. A p-value of 1% means that if multiple polls were conducted at the same time, with the same methodology and with the only difference being the people randomly chosen to participate in the polls and the assumption that there is no difference in support for the candidates, then we would expect 99% of the polls to have less than the observed difference. That is, the observed difference is big, so it suggests a real difference in support for the candidates in the overall population. If the p-value were 50%, then even though the difference is noticeable in the poll, it says very little about which candidate has greater support.

## Normal Distribution

The normal distribution, also called the bell curve and the Gaussian distribution, plays a special role in statistics. In many situations, the normal distribution can answer the following question: Given an observed measure on a sample (such as a poll), what confidence do we have that the actual measure for the whole population falls within a particular range? For instance, if 50% of poll respondents say they support Candidate A, what does this mean about Candidate A's support in the whole population? Pollsters report something like "There is a 95% confidence that the candidate's support is between 47.5% and 52.5%."

In this particular case, the *confidence interval* is 47.5% to 52.5% and the *confidence* is 95%. A different level of confidence would produce a different interval. So the interval for 99.9% confidence would be wider. The interval for 90% would be narrower.

## MONTY HALL PARADOX

Monty Hall was the famous host of the television show *Let's Make a Deal* from 1963 through 1986. This popular show offered prizes, which were hidden behind three doors. One of the doors contained a grand prize, such as a car or vacation. The other two had lesser prizes, such as a goat or rubber chicken. In this simplification of the game show, a contestant is asked to choose one of the doors and can keep the prize behind it. One of the remaining two doors is then opened, revealing perhaps a rubber chicken, and the contestant is asked whether he or she wants to keep the unseen prize behind the chosen door or switch to the other unopened one.

Assuming that the contestant is asked randomly regardless of whether the chosen door has the prize, should he or she keep the original choice or switch? Or, does it not make a difference? The rest of this aside gives the answer, so stop here if you want to think about it.

A simple analysis of the problem might go as follows. When the contestant first makes a choice, there are three doors, so the odds of getting the prize are initially one in three (or 33.3% probability). After the other door is opened, though, there are only two doors remaining, so the probability of either door having the prize is 50%. Because the probabilities are the same, switching does not make a difference. It is equally likely that the prize is behind either door.

Although an appealing and popular analysis, this is not correct for a subtle reason that involves a distinction similar to the distinction between confidence and probability: Just because there are two doors does not mean that the probabilities are equal.

Monty knows where the prize is. So, after the contestant chooses a door, any door, Monty can always open one of the remaining two and show a booby prize. Opening one door and showing that there is no grand prize behind it adds no new information. This is always possible, regardless of where the grand prize is. Because opening some door with no grand prize offers no new information, showing a booby prize does not change the original probabilities.

What are those probabilities? The probabilities are 33.3% that the prize is behind the door the contestant originally chose and 66.7% that the prize is behind one of the other two. These do not change, so the contestant doubles his or her chances of winning by switching.

Confidence levels can help us understand this problem. At the beginning, the contestant should be 33.3% confident that the prize is behind the chosen door and 66.7% confident that the prize is behind one of the other two. This confidence does not change when another door without the prize is opened, because the contestant should realize that it is always possible to show a door with no prize. Nothing has changed. So given the opportunity to switch, the contestant should do so, and double his or her chances of winning.

Measuring the confidence interval uses the normal distribution, shown in Figure 3-1 for the data corresponding to the polling example. In this example, the average is 50%, and the range from 47.5% and 52.5% has 95% confidence.

The two points define the ends of the confidence interval, and the area under the curve, between the two points, measures the confidence. The units on the vertical axis are shown, but they are not important. They just guarantee that the area under the entire curve equals 100%.

The normal distribution is a family of curves, defined by two numbers, the average and standard deviation. The average determines where the center of the distribution is, so smaller averages result in curves shifted to the left, and larger averages have curves shifted to the right. The standard deviation determines how narrow and high or how wide and flat the hump is in the middle. Small standard deviations make the curve spikier; larger standard deviations spread it out. Otherwise, the shape of the curve remains the same, and the area under all these curves is always one.

Properties of the normal distribution are well understood. So, about 68% of the averages from samples fall within one standard deviation of the overall average. About 95.5% fall within two standard deviations, and 99.73% fall within three standard deviations. By tradition, statistical significance is often taken at the 95% level, and this occurs at the not-so-intuitive level of 1.96 standard deviations from the average.

Table 3-1 shows the confidence for various confidence intervals measured in terms of standard deviations. The distance from a value to the average, measured in standard deviations, is called the *z-score*. This is actually a simple transformation on any set of data, where the difference between the value and average is divided by the standard deviation. Z-scores are particularly useful when comparing variables that have different ranges, such as the average age and average income of a group of people. Z-scores are also useful for transforming variables for data mining modeling.

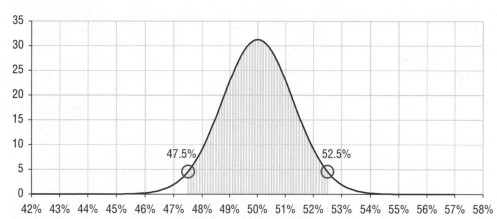

**Figure 3-1:** The area under the normal distribution, between two points, is the confidence that the measurement on the entire population falls in that range.

**Table 3-1:** Confidence Levels Associated with Various Z-Scores (which is half the width of the confidence interval measured in standard deviations)

| Z-SCORE | CONFIDENCE |
| --- | --- |
| 1.00 | 68.269% |
| 1.64 | 89.899% |
| 1.96 | 95.000% |
| 2.00 | 95.450% |
| 2.50 | 98.758% |
| 3.00 | 99.730% |
| 3.29 | 99.900% |
| 3.89 | 99.990% |
| 4.00 | 99.994% |
| 4.42 | 99.999% |
| 5.00 | 100.000% |

The values in Table 3-1 were calculated using the Excel formula:

```
<confidence> = NORMSDIST(<z-score>) - NORMSDIST(- <z-score>)
```

In Excel, the function NORMSDIST() calculates the area under the normal distribution up to a particular z-score. That is, it defines the confidence interval from minus infinity to the z-score. To get a finite confidence interval on either side of the average, calculate the one from minus infinity to <value> and then subtract out the one from minus infinity to minus z-score, as shown in Figure 3-2.

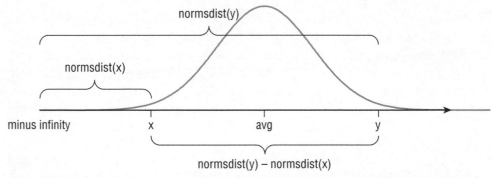

**Figure 3-2:** The Excel function NORMSDIST() can be used to calculate the confidence for an interval around the average.

The preceding formula works for z-scores that are positive. A slight variation works for all z-scores:

```
<confidence> = ABS(NORMSDIST(<z-score>) - NORMSDIST(- <z-score>))
```

From the preceding polling example, the standard deviation can be reverse engineered. The confidence is 95%, implying that the confidence interval ranges 1.96 times the standard deviation on either side of the average. Because the confidence interval is 2.5% on either side of the average, the standard deviation is 2.5%/1.96 or 1.276%. This information can be used to calculate the 99.9% confidence interval. It is 3.29 times the standard deviation. So, the confidence interval for the poll with 99.9% confidence ranges from 50% − 3.29*1.276% to 50% + 3.29*1.276%, or 45.8% to 54.2%.

As a final note, the normal distribution depends on knowing the average and standard deviation. All we have is data, which does not include this information directly. Fortunately, statistics provides some methods for estimating these values from data, as explained in examples throughout this chapter.

## How Different Are the Averages?

The retail purchase data has purchases from all fifty states, and then some. This section addresses the question of whether the average purchase amount (in the column TOTALPRICE) differs in different states. Statistics answers this question, and most of the calculations can be done using SQL queries.

Let's start with the observation that the average purchase amount for the 17,839 purchases from California is $85.48 and the average purchase amount for the 53,537 purchases from New York is $70.14. Is this difference significant?

### The Approach

The approach to answering the question starts by putting all the orders from New York and California into one big bucket whose overall average total price is $73.98. The question is: *What is the likelihood that a random subset of 17,839 purchases from this bucket has an average TOTALPRICE of $85.48?* If this probability is largish, then orders from California look like a random sample, and there is nothing special about them. On the other hand, if the p-value is small, there is evidence that orders from California are different from a random sample of orders from the two states, leading to the conclusion that California orders are different.

Looking at extreme cases can help shed light on this approach. Assume that all orders from California are exactly $85.48 and all orders from New York are exactly $70.14. In this case, there is only one group of orders from the bucket whose average amount is $85.48 — the group that consists of exactly the California orders. If the orders took on only these two values, it would be safe to say that distinction between New York and California is not due just to chance. It is due to some other factor.

A cursory look at the data shows that this is not the case. Given that TOTAL-PRICE runs the gamut of values from $0 to $10,000, can we say anything about whether the difference in average order size in New York and California is due to randomness, or due to a difference in the markets?

## Standard Deviation for Subset Averages

The preceding question is about averages of samples. Something called the Central Limit Theorem in statistics sheds light on precisely the subject of the average of a subset of values randomly selected from a larger group. This theorem says that if we repeatedly take samples of a given size, then the distribution of the averages of these samples approximates a normal distribution, whose average and standard deviation are based on exactly three factors:

- ▪ The average of the original data;
- ▪ The standard deviation of the original data; and,
- ▪ The size of the sample.

Notice that the Central Limit Theorem says nothing about the distribution of the original values. The wonder of this theorem is that it works for basically any distribution of the original values. The Central Limit Theorem tells us about the distribution of the averages of the samples, not the distribution of the original values.

Consider the average TOTALPRICE of ten orders taken randomly. If this process is repeated, the averages approximate a normal distribution. If instead we were to take one hundred orders repeatedly rather than ten, the averages also follow a normal distribution, but one whose standard deviation is a bit smaller. As the size of the samples increases, the distribution of the average forms a narrower band around the actual average in the original data. Figure 3-3 shows some distributions for the average value of TOTALPRICE for different sized groups coming from the California–New York orders.

The Central Limit Theorem says that the average of the distribution is the average of the original data and the standard deviation is the standard deviation of the original data divided by the square root of the sample size. As the sample size gets larger, the standard deviation gets smaller, and the distribution becomes taller and narrower and more centered on the average. This means that the average of a larger sample is much more likely to be very close to the overall average, than the average of a smaller sample. In statistics-speak, the standard deviation of the average of a sample is called the *standard error* (of the sample). So, the previous formulation says that the standard error of a sample is equal to the standard deviation of the population divided by the square root of the sample size.

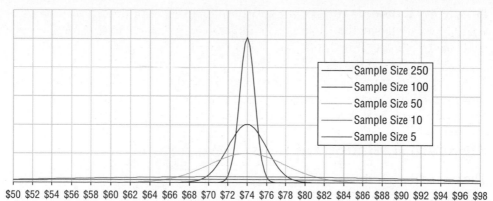

**Figure 3-3:** The theoretical distributions of TOTALPRICE for different sample sizes follow the normal distribution.

Now, the question about the average values of California and New York gets a little tricky. It is trivial to calculate the average and standard deviation of the New York and California orders, using the SQL aggregation functions AVG() and STDDEV(). However, the question that we want to answer is slightly different. The question is: *What is the likelihood that taking the average of 17,839 values randomly chosen from the population results in an average of $85.48 and taking a sample of 53,537 values results in $70.14?*

Looking at the distribution of values from each state helps to understand what is happening. The following SQL query returns the counts of the TOTAL-PRICE column in five-dollar increments:

```
SELECT 5*FLOOR(totalprice/5),
       SUM(CASE WHEN state = 'CA' THEN 1 ELSE 0 END) as CA,
       SUM(CASE WHEN state = 'NY' THEN 1 ELSE 0 END) as NY
FROM orders o
WHERE o.state IN ('CA', 'NY')
GROUP BY 5*FLOOR(totalprice/5)
```

A histogram of the results is shown in Figure 3-4, which has the averages for each state in the legend. Visually, the two histograms look quite similar, suggesting that the average sizes for each state might well be within the margin of error. However, the analysis is not yet complete.

## Three Approaches

There are at least three statistical approaches to determining whether the average purchase sizes in New York and California are the same or different.

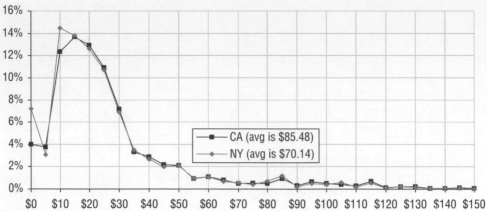

**Figure 3-4:** This chart shows the distribution of the TOTALPRICE of orders from New York and California.

The first approach is to treat the orders as two samples from the same population and ask a question that is perhaps now familiar: *What is the likelihood that the differences are due just to random variation?* The second approach is to take the difference between the two means and ask: *How likely it is that the difference could be zero?* If the difference could reasonably be zero, then the two observed values are too close and should be treated as equivalent to each other.

The third approach is to list out all the different possible combinations of purchases and to calculate the averages for all of them. The information from all possible combinations makes it possible to determine how often the average in two groups exceeds the observed averages. This direct counting approach is too computationally intensive in this case, so this section does not go into detail into this approach. Later in this chapter, though, the counting approach is used for a different problem.

## Estimation Based on Two Samples

There are 71,376 orders in New York and California, with an average order size of $73.98 and a standard deviation of $197.23. The orders from California are a subgroup of this population, comprising 17,839 orders with an average order size of $85.48. *What is the confidence that this subgroup is just a random sample pulled from the data (meaning that the observed difference is due only to chance)?*

As mentioned earlier, the standard deviation of the sample average is the standard deviation of the overall data divided by the square root of the sample size. For instance, the 17,839 orders from California constitute a sample from the original population. Based on the overall data the average expected value should be $73.98 and the standard deviation $197.23 divided by the square root of 17,839, which is about $1.48.

An average of $85.48 seems quite far from $73.98, so it seems unlikely that the results for California are just "random" error. There is probably some cause for the difference. Perhaps Californians are different from New Yorkers in their affinity for various products. Perhaps marketing campaigns are different in the two states. Perhaps brand awareness differs in the two states.

The NORMDIST() function in Excel makes it possible to quantify the confidence. The first argument to NORMDIST() is the observed average, the second is the expected average, and then the standard deviation. The last argument tells NOR-MDIST() to return the cumulative area from minus infinity to the observed value.

Quantifying the confidence requires explaining what to look for. Getting any particular value for the average — whether $85.48 or $73.98 or $123.45 or whatever — is highly unlikely. Instead, the question is: *What is the probability that a random sample's average value is at least as far from the overall average as the observed sample average?* Notice that this statement does not say whether the value is bigger or smaller than the average, just the distance away. The expression to do this is:

```
=2*MIN(1-NORMDIST(85.14, 73.98, 1.48, 1), NORMDIST(85.14, 73.98, 1.48, 1))
```

This expression calculates the probability of a random sample's average being in the tail of the distribution of averages — that is, as far away as or farther away from the overall average than the observed sample average.

The multiplication by two is because the tail can be on either side of the overall average. The MIN() is needed because there are two cases. When the observed sample average is less than the overall average, the tail is from minus infinity to the observed value; NORMDIST() calculates this value. When the observed sample average is greater than the overall average, then the tail is on the other side and goes from the observed value to positive infinity; 1-NOR-MDIST() calculates this value.

For the case at hand, the calculated result gives a probability, a p-value, that is indistinguishable from zero, meaning that the high value for California relative to New York is not due to chance.

Another way of looking at this is using the z-score, which measures the distance from the average to the observed value, in multiples of standard deviations. The expression to calculate the z-score is ($84.48 – $73.98)/$1.48, which comes to 7.8 standard deviations away. That is a long way away, and it is very, very, very unlikely that the average order size for California is due to nothing more than chance.

**TIP** The z-score measures how far away an observed value is from the mean, in units of standard deviations. It is the difference divided by the standard deviation. The z-score can be turned into a probability using the Excel formula `2*MIN(1-NORMSDIST(z-score), NORMSDIST(z-score))`.

### Estimation Based on Difference

The previous calculation compared the results of one state to the combined orders from both states. The following series of questions is a chain of reasoning that shows another way to think about this problem:

- Does the average TOTALPRICE differ between New York and California?

- Could the difference between the average TOTALPRICE for the two states be zero?

- What is the confidence of the Null Hypothesis that the difference between the TOTALPRICE of New York and the TOTALPRICE of California is zero?

That is, we can compare New York and California by looking at the difference between the two values rather than looking at the values themselves. The difference is \$15.34 = \$85.48 − \$70.14. Given the information about the two groups, is this statistically significant?

Once again, the differences between the averages follow a distribution, whose average is zero (because samples from the same distribution have the same expected average). Calculating the standard deviation requires borrowing another formula from statistics. The standard deviation of the difference is the square root of the sum of the squares of the standard deviations of each sample. This formula is similar to the Pythagorean formula from high school geometry. Instead of sides of a right triangle, though, the formula is about standard deviations.

In the example, the standard deviation for California is \$1.48 and for New York it is \$0.85. The square root of the sum of the squares yields \$1.71.

The observed difference of \$15.34 corresponds to about nine standard deviations from zero. The corresponding p-value is essentially zero, meaning that the observed difference is likely to be significant. This produces the same result as before; orders from California and New York have differences that are not due merely to chance.

Investigating the distributions of the orders highlights some differences. New York has twice the proportion of orders whose TOTALPRICE is zero, which suggests that there is a difference between the states. For orders less than \$100, the two states look identical. On the other hand, California has relatively more orders greater than \$100.

## Counting Possibilities

Averages are interesting, but many of the comparisons between customers involve counts, such as the number of customers who have responded to an offer, or who have stopped, or who prefer particular products. Counting is a simple process, and one that computers excel at.

Counting is not just about individuals, it is also about counting combinations. For instance, if there are ten teams in a baseball league, how many different possible games are there? Figure 3-5 illustrates the 45 different possible games between two teams in the league; each possible game is a line segment connecting two boxes. This type of chart is called a link chart, and it can be created in Excel as explained in the aside "Creating a Link Chart Using Excel Charts."

The study of such combinations is called *combinatorics*, a field that straddles the boundary between probability and statistics. The rest of the chapter looks at statistical approximations to questions about combinations, approximations that are good enough for everyday use.

This section starts with a small example that can easily be illustrated and counted by hand. The ideas are then extended to the larger numbers found in customer databases, along with the SQL and Excel code needed for doing the calculations.

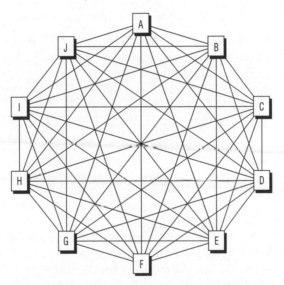

**Figure 3-5:** There are 45 different possible games in a Little League club with ten teams. In this chart, each line connecting two boxes represents one possible game.

## How Many Men?

This first counting example asks the following two questions about a committee that has five members:

- What is the probability that the committee has exactly two men?
- What is the probability that the committee has at most two men?

For the purposes of this example, men and women are equally likely to be on the committee.

## CREATING A LINK CHART USING EXCEL CHARTS

The chart in Figure 3-5 is a link chart that shows connections between pairs of things (in this case teams). Perhaps surprisingly, this is an Excel scatter plot. There are two advantages to doing this in Excel rather than manually in PowerPoint or another tool. First, the boxes and lines can be placed precisely where they need to be, which gives the chart a cleaner and more professional look. Second, making small changes, such as moving a box or changing a label, should be easier, because everything in the chart is created from data that describes what the chart looks like.

When thinking about making a complicated, non-traditional chart, it is important to divide the problem into manageable pieces. This chart has three such pieces:

- The ten teams, which are represented as squares, arrayed around a circle;

- The letter representing each team, inside the squares; and,

- The lines connecting the teams together.

The first step is to place the squares representing the teams. For this, we dip into trigonometry, and set the X-coordinates using the sine of an angle and the Y-coordinate using the cosine. The basic formula for the $n^{th}$ team is:

```
<x-coordinate> = SIN(2*PI()/<n>)
<y- coordinate > = COS(2*PI()/<n>)
```

In the actual chart, these are rotated by a fraction, by adding an offset inside the `SIN()` and `COS()` functions. These formulas give the positions of the teams, as X- and Y-coordinates.

Labeling the points with the team names is a bit more challenging. There are three options for labeling points. Two of them use the X- and Y-coordinates, but these are always numbers. The third option, the "Series name" option, is the only way to get a name. This unfortunately requires creating a separate series for each point, so each has a unique name. The following steps accomplish this:

- Put the X-coordinate in one column.

- Label the columns to the right sequentially with the desired names (A, B, C, and so on). These columns contain the Y-coordinate for the points.

- In the column for team "A," all the values are `NA()`, except for the one corresponding to the A value, and so on for the other columns.

A useful formula to set the values in this table is something like:

```
=IF($G3=J$2, $E3, NA())
```

**CREATING A LINK CHART USING EXCEL CHARTS** *(CONTINUED)*

This formula assumes that the Y-coordinates are in column E, and the team labels are in both row 2 as column headers and in column G as row labels. By careful use of absolute and relative references (the use of "$" in the cell reference), this formula can be copied through the whole range of cells.

The result is an array of cells with values shown in Table 3-2. The first column is the X-coordinate, the second is the Y-coordinate, and the rest are the Y-coordinates for a single team, with other values in the columns being #N/A.

**Table 3-2:** Pivoting the Y-Values for a Circular Link Chart

| Y | X-VALUE | Y-VALUE | | | | | | |
|---|---------|---------|------|------|------|------|-----|------|
|   |         | ALL     | A    | B    | C    | D    | ... | J    |
| A | 0.00    | 1.00    | 1.00 | #N/A | #N/A | #N/A |     | #N/A |
| B | 0.59    | 0.81    | #N/A | 0.81 | #N/A | #N/A |     | #N/A |
| C | 0.95    | 0.31    | #N/A | #N/A | 0.31 | #N/A |     | #N/A |
| D | 0.95    | -0.31   | #N/A | #N/A | #N/A | -0.31|     | #N/A |
| E | 0.59    | -0.81   | #N/A | #N/A | #N/A | #N/A |     | #N/A |
| F | 0.00    | -1.00   | #N/A | #N/A | #N/A | #N/A |     | #N/A |
| G | -0.59   | -0.81   | #N/A | #N/A | #N/A | #N/A |     | #N/A |
| H | -0.95   | -0.31   | #N/A | #N/A | #N/A | #N/A |     | #N/A |
| I | -0.95   | 0.31    | #N/A | #N/A | #N/A | #N/A |     | #N/A |
| J | -0.59   | 0.81    | #N/A | #N/A | #N/A | #N/A |     | 0.81 |

With this arrangement, select the whole table starting from the X-value and insert a scatter plot with no lines. The first series represents all ten teams. For these, set the marker to squares with a white background and shadow; this chart uses a size of 15 for the marker. The rest of the series are for the labels, which have to be inserted individually. To do this, select the series on the chart and set the line and marker patterns to "None." Then click the "Data Labels" tab and choose "Series name" and click "OK." When the label appears, right-click it and choose "Format Data Labels." On the "Alignment" tab, set the "Label Position" to be "Center." With this process, the boxes and their labels are on the chart.

The final step is to include the lines that connect the squares. The idea is to have a table of X- and Y-coordinates and to add a new series into the scatter plot that has lines between the points, but no markers. Unfortunately, the scatter plot connects all points, one after the other, which is like trying to draw the lines without lifting a pencil from the paper. This is hard. Fortunately, when a point has an #N/A value, the scatter plot does not draw the lines going to or

*Continued on next page*

---

**CREATING A LINK CHART USING EXCEL CHARTS** *(CONTINUED)*

from the point; this is like lifting the pencil off the paper. So, each pair of points that defines a connection needs to be interspersed with #N/A values.

There are forty-five unique line segments in the chart, because each team only needs to be connected to the teams after it alphabetically. "A" gets connected to "B" and "C" and so on. However, "I" only gets connected to "J." These segments are placed in a table, where three rows define the segment. Two rows define the beginning and ending of the line, and the third contains the function NA(). There is no redundancy in these line segments, so removing a point from the table makes the line disappear from the chart.

The resulting chart uses twelve different series. One series defines the points, which are placed as boxes. Ten define the labels inside the boxes. And the twelfth series defines the line segments that connect them together.

---

Table 3-3 lists the 32 possible combinations of people that could be on the committee, in terms of gender. One combination has all males. One has all females. Five each have exactly one male or exactly one female. In all, there are 32 combinations, which is two raised to the fifth power: "Two," because there are two possibilities, male or female; "Fifth power," because there are five people on the committee.

All these combinations are equally likely, and they can be used to answer the original questions. Ten rows in the table have exactly two males: rows 8, 12, 14, 15, 20, 22, 23, 26, 27, and 29. That is, 10/32 or about 31% of the combinations have exactly two males. There are an additional six rows that have zero or one males, for a total of sixteen combinations with two or fewer males. So, exactly half of all possible committees have two or fewer men.

Listing the combinations provides insight, but is cumbersome for all but the simplest problems. Fortunately, there are two functions in Excel that do the work for us. The function COMBIN(n, m) calculates the number of combinations of $m$ things taken from $n$ things. The question "How many committees of five people have two males" is really asking "How many ways are there to choose two things (male) from five (the committee size)." The Excel formula is "=COMBIN(5, 2)".

This function returns the number of combinations, but the original questions asked for the proportion of possible committees having exactly two, or two or fewer, males. This proportion is answered using something called the binomial formula, which is provided in Excel as the function BINOMDIST(). This function takes four arguments:

- The size of the group (the bigger number);
- The number being chosen (the smaller number);
- The probability (50%, in this case) of being chosen; and,
- A flag that is 0 for the exact probability and 1 for the probability of less than or equal to the number chosen.

**Table 3-3:** Thirty-two Possibilities of Gender on a Committee of Five

|  | PERSON #1 | PERSON #2 | PERSON #3 | PERSON #4 | PERSON #5 | # M | # F |
|---|---|---|---|---|---|---|---|
| 1 | M | M | M | M | M | 5 | 0 |
| 2 | M | M | M | M | F | 4 | 1 |
| 3 | M | M | M | F | M | 4 | 1 |
| 4 | M | M | M | F | F | 3 | 2 |
| 5 | M | M | F | M | M | 4 | 1 |
| 6 | M | M | F | M | F | 3 | 2 |
| 7 | M | M | F | F | M | 3 | 2 |
| 8 | M | M | F | F | F | 2 | 3 |
| 9 | M | F | M | M | M | 4 | 1 |
| 10 | M | F | M | M | F | 3 | 2 |
| 11 | M | F | M | F | M | 3 | 2 |
| 12 | M | F | M | F | F | 2 | 3 |
| 13 | M | F | F | M | M | 3 | 2 |
| 14 | M | F | F | M | F | 2 | 3 |
| 15 | M | F | F | F | M | 2 | 3 |
| 16 | M | F | F | F | F | 1 | 4 |
| 17 | F | M | M | M | M | 4 | 1 |
| 18 | F | M | M | M | F | 3 | 2 |
| 19 | F | M | M | F | M | 3 | 2 |
| 20 | F | M | M | F | F | 2 | 3 |
| 21 | F | M | F | M | M | 3 | 2 |
| 22 | F | M | F | M | F | 2 | 3 |
| 23 | F | M | F | F | M | 2 | 3 |
| 24 | F | M | F | F | F | 1 | 4 |
| 25 | F | F | M | M | M | 3 | 2 |
| 26 | F | F | M | M | F | 2 | 3 |
| 27 | F | F | M | F | M | 2 | 3 |
| 28 | F | F | M | F | F | 1 | 4 |
| 29 | F | F | F | M | M | 2 | 3 |
| 30 | F | F | F | M | F | 1 | 4 |
| 31 | F | F | F | F | M | 1 | 4 |
| 32 | F | F | F | F | F | 0 | 5 |

So, the following two formulas provide the answers to the original questions:

```
=BINOMDIST(5, 2, 50%, 0)
=BINOMDIST(5, 2, 50%, 1)
```

These formulas simplify the calculations needed to answer each question to a single function call. The purpose here is not to show the actual steps that `BINOMDIST()` uses to make the calculation (which is just a lot of messy arithmetic). Instead, the purpose is to describe intuitively what's happening in terms of combinations of people. The binomial distribution function merely simplifies the calculation.

## How Many Californians?

The second example asks a very similar question about a group of five people. In this case, the question is about where people are from. Let's assume that one in ten people who could be on the committee are from California (because very roughly about one in ten Americans are from California).

- What is the probability that the committee has exactly two Californians?
- What is the probability that the committee has at most two Californians?

Table 3-4 lists all the possibilities. This table is similar to the example for gender, but with two differences. First, each possibility consists of five probabilities, one for each person in the group. The probability is either 10% for the possibility that someone is from California or 90% for the possibility that the person is from somewhere else.

In addition, the overall probability for that occurrence is included as an additional column. In the gender example, each gender was equally likely, so all rows had equal weights. In this case, being from California is much less likely than not being from California, so the rows have different weights. The overall probability for any given row is the product of that row's probabilities. The probability that all five people are from California is 10%*10%*10%*10%*10%, which is 0.001%. The probability that none of the five are from California is 90%*90%*90%*90%*90%, or about 59%. The possibilities are no longer equally likely.

Once again, the detail is interesting. In such a small example, it is possible to count all the different possibilities to answer questions. For example, Table 3-5 shows the probabilities for having zero to five Californians in the group. These numbers can be readily calculated in Excel using the `BINOMDIST()` function, using an expression such as `BINOMDIST(5, 2, 10%, 0)` to calculate the probability that the committee has exactly two Californians.

**Table 3-4:** Thirty-two Possibilities of State of Origin on a Committee of Five

|     | #1   | #2   | #3   | #4   | #5   | PROB    | # CA | # NOT CA |
|-----|------|------|------|------|------|---------|------|----------|
| 1   | 10%  | 10%  | 10%  | 10%  | 10%  | 0.001%  | 5    | 0        |
| 2   | 10%  | 10%  | 10%  | 10%  | 90%  | 0.009%  | 4    | 1        |
| 3   | 10%  | 10%  | 10%  | 90%  | 10%  | 0.009%  | 4    | 1        |
| 4   | 10%  | 10%  | 10%  | 90%  | 90%  | 0.081%  | 3    | 2        |
| 5   | 10%  | 10%  | 90%  | 10%  | 10%  | 0.009%  | 4    | 1        |
| 6   | 10%  | 10%  | 90%  | 10%  | 90%  | 0.081%  | 3    | 2        |
| 7   | 10%  | 10%  | 90%  | 90%  | 10%  | 0.081%  | 3    | 2        |
| 8   | 10%  | 10%  | 90%  | 90%  | 90%  | 0.729%  | 2    | 3        |
| 9   | 10%  | 90%  | 10%  | 10%  | 10%  | 0.009%  | 4    | 1        |
| 10  | 10%  | 90%  | 10%  | 10%  | 90%  | 0.081%  | 3    | 2        |
| 11  | 10%  | 90%  | 10%  | 90%  | 10%  | 0.081%  | 3    | 2        |
| 12  | 10%  | 90%  | 10%  | 90%  | 90%  | 0.729%  | 2    | 3        |
| 13  | 10%  | 90%  | 90%  | 10%  | 10%  | 0.081%  | 3    | 2        |
| 14  | 10%  | 90%  | 90%  | 10%  | 90%  | 0.729%  | 2    | 3        |
| 15  | 10%  | 90%  | 90%  | 90%  | 10%  | 0.729%  | 2    | 3        |
| 16  | 10%  | 90%  | 90%  | 90%  | 90%  | 6.561%  | 1    | 4        |
| 17  | 90%  | 10%  | 10%  | 10%  | 10%  | 0.009%  | 4    | 1        |
| 18  | 90%  | 10%  | 10%  | 10%  | 90%  | 0.081%  | 3    | 2        |
| 19  | 90%  | 10%  | 10%  | 90%  | 10%  | 0.081%  | 3    | 2        |
| 20  | 90%  | 10%  | 10%  | 90%  | 90%  | 0.729%  | 2    | 3        |
| 21  | 90%  | 10%  | 90%  | 10%  | 10%  | 0.081%  | 3    | 2        |
| 22  | 90%  | 10%  | 90%  | 10%  | 90%  | 0.729%  | 2    | 3        |
| 23  | 90%  | 10%  | 90%  | 90%  | 10%  | 0.729%  | 2    | 3        |
| 24  | 90%  | 10%  | 90%  | 90%  | 90%  | 6.561%  | 1    | 4        |
| 25  | 90%  | 90%  | 10%  | 10%  | 10%  | 0.081%  | 3    | 2        |
| 26  | 90%  | 90%  | 10%  | 10%  | 90%  | 0.729%  | 2    | 3        |
| 27  | 90%  | 90%  | 10%  | 90%  | 10%  | 0.729%  | 2    | 3        |
| 28  | 90%  | 90%  | 10%  | 90%  | 90%  | 6.561%  | 1    | 4        |
| 29  | 90%  | 90%  | 90%  | 10%  | 10%  | 0.729%  | 2    | 3        |
| 30  | 90%  | 90%  | 90%  | 10%  | 90%  | 6.561%  | 1    | 4        |
| 31  | 90%  | 90%  | 90%  | 90%  | 10%  | 6.561%  | 1    | 4        |
| 32  | 90%  | 90%  | 90%  | 90%  | 90%  | 59.049% | 0    | 5        |

**Table 3-5:** Probability of Having $n$ Californians on a Committee of Five

| # CA | # NON-CA | PROBABILITY |
|------|----------|-------------|
| 0 | 5 | 59.049% |
| 1 | 4 | 32.805% |
| 2 | 3 | 7.290% |
| 3 | 2 | 0.810% |
| 4 | 1 | 0.045% |
| 5 | 0 | 0.001% |

## Null Hypothesis and Confidence

Let's return to the gender breakdown of five people on a committee. This example shows that even when there is a 50% chance of members being male or female, there is still a chance of finding a unisex committee (either all male or all female). In fact, 6.2% of the time the committee is unisex assuming that the participants are chosen randomly. Another way of looking at this is that if there were enough committees, about 6.2% of them would be unisex, assuming the members are chosen randomly from a pool that is half women and half men.

Does one committee that is unisex support that idea that gender was used to select the members? Or, is it reasonable that the committee was selected randomly? Intuitively we might say that it is obvious that gender was used as a selection criterion. Because people of only one gender were included, it seems obvious that people of the other gender were excluded. This intuition would be wrong over 6% of the time. And without any other information, whether we think the committee shows bias or not depends on our own personal confidence thresholds.

The Null Hypothesis is that the committee members are chosen randomly, without regard to gender. *What is the confidence that the Null Hypothesis is true, assuming that there is one committee and that committee is unisex?* Out of 32 possible gender combinations, two are unisex. Randomly, unisex committees would be chosen 2/32 or 6% of the time. A common statistical test is 5%, so this exceeds the statistical threshold. Using this level of statistical significance, even a unisex committee is not evidence of bias.

On the other hand, a unisex committee is either all female or all male. Looking at the particular gender reduces the possibilities to one out of 32 (that is, one out of 32 possible committees are all female; and one out of 32 are all male). Including the gender changes the confidence to about 3%, in which case an all-male or all-female committee suggests that the Null Hypothesis is false, using the standard statistic level of significance. The fact that looking at the problem in two slightly different ways produces different results is a good lesson to remember when facing problems in the real world.

**WARNING** Slightly changing the problem (such as looking at unisex committees versus all-male or all-female committees) can change the answer to a question. Be clear about stating the problem being solved.

Let's now look at the second example of Californians. What if all members were from California? The Null Hypothesis is that people in the committee are chosen irrespective of their state of origin. However, there is only a 0.001% chance that a randomly selected committee of five would consist only of Californians. In this case, we would be quite confident that the Null Hypothesis is false. And that in turn suggests some sort of bias in the process of choosing members in the committee. In this case, we would be right in assuming a bias 99.999% of the time.

## How Many Customers Are Still Active?

Analyzing committees of five members gives insight into the process of counting possibilities to arrive at probabilities and confidence levels. More interesting examples use customer data. Let's consider the customers in the subscription database who started exactly one year before the cutoff date, and of them, the proportion that stopped in the first year. In this table, active customers are identified by having the STOP_TYPE column set to a value other than NULL. The following SQL calculates this summary information:

```
SELECT COUNT(*) as numstarts,
       SUM(CASE WHEN stop_type IS NOT NULL THEN 1 ELSE 0 END) as numstops,
       AVG(CASE WHEN stop_type IS NOT NULL THEN 1.0 ELSE 0 END
          ) as stoprate
FROM subs
WHERE start_date = '2005-12-28'
```

Notice that the query uses the floating-point constant 1.0 for the average rather than the integer 1. This ensures that the average is a floating-point average, regardless of the database.

This query returns the following results:

- Exactly 2,409 customers started one year before the cutoff date.
- Of these, 484 were stopped on the cutoff date.
- The stop rate is 20.1%.

Both the number stopped and the stop rate are accurate measurements about what happened to the 2,409 customers who started on Dec 28, 2005. How much confidence do we have in these numbers as representative of all customers one year after they start? The idea in answering this question is that there is a process that causes customers to stop. This process is random and behaves like a lottery. Customers who have the right lottery ticket stop (or perhaps customers that have the wrong ticket?); everyone else remains active. Our goal is to understand this process better.

The first question assumes that the number of stops is fixed. *Given the number of stops, what range of stop rates is likely to cause exactly that number of stops?*

The second question assumes that the stop rate is really fixed at 20.1%. *If this is the case, how many customers would we expect to stop?* Remember the committee example. Even though the members have an equal probability of being male or female, the committee can still take on any combination of genders. The same is true here. The next two subsections examine these questions in more detail. The methods are similar to the methods used for understanding the committee; however, the details are a bit different because the sizes are much larger.

### Given the Count, What Is the Probability?

The observed stop rate is 20.1% for the one-year subscribers. Let's propose a hypothesis, that the stop process actually has a stop rate of 15% in the first year rather than the observed rate. The observed 484 stops are just an outlier, in the same way that five people chosen for a committee, at random, all turn out to be women.

Figure 3-6 shows the distribution of values for the number of stops, given that the stop rate is 15%, both as a discrete histogram and as a cumulative distribution. The discrete histogram shows the probability of getting exactly that number of stops; this is called the *distribution*. The *cumulative distribution* shows the probability of getting up to that many stops.

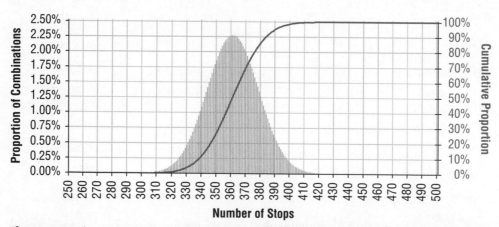

**Figure 3-6:** The proportion of combinations with a given number of stops, assuming a 15% stop rate and 2,409 starts, follows a binomial distribution.

A 15% stop rate should produce, on average, 361 stops (15% of 2,409); this overall average is called the *expected value*. The 484 stops are actually 123 more stops than the expected value, leading to the question: *What is the probability (p-value) of being 123 or more stops away from the expected value?* And this question has an answer. To a very close approximation, the probability is 0%. The actual number is more like 0.0000000015%; calculated using the formula `2*MIN(1-BINOMDIST(484, 2409, 15%, 1), BINOMDIST(484, 2409, 15%, 1))`. The p-value is twice the size of the tail of the distribution.

So, it is very, very, very unlikely that the original stop rate was 15%. In fact, it is so unlikely that we can simply ignore the possibility and assume that the stop rate was higher. Okay, so the stop rate is not 15%. What about 16%? Or 17%? Table 3-6 shows the probability of being in the tail of the distribution for a range of different stop rates. Based on this table, it is reasonable to say that the stop rate for the underlying stop process could really be anywhere from about 18.5% to about 21.5%.

**Table 3-6:** Probability of Having 484 Stops on 2,409 Starts Given Various Hypothetical Stop Rates

| STOP RATE | EXPECTED STOPS | DIFFERENCE | PROBABILITY OF THAT FAR OFF |
|---|---|---|---|
| 17.00% | 409.5 | -74.5 | 0.01% |
| 18.00% | 433.6 | -50.4 | 0.77% |
| 18.50% | 445.7 | -38.3 | 4.33% |
| 18.75% | 451.7 | -32.3 | 8.86% |
| 19.00% | 457.7 | -26.3 | 16.56% |
| 19.25% | 463.7 | -20.3 | 28.35% |
| 19.50% | 469.8 | -14.2 | 44.70% |
| 19.75% | 475.8 | -8.2 | 65.23% |
| 19.90% | 479.4 | -4.6 | 79.06% |
| 20.00% | 481.8 | -2.2 | 88.67% |
| 20.10% | 484.2 | 0.2 | 98.42% |
| 20.25% | 487.8 | 3.8 | 87.01% |
| 20.50% | 493.8 | 9.8 | 64.00% |
| 20.75% | 499.9 | 15.9 | 44.12% |
| 21.00% | 505.9 | 21.9 | 28.43% |
| 21.25% | 511.9 | 27.9 | 17.08% |

*Continued on next page*

**Table 3-6** *(continued)*

| STOP RATE | EXPECTED STOPS | DIFFERENCE | PROBABILITY OF THAT FAR OFF |
|---|---|---|---|
| 21.50% | 517.9 | 33.9 | 9.56% |
| 21.75% | 524.0 | 40.0 | 4.97% |
| 22.00% | 530.0 | 46.0 | 2.41% |
| 22.50% | 542.0 | 58.0 | 0.45% |
| 23.00% | 554.1 | 70.1 | 0.06% |

This is a very important idea, so it is worth reconstructing the thought process. First, there was a hypothesis. This hypothesis stated that the actual stop process stop rate is 15% rather than the observed value of 20.1%. Assuming this hypothesis to be true, we then looked at all the different possible combinations of stops that a 15% stop rate would result in. Of course, listing out all the combinations would be too cumbersome; fortunately, the binomial formula simplifies the calculations. Based on these counts, we saw that the observed number of stops — 484 — was quite far from the expected number of stops, 361. In fact, there is essentially a 0% probability that an observation 123 or more stops away from the average would be observed.

There is nothing magic or general about the fact that 15% does not work and values roughly in the range 19%–21% do work. The confidence depends on the number of starts in the data. If there were only 100 starts, the difference between 15% and 20% would not be statistically significant.

## Given the Probability, What Is the Number of Stops?

The second question is the inverse of the first one: *Given that the underlying stop process has stop rate of 20.1%, what is the likely number of stops?* This is a direct application of the binomial formula. The calculation, BINOMDIST(484, 2409, 20.1%, 0) returns 2.03%, saying that only about one time in fifty do exactly 484 stops result. Even with a stop rate of exactly 20.1%, the expected value of 484 stops is achieved only 2% of the time by a random process. With so many starts, getting a few more or a few less is reasonable assuming that the underlying process is random.

The expected range accounting for 95% of the number of stops can be calculated using the binomial formula. This range goes from 445 stops to 523 stops, which in turn corresponds to a measured stop rate between 18.5% and 21.7%. Table 3-7 shows the probability of the number of stops being in particular ranges around 484 stops.

**Table 3-7:** Probability of a 20% Stop Rate Resulting in Various Ranges Around the Expected Value of 484 Stops

| WIDTH | LOWER BOUND | HIGHER BOUND | PROBABILITY |
|---|---|---|---|
| 3 | 483.0 | 485.0 | 4.42% |
| 15 | 477.0 | 491.0 | 27.95% |
| 25 | 472.0 | 496.0 | 45.80% |
| 51 | 459.0 | 509.0 | 79.46% |
| 75 | 447.0 | 521.0 | 93.91% |
| 79 | 445.0 | 523.0 | 95.18% |
| 101 | 434.0 | 534.0 | 98.88% |
| 126 | 421.0 | 546.0 | 99.86% |
| 151 | 409.0 | 559.0 | 99.99% |

## The Rate or the Number?

Time for a philosophy break. This analysis started with very hard numbers: exactly 484 out of 2,409 customers stopped in the first year. After applying some ideas from statistics and probability, the hard numbers have become softer. What was an exact count becomes a confidence of a value within a certain interval. Are we better off with or without the statistical analysis?

The situation is more reasonable than it appears. The first observation is that the range of 445 stops to 523 stops might seem wide. In fact, it is rather wide. However, if there were a million customers who started, with a stop rate of 20.1%, then the corresponding range would be much tighter. The equivalent confidence range would be from about 200,127 to 201,699 stops — or from 20.01% to 20.17%. More data implies narrower confidence intervals.

Why is there a confidence interval at all? This is an important question. The answer is that we are making an assumption, and the assumption is that customers stop because of some unseen process that affects all customers. This process causes some percentage of customers to stop in the first year. However, the decision of whether one particular customer stops is like rolling dice or tossing a coin, which means that there might be unusual lucky streaks (lower stop rates) or unusually unlucky streaks (higher stop rates), in the same way that a randomly chosen committee could have five men or five women.

A random process is different from a deterministic process that says that every fifth customer is going to stop in the first year, or that we'll cancel the accounts of everyone named "Pat" at day 241. The results from a deterministic process are exact, ignoring the small deviations that might arise due to operational error. For instance, for customers who have already started, the start process is deterministic; 2,409 customers started. There is no confidence interval on this. The number really is 2,409. The statistics measure the "decision-to-stop" process, something that is only observed by its actual effects on stops.

This section started with an example of a committee with five members and moved to a larger example on thousands of starts. As the size of the population increases, confidence in the results increases as well, and the corresponding confidence intervals become narrower. As the population gets larger, whether we look at the ratio or the absolute number becomes less important, simply because both appear to be quite accurate. Fortunately, there is a lot of data stored in databases, so corresponding confidence intervals are often small enough to ignore.

**TIP** On large datasets, charts that show visible differences between groups of customers are usually showing differences that are statistically significant.

## Ratios, and Their Statistics

The binomial distribution really just counts up all the different combinations and determines which proportion of them meets particular conditions. This is very powerful for finding confidence intervals for a random process, as shown in the previous section. This section introduces an alternative method that estimates a standard deviation for a ratio, and uses the normal distribution to approximate confidence ratios.

Using the normal distribution has two advantages over the binomial distribution. First, it is applicable in more areas than the binomial distribution; for instance, the methods here are more suited for comparing two ratios and asking whether they are the same. Second, SQL does not support the calculations needed for the binomial distribution, but it does support almost all the calculations needed for this method.

This section introduces the method for estimating the standard deviation of a ratio (which is actually derived from the *standard error of a proportion*). This is then applied to comparing two different ratios. Finally, the section shows how to use these ideas to produce lower bounds for ratios that might be more appropriate for conservative comparisons of different groups.

### Standard Error of a Proportion

Remember that a standard error is just the standard deviation of some statistic that has been measured on some subgroup of the overall data. In this case, the statistic is a proportion of two variables, such as the number of stops divided by the number of starts. The formula for the standard error in this case is simple and can easily be expressed in SQL or Excel:

```
STDERR = SQRT(<ratio> * (1-<ratio>) / <number of data points>)
```

That is, the standard error is the square root of the product of the observed probability times one minus the observed probability divided by the sample size.

The following SQL query calculates both the standard error and the lower and upper bounds of the 95% confidence interval:

```
SELECT stoprate - 1.96 * stderr as conflower,
       stoprate + 1.96 * stderr as confupper,
       stoprate, stderr, numstarts, numstops
FROM (SELECT SQRT(stoprate * (1 - stoprate)/numstarts) as stderr,
             stoprate, numstarts, numstops
      FROM (SELECT COUNT(*) as numstarts,
                   SUM(CASE WHEN stop_type IS NOT NULL THEN 1 ELSE 0
                       END) as numstops,
                   AVG(CASE WHEN stop_type IS NOT NULL THEN 1.0 ELSE 0
                       END) as stoprate
            FROM subs
            WHERE start_date = '2005-12-28') s
     ) s
```

This SQL query uses two nested subqueries to define the columns NUM-STOPS, STOPRATE, and STDERR. The overall expression could be written without subqueries, but that would result in a much messier query.

This query uses the constant 1.96 to define the 95% confidence bounds for the interval. The result is the interval from 18.5% to 21.7%. Recall that using the binomial distribution, the exact confidence interval was 18.5% to 21.7%. The results are, fortunately and not surprisingly, remarkably close. Even though the standard error of proportions is an approximation that uses the normal distribution, it is a very good approximation.

The standard error can be used in reverse as well. In the earlier polling example, the standard error was 1.27% and the expected probability was 50%. What does this say about the number of people who were polled? For this, the calculation simply goes in reverse. The formula is:

```
<number> = <ratio>*(1-<ratio>)/(<stderr>^2)
```

For the polling example, it gives the value of 1,552, which is a reasonable size for a poll.

One important observation about the standard error and the population size is that halving the standard error corresponds to increasing the population size by a factor of four. In plainer language, there is a trade-off between cost and accuracy. Reducing the standard error on the poll to 0.635%, half of 1.27%, would require polling four times as many people, over 6,000 people instead of

1,500. This would presumably increase costs by a factor of four. Reducing the standard error increases costs.

## Confidence Interval on Proportions

Confidence intervals can be derived from the standard error. For instance, there are three markets in the subscription data: Gotham, Metropolis, and Smallville. These three markets have the following stop rates for customers who started on 26 Dec 2005 (this example uses a slightly different stop rate from the previous example):

- Gotham, 35.2%
- Metropolis, 34.0%
- Smallville, 20.9%

Are we confident that these stop rates are different? Or, might they all be the same? Although it seems unlikely that they are the same, because Smallville is much smaller than the others, remember that a group of five people drawn at random will all have the same genders over 5% of the time. Even though Smallville has a lower stop rate, it might still be just another reasonable sample.

The place to start is with the confidence intervals for each market. The following query does this calculation:

```
SELECT market, stoprate - 1.96 * stderr as conflower,
       stoprate + 1.96 * stderr as confupper,
       stoprate, stderr, numstarts, numstops
FROM (SELECT market,
             SQRT(stoprate * (1 - stoprate)/numstarts) as stderr,
             stoprate, numstarts, numstops
      FROM (SELECT market, COUNT(*) as numstarts,
                   SUM(CASE WHEN stop_type IS NOT NULL THEN 1 ELSE 0
                       END) as numstops,
                   AVG(CASE WHEN stop_type IS NOT NULL THEN 1.0 ELSE 0
                       END) as stoprate
            FROM subs
            WHERE start_date in ('2005-12-26')
            GROUP BY market) s
     ) s
```

This query is very similar to the query for the overall calculation, with the addition of the aggregation by market.

The results in Table 3-8 make it clear that the stop rate for Smallville is different from the stop rate for Gotham and Metropolis. The 95% confidence interval for Smallville does not overlap with the confidence intervals of the other two markets, as shown in Figure 3-7. This is a strong condition. When the confidence intervals do not overlap, there is a high confidence that the ratios are different.

**Table 3-8:** Confidence Intervals by Markets for Starts on 26 Dec 2005

| | | STOPS | | 95% CONFIDENCE | | |
| | | # | RATE | LOWER BOUND | UPPER BOUND | STANDARD ERROR |
| MARKET | STARTS | | | | | |
| --- | --- | --- | --- | --- | --- | --- |
| Gotham | 2,256 | 794 | 35.2% | 33.2% | 37.2% | 1.0% |
| Metropolis | 1,134 | 385 | 34.0% | 31.2% | 36.7% | 1.4% |
| Smallville | 666 | 139 | 20.9% | 17.8% | 24.0% | 1.6% |

Figure 3-7, by the way, is an Excel scatter plot. The X-axis has the stop rate for each market. The Y-values are simply 1, 2, and 3 (because Excel does not allow names to be values for a scatter plot); the Y-axis itself has been removed, because it adds no useful information to the chart. The intervals use the X-Error Bar feature, and the labels on the points were added manually, by typing in text and placing the labels where desired.

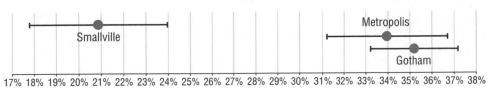

**Figure 3-7:** When confidence intervals do not overlap, there is a high level of confidence that the observed values really are different. So Smallville is clearly different from Gotham and Metropolis.

## Difference of Proportions

For Metropolis and Gotham, the situation is different, because their confidence intervals do overlap. The difference between their observed stop rates is 1.2%. *How likely is it that this difference is due just to chance, if we assume the Null Hypothesis that the two values are really equal?*

There is another estimate of the standard error that is used for the difference between two proportions, which is quite reasonably called the *standard error of the difference of proportions*. The formula for this is easily calculated in Excel or SQL:

```
STDERR = SQRT((<ratio1>*(1-<ratio1>)/<size1>) +
              (<ratio2>*(1-<ratio2>)/<size2>)
```

That is, the standard error of the difference of two proportions is the square root of the sum of the squares of the standard errors of each proportion (this is basically the same as the standard error of a difference of two values). The calculation yields a standard error of 1.7% for the difference. The observed difference is 1.2%, resulting in a z-score of 0.72 (the z-score is 1.2%/1.7%). Such a small z-score is well within a reasonable range, so the difference is not significant.

Another way of looking at this is using the 95% confidence interval. The lower bound is at the observed difference minus 1.96*1.7% and the upper bound is the observed difference plus 1.96*1.7%, which comes to a range from −2.2% to 4.6%. Because the confidence interval is both positive and negative, it includes zero. That is, Gotham and Metropolis could actually have the same stop rate, or Metropolis's stop rate could even be bigger than Gotham's (the opposite of the observed ordering). The observed difference could easily be due to randomness of the underlying stop process.

This example shows the different ways that the standard error can be used. When confidence intervals do not overlap, the observed values are statistically different. It is also possible to measure the confidence of the difference between two values, using the standard error of the difference of proportions. This calculation uses similar methods. When the resulting confidence interval contains zero, the difference is not significant.

The techniques are only measuring a certain type of significance, related to the randomness of underlying processes. The observed values can still provide guidance. There is some evidence that Gotham has a higher stop rate than Metropolis, some evidence but not enough to be confident in the fact. If we had to choose one market or the other for a retention program to save customers, Gotham would be the likely candidate, because its stop rate is larger. However, the choice of Gotham over Metropolis is based on weak evidence, because the difference is not statistically significant.

## Conservative Lower Bounds

Notice that the confidence intervals for the three markets all have different standard errors. This is mostly because the size of each market is different (and to a much lesser extent to the fact that the measured stop rates are different). To be conservative, it is sometimes useful to use the observed value minus one standard error, rather than the observed value. This can change the relative values of different groups, particularly because the standard error on a small group is larger than the standard error on a larger group. In some cases, using a conservative estimate changes the ordering of the different groups, although that is not true in this case.

**TIP** When comparing ratios on different groups that are different sizes, a conservative estimate for the comparison is the observed ratio minus one standard deviation.

# Chi-Square

The chi-square test (pronounced to rhyme with "guy" and starting with a hard "c" sound) provides another method for addressing the question "how different is different?" The chi-square test is appropriate when there are multiple dimensions being compared to each other. Instead of just looking at the "stop rate" for customers, for instance, the customers are divided into two distinct groups, those who stopped and those who are active. These groups can then be compared across different dimensions, such as channel, market, or the period when they started.

The chi-square test does not create confidence intervals, because confidence intervals do not make as much sense across multiple dimensions. Instead, it calculates the confidence that the observed counts are due to chance, by comparing the observed counts to expected counts. Because the chi-square test does not use confidence intervals, it avoids some of the logical conundrums that occur at the edges, such as when the confidence interval for a ratio crosses the 0% or 100% thresholds. Proportions are in the range of 0% to 100%, and so too should be their confidence intervals.

## Expected Values

Consider customers who started on December 26, 2005. What is the number of stops expected for each of the three markets? A simple way to calculate these expected values is to observe that the overall stop rate is 32.5% for starts from that day. So, given that Gotham had 2,256 starts, there should be about 733.1 stops (32.5% * 2,256). In other words, assuming that all the markets behave the same way, the stops should be equally distributed.

In actual fact, Gotham has 794 stops, not 733.1. It exceeds the expected number by 60.9 stops. The difference between the observed value and the expected value is the *deviation*; Table 3-9 shows the observed values, expected values, and deviations for stops in all three markets.

**Table 3-9:** Observed and Expected Values of Active and Stopped Customers, by Market

|  | OBSERVED | | EXPECTED | | DEVIATION | |
|---|---|---|---|---|---|---|
|  | **ACTIVE** | **STOP** | **ACTIVE** | **STOP** | **ACTIVE** | **STOP** |
| Gotham | 1,462 | 794 | 1,522.9 | 733.1 | -60.9 | 60.9 |
| Metropolis | 749 | 385 | 765.5 | 368.5 | -16.5 | 16.5 |
| Smallville | 527 | 139 | 449.6 | 216.4 | 77.4 | -77.4 |

The expected values have some useful properties. For instance, the sum of the expected values is the same as the sum of the observed values. In addition, the total number of expected stops is the same as the number of observed stops; and the totals in each market are the same. The expected values have the same numbers of actives and stops; they are just arranged differently.

The deviations for each row have the same absolute values, but one is positive and the other negative. For Gotham, the "active customer" deviation is −60.9 and the "stopped customer" deviation is +60.9, so the row deviations sum to zero. This property is not a coincidence. The sum of the deviations along each row and each column always adds up to zero, regardless of the number of rows and columns.

Calculating the expected values from the raw tabular data is quite simple. Figure 3-8 shows the Excel formulas. First, the sums of the counts in each row and each column are calculated, as well as the sum of all cells in the table. The expected value for each cell is the row sum total times the column sum divided by the overall sum. With good use of relative and absolute cell range references, it is easy to write this formula once, and then copy it to the other five cells.

With this background, the chi-square question is: *What is the likelihood that the deviations are due strictly to chance?* If this likelihood is very low, then we are confident that there is a difference among the markets. If the likelihood is high (say over 5%), then there may be a difference among the markets, but the observed measurements do not provide enough evidence to draw that conclusion.

## Chi-Square Calculation

The chi-square measure of a single cell is the deviation squared divided by the expected value. The chi-square measure for the entire table is the sum of the chi-square measures for all the cells in the table.

Table 3-10 extends Table 3-9 with the chi-square values of the cells. The sum of the chi-square values for all cells is 49.62. Notice that the chi-square values no longer have the property that the sum of each row is zero and the sum of each column is zero. This is obvious, because the chi-square value is never negative. The two divisors are always positive: variance squared is positive, and the expected value of a count is always positive.

| | C | D | E | F | G | H | I | J | K | L |
|---|---|---|---|---|---|---|---|---|---|---|
| 3 | FROM SQL | | | EXCEL CALCULATION FOR EXPECTED, DEVIATION, AND CHI-SQUARE | | | | | | |
| 4 | | | | | Expected | | Deviation | | CHI-Square | |
| 5 | | Actives | Stops | Total | Actives | Stops | Active | Stops | Active | Stops |
| 6 | Gotham | 1462 | 794 | =SUM(D6:E6) | =$F6*D$9/ $F$9 | =$F6*E$9/ $F$9 | =D6-G6 | =E6-H6 | =I6^2/G6 | =J6^2/H6 |
| 7 | Metropolis | 749 | 385 | =SUM(D7:E7) | =$F7*D$9/ $F$9 | =$F7*E$9/ $F$9 | =D7-G7 | =E7-H7 | =I7^2/G7 | =J7^2/H7 |
| 8 | Smallville | 527 | 139 | =SUM(D8:E8) | =$F8*D$9/ $F$9 | =$F8*E$9/ $F$9 | =D8-G8 | =E8-H8 | =I8^2/G8 | =J8^2/H8 |
| 9 | TOTAL | =SUM(D6:D8) | =SUM(E6:E8) | =SUM(F6:F8) | =SUM(G6:G8) | =SUM(H6:H8) | =SUM(I6:I8) | =SUM(J6:J8) | =SUM(K6:K8) | =SUM(L6:L8) |

**Figure 3-8:** Expected values are easy to calculate in Excel.

The chi-square value is interesting, but it does not tell us if the value is expected or unexpected. For this, we need to compare the value to a distribution, to turn the total chi-square of 49.62 into a p-value. Unfortunately, chi-square values do not follow a normal distribution. They do, however, follow another well-understood distribution.

**Table 3-10:** Chi-Square Values by Market

| | OBSERVED | | EXPECTED | | DEVIATION | | CHI-SQUARE | |
|---|---|---|---|---|---|---|---|---|
| | ACT | STOP | ACT | STOP | ACT | STOP | ACT | STOP |
| Gotham | 1,462 | 794 | 1,522.9 | 733.1 | -60.9 | 60.9 | 2.4 | 5.1 |
| Metropolis | 749 | 385 | 765.5 | 368.5 | -16.5 | 16.5 | 0.4 | 0.7 |
| Smallville | 527 | 139 | 449.6 | 216.4 | 77.4 | -77.4 | 13.3 | 27.7 |
| TOTAL | 2,738 | 1,318 | 2,738.0 | 1,318.0 | 0.0 | 0.0 | 16.1 | 33.5 |

## Chi-Square Distribution

The final step in the calculation is to translate the chi-square value into a p-value. Like the standard error, this is best understood by referring to an underlying distribution. In this case, the distribution is not the normal distribution. It is the appropriately named *chi-square distribution*.

Actually, the chi-square distribution is a family of distributions, based on one parameter, called the *degrees of freedom*. The calculation of the degrees of freedom of a table is simple. It is one less than the number of rows in the table times one less than the number of columns in the table. This example has three rows (one for each market) and two columns (one for actives and one for stops), so the degrees of freedom is (3–1)*(2–1) which equals 2. The aside "Degrees of Freedom for Chi-Square" discusses what the concept means in more detail.

Figure 3-9 shows the chi-square distributions for various degrees of freedom. As the degrees of freedom gets larger, the bump in the distribution moves to the left. In fact, the bump is at the value degrees of freedom minus two. The 95% confidence level for each of the curves is in parentheses. If the chi-square value exceeds this confidence level, it is reasonable to say that the distribution of values is not due to chance.

The Excel function CHIDIST() calculates the confidence value associated with a chi-square value for a particular degrees of freedom. CHIDIST(49.62, 2) returns the miniscule value of 0.0000000017%. This number is exceedingly small, which means that we have very little confidence that the actives and stops are randomly distributed by market. In other words, something else seems to be going on.

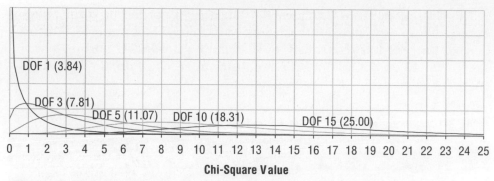

**Figure 3-9:** The chi-square distribution becomes flatter as the number of degrees of freedom increases; the 95% confidence bound is in parentheses.

As shown earlier in Figure 3-8, the sequence of calculations from the expected value to the variance to the chi-square calculation can all be done in Excel. The formula for the degrees of freedom uses functions in Excel that return the number of rows and columns in the table, so the degrees of freedom of a range of cells is `(ROWS(<table>)-1)*(COLUMNS(<table>)-1)`. The `CHIDIST()` function with the appropriate arguments then calculates the associated probability.

**DEGREES OF FREEDOM FOR CHI-SQUARE**

The degrees of freedom for the chi-square calculation is not a difficult idea, although understanding it requires some algebra. Historically, the first person to investigate degrees of freedom was the British statistician Sir Ronald Fisher, perhaps the greatest statistician of the twentieth century. He was knighted for his contributions to statistics and science.

The idea behind degrees of freedom addresses the question of how many independent variables are needed to characterize the observed data, given the expected values and the constraints on the rows and columns. This may sound like an arcane question, but it is important for understanding many types of statistical problems. This section shows how the particular formula in the text is calculated.

The first guess is that each observed value is an independent variable. That is, the number of degrees of freedom is $r*c$, where $r$ is the number of rows and $c$ is the number of columns in the data. However, the constraints mean that there are some relationships among the variables. For instance, the sum of each row has to be equal to the sum of each corresponding row in the expected values. So, the number of variables needed to describe the observed values is reduced by the number of rows. Taking into account the row constraints reduces the degrees of freedom to $r*c-r$. Because similar constraints apply to the columns, the degrees of freedom becomes $r*c - r - c$.

**DEGREES OF FREEDOM FOR CHI-SQUARE *(CONTINUED)***

However, the constraints on the rows and columns are themselves redundant, because the sum of all the rows is the same as the sum of the columns — in both cases, the sum is equal to total sum of all the cells. One of the constraints is unnecessary; the preceding formula has overcounted by 1. The formula for the degrees of freedom is $r*c - r - c + 1$. This is equivalent to $(r-1) * (c-1)$, the formula given in the text.

An example should help clarify this. Consider the general 2x2 table, where $a$, $b$, $c$, and $d$ are the expected values in the cells, and R1, R2, C1, C2, and T are the constraints. So R1 refers to the fact that the sum of the observed values in the first row equals the sum of the expected values, a+b.

The degrees of freedom for this example is one. That means that knowing one of the observed values along with the expected values defines all the other observed values. Let's call the observed values $A$, $B$, $C$, and $D$ and assume the value of $A$ is known. What are the other values?

The following formulas give the answer:

- $B = R1 - A$
- $C = C1 - A$
- $D = C2 - B = C2 - R1 + A$

The degrees of freedom are the number of variables we need to know in order to derive the original data from the expected values.

For the mathematically inclined, the degrees of freedom is the dimension of the space of observed values, subject to the row and column constraints. The precise definition is not needed to understand how to apply the ideas to the chi-square calculation. But it is interesting that the degrees of freedom characterizes the problem in a fundamental way.

## Chi-Square in SQL

Calculating the chi-square value uses basic arithmetic, so it can be readily calculated in SQL. The challenge is keeping track of the intermediate values, such as the expected values and the variances.

There are two dimensions in the chi-square table, the rows and the columns. The calculation in SQL uses four summaries along these dimensions:

- An aggregation along both the row and column dimensions. This calculates the values observed in each cell.

- An aggregation along the row dimension. This calculates the sum for each row and is used for the expected value calculation.

- An aggregation along the column dimension. This calculates the sum for each column and is used for the expected value calculation.

- The sum of everything.

The following SQL shows the calculation, liberally using subqueries for each of the preceding aggregations:

```
SELECT market, isstopped, val, exp, SQUARE(val - exp) / exp as chisquare
FROM (SELECT cells.market, cells.isstopped,
             1.0*r.cnt * c.cnt /
                  (SELECT COUNT(*) FROM subs
                   WHERE start_date in ('2005-12-26')) as exp,
             cells.cnt as val
      FROM (SELECT market,
                   (CASE WHEN stop_type IS NOT NULL THEN 1 ELSE 0 END
                   ) as isstopped, COUNT(*) as cnt
            FROM subs
            WHERE start_date in ('2005-12-26')
            GROUP BY market,
                   (CASE WHEN stop_type IS NOT NULL THEN 1 ELSE 0 END)
            ) cells LEFT OUTER JOIN
            (SELECT market, COUNT(*) as cnt
             FROM subs
             WHERE start_date in ('2005-12-26')
             GROUP BY market
             ) r
            ON cells.market = r.market LEFT OUTER JOIN
            (SELECT (CASE WHEN stop_type IS NOT NULL THEN 1 ELSE 0 END
                    ) as isstopped, COUNT(*) as cnt
             FROM subs
             WHERE start_date in ('2005-12-26')
             GROUP BY (CASE WHEN stop_type IS NOT NULL THEN 1 ELSE 0 END)
             ) c
            ON cells.isstopped = c.isstopped) a
ORDER BY 1, 2
```

This SQL follows the same logic as the Excel method for calculating the chi-square value. The row totals are in the query whose alias is R. The column totals are in the table whose alias is C. The expected value is then R.CNT times C.CNT divided by the sum for the entire table.

## What States Have Unusual Affinities for Which Types of Products?

The overall chi-square value tells us how unlikely or likely the values in each cell are. The values for each cell can be used as a measure of likelihood for that particular combination. The purchases data contains eight product groups and over fifty states. The question is: *Which states (if any) have an unusual affinity (positive or negative) for product groups?* That is, is there a geographical component to product preferences at the product group level?

Imagine the orders data summarized into a table, with product groups going across and states going down, and each cell containing the number of customers ordering that product group in that state. This looks like the tables used for chi-square calculations. *Which cells have the largest chi-square values?*

## Data Investigation

The first step in addressing a question such as this is investigating features of the data. Chapter 2 shows the distribution of orders by state. Figure 3-10 shows the distribution of orders by product group. A typical query to produce this distribution is:

```
SELECT productgroupname, COUNT(*) as numorderlines,
       COUNT(DISTINCT o.orderid) as numorders,
       COUNT(DISTINCT o.customerid) as numcustomers
FROM orders o LEFT OUTER JOIN
     orderline ol
     ON o.orderid = ol.orderid LEFT OUTER JOIN
     product p
     ON ol.productid = p.productid
GROUP BY productgroupname
ORDER BY 1
```

The results show that books are the most popular product group. Is this true on a state-by-state basis? It is indeed true that with very few exceptions, the most popular items in each state are books.

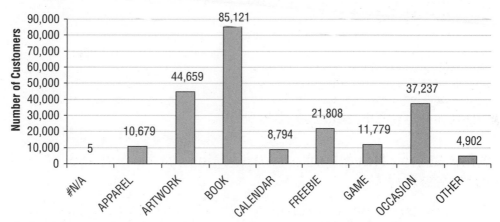

**Figure 3-10:** Some product groups attract more customers than other groups.

The following SQL answers this question, by calculating the number of customers in each state that have ordered books, and then choosing the one that is largest for each state. Chapter 2 discussed various methods of pulling the largest value out from a list. This example converts the frequency to a zero-padded number, concatenates the product group name to it, and takes the maximum.

```
SELECT state,
       SUBSTRING(MAX(RIGHT('0000000'+CAST(numcustomers as VARCHAR), 7)+
                   productgroupname), 8, 100) as prodgroup,
       MAX(numcustomers) as numcustomers
FROM (SELECT o.state, productgroupname,
             COUNT(DISTINCT o.customerid) as numcustomers
      FROM orders o LEFT OUTER JOIN
           orderline ol
           ON o.orderid = ol.orderid LEFT OUTER JOIN
           product p
           ON ol.productid = p.productid
      GROUP BY o.state, productgroupname) a
GROUP BY state
ORDER BY 3 DESC
```

The result confirms the hypothesis that books are, by far, the most popular product in most states. The first exception is the state "AE," which has nine customers buying ARTWORK. By the way, the state "AE" is not a mistake. It refers to military post offices in Europe.

### SQL to Calculate Chi-Square Values

Calculating the chi-square calculations for the state-group combinations requires a long SQL query. This query follows the same form as the earlier chi-square calculation, where there are three subqueries for the three aggregations of interest: by state and product group, by state alone, and by product group alone. The query itself joins these three tables and then does the appropriate aggregations.

```
SELECT state, productgroupname, val, exp,
       SQUARE(val - exp) / exp as chisquare
FROM (SELECT cells.state, cells.productgroupname,
             1.0*r.cnt * c.cnt /
                  (SELECT COUNT(DISTINCT customerid) FROM orders) as exp,
             cells.cnt as val
      FROM (SELECT state, productgroupname,
                   COUNT(DISTINCT o.customerid) as cnt
            FROM orders o LEFT OUTER JOIN
                 orderline ol
                 ON o.orderid = ol.orderid LEFT OUTER JOIN
                 product p
                 ON ol.productid = p.productid
            GROUP BY state, productgroupname
           ) cells LEFT OUTER JOIN
           (SELECT state, COUNT(DISTINCT customerid) as cnt
            FROM orders o
            GROUP BY state
           ) r
```

```
                 ON cells.state = r.state LEFT OUTER JOIN
                 (SELECT productgroupname,
                        COUNT(DISTINCT customerid) as cnt
                  FROM orders o LEFT OUTER JOIN
                       orderline ol
                       ON o.orderid = ol.orderid LEFT OUTER JOIN
                       product p
                       ON ol.productid = p.productid
                  GROUP BY productgroupname
                 ) c
                 ON cells.productgroupname = c.productgroupname) a
ORDER BY 5 DESC
```

The subquery for Cells calculates the observed value in each cell. The subquery called R calculates the row summaries, and the one called C calculates the column summaries. With this information, the chi-square calculation is just a matter of arithmetic.

## Affinity Results

Table 3-11 shows top ten combinations of state and product group that are most unexpected, based on the chi-square calculation. The first row in the table says that the most unexpected combination is GAMES in New York. Based on the information in the database, we would expect to have 3,306.1 customers purchasing games in that state. Instead, there are only 2,598, a difference of 708 customers. On the other hand, customers in Massachusetts are more likely to purchase games than we would expect.

**Table 3-11:** Unexpected Product-Group/State Combinations

| STATE | GROUP | OBSERVED | EXPECTED | CHI-SQUARE |
|-------|-------|----------|----------|------------|
| NY | GAME | 2,599 | 3,306.4 | 151.4 |
| FL | ARTWORK | 1,848 | 2,391.6 | 123.5 |
| NY | FREEBIE | 5,289 | 6,121.4 | 113.2 |
| NY | ARTWORK | 13,592 | 12,535.2 | 89.1 |
| NJ | ARTWORK | 5,636 | 4,992.6 | 82.9 |
| NY | OCCASION | 9,710 | 10,452.0 | 52.7 |
| NJ | GAME | 1,074 | 1,316.9 | 44.8 |
| AP | OTHER | 5 | 0.5 | 44.2 |
| FL | APPAREL | 725 | 571.9 | 41.0 |
| MA | GAME | 560 | 428.9 | 40.1 |
| NJ | CALENDAR | 785 | 983.2 | 40.0 |

This table cannot tell us that the results themselves are significant, simply that the differences exist. It does suggest asking about the differences between New York and Massachusetts that would explain why games are more popular in one state than the other. Or why ARTWORK is less popular is Florida than in New Jersey. Perhaps by changing marketing practices, there is opportunity to sell more products in the games category in New York, and more ARTWORK in Florida.

## Lessons Learned

This chapter strives to answer the questions of the genre "how different is different." Such questions necessarily bring up the subject of statistics, which has been studying ways to answer such questions for almost two centuries.

The normal distribution, which is defined by its average and standard deviation, is very important in statistics. Measuring how far a value is from the average, in terms of standard deviations, is the z-score. Large z-scores (regardless of sign) have a very low confidence. That is, the value is probably not produced by a random process, so *something* is happening.

Counts are very important in customer databases. There are three approaches to determining whether counts for different groups are the same or different. The binomial distribution counts every possible combination, so it is quite precise. The standard error of proportions is useful for getting z-scores. And, the chi-square test directly compares counts across multiple dimensions. All of these are useful for analyzing data.

The chi-square value and the z-score can both be informative. Although they use different methods, they can both find groups in the data where particular measures are unexpected. This can in turn lead to understanding things such as where certain products are more or less likely to be selling.

The next chapter moves from statistical measures of difference to geography, because geography is one of the most important factors in differentiating between customer groups.

# Where Is It All Happening?
# Location, Location, Location

From foreign policy to politics to real estate and retailing, many would agree with Napoleon's sentiment that "geography is destiny." Where customers reside and the attributes of that area are among customers' most informative characteristics: East coast, west coast, or in-between? Red state or blue state? Urban, rural, or suburban? Sun belt or snow belt? Good school district or retirement community? Geography is important.

Incorporating this rich source of information into data analysis poses some challenges. One is *geocoding*, the process of identifying where addresses are physically located, based on information in databases. Location information typically includes latitude and longitude, as well as the identification of multiple geographic areas, such as zip code, county, and state. This information makes it possible to determine who are neighbors and who are not.

Another challenge is incorporating the wealth of information about geographic areas. In the United States, the Census Bureau provides demographic and economic information about various levels of geography. The Bureau divides the country into very specific geographic pieces, such as census tracts and block groups and zip code tabulation areas (ZCTAs, which are like zip codes). The Bureau then summarizes information for these areas, information such as the number of households, the median household income, and the percent of housing units that use solar heat. The best thing about census data is that it is free and readily accessible on the web.

The Zipcode table contains just a small fraction of the available census variables. These are interesting by themselves. More importantly, such demographic data complements customer data. Combining the two provides new insight into customers.

This chapter introduces the information provided by geocoding and how to use this information in databases. The chapter continues by adding customer data into the mix. The examples in the chapter use the purchase dataset, because it has zip codes. Matching zip codes to census zip codes (actually zip code tabulation areas) serves as a rudimentary form of geocoding.

No discussion of geography would be complete without including maps, which are a very powerful way of communicating information. Once upon a time (prior to Excel 2002), Excel had built-in mapping capabilities; unfortunately, such capabilities now require purchasing additional products. Nevertheless, there are some clever things to do in Excel to visualize data, and it is even possible to connect Excel to maps on the web. This chapter starts with a discussion of geographic data and ends with an overview of the role that mapping can play in data analysis.

## Latitude and Longitude

Each point on the earth's surface is described by a latitude and a longitude. Because the earth is basically a sphere and not a flat plane, latitudes and longitudes behave a bit differently from high school geometry. This section uses the Zipcode table to investigate latitudes and longitudes.

### Definition of Latitude and Longitude

The "lines" of latitude and longitude are actually circles on the earth's globe. All "lines" of longitude go through the north and south poles. All "lines" of latitude are circles parallel to the equator. The actual measurements are angles, measured from the center of the earth to the Greenwich meridian (for longitude) or to the equator (for latitude). Figure 4-1 shows examples of latitudes and longitudes.

Although the two seem quite similar, there are some important and interesting differences between them. One difference is historical. Longitude (how far east and west) is difficult to measure without accurate time-keeping devices, which are a relatively modern invention.

Latitude (how far north or south) has been understood for thousands of years and can be measured by the angle of stars in the sky or the position of the sun when it is directly overhead. By observing the position of the sun at noon on the summer solstice several thousand years ago, the ancient Greek astronomer Eratosthenes estimated the circumference of the earth. He noted three facts. At noon on the summer solstice, the sun was directly overhead in the town of Syene. At the same time, the sun was at an angle of 7.2 degrees from the vertical in his town of Alexandria. And, Syene was located a certain distance south of Alexandria. According to modern measurements, his estimate of the circumference was accurate within two percent — pretty remarkable accuracy for work done twenty-five centuries ago.

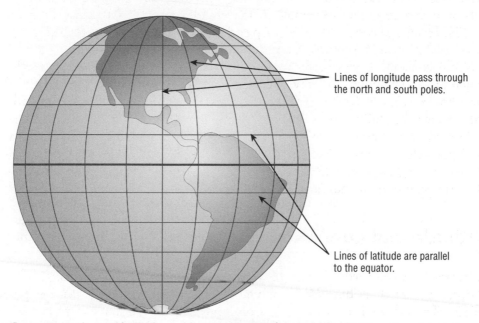

Lines of longitude pass through the north and south poles.

Lines of latitude are parallel to the equator.

**Figure 4-1:** Lines of latitude and longitude make it possible to locate any point on the earth's surface.

Unlike lines of longitude, lines of latitude do not intersect. The distance between two lines of latitude separated by one degree is always about 68.7 miles (the earth's circumference divided by 360 degrees). The distance between two lines of longitude separated by one degree varies by latitude, being about 68.7 miles at the equator and diminishing to zero at the poles.

Recall from high school geometry that one definition of a line is the shortest distance between two points. On a sphere, lines of longitude have this property. So for two locations, one directly north or south of the other, following the line of longitude is the shortest path between the two points.

Lines of latitude do not have this property (so they are not strictly lines in the sense of spherical geometry). For two locations at the same latitude, such as Chicago, IL and Providence, RI or Miami, FL and Brownsville, TX, the latitude line connecting them is not the shortest distance. This is one reason why airplanes flying between the East Coast and West Coast often go into Canadian airspace, and why flights from the United States to Asia and Europe often go far north near the North Pole. The airplanes are following a shorter path by going farther north.

## Degrees, Minutes, Seconds, and All That

Latitude and longitude are measured in degrees, usually ranging from minus 180 degrees to positive 180 degrees. For latitude, the extremes are the South and North Poles, respectively. Negative degrees are traditionally south of the equator, and positive degrees are north of the equator, probably due to the fact that people living in the northern hemisphere invented the whole system in the first place.

Longitudes also range from minus 180 degrees to positive 180 degrees. Traditionally, locations west of Greenwich, England have negative longitudes and those east of Greenwich have positive longitudes, so all of North and South America, with the exception of very small parts of far western Alaska, have negative longitudes. People in Europe — which mostly has positive longitudes — invented the numbering scheme rather than people in the Americas.

Angles are traditionally measured in degrees, minutes, and seconds. One degree consists of sixty minutes. One minute consists of sixty seconds, regardless of whether the minute is a fraction of a degree or a fraction of an hour. This is not a coincidence. Thousands of years ago, the ancient Babylonians based their number system on multiples of sixty (which they in turn may have borrowed from the more ancient Sumerians), rather than the multiples of ten that we are familiar with. They divided time and angles into sixty equal parts, which is why there are sixty minutes in both one hour and one degree. Such a system is called a sexagesimal number system, a piece of trivia otherwise irrelevant to data analysis.

When working with degrees, both databases and Excel prefer to work with decimal degrees. *How can we convert degrees/minutes/seconds to decimal degrees and vice versa?* The first part of this question is easy to answer. The author was born at approximately at 25° 43′ 32″ degrees north and 80° 16′ 22″ degrees west. To convert this to decimal degrees, simply divide the minutes by 60 and the seconds by 3600 to arrive at 25.726° N and 80.273° W. This is easily done in either Excel or SQL.

Although decimal degrees are quite sufficient for our purposes, it is worth considering the reverse computation. The following expressions calculate the degrees, minutes, and seconds from a decimal degree using Excel functions (assuming the decimal degrees are in cell A1):

```
<degrees> = TRUNC(A1)
<minutes> = MOD(TRUNC(ABS(A1)*60), 60)
<seconds> = MOD(TRUNC(ABS(A1)*3600), 60)
```

The MOD() function returns the remainder when the second argument is divided by the first. For instance, when the second argument is two, MOD() returns zero for even numbers and one for odd numbers. The TRUNC() function removes the fractional part of a number for both positive and negative values.

Unfortunately, Excel does not have a number format that supports degrees, minutes, and seconds. However, the following expression takes degrees, minutes, and seconds and creates an appropriate string:

```
<degrees>&CHAR(176)&" "&<minutes>&"' "&<seconds>&""""
```

The function CHAR(176) returns the degree symbol. The symbol for minutes is a single quote. The symbol for seconds is a double quote. Putting a double quotation mark in a string requires using four double quotes in a row.

**TIP**  Any character can be included in an Excel text value. One way to add a character is with the CHAR() function. Another way is to use the Insert ➪ Symbol menu option.

## Distance between Two Locations

Longitudes and latitudes make it possible to calculate the distance between two locations. This section introduces two methods for calculating the distance, a less accurate but easier way, and a more accurate method. The distances are then used to answer some questions about zip codes, because the latitude and longitude of the center of each zip code is available in the Zipcensus table.

This section uses trigonometric functions, which expect their arguments to be in units called radians rather than the more familiar degrees. There is a simple conversion from degrees to radians and back again:

```
<radians> = <degrees>*PI()/180
<degrees> = <radians>*180/PI()
```

The conversion is simple because pi radians equal exactly 180 degrees. Both SQL and Excel support the function PI(), which is used for the conversion. Excel also has the function RADIANS() that also does the conversion.

**WARNING**  When working with angles, be careful whether the measurements should be in degrees or radians. Usually, functions that operate on angles expect the angles in radians.

### Euclidian Method

The Pythagorean formula calculates the length of the long side of a right triangle as the square root of the sum of the squares of the lengths of the two shorter sides. An equivalent formulation is that the distance between two points is the square root of the sum of the squares of the X-coordinate difference and the Y-coordinate difference. These are handy formulas when two points lie on a flat plane.

The same formula could be applied directly to latitudes and longitudes, but the result does not make sense — latitudes and longitudes are measured in degrees, and distance in degrees does not make sense. The distance should be measured in miles or kilometers.

The degrees need to be converted to miles before applying the formula. The north-south distance between two lines of latitude is simply the difference in degrees times 68.7 miles, regardless of the longitude. The east-west distance between two lines of longitude depends on the latitude; the distance is the difference in degrees of longitude times 68.7 times the cosine of the bigger latitude.

For two points on the surface of the earth, the north-south distance and east-west distance are the sides of a right triangle, as shown in Figure 4-2. Note that a right triangle on the earth's surface does not necessarily look like one in a picture.

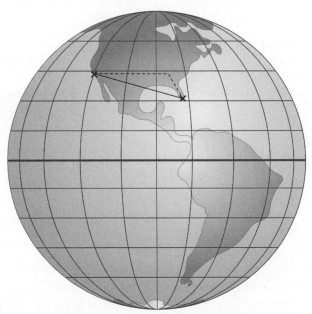

**Figure 4-2:** The distance between two points on the earth's surface can be approximated by converting the latitude and longitudes to miles and then using the Pythagorean Theorem.

The geographic center of the continental United States is in the middle of Kansas and has a longitude of –98.6° and a latitude of 39.8°. By converting the differences in coordinates to miles, the following query finds the ten closest zip codes to the geographic center:

```
SELECT TOP 10 zipcode, state, population, latitude, longitude, disteuc
FROM (SELECT zc.*,
            (CASE WHEN latitude > 39.8
                THEN SQRT(SQUARE(difflat*68.9) +
```

```
                        SQUARE(difflong*SIN(latrad)*68.9))
            ELSE SQRT(SQUARE(difflat*68.9) +
                        SQUARE(difflong*SIN(centerlatrad)*68.9))
         END) as disteuc
  FROM (SELECT zc.*, latitude - 39.8 as difflat,
            longitude - (-98.6) as difflong,
            latitude*PI()/180 as latrad,
            39.8*PI()/180 as centerlatrad
      FROM zipcensus zc) zc) zc
ORDER BY disteuc
```

The innermost subquery defines useful variables, such as the latitude and longitude in radians (perhaps the trickiest part of the calculation). The next subquery calculates the distance. The CASE statement chooses the larger latitude to get the smaller distance. The ten zip codes closest to the geographic center of the continental United States are in Table 4-1.

**Table 4-1:** The Closest Zip Codes by Euclidean Distance to the Geometric Center of the United States

| ZIP CODE | STATE | LONGITUDE | LATITUDE | EUCLIDIAN DISTANCE | CIRCULAR DISTANCE |
|----------|-------|-----------|----------|--------------------|--------------------|
| 66952 | KS | -98.59 | 39.84 | 2.5 | 2.5 |
| 66941 | KS | -98.44 | 39.83 | 7.2 | 8.5 |
| 66967 | KS | -98.80 | 39.79 | 8.6 | 10.4 |
| 66932 | KS | -98.92 | 39.76 | 14.5 | 17.3 |
| 67638 | KS | -98.85 | 39.64 | 15.4 | 17.0 |
| 66936 | KS | -98.29 | 39.91 | 15.4 | 17.8 |
| 67474 | KS | -98.70 | 39.58 | 15.8 | 16.1 |
| 66956 | KS | -98.21 | 39.79 | 17.3 | 20.8 |
| 67628 | KS | -98.97 | 39.65 | 19.4 | 22.2 |
| 66951 | KS | -99.04 | 39.79 | 19.4 | 23.2 |

### Accurate Method

This formula for distance between two locations is not accurate because the calculation uses formulas from flat geometry. The distance does not take the curvature of the earth into account.

There is a formula for the distance between two points on a sphere, based on a simple idea. Connect the two points to the center of the earth. This forms an angle. The distance is the angle measured in radians times the radius of the earth. A simple idea, but it leads to a messy formula. The following SQL query uses this formula to find the ten zip codes closest to the center of the continental United States using the more accurate method:

```
SELECT TOP 10 zipcode, state, population, latitude, longitude, disteuc,
       distcirc
FROM (SELECT zc.*,
           ACOS(COS(centerlatrad)*COS(latrad)*
                               COS(centerlongrad - longrad) +
             SIN(centerlatrad)*SIN(latrad))*radius as distcirc,
           (CASE WHEN latitude > 39.8
               THEN SQRT(SQUARE(difflat*68.9) +
                       SQUARE(difflong*SIN(latrad)*68.9))
               ELSE SQRT(SQUARE(difflat*68.9) +
                       SQUARE(difflong*SIN(centerlatrad)*68.9))
           END) as disteuc
       FROM (SELECT zc.*, latitude - 39.8 as difflat,
               longitude - (-98.6) as difflong,
               latitude*PI()/180 as latrad,
               39.8*PI()/180 as centerlatrad,
               longitude*PI()/180 as longrad,
               (-98.6)*PI()/180 as centerlongrad,
               3949.9 as radius
           FROM zipcensus zc) zc) zc
ORDER BY disteuc
```

This formula uses several trigonometric functions, so the innermost query converts all the latitudes and longitudes to radians. In addition, this method uses the radius of the earth, which is taken to be 3,949.9 miles.

Table 4-1 shows the circular distance as well as the Euclidean distance. Although the results are similar, there are some discrepancies. For points due north or south of the center, such as zip codes 68970 and 67437, the two methods produce similar distances, down to a fraction of a mile. Both are measuring the distance along the shortest path between the two points.

However, for points that lie due east or west of the center point, the two methods produce different results. For zip code 66956 the Euclidean method produces a distance of 17.3 miles and the circular produces a distance of 20.8 miles. Overall, the two methods are usually within about 10%–20% of each other.

The spherical method is not perfect, because the earth is not a perfect sphere. A better approximation could take into account the bulges around the equator. Improvements might take into account altitude, because not all locations are at sea level. And finally, the travel distance along roads rather than the theoretical distance between two locations may be the right distance. Such a calculation requires special-purpose tools and databases of roads and is not feasible in Excel and SQL.

## Finding All Zip Codes within a Given Distance

Being able to find the distance between two locations can be useful. It makes it possible to find the nearest Wal-Mart to where a customer lives or the closest repair center to where a car broke down or the distance from home to where a customer paid for a restaurant dinner. Each of these applications assumes that the locations (customers' and otherwise) are available as latitudes and longitudes, typically through the process of geocoding or through the use of global positioning systems (GPS).

Finding the zip codes within a certain distance of a location is another application. Once upon a time, a newspaper was interested in areas where it could provide home delivery copies. One part of the newspaper delivered copies to university campuses. Another part arranged for home delivery. Some universities received newspapers, even though the surrounding areas were not routable for home delivery. Why not also offer home delivery in the surrounding area? A brilliant idea that led to the question: *Which zip codes are within eight miles of a specific set of university zip codes?*

One way to answer the question is with a big map, or with a mapping web site (such as Google Maps, MapQuest, Yahoo! Maps, or Microsoft Live). This would be a manual process of looking up each zip code to find the neighboring ones. Manual solutions are prone to error. Because the Census Bureau provides the latitude and longitude of the center of each zip code, why not use this information instead?

The actual solution was an Excel worksheet that used the census information to find the distance from each zip code to the chosen zip code. The spreadsheet then created a table with the zip codes within eight miles.

Such a spreadsheet is useful for manual processing, but the processing can also be done in SQL. The following query calculates all zip codes within eight miles of Dartmouth University in Hanover, NH:

```
SELECT z.zipcode, z.state, zco.poname, distcirc, population, hh,
       hhmedincome
FROM (SELECT zips.*,
             ACOS(COS(comp.latrad)*COS(zips.latrad)*
                                 COS(comp.longrad - zips.longrad) +
                 SIN(comp.latrad)*SIN(zips.latrad))*radius as distcirc
      FROM (SELECT zc.*, latitude*PI()/180 as latrad,
                   longitude*PI()/180 as longrad, 3949.9 as radius
            FROM zipcensus zc) zips CROSS JOIN
           (SELECT zc.*, latitude*PI()/180 as latrad,
                   longitude*PI()/180 as longrad
            FROM zipcensus zc
            WHERE zipcode IN ('03755')) comp) z LEFT OUTER JOIN
     zipcounty zco
     ON z.zipcode = zco.zipcode
WHERE distcirc < 8
ORDER BY distcirc
```

The two innermost subquerys, Zips and Comp, convert latitudes and longitudes to radians. These two subqueries are joined using CROSS JOIN because Comp has only one row, the zip code for Dartmouth (03755). This join provides the data for calculating the distance, and then the Zipcounty table is joined in for the post office name. More zip codes can be included by expanding the list in the Comp subquery.

The closest zip codes are shown in Table 4-2. Some are in New Hampshire and some are in Vermont, because Hanover is near the border between these states.

**Table 4-2:** Zip Codes within Eight Miles of Hanover, NH

| ZIP CODE | PO NAME AND STATE | DISTANCE | POPULATION | HOUSEHOLDS # | MEDIAN INCOME |
|---|---|---|---|---|---|
| 03755 | Hanover, NH | 0.0 | 9,877 | 2,504 | $69,430 |
| 05055 | Norwich, VT | 2.3 | 3,500 | 1,348 | $66,214 |
| 03750 | Etna, NH | 2.8 | 962 | 319 | $86,421 |
| 05088 | Wilder, VT | 4.1 | 777 | 316 | $34,444 |
| 03766 | Lebanon, NH | 5.3 | 8,628 | 3,759 | $42,693 |
| 03784 | West Lebanon, NH | 5.6 | 3,701 | 1,594 | $42,397 |
| 05043 | East Thetford, VT | 5.6 | 596 | 247 | $49,750 |
| 05074 | Thetford, VT | 6.8 | 166 | 49 | $68,250 |
| 05001 | White River Junction, VT | 7.0 | 9,172 | 3,939 | $43,125 |
| 05075 | Thetford Center, VT | 7.8 | 1,487 | 597 | $47,321 |

It is tempting to extend the find-the-nearest-zip-code query to find the nearest zip code to every zip code in the table. As a query, this is a slight modification of the Dartmouth query (Comp would choose all zip codes). However, such a query is going to take a long time to complete. The problem is that the distance between every possible pair of all 32,038 zip codes needs to be calculated — over one billion distance calculations. The distances between zip codes in Florida and zip codes in Washington (state) have to be calculated, even though no zip code in Washington is close to any zip code in Florida.

Unfortunately, SQL does not, in general, have the ability to make these queries run faster. Using indexes does not help, because the distance calculation requires two columns, both latitude and longitude. Indexes speed up access to one column at a time, not both at once. There are special-purpose databases that use special-purpose data structures to store geographic information and make such queries much more feasible; however, these are not part of standard SQL.

### Finding Nearest Zip Code in Excel

This section does a very similar calculation in Excel, finding the nearest zip code to a given zip code. The Excel spreadsheet consists of the following areas:

- The input area is for typing in a zip code.
- The output area for the nearest zip code and distance.
- The table contains all the zip codes, each with its latitude and longitude.

The user types a zip code in the spreadsheet in the input area. The spreadsheet looks up the latitude and longitude using the VLOOKUP() function. The distance from every zip code to the chosen zip code is then calculated as an additional column.

Figure 4-3 shows the functions in the worksheet. The nearest zip code is chosen using the MIN() function, with a small caveat. The minimum distance is clearly going to be zero, which is the distance from any given zip code to itself. The minimum uses a nested IF() to exclude the input zip code. This is an example of an array function, discussed in the aside "Array Functions in Excel." With the minimum distance, the actual zip code is found using a combination of MATCH() to find the row with the zip code and then OFFSET() to return the value in the correct column.

| | F5 | | | ▼ | fx | {=MIN(IF($B$13:$B$32050<>$F$2, $F$13:$F$32050))} | |
|---|---|---|---|---|---|---|---|

| | A | B | C | D | E | F |
|---|---|---|---|---|---|---|
| 1 | | | | | | |
| 2 | | | | | INPUT ZIP | 10011 |
| 3 | | | | | LATITUDE | =VLOOKUP(F2, $B$13:$E$32050, 3, 0) |
| 4 | | | | | LONGITUDE | =VLOOKUP(F2, $B$13:$E$32050, 4, 0) |
| 5 | | | | | MIN DIST | =MIN(IF($B$13:$B$32050<>$F$2, $F$13:$F$32050)) |
| 6 | | | | | ZIP | =OFFSET($B$12, MATCH($F$5, $F$13:$F$32050, 0), 0) |
| 7 | | | | | RADIUS | 3949.9 |
| 8 | | | | | LAT RADIAN | =RADIANS($F$3) |
| 9 | | | | | | |
| 10 | | | | | | |
| 11 | | | FROM SQL | | | |
| 12 | | ZIP | STATE | LAT | LONG | DISTANCE FROM INPUT ZIP |
| 13 | | 601 | PR | 18.1801 | -66.74947 | =ACOS(SIN(RADIANS(D13))*SIN($F$8)+COS(RADIANS(D13))*COS($F$8)*COS(RADIANS($F$4-E13)))*$F$7 |
| 14 | | 602 | PR | 18.36329 | -67.18024 | =ACOS(SIN(RADIANS(D14))*SIN($F$8)+COS(RADIANS(D14))*COS($F$8)*COS(RADIANS($F$4-E14)))*$F$7 |
| 15 | | 603 | PR | 18.44862 | -67.13422 | =ACOS(SIN(RADIANS(D15))*SIN($F$8)+COS(RADIANS(D15))*COS($F$8)*COS(RADIANS($F$4-E15)))*$F$7 |
| 16 | | 604 | PR | 18.49899 | -67.13699 | =ACOS(SIN(RADIANS(D16))*SIN($F$8)+COS(RADIANS(D16))*COS($F$8)*COS(RADIANS($F$4-E16)))*$F$7 |
| 17 | | 606 | PR | 18.18215 | -66.95881 | =ACOS(SIN(RADIANS(D17))*SIN($F$8)+COS(RADIANS(D17))*COS($F$8)*COS(RADIANS($F$4-E17)))*$F$7 |
| 18 | | 610 | PR | 18.28832 | -67.13605 | =ACOS(SIN(RADIANS(D18))*SIN($F$8)+COS(RADIANS(D18))*COS($F$8)*COS(RADIANS($F$4-E18)))*$F$7 |
| 19 | | 612 | PR | 18.44973 | -66.6988 | =ACOS(SIN(RADIANS(D19))*SIN($F$8)+COS(RADIANS(D19))*COS($F$8)*COS(RADIANS($F$4-E19)))*$F$7 |
| 20 | | 616 | PR | 18.42675 | -66.67669 | =ACOS(SIN(RADIANS(D20))*SIN($F$8)+COS(RADIANS(D20))*COS($F$8)*COS(RADIANS($F$4-E20)))*$F$7 |
| 21 | | 617 | PR | 18.4555 | -66.55576 | =ACOS(SIN(RADIANS(D21))*SIN($F$8)+COS(RADIANS(D21))*COS($F$8)*COS(RADIANS($F$4-E21)))*$F$7 |

**Figure 4-3:** This Excel spreadsheet calculates the closest zip code to any other zip code. The curly braces in the formula line indicate that this particular formula is an array function.

## ARRAY FUNCTIONS IN EXCEL

Many functions in Excel, such as SUM() and COUNT(), accept ranges of cells. This is quite useful for choosing the rows for a calculation according to some condition. Excel offers two functions that do this, SUMIF() and COUNTIF(). However, this functionality may not be enough. The conditions are limited to simple comparisons, and the functions are limited to summation and counting.

To extend this functionality, Excel has the concept of array functions. These are functions that operate on arrays of spreadsheet values, typically columns. Array functions can be nested, so they have the full power of Excel functions. Some of them can even return values in multiple cells, although these are not discussed until Chapter 11.

An example perhaps explains this best. The following are two ways of taking the sum of the product of the values in two columns of cells:

```
=SUMPRODUCT($A$2$A$10, $B$2$B$10)
{=SUM($A$2$A$10 * $B$2$B$10)}
```

These two methods are equivalent. The first uses the built-in function SUMPRODUCT() that does exactly what we want. The second combines the SUM() function and the multiplication operator as an array function. It says to multiply the values in the two columns row-by-row and then to take the sum. Think of the expression as reading each row, multiplying together the corresponding values in columns A and B and saving all these products somewhere. This somewhere is then an array of values passed to SUM().

Entering an array function takes a sleight of hand. The expression is typed in just like any other expression. Instead of hitting the <return> key after entering the formula, hit <control><shift><return> at the same time. Excel encloses the formula in curly braces on the formula bar to indicate that it is an array function. The curly braces are not entered as part of the function, though.

One particularly useful application of array functions is combining them with IF(). In the text, the problem is to find the minimum distance, where the zip code is not the given zip code. The formula for this is:

```
{=MIN(IF($A$7:$A$32044<>B2, $E$7:$E$32044))}
```

This says to take the minimum of the values in column E, but only where the corresponding value in column A is not equal to the value in cell B2.

Array functions can be as complicated as other Excel functions. Although they are easy to express, a column filled with thousands of array functions can take a while to calculate.

And they come with one small warning. The functions AND() and OR() do not always work as expected. Instead, just use nested IF() statements to achieve the same logic.

## Pictures with Zip Codes

Latitudes and longitudes are coordinates, and these can be plotted using scatter plots. Such plots are a poor-man's geographic information system (GIS). This section introduces the idea, along with some caveats about the process.

### The Scatter Plot Map

There are enough zip codes in the United States that just the center points form a recognizable outline of the country. Figure 4-4 shows a zip code map of the continental United States, where each zip code is represented as a small hollow circle. The reason for using a hollow circle is to see where zip codes overlap each other.

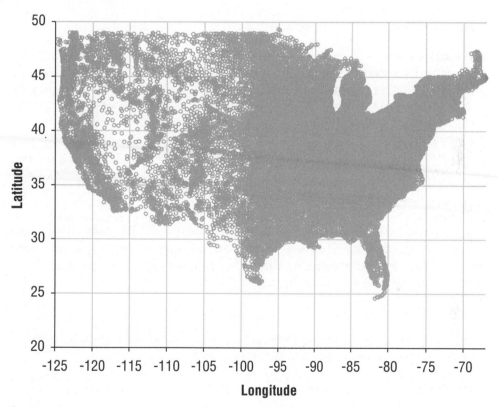

**Figure 4-4:** The center of zip codes form a recognizable map of the United States.

This map is based on the same latitude and longitude data used for the distance calculations. The latitude is assigned as the Y-axis in a scatter plot and the longitude is assigned as the X-axis. To focus on the continental United States, the horizontal scale goes from −65 to −125 and the vertical scale from 20 to 50. Lines are drawn every five degrees on both scales. Although far from perfect, the zip code centers do form a blob that is recognizable as the continental United States.

Cartographers — the people who study maps and how to convey information on them — have many standards for what makes a good map. This simple zip code scatter plot fails almost all of them. It distorts distances and areas. For instance, small land areas in the north appear bigger, and larger land areas near the equator appear smaller. It does not have boundaries or features, such as mountains, cities, and roads. And, if the dimensions of the chart are not right, the map is stretched in unusual ways.

Nonetheless, the result is recognizable and actually useful for conveying information. It is also easy to create. Even the simple zip code map shows area where there are many zip codes (along the coasts) and where there are few (in the mountainous states of the west, in the Everglades in South Florida).

## Who Uses Solar Power for Heating?

The census provides many attributes about people, households, families, and housing units. One of them, for instance, happens to be the source of heat. The column HHUFUELSOLAR contains the proportion of housing units using solar power in a zip code. To convert this to a count, multiply by HHUOCCUPIED, the number of occupied housing units.

In 2000, solar power was not particularly widespread, but a simple zip code map can show where it existed. *Which zip codes have any household with solar power?* Figure 4-5 shows a map with this information. The faint grey areas are zip codes that do not have solar power; the larger darker triangles show zip codes that do.

Arranging the data in the spreadsheet can make it easier to create the map. The first column is the X-value for the chart and the second two columns are the Y-values for two series in the chart. The data should be laid out as:

- Longitude, which is along the X-axis;
- Latitude for non-solar zip codes; and,
- Latitude for solar zip codes.

Each row has exactly one value for latitude, in one of the two columns, with the latitude only in the appropriate column. The following query returns the data in this format:

```
SELECT zipcode, longitude,
       (CASE WHEN hhuofuelsolar = 0 THEN latitude END) as nosolarlat,
       (CASE WHEN hhuofuelsolar > 0 THEN latitude END) as solarlat
FROM zipcensus
WHERE latitude BETWEEN 20 and 50 AND
      longitude BETWEEN -135 AND -65
```

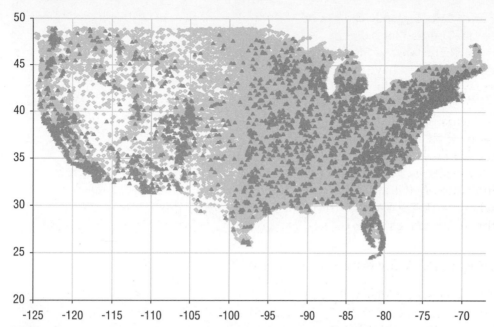

**Figure 4-5:** This map shows the zip codes that have housing units with solar power, based on the 2000 Census.

An alternative approach would be to have the query provide a "solar" indicator along with the longitude and latitude. The data would be put into the right format using the IF() function in Excel. Both methods work, but there is no reason to do the extra work in Excel when it can be done in SQL.

> **TIP** Pulling the data in the right format using SQL can often save time and effort in Excel.

The little triangles in the chart are the zip codes that have solar power. Not surprisingly, Florida and California have a high concentration of these, because these are two states that are both sunny and highly populated. The cloudy northeast has many solar zip codes, but this is probably because there are so many zip codes in such a densely populated area. Some states in the west, such as New Mexico, Arizona, and Colorado have a relatively high number of solar zip codes, but because these states are less dense, there are not as many triangles.

A map is useful for seeing what is happening. The data itself can be verified by asking: *What proportion of zip codes in each state have at least one solar powered residence?* The following query answers this question, using the Census Bureau definition of a state:

```
SELECT TOP 10 state,
       SUM(CASE WHEN hhuofuelsolar > 0 THEN 1.0 END)/COUNT(*) as propzips,
       SUM(hhuofuelsolar*hhuoccupied)/SUM(hhuoccupied) as prophhu
```

```
FROM zipcensus zc
GROUP BY state
ORDER BY 3 DESC
```

This query actually calculates two numbers: the proportion of zip codes with solar power and the proportion of households. For most states, there is a strong correlation between these as shown in Table 4-3. However, for some states such as Wyoming, solar power is concentrated in a few zip codes (fewer than 14%), but a relatively high proportion of housing units have it (0.10%).

**Table 4-3:** The Top Ten States by Penetration of Solar Power in Housing Units

| STATE | PROPORTION ZIPS SOLAR | PROPORTION HOUSING UNITS SOLAR |
|-------|-----------------------|-------------------------------|
| HI | 87.64% | 1.51% |
| PR | 97.60% | 1.31% |
| NM | 30.35% | 0.37% |
| CO | 35.48% | 0.14% |
| CA | 37.09% | 0.12% |
| WY | 13.61% | 0.10% |
| AZ | 33.70% | 0.06% |
| NV | 17.69% | 0.05% |
| MT | 10.60% | 0.05% |
| NC | 16.60% | 0.04% |

## Where Are the Customers?

Questions about zip codes are not limited to the census information. The Orders table contains information about where customers place orders. The following query summarizes the number of orders in each zip code and then joins this information to the latitude and longitude in the Zipcensus table:

```
SELECT zc.zipcode, longitude, latitude, numords,
       (CASE WHEN hh = 0 THEN 0.0 ELSE numords*1.0/hh END) as penetration
FROM zipcensus zc JOIN
     (SELECT zipcode, COUNT(*) as numords
      FROM orders
      GROUP BY zipcode) o
     ON zc.zipcode = o.zipcode
WHERE latitude BETWEEN 20 and 50 AND
      longitude BETWEEN -135 AND -65
```

The results are shown in Figure 4-6 as a bubble chart. The size of the bubbles is the number of orders placed in the zip code; the X-axis is the longitude, and the Y-axis is the latitude. Like the scatter plot, this bubble chart is a rudimentary map; however, bubble charts have fewer formatting options available than scatter plots (for instance, the shape of the bubbles cannot be changed). The bubbles in this chart are disks, colored on the outside and transparent inside. This is important because bubbles may overlap each other.

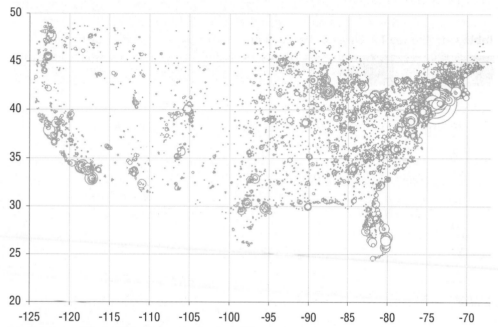

**Figure 4-6:** This bubble chart shows the order penetration in each zip code.

This map has fewer zip codes than the previous ones, because only about 11,000 zip codes have orders. Many of these zip codes are in the northeast, so that region of the country is overrepresented.

Such a map conveys interesting information about customers. By using multiple series, for instance, orders could be classified by the products they contain, or customers by the number of purchases they make.

## Census Demographics

Solar power is interesting, but not as useful as economic information for understanding customers. This section looks at some other types of information available, and at ways of combining this information with the purchase data. Of course, the Zipcensus table contains only a subset of all the possible information available (for free) from the census web site.

## The Extremes: Richest and Poorest

There are several columns in the data related to wealth, which is very valuable information for understanding customers. You may not know how wealthy your customers are, but you can know how wealthy their neighbors are.

### Median Income

The median household income in a zip code is the income in the middle, where half the households earn more than the median and half earn less. The median income is a very useful measure for understanding whether a given area is relatively wealthy or relatively poor. Households are a reasonable unit because they tend to correspond to an economic marketing unit — groups in the population bound together economically.

However, median household income is not the only measure available. The Census Bureau also provides the average household income, as well as dividing income into ranges (how many households earned $45,000 to $50,000 dollars, for instance). This information is provided at the household level, at the family level, and for individuals. There is even information about sources of income, separating out earned income, social security income, and government benefits. There is a wealth of variables just describing wealth, but we'll generally stick with median household income.

One query for finding the zip code with the highest median household income is:

```
SELECT TOP 1 zipcode, hhmedincome
FROM zipcensus
ORDER BY hhmedincome DESC
```

To find the poorest, the sort order is changed to ASC rather than DESC.

This query is simple, but it has a flaw: more than one zip code could be tied for the richest or the poorest. A better approach finds all zip codes that match the extreme values. The following query counts the number of matching zip codes:

```
SELECT hhmedincome, COUNT(*) as numzips,
       SUM(CASE WHEN population = 0 THEN 1 ELSE 0 END) as pop0,
       SUM(CASE WHEN hh = 0 THEN 1 ELSE 0 END) as hh0,
       AVG(population*1.0) as avgpop, AVG(hh*1.0) as avghh
FROM zipcensus zc JOIN
     (SELECT MAX(hhmedincome) as hhmax, MIN(hhmedincome) as hhmin
      FROM zipcensus) minmax
     ON zc.hhmedincome IN (minmax.hhmax, minmax.hhmin)
GROUP BY hhmedincome
```

This query returns some additional information, such as the number of zip codes where the population is zero, where the number of households is zero, and the average population of the zip code.

Table 4-4 shows that 149 zip codes have zero median income. Although some people live in these zip codes, there are no households. These zip codes probably contain institutions of some sort, where everyone is in group housing, rather than private residences (for example, prisons and college dorms). Because there are no households, the household income is zero, which appears to be a placeholder for NULL.

**Table 4-4:** Information About the Wealthiest and Poorest Zip Codes

| HOUSE-HOLD MEDIAN INCOME | NUMBER OF ZIPS | NO POPU-LATION | NO HOUSE-HOLDS | AVERAGE POPU-LATION | AVERAGE HOUSE-HOLDS |
|---|---|---|---|---|---|
| $0 | 149 | 55 | 149 | 710.4 | 0.0 |
| $200,001 | 10 | 0 | 0 | 1,057.9 | 339.3 |

The ten zip codes with the maximum median income are shown in Table 4-5. These are almost all small, except for one in Illinois and one in California.

**Table 4-5:** The Wealthiest Zip Codes by Household Income in the 2000 Census

| ZIP CODE | PO NAME AND STATE | POPU-LATION | HOUSE-HOLDS | FAMI-LIES | MEDIAN INCOME HOUSE-HOLDS | FAMILY |
|---|---|---|---|---|---|---|
| 12429 | Esopus, NY | 15 | 7 | 7 | $200,001 | $200,001 |
| 38157 | Memphis, TN | 95 | 5 | 5 | $200,001 | $200,001 |
| 33109 | Miami Beach, FL | 339 | 204 | 118 | $200,001 | $200,001 |
| 60043 | Kenilworth, IL | 2,550 | 820 | 732 | $200,001 | $200,001 |
| 19736 | Yorklyn, DE | 66 | 22 | 22 | $200,001 | $200,001 |
| 32447 | Marianna, FL | 236 | 19 | 7 | $200,001 | $28,750 |
| 19710 | Montchanin, DE | 26 | 16 | 8 | $200,001 | $200,001 |
| 94027 | Atherton, CA | 6,872 | 2,258 | 1,859 | $200,001 | $200,001 |
| 19732 | Rockland, DE | 46 | 26 | 19 | $200,001 | $200,001 |
| 28378 | Rex, NC | 33 | 16 | 16 | $200,001 | $200,001 |

### Proportion of Wealthy and Poor

Median household income is interesting, but, like all medians, it provides information about only one household, the one whose income is in the middle. An alternative approach is to consider the distribution of incomes, by looking at the proportion of the very rich or very poor in the zip codes. The column FAMINC000_010 identifies for the poorest group, those whose family income is less than ten thousand dollars per year. At the other extreme are the wealthiest whose income exceeds two hundred thousand dollars per year, counted by FAMINC200. The resulting query looks like:

```
SELECT zipcode, state, hhmedincome, fammedincome, pop, hh
FROM zipcensus zc CROSS JOIN
    (SELECT MAX(faminc200) as richest, MAX(faminc000_010) as poorest
     FROM zipcensus
     WHERE hh >= 1000 AND state <> 'PR') minmax
WHERE (zc.faminc200 = richest OR zc.faminc000_010 = poorest) AND
      zc.hh >= 1000
```

One thing notable about this query are the parentheses in the outer WHERE clause. Without the parentheses, the clause would be evaluated as:

```
WHERE (zc.faminc200 = richest) OR (zc.faminc000_010 = poorest AND
      zc.hh >= 1000)
```

That is, the condition on the number of households would apply only to the poorest condition and not the richest, which is not the intended behavior. Misplaced or missing parentheses can alter the meaning and performance of a query.

**TIP** In WHERE **clauses that mix** ANDs **and** ORs, **be sure to use parentheses to ensure that the clauses are interpreted correctly.**

The results are similar to the previous results. The poorest zip code has now switched to an inner city neighborhood of another city. At the time of the 2000 Census, 70112 was a poor district in New Orleans, but this data predates Hurricane Katrina, so this zip code is probably very sparsely populated now.

### Income Similarity and Dissimilarity Using Chi-Square

The distribution of income is another level of information that goes beyond median or average income. The Census Bureau breaks income into sixteen buckets, the poorest being family income less than $10,000 and the wealthiest being family income in excess of $200,000. The proportion of families in each of these sixteen buckets is available at the zip code level, and this is a good description of the income distribution.

In which zip codes does the income distribution match the country as a whole? These zip codes are all over the entire United States. Such representative areas can be useful. What works well in these areas may work well across the whole country. At the other extreme are zip codes that differ from the national distribution, the most unrepresentative areas.

The chi-square calculation is one way to measure both these extremes. To use the chi-square, an expected value is needed, and this is the income distribution at the national level. The key to calculating the national numbers is to multiply the proportions in each of the buckets by the total number of families to obtain counts of families. This total number can be aggregated across all zip codes, and then divided by the number of families to get the distribution at the national level. The following query provides an example of this calculation for zip codes having a population of more than one thousand:

```
SELECT SUM(faminc000_010*fam)/SUM(fam) as faminc000_010,
       . . .
       SUM(faminc150_200*fam)/SUM(fam) as faminc150_175,
       SUM(faminc200*fam)/SUM(fam) as faminc200
FROM zipcensus
WHERE pop >= 1000
```

Which zip codes are most similar (or most dissimilar) can be expressed as a question: *What is the likelihood that the income distribution seen in a given zip code is due to chance, relative to the national average?* Or, to slightly simplify the calculation: *What is the chi-square value of the income distribution of the zip code compared to the national income distribution?* The closer the chi-square value is to zero, the more representative the zip code. Higher chi-square values suggest that the observed distribution is not due to chance.

The calculation requires a lot of arithmetic. The chi-square value for a given income column, such as FAMINC000_010, is the square of the difference between the variable and the expected value divided by the expected value. For each of the sixteen buckets, the following expression calculates its contribution to the total chi-square value:

```
POWER(zc.FAMINC000_010 - usa.FAMINC000_010, 2)/usa.FAMINC000_010
```

The total chi-square is the sum of the chi-square values for all the bins.

As an example, the following query finds the top ten zip codes most similar to the national distribution of incomes and having a population greater than 1000:

```
SELECT TOP 10 zipcode, state,
       (SQUARE(zc.faminc000_010 - usa.faminc000_010)/usa.faminc000_010 +
        . . .
        SQUARE(zc.faminc150_200 - usa.faminc150_175)/usa.faminc150_175 +
        SQUARE(zc.faminc200 - usa.faminc200)/usa.faminc200
       ) as chisquare,
```

*(continued)*

```
        pop, fammedincome
FROM zipcensus zc CROSS JOIN
     (SELECT SUM(faminc000_010*fam)/SUM(fam) as faminc000_010,
            . . .
            SUM(faminc150_200*fam)/SUM(fam) as faminc150_175,
            SUM(faminc200*fam)/SUM(fam) as faminc200
     FROM zipcensus
     WHERE pop > 1000) usa
WHERE pop >= 1000
ORDER BY 3 DESC
```

This uses a subquery to calculate the distribution at the national level, which is joined in using the CROSS JOIN. The actual chi-square value is calculated as a long expression in the outermost query.

The zip codes most similar to the national income distribution are dispersed across the United States, as shown in Table 4-6.

**Table 4-6:** Top Ten Zip Codes by Chi-Square Income Similarity

| ZIP CODE | STATE | INCOME CHI-SQUARE | POPU-LATION | FAMILY MEDIAN INCOME |
|----------|-------|-------------------|-------------|----------------------|
| 87505 | NM | 0.007 | 69,700 | $51,062 |
| 70065 | LA | 0.008 | 53,565 | $52,001 |
| 95076 | CA | 0.009 | 81,131 | $47,365 |
| 95670 | CA | 0.009 | 50,135 | $51,105 |
| 55104 | MN | 0.010 | 46,169 | $50,165 |
| 30263 | GA | 0.010 | 41,393 | $50,525 |
| 93277 | CA | 0.010 | 44,788 | $50,461 |
| 72205 | AR | 0.011 | 23,892 | $50,432 |
| 97202 | OR | 0.011 | 37,407 | $51,968 |
| 29407 | SC | 0.011 | 36,515 | $47,323 |

Table 4-7 shows the ten zip codes with the highest deviation from the national income distribution. Visualizing the income variables for these ten zip codes helps explain why these are different. Figure 4-7 is an example of a parallel dimension plot, where each zip code is a line on the chart, and each point on a line is the value of one of the income variables. The thickest line is the average for the United States. The plot shows that there are five zip codes that differ from the national distribution because everyone earns the same amount of money — so 100% of families in those zip codes are in one income bucket. One of these, 75207, happens to have a family median income very close to the national average.

**Table 4-7:** Top Ten Zip Codes by Chi-Square Income Disparity

| ZIP CODE | STATE | INCOME CHI-SQUARE | POPU-LATION | FAMILY MEDIAN INCOME |
|---|---|---|---|---|
| 53706 | WI | 21.6 | 5,217 | $11,250 |
| 75207 | TX | 17.8 | 8,121 | $48,750 |
| 46556 | IN | 15.9 | 6,731 | $26,250 |
| 24142 | VA | 15.5 | 2,765 | $31,250 |
| 97331 | OR | 15.5 | 1,390 | $31,250 |
| 60043 | IL | 10.8 | 2,550 | $200,001 |
| 94027 | CA | 10.6 | 6,872 | $200,001 |
| 92067 | CA | 9.8 | 7,250 | $200,001 |
| 07078 | NJ | 9.0 | 12,888 | $200,001 |
| 60022 | IL | 8.5 | 8,602 | $200,001 |

The remaining five zip codes all differ from the national average because they have a lot of wealthy people. These all have very similar distributions, with about half the households at the highest income levels.

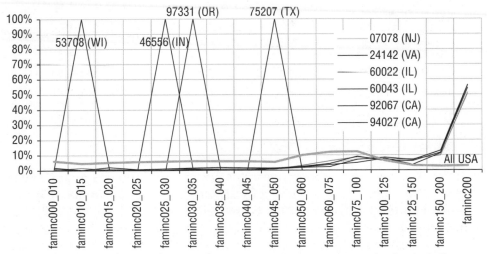

**Figure 4-7:** This parallel dimension plot compares the top ten zip codes least similar to the United States by income distribution.

The query that returns this information is a modification of the chi-square query. It replaces the CROSS JOIN with UNION ALL, does not have the chi-square calculation, and lists the zip codes explicitly:

```
(SELECT CAST(zipcode as varchar), state, fammedincome, zc.faminc000_010
        . . .
        zc.faminc200
 FROM zipcensus zc
 WHERE zipcode in ('53706', '75207', '46556', '24142', '97331', '60043',
                   '94027', '92067', '07078', '60022')
) UNION ALL
(SELECT CAST('XXXXX' as varchar) as zipcode, NULL as state,
        SUM(fammedincome*fam)/SUM(fam) as fammedincome,
        SUM(faminc000_010*fam)/SUM(fam) as faminc000_010,
        . . .
        SUM(faminc200*fam)/SUM(fam) as faminc200
 FROM zipcensus)
```

The difference between the UNION ALL and the CROSS JOIN is that the UNION ALL adds a new row into the data with the same columns, so the result here has eleven rows, ten for the zip codes and one for the entire United States. The CROSS JOIN, by contrast, does not add new rows (assuming there is one row in the second table). Instead, it adds additional columns to the result. As a result, the overall values for the United States are added onto the row for each zip code, so the two sets of values can be compared within a single row.

## Comparison of Zip Codes with and without Orders

The orders in the purchases database have zip codes assigned to them. Many of these zip codes have demographic data. Others have no corresponding census zip code, are mistakes, or are for non-US addresses. This section investigates the intersection of orders in zip codes and zip code demographic data.

### Zip Codes Not in Census File

There are two lists of zip codes, one in the Orders table and one in the Zipcensus table. *How many zip codes are in each table and how many are in both?* This is a question about the relationship between two sets of zip codes. The right way to answer it is by comparing the zip codes in the two tables using the UNION ALL technique:

```
SELECT inorders, incensus, COUNT(*) as numzips,
       SUM(numorders) as numorders, MIN(zipcode), MAX(zipcode)
FROM (SELECT zipcode, MAX(inorders) as inorders,
             MAX(incensus) as incensus, MAX(numorders) as numorders
      FROM ((SELECT zipcode, 1 as inorders, 0 as incensus,
```

```
                COUNT(*) as numorders
        FROM orders o
        GROUP BY zipcode)
        UNION ALL
        (SELECT zipcode, 0 as inorders, 1 as incensus, 0 as numorders
        FROM zipcensus zc)
      ) a
   GROUP BY zipcode
   ) b
GROUP BY inorders, incensus
```

The first subquery in the UNION ALL sets a flag for all zip codes in the Orders table and counts the number of orders in the zip code. The second subquery sets a flag for all zip codes in the Zipcensus table. These are aggregated by zip code to produce two flags for each zip code, one indicating whether it is in Orders and the other indicating whether it is in Zipcensus. Each zip code also has a count of the number of orders. These flags are summarized again in the outer query to obtain information about the overlap of zip codes in the two tables.

The results in Table 4-8 show that most zip codes in Zipcensus do not have orders. On the other hand, most order zip codes are in Zipcensus. And, by far most orders are in recognized zip codes. It is quite likely that many of the unrecognized zip codes are for foreign orders.

**Table 4-8:** Overlaps of Zip Codes between Census Zips and Purchase Zips

| IN ORDERS | IN CENSUS | COUNT | NUMBER ORDERS | MINIMUM ZIP | MAXIMUM ZIP |
| --- | --- | --- | --- | --- | --- |
| 0 | 1 | 20,501 | 0 | 00601 | 99950 |
| 1 | 0 | 4,042 | 7,565 | 00000 | Z5B2T |
| 1 | 1 | 11,537 | 185,418 | 00646 | 99901 |

## Profiles of Zip Codes with and without Orders

*Are the zip codes with orders different from the zip codes without orders?* Information such as the following can distinguish between these two groups:

- Estimated number of households;
- Estimated median income;
- Percent of households on public assistance;
- Percent of population with a college degree; and,
- Percent of housing units that are owned.

Table 4-9 shows summary statistics for the two groups. Zip codes without orders are smaller, poorer, and have more home owners. Zip codes with orders are more populous, richer, and better educated. Given that the numbers of zip codes in the two groups are so large, these differences are statistically significant.

**Table 4-9:** Some Demographic Information about Zip Codes with and without Purchases

| | HAS ORDER | |
| --- | --- | --- |
| MEASURE | NO | YES |
| Number of Zip Codes | 20,501 | 11,537 |
| Average Number of Households | 1,201.4 | 7,121.3 |
| Average Median Income | $34,417 | $48,238 |
| Households on Public Assistance | 4.6% | 3.4% |
| Population with College Degree | 12.9% | 27.8% |
| Owner Occupied Households | 74.0% | 63.9% |

The following query was used to calculate the information in the table:

```
SELECT (CASE WHEN o.zipcode IS NULL THEN 'NO' ELSE 'YES' END) as hasorder,
       COUNT(*) as cnt, AVG(hh*1.0) as avg_hh,
       AVG(hhmedincome) as avg_medincome,
       SUM(numhhpubassist) / SUM(hh) as hhpubassist,
       SUM(numcoll) / SUM(popedu) as popcollege,
       SUM(numhhowner) / SUM(hhuoccupied) as hhowner
FROM (SELECT zc.*, hhpubassist*hh as numhhpubassist,
             (popedubach + popedumast + popeduprofdoct)*popedu as numcoll,
             hhuowner*hhuoccupied as numhhowner
      FROM zipcensus zc) zc LEFT OUTER JOIN
     (SELECT DISTINCT zipcode FROM orders o) o
     ON zc.zipcode = o.zipcode
GROUP BY (CASE WHEN o.zipcode IS NULL THEN 'NO' ELSE 'YES' END)
```

This query uses a LEFT OUTER JOIN in order to retain all the information in the Zipcensus table. From the Orders table, only the distinct zip codes are needed; use of the DISTINCT keyword eliminates the need for an explicit GROUP BY and ensures that no duplicate rows are inadvertently created.

The census values are ratios. To calculate overall ratios at the group levels, it might be tempting to use something like AVG(HHPUBASSIST). However, this is not correct, because different zip codes have different sizes. The correct way is to convert the ratios to counts by multiplying by the appropriate factor, sum the counts, and then divide by the sum of the factor. For instance, the ratio of the households on public assistance, HHPUBASSIST, is multiplied by HH to get the number of households on public assistance. Dividing this product by SUM(HH) gets the ratio at the aggregated level.

The preceding analysis shows that zip codes that place orders are indeed more likely to be richer and larger. However, there is a subtle bias in this analysis. Orders are more likely to come from larger zip codes, simply because there are more people in larger zip codes who could place the order. Smaller zip codes are more likely to be rural and poor than larger ones. This is an example of a sampling bias. The zip codes vary by size, and characteristics of zip codes are sometimes related to their sizes.

Restricting the query to largish zip codes helps eliminate this bias. For instance, any area with one thousand households has a reasonable opportunity to have someone who would place an order, because the national rate is about 0.23%. Table 4-10 shows the zip code characteristics with this restriction. Even among these zip codes, the same pattern holds of richer, larger, better educated areas placing orders.

**Table 4-10:** Some Demographic Information about Zip Codes with and without Purchases with More Than 1000 Households

| MEASURE | HAS ORDER | |
|---|---|---|
| | NO | YES |
| Number of Zip Codes | 6,244 | 9,947 |
| Average Number of Households | 3,168.7 | 8,182.1 |
| Average Median Income | $35,815 | $48,660 |
| Households on Public Assistance | 4.9% | 3.4% |
| Population with College Degree | 13.1% | 27.8% |
| Owner Occupied Households | 72.5% | 63.8% |

## Classifying and Comparing Zip Codes

Wealthier zip codes place orders and less wealthy zip codes do not place orders. Extending this observation a step further leads to the question: *Among zip codes that place orders, do wealthier ones place more orders than less wealthy ones?* This is a reasonable extrapolation, so it is worth investigating.

One approach is to classify the zip codes by the penetration of orders within them. Penetration is the number of orders in the zip code divided by the number of households. Based on the previous analysis, we would expect the average median household income to increase as penetration increases. Similarly, we would expect the proportion of college educated people to increase, and the proportion of households on public assistance to decrease. These expectations are all extensions of trends seen for zip codes with and without orders.

First, let's look at the median household income. Figure 4-8 shows a scatter plot of zip code penetration by household median income, along with the best fit line (these are discussed in more detail in Chapter 11) and its equation. Each point on this chart is a zip code. Although the data looks like a big blob, it does show that higher penetration zip codes tend to be on the higher income side.

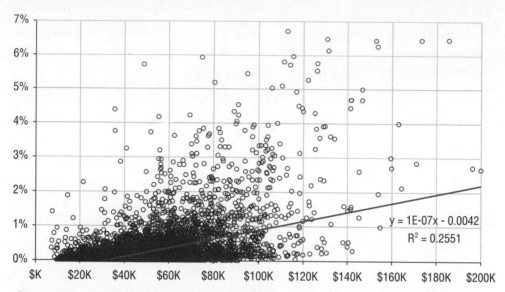

**Figure 4-8:** This plot shows household median income and penetration by zip code, for zip codes with more than 1,000 households. This pattern is noticeable but not overwhelming.

The horizontal scale uses a clever trick to remove the last three zeros of the median income and replace them with the letter "K." This is accomplished using the number format "$#,K". The best fit line shows both the equation and the $R^2$ value, which is a measure of how good the line is (Chapter 11 discusses both the best fit line and the $R^2$ value in more detail). The value of 0.26 indicates some relationship between the median income and the penetration, but the relationship is not overpowering.

**TIP** The number format "$#,K" will drop the last three zeros from a number and replace them with the letter "K."

The query that produces the data for this chart is:

```
SELECT zc.zipcode, hhmedincome,
       (CASE WHEN o.numorders IS NULL OR zc.hh = 0 THEN 0
             ELSE o.numorders * 1.0/ zc.hh END) as pen
FROM zipcensus zc LEFT OUTER JOIN
     (SELECT zipcode, COUNT(*) as numorders
      FROM orders o
```

```
      GROUP BY zipcode) o
    ON zc.zipcode = o.zipcode
WHERE zc.hh >= 1000 AND state <> 'PR'
```

An alternative approach is to classify zip codes by penetration, and to compare demographic variables within these groups. Overall, there is 0.23% order penetration at the national level by households. All zip codes fall into one of five groups:

- Zip codes with no orders (already seen in the previous section);
- Zip codes with fewer than 1,000 households;
- Zip codes with penetration less than 0.1% (low penetration);
- Zip codes with penetration between 0.1% and 0.3% (medium penetration); or,
- Zip codes with penetration greater than 0.3% (high penetration).

The following query summarizes information about these groups:

```
SELECT (CASE WHEN o.zipcode IS NULL THEN 'ZIP MISSING'
             WHEN zc.hh < 1000 THEN 'ZIP SMALL'
             WHEN 1.0*o.numorders / zc.hh < 0.001 THEN 'SMALL PENETRATION'
             WHEN 1.0*o.numorders / zc.hh < 0.003 THEN 'MED PENETRATION'
             ELSE 'HIGH PENETRATION' END) as ziptype,
       SUM(numorders) as numorders,
       COUNT(*) as numzips,
       AVG(1.0*hh) as avg_hh,
       AVG(hhmedincome) as avg_medincome,
       SUM(numhhpubassist) / SUM(hh) as hhpubassist,
       SUM(numcoll) / SUM(popedu) as popcollege,
       SUM(numhhowner) / SUM(hhuoccupied) as hhowner
FROM (SELECT zc.*,
             hhpubassist*hh as numhhpubassist,
             (popedubach + popedumast + popeduprofdoct)*popedu as numcoll,
             hhuowner*hhuoccupied as numhhowner
      FROM zipcensus zc) zc LEFT OUTER JOIN
     (SELECT zipcode, COUNT(*) as numorders
      FROM orders o
      GROUP BY zipcode) o
     ON zc.zipcode = o.zipcode
GROUP BY (CASE WHEN o.zipcode IS NULL THEN 'ZIP MISSING'
               WHEN zc.hh < 1000 THEN 'ZIP SMALL'
               WHEN 1.0*o.numorders / zc.hh < 0.001 THEN 'SMALL PENETRATION'
               WHEN 1.0*o.numorders / zc.hh < 0.003 THEN 'MED PENETRATION'
               ELSE 'HIGH PENETRATION' END)
ORDER BY 1 DESC
```

This query is similar to the previous query with two differences. First, the inner subquery on the Orders table uses an aggregation, because now the number of orders is needed as well as the presence of any order. And, the outer aggregation is a bit more complicated, defining the five groups just listed.

The results in Table 4-11 confirm what we expected to see. As penetration increases, the zip codes become wealthier, better educated, and have fewer households on public assistance.

**Table 4-11:** As Penetration Increases, Zip Codes Become Wealthier and Better Educated

|  | ZIP CODE GROUP | | | | |
| MEASURE | ZIP SMALL | ZIP MISSING | SMALL PEN | MIDDLE PEN | HIGH PEN |
| --- | --- | --- | --- | --- | --- |
| Number of Orders | 4,979 | 0 | 19,462 | 33,117 | 127,860 |
| Number of Zip Codes | 1,590 | 20,501 | 5,765 | 2,326 | 1,856 |
| Average Number of Households | 484.5 | 1,201.4 | 8,407.6 | 8,165.1 | 7,503.1 |
| Average Median Income | $45,592 | $34,417 | $42,388 | $50,720 | $65,562 |
| Households on Public Assistance | 2.4% | 4.6% | 3.9% | 2.9% | 2.1% |
| Population with College Degree | 25.5% | 12.9% | 20.5% | 33.3% | 45.7% |
| Owner Occupied Households | 76.4% | 74.0% | 65.5% | 62.3% | 60.1% |

# Geographic Hierarchies

The zip code information has a natural hierarchy in it: zip codes are in counties, and counties are in states, for instance. Such hierarchies are important for understanding and effectively using geographic information. This section discusses information at different levels of geographic hierarchies.

## Wealthiest Zip Code in a State?

Wealth is spread unevenly across the United States. Relative wealth is often more important than absolute wealth, although actual income levels may differ considerably. This inspires a question: *What is the wealthiest zip code in each state?*

This question is about geographic hierarchies. Locations are simultaneously in multiple geographic areas, so zip codes are in counties and counties are in states. Someone residing in zip code 10011 in Manhattan is also living in New York County, and in New York City, and in New York State, and in the United States. Of course, some zip codes do straddle state and county borders, as explained in Chapter 1. However, there is a predominant state and county assigned to each zip code.

The following query finds the wealthiest zip code in each state:

```
SELECT zc.*
FROM zipcensus zc JOIN
     (SELECT state, MAX(hhmedincome) as maxincome
      FROM zipcensus zc
      GROUP BY state) hhmax
     ON zc.state = hhmax.state AND
        zc.hhmedincome = hhmax.maxincome
```

It uses a subquery to calculate the zip code with the maximum income, and then joins this back to the zip code table to get information about the zip code.

Figure 4-9 shows a scatter plot of zip codes that have the maximum median household income in each state. Some states, such as Florida, have more than one zip code that matches the maximum. In this case, all are shown. This chart includes state boundaries, which are explained later in this chapter.

**Figure 4-9:** The wealthiest zip codes in each state are scattered across the map. Here they are shown placed into four income buckets.

The chart places the zip codes into four buckets based on the maximum median household income:

- Greater than $200,000;
- $150,000 to $200,000;
- $100,000 to $150,000; and,
- $50,000 to $100,000.

The chart is created using four different series for each of these groups. The first series — the very wealthiest zip codes — are labeled with the name of the state and the zip code. Unfortunately, Excel does not make it possible to label scatter plots. Fortunately, there is a simple add-in that enables this functionality, as explained in the aside "Labeling Points on Scatter Plots."

The spreadsheet shown in Figure 4-10 pivots the data for the chart. The data starts out as a table describing zip codes with columns for zip code, state, longitude, latitude, and median household income. The data for the chart is in an adjacent five columns, with longitude in the first. The next four contain the latitude for the bucket the zip code belongs in or NA(). Column titles are constructed from the ranges defining the buckets. The scatter plot can then be created by selecting the five columns and inserting the chart.

| | C | D | E | F | G | H | I | J | K | |
|---|---|---|---|---|---|---|---|---|---|---|
| 12 | | | | | | | | Lower | 200001 | 1500 |
| 13 | | | | | | | | Upper | =K12+1 | =K12 |
| 14 | | | | | | | | | | |
| 15 | | | FROM SQL | | | | | | | |
| 16 | Zip | State | Long | Lat | Med Inc | Pop | | Long | =TEXT(K12, "$#,K")&IF(K13>K12+1, " to "&TEXT(K13, "$#,K"), "") | =TE) |
| 17 | 966 | PR | -66.11523 | 18.39851 | 49354 | 15340 | | =E17 | =IF(AND($G17>=K$12, $G17 < K$13), $F17, NA()) | =IF(/ |
| 18 | 2493 | MA | -71.28831 | 42.35866 | 153918 | 11469 | | =E18 | =IF(AND($G18>=K$12, $G18 < K$13), $F18, NA()) | =IF(/ |
| 19 | 2836 | RI | -71.62146 | 41.44884 | 80611 | 138 | | =E19 | =IF(AND($G19>=K$12, $G19 < K$13), $F19, NA()) | =IF(/ |
| 20 | 3087 | NH | -71.29879 | 42.80519 | 94794 | 10709 | | =E20 | =IF(AND($G20>=K$12, $G20 < K$13), $F20, NA()) | =IF(/ |
| 21 | 4110 | ME | -70.19682 | 43.76037 | 100279 | 1206 | | =E21 | =IF(AND($G21>=K$12, $G21 < K$13), $F21, NA()) | =IF(/ |
| 22 | 5074 | VT | -72.22276 | 43.81562 | 68250 | 166 | | =E22 | =IF(AND($G22>=K$12, $G22 < K$13), $F22, NA()) | =IF(/ |
| 23 | 6820 | CT | -73.48295 | 41.07566 | 146755 | 19607 | | =E23 | =IF(AND($G23>=K$12, $G23 < K$13), $F23, NA()) | =IF(/ |
| 24 | 7078 | NJ | -74.32749 | 40.73915 | 185466 | 12849 | | =E24 | =IF(AND($G24>=K$12, $G24 < K$13), $F24, NA()) | =IF(/ |
| 25 | 12429 | NY | -73.97825 | 41.81663 | 200001 | 51 | | =E25 | =IF(AND($G25>=K$12, $G25 < K$13), $F25, NA()) | =IF(/ |
| 26 | 16155 | PA | -80.50611 | 41.07494 | 177361 | 124 | | =E26 | =IF(AND($G26>=K$12, $G26 < K$13), $F26, NA()) | =IF(/ |

**Figure 4-10:** This Excel spreadsheet pivots the data and assigns the names of the series for the chart in the previous figure (formulas for first bin are shown).

The spreadsheet creates reasonable names for each of the series. The bucket is defined by two values, the minimum and maximum of the income range. The label is created using string functions in Excel:

```
=TEXT(L7, "$#,K")&IF(L8>L7+1, " to "&TEXT(L8, "$#,K"), "")
```

This formula uses the TEXT() function to transform a number into a string. The second argument is a number format that drops the last three digits and replaces them with a "K" ("$#,K"). The IF() takes care of the bucket that does not have an upper bound.

The following query obtains the data for the chart:

```
SELECT zc.zipcode, zc.state, zc.longitude, zc.latitude, zc.hhmedincome
FROM zipcensus zc JOIN
    (SELECT state, MAX(hhmedincome) as maxincome
     FROM zipcensus zc
     GROUP BY state) hhmax
   ON zc.state = hhmax.state AND
      zc.hhmedincome = hhmax.maxincome
```

This query calculates the maximum median income for zip codes in each state, and then joins in the zip code information by matching to the maximum value.

---

**LABELING POINTS ON SCATTER PLOTS**

The ability to label points in scatter plots and bubble plots (as in Figure 4-9) is very useful, but not part of Excel. Fortunately, Rob Bovey has written a small application to do this. Better yet, this application is free for download from `http://www.appspro.com/Utilities/ChartLabeler.htm`.

The XY-Labeler installs new functionality in Excel by adding a new menu item called "XY Chart Labels" to the "Tools" menu, which makes it possible to:

- Add labels to a chart, where the labels are defined by a column in the spreadsheet;
- Modify existing labels; and,
- Add labels to individual points in any series.

In the chart, the labels behave like labels on any other series. Just like other text, they can be formatted as desired, with fonts, colors, backgrounds, and orientations. They can be deleted by clicking them and hitting the `<delete>` key.

When inserting the labels, the chart labeler asks for several items of information. First, it needs the series to label. Second, it needs the labels, which are typically in a column in the same table. And third, it needs to know where to place the labels: above, below, to the right, to the left, or on the data points.

The labels themselves are values in a column, so they can be arbitrary text and as informative as needed. In this case, the label for each point consists of the state abbreviation with the zip code in parentheses, created using the following formula:

```
=D10&" ("&TEXT(C10, "00000")&")"
```

where D10 contains the state and C10 contains the zip code. The TEXT() function adds zeros to the beginning of the zip codes to ensure that zip codes starting with "0" look correct.

---

## Zip Code with the Most Orders in Each State

Of course, there is no reason to limit examples to demographic features of the zip codes. The same ideas can be used to identify the zip code in each state that has the most orders and the most orders per household.

Figure 4-11 shows a map showing the zip codes with the most orders in each state. Zip codes with the most orders are typically large, urban zip codes. If the measure were penetration, the zip codes with the most orders per household would be small zip codes that have very few households.

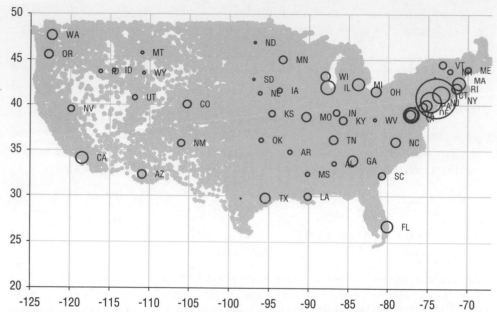

**Figure 4-11:** This map shows the zip code with the largest number of orders. The size of the circles represents the number of orders.

The query that generates the information for this chart finds the zip code with the most orders in each state. Figure 4-12 shows a dataflow diagram that describes how the query processes the data, using the following steps:

1. The number of orders for each zip code in each state is calculated, by counting the orders and aggregating by state and zip code.

2. The maximum number of orders is determined, by calculating the maximum value of number of orders in each state, from step (1).

3. The zip code associated with the maximum number of orders in each state is calculated by finding the zip code from (1) whose number of orders matches the maximum from (2).

The resulting query looks like:

```
SELECT zc.zipcode, zc.state, longitude, latitude, numorders
FROM (SELECT zipcode, state, COUNT(*) as numorders
      FROM orders
      GROUP BY zipcode, state) ozip JOIN
     (SELECT state, MAX(numorders) as maxorders
      FROM (SELECT zipcode, state, COUNT(*) as numorders
            FROM orders
            GROUP BY zipcode, state) o
      GROUP BY state) ostate
```

```
      ON ozip.state = ostate.state AND
         ozip.numorders = ostate.maxorders JOIN
      zipcensus zc
      ON zc.zipcode = ozip.zipcode
WHERE latitude BETWEEN 20 and 50 AND longitude BETWEEN -135 AND -65
ORDER BY 2
```

This query uses multiple levels of subqueries to find the zip code with the most orders. Standard SQL does not make it easy to answer such questions. However, there are SQL extensions that facilitate these calculations. The window function extensions are discussed in more detail in Chapter 8.

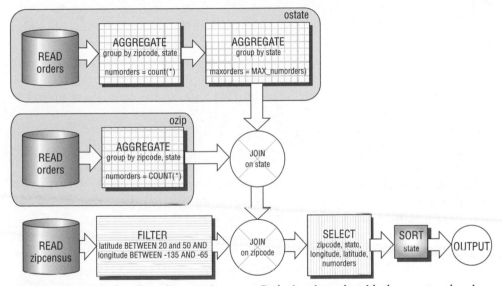

**Figure 4-12:** This dataflow diagram for query finds the zip code with the most orders in each state.

## Interesting Hierarchies in Geographic Data

Zip codes within states are only one example of geographic levels nestling inside each other. This section discusses some other geographic levels, even though most of these are not in the datasets.

### Counties

Every state is divided into counties. Some states such as Texas have hundreds of counties (254). By contrast, Delaware and Hawaii have only three. Counties are useful precisely because every address has some county associated with it, even though the location may not be in a village, town, or city. The table Zip-county maps zip codes to counties.

Counties in different states can have the same name. Once upon a time, the author was surprised to see a map highlighting two counties in northern Minnesota as having very large marketing potential. Between them, these counties have a population of less than fifteen thousand people, which is not very big at all. Although Lake County and Cook County are small and out of the way in Minnesota, their namesakes in Illinois are two of the most populous counties in the country.

To prevent such confusion, the Census Bureau has a numbering system for geographic areas called FIPS (Federal Information Processing Standard). The FIPS county codes consist of five digits. The first two digits are for the state and the last three are for the counties. In general, the state number is obtained by alphabetizing the states and assigning sequential numbers, starting with 01 for Alabama. The counties in each state are similarly numbered, so Alabaster County in Alabama has the FIPS code of 01001.

Counties are useful for other purposes as well. For instance, sales taxes are often set at the county level.

## Designated Marketing Areas (DMAs)

Designated marketing areas are the invention of Nielsen Market Research and were originally designed as the markets for television advertising. These are groups of counties that form marketing regions, and are good approximations to metropolitan areas. There are 210 DMAs in the United States. The largest DMA by population is the one containing New York City with about 7.4 million households (in 2004) and it has twenty-nine counties spread over four states.

A big advantage of DMAs is that they are defined as groups of counties, because all areas in the United States are in some county. Hence, every location is in some DMA. Unfortunately, the definition is privately owned, so the mapping from county to DMA or zip code to DMA needs to be purchased for a nominal amount of money.

Each company may have its own definition of its marketing area. Newspapers and radio stations also have designated marketing areas. This is the area where they compete for readers and advertising in the "local" market.

## Census Hierarchies

The Census Bureau in the United States has quite a challenge. As mandated by the Constitution, the Bureau is responsible for "enumerating" the population of every state in the United States every ten years. The purpose is to determine the number of seats assigned to each state in the House of Representatives. In addition to counting residents, the census also estimates various demographic and economic statistics.

The Census Bureau divides the United States into a mosaic of small geographic entities, such as:

- Census block;
- Census block group; and,
- Census tract.

The *census block* is the smallest unit and typically has a population of a few dozen people in a small area (such as along one side of a street). The United States is divided into over eight million census blocks. The Bureau publishes very few statistics at the block level, because such statistics could compromise the privacy of the individuals living in such a small area.

*Block groups* are collections of census blocks that typically have up to about four thousand people. Both census blocks and block groups change at the whims and needs of the Census Bureau, as populations grow and shrink, and shift.

*Census tracts* are intended to be more permanent statistical subdivisions, with about two to eight thousand people each (although the largest can be much larger). Unlike zip codes, census tracts are designed to be statistically homogeneous and relevant to local governments. This is in contrast to post offices that are intended to serve diverse areas. Further information about the census divisions is available at www.census.gov.

The low-level census hierarchies are then aggregated into a cornucopia of other groupings, such as:

- Metropolitan Statistical Area (MSA);
- Consolidated Metropolitan Statistical Area (CMSA); and,
- New England Consolidated Metropolitan Areas (NECMAs).

And more! The problem with these hierarchies boils down to one word, politics. The funding for various federal programs is tied to populations. Perhaps for this reason, these are defined by the Office of Management and Budget (OMB) rather than the Census Bureau. For instance, in the 2000 Census, Worcester, MA was included in the Boston metropolitan statistical area. By 2003, it had been split out into its own area.

## Other Geographic Subdivisions

There are a host of other geographic subdivisions, which might be useful for special purposes. The following discusses some of these.

### Zip+2 and Zip+4

The five-digit zip code in the United States has been augmented with four additional digits, commonly known as zip+4. The first two are the carrier route code and the second two are the stop along the route. Because zip+4s change at the whim of the post office, they are not particularly useful for comparisons over time.

### Electoral Districts

People vote. And the wards and precincts where they vote are located in Congressional districts and state-wide office districts. Such information is particularly useful for political campaigns. However, the districts change at least every ten years, so these are not so useful for other purposes.

### School Districts

School districts are another geographic grouping. School districts can be useful, because each school district has its own schedule. When do you want to send customers "back-to-school" messages? Some districts start the school year in early August. Others start a month later. Similarly, some end in early May and some continue well into June.

### Catchment Areas

A catchment area is the area from where a retail establishment draws its customers. The definition of a catchment area can be quite complicated, taking into account store locations, road patterns, commuting distances, and competitors. Retailing companies often know about their catchment areas and the competition inside them.

## Calculating County Wealth

This section looks at wealth in counties, which provides an opportunity to make comparisons across different levels of geography. The place to begin is in identifying the counties.

### Identifying Counties

If the Orders table contained complete addresses and the addresses were geocoded, the county would be available as well as the zip code (and census tract and other information). However, the data contains zip codes, rather than geocoded addresses. The county for a zip code can be looked up using Zipcounty. This is an approximate mapping, based on the zip codes existing in 1999. Even though zip codes can span both state and county borders, this table assigns one single county to each zip code.

*What is the overlap between these tables?* This question is quite similar to the question about the overlap between zip codes in Orders and Zipcensus. The way to determine the overlap is with the following UNION BY query:

```
SELECT inzc, inzco, COUNT(*) as numzips, MIN(zipcode), MAX(zipcode),
       MIN(countyname), MAX(countyname)
FROM (SELECT zipcode, MAX(countyname) as countyname, SUM(inzc) as inzc,
             SUM(inzco) as inzco
      FROM ((SELECT zipcode, '' as countyname, 1 as inzc, 0 as inzco
             FROM zipcensus)
            UNION ALL
            (SELECT zipcode, countyname, 0 as inzc, 1 as inzco
             FROM zipcounty)) z
      GROUP BY zipcode) a
GROUP BY  inzc, inzco
```

This query is typical of queries that determine the overlap of two or more tables, with the addition of the county name as well as the zip code. The county name is for informational purposes, because discrepancies might occur at the county level.

Table 4-12 shows that almost all zip codes in Zipcensus are also in Zipcounty; the exceptions being zip codes in Puerto Rico (which, technically speaking, has "municipios" rather than "counties"). There are over ten thousand zip codes in Zipcounty that are not in Zipcensus, because Zipcensus consists of zip code tabulation areas maintained by the Census Bureau. They define zip code tabulation areas for only a subset of zip codes that would be expected to have a residential population.

**Table 4-12:** Overlap of Zip Codes in Zipcensus and Zipcounty

| IN ZIP CENSUS | IN ZIP COUNTY | NUMBER OF ZIPS | MIN ZIP | MAX ZIP | MINIMUM COUNTY | MAXIMUM COUNTY |
|:---:|:---:|---:|:---:|:---:|:---|:---|
| 1 | 0 | 77 | 00601 | 00772 | | |
| 1 | 1 | 31,961 | 00773 | 99950 | Abbeville | Ziebach |
| 0 | 1 | 10,131 | 00785 | 99928 | Ziebach | |

## Measuring Wealth

The typical attribute for wealth is HHMEDINCOME, the median household income. Unfortunately, this is not available at the county level in the data. Fortunately, a reasonable approximation is the average of the median incomes in all zip codes in the county. The average of a median is an approximation, but it is good enough. The following query calculates the average median household income for each county:

```
SELECT zco.countyfips, zco.poname,
       (CASE WHEN SUM(hh) = 0 THEN NULL
             ELSE SUM(hhmedincome * hh) / SUM(hh) END)
FROM zipcensus zc JOIN zipcounty zco ON zc.zipcode = zco.zipcode
GROUP BY zco.countyfips, zco.poname
```

Notice that this query uses the weighted average (weighted by the number of households), rather than just the average. The alternative formulation, AVG(hhmedincome), would calculate a different value; each zip code would have the same weight regardless of its population.

This query takes into account the fact that counties might have zero households, an unusual situation. The only example in the data is Williamsburg, VA, an independent city in Virginia (meaning it is its own county). Three of its five zip codes are in neighboring counties. The only two zip codes assigned to Williamsburg are for the College of William and Mary, which has "group housing" but no "households." Such is the census data, accurate and detailed, and sometimes surprising.

## Distribution of Values of Wealth

The distribution of median household income for both zip codes and counties is in Figure 4-13. This distribution is a histogram, with the values in thousand-dollar increments. The vertical axis shows the proportion of zip codes or counties whose median household income falls into each range. Overall the distribution looks like a normal distribution, although it is skewed a bit to the left meaning that there are more very rich areas than very poor areas. One reason for the skew is that the median household income is never negative, so it cannot fall too low.

The peak for both zip codes and counties is in the range of $30,000–$31,000. However, the peak for counties is higher than the peak for zip codes. And, the curve for counties is narrower, with fewer very large values or very small values. Does this tell us anything interesting about counties?

Actually not. We can think of counties as being samples of zip codes. As explained in the previous chapter, the distribution of the average of a sample is narrower than the original data, clustering more about the overall average. Geographic hierarchies usually follow this pattern.

The data in Figure 4-13 was calculated in SQL and Excel. The SQL query summarizes the counts by bin, which Excel then converts to ratios for the chart:

```
SELECT bin, SUM(numzips) as numzips, SUM(numcounties) as numcounties
FROM ((SELECT FLOOR(hhmedincome/1000)*1000 as bin, COUNT(*) as numzips,
              0 as numcounties
       FROM zipcensus zc
```

```
      WHERE hh > 0
      GROUP BY FLOOR(hhmedincome/1000)*1000)
    UNION ALL
    (SELECT FLOOR(countymedian/1000)*1000 as bin, 0 as numzips,
            COUNT(*) as numcounties
     FROM (SELECT countyfips,
                  SUM(hhmedincome*hh*1.0) / SUM(hh) as countymedian
           FROM zipcensus zc JOIN
                zipcounty zco
                ON zc.zipcode = zco.zipcode AND
                   hh > 0
           GROUP BY countyfips) c
     GROUP BY FLOOR(countymedian/1000)*1000)
    ) a
GROUP BY bin
ORDER BY 1
```

This query creates a bin for median income by taking only the thousands component of the number. So, an income of $31,948 is placed into the $31,000 bin. The calculation for this is simple arithmetic that uses the FLOOR() function. The query calculates this bin both at the zip code level and at the county level.

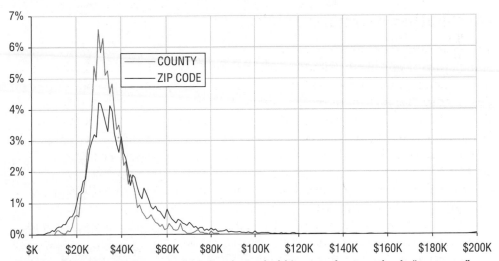

**Figure 4-13:** The distribution of median household income for counties is "narrower" than for zip codes.

## Which Zip Code Is Wealthiest Relative to Its County?

Local areas that are significantly different from their surrounding areas are interesting: *What is the wealthiest zip code relative to its county?*

Answering this question requires understanding what it really means. Does it mean that the difference between the median incomes is the largest possible? Does it mean that the ratio is as large as possible? Both of these are reasonable interpretations. The second leads to the idea of indexing values between different geographic levels, which is a good idea.

**TIP** Dividing the value of a variable in one geographic level by the value in a larger area is an example of indexing. This can find interesting patterns in the data, such as the wealthiest zip code in a county.

The following query finds the ten zip codes with more than one thousand households whose index relative to their county is the largest in the country:

```
SELECT TOP 10 zc.zipcode, zc.state, zc.countyname, zc.hhmedincome,
       c.countymedian, zc.hhmedincome / c.countymedian, zc.hh, c.hh
FROM (SELECT zc.*, countyfips, countyname
      FROM zipcensus zc JOIN
           zipcounty zco
           ON zc.zipcode = zco.zipcode) zc JOIN
     (SELECT countyfips, SUM(hh) as hh,
             SUM(hhmedincome*hh*1.0) / SUM(hh) as countymedian
      FROM zipcensus zc JOIN
           zipcounty zco
           ON zc.zipcode = zco.zipcode AND
              hh > 0
      GROUP BY countyfips) c
     ON zc.countyfips = c.countyfips
WHERE zc.hh > 1000
ORDER BY zc.hhmedincome / c.countymedian DESC
```

This query has two subqueries. The first appends the FIPS county code onto each row in Zipcensus. The second calculates the median household income for the county. These are joined together using the FIPS code. The ORDER BY clause then supplies the intelligence behind the query, by ordering the result by the ratio in descending order.

These wealthy zip codes (in Table 4-13) all seem to be in counties whose income is a bit above average and whose population is quite large (they have hundreds of thousands or millions of households). These are wealthy enclaves in highly urban counties.

**Table 4-13:** Wealthiest Zip Codes Relative to Their Counties

| ZIP CODE | COUNTY NAME | MEDIAN INCOME | | | HOUSEHOLDS | |
|----------|-------------|------|--------|-------|------|--------|
| | | ZIP | COUNTY | INDEX | ZIP | COUNTY |
| 92067 | San Diego, CA | $196,298 | $49,499 | 3.97 | 2,543 | 995,487 |
| 07078 | Essex, NJ | $185,466 | $51,099 | 3.63 | 4,279 | 283,825 |

**Table 4-13**  *(continued)*

| ZIP CODE | COUNTY NAME | MEDIAN INCOME | | | HOUSEHOLDS | |
|---|---|---|---|---|---|---|
| | | ZIP | COUNTY | INDEX | ZIP | COUNTY |
| 60022 | Cook, IL | $171,063 | $47,998 | 3.56 | 2,955 | 1,965,876 |
| 33158 | Miami-Dade, FL | $118,410 | $37,974 | 3.12 | 2,094 | 777,378 |
| 90077 | Los Angeles, CA | $141,527 | $45,737 | 3.09 | 4,165 | 3,132,861 |
| 44040 | Cuyahoga, OH | $123,980 | $41,485 | 2.99 | 1,071 | 574,086 |
| 19085 | Delaware, PA | $159,538 | $55,292 | 2.89 | 1,902 | 224,026 |
| 38139 | Shelby, TN | $116,200 | $42,586 | 2.73 | 4,656 | 341,743 |
| 76092 | Tarrant, TX | $130,655 | $48,381 | 2.70 | 6,280 | 524,833 |
| 90272 | Los Angeles, CA | $122,877 | $45,737 | 2.69 | 9,272 | 3,132,861 |

## County with Highest Relative Order Penetration

Geographic hierarchies can also be used for customer-related information. For instance: *Which counties in each state have the highest order penetration relative to the state?*

Order penetration is orders per household. In addition to order penetration, the query also calculates some other statistics about the counties and states:

- Estimated number of households;
- Estimated median income;
- Percent of households on public assistance;
- Percent of population with a college degree; and,
- Percent of housing units that are owned.

These are interesting demographics. The purpose is to compare the highest penetration county to the state, to see if other factors might be correlated with high penetration.

Table 4-14 shows the top ten counties whose order penetration is highest relative to their states. For the most part, these consist of small counties with a smallish number of orders. However, the penetration by household is quite high. Interestingly, the larger counties with high relative penetration are wealthier than their states. However, some of the smaller counties are poorer. In general, these counties do seem to be better educated and have fewer people on public assistance.

**Table 4-14:** Counties with Highest Order Penetration Relative to Their State

| COUNTY FIPS/ STATE | NUMBER | MEDIAN INCOME | HOUSEHOLDS | | | ORDER | PEN IND-EX |
| | | | ON PUBLIC ASSIST-ANCE | OWNER OCCU-PIED | % WITH COLLEGE DEGREE | | |
|---|---|---|---|---|---|---|---|
| 16013 | 7,754 | $50,609 | 1.1% | 68.9% | 43.1% | 0.46% | 11.2 |
| ID | 469,521 | $38,416 | 3.4% | 72.7% | 21.7% | 0.04% | |
| 56039 | 7,523 | $55,571 | 1.3% | 55.8% | 45.6% | 0.45% | 9.7 |
| WY | 193,787 | $38,664 | 2.6% | 70.1% | 21.9% | 0.05% | |
| 46027 | 4,988 | $27,847 | 2.9% | 54.9% | 38.4% | 0.20% | 9.7 |
| SD | 290,246 | $35,783 | 3.0% | 68.4% | 21.5% | 0.02% | |
| 08097 | 5,788 | $58,962 | 1.0% | 56.6% | 59.6% | 1.02% | 8.3 |
| CO | 1,659,224 | $48,967 | 2.5% | 67.3% | 32.7% | 0.12% | |
| 16081 | 2,065 | $42,878 | 0.6% | 74.6% | 28.5% | 0.34% | 8.2 |
| ID | 469,521 | $38,416 | 3.4% | 72.7% | 21.7% | 0.04% | |
| 72061 | 34,673 | $30,490 | 13.5% | 76.7% | 36.3% | 0.07% | 7.6 |
| PR | 1,261,816 | $15,373 | 20.1% | 72.9% | 18.3% | 0.01% | |
| 45013 | 45,089 | $49,158 | 1.8% | 74.4% | 33.4% | 0.40% | 7.3 |
| SC | 1,534,207 | $37,808 | 2.5% | 72.4% | 20.4% | 0.05% | |
| 51610 | 5,831 | $76,806 | 1.1% | 71.6% | 60.0% | 1.06% | 7.1 |
| VA | 2,700,238 | $49,960 | 2.5% | 68.2% | 29.5% | 0.15% | |
| 37135 | 46,973 | $45,882 | 1.4% | 56.0% | 56.8% | 0.51% | 7.1 |
| NC | 3,133,265 | $40,355 | 2.8% | 69.6% | 22.5% | 0.07% | |
| 28071 | 13,454 | $27,935 | 1.5% | 59.2% | 32.8% | 0.13% | 7.0 |
| MS | 1,047,140 | $31,929 | 3.5% | 72.4% | 16.9% | 0.02% | |

The query that finds these counties is:

```
SELECT TOP 10 c.*, s.*, c.orderpen / s.orderpen
FROM (SELECT zcounty.*, ocounty.numorders,
             (CASE WHEN numhh > 0 THEN numorders*1.0/numhh ELSE 0
              END) as orderpen
      FROM (SELECT zco.countyfips, zco.state,
                   MIN(countyname) as countyname, COUNT(*) as numorders
            FROM orders o JOIN zipcounty zco ON o.zipcode = zco.zipcode
            GROUP BY countyfips, zco.state) ocounty JOIN
           (SELECT zco.countyfips, zco.state, SUM(hh) as numhh,
```

```
                        SUM(hhmedincome*hh)/SUM(hh) as hhmedincome,
                        SUM(hhpubassist*hh)/SUM(hh) as hhpubassist,
                        (SUM((popedubach+popedumast+popeduprofdoct)*popedu)/
                         SUM(popedu)) as popcollege,
                        SUM(hhuowner*hhunits)/SUM(hhunits) as hhuowner
               FROM zipcensus zc JOIN
                    zipcounty zco
                    ON zc.zipcode = zco.zipcode
               WHERE hh > 0
               GROUP BY zco.countyfips, zco.state) zcounty
             ON ocounty.countyfips = zcounty.countyfips) c JOIN
         (SELECT zstate.*, ostate.numorders, numorders*1.0/numhh as orderpen
          FROM (SELECT o.state, COUNT(*) as numorders
                FROM orders o
                WHERE zipcode IN (SELECT zipcode FROM zipcensus WHERE hh > 0)
                GROUP BY o.state) ostate JOIN
               (SELECT zc.state, SUM(hh) as numhh,
                        SUM(hhmedincome*hh)/SUM(hh) as hhmedincome,
                        SUM(hhpubassist*hh)/SUM(hh) as hhpubassist,
                        (SUM((popedubach+popedumast+popeduprofdoct)*popedu)/
                         SUM(popedu)) as popcollege,
                        SUM(hhuowner*hhunits)/SUM(hhunits) as hhuowner
                FROM zipcensus zc
                WHERE hh > 0
                GROUP BY zc.state) zstate
               ON ostate.state = zstate.state) s
          ON s.state = c.state
    ORDER BY c.orderpen / s.orderpen DESC
```

This is a complicated query built around four subqueries. The first two calculate the number of orders and the number of households in each county, in order to calculate the order penetration by county. The second does the same thing for states. These are then combined to calculate the order penetration index. The dataflow for this query in Figure 4-14 shows how these four subqueries are combined together.

The calculation of the demographic ratios at the county and state level follows the same methods seen earlier in the chapter. The percentages are multiplied by the appropriate factors to get counts (number of households, population, educated population). The counts are aggregated and then divided by the sum of the factors.

## Mapping in Excel

Maps are very useful when working with geographic data. This section discusses the issue of creating maps in Excel. The short answer is that if mapping is important, Excel is not the right tool. However, the longer answer is that there are some useful things to do before purchasing more expensive software.

## Why Create Maps?

The purpose of mapping is to visualize trends and data, making it easier to understand where things are and are not happening. The zip code maps seen earlier in the chapter (for solar power or wealthy zip codes) contain tens of thousands of zip codes in a format readily understandable by most people. A map summarizes information at different levels — it is possible to see differences across regions, between urban and rural areas, and for particular geographic areas. And this is just from rudimentary zip code maps.

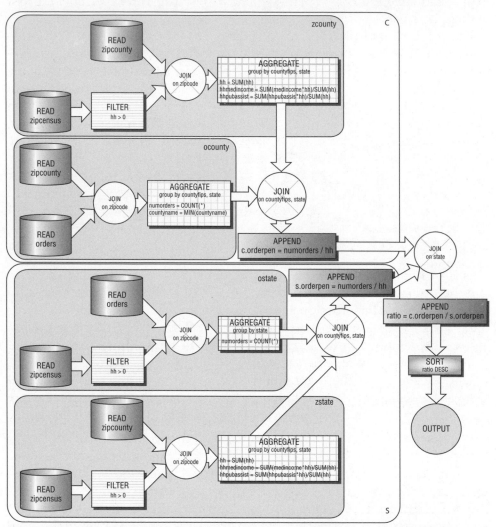

**Figure 4-14:** This dataflow calculates index of order penetration in a county to its state; this is the ratio between the order penetration in the county to the order penetration in its state.

Beyond this, there are several things that mapping software should do. Mapping software should be able to show different levels of geography. In the United States, this means the ability to see the boundaries of states, counties, and zip codes, at a minimum. In other parts of the world, this means the ability to see different countries, regions in countries, and different linguistic areas.

Another important capability is being able to color and highlight different geographic regions based on data, whether this is derived from business data (the number of orders) or census data (population and wealth). Fancy mapping software allows you to include specific markers for specific types of data, to use graduated colors, and to fill regions with textures. In Excel, only the first of these is possible.

The maps should include data available for geographic areas. This especially includes census population counts, so it is possible to measure penetration. Other census variables, such as wealth and education, types of home heating systems, and commuting times, are also useful. And this additional data should not be particularly expensive, because it is available for free from the census web site. It is also nice to see other features on maps, such as roads, rivers, and lakes. These make it easier to identify specific locations, and are readily available on web mapping tools.

This list is intended to be a bare-bones discussion of what is needed for data visualization. Advanced mapping software has many other capabilities. For instance, mapping software often has the ability to integrate into GPS (global positioning services) systems to trace a route between different points, to incorporate satellite imagery, to overlay many different features, and other advanced capabilities.

## It Can't Be Done

Once upon a time, Excel did include mapping capabilities similar to the charting capabilities. Excel was able to create maps and color and highlight states and countries based on data attributes. This product was a trimmed-down version of a product from Mapinfo (www.mapinfo.com). However, Microsoft removed this functionality in Excel 2002, separating out the mapping tool into a separate product called MapPoint. MapPoint is one of several products on the market; others include products from Mapinfo and ESRI's ArcView.

Because the mapping product is separate, Excel cannot be readily used for creating and manipulating maps without purchasing additional products. This chapter has shown basic maps for data visualization, and often these are sufficient for analytic purposes, although prettier maps are often better for presentations. For data visualization, the needs are often more basic than the more advanced geographic manipulations provided by special-purpose software.

## Mapping on the Web

There are various map sites on the web, such as Yahoo!, Google, MapQuest, MapBlaster, and Microsoft Live. These web sites are probably familiar to most readers for finding specific addresses and directions between addresses. They also include nifty capabilities, such as satellite images and road networks and are rapidly including other features, such as local businesses on the maps.

Perhaps less familiar is the fact that these web sites have application programming interfaces (APIs), which make it possible to use the maps for other purposes. A good example is www.wikimapia.org, which shows the ability to annotate features on maps is built using Google Maps. Wikimapia incorporates Google Maps using an API, which can also be called from other web applications and from Excel.

The upside to interfacing with online maps is the ability to create cool graphics that can even be updated in real time. The downside to using then is that they require programming, which often distracts from data analysis. These systems are designed to make maps for web sites, rather than for visualizing data. It is possible to use them for data visualization, but that is not what they are designed for.

**WARNING**  Having to use programming to visualize data (such as using an API to web mapping software) often distracts from data analysis. It is all too easy for analysis efforts to become transformed into programming projects.

## State Boundaries on Scatter Plots of Zip Codes

Scatter plots of zip codes make functional maps, and they have the ability to annotate specific points on them. One of the features that would make them more useful is the ability to see boundaries between states. This section discusses two methods for doing this. Both methods highlight powerful features of Excel.

### Plotting State Boundaries

The boundaries between states are defined by geographic positions — longitude and latitude. Excel scatter plots have the ability to connect the points in the scatter plot. For instance, Figure 4-15 shows the boundary of the state of Pennsylvania, where the boundary really connects a handful of points. Some parts of the boundary have very few points (because the boundary is a line). Some parts of the boundary have many points, usually because the boundary follows natural features such as rivers. The Pennsylvania border does have an unusual feature. The boundary between Pennsylvania and Delaware is actually defined as a semicircle, the only such circular-arc state border in the country. However, in this map, the arc is approximated by line segments.

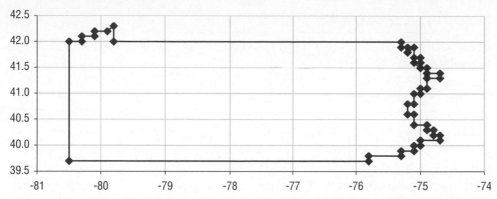

**Figure 4-15:** The outline for Pennsylvania consists of a set of points connected by lines.

The points defining the outline of the states are defined by their latitude and longitude. For instance, Colorado is a particularly simple state, because it is shaped like a rectangle. Table 4-15 shows the boundary data for Colorado; the first and last points on the boundary are the same, so there is a complete loop. To create the map of Colorado, these points are plotted as a scatter plot, with lines connecting the points, and no markers shown at each point. These options are on the "Patterns" tab of the "Format Data Series" dialog box.

**Table 4-15:** Latitude and Longitude of Points Defining Colorado State Border

| STATE | LONGITUDE | LATITUDE |
|-------|-----------|----------|
| CO | -107.9 | 41.0 |
| CO | -102.0 | 41.0 |
| CO | -102.0 | 37.0 |
| CO | -109.0 | 37.0 |
| CO | -109.0 | 41.0 |
| CO | -107.9 | 41.0 |

Adding more states requires getting the latitude and longitude, and making sure that extraneous lines do not appear. For instance, Figure 4-16 shows what happens when the outline of Wyoming is added to the Colorado outline. An extraneous line appears. Excel connects the points in the scatter plot without picking up the pen, so an extra line segment appears where Colorado ends and Wyoming begins. Fortunately, Excel makes it easy to eliminate this extraneous segment, merely by including empty cells between the two boundaries. This makes it possible to plot discrete entities on a scatter plot, without having a separate series for each one. Figure 4-9 used this technique to include state boundaries on the maps.

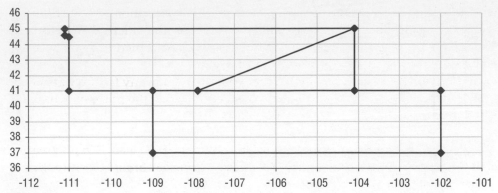

**Figure 4-16:** The outline for Colorado and Wyoming; drawn using the scatter plot, has an extraneous line.

**TIP** To make a particular line segment disappear from a scatter plot, simply insert a blank line in the data between the two points. The scatter plot skips the lines in the chart.

The boundary data was manually modified from detailed outlines of the states. It consists of several thousand points rounded to the nearest tenth of a degree. This scale captures the zigs and zags of the state boundaries to within ten miles or so, which is quite sufficient for a map of the country. However, the boundaries are not accurate at the finest levels.

## Pictures of State Boundaries

An alternative method of showing state boundaries is to use a real map as the background for the scatter plot. The first challenge is finding an appropriate map. Plotting latitudes and longitudes as straight lines on graph paper is not the recommended way of showing maps in the real world, because such maps distort distances and areas. Unfortunately, this is how most maps appear on the web. An exception is the national atlas at www.nationalatlas.com, which has curved lines for latitude and longitude.

The maps on web sites cannot generally be copied as convenient image files. Instead, capture the screen image (using <print screen>), paste it into a program such as PowerPoint, and crop the image to the appropriate size. Power-Point then allows you to save just the image as a picture file (right-click the image and choose "Save as").

The second challenge is setting the scale for the map. This is a process of trial and error, made easier by lining up the state boundaries on both maps.

Figure 4-17 shows an example using a map from Wikimapia that mimics the data from Figure 4-9. The map is copied into the chart by right-clicking the chart and choosing "Format Plot Area." On the right side is an option for "Fill Effects," which brings up the "Fill Effects" dialog box. Under the "Picture" tab, there is the option to select a picture, which in this case is a map copied from the web. Of course, this works for any picture, not just a map.

The advantage of a picture is that that you can include any features available in the map. One disadvantage is that you cannot rescale the map to focus in on particular areas.

> **TIP** The background of a chart can be any picture that you want. Simply insert it through the "Picture" tab on the "Fill Effects" dialog box brought up through the "Format Plot Area" option.

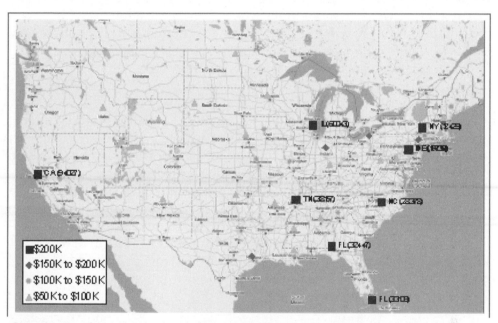

**Figure 4-17:** This example shows data points plotted on top of a map (from Wikimapia). The challenge in doing this is aligning the latitudes and longitudes so the points are properly placed.

## Lessons Learned

This chapter discusses one of the most important characteristics of customers — where they live. Geography is a complicated topic; this chapter shows how to use geographic data in SQL and Excel.

Using geography starts with geocoding addresses to locate them in the world. Geocoding translates points into latitudes and longitudes, and identifies census blocks, and tracks, and counties, and other geographic entities. Using the scatter plot mechanism in Excel, the latitudes and longitudes can even be charted, in a way that resembles a map.

One of the advantages of using geography is that data from the Census Bureau makes it possible to know about customers' neighborhoods. The census provides demographic and other information about regions in the country. Fortunately, one level of the census geography is called the zip code tabulation area (ZCTA) and these match most of the zip codes in databases. Information such as the population of the area, the median income, the type of heating, the level of education — and much more — is available from the Census Bureau, for free.

Any given location is in multiple geographies. A location lies within a zip code, within a county, within a state, within the country. This is a hierarchy of locations. Comparing information at different levels of the hierarchy can be quite informative. One method is to create an index of the wealthiest zip code in each state, or the highest penetration county in each state. Such questions use geographic hierarchies.

No discussion of geography would be complete without some discussion of mapping. Unfortunately, the simple answer is that Excel does not support maps, so use other software. For simply locating a point, there are resources on the web. For fancy maps, there are more sophisticated mapping packages.

However, rudimentary mapping is quite useful and often sufficient for data analysis. For this purpose, Excel can be a useful visualization tool, because it can use latitude and longitude to display locations and boundaries. By using background maps, it is even possible to include many other features in the maps.

The next chapter steps away from geography and moves to the other critical component for understanding customers: time.

# It's a Matter of Time

Along with geography, time is a critical dimension describing customers and business. This chapter introduces dates and times as tools for understanding customers. This is a broad topic. The next two chapters extend these ideas by introducing survival analysis, the branch of statistics also known as time-to-event analysis.

This chapter approaches time from several different vantage points. There is the perspective of what is actually stored in the columns representing dates and times, the years, months, days, hours, and minutes themselves. There is the perspective of when things happen, along with ways to visualize changes over time and year-over-year variation. Another perspective is duration, the difference between two dates, and even how durations change over time.

The two datasets used for examples — purchases and subscribers — have date stamps accurate to the day, rather than time stamps accurate to the minute, second, or fraction of a second. This is not an accident. Typically for business purposes, the date component is the most important part, so this chapter focuses on whole dates. The ideas can readily be extended from dates to times with hours, minutes, and seconds.

Times and dates are complex data types, comprised of six different components and an optional seventh. Years, months, days, hours, minutes, and seconds are the six. In addition, time zone information may or may not be present. Fortunately, databases handle dates and times consistently, with functions extracting components and operating on them. Unfortunately, each database has its own set of functions and peculiarities. The analyses presented in this chapter do not rely on any one particular database's methods for doing things; instead, the analyses offer an approach that works broadly on many systems. The syntax is the syntax for SQL Server. Appendix A provides equivalent syntax for other databases.

The chapter starts with an overview of date and time data types in SQL and basic types of questions to ask about such data. It continues by looking at other columns and how their values change over time, with tips on how to do year-over-year comparisons. The difference between two dates represents duration; durations tie together events for each customer over a span of time. Analyzing data over time introduces new questions, so the chapter includes forays into questions suggested by the time-based analysis.

The chapter finishes with two useful examples. The first is determining the number of customers active at a given point in time. The second relies on simple animations in Excel to visualize changes in durations over time. After all, animating charts incorporates the time dimension directly into the presentation of the results. And, such animations can be quite powerful, persuasive, and timely.

## Dates and Times in Databases

The place to start is the timekeeping system, which measures the passage of time. For times of the day, the system is rather standardized, with twenty-four hour days divided into sixty minutes each and each minute divided into sixty seconds. The big issue is the time zone, and even that has international standards.

For dates, the Gregorian calendar is the calendar prevalent in the modern world. February follows January, school starts in August or September, and pumpkins are ripe at the end of October (in much of the Northern Hemisphere at least). Leap years occur just about every four years by adding an extra day to the miniature winter month of February. This calendar has been somewhat standard in Europe for several centuries. But it is not the only calendar around.

Over the course of millennia, humans have developed thousands of calendars based on the monthly cycles of the moon, the yearly cycles of the sun, cycles of the planet Venus (courtesy of the Mayans), logic, mere expediency, and the frequency of electrons on cesium atoms. Even in today's rational world with instant international communications and where most people use the Gregorian calendar, there are some irregularities. Some Christian holidays float around a bit from year to year, and Orthodox Christian holidays vary from other branches of the religion. Jewish holidays jump around by several weeks from one year to the next, while Muslim holidays cycle through the seasons, because the Islamic year is shorter than the solar year. Chinese New Year is a month later than the Gregorian New Year.

Even rational businesses invent their own calendars. Many companies observe fiscal years that start on days other than the first of January, and some use a 5-4-4 system as their fiscal calendar. The 5-4-4 system describes the number of weeks in a month, regardless of whether the days actually fall in the calendar month. All of these are examples of calendar systems, whose differences strive to meet different needs.

Given the proliferation of calendars, perhaps it shouldn't be surprising that databases handle and manage dates and times in different ways. Each database stores dates in its own internal format. What is the earliest date supported by the database? How much storage space does a date column require? How accurate is a time stamp? The answers are specific to the database implementation. However, databases do all work within the same framework, the familiar Gregorian calendar, with its yearly cycle of twelve months. The next few sections discuss some of the particulars of using these data types.

## Some Fundamentals of Dates and Times in Databases

In databases, dates and times have their own data types. The ANSI standard types are DATETIME and INTERVAL, depending on whether the value is absolute or a duration. Each of these can also have a specified precision, typically in days, seconds, or fractions of a second. The ANSI standard provides a good context for understanding the data types, but every database handles them differently. The aside "Storing Dates and Times in Databases" discusses different ways that date and time values are physically stored.

This section discusses various aspects of dates and times that are fundamental to the data types. These include the topics of extracting components, measuring intervals, and time zones. In addition, this section introduces the Calendar table, which can be used to describe days and is included on the companion web site.

### Extracting Components of Dates and Times

There are six important components of date and time values: year, month, day of month, hour, minute, and second. For understanding customers, year and month are typically the most important components. The month captures seasonality in customer behavior, and the year makes it possible to look at changes in customers over longer periods of time.

Most databases and Excel support functions to extract components from dates, where the function name is the same as the date part: YEAR(), MONTH(), DAY(), HOUR(), MINUTE(), and SECOND(). Actually, only the first three are common to all databases (Excel supports all six). These functions return numbers, rather than a special date-time value or string.

## STORING DATES AND TIMES IN DATABASES

Date and time values are generally presented in human-readable format. For instance, some dispute whether the new millennium started on "2000-01-01" or on "2001-01-01," but we can agree on what these dates mean. Incidentally, this format for representing dates conforms to the international standard called ISO 8601 (`http://www.iso.org/iso/en/prods-services/popstds/datesandtime.html`) and is used throughout this book. Fortunately, most databases understand date constants in this format.

Under the hood, databases store dates and times in many different ways, almost all of which look like meaningless strings of bits. One common way is to store a date as the number of days since a specific reference date, such as 1899-12-31. In this scheme, the new millennium started 36,526 days after the reference date. Or was that 36,892 days? To the human eye, both numbers are incomprehensible as dates. Excel happens to use this mechanism, and the software knows how to convert between the internal format and readable dates, especially for users familiar with setting "Number" formats on cells.

One way to store time is as fractions of a day, so noon on the first day of the year 2000 is represented as 36,526.5. Microsoft Excel also uses this format, representing dates and times as days and fractional days since 1899-12-31.

An alternative method for both dates and times is to store the number of seconds since the reference date. Using the same reference day as Excel, noon on the first day of 2000 would be conveniently represented by the number 3,155,889,600. Well, what's convenient for software makes no sense to people.

Another approach eschews the reference date, storing values as they are in the Gregorian calendar. That is, the year, month, day, and so on are stored separately, typically each as half-byte or one-byte numbers. In the business world, a date two thousand years ago is safely before the data that we work with. Even so, as more information is stored in databases, there are some uses for dates in ancient times, and some databases do support them.

SQL Server has two data types for dates and times. The more accurate one, `DATETIME`, can represent dates from the year 1753 through the year 9999. The less accurate `SMALLDATETIME` supports dates from 1900 through 2079-06-06. In both cases, the internal format consists of two components: the date is the number of days since a reference date and the time is the number of milliseconds or minutes since midnight. Durations are stored using the same data types. Other databases store dates and times in entirely different ways.

The variety of internal coding systems is a testament to the creativity of software designers. More important than the internal coding system is the information derived from dates and times and that information gets used. Different databases offer similar functionality with the caveat that the syntax may vary from product to product. Appendix A shows different syntax for some databases for the constructs used throughout this chapter and the book.

## Converting to Standard Formats

The ISO (International Standards Organization) standard form for dates is "YYYY-MM-DD," where each component is prepended by zeros if necessary. So, the first day of 2000 is "2000-01-01" rather than "2000-1-1." There are two good reasons for including the zeros. First, all dates have the same length as strings. The second reason is that the alphabetical ordering is the same as the time ordering. Alphabetically, the string "2001-02-01" follows "2001-01-31," just as February 1st follows January 31st. However, alphabetically the string "2001-1-31" would be followed by "2001-10-01" rather than by "2001-2-01," even though October does not immediately follow January.

The simplest way to convert a value in Excel to a standard date is TEXT(NOW(), "YYYY-MM-DD"). The function NOW() returns the current date and time on the computer, as the number of days and partial days since 1899-12-31.

Unfortunately, the syntax for similar conversions in SQL depends on the database. One way to get around the peculiarities of each database and still get a common format is to convert the date to a number that looks like a date:

```
SELECT YEAR(orderdate)*10000+MONTH(orderdate)*100+DAY(orderdate)
FROM orders
```

The results are numbers like 20040101, which is recognizable as a date when written without commas. In Excel, such a number can even be given the custom number format of "0000-00-00" to make it look even more like a date.

This convert-to-a-number method can be used for any combination of date parts, such as year with month, month with day, or hour with minute. For instance, the following query returns the number of orders and average order size in dollars for each calendar day of the year:

```
SELECT MONTH(orderdate)*100+DAY(orderdate) as monthday,
       COUNT(*) as numorders, AVG(totalprice) as avgtotalprice
FROM orders
GROUP BY MONTH(orderdate)*100+DAY(orderdate)
ORDER BY 1
```

Figure 5-1 shows the result as a line chart for each day in the year, with the number of orders on the left axis and the average dollars on the right axis. The average order size does not vary much during the year, although it appears a bit higher before August than after. On the other hand, the chart shows the expected seasonality in the number of orders, with more orders appearing in December than in any other month. The peak in early December suggests a lead time for the products and shipping, with customers ordering earlier to ensure delivery by the holiday. This curve suggests that reducing the lead times might increase impulse sales in the two or three weeks before Christmas.

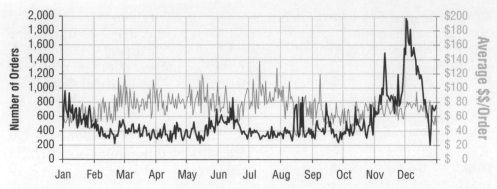

**Figure 5-1:** This chart uses a line chart to show the number of orders and average order size by calendar day.

The challenge in making this chart is the scale on the horizontal axis. It is tempting to make a scatter plot, but such a chart looks quite awkward, because the "date" values are really numbers. There is a big gap between the values; 0131 and 0201. These would be 70 units apart on a scatter plot, even though the corresponding dates are one day apart.

> **TIP** Dates or times on the horizontal axis suggest using a line chart or column chart, rather than a scatter plot. A scatter plot treats the values as numbers, whereas the line and column charts understand date components.

The fix is to convert the numbers back into dates in Excel, using:

```
=DATE(2000, FLOOR(<datenum>/100, 1), MOD(<datenum>, 100))
```

This formula extracts the month and day portions from the number, and puts them into a date with the year 2000. The year is arbitrary, because the chart does not use it. The line chart does recognize dates on the horizontal axis, so the "Number format" can be set to "Mmm" and the axis labels placed at convenient intervals, such as one month apart.

The right-hand axis (secondary axis) also uses an Excel trick. Notice that the numbers line up on the decimal point, so all the "0"s are neatly stacked. This occurs because there are spaces between the "$" and the digits for numbers under $100. The format for this is "$??0".

## Intervals (Durations)

The difference between two dates or two times is a duration. ANSI SQL represents durations using the INTERVAL data type with a specified precision up to any date or time part. Most databases, however, use the same data types for durations as for dates and times.

Logically, there are some differences between durations and dates. For instance, durations can be negative (four days ago rather than four days in the future). They can also take values larger than would be expected for a date or time value. A difference between two times, for instance, might be measured in hours and there might be more than twenty-four hours between them. Also, durations at the level of hours might measure differences in fractions of an hour rather than hours, minutes, and seconds.

For the purposes of analyzing customer data, these distinctions are not important. Most analysis is at the level of dates, and durations measured in days are sufficient. Durations in a single unit, such as days, can simply be measured as numbers.

### Time Zones

Dates and times in the real world occur in a particular time zone. ANSI SQL offers full support of time zones within the date and time values themselves, so values in the same column on different rows can be in different time zones. For some types of data, this is quite useful. For instance, when java scripts return time and date information on web site visitors' machines, the results may be in any time zone. However, in most databases, time zone information, if present at all, is stored in a separate column.

In practice, dates and times rarely need time zone information. Most time stamp values come from operational systems, so all values are from the same time zone anyway, typically the location of the operational system or the company headquarters. It is worth remembering, though, that an online purchase made at midnight might really be a lunch time order from a customer in Singapore.

### Calendar Table

The companion web site includes a table called Calendar that describes dates from Jan 1, 1950 to Dec 31, 2050. The table includes columns such as the following:

- Date
- Year
- Month as both a string and abbreviation
- Day of the week
- Number of days since the beginning of the year
- Holiday names for various holidays
- Holiday categories for various categories

This table is intended to be an example of what a calendar table might contain. Throughout the chapter, various queries that use features of dates, such as day of the week or month, can be accomplished either using SQL functions or by joining to the Calendar table. The purpose of including the Calendar table is because it is useful, but not absolutely necessary, for querying purposes. However, within a single business, a Calendar table can play a more important role, by maintaining important information about the business such as when the fiscal year ends, important holidays, dates of marketing campaigns, and so on. The source of most of the holidays and categories comes from an editor called emacs, which supports a command called "list-holidays". Emacs is distributed by the Free Software Foundation through the GNU project (`http://www.gnu.org/software/emacs`).

## Starting to Investigate Dates

This section covers some basics when looking at date columns. There are several such columns in the companion datasets. The Subscription table contains the start date and stop date of subscriptions. The Orders table contains the order date, and the related Orderline table contains the billing date and shipping date for each line item in the order. Throughout this chapter, all these dates are used in examples. This section starts by looking at the date values themselves, and continues from there.

### Verifying that Dates Have No Times

When the result of a query contains a date-time value, the results sometimes show only the date components, and not the time components. After all, the date part is usually more interesting; and, leaving out the time reduces the width needed for output. This means that non-zero time values are often not visible, which can be misleading. For instance, two dates might look equal, with each looking like, say, 2004-01-01. In a comparison, the two dates might not be equal because one is for noon and the other for midnight. Also, when aggregating date columns, a separate row is created for every unique time value — something that can result in unexpectedly voluminous results if every date has an associated time.

Verifying that date columns have only dates is a good idea: *Does this date column have any unexpected time values?* The solution is to look at the hour, minute, and second components of the date. When any of these are not zero, the date is categorized as "MIXED"; otherwise the date is "PURE". The following query counts the number of mixed and pure values in SHIPDATE in the Orderline table:

```
SELECT (CASE WHEN DATEPART(hh, shipdate) = 0 AND
                 DATEPART(mi, shipdate) = 0 AND
                 DATEPART(ss, shipdate) = 0
           THEN 'PURE' ELSE 'MIXED' END) as datetype,
        COUNT(*), MIN(orderlineid), MAX(orderlineid)
FROM orderline ol
GROUP BY (CASE WHEN DATEPART(hh, shipdate) = 0 AND
                   DATEPART(mi, shipdate) = 0 AND
                   DATEPART(ss, shipdate) = 0
             THEN 'PURE' ELSE 'MIXED' END)
```

This query returns only one row, indicating that all the values in the SHIP-DATE column are pure dates. If any were mixed, the ORDERLINEIDs could be investigated further. In fact, all the date columns in the companion database tables are pure. If, instead, some dates were mixed, we would want to eliminate the time values before using them in queries designed for dates.

## Comparing Counts by Date

Often, just looking at the number of things that happen on a particular date is useful. The following SQL query counts the number of order lines shipped on a given day:

```
SELECT shipdate, COUNT(*)
FROM orderline
GROUP BY shipdate
ORDER BY 1
```

This is a basic histogram query for the shipping date, which was discussed in Chapter 2. A similar query generates the histogram for the billing date. The next sections look at counting more than one date column in a single query, and counting different things, such as customers rather than order lines.

### Orderlines Shipped and Billed

A follow-on question is: *How many orderlines shipped each day and how many billed each day?* The ship date and bill date are both columns in the Orderline table. At first, this might seem to require two queries. Although a possible solution, that method is messy, because the results then have to be combined in Excel.

A better approach is to get the results in a single query, which might suggest a self-join, such as:

```
SELECT shipdate, numship, numbill
FROM (SELECT shipdate, COUNT(*) as numship
      FROM orderline
      GROUP BY shipdate) s LEFT OUTER JOIN
     (SELECT billdate, COUNT(*) as numbill
      FROM orderline
      GROUP BY billdate) b
     ON s.shipdate = b.billdate
ORDER BY 1
```

This query is incorrect, though. Some dates might have bills but no shipments; if so, these dates are lost in the join operation. The opposite problem, dates with shipments but no bills, is handled by the LEFT OUTER JOIN. One solution is to replace the LEFT OUTER JOIN with a FULL OUTER JOIN. This keeps rows in both tables; however, the FULL OUTER JOIN works only because both subqueries are summarized by date.

**TIP** LEFT **and** RIGHT OUTER JOIN **keeps rows from one table but not both. When you need rows from both tables, the right solution is probably** UNION ALL **or** FULL OUTER JOIN**.**

Another solution is to use the UNION ALL operator, which brings together all the rows from two tables:

```
SELECT thedate, SUM(isship) as numships, SUM(isbill) as numbills
FROM ((SELECT shipdate as thedate, 1 as isship, 0 as isbill
       FROM orderline
      ) UNION ALL
      (SELECT billdate as thedate, 0 as isship, 1 as isbill
       FROM orderline)) a
GROUP BY thedate
ORDER BY 1
```

The first subquery chooses the shipping date, setting the ISSHIP flag to one and the ISBILL flag to zero. The second chooses the billing date, setting the flags in the reverse way. The aggregation then counts the number of shipments and bills on each date. If nothing is shipped on a particular date and something is billed, the date appears with the value of NUMSHIPS set to zero. If nothing is shipped or billed on a particular date, that date does not appear in the output.

To include all dates between the first and last, we would need a source of dates when nothing happens. Including the Calendar table as an additional subquery would accomplish this; the subquery would have both ISSHIP and ISBILL set to zero.

By the way, this is the type of question where it makes a difference whether the dates have a time component. With time components, two order lines shipped or billed on the same date, but at different times, would appear as two rows in the output rather than one.

Figure 5-2 shows the resulting chart for just the year 2015 as a line chart (because the horizontal axis is a date). This chart is difficult to read, because the number shipped and number billed track each other so closely. In fact, there is a one-day lag between the two, which makes patterns very difficult to see.

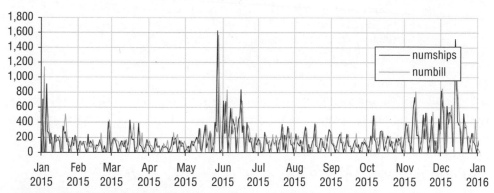

**Figure 5-2:** The number of items in an order and the number billed so closely track each other that the chart is difficult to read.

One way to see how closely correlated two curves are is to use the CORREL() function in Excel to calculate the correlation coefficient, a value between minus one and one, with zero being totally uncorrelated, minus one negatively correlated, and one positively correlated. The correlation coefficient for the two series is 0.46, which is high, but not that high. On the other hand, the correlation coefficient between NUMSHIPS lagged by one day and NUMBILLS is 0.95, which says that the value of SHIPDATE is highly correlated with BILLDATE minus one.

## Customers Shipped and Billed

Perhaps more interesting than the number of order lines shipped each day is the question: *How many customers were sent shipments and bills on each day?* For this query, a customer might have an order with multiple shipping and billing dates. Such customers would be counted multiple times, once for each date.

The approach to this query is similar to the previous query. However, the subqueries in the UNION ALL statement are aggregated prior to the UNION ALL operation, and the aggregations count the number of distinct customers:

```
SELECT thedate, SUM(numship) as numships, SUM(numbill) as numbill,
       SUM(numcustship) as numcustship, SUM(numcustbill) as numcustbill
```

*(continued)*

```
FROM ((SELECT shipdate as thedate, COUNT(*) as numship, 0 as numbill,
              COUNT(DISTINCT customerid) as numcustship,
              0 as numcustbill
       FROM orderline ol JOIN orders o ON ol.orderid = o.orderid
       GROUP BY shipdate
      ) UNION ALL
      (SELECT billdate as thedate, 0 as numship, COUNT(*) as numbill,
              0 as numcustship,
              COUNT(DISTINCT customerid) as numcustbill
       FROM orderline ol JOIN orders o ON ol.orderid = o.orderid
       GROUP BY billdate)) a
GROUP BY thedate
ORDER BY 1
```

The results for this query look essentially the same as the results for the previous query, because for most customers, there is only one order with one ship date and bill date.

## Number of Different Bill and Ship Dates per Order

That last statement is worth verifying: *How many different order and ship dates are there for a given order?* This question is not about time sequencing, but it is interesting nonetheless:

```
SELECT numbill, numship, COUNT(*) as numorders, MIN(orderid), MAX(orderid)
FROM (SELECT orderid, COUNT(DISTINCT billdate) as numbill,
             COUNT(DISTINCT shipdate) as numship
      FROM orderline
      GROUP BY orderid) a
GROUP BY numbill, numship
ORDER BY 1, 2
```

This query uses COUNT(DISTINCT) in the subquery to get the number of bill dates and ship dates for each order. These are then summarized for all orders.

The results in Table 5-1 confirm that almost all orders have a single value for order date and a single value for ship date. This makes sense, because most orders have only one order line. The table also shows that when there are multiple dates, there are typically the same number of bill dates and ship dates. The policy on billing is that customers only get billed when the items are shipped. In other words, every date that something is shipped results in a bill. There are 61 exceptions. In actual practice, it might be worth investigating further to determine whether there is an occasional violation of this policy.

**Table 5-1:** Number of Orders Having *b* Bill Dates and *s* Ship Dates

| # BILL DATES | # SHIP DATES | # ORDERS | % OF ORDERS |
|---|---|---|---|
| 1 | 1 | 181,637 | 94.1% |
| 1 | 2 | 8 | 0.0% |
| 2 | 1 | 35 | 0.0% |
| 2 | 2 | 10,142 | 5.3% |
| 2 | 3 | 1 | 0.0% |
| 3 | 2 | 10 | 0.0% |
| 3 | 3 | 999 | 0.5% |
| 3 | 4 | 2 | 0.0% |
| 4 | 3 | 3 | 0.0% |
| 4 | 4 | 111 | 0.1% |
| 5 | 4 | 1 | 0.0% |
| 5 | 5 | 23 | 0.0% |
| 6 | 4 | 1 | 0.0% |
| 6 | 6 | 9 | 0.0% |
| 17 | 17 | 1 | 0.0% |

## Counts of Orders and Order Sizes

Business changes over time, and understanding these changes is important for managing the business. Two typical questions are: *How many customers place orders in each month? How does an average customer's monthly order size change over time?* The first question is unambiguous, and answered by the following query:

```
SELECT YEAR(orderdate) as year, MONTH(orderdate) as month,
       COUNT(DISTINCT customerid) as numcustomers
FROM orders o
GROUP BY YEAR(orderdate), MONTH(orderdate)
ORDER BY 1
```

The second question is ambiguous. How many "items" as measured by the number of units in each customer's purchases? How many distinct products, as measured by distinct product IDs in each customer's order? How has the average amount spent per customer order changed? The next three subsections address each of these questions.

### Items as Measured by Number of Units

Determining the number of units is easily answered using the Orders table and is a simple modification to the customer query. The SELECT statement needs to include the following additional variables:

```
SELECT SUM(numunits) as numunits,
       SUM(numunits) / COUNT(DISTINCT customerid) as unitspercust
```

This query combines all orders from a single customer during a month, rather than looking at each order individually. So, if a customer places two orders in the same month, and each has three units, the query returns an average of six units for that customer, rather than three. The original question is unclear on how to treat customers who have multiple orders during the period.

If instead we wanted the customer to count as having three units, the query would look like:

```
SELECT SUM(numunits) as numunits,
       SUM(numunits) / COUNT(*) as unitspercustorder
```

This takes all the units and divides them by the number of orders, rather than the number of customers. There is a subtle distinction between counting the average units per order and the average per customer. Both are equally easy to calculate, but they result in different numbers.

### Items as Measured by Distinct Products

In Chapter 2, we saw that some orders contain the same product on multiple order lines. With this in mind, another way to approach the original question might be by calculating two values. The first is the average number of products per order in a month. The second is the average number of products per customer per month. These quantities can be calculated by first aggregating the order lines at the order level and then aggregating again by year and month:

```
SELECT YEAR(orderdate) as year, MONTH(orderdate) as month,
       COUNT(*) as numorders, COUNT(DISTINCT customerid) as numcusts,
       SUM(prodsperord) as sumprodsperorder,
       SUM(prodsperord)*1.0/COUNT(*) as avgperorder,
       SUM(prodsperord)*1.0/COUNT(DISTINCT customerid) as avgpercust
FROM (SELECT o.orderid, customerid, orderdate,
             COUNT(DISTINCT productid) as prodsperord
      FROM orders o JOIN orderline ol ON o.orderid = ol.orderid
      GROUP BY o.orderid, customerid, orderdate ) a
GROUP BY YEAR(orderdate), MONTH(orderdate)
ORDER BY 1, 2
```

One notable feature in this query is the multiplication by 1.0. This ensures that the division operation is done on floating-point numbers rather than integers, so three divided by two is 1.5 rather than 1.

It turns out that the average products per order and per customer are pretty much the same on a monthly basis. Figure 5-3 shows the results of the query, with the number of customers plotted on the left axis and the average products per order plotted on the right. This chart shows peaks in the average products in an order. Most months have a bit over one product per order, but October 2014 and May 2015 peak at twice that value.

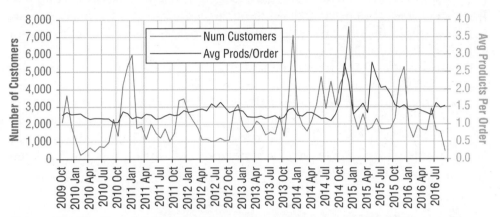

**Figure 5-3:** The size of orders as measured by average number of products per order changes from month to month.

Such unexpected peaks suggest further analysis: *Is there anything different about the products being ordered in different months?* One way to answer this question is to look at information about the most popular product in each month. The new question is: *What is the product group of the most popular product during each month?*

To find the most popular product, the frequencies of all products in each month are compared to the maximum frequency for that month, as shown by the dataflow diagram in Figure 5-4 and by the following query:

```
SELECT prodmon.yr, prodmon.mon, prodmon.cnt, p.productgroupname
FROM (SELECT YEAR(orderdate) as yr, MONTH(orderdate) as mon,
             productid, COUNT(*) as cnt
      FROM orders o JOIN orderline ol ON o.orderid = ol.orderid
      GROUP BY YEAR(orderdate), MONTH(orderdate), productid
     ) prodmon JOIN
     (SELECT yr, mon, MAX(cnt) as maxcnt
      FROM (SELECT YEAR(orderdate) as yr, MONTH(orderdate) as mon,
             productid, COUNT(*) as cnt
            FROM orders o JOIN orderline ol ON o.orderid = ol.orderid
            GROUP BY YEAR(orderdate), MONTH(orderdate), productid) c
```

*(continued)*

```
    GROUP BY yr, mon
  ) prodmax
  ON prodmon.yr = prodmax.yr AND prodmon.mon = prodmax.mon AND
     prodmon.cnt = prodmax.maxcnt JOIN
  product p
  ON prodmon.productid = p.productid
ORDER BY 1, 2
```

The first subquery for Prodmon calculates the frequency of each product during each month. The second subquery for Prodmax calculates the maximum frequency in each month, where the first subquery is repeated as a sub-subquery. These are joined together to get the most frequent product id for each month. The final join to the product table looks up the name of the product group for this product.

Figure 5-5 shows the frequency and product group of the most frequent product for each month. In October 2014 the FREEBIE product group appears for the first time, and the high peaks in November and December are for FREEBIE products. Presumably, there was a marketing offer during this time giving customers a free product in many orders. This also explains why the average order size increases by about one product during this time. It looks like a similar offer was tried again six months later, but to lesser effect.

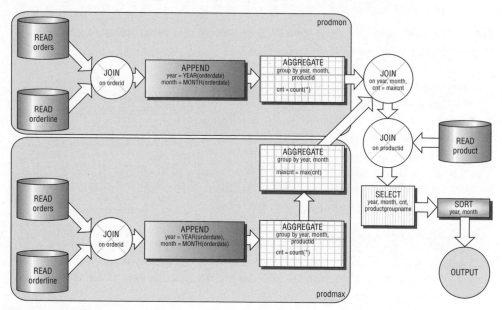

**Figure 5-4:** This dataflow diagram shows the processing for finding the most popular product in each month and returning its product group name.

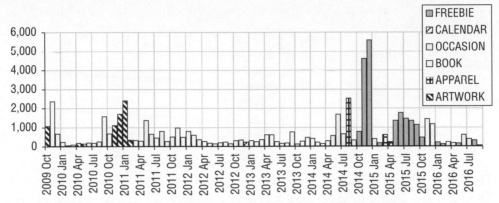

**Figure 5-5:** The most popular product group varies from month to month.

The chart in Figure 5-5 is a stacked column chart. The original data is in a tabular format, with columns for year, month, the product category, and the frequency. In Excel, an additional column is added for each product; the value in the cells is the frequency for the product group that matches the column and zero otherwise. When plotted as a stacked column chart, the groups with zero counts disappear, so only the most popular is shown. Figure 5-6 shows a screen shot of the Excel formulas that accomplish this.

**TIP** Stacked column charts can be used to show one value for each category — such as information about the most popular product for each month.

| | B | C | D | E | F | G | H | I |
|---|---|---|---|---|---|---|---|---|
| 27 | | | | FROM SQL | | | EXCEL CALCULATION | |
| 28 | DATE | yr | mon | cnt | productgroupname | | ARTWORK | APPAREL |
| 29 | =DATE(C29, D29, 1) | 2009 | 10 | 1063 | ARTWORK | | =IF($F29=H$28, $E29, 0) | =IF($F29=I$28, $E29, 0) |
| 30 | =DATE(C30, D30, 1) | 2009 | 11 | 2353 | BOOK | | =IF($F30=H$28, $E30, 0) | =IF($F30=I$28, $E30, 0) |
| 31 | =DATE(C31, D31, 1) | 2009 | 12 | 658 | BOOK | | =IF($F31=H$28, $E31, 0) | =IF($F31=I$28, $E31, 0) |
| 32 | =DATE(C32, D32, 1) | 2010 | 1 | 226 | BOOK | | =IF($F32=H$28, $E32, 0) | =IF($F32=I$28, $E32, 0) |
| 33 | =DATE(C33, D33, 1) | 2010 | 2 | 47 | OCCASION | | =IF($F33=H$28, $E33, 0) | =IF($F33=I$28, $E33, 0) |
| 34 | =DATE(C34, D34, 1) | 2010 | 3 | 97 | BOOK | | =IF($F34=H$28, $E34, 0) | =IF($F34=I$28, $E34, 0) |
| 35 | =DATE(C35, D35, 1) | 2010 | 4 | 180 | ARTWORK | | =IF($F35=H$28, $E35, 0) | =IF($F35=I$28, $E35, 0) |
| 36 | =DATE(C36, D36, 1) | 2010 | 5 | 145 | ARTWORK | | =IF($F36=H$28, $E36, 0) | =IF($F36=I$28, $E36, 0) |
| 37 | =DATE(C37, D37, 1) | 2010 | 6 | 202 | OCCASION | | =IF($F37=H$28, $E37, 0) | =IF($F37=I$28, $E37, 0) |
| 38 | =DATE(C38, D38, 1) | 2010 | 7 | 184 | BOOK | | =IF($F38=H$28, $E38, 0) | =IF($F38=I$28, $E38, 0) |
| 39 | =DATE(C39, D39, 1) | 2010 | 8 | 255 | OCCASION | | =IF($F39=H$28, $E39, 0) | =IF($F39=I$28, $E39, 0) |

**Figure 5-6:** This Excel screen shot shows the formulas used to pivot the product group data for the groups ARTWORK and APPAREL for the stacked column chart in the previous figure. Formulas for other groups are similar.

## Size as Measured by Dollars

Back to measuring the order size. Perhaps the most natural measurement is dollars. Because the Orders table contains the TOTALPRICE column, it is easy to calculate the average dollars per order or the average per customer on a monthly basis:

```
SELECT YEAR(orderdate) as year, MONTH(orderdate) as month,
       COUNT(*) as numorders, COUNT(DISTINCT customerid) as numcust,
       SUM(totalprice) as totspend,
       SUM(totalprice)*1.0/COUNT(*) as avgordersize,
       SUM(totalprice)*1.0/COUNT(DISTINCT customerid) as avgcustorder
FROM orders o
GROUP BY YEAR(orderdate), MONTH(orderdate)
ORDER BY 1, 2
```

Figure 5-7 shows a "cell" chart of the results. The order size tends to increase over time, although there were some months with large average order sizes early on.

| | C | D | E | F | G | H | I | J |
|---|---|---|---|---|---|---|---|---|
| 11 | YEAR | MONTH | ORDERS | CUSTS | $$ | $$/ORDER | $$/CUST | |
| 39 | 2012 | 1 | 2,676 | 2,653 | $116,203.10 | $43.42 | $43.80 | |||||||||||||||||||||||||||||||| |
| 40 | 2012 | 2 | 2,227 | 2,202 | $106,719.55 | $47.92 | $48.46 | |||||||||||||||||||||||||||||| |
| 41 | 2012 | 3 | 1,822 | 1,797 | $89,272.70 | $49.00 | $49.68 | |||||||||||||||||||||||||||| |
| 42 | 2012 | 4 | 1,125 | 1,110 | $64,056.72 | $56.94 | $57.71 | |||||||||||||||||||||||||||||| |
| 43 | 2012 | 5 | 1,150 | 1,137 | $62,787.74 | $54.60 | $55.22 | |||||||||||||||||||||||||||| |
| 44 | 2012 | 6 | 1,033 | 1,024 | $71,591.29 | $69.30 | $69.91 | |||||||||||||||||||||||||||||||||||| |
| 45 | 2012 | 7 | 1,080 | 1,066 | $70,964.26 | $65.71 | $66.57 | |||||||||||||||||||||||||||||||| |
| 46 | 2012 | 8 | 1,221 | 1,203 | $88,913.55 | $72.82 | $73.91 | ||||||||||||||||||||||||||||||||||| |
| 47 | 2012 | 9 | 1,082 | 1,063 | $78,597.14 | $72.64 | $73.94 | ||||||||||||||||||||||||||||||||||| |
| 48 | 2012 | 10 | 1,138 | 1,109 | $75,874.69 | $66.67 | $68.42 | |||||||||||||||||||||||||||||||| |
| 49 | 2012 | 11 | 2,803 | 2,760 | $265,415.97 | $94.69 | $96.17 | ||||||||||||||||||||||||||||||||||||||||||||| |
| 50 | 2012 | 12 | 3,171 | 3,130 | $313,752.39 | $98.94 | $100.24 | ||||||||||||||||||||||||||||||||||||||||||||||||| |
| 51 | 2013 | 1 | 1,962 | 1,941 | $173,661.90 | $88.51 | $89.47 | |||||||||||||||||||||||||||||||||||||||||| |
| 52 | 2013 | 2 | 1,575 | 1,548 | $100,720.61 | $63.95 | $65.06 | |||||||||||||||||||||||||||||| |
| 53 | 2013 | 3 | 1,721 | 1,698 | $117,781.27 | $68.44 | $69.36 | |||||||||||||||||||||||||||||||| |
| 54 | 2013 | 4 | 2,194 | 2,172 | $146,362.30 | $66.71 | $67.39 | |||||||||||||||||||||||||||||||| |
| 55 | 2013 | 5 | 1,975 | 1,949 | $130,189.96 | $65.92 | $66.80 | |||||||||||||||||||||||||||||||| |
| 56 | 2013 | 6 | 1,407 | 1,389 | $123,239.12 | $87.59 | $88.73 | |||||||||||||||||||||||||||||||||||||||| |
| 57 | 2013 | 7 | 1,593 | 1,556 | $138,443.67 | $86.91 | $88.97 | |||||||||||||||||||||||||||||||||||||||| |
| 58 | 2013 | 8 | 1,467 | 1,427 | $106,110.48 | $72.33 | $74.36 | ||||||||||||||||||||||||||||||||||| |
| 59 | 2013 | 9 | 2,524 | 2,452 | $122,590.80 | $48.57 | $50.00 | |||||||||||||||||||||||| |
| 60 | 2013 | 10 | 1,340 | 1,300 | $99,943.43 | $74.58 | $76.88 | |||||||||||||||||||||||||||||||||| |
| 61 | 2013 | 11 | 3,617 | 3,559 | $300,619.88 | $83.11 | $84.47 | |||||||||||||||||||||||||||||||||||||| |
| 62 | 2013 | 12 | 7,190 | 7,099 | $582,263.34 | $80.98 | $82.02 | ||||||||||||||||||||||||||||||||||||| |
| 63 | 2014 | 1 | 2,790 | 2,740 | $198,081.37 | $71.00 | $72.29 | ||||||||||||||||||||||||||||||||| |
| 64 | 2014 | 2 | 1,979 | 1,933 | $125,088.95 | $63.21 | $64.71 | |||||||||||||||||||||||||||||| |
| 65 | 2014 | 3 | 1,636 | 1,596 | $171,355.72 | $104.74 | $107.37 | |||||||||||||||||||||||||||||||||||||||||||||||||||| |
| 66 | 2014 | 4 | 2,254 | 2,221 | $188,072.17 | $83.44 | $84.68 | |||||||||||||||||||||||||||||||||||||| |
| 67 | 2014 | 5 | 3,168 | 3,112 | $239,294.02 | $75.53 | $76.89 | |||||||||||||||||||||||||||||||||| |
| 68 | 2014 | 6 | 4,793 | 4,719 | $250,800.68 | $52.33 | $53.15 | |||||||||||||||||||||||| |
| 69 | 2014 | 7 | 2,935 | 2,884 | $206,480.10 | $70.35 | $71.60 | ||||||||||||||||||||||||||||||||| |

**Figure 5-7:** This bar chart is shown in Excel cells rather than as a chart. This is a good approach when there are too many rows to fit easily into a chart.

The results use a clever mechanism for creating bar charts directly in spreadsheet cells, rather than in a separate chart. Such a mechanism is useful for showing summaries next to a row of data. The idea is credited to the folks at Juice Analytics through their blog at `http://www.juiceanalytics.com/weblog/?p=236`.

The idea is quite simple. The bar chart consists of repeated strings of vertical bars, where the bars are formatted to be in the Ariel 8-point font (another option Webdings font at about 4-points for a solid bar). The specific formula is "`=REPT("|", <cellvalue>)`". The function `REPT()` creates a string by repeating a character the number of times specified in the second argument. Because only the integer portion of the count is used, fractions are not represented in the length of the bars.

## Days of the Week

Many business events occur on weekly cycles, with different days of the week (DOWs) having different characteristics. Monday might be a busy time for starts and stops, because of pent-up demand over the weekend. Business operations can determine day of week effects as well. Customers are usually identified as late payers (and forced to stop, for instance) during the billing processing, which may be run on particular days of the month or on particular days of the week. This section looks at various ways of analyzing days of the week. Later in the chapter we'll look at how to count the number of times a given day occurs between two dates.

### Billing Date by Day of the Week

*How many order lines are billed on each day of the week?* This seems like an easy question, but it has a twist: there is no standard way to determine the DOW in SQL. One way around this is to do the summaries in Excel. Histograms for billing dates were calculated earlier. In Excel, the following steps summarize by day of the week:

- Determine the day of the week for each date, using the `TEXT()` function. (`TEXT(<date>, "Ddd")` returns the three-letter abbreviation.)
- Summarize the data, using `SUMIF()` or pivot tables.

Table 5-2 shows that Tuesday is the most common day for billing and Monday the least common. Calculating these results is also possible in SQL. The simplest method is to use an extension to get the day of the week, such as this version using SQL Server syntax:

```
SELECT billdow, COUNT(*) as numbills
FROM (SELECT o.*, DATENAME(dw, billdate) as billdow FROM orderline o) o
GROUP BY billdow
ORDER BY (CASE WHEN billdow = 'Monday' THEN 1
               WHEN billdow = 'Tuesday' THEN 2
               WHEN billdow = 'Wednesday' THEN 3
```

*(continued)*

```
                    WHEN billdow = 'Thursday' THEN 4
                    WHEN billdow = 'Friday' THEN 5
                    WHEN billdow = 'Saturday' THEN 6
                    WHEN billdow = 'Sunday' THEN 7 END)
```

The most interesting part of the SQL statement is the ORDER BY clause. Ordering the days of the week alphabetically would result in: Friday, Monday, Saturday, Sunday, Thursday, Tuesday, Wednesday — a nonsensical ordering. SQL does not understand the natural ordering to the names. The solution is to use the CASE statement in the ORDER BY clause to assign the days of the week numbers that can be sorted correctly.

**TIP** Using a CASE statement in an ORDER BY clause allows you to order things, such as days of the week, the way you want to see them.

**Table 5-2:** Number of Units Billed by Day of the Week

| DAY OF WEEK | NUMBER OF BILLS |
| --- | --- |
| Monday | 17,999 |
| Tuesday | 61,019 |
| Wednesday | 61,136 |
| Thursday | 54,954 |
| Friday | 49,735 |
| Saturday | 32,933 |
| Sunday | 8,241 |

## Changes in Day of the Week by Year

A natural extension is looking at changes over time: *Has the proportion of bills by day of the week changed over the years?* This can be answered by manipulating the day-by-day data in Excel. It is also possible to answer the question directly using SQL. The following query outputs a table with rows for years and columns for days of the week:

```
SELECT YEAR(billdate) as theyear,
       AVG(CASE WHEN dow = 'Monday' THEN 1.0 ELSE 0 END) as Monday,
       . . .
       AVG(CASE WHEN dow = 'Sunday' THEN 1.0 ELSE 0 END) as Sunday
FROM (SELECT ol.*, DATENAME(dw, billdate) as dow FROM orderline ol) ol
GROUP BY YEAR(billdate)
ORDER BY 1
```

Table 5-3 shows the results. Monday and Saturday stand out as having the largest variance from one year to the next. It suggests that something has changed from year to year, such as operations changing to prefer one day over another. Or, perhaps the date recorded as the billing date is changing due to systems issues, and the underlying operations remain the same. The results only show that something is changing; they do not explain why.

**Table 5-3:** Proportion of Order Lines Billed on Each Day of the Week, by Year

| YEAR | MON | TUE | WED | THU | FRI | SAT | SUN |
| --- | --- | --- | --- | --- | --- | --- | --- |
| 2009 | 0.1% | 21.1% | 22.0% | 15.2% | 25.5% | 14.1% | 2.1% |
| 2010 | 1.4% | 27.5% | 17.1% | 22.0% | 17.5% | 13.1% | 1.5% |
| 2011 | 11.2% | 21.9% | 25.9% | 18.4% | 13.6% | 5.0% | 4.1% |
| 2012 | 4.8% | 22.9% | 19.3% | 18.5% | 17.2% | 14.7% | 2.6% |
| 2013 | 1.4% | 20.2% | 19.3% | 16.3% | 20.8% | 17.3% | 4.7% |
| 2014 | 1.5% | 18.6% | 22.5% | 21.0% | 18.5% | 15.5% | 2.4% |
| 2015 | 16.1% | 22.8% | 19.7% | 19.8% | 14.2% | 4.0% | 3.3% |
| 2016 | 4.7% | 19.5% | 24.7% | 18.4% | 19.2% | 13.1% | 0.3% |

## Comparison of Days of the Week for Two Dates

The STARTDATE and STOPDATE columns in the Subs table contain the start and stop dates of customers of a mobile telephone company. When there are two dates that describe such customer behaviors, a natural question is: *What is the relationship between the days of the week when customers start and the days of the week when customers stop?* The following SQL query answers this question:

```
SELECT startdow,
       AVG(CASE WHEN stopdow = 'Monday' THEN 1.0 ELSE 0 END) as Mon,
       . . .
       AVG(CASE WHEN stopdow = 'Sunday' THEN 1.0 ELSE 0 END) as Sun
FROM (SELECT s.*, DATENAME(dw, start_date) as startdow,
             DATENAME(dw, stop_date) as stopdow
      FROM subs s) s
WHERE startdow IS NOT NULL AND stopdow IS NOT NULL
GROUP BY startdow
ORDER BY (CASE WHEN startdow = 'Monday' THEN 1
             . . .
              WHEN startdow = 'Sunday' THEN 7 END)
```

The results in Table 5-4 show very little correlation between the start dates and stop dates of customers. Each row in the table is for all customers who start on a particular day of the week, broken out by the day of the week of the stops. More customers are likely to stop on a Thursday than any other day, regardless of the day they started. And fewer customers are likely to stop on a Wednesday, regardless of the day they started.

**Table 5-4:** Proportion of Stops by Day of Week Based on Day of Week of Starts

| START DAY OF WEEK | STOP DAY OF WEEK | | | | | | |
|---|---|---|---|---|---|---|---|
| | **MON** | **TUE** | **WED** | **THU** | **FRI** | **SAT** | **SUN** |
| Monday | 13.7% | 11.0% | 5.2% | 22.4% | 18.7% | 15.0% | 13.9% |
| Tuesday | 12.9% | 10.7% | 7.6% | 22.9% | 18.2% | 14.5% | 13.2% |
| Wednesday | 12.6% | 9.9% | 7.4% | 23.9% | 18.6% | 14.7% | 13.0% |
| Thursday | 13.5% | 9.5% | 4.4% | 21.5% | 20.4% | 16.1% | 14.4% |
| Friday | 13.9% | 9.6% | 4.2% | 21.3% | 18.6% | 16.9% | 15.5% |
| Saturday | 14.7% | 9.8% | 4.4% | 21.5% | 18.4% | 15.2% | 16.0% |
| Sunday | 15.4% | 10.3% | 4.6% | 21.9% | 18.5% | 15.0% | 14.3% |

# How Long between Two Dates?

The previous section looked at two dates and some relationships between them. Perhaps the most natural relationship is the duration between them. This section looks at differences between dates in different time units: days, months, years, and by the number of specific days of the week. Surprisingly, durations at each of these levels is interesting, because the different levels reveal different types of information.

## Duration in Days

The BILLDATE and SHIPDATE columns provide a good place to start with investigating duration, particularly in conjunction with the ORDERDATE column in Orders. Two natural questions are: *How long after the order is placed are items shipped? How long after the order is placed are items billed?*

These questions are about durations. In most dialects of SQL, simply subtracting one date from the other calculates the duration between them. This also works in Excel, but Microsoft SQL uses the DATEDIFF() function instead. The following answers the first question about shipping dates:

```
SELECT DATEDIFF(dd, o.orderdate, ol.shipdate) as days, COUNT(*) as numol
FROM orders o JOIN orderline ol ON o.orderid = ol.orderid
GROUP BY DATEDIFF(dd, o.orderdate, ol.shipdate)
ORDER BY 1
```

Notice that this query is actually counting order lines, which makes sense because a single order has multiple ship dates.

The results are shown in Figure 5-8. In a handful of cases the ship date is before the order date. Perhaps this is miraculous evidence of customer insight and service — sending customers what they want even before the orders are placed. Or, perhaps the results are preposterous, suggesting a problem in the data collection for the twenty-eight orders where this happens. At the other extreme, the delay from ordering to shipping for a handful of orders is measured in hundreds of days, a very long lead time indeed.

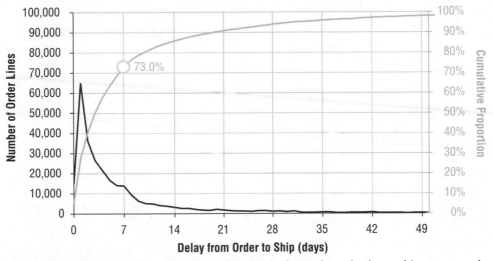

**Figure 5-8:** The delay from ordering to shipping is shown here, both as a histogram and a cumulative proportion.

The cumulative proportion in the chart shows that about three quarters of order lines are fulfilled within a week. This fulfillment time is an important measure for the business. However, an order should be considered fulfilled only when the last item has been shipped, not the first. Calculating the time to fulfill the entire order requires an additional aggregation:

```
SELECT DATEDIFF(dd, orderdate, fulfilldate) as days, COUNT(*) as numorders
FROM (SELECT o.orderid, o.orderdate, MAX(ol.shipdate) as fulfilldate
      FROM orders o JOIN orderline ol ON o.orderid = ol.orderid
```

*(continued)*

```
        GROUP BY o.orderid, o.orderdate) o
GROUP BY DATEDIFF(dd, orderdate, fulfilldate)
ORDER BY 1
```

This query summarizes the orders in the subquery to get the fulfillment date. It aggregates by both ORDERID and ORDERDATE. Strictly speaking, only ORDERID is necessary because there is only one date per order. However, including ORDERDATE in the GROUP BY is simpler than including MIN(ORDERDATE) as ORDERDATE.

Table 5-5 shows the cumulative fulfillment by days after the order for the first ten days. One column is by order (that is, when the last item is fulfilled) and the other is by item. Although 73% of items are shipped within a week, 70% of orders have all their items shipped within a week.

**Table 5-5:** Days to Fulfill Entire Order

| DAYS | COUNT | CUMULATIVE PROPORTION |
|------|-------|-----------------------|
| 0 | 10,326 | 5.4% |
| 1 | 42,351 | 27.3% |
| 2 | 22,513 | 39.0% |
| 3 | 17,267 | 47.9% |
| 4 | 14,081 | 55.2% |
| 5 | 11,115 | 61.0% |
| 6 | 9,294 | 65.8% |
| 7 | 8,085 | 70.0% |
| 8 | 5,658 | 72.9% |
| 9 | 4,163 | 75.1% |
| 10 | 3,373 | 76.8% |

## Duration in Weeks

Duration in weeks is calculated directly from days. The number of weeks is the number of days divided by seven:

```
SELECT FLOOR(DATEDIFF(dd, orderdate, fulfilldate)/7) as weeks, . . .
    . . .
GROUP BY FLOOR(DATEDIFF(dd, orderdate, fulfilldate)/7)
```

Notice that this query uses the FLOOR() function to eliminate any fractional part. One advantage of using weeks is when data is relatively sparse, because a week brings together more instances than a day. Another advantage is when there is a natural weekly cycle to the data. For instance, if orders were not shipped or billed on weekends, then that would introduce a weekly cycle. Summarizing by weeks removes the extraneous cycle within a week, making longer-term patterns more visible.

## Duration in Months

Measuring the number of months between two dates is more challenging than measuring the number of day or weeks. The problem is that two dates might differ by 30 days and be one month apart (say, 15 April and 15 May) or might be zero months apart (say, 1 Jan and 31 Jan). A good approximation is to divide the difference in days by 30.4, the average number of days in a month. Another approach is to do an exact calculation, based on the following rules:

- The duration in months between two dates in the same month is zero. So, the duration between 2000-01-01 and 2000-01-31 is zero months.

- The duration in months between a date in one month and a date in the next month depends on the day of the month. The duration is zero when the day in the second month is less than the day in the first month. So, the duration between 2000-01-01 and 2000-02-01 is one month. The duration between 2000-01-31 and 2000-02-01 is zero months.

The following query does the duration calculation, using the start dates and stop dates in the subscription table:

```
SELECT ((YEAR(s.stop_date)*12+MONTH(s.stop_date)) -
        (YEAR(s.start_date)*12+MONTH(s.start_date)) -
        (CASE WHEN DAY(s.stop_date) < DAY(s.start_date)
              THEN 1 ELSE 0 END)
       ) as tenuremonths, s.*
FROM subs s
WHERE s.stop_date IS NOT NULL
```

The calculation uses the idea of calculating the number of months since the year zero and then taking the difference. The number of months since year zero is the year times twelve plus the month number. One adjustment is needed. This adjustment takes care of the situation when the start date is later in the month than the stop date. The extra month has not gone by, so the difference has over-counted by one.

An alternative is to use built-in functions, if they are available. In Microsoft SQL, the expression DATEDIFF(m, start_date, stop_date) calculates the number of months between two dates.

## How Many Mondays?

Normally, durations are measured in units of time, such as the days, weeks, and months between two dates. Sometimes, though, understanding milestones between two dates, such as the number of birthdays or the number of school days, is important.

This section goes into detail on one particular example, finding the number of times that a specific day of the week occurs between two dates. This is motivated by a specific business problem. In addition, this section illustrates taking a business problem and some observations on how to solve it, converting the observations into rules, and implementing the rules in SQL to address the problem.

### A Business Problem about Days of the Week

This example originated at a newspaper company studying its home delivery customers. The newspaper customer database typically contains the start and stop dates of each customer's subscription, similar to the information in the Subs table. In the newspaper industry, though, not all days of the week are created equal. In particular, Sunday papers are more voluminous and more expensive, filled with more advertising, and their circulation is even counted differently by the organization that audits newspaper circulation, the aptly named Audit Bureau of Circulation.

This newspaper was interested in knowing: *How many Sunday copies did any given home delivery customer receive?* This question readily extends to the number of copies received on any day of the week, not just Sunday. And more generally, for any two dates, the same techniques can count the number of Sundays and Mondays and Tuesdays and so on between them. This section shows how to do this calculation in SQL using the subscription data. Why SQL and not Excel? The answer is that there are many start dates, and many stop dates, and many, many combinations of the two. The data simply does not fit into a worksheet, so SQL is needed to do the heavy lifting.

### Outline of a Solution

The approach relies on several observations. The first is that complete weeks are easy, so customers whose start and stop dates differ by a multiple of seven days have equal numbers of Sundays and Mondays and Tuesdays and so on between the dates. And, that number is the number of weeks between the dates. For any two dates, we can subtract complete weeks from the later one until there are zero to six days left over. The problem is half solved.

When complete weeks are subtracted out, the problem reduces to the following. *Given a start date and a period of zero to six days, how often does each day of the week occur during this period?* Periods longer than six days have been taken care of by subtracting out complete weeks.

Table 5-6 is a lookup table that answers this question for Wednesdays. The first row says that if the start date is Sunday, there have to be at least four days left over in order to have a Wednesday in the period. Notice that the first column is all zeros, which occurs when the difference between the dates is a whole number of weeks. In this case, all the days are accounted for in the first part of the calculation.

**Table 5-6:** Extra Wednesday Lookup Table, Given Start Day of Week and Days Left Over

| START DAY OF WEEK | DAYS LEFT OVER | | | | | | |
|---|---|---|---|---|---|---|---|
| | **0** | **1** | **2** | **3** | **4** | **5** | **6** |
| Sunday (1) | NO | NO | NO | NO | YES | YES | YES |
| Monday (2) | NO | NO | NO | YES | YES | YES | YES |
| Tuesday (3) | NO | NO | YES | YES | YES | YES | YES |
| Wednesday (4) | NO | YES | YES | YES | YES | YES | YES |
| Thursday (5) | NO | NO | NO | NO | NO | NO | NO |
| Friday (6) | NO | NO | NO | NO | NO | NO | YES |
| Saturday (7) | NO | NO | NO | NO | NO | YES | YES |

Unfortunately, there is a separate table for each day of the week. Can we determine this information without a plethora of lookup tables? There is a way, and although it is a bit cumbersome arithmetically it provides a nice illustration of observing rules and implementing them in SQL. This method rests on two additional rules, which in turn need two variables. The first is LEFTOVER, the number of days left over after all the complete weeks have been counted. The second is the day of the week as a number, which for convention we are taking to start on Sunday as one through Saturday as seven (this is the default convention for the Excel function WEEKDAY()). With this information, the following rules tell us whether a Wednesday, whose number is four, is included in the leftover days:

- If the start day of the week falls on or before Wednesday, then Wednesday is included when the start day of the week number plus the leftover days is greater than five. For example, if someone starts on a Sunday (value one), then leftover days needs to be at least four.

- If the start day of the week is after Wednesday, then Wednesday is included when the start day of the week number plus the leftover days is greater than eleven. For instance, if someone starts on a Saturday (value seven), then leftover days needs to be at least five.

These generalize to the following rules, where DOW is the day we are looking for:

- If the start day of the week is on or before DOW, then DOW is included when the start day of the week number plus the leftover days is greater than the DOW number.

- If the start day of the week is after DOW, then DOW is included when the start day of the week number plus the leftover days is greater than seven plus the DOW number.

The next section builds the rules in SQL.

## Solving It in SQL

To implement this in SQL, three columns need to be defined. WEEKSBETWEEN is the number of complete weeks between the two dates; this is calculated by taking the duration in days, dividing by seven, and ignoring the remainder. LEFTOVER is the days left over after all the weeks have been counted. DOWNUM is the day of week number determined using a CASE statement on the day of week name. These columns are defined using nested subqueries:

```
SELECT s.*, (weeksbetween +
            (CASE WHEN (downum <= 1 AND downum + leftover > 1) OR
                        (downum > 1 AND downum + leftover > 7+1)
                  THEN 1 ELSE 0 END)) as Sundays,
      (weeksbetween +
        (CASE WHEN (downum <= 2 AND downum + leftover > 2) OR
                    (downum > 2 AND downum + leftover > 7+2)
              THEN 1 ELSE 0 END)) as Mondays
FROM (SELECT daysbetween, FLOOR(daysbetween/7) as weeksbetween,
            daysbetween - 7*FLOOR(daysbetween/7) as leftover,
            (CASE WHEN startdow = 'Monday' THEN 1
                    . . .
                  WHEN startdow = 'Sunday' THEN 7 END) downum
        FROM (SELECT s.*, DATENAME(dw, start_date) as startdow,
                DATEDIFF(dd, stop_date, start_date
                            ) as daysbetween
            FROM subs s
            WHERE s.stop_date IS NOT NULL
            ) s
    ) s
```

The outermost query calculates the number of Sundays and Mondays between the start date and stop date using the two rules. Other days of the week follow the same logic as these counts.

### *Using a Calendar Table Instead*

An alternative method would be to use the Calendar table, if one is available. So the following query expresses what needs to be done:

```
SELECT s.customerid,
       SUM(CASE WHEN c.dow = 'Mon' THEN 1 ELSE 0 END)as Monday
FROM subs s JOIN
     calendar c
     ON c.date BETWEEN s.start_date AND s.stop_date - 1
WHERE s.stop_date IS NOT NULL
GROUP BY s.customerid
```

This query has many advantages in terms of readability and understandability. The only downside is performance. The join operation creates an intermediate table with one row for every calendar date between the start date and stop date, potentially multiplying the number of rows by hundreds or thousands. This query has very poor performance.

If counting weekdays is important, there is a more efficient method both in terms of representation and performance. The Calendar table has seven additional columns, which count the number of each day of the week since some reference date. So, MONDAYS is the number of Mondays since the reference date. The following query uses these columns:

```
SELECT s.*, (cstop.mondays - cstart.mondays) as mondays
FROM subs s JOIN calendar cstart ON cstart.date = s.start_date JOIN
     calendar cstop ON cstop.date = s.stop_date
WHERE s.stop_date IS NOT NULL
```

This method joins the Calendar table twice to the Subs table to look up the MONDAYS value for both the start and stop dates. The number of Mondays between them is just the difference between these values.

## Year-over-Year Comparisons

The previous year usually provides the best comparison for what is happening the following year. This section talks about such comparisons, with particular emphasis on one of the big challenges. This year's data is usually not complete, so how can we make a valid comparison?

### Comparisons by Day

The place to start is with day-by-day comparisons from one year to the next. Here is a method where much of the work is done in Excel:

1. Query the database and aggregate by date.

2. Load the data into Excel, with all the dates in one column.

3. Pivot the data, so there are 366 rows (for each day in the year) and a separate column for each year.

This is actually more work than necessary. An easier way is to use the MONTH(), DAY(), and YEAR() functions in SQL to create the resulting table directly, as in the following example using starts from the subscription database:

```
SELECT MONTH(start_date) as mon, DAY(start_date) as dom,
       SUM(CASE WHEN startyear = 2004 THEN 1 ELSE 0 END) as n2004,
       SUM(CASE WHEN startyear = 2005 THEN 1 ELSE 0 END) as n2005,
       SUM(CASE WHEN startyear = 2006 THEN 1 ELSE 0 END) as n2006
FROM (SELECT s.*, YEAR(start_date) startyear FROM subs s) s
WHERE startyear in (2004, 2005, 2006)
GROUP BY MONTH(start_date), DAY(start_date)
ORDER BY 1, 2
```

Figure 5-9 shows the results as a line chart with three series. There is a weekly cycle of peaks and valleys for all three years. The chart illustrates that starts in 2006 are lower than in the other years during most months.

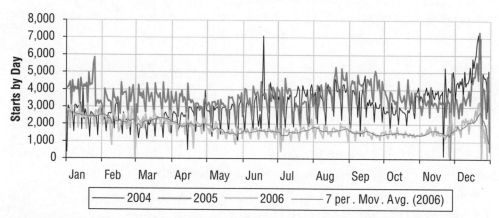

**Figure 5-9:** This line chart shows the pattern of starts by day throughout the year for three years.

The chart is a line chart so the horizontal axis can be a date. The date is calculated in Excel as a new column, using the DATE() function on the month and day values in each row. In the chart, the horizontal axis is this date column, whose "Number" format is set to "Mmm" to display only the month. The scale is set to show tick marks every month.

## Adding a Moving Average Trend Line

A pattern of starts by within weeks (by weekday) can interfere with seeing larger trends. One way to fix this is by adding a trend line with a seven-day moving average. Figure 5-9 also shows the trend line along with the original data. The seven-day moving average eliminates the weekly cycle.

To add the trend line, left-click a series to select it. Then right-click and choose the "Add Trendline" option. In the dialog box, "Moving Average" is the option on the lower right, with the width of the moving average in the "Period" box. Change the default value to seven to eliminate weekly cycles, and then click "OK" to finish.

## Comparisons by Week

An alternative way of eliminating the bumpiness is to aggregate the data at the weekly level rather than at the daily level. This is a little bit tricky, because SQL does not have a function that returns the week number of the year, so we have to calculate it by calculating the number of days since the beginning of the year and dividing by seven:

```
SELECT (CASE WHEN startyear = 2004
             THEN FLOOR(DATEDIFF(dd, '2004-01-01', start_date)/7)
             WHEN startyear = 2005
             THEN FLOOR(DATEDIFF(dd, '2005-01-01', start_date)/7)
             WHEN startyear = 2006
             THEN FLOOR(DATEDIFF(dd, '2006-01-01', start_date)/7)
        END) as weekofyear,
        SUM(CASE WHEN startyear = 2004 THEN 1 ELSE 0 END) as n2004,
        SUM(CASE WHEN startyear = 2005 THEN 1 ELSE 0 END) as n2005,
        SUM(CASE WHEN startyear = 2006 THEN 1 ELSE 0 END) as n2006
FROM (SELECT s.*, YEAR(start_date) as startyear FROM subs s) s
WHERE startyear in (2004, 2005, 2006)
GROUP BY (CASE WHEN startyear = 2004
               THEN FLOOR(DATEDIFF(dd, '2004-01-01', start_date)/7)
               WHEN startyear = 2005
               THEN FLOOR(DATEDIFF(dd, '2005-01-01', start_date)/7)
               WHEN startyear = 2006
               THEN FLOOR(DATEDIFF(dd, '2006-01-01', start_date)/7)
          END)
ORDER BY 1
```

The SQL statement explicitly lists each year when calculating WEEKOFYEAR; being explicit has the advantage of being more understandable.

An alternative method is perhaps more cryptic, but is preferable because the years do not all need to be specified:

```
FLOOR(DATEDIFF(dd, CAST(REPLACE('<YEAR>-01-01', '<YEAR>', startyear)
                   as DATETIME), start_date)/7) as weekofyear
```

This formulation follows the same logic as the previous one. Here, though, the first day of the year is calculated on the fly, by constructing a string form of the date which is then converted to a DATETIME. In some dialects of SQL, the CAST() is unnecessary, because the SQL engine recognizes date arithmetic and does the conversion automatically.

Creating a chart from this data follows a similar line of reasoning as for comparison by days. The idea is to add a new column with a date from some specific year. Instead of using the DATE() function, though, the date is created by adding 7*WEEKOFYEAR to a base date, such as 2000-01-01.

Of course, Excel can also handle the transformation from daily data to weekly data, using the same method of subtracting the first day of the year, dividing by seven, and then summing the results using SUMIF().

## Comparisons by Month

A year-over-year comparison by month can follow the same structure as the comparison by day or week. The following SQL shows the summaries by month:

```
SELECT MONTH(start_date) as month,
       SUM(CASE WHEN startyear = 2004 THEN 1 ELSE 0 END) as n2004,
       SUM(CASE WHEN startyear = 2005 THEN 1 ELSE 0 END) as n2005,
       SUM(CASE WHEN startyear = 2006 THEN 1 ELSE 0 END) as n2006
FROM (SELECT s.*, YEAR(start_date) as startyear FROM subs s) s
WHERE startyear IN (2004, 2005, 2006)
GROUP BY MONTH(start_date)
ORDER BY 1
```

Monthly data is often better represented by column charts with the different years side-by-side, as shown in Figure 5-10.

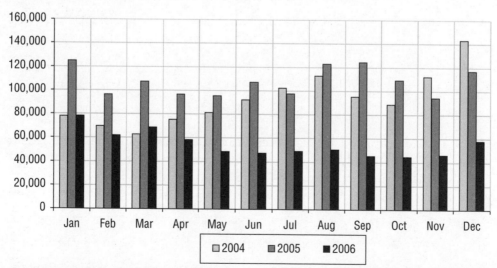

**Figure 5-10:** Column charts are useful for showing monthly data, year over year, such as this example showing subscription starts.

The next example examines TOTALPRICE in the Orders table. This differs from the examples so far for two reasons. First, the results are not just counts but dollars. Second, the last day of data has a date of September 20th, although there is missing data after September 7th. The incomplete September data poses a challenge. The following SQL query extracts the information by month:

```
SELECT MONTH(orderdate) as month,
       SUM(CASE WHEN ordyear = 2014 THEN totalprice END) as r2014,
       SUM(CASE WHEN ordyear = 2015 THEN totalprice END) as r2015,
       SUM(CASE WHEN ordyear = 2016 THEN totalprice END) as r2016
FROM (SELECT o.*, YEAR(orderdate) as ordyear FROM orders o) o
WHERE orderdate <= '2016-09-07'
GROUP BY MONTH(orderdate)
ORDER BY 1
```

Table 5-7 shows the results, which suggest that sales have dropped precipitously in the month of September. This is misleading, of course, because only the first few days of September are included for the third year. There are two approaches to getting valid comparison information. The first is to look at month-to-date (MTD) comparisons for previous years. The second is to extrapolate the values to the end of the month.

**Table 5-7:** Revenue by Month for Orders

| MONTH | 2014 | 2015 | 2016 |
|---|---|---|---|
| 1 | $198,081.37 | $201,640.63 | $187,814.13 |
| 2 | $125,088.95 | $191,589.28 | $142,516.49 |
| 3 | $171,355.72 | $215,484.26 | $251,609.27 |
| 4 | $188,072.17 | $140,299.76 | $193,443.75 |
| 5 | $239,294.02 | $188,226.96 | $247,425.25 |
| 6 | $250,800.68 | $226,271.71 | $272,784.77 |
| 7 | $206,480.10 | $170,183.03 | $250,807.38 |
| 8 | $160,693.87 | $157,961.71 | $164,388.50 |
| 9 | $234,277.87 | $139,244.44 | $26,951.14 |
| 10 | $312,175.19 | $170,824.58 | |
| 11 | $394,579.03 | $409,834.57 | |
| 12 | $639,011.54 | $466,486.34 | |

## Month-to-Date Comparison

The month-to-date comparison is shown in the upper chart in Figure 5-11. The bars for September in 2014 and 2015 have overlapping columns, with the shorter ones in September being the month-to-date values and the taller ones being the total revenue. These month-to-date numbers are the appropriate level of comparison for September.

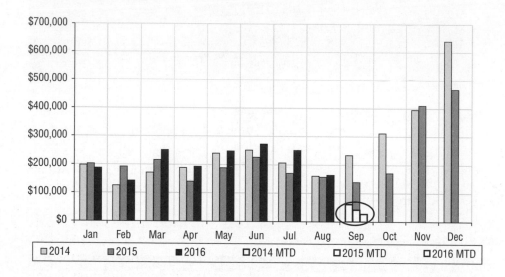

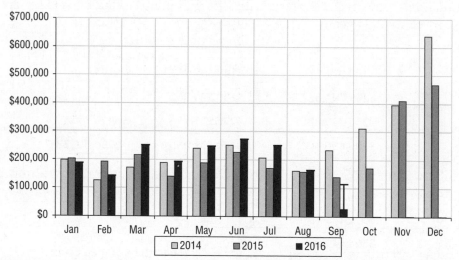

**Figure 5-11:** The upper chart shows month-to-date comparisons using overlapping column charts. The lower chart shows the end-of-month estimate using Y-error bars.

How are these overlapping columns created? Unfortunately, Excel does not have an option for column charts that are both stacked and side-by-side, but we can improvise by having two sets of three series. The first three are plotted on the primary axis and contain the full month revenue numbers. The second set is plotted on the secondary axis and contains only the month-to-date revenue numbers for September. Both groups need to contains the same number of columns, to ensure that the column widths are the same, and the columns overlap completely. The data for this chart is calculated by adding the following three columns to the previous SQL statement:

```
SUM(CASE WHEN ordyear = 2014 AND ordmon = 9 AND orderdate <= '2014-09-07'
         THEN totalprice END) as rev2014mtd,
SUM(CASE WHEN ordyear = 2015 AND ordmon = 9 AND orderdate <= '2015-09-07'
         THEN totalprice END) as rev2015mtd,
SUM(CASE WHEN ordyear = 2016 AND ordmon = 9 AND orderdate <= '2016-09-07'
         THEN totalprice END) as rev2016mtd
```

The subquery also needs to define ORDMON.

These additional columns calculate the month-to-date numbers for September, returning NULL for all other months. Although the last column is redundant (because it contains the same data as the corresponding full month column), having it simplifies the charting procedure, by providing the third series on the secondary axis.

Creating the chart starts by pasting the results in Excel. The horizontal axis uses the month name; although we could type in the month abbreviations, an alternative method is to use dates: create a date column by copying the formula "DATE(2000, <monthnum>, 1)" down a column, use that column as the horizontal axis, and then format it with just the month name by setting its "Number" format to "Mmm".

Next, a column chart is created with the following columns:

- The new date column goes on the horizontal axis.
- The three full revenue columns are data columns, for the first three series on the primary axis.
- The three month-to-date-revenue columns are data columns, for the second three series for the secondary axis.

Now the chart needs to be customized. First, the three month-to-date columns need to be switched to the secondary axis. To do this, click each series, go to the "Axis" tab, and choose "Secondary axis."

The final step is cleaning up the secondary axis:

- The month-to-date numbers need to be on the same scale as on the other axis. Click the secondary vertical axis and make the maximum value the same as the maximum value on the primary axis.
- The secondary axis labels and tick marks need to be removed, by clicking them and hitting <delete>.

Finally, the month-to-date series should be colored similarly so they can be seen.

**TIP** If you make a mistake in Excel, just hit `<control>-Z` to undo it. You can always experiment and try new things, and undo the ones that don't look right.

### Extrapolation by Days in Month

The lower chart in Figure 5-11 shows a different approach. Here, the comparison is to the estimated value for the end of the month, rather than to the past month-to-date values. The simplest end-of-month estimate is a linear trend, calculated by multiplying the current value for the month times the number of days in the month and dividing by the number of days that have data. For instance, for the September data, multiply the $26,951.14 by 30 and divide by 7, to get $115,504.89.

The chart shows this difference using Y-error bars. The length of the bar is the difference from the end-of-month estimate and the current value; that is $88,553.75 = $115,504.89 – $26,951.14. Starting with the column chart that has three series for each year, adding the Y-error bar has the following steps:

1. Add a column to the table in Excel where all the cells are blank except for the one for September. This one gets the difference value.

2. Add the error bars by double-clicking the series for 2016 to bring up the "Format Data Series" dialog box. On the "Y-Error Bars" tab, choose "Plus" (the second option) and click by "Custom," the bottom option. Set the "+" series to refer to the difference column.

3. Format the error bar by double-clicking it.

Calculating the difference column in Excel is feasible. However, doing it in SQL is instructive because it shows the power of manipulating dates in the database. Unfortunately, SQL lacks a simple way to calculate the number of days in the month. The solution starts with the following two rules:

- If the month number is 12 (December), then the number of days is 31.

- Otherwise, it is the difference between the first day of the current month and the first day of the next month.

The dates for the first date of the current month and the first date of the next month are calculated using the CAST() and REPLACE() trick that we saw earlier. Combined into a query, this looks like:

```
SELECT mon,
       SUM(CASE WHEN ordyear = 2014 THEN totalprice END) as r2014,
       SUM(CASE WHEN ordyear = 2015 THEN totalprice END) as r2015,
```

```
        SUM(CASE WHEN ordyear = 2016 THEN totalprice END) as r2016,
        (SUM(CASE WHEN ordyear = 2016 AND mon = 9 THEN totalprice END)*
         ((MAX(daysinmonth)*1.0/MAX(CASE WHEN ordyear= 2016 AND mon = 9
                                    THEN DAY(orderdate) END)) - 1)
        ) as IncrementToMonthEnd
FROM (SELECT o.*, DATENAME(dw, orderdate) as dow,
             (CASE WHEN mon = 12 THEN 31
                   ELSE DATEDIFF(dd,
                                 CAST(REPLACE(REPLACE('<Y>-<M>-01',
                                                      '<Y>', ordyear),
                                      '<M>', mon) as DATETIME),
                                 CAST(REPLACE(REPLACE('<Y>-<M>-01',
                                                      '<Y>', ordyear),
                                      '<M>', mon + 1) as DATETIME))
              END) as daysinmonth
      FROM (SELECT o.*, YEAR(orderdate) as ordyear,
                   MONTH(orderdate) as mon
            FROM orders o) o
     ) o
WHERE orderdate <= '2016-09-07'
GROUP BY mon
ORDER BY 1
```

The query is not pretty, but it does the job of calculating the linear trend to the end of the month. The subquery calculates the number of days in the month (some databases have simpler methods of doing this). The column INCRE-MENTTOMONTHEND is then calculated by taking the total for the month so far, multiplying by one less than the days in the month divided by the maximum day seen in the month. The "one less" is because we want the increment over the current value, rather than the month-end estimate itself.

## Estimation Based on Day of Week

There may be more accurate methods to estimate the end-of-month value than linear extrapolation. If there is a weekly cycle, a method that takes into account days of the week should do a better job. In the previous instance, there are seven days of data for September 2016. If weekdays have one set of start behavior and weekends another set, how could we use this information to extrapolate the $26,952.14 to the end of the September? Notice that this estimation is only possible after at least one weekday and at least one weekend day has passed, unless we borrow information from previous months.

There are two parts to this calculation. The first is calculating the average weekday and the average weekend contribution for September. The second is calculating the number of weekdays and number of weekend days during the month. We'll do the first calculation in SQL and the second calculation in

Excel. The following additional two columns contain the averages for week-days and weekends in September 2016:

```
(SUM(CASE WHEN ordyear = 2016 AND mon = 9 AND
          dow NOT IN ('Saturday', 'Sunday')
     THEN totalprice END) /
 COUNT(DISTINCT (CASE WHEN ordyear = 2016 AND mon = 9 AND
                      dow NOT IN ('Saturday', 'Sunday')
                 THEN orderdate END)) ) as weekdayavg,
 (SUM(CASE WHEN ordyear = 2016 AND mon = 9 AND
          dow IN ('Saturday', 'Sunday') THEN totalprice END) /
 COUNT(DISTINCT (CASE WHEN ordyear = 2016 AND mon = 9 AND
                      dow IN ('Saturday', 'Sunday')
                 THEN orderdate END)) )  as weekendavg
```

Notice that the average calculation for weekdays takes the sum of all the orders on weekdays and divides by the number of distinct days when orders were placed. This gives the average total order volume on weekdays. By contrast, the AVG() function would calculate something different, the average order size.

Without a calendar table, it is rather complex to determine the number of weekdays and weekend days in a given month using SQL. Excel has the advantage of being able to define a lookup table, such as the one in Table 5-8. This table has the number of weekend days in a month, given the start date and number of days in the month.

**Table 5-8:** Weekdays and Weekend Days by Start of Month and Length of Month

| MONTH START DAY OF WEEK | WEEKDAYS | | | | WEEKEND DAYS | | | |
|---|---|---|---|---|---|---|---|---|
| | 28 | 29 | 30 | 31 | 28 | 29 | 30 | 31 |
| Monday | 20 | 21 | 22 | 23 | 8 | 8 | 8 | 8 |
| Tuesday | 20 | 21 | 22 | 23 | 8 | 8 | 8 | 8 |
| Wednesday | 20 | 21 | 22 | 23 | 8 | 8 | 8 | 8 |
| Thursday | 20 | 21 | 22 | 22 | 8 | 8 | 8 | 9 |
| Friday | 20 | 21 | 21 | 21 | 8 | 8 | 9 | 10 |
| Saturday | 20 | 20 | 20 | 21 | 8 | 9 | 10 | 10 |
| Sunday | 20 | 20 | 21 | 22 | 8 | 9 | 9 | 9 |

The following Excel formula calculates the number of days in a month:

```
days in month = DATE(<year>, <mon>+1, 1) - DATE(<year>, <mon>, 1)
```

This works in Excel even for December because Excel interprets month 13 as January of the following year. The day of the week when the month starts is calculated using:

```
startdow = TEXT(DATE(<year>, <mon>, 1), "Dddd")
```

Using this information, the number of weekdays can be looked up in the preceding table using the following formula:

```
VLOOKUP(<startdow>, <table>, <daysinmonth>-28+2, 0)
```

Figure 5-12 shows a screen shot of Excel with these formulas. Taking weekdays and weekends into account, the end-of-month estimate is $109,196.45, which is only slightly less than the $115,504.89 linear estimate.

| | B | C | D | E | F | G | H | I | J |
|---|---|---|---|---|---|---|---|---|---|
| 1 | | FROM SQL | | | | EXCEL CALCULATION FOR WEEKDAYS AND WEEKEND DAYS IN MONTH | | | |
| 2 | Month Start | ordmon | 2016 | weekdays | weekends | Days in Month | Start DOW | Weekdays | Weekend |
| 3 | =DATE($D$2, C3, 1) | 1 | 187814.13 | | | =DATE($D$2, C3+1, 1)-$B3 | =TEXT($B3, "ddd") | =VLOOKUP(H3, $B$20:$F$26, $G3-28+2, 0) | =G3-I3 |
| 4 | =DATE($D$2, C4, 1) | 2 | 142516.49 | | | =DATE($D$2, C4+1, 1)-$B4 | =TEXT($B4, "ddd") | =VLOOKUP(H4, $B$20:$F$26, $G4-28+2, 0) | =G4-I4 |
| 5 | =DATE($D$2, C5, 1) | 3 | 251609.27 | | | =DATE($D$2, C5+1, 1)-$B5 | =TEXT($B5, "ddd") | =VLOOKUP(H5, $B$20:$F$26, $G5-28+2, 0) | =G5-I5 |
| 6 | =DATE($D$2, C6, 1) | 4 | 193443.75 | | | =DATE($D$2, C6+1, 1)-$B6 | =TEXT($B6, "ddd") | =VLOOKUP(H6, $B$20:$F$26, $G6-28+2, 0) | =G6-I6 |
| 7 | =DATE($D$2, C7, 1) | 5 | 247425.25 | | | =DATE($D$2, C7+1, 1)-$B7 | =TEXT($B7, "ddd") | =VLOOKUP(H7, $B$20:$F$26, $G7-28+2, 0) | =G7-I7 |
| 8 | =DATE($D$2, C8, 1) | 6 | 272784.77 | | | =DATE($D$2, C8+1, 1)-$B8 | =TEXT($B8, "ddd") | =VLOOKUP(H8, $B$20:$F$26, $G8-28+2, 0) | =G8-I8 |
| 9 | =DATE($D$2, C9, 1) | 7 | 250807.38 | | | =DATE($D$2, C9+1, 1)-$B9 | =TEXT($B9, "ddd") | =VLOOKUP(H9, $B$20:$F$26, $G9-28+2, 0) | =G9-I9 |
| 10 | =DATE($D$2, C10, 1) | 8 | 164388.5 | | | =DATE($D$2, C10+1, 1)-$B10 | =TEXT($B10, "ddd") | =VLOOKUP(H10, $B$20:$F$26, $G10-28+2, 0) | =G10-I10 |
| 11 | =DATE($D$2, C11, 1) | 9 | 26951.14 | 4719.616 | 1676.53 | =DATE($D$2, C11+1, 1)-$B11 | =TEXT($B11, "ddd") | =VLOOKUP(H11, $B$20:$F$26, $G11-28+2, 0) | =G11-I11 |
| 12 | =DATE($D$2, C12, 1) | 10 | | | | =DATE($D$2, C12+1, 1)-$B12 | =TEXT($B12, "ddd") | =VLOOKUP(H12, $B$20:$F$26, $G12-28+2, 0) | =G12-I12 |
| 13 | =DATE($D$2, C13, 1) | 11 | | | | =DATE($D$2, C13+1, 1)-$B13 | =TEXT($B13, "ddd") | =VLOOKUP(H13, $B$20:$F$26, $G13-28+2, 0) | =G13-I13 |
| 14 | =DATE($D$2, C14, 1) | 12 | | | | =DATE($D$2, C14+1, 1)-$B14 | =TEXT($B14, "ddd") | =VLOOKUP(H14, $B$20:$F$26, $G14-28+2, 0) | =G14-I14 |
| 15 | This is the first day of the month for the year in $D$2 and the month in column D. | Month number | Dollars Spent in month in 2016 | Week-day average so far | Week-end average so far | Number of days in the month is the difference between the start of the next month and the start of this month. | The TEXT function returns the day of the week when month starts. | Number of weekdays in the month comes from the weekday lookup table determined by START DOW; the column by the number of days in the month. | Weekend days are total days minus week-days. |
| 16 | | | | | | | | | |
| 17 | | WEEKDAYS LOOKUP TABLE | | | | | | | |
| 18 | Month | | Days in Month | | | | | | |
| 19 | Starts on ... | 28 | 29 | 30 | 31 | | | | |
| 20 | Mon | 20 | 21 | 22 | 23 | | | | |
| 21 | Tue | 20 | 21 | 22 | 23 | | | | |
| 22 | Wed | 20 | 21 | 22 | 23 | | | | |
| 23 | Thu | 20 | 21 | 22 | 22 | | | | |
| 24 | Fri | 20 | 21 | 21 | 21 | | | | |
| 25 | Sat | 20 | 20 | 20 | 21 | | | | |
| 26 | Sun | 20 | 20 | 21 | 22 | | | | |

**Figure 5-12:** This screen shot of Excel shows the calculation of the number of days in the month, the number of weekdays, and the number of weekend days, which can then be used to estimate the end-of-month average taking into account the day of the week.

## Estimation Based on Previous Year

Another way to estimate the end of the month value uses the ratio of the previous year month-to-date and previous year month total. Applying this ratio to the current month gives an estimate of the end-of-month value. This calculation has the advantage of taking into account holidays, because the same month period the year before probably had the same holidays. Of course, this doesn't work well for floating holidays such as Easter and Rosh Hashanah.

For instance, in the previous year, the monthly total was $139,244.44. The total for the first seven days during that month was $41,886.47, which is about 30.1% of the total. The current month to date is $26,951.14. This is 30.1% of $89,594.48. The estimate for the entire month calculated using this approach is considerably smaller than using the linear trend.

# Counting Active Customers by Day

Calculating the number of active customers as of the database cut-off date is easy, by simply counting those whose status code indicates that they are active. This section extends this simple counting mechanism to historical time periods, by progressing from counting the active customers on any given day in the past, to counting active customers on all days, and finally, to breaking customers into tenure groups and counting the sizes of those groups on any given day.

## How Many Customers on a Given Day?

On a given day in the past, the customers who are active have two characteristics:

- They started on or before the given day.
- They stopped after the given day.

For instance, the following query answers the question: *How many subscriptions customers were active on Valentine's Day in 2005?*

```
SELECT COUNT(*)
FROM subs
WHERE start_date <= '2005-02-14' AND
      (stop_date > '2005-02-14' OR stop_date IS NULL)
```

The WHERE clause implements the logic that selects the right group of customers.

The query returns the value of 2,387,765. By adding GROUP BY clauses, this number can be broken out by features such as market, channel, rate plan, or any column that describes customers when they started.

The data in the Subs table does not contain any accounts that stopped prior to 2004-01-01. Because these accounts are missing, it is not possible to get accurate counts prior to this date.

## How Many Customers Every Day?

Calculating the number of active customers on one day only provides information about one day. A more useful question is: *How many customers were active on any given day in the past?* For the subscriptions data, this question has to be tempered, because it is only possible to get an accurate count since 2004-01-01, because of the missing stops prior to that date.

The answer to this question relies on an observation: the number of customers who are active on a given day is the number who started on or before that day minus the customers who stopped on or before that day. The preceding question simplifies into two other questions: *How many customers started as of a given day? How many customers stopped as of a given day?*

These questions are readily answered with the combination of SQL and Excel. The mechanism is to count the number of starts and stops on each day using SQL. Excel is then used to accumulate the numbers up to any given date, and then to subtract the cumulative number of stops from the cumulative number of starts. The following SQL finds all the starts by day, grouping all the pre-2004 starts into one bucket:

```
SELECT thedate, SUM(nstarts) as nstarts, SUM(nstops) as nstops
FROM ((SELECT (CASE WHEN start_date >= '2003-12-31' THEN start_date
                    ELSE '2003-12-31' END) as thedate,
             COUNT(*) as nstarts, 0 as nstops
      FROM subs
      WHERE start_date IS NOT NULL
      GROUP BY (CASE WHEN start_date >= '2003-12-31' THEN start_date
                    ELSE '2003-12-31' END) )
     UNION ALL
     (SELECT (CASE WHEN stop_date >= '2003-12-31'
                    THEN stop_date ELSE '2003-12-31' END) as thedate,
             0 as nstarts, COUNT(*) as nstops
      FROM subs
      WHERE start_date IS NOT NULL AND stop_date IS NOT NULL
      GROUP BY (CASE WHEN stop_date >= '2003-12-31'
                    THEN stop_date ELSE '2003-12-31' END) )
    ) a
GROUP BY thedate
ORDER BY 1
```

The query works by separately counting starts and stops, combining the results using UNION ALL, and then reporting the start and stop numbers for each date. Starts and stops prior to 2004 are placed in the 2003-12-31 bucket. The query uses UNION ALL rather than a JOIN because there may be dates that have no starts and there may be dates that have no stops.

The Subs table has 181 records where the START_DATE is set to NULL. With no start date, these rows could either be excluded (the choice here) or the start date replaced with some reasonable value (if one is known). Notice that both subqueries have the restriction on start date not being NULL, even though one subquery counts starts and the other stops. Both subqueries need to include the same group of customers. Because the second subquery counts stops, it has an additional restriction that customers have stopped.

Excel then does the cumulative sums of the starts and stops, as shown in Figure 5-13. The difference between the cumulative starts and the cumulative stops is the number of active customers on each day since the beginning of 2004.

| | C | D | E | F | G | H |
|---|---|---|---|---|---|---|
| 32 | FROM SQL | | | EXCEL CALCULATION | | |
| 33 | thedate | numstarts | numstops | cum starts | cum stops | actives |
| 34 | 37986 | 2006134 | 0 | =SUM(D$34:D34) | =SUM(E$34:E34) | =F34-G34 |
| 35 | 37987 | 349 | 1691 | =SUM(D$34:D35) | =SUM(E$34:E35) | =F35-G35 |
| 36 | 37988 | 3062 | 2853 | =SUM(D$34:D36) | =SUM(E$34:E36) | =F36-G36 |
| 37 | 37989 | 2865 | 5138 | =SUM(D$34:D37) | =SUM(E$34:E37) | =F37-G37 |
| 38 | 37990 | 2653 | 2737 | =SUM(D$34:D38) | =SUM(E$34:E38) | =F38-G38 |
| 39 | 37991 | 2561 | 2104 | =SUM(D$34:D39) | =SUM(E$34:E39) | =F39-G39 |
| 40 | 37992 | 2710 | 1276 | =SUM(D$34:D40) | =SUM(E$34:E40) | =F40-G40 |
| 41 | 37993 | 1545 | 706 | =SUM(D$34:D41) | =SUM(E$34:E41) | =F41-G41 |
| 42 | 37994 | 3094 | 4138 | =SUM(D$34:D42) | =SUM(E$34:E42) | =F42-G42 |

**Figure 5-13:** This Excel screen shot shows a worksheet that calculates the number of customers on each day.

## How Many Customers of Different Types?

The overall number of customers on any given day can be broken out by customer attributes. The following query is a modification of the previous query for the breakdown by market:

```
SELECT thedate, SUM(numstarts) as numstarts,
       SUM(CASE WHEN market = 'Smallville' THEN numstarts ELSE 0
           END) as smstarts,
       . . .
       SUM(numstops) as numstops,
       SUM(CASE WHEN market = 'Smallville' THEN numstops ELSE 0
           END) as smstops,
       . . .
FROM ((SELECT (CASE WHEN start_date >= '2003-12-31' THEN start_date
                  ELSE '2003-12-31' END) as thedate,
          market, COUNT(*) as numstarts, 0 as numstops
       FROM subs
       WHERE start_date IS NOT NULL
       GROUP BY (CASE WHEN start_date >= '2003-12-31' THEN start_date
                  ELSE '2003-12-31' END), market )
      UNION ALL
      (SELECT (CASE WHEN stop_date >= '2003-12-31'
                  THEN stop_date ELSE '2003-12-31' END) as thedate,
          market, 0 as numstarts, COUNT(*) as numstops
```

```
        FROM subs
        WHERE start_date IS NOT NULL AND stop_date IS NOT NULL
        GROUP BY (CASE WHEN stop_date >= '2003-12-31'
                       THEN stop_date ELSE '2003-12-31' END), market )
      ) a
GROUP BY thedate
ORDER BY 1
```

Each subquery aggregates by date and also market. In addition, the outer query sums the starts and stops separately for each market. The data is handled the same way in Excel, with the starts and stops being accumulated, and the difference between them being the number active in each market on any given day.

Figure 5-14 shows the results of the query. The results show that Gotham is always the largest market and Smallville the smallest. It appears, though, that Smallville is catching up to Gotham. In addition, there also seems to be an increase in all three markets at the end of 2005, and a decrease in 2006. The decrease for Gotham is larger than for the other two markets. Interestingly, there are no Smallville stops until Oct 26, 2004. Apparently, the different markets have different cut-off dates.

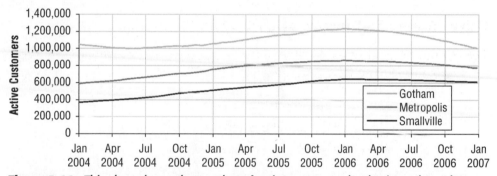

**Figure 5-14:** This chart shows the number of active customers by day in each market.

## How Many Customers by Tenure Segment?

A tenure segment specifies how long customers have been active. For instance, customers might be divided into three such segments: the first-year segment, consisting of those who have been around less than one year; the second-year segment, consisting of those who have been around between one and two years; and the long-term segment.

This section extends the counting of active customers over time to active customers by tenure segment. Of course, the definition of the groups of interest can vary, because there is nothing sacrosanct about milestones at one and two years. The specific question is: *On any given date, how many subscribers have been around for one year, for two years, and for more than two years?*

The answer to this question relies on a few observations about the relationship between the size of a tenure segment on the day and the size on the day before. This logic uses a mathematical technique called induction.

The number of customers in the first-year segment on a particular date consists of:

- All the customers in the first-year segment the day before,
- Minus the first-year segment customers who graduated (by passing the one year milestone) on that date,
- Minus the first-year segment customers who stopped on that date,
- Plus new customers who started on that date.

The number of customers in the second-year segment consists of:

- All the second-year segment customers who were around the day before,
- Minus the second-year segment customers who graduated (by passing the two year milestone),
- Minus the second-year segment customers who stopped on that date,
- Plus customers who graduated from the first-year segment on that date.

Finally, the number of customers in the long-term segment is determined by:

- All the long-term segment customers who were around the day before,
- Minus the long-term segment customers who stopped,
- Plus customers who graduated from the second-year segment.

These rules suggest the information that is needed to keep track of the segments on a day-by-day basis. The first is the number of customers who enter each segment on each day. For the first-year segment, this is the number of customers who start. For the second-year segment, it is the customers who pass their 365-day milestone. For the long-term customers, it is the customers who pass their 730-day milestone. Also needed is the number of customers within each segment who stop.

Figure 5-15 shows the dataflow processing for this calculation. The first three subqueries calculate the number of customers that enter each segment at a given unit of time. The last row calculates the segment when customers stop. These are then combined using UNION ALL and then summarized for output.

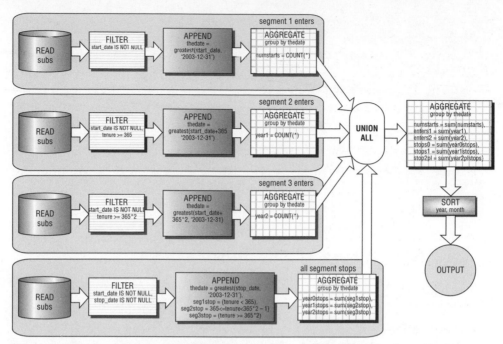

**Figure 5-15:** The dataflow processing shows how to calculate the number of customers that enter and leave each tenure segment.

The following SQL corresponds to this dataflow:

```sql
SELECT thedate, SUM(numstarts) as numstarts, SUM(year1) as enters1,
       SUM(year2) as enters2, SUM(year0stops) as stops0,
       SUM(year1stops) as stops1, SUM(year2plstops) as stops2pl
FROM ((SELECT (CASE WHEN start_date >= '2003-12-31' THEN start_date
                    ELSE '2003-12-31' END) as thedate,
             COUNT(*) as numstarts, 0 as YEAR1, 0 as YEAR2,
             0 as year0stops, 0 as year1stops, 0 as year2plstops
      FROM subs
      WHERE start_date IS NOT NULL
      GROUP BY (CASE WHEN start_date >= '2003-12-31' THEN start_date
                    ELSE '2003-12-31' END))
     UNION ALL
     (SELECT (CASE WHEN start_date >= '2002-12-31'
                    THEN DATEADD(day, 365, start_date)
                    ELSE '2003-12-31' END) as thedate,
             0 as numstarts, COUNT(*) as YEAR1, 0 as YEAR2,
             0 as year0stops, 0 as year1stops, 0 as year2plstops
      FROM subs
      WHERE start_date IS NOT NULL AND tenure >= 365
      GROUP BY (CASE WHEN start_date >= '2002-12-31'
```

*(continued)*

```
                              THEN DATEADD(day, 365, start_date)
                              ELSE '2003-12-31' END))
          UNION ALL
          (SELECT (CASE WHEN start_date >= '2001-12-31'
                        THEN DATEADD(day, 365*2, start_date)
                        ELSE '2003-12-31' END) as thedate,
                  0 as numstarts, 0 as year1, COUNT(*) as year2,
                  0 as year0stops, 0 as year1stops, 0 as year2plstops
           FROM subs
           WHERE start_date IS NOT NULL AND tenure >= 365*2
           GROUP BY (CASE WHEN start_date >= '2001-12-31'
                        THEN DATEADD(day, 365*2, start_date)
                        ELSE '2003-12-31' END))
          UNION ALL
          (SELECT (CASE WHEN stop_date >= '2003-12-31' THEN stop_date
                        ELSE '2003-12-31' END) as thedate,
                  0 as numstarts,  0 as YEAR0, 0 as YEAR1,
                  SUM(CASE WHEN tenure < 365 THEN 1 ELSE 0 END
                      ) as year0stops,
                  SUM(CASE WHEN tenure BETWEEN 365 AND 365*2 - 1
                          THEN 1 ELSE 0 END) as year1stops,
                  SUM(CASE WHEN tenure >= 365*2 THEN 1 ELSE 0 END
                      ) as year2plstops
           FROM subs
           WHERE start_date IS NOT NULL AND stop_date IS NOT NULL
           GROUP BY (CASE WHEN stop_date >= '2003-12-31'
                        THEN stop_date ELSE '2003-12-31' END) )
          ) a
    GROUP BY thedate
    ORDER BY 1
```

This query follows the same logic as the dataflow. The first three subqueries calculate the number of customers who enter each segment. Separate subqueries are needed because the entry dates are different. A customer who starts on 2005-04-01 enters the first-year segment on that date. The same customer enters the second-year segment on 2006-04-01, one year later. Each of these subqueries selects the appropriate group using the WHERE clause and the TENURE column. For the first segment, there is no restriction. For the second, the tenure is at least one year. For the third, the tenure is at least two years.

The fourth subquery handles the stops for all three segments. Because the stop date does not change, only one subquery is needed for the three calculations. The Excel calculation then follows the rules described at the beginning of this section.

Figure 5-16 shows the three segments of customers using stacked area charts. This chart makes it possible to see the total number of customers as well as the breakdown between the different tenure segments over time.

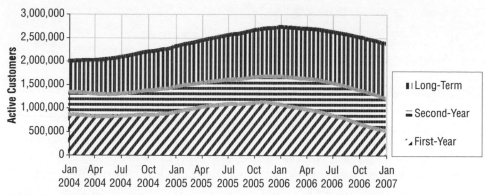

**Figure 5-16:** This chart shows the number of active customers broken out by one-year tenure segments.

## Simple Chart Animation in Excel

This section goes back to the purchases dataset to investigate the delay between the date when an order is placed and when the last item is shipped, the fulfillment date. Investigating the fulfillment date gets rather complicated, because other features (such as the size of the order) undoubtedly have an effect on the delay. Visualizing the results is challenging, because there are two time dimensions, the duration and order date.

This example provides an opportunity to show rudimentary chart animation in Excel, using a Visual Basic macro. This is the only place in the book that uses macros, because even without them SQL and Excel are quite powerful for data analysis and visualization. However, the macro is quite simple and easy to implement.

### Order Date to Ship Date

*What is the delay between the order date and the fulfillment date?* The following SQL query answers this question, breaking out the delay by number of units in the order:

```
SELECT DATEDIFF(dd, orderdate, fulfilldate) as delay, COUNT(*) as cnt,
       SUM(CASE WHEN numunits = 1 THEN 1 ELSE 0 END) as un1,
       . . .
       SUM(CASE WHEN numunits = 5 THEN 1 ELSE 0 END) as un5,
       SUM(CASE WHEN numunits >= 6 THEN 1 ELSE 0 END) as un6pl
FROM orders o JOIN
     (SELECT orderid, MAX(shipdate) as fulfilldate
      FROM orderline
      GROUP BY orderid) ol
```

*(continued)*

```
        ON o.orderid = ol.orderid
WHERE orderdate <= fulfilldate
GROUP BY DATEDIFF(dd, orderdate, fulfilldate)
ORDER BY 1
```

This query summarizes Orderline to get the last shipment date. As a reminder, the number of units is different from the number of distinct items. If a customer orders ten copies of the same book, that is one item but ten units.

There are a handful of anomalies in the data, such as the twenty-two orders that completely shipped before the order was placed. There is obviously some reason for this, such as a mistake in the order date. For this discussion, these few extraneous cases are not of interest, so a WHERE clause eliminates them. It should also be noted that pending orders are not in the database, which is evident because all rows in Orderline have valid SHIPDATEs.

Figure 5-17 shows the cumulative proportion of orders shipped for different numbers of units. For all groups, over half the orders have been completely fulfilled within a week. The most common orders have one unit, and over 70% of these are fulfilled within one week.

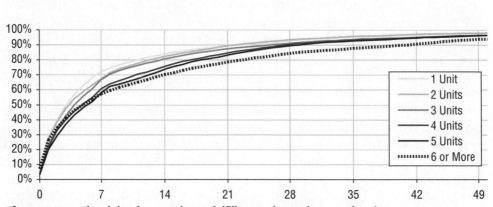

**Figure 5-17:** The delay from order to fulfillment depends on order size.

As the curves stretch out into longer and longer delays, orders with more units do take longer to fulfill. At 50 days, about 98% of the smaller orders have been fulfilled, compared to 94% of the large orders. Looking at it the other way, fewer than 2% of the smaller orders have such a long delay, whereas about 6% of the larger orders do.

Although it is difficult to see on the chart, something interesting happens in the first few days. Of all the groups, orders with six or more units actually have the largest proportion shipping on the day the order is placed. This means that the curve for the largest orders crosses all the other curves. Curves that cross like this are often interesting. Is something going on?

> **TIP** Curves that intersect are often a sign that something interesting is happening, suggesting ideas for further investigation.

To investigate this, let's ask the question: *What is the relationship between the number of units in an order and the number of distinct products?* The hypothesis is that larger orders are actually more likely to have only one product, so they can ship efficiently. Of course, orders with only one unit have only one product, so these don't count for the comparison. The following SQL calculates the proportion of orders having one product among the orders with a given number of units:

```
SELECT numunits, COUNT(*),
       AVG(CASE WHEN numprods = 1 THEN 1.0 ELSE 0 END) as prop1prod
FROM (SELECT orderid, SUM(numunits) as numunits,
             COUNT(DISTINCT productid) as numprods
      FROM orderline ol
      GROUP BY orderid) a
WHERE numunits > 1
GROUP BY numunits
ORDER BY 1
```

The subquery counts the number of units and the number of distinct products in each order. Notice that the number of units is calculated from Orderline by summing the NUMUNITS column. An alternative would be to use the NUMUNITS column in Orders, but that would require joining the tables together.

Figure 5-18 shows a bubble plot of the results. The horizontal axis is the number of units in the order. The vertical is the proportion of the orders that consists of only one product. The size of each bubble is the log of the number of orders (calculated in Excel using the LOG() function). Larger bubbles account for even more orders than the bubbles suggest because the bubble size is based on the log.

The first and largest bubble is missing, because all orders with only one unit have only one product. For larger orders, the proportion of one-product orders starts off fairly low. For orders with two units, it is 21.8%; for three, 13.9%. However, the proportion then starts increasing. For orders with six or more units, almost one third (32.1%) have only one product. These one-product orders are the ones that ship quickly, often on the same day they are placed. The orders with more products take longer to fulfill.

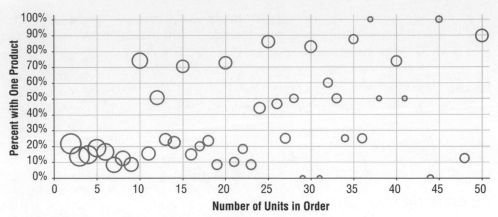

**Figure 5-18:** This bubble chart shows that as the number of units increases in an order, more orders have only one product.

## Order Date to Ship Date by Year

The previous section showed the overall situation with delays in shipping orders. The question now includes changes over time: *Does the delay between the order date and fulfillment date change from year to year?* To calculate the delay for any given year, extend the WHERE clause in the delay query, restricting the results to a particular year; something like "AND YEAR(ORDERDATE) = 2014".

This section proposes another solution where the data for all years is brought into Excel. Then, a subset of the data is placed into another group of cells, a "one-year" table, which in turn is used for generating a chart. This makes it possible to flip between the years, simply by changing the contents of one cell in the spreadsheet.

### Querying the Data

The query to fetch the results simply adds YEAR(ORDERDATE) as an aggregation on the query that calculates the delays:

```
SELECT YEAR(orderdate) as yr,
       DATEDIFF(dd, orderdate, fulfilldate) as delay,
       COUNT(*) as cnt,
       SUM(CASE WHEN numunits = 1 THEN 1 ELSE 0 END) as un1,
       . . .
       SUM(CASE WHEN numunits = 5 THEN 1 ELSE 0 END) as un5,
       SUM(CASE WHEN numunits >= 6 THEN 1 ELSE 0 END) as un6pl
FROM orders o JOIN
     (SELECT orderid, MAX(shipdate) as fulfilldate
      FROM orderline
      GROUP BY orderid) ol
```

```
        ON o.orderid = ol.orderid AND o.orderdate <= ol. fulfilldate
  GROUP BY  YEAR(orderdate), DATEDIFF(dd, orderdate, fulfilldate)
  ORDER BY 1, 2
```

These results pose a challenge for charting. There are almost one thousand rows. The data could be plotted on a single chart, but it is not clear how to make the chart intelligible. There are already several different curves for the number of units, leaving year and delay on the horizontal axis. A separate graph for each year, such as shown already in Figure 5-16, would be much easier to interpret.

### Creating the One-Year Excel Table

The one-year table is a group of cells that contains the delay information for a single year. It has the same columns and rows as the original data, except for the year column because the year is in a special cell, which we'll call the *year-cell*. The data in the table is keyed off of this cell, so when the value is updated, the table is updated for that year.

One column in the one-year table is the delay. This starts at zero and is incremented by one until it reaches some large number (the maximum delay in the data is 625). The one-year table finds the appropriate value in the overall data using the year in the year-cell and the delay on the row. There are three steps needed to make this work.

First, a lookup key is added to the query results to facilitate finding the appropriate row in the original data by the combination of year and delay. This additional column consists of the year and delay concatenated together to create a unique identifier:

```
<key> = <year>&":"&<delay>
```

The first value, for instance, is "2009:1" — a colon is used to separate the two values.

The second step is to find the offset into the table by matching each row in the one-year table to this column. The Excel function MATCH() looks up the value in its first argument in a list and returns the offset where the value is found in the list. If the value is not found, it returns NA() (when the third argument is FALSE):

```
<offset> = MATCH(<year cell>&":"&<delay>, <key column>, FALSE)
```

The third step is to get the right data for each cell in the one-year table by using the OFFSET() function to skip down <offset>-1 rows from the top of each column. Figure 5-19 shows a screen shot of Excel with the formulas for the "1 Unit" column.

The one-year table is now keyed off of the year-cell. Changing the value in that cell causes the table to be updated.

| | B | C | D | E | F | M | N | O |
|---|---|---|---|---|---|---|---|---|
| 21 | | | | | | | ANIMATION VARIABLES | |
| 22 | | | | | | | Year | Start | End |
| 23 | | | | | | 2009 | 2009 | 2016 |
| 24 | | | | | | ="Days from Order to Fulfillment by Units for "&M2‹ | | |
| 25 | | | | | | | | |
| 26 | | | FROM SQL | | | EXCEL CALCULATION | | |
| 27 | Key | yr | delay | cnt | un1 | Offset | Delay | 1 Unit |
| 28 | =C28&":"&D28 | 2009 | 0 | 27 | 12 | =MATCH($M$23&":"&N28, $B$28:$B$974, 0) | 0 | =OFFSET(F$27, $M28, 0) |
| 29 | =C29&":"&D29 | 2009 | 1 | 728 | 545 | =MATCH($M$23&":"&N29, $B$28:$B$974, 0) | =N28+1 | =OFFSET(F$27, $M29, 0) |
| 30 | =C30&":"&D30 | 2009 | 2 | 342 | 228 | =MATCH($M$23&":"&N30, $B$28:$B$974, 0) | =N29+1 | =OFFSET(F$27, $M30, 0) |
| 31 | =C31&":"&D31 | 2009 | 3 | 275 | 177 | =MATCH($M$23&":"&N31, $B$28:$B$974, 0) | =N30+1 | =OFFSET(F$27, $M31, 0) |
| 32 | =C32&":"&D32 | 2009 | 4 | 272 | 181 | =MATCH($M$23&":"&N32, $B$28:$B$974, 0) | =N31+1 | =OFFSET(F$27, $M32, 0) |
| 33 | =C33&":"&D33 | 2009 | 5 | 302 | 166 | =MATCH($M$23&":"&N33, $B$28:$B$974, 0) | =N32+1 | =OFFSET(F$27, $M33, 0) |
| 34 | =C34&":"&D34 | 2009 | 6 | 476 | 344 | =MATCH($M$23&":"&N34, $B$28:$B$974, 0) | =N33+1 | =OFFSET(F$27, $M34, 0) |
| 35 | =C35&":"&D35 | 2009 | 7 | 483 | 359 | =MATCH($M$23&":"&N35, $B$28:$B$974, 0) | =N34+1 | =OFFSET(F$27, $M35, 0) |
| 36 | =C36&":"&D36 | 2009 | 8 | 312 | 192 | =MATCH($M$23&":"&N36, $B$28:$B$974, 0) | =N35+1 | =OFFSET(F$27, $M36, 0) |
| 37 | =C37&":"&D37 | 2009 | 9 | 273 | 167 | =MATCH($M$23&":"&N37, $B$28:$B$974, 0) | =N36+1 | =OFFSET(F$27, $M37, 0) |
| 38 | =C38&":"&D38 | 2009 | 10 | 304 | 144 | =MATCH($M$23&":"&N38, $B$28:$B$974, 0) | =N37+1 | =OFFSET(F$27, $M38, 0) |

**Figure 5-19:** These Excel formulas show the formulas for constructing the intermediate table for one year of data for the "1 Unit" column.

## Creating and Customizing the Chart

Figure 5-20 shows the resulting chart for one year. Notice that this chart has a title that incorporates the year. This is accomplished by pointing the title box to a cell that has a formula for the title, using the following steps:

1. Place the desired title text in a cell, which can be a formula: `="Days from Order to Fulfillment by Units for "&<year-cell>`.

2. Add an arbitrary title to the chart by right-clicking inside the chart, choosing "Chart Option," going to the "Titles" tab, and inserting some text in the "Chart Title" box. Then exit the dialog box.

3. Click once on the chart title to select the text. Then type "=" and point to the cell with the title. Voila! The cell contents become the chart title.

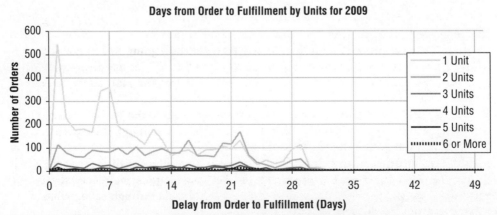

**Figure 5-20:** This chart shows the delay information for one year.

## SIMPLE ANIMATION USING EXCEL MACROS

Excel macros are a very powerful component of Excel. They provide the capability to customize Excel using the power of a full programming language, Visual Basic. Because the focus of this book is on analyzing data, macros are generally outside the scope. However, one is so useful, simple, and impressive that it is worth including. The one is the animation macro.

The text describes the ability to create a chart whose contents are determined by the value in the year-cell. Animating the chart just requires automatically incrementing the year cell, starting at one value, ending at another, and waiting for a small number of seconds in between. To set this up, we'll put the start value, the end value, and the time increment in the three cells adjacent to the year cell, so they look something like:

| YEAR | START | END | SECONDS |
|------|-------|-----|---------|
| 2009 | 2009 | 2016 | 1 |

The macro automatically increments the year-cell. First, create a macro by going to the Tools ⇨ Macro ⇨ Macros menu. In the "Macro Name" box, type in a name, such as "animate," and then click the "Create" menu button. This brings up the Visual Basic editor. The following macro code then creates the macro (the template that automatically appears consists of the first and last lines of this code):

```
Sub animate()
    Dim startval As Integer, endval As Integer
    startval = ActiveCell.Offset(0, 1).Value
    endval = ActiveCell.Offset(0, 2).Value
    For i = startval To endval
        ActiveCell.Value = i
        Application.Wait(Now() +
            TimeValue(ActiveCell.Offset(0, 3).Text))
    Next i
End Sub
```

When the code appears, leave the Visual Basic editor by going to the "File" menu and choosing "Close and Return to Microsoft Excel" (or use the key <alt>Q). This adds the macro into the current Excel file. The macro gets saved with the workbook.

To use the macro, place the cursor on the year-cell, go to the Tools ⇨ Macro ⇨ Macros dialog box, and choose "Run." It is also possible to assign the macro to a keystroke through the "Options" on the dialog box.

This example uses animation to walk through time values, which changes both the chart and the corresponding table. The more impressive demonstration is to just watch the chart. Animation can be used to walk through other values, such as products, number of units, and so on.

With this mechanism, the chart title and chart contents both update when the value in the year-cell changes. The aside "Simple Animation Using Excel Macros" discusses how to take this one step further with a rudimentary animation.

## Lessons Learned

Time is important for understanding the universe and time is important for data analysis. In databases, times and dates are stored with six components: years, months, days, hours, minutes, and seconds. In addition, dates can also have a time zone attached. The structure is complicated, but within one database, times and dates tend to be from one time zone and at the same level of precision.

As with other data types, dates and times need to be validated. The most important validations are checking the range of values and verifying that dates have no extraneous time component.

Analyzing dates starts with the values and the counts themselves. Looking at counts and aggregations over time is valuable, whether the number of customers, or the order size, or the amount spent. Seasonal patterns appear in the data, further showing what customers are really doing. Many businesses have weekly cycles. For instance, stops may be higher on weekdays than on weekends. Comparisons at the day level show these differences. Trend lines or weekly summaries remove them, highlighting longer-term patterns instead.

Individual time values are interesting, more so are durations between two values. Duration can be measured in many different ways, such as days between two dates or months between two dates. One challenge is determining the number of a particular day of the week, such as Mondays, between two dates. However, even this is possible with SQL and Excel.

This chapter presents two important applications involving dates. The first is calculating the number of customers active on a particular date, which is simply the number who started as of that date minus the number who stopped before that date. This can be broken out by different groups, including tenure groups.

The last example looks at changes over time in a duration value — the delay from when a customer places an order to when the order is fulfilled. With two time dimensions, the best way to visualize this is through a simple Excel animation, which requires just a dab of macro programming.

The next chapter continues the exploration of time through survival analysis, the part of statistics that deals with time-to-event problems.

# How Long Will Customers Last? Survival Analysis to Understand Customers and Their Value

How long will a lightbulb last? What factors influence a cancer patient's prognosis? What is the mean time to failure (MTTF) of a disk drive? These questions may seem to have little relationship to each other, but they do have one thing in common. They are all questions that can be answered using survival analysis, because they involve time-to-event estimations. And, if we think about customers instead of lightbulbs, patients, and disk drives, they readily translate into important questions about customers, their tenures, and their value.

The scientific and industrial origins of survival analysis explain the terminology. Its emphasis on "failure" and "risk," "mortality" and "recidivism" may explain why, once upon a time, survival analysis did not readily catch on in the business and marketing world. That time has passed, and survival analysis is recognized as a powerful set of analytic techniques for understanding customers. And, the combination of SQL and Excel is sufficiently powerful to apply many of these techniques to large customer databases.

Survival analysis estimates how long it takes for a particular event to happen. A customer starts; when will that customer stop? By assuming that the future will be similar to the past (the *homogeneity assumption*), the wealth of data about historical customer behavior can help us understand what will happen and when.

For customers that have a well-defined beginning and end, the most important time-to-event question is when the customers will stop. These are subscription relationships. Examples abound:

- Customers get a mortgage, and are customers until they pay the mortgage off (or default).

- Customers get a credit card, and are customers until they stop using the card (or stop paying).

- Customers get a telephone, and are customers until they cancel the phone service (or stop paying).

- Customers subscribe to a magazine, and are customers until they cancel the delivery (or stop paying).

This chapter focuses on these types of relationships. Chapter 8 looks at time-to-event problems in other areas, such as retailing relationships where customers return, but there is no explicit end to the relationship.

Survival analysis is a broad, multifaceted subject. This chapter is intended as an introduction to the important concepts and their application to customer data using SQL and Excel. It starts with a bit of history. The history is not only interesting but also puts the topics in a good context for understanding time-to-event analysis. Examples are then provided to give a qualitative feel for how survival analysis provides information, because this type of analysis is a powerful way of gaining insight into customer behavior, both qualitatively and quantitatively.

Of course, survival analysis is more than history and description. The quantitative sections describe how to do the calculations, starting with the hazard, moving to survival, and then extracting useful measures from the survival probabilities. The final example is using survival analysis to estimate customer value, or at least estimate future revenue. The next chapter picks up where this one leaves off, covering some more advanced topics in survival analysis.

# Background on Survival Analysis

The origins of survival analysis can be traced back to a paper published in 1693 by Edmund Halley, as described in the aside "An Early History of Survival Analysis." The techniques were developed further in the late 19th and 20th centuries, particularly for applications in social sciences, industrial process control, and medical research. These applications necessarily used a small amount of data, because all data had to be collected by hand. A typical medical study, for instance, has dozens or hundreds of participants, rather than the multitudes of customers whose information is stored in today's databases.

## AN EARLY HISTORY OF SURVIVAL ANALYSIS

Survival analysis predates what we call statistics by about two centuries. Much of what we call statistics was invented in the 19th and 20th centuries; however, the origins of survival analysis go back to the 17th century, specifically to a paper presented in 1693 to the Royal Society in London. This paper, published in the Royal Society's *Philosophical Transactions,* was *"An Estimate of the Degrees of the Mortality of Mankind, drawn from curious Tables of the Births and Funerals at the City of Breslaw, with an Attempt to ascertain the Price of Annuities."* It is available online at http://www.pierre-marteau.com/ editions/1693-mortality.html.

The paper's author, Edmund Halley, is now famous for quite another reason. In 1758, sixteen years after his death, a comet he predicted to return did indeed return. And Halley's comet has continued to return every 76 or so years.

In the paper, Halley presents the basic calculations for survival analysis using mortality data collected from Breslau (now called by its Polish name Wroclaw, located in southeastern Poland). These techniques are still used today. And, in other ways, the paper is quite modern.

For one thing, technological innovations in computing enabled Halley's analysis. No, not the calculator or electronic computer. Logarithms and the slide rule were invented earlier in the 1600s. These innovations made it possible to do lots of multiplications and divisions much more efficiently than ever.

Halley was also responding to the availability of data. The "curious tables of births and funerals" refers to the fact that Breslau was keeping track of births and deaths at the time. Why Breslau and not some other city? The reason is unknown. Perhaps Breslau was keeping accurate records of births and deaths in response to the counter-reformation. Mandating records strengthened the Catholic churches that gathered these vital statistics, helping to ensure that everyone was born and died a Catholic.

And what was the application of the new techniques, calculated using the new technology, on the newly available data? Financial calculations for life insurance. This is surely an application we can relate to today. In fact, this particular method of calculating survival values is now called the *life table method*, because actuaries in life insurance companies have been using the same techniques for about 200 years.

Some things do change, however, such as his opinion that "four of six [women] should bring a Child every year" and "Celibacy ought to be discouraged . . . by extraordinary Taxing and Military Service." The paper also includes what is, perhaps, the earliest reference to infant morality rates. At the time, Breslau had a rate of 281 infant deaths per 1000 births. By comparison, the country with the worst infant mortality in the modern world, Angola, had an estimated rate of 185 per 1000 in 2006, and Poland had improved to a very respectable 7 per 1000. Some things do fortunately change for the better.

This section shows some examples of survival analysis without strictly defining terms such as hazard probabilities and survival. The purpose is to present ideas and show how survival analysis can be used qualitatively, for explaining what is happening. The examples start with life expectancy, then an explanation of survival in the medical realm, and finally ending with an example of hazard probabilities and how they shed light on customer behavior.

## Life Expectancy

Life expectancy is a natural application of survival analysis, because it answers the question how long people will survive. Figure 6-1 shows life expectancy curves for the U.S. population broken out by gender and race (`http://www.cdc.gov/nchs/data/nvsr/nvsr54/nvsr54_14.pdf`), as calculated by the U.S. Census Bureau in 2003. For instance, the curves show that only 90% of black males survive to about 45 years old. By comparison, 90% of white women survive to their early sixties. About 3% of females — whether black or white — are expected to survive to age 100. On the other hand, only about half as many males are expected to survive to that age.

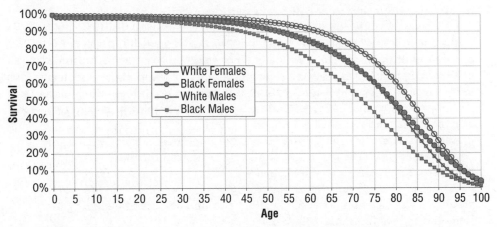

**Figure 6-1:** Life expectancy curves are an example of survival curves.

Life expectancy curves are examples of survival curves. One property is that they always start at 100% and decline toward 0%. They also provide information, such as the fact that almost everyone survives to age 50 or so. After that, the curves decline more sharply, because as people age, their risk of dying increases. Even at age 50, it is apparent that the different groups behave differently, with black men having noticeably lower survival than the other groups.

The point where half the population survives differs for the four groups:

- For black males, half survive to about age 73.5;
- For white males, half survive to about age 79;

- For black females, half survive to about age 80.5; and,
- For white females, half survive to about age 84.

This age, where half survive, is called the *median age*, and it is a useful measure for comparing different groups.

## Medical Research

Purportedly, one of the ten most cited scientific papers of all time is a classic paper on survival analysis published in 1972. This paper, by Sir David Cox — the "Sir" was added because of his renown as a statistician — was called "Regression Models and Life Tables (with Discussion)." It introduced a technique, now called Cox proportional hazards regression, which provides a way of measuring the effects of various factors on survival.

As an example, consider what happens to prisoners after they are released from prison. *Longitudinal* studies follow groups of prisoners over time to determine what happens to them. These studies are for research into recidivism, a fancy word used to describe prisoners who return to their criminal behavior. Some prisoners return to a life of crime. Others are rehabilitated. Others are lost to follow-up for some reason.

What factors affect the ultimate outcome? Is it the length of time they were in prison? Is it the crime that they committed? Is it their gender, previous criminal history, availability of counseling after release? Data from longitudinal studies is analyzed to understand which factors are most important in determining who goes back to prison, and who doesn't. And the analysis that researchers use is often based on the techniques invented by Sir David Cox back in 1972 (and so the paper describing the study often cites the original paper).

These ideas have been applied in many different areas, from the effect of smoking and diabetes on longevity to the factors that affect the length of time people remain unemployed, from the factors that affect the length of business cycles to the impact of a drug such as Vioxx on cardiovascular disease. Determining which factors affect survival — for better or worse — is quite useful.

## Examples of Hazards

Survival is the probability that someone survives to a given point in time. A related concept, the hazard, is the probability that someone succumbs to a risk at a given point in time. Figure 6-2 shows two examples of hazard probability curves.

The top chart in Figure 6-2 is the overall risk of dying, based on the 2003 data for the U.S. population. This chart shows the risk at yearly intervals, and reveals interesting facts. During the first year, the hazard is relatively large. The *infant mortality rate*, as this number is called, is about 0.7% (which is many times less than in Angola in 2006 or Breslau in the 1680s). After the first year, the risk of dying falls considerably, rising a bit as teens learn how to drive, and then more as people age. The shape of this curve, where it starts a bit high, falls, and then increases again is called the "bathtub-shaped" hazard. The name comes from the shape of the curve, which follows the contours of a bathtub. Imagine the drain on the left side.

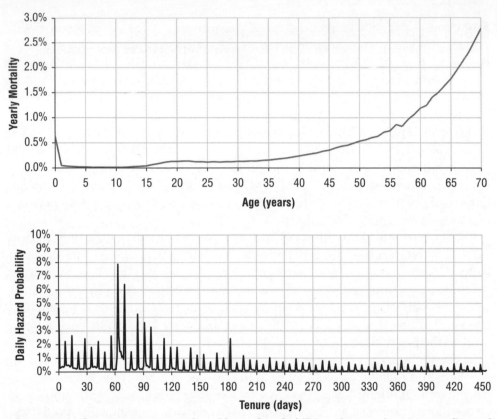

**Figure 6-2:** These are two examples of hazard probabilities: the top chart is mortality and the bottom chart is stopped subscriptions.

The bottom chart in Figure 6-2 shows the more complicated hazard probabilities for the risk of customers stopping a subscription a certain number of days after they start. This chart also has several features. First, the hazard at tenure 0 is quite high because many customers are recorded as starting but are not able to start — perhaps their credit cards didn't go through, or their addresses were incorrect, or they immediately changed their mind. There are another two peaks between 60 and 90 days out. These peaks correspond to customers not paying and to customers stopping after the end of the initial promotional period.

The hazard curve also has a bumpiness, with an evident weekly pattern and also peaks about every thirty days. The explanation is the billing period: customers are more likely to stop shortly after receiving a bill. Finally, the long-term trend in the hazard probabilities is downwards, indicating that as customers stay longer, their chance of leaving decreases. This long-term downward trend is a good measure of loyalty; it shows that as customers stay around longer, they are less likely to leave.

> **TIP** The long-term trend in the hazard probabilities is a good measure of loyalty, because it shows what happens as customers become more familiar with you.

# The Hazard Calculation

The rest of this chapter explores and explains various calculations used in survival analysis, with particular emphasis on using SQL and Excel to do them. The examples in the rest of the chapter use the subscription dataset, which consists of customers of a mobile phone company in three markets.

The hazard calculation is the foundation of survival analysis. It is tempting to say that calculating hazards is easy, but estimating unbiased hazards is hard. The hazards, in turn, lead to survival probabilities, and these, in turn, to informative charts and useful measures. The survival calculations use data, particularly the start date, stop date, and stop type columns. This section first explores these columns and then goes into the calculation of the hazard itself.

## Data Investigation

Survival analysis fundamentally relies on two pieces of information about each customer, the *stop flag* (whether the customer is stopped or active) and the *tenure* (how long the customer was active). Often, these columns must be derived from other columns in the database. In the Subs table, for instance, the tenure is already calculated but the stop flag must be derived from other columns.

Because this information is so important, a good place to start is with data exploration. This is true even when the fields are precalculated, because the definitions in the data may not match exactly the definitions that we need.

### Stop Flag

The stop flag specifies which customers are active and which are stopped, as of the cutoff date. What happens to customers after the cutoff date is unknown. The STOP_TYPE column contains the stop reasons. *What values does this column take on?* A simple aggregation query answers this question:

```
SELECT stop_type, COUNT(*), MIN(customer_id), MAX(customer_id)
FROM subs
GROUP BY stop_type
```

Table 6-1 shows three stop types that are expected, and NULL which indicates that customers area still active. The query includes the minimum and maximum customer ID, which is useful for finding rows that contain each value.

The stop types have the following meanings:

- NULL means that the customer is still active.
- "I" stands for "involuntary" and means the company initiated the stop, usually due to nonpayment on bills.
- "V" stands for "voluntary" and means the customer initiated the stop.
- "M" stands for "migration" and means the customer switched to another product.

A customer is active when the stop type is NULL. Otherwise, the customer has stopped. This rule is expressed in SQL as:

```
SELECT (CASE WHEN stop_type IS NOT NULL THEN 1 ELSE 0 END) as isstop
```

The inverse of the stop flag is the active flag, which is simply one minus the stop flag. In statistics, survival analysis often focuses on the active flag rather than the stop flag, calling it the *censor flag*. The two are related in a simple manner, and either can be used for the calculations.

The stop type originally stored in the data took on dozens of different values, indicating the myriad of particular reasons why someone might stop ("bad service," "no service at home," "billing dispute," and so on). These specific reasons were then mapped into the voluntary and involuntary categories in the STOP_TYPE column.

**Table 6-1**: Stop Types in the Subscription Data

| STOP_TYPE | COUNT | MINIMUM CUSTOMERID | MAXIMUM CUSTOMERID |
|:---:|---:|:---:|:---:|
| NULL | 2,390,959 | 2 | 115985522 |
| I | 790,457 | 217 | 115960366 |
| M | 15,508 | 9460 | 115908229 |
| V | 1,871,111 | 52 | 115962722 |

## *Tenure*

The *tenure* is the length of time between a customer's start date and stop date. Usually, the tenure needs to be calculated, using differences between the dates. The subscription table, though, already has tenure defined. Using the Microsoft SQL function for subtracting dates, the definition is:

```
SELECT DATEDIFF(day, start_date,
               (CASE WHEN stop_type IS NOT NULL THEN '2006-12-28'
                     ELSE stop_date END)) as tenure
```

This expression follows the logic that a customer's tenure is known when the customer has already stopped. However, if the customer has not stopped, the tenure is as of the cutoff date (in a working database, this might be the current date or the most recent load date).

**WARNING** A stop date can be the first day a customer is no longer active. Or, it can be the last day a customer is active — the particular definition depends on the database. The tenure calculation is slightly different for these two cases. In the first case, the tenure is the difference between the start and stop dates. In the second, it is one more than the difference.

In order to have unbiased calculations for the hazard and survival probabilities, the start and stop dates need to be accurate. There are many things that can affect the accuracy of dates, particularly older dates:

- Customer records for stopped customers fail to be loaded into the database.
- The start date gets replaced with another date, such as the date the account was loaded into the database.
- The stop date gets overwritten with dates that occur after the stop date, such as the date an unpaid account was written off.
- The start date gets overwritten with another date, such as the date the customer switched to another product.

Investigating dates is definitely important. The place to start is with a histogram of the starts and stops over time. The following query produces a histogram by year:

```
SELECT YEAR(thedate) as year, SUM(isstart) as starts, SUM(isstop) as stops
FROM ((SELECT start_date as thedate, 1 as isstart, 0 as isstop
       FROM subs s)
      UNION ALL
      (SELECT stop_date, 0 as isstart, 1 as isstop
       FROM subs s)
     ) s
GROUP BY YEAR(thedate)
ORDER BY 1
```

The results from this query are in Table 6-2. Notice that there are over two million customers that have NULL stop dates; these customers are still active. The first two rows of the table also show that there are 182 customers with questionable start dates — either NULL or in 1958. The data for these customers is invalid. There should be no customers that predate the invention of wireless phones. Because there are so few, the best thing to do is just filter them out.

**Table 6-2:** Start and Stop Date by Year

| YEAR | STARTS | STOPS |
|------|--------|-------|
| <NULL> | 181 | 2,390,959 |
| 1958 | 1 | 0 |
| 1988 | 70 | 0 |
| 1989 | 213 | 0 |
| 1990 | 596 | 0 |
| 1991 | 1,011 | 0 |
| 1992 | 2,288 | 0 |
| 1993 | 3,890 | 0 |
| 1994 | 7,371 | 0 |
| 1995 | 11,638 | 0 |
| 1996 | 22,320 | 0 |
| 1997 | 42,462 | 0 |
| 1998 | 66,701 | 0 |
| 1999 | 102,617 | 0 |
| 2000 | 146,975 | 0 |
| 2001 | 250,471 | 0 |
| 2002 | 482,291 | 0 |
| 2003 | 865,219 | 0 |
| 2004 | 1,112,707 | 793,138 |
| 2005 | 1,292,819 | 874,845 |
| 2006 | 656,194 | 1,009,093 |

A very important feature of the data is that there are no stops prior to 2004. Was this because superior business practices during that time resulted in no stops? Probably not. Was this because the company forgot to record stops in the database? Probably not. The most likely reason is that the data was loaded in 2004, and only active customers were loaded. This data is an example of *left truncation*, because rows have been filtered out based on the stop date. The next chapter explains how to handle left truncation.

In order to get unbiased estimates of the hazard and survival probabilities, the start and stop dates need to come from the same time period. For now, the solution is to filter the data, removing any starts that happened prior to 2004. In addition, one customer has a negative tenure. Throughout this chapter, the expression "WHERE start_date >= '2004-01-01' AND tenure >= 0" is part of most of the queries on the subscription table.

## Hazard Probability

The hazard probability at tenure *t* is the ratio between two numbers: the number of customers who succumb to the risk divided by everyone who could have succumbed to the risk. The denominator is called the *population at risk at tenure t*. The hazard probability is always between 0% and 100%. It is never negative, because the population at risk and the population that succumb to the risk are counts and neither is ever negative. It is not greater than 100%, because the population at risk always includes at least everyone who succumbs to the risk. The calculation is easy; for any given tenure, we simply divide two numbers. Getting the right numbers is the challenge.

As a simple example, consider 100 customers who start on January 1$^{st}$ and are still active on January 31$^{st}$. If two of these customers stop on February 1$^{st}$, then the 31-day hazard is 2%. There are 100 customers in the population at risk and two who succumb. The ratio is 2%.

The 31-day hazard remains the same regardless of how many customers actually start on January 1$^{st}$, so long as all but 100 stop during the month of January. The customers who stop in January are not at risk on day 31, because they are no longer active. These stopped-too-early customers do not affect the 31-day hazard.

The following SQL query calculates the hazard at tenure 100 in the subscription table:

```
SELECT 100 as TENURE, COUNT(*) as popatrisk,
       SUM(CASE WHEN tenure = 100 AND stop_type IS NOT NULL
              THEN 1 ELSE 0 END) as succumbtorisk,
       AVG(CASE WHEN tenure = 100 AND stop_type IS NOT NULL
              THEN 1.0 ELSE 0 END) as h_100
FROM subs
WHERE start_date >= '2004-01-01' AND tenure >= 100
```

The population at risk consists of all customers whose tenure is greater than or equal to 100. Of the 2,589,423 customers at risk, 2,199 of them stopped at tenure 100. This gives a 100-day hazard of 0.085%. Notice that this calculation considers only customers since 2004, because of the left truncation issue in the data.

## Visualizing Customers: Time versus Tenure

Figure 6-3 shows two pictures of the same group of customers. In each picture, one customer is represented by a line, with a vertical bar indicating where a customer starts and a circle indicating the stop date or current date (for active customers). An open circle means that the customer is still active, suggesting an open account. A filled circle means the customer has stopped, suggesting a closed account.

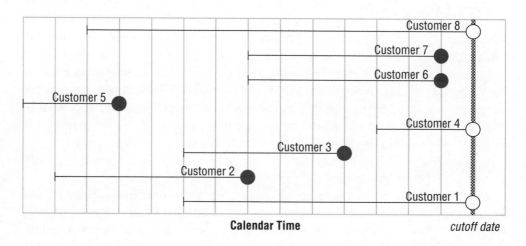

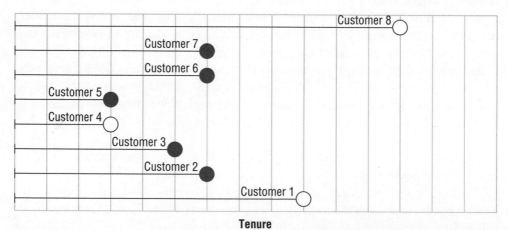

**Figure 6-3:** This is a picture of customers on the calendar time and tenure timelines.

The two charts show the same customers from two different perspectives. The top one shows the customers based on when they start and stop in calendar time. All customers that are active are active until the cutoff date. The bottom shows the same customers on the tenure timeline. The customers have been shifted to the left, so they all start at the same time, tenure zero. On the calendar time, all the active customers were aligned on the right, because they are all active on the cutoff date. On the tenure chart, the active customers are interspersed at all tenures. Some long tenure customers are no longer active, and some are active. Some short tenure customers are active, some are not. The aside, "Visualizing Survival Customers Using Excel" explains how these charts were made using Excel charts.

The calendar time frame and tenure time both show customers and their tenures. Survival analysis focuses on the tenure time frame, because tenure generally has the greater effect on customer retention. After all, the fact that customers can only stop after they have started puts a condition on the tenure, but not on the calendar time. Also, a myriad of events happen on the tenure time frame, such as monthly bills, contract renewals, and the end of the initial promotion.

However, the calendar time frame is also important. The calendar time frame has seasonality and other things that affect all customers at the same time. One of the challenges in survival analysis is incorporating all the available information from these two time frames.

## Censoring

Figure 6-3, the visualization of customers in the two time frames, also hints at one of the most important concepts in survival analysis. The tenure of customers who have stopped is known, because these customers have both a start date and a stop date. However, customers who are still active have an unknown tenure. Of course, their tenure is at least as long as they have been around, but the ultimate value is unknown. Any given active customer could stop tomorrow, or ten years from now.

Tenure is an example of *censored* data values. In Figure 6-3, censored customers are represented by empty circles on the right end. In this diagram, censoring is synonymous with being active, although this is not always the case. Censoring can have other causes, as we will see in the later in this chapter and in the next chapter.

Censored data values are central to survival analysis. There are three different types of censoring.

The type just described is, strictly speaking, *right censoring*. This occurs when the tenure is known to be greater than some value $T$. Right censoring is the most common type of censoring.

## VISUALIZING SURVIVAL CUSTOMERS USING EXCEL

The charts in Figure 6-3 were created using Excel. Each chart includes two series plotted using a scatter plot. One series is for all customers. This series has the tail, which is really an X-error bar. The other series fills in some of the circles for the active customers.

The following data was used for the empty circles on the top chart:

| NAME | ID | Y-VALUE | X START | X-END | LENGTH |
|------|-----|---------|---------|-------|--------|
| Ann | 8 | 7.5 | 12 | 14 | 2 |
| Bob | 7 | 6.5 | 6 | 13 | 7 |
| Cora | 6 | 5.5 | 6 | 13 | 7 |
| Diane | 5 | 4.5 | 3 | 3 | 0 |
| Emma | 4 | 3.5 | 3 | 14 | 11 |
| Fred | 3 | 2.5 | 5 | 10 | 5 |
| Gus | 2 | 1.5 | 6 | 7 | 1 |
| Hal | 1 | 0.5 | 9 | 14 | 5 |

The Y-Value is the vertical position of the line. The reason for starting at 0.5 and incrementing by 1 is purely aesthetic. These values control the spacing of the lines on the chart and the distance from the customers to the top and bottom of the chart. This can also be done by adjusting the Y-axis, but the fraction 0.5 makes it work without such meddling.

The points are plotted using the X-END values rather than the X-START values. The symbol is a circle, with a size of 10 pts and a white background (if no background color is set, the gridline shows through). To set the symbol, right-click the series, choose "Format Data Series," and go to the "Patterns" tab. The appropriate selections are on the right.

The tail is added by going to the "X error bars" tab and clicking the "Minus" option. The length is in the "Length" column. This is set by clicking "Custom" and putting in the appropriate series reference by the "-" sign.

The labels on the lines are data labels. Add these by going to the "Data Labels" tab and clicking next to "Y-Value." When the values appear, select one value by left-clicking, then right-click and choose "Format Data Labels." There is not a great deal of flexibility on the placement of data labels, so we have to improvise. On the "Alignment" tab, set the "Label position" to "Left," so the text goes to the left of the circle. On the "Font" tab, set the "Effects" to "Superscript" so the text is above the line. And, on the "Number" tab, click "Customer" and type in "'Customer"0' (include the double quotes, but not the single quotes). This gives the "Customer X" label. The font is 12-pt Arial. Alternatively, the XY-Labeler introduced in Chapter 4 can be used to label the lines with actual customer names.

**VISUALIZING SURVIVAL CUSTOMERS USING EXCEL *(CONTINUED)***

Add the filled circles using another data series, setting the options on "Patterns" to fill in the circle. Copy the data for the three customers who are active (customers 1, 4, and 8) and add the series. The X-error bar and data labels do not need to be set in this case.

The final step is to add the vertical gridlines and to remove two axes (by clicking on each of them and typing `<delete>`).

Voila! The end result is a chart that depicts customers using Excel charting — certainly an unexpected application for charting.

*Left censoring* is the opposite of right censoring. This occurs when the tenure is known to be less than some value *T*. Left censoring is not very common, but it can occur when we have forgotten the start date of a customer but we know it was after some date. Another example occurs when the data is a current snapshot of a group of customers, where there is a stop flag but not a stop date. So, a row in the data specifies that a customer has stopped. It also has the start date and the snapshot date. All we know is the customer stopped before the snapshot date.

*Interval censoring* is the combination of left censoring and right censoring. It is basically the left censoring case when customers are still active, so they are right censored in addition to being left censored. Interval censoring can also occur when data is being collected at long intervals. For instance, researchers studying prisoners after they are released may check in on the prisoners every year. If a prisoner drops out of the study, the tenure is known only to the nearest year.

In customer databases, the start date is usually known. As an example of a situation where the start date is not known, consider the question of how long patients survive after cancer appears. The only date that is known is the diagnosis date of the cancer, not when the cancer first appeared. The age of the cancer is right censored because the start date is not known, but is known to be before the diagnosis date. Ironically, one result of relying on the detection date is that better cancer detection can result in better five-year survival after diagnosis, even for the same treatment. The cancer is simply diagnosed earlier so the patient survives longer after the diagnosis.

Left censoring and interval censoring are unusual in customer databases. The typical situation with customer databases is that the start date is known, and active customers are right censored.

# Survival and Retention

Hazard probabilities measure the probability that someone succumbs to a risk at a given time. Survival is the probability that someone has not succumbed to the risk up to that time. In other words, survival accumulates information about hazards.

## Point Estimate for Survival

Survival at time *t* is the proportion of customers who are active at tenure *t*. For a given tenure, the survival question is: *What proportion of customers survived to at least tenure t?* This question is easy to answer in SQL for any given tenure:

```
SELECT 100 as tenure, COUNT(*) as popatrisk,
       SUM(CASE WHEN tenure < 100 AND stop_type IS NOT NULL
                THEN 1 ELSE 0 END) as succumbtorisk,
       AVG(CASE WHEN tenure >= 100 OR stop_type IS NULL
                THEN 1.0 ELSE 0 END) as s_100
FROM subs
WHERE start_date >= '2004-01-01' AND tenure >= 0 AND
      start_date <= DATEADD(dd, -100, '2006-12-28')
```

This calculation is similar to the point estimate for the hazard. The population at risk is everyone who started more than 100 days before the cutoff date, because these are the only customers in the data who could have survived to 100 days. The ones who survived are those who are either still active or whose tenure is greater than 100 days. The survival is the ratio of those who survived to the population at risk.

## Calculating Survival for All Tenures

The customers who survive to tenure *t* are those customers that have not yet succumbed to the risk of stopping. Mathematically, the survival at tenure *t* is the product of one minus the hazards for all tenures less than *t*. One minus the hazard is the probability that someone did not succumb to the risk at that point in time. It could also be called the *incremental survival*, because it corresponds to the survival from tenure *t* to tenure *t+1*. Overall survival at tenure *t*, then, is the product of the incremental survivals up to *t*.

This type of cumulative product is, alas, not readily supported in standard SQL. Fortunately, the combination of SQL and Excel makes the calculation easy. The first step is to calculate the hazards for all tenures, then to calculate the incremental survival, and then the cumulative product.

The calculation of the hazard probability uses two items of information:

- Population that succumbed to the risk: the number of customers who stopped at exactly tenure *t*.

- Population at risk: the number of customers whose tenure is greater than or equal to *t*.

The population at risk at tenure *t* is an example of a cumulative sum, because it is the sum of all customers whose tenure is greater than or equal to *t*. Excel is the tool of choice for the calculation.

The calculation requires two values for all tenures: the number of customers whose tenure is exactly $t$ and the number of customers that stopped at exactly tenure $t$:

```
SELECT tenure, COUNT(*) as popt,
       SUM(CASE WHEN stop_type IS NOT NULL THEN 1 ELSE 0 END) as stopt
FROM subs
WHERE start_date >= '2004-01-01' AND tenure >= 0
GROUP BY tenure
ORDER BY 1
```

When the results are copied into Excel, one column has TENURE, one column POPT, and the third STOPT. Assume that the results are copied, with the data starting at cell C29. What is the population at risk at a given tenure? The population at risk is the sum of the POPT values (in column D) for that tenure and higher.

To do the calculation without typing in a separate formula for all 1,093 rows, use a formula that changes when it is copied down the column. Such a formula for cell F29 is "=SUM($D29:$D$1121)". This formula has the range "$D29:$D$1121", so the sum starts at D29 and continues through D1121. The prefix "$" holds that portion of the cell reference constant. Copying the formula down (by highlighting the region and typing <control>-D) modifies the first cell reference in the range. Cell F30 gets the formula "=SUM($D30:$D$1121)", and so on to "=SUM($D1121:$D$1121)".

The hazard is then the ratio between the stops and the population at risk, which for cell G29 is "=E29/F29". Figure 6-4 shows an Excel spreadsheet with these formulas.

| | C | D | E | F | G | H |
|---|---|---|---|---|---|---|
| 27 | | FROM SQL | | | CALCULATED IN EXCEL | |
| 28 | tenure | popt | stopt | POPCUM | h | S |
| 29 | 0 | 2383 | 508 | =SUM($D29:$D$1121) | =E29/F29 | =IF($C29=0, 1, H28*(1-G28)) |
| 30 | 1 | 18354 | 17306 | =SUM($D30:$D$1121) | =E30/F30 | =IF($C30=0, 1, H29*(1-G29)) |
| 31 | 2 | 16730 | 15091 | =SUM($D31:$D$1121) | =E31/F31 | =IF($C31=0, 1, H30*(1-G30)) |
| 32 | 3 | 13283 | 11346 | =SUM($D32:$D$1121) | =E32/F32 | =IF($C32=0, 1, H31*(1-G31)) |
| 33 | 4 | 9544 | 9500 | =SUM($D33:$D$1121) | =E33/F33 | =IF($C33=0, 1, H32*(1-G32)) |
| 34 | 5 | 11746 | 9152 | =SUM($D34:$D$1121) | =E34/F34 | =IF($C34=0, 1, H33*(1-G33)) |
| 35 | 6 | 12649 | 9409 | =SUM($D35:$D$1121) | =E35/F35 | =IF($C35=0, 1, H34*(1-G34)) |
| 36 | 7 | 13466 | 10298 | =SUM($D36:$D$1121) | =E36/F36 | =IF($C36=0, 1, H35*(1-G35)) |
| 37 | 8 | 11862 | 9560 | =SUM($D37:$D$1121) | =E37/F37 | =IF($C37=0, 1, H36*(1-G36)) |
| 38 | 9 | 12265 | 9449 | =SUM($D38:$D$1121) | =E38/F38 | =IF($C38=0, 1, H37*(1-G37)) |
| 39 | 10 | 12017 | 9477 | =SUM($D39:$D$1121) | =E39/F39 | =IF($C39=0, 1, H38*(1-G38)) |
| 40 | 11 | 11104 | 9041 | =SUM($D40:$D$1121) | =E40/F40 | =IF($C40=0, 1, H39*(1-G39)) |
| 41 | 12 | 10441 | 8286 | =SUM($D41:$D$1121) | =E41/F41 | =IF($C41=0, 1, H40*(1-G40)) |

**Figure 6-4:** These formulas in an Excel spreadsheet calculate hazards and survival.

The next step is to calculate the survival as the cumulative product of one minus the hazards. The following formula in cell H29 is the survival formula: "=IF($C29=0, 1, H28*(1-G28))". The "if" part of the formula takes care of the case when the tenure is zero and the survival is 100%. Each subsequent survival value is the previous survival value multiplied by one minus the previous hazard. This type of formula, where the formulas in a column of cells refer to the values calculated in previous rows in the same column is called a *recursive formula*. When this formula is copied down the column, the formula calculates the survival value for all tenures. The resulting survival curve is shown in Figure 6-5.

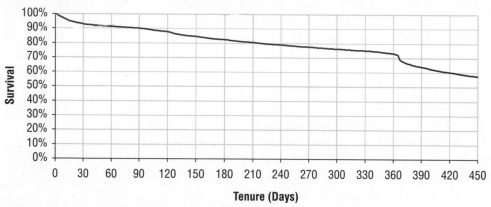

**Figure 6-5:** This is the survival curve for the subscription data.

In this case, all tenure values appear in the table (there are no gaps in the tenure column). However, this is not necessarily true. When this happens, it means that no stopped or active customers have exactly that particular tenure. The hazard is zero for the missing tenure, and the survival is the same as the previous survival. This does not cause any problems with the calculation. It does, however, make scatter plots preferable for survival curves rather than line charts. When values are skipped, the scatter plot does a better job labeling the X-axis.

## Calculating Survival in SQL

Having the hazard and survival probabilities in SQL tables, rather than in Excel, is sometimes convenient. One approach is to do the calculations in Excel, save the results out as text files, and re-import them into SQL. However, it is possible to do the calculations directly in SQL in a multi-step approach:

1. Create the survival table with the appropriate columns.

2. Load the survival table with STOPT and POPT.

3. Calculate the cumulative population and ENDTENURE.

4. Calculate the hazard and NUMDAYS.

5. Calculate SURVIVAL.

6. Fix ENDTENURE and NUMDAYS in last row.

This processing requires using SQL data manipulation language (DML), which includes INSERT and UPDATE. The syntax for these expressions varies more between databases than the syntax for the SELECT. Also, when doing the processing, some steps are easier and much more efficient using database extensions, particularly those that allow cumulative sums. However, in this section, the calculations are shown using self-joins, an alternative approach supported by standard SQL.

## Step 1. Create the Survival Table

The following SQL creates the survival table:

```
CREATE TABLE survival (
     tenure        INT,
     popt          INT,
     stopt         INT,
     cumpopt       INT,
     hazard        FLOAT,
     survival      FLOAT,
     endtenure     INT,
     numdays       INT
)
```

Most of these columns are similar to the Excel version. The purpose of ENDTENURE and NUMDAYS is to take care of the situation where tenures are skipped because there are no active or stopped customers with exactly that tenure. The survival for a skipped tenure value is the same as the survival for the previous tenure. The idea is that we can look up survival values using the expression: "WHERE tenure BETWEEN survival.tenure AND survival.endtenure" and this works for skipped tenures as well as other tenures.

## Step 2: Load POPT and STOPT

Loading the table with the base information uses the insert statement:

```
INSERT INTO survival
    SELECT tenure,
           COUNT(*) as popt,
           SUM(CASE WHEN stop_type IS NOT NULL THEN 1 ELSE 0 END
              ) as stopt,
           NULL as cumpopt, NULL as hazard, NULL as survival,
           NULL as endtenure, NULL as numdays
```

*(continued)*

```
    FROM subs
    WHERE start_date >= '2004-01-01' AND
          tenure >= 0
    GROUP BY tenure
```

This is the same basic query used that prepares the data for the Excel calculation. Here, an INSERT statement is wrapped around the query to add rows into the survival table.

### Step 3: Calculate Cumulative Population

The next step is to calculate the cumulative population and ENDTENURE. The self-join query that calculates these columns is:

```
SELECT s1.tenure, SUM(s2.popt) as cumopt,
       MIN(CASE WHEN s2.tenure > s1.tenure THEN s2.TENURE-1 END
           ) as endtenure
FROM survival s1 LEFT OUTER JOIN
     survival s2
     ON s1.tenure <= s2.tenure
GROUP BY s1.tenure
```

The challenge is expressing this as an update statement. This is a challenge because this query is updating the same table that's generating the values. One solution that works for all databases is to place the results of the query in a temporary table and do the update from there. Another is to use syntax specific to a particular database. The following is the statement in Microsoft SQL:

```
UPDATE survival
    SET survival.cumopt = ssum.cumopt,
        survival.endtenure = ssum.endtenure
    FROM (SELECT s1.tenure, SUM(s2.popt) as cumopt,
          MIN(CASE WHEN s2.tenure > s1.tenure THEN s2.TENURE-1 END
              ) as endtenure
          FROM survival s1 LEFT OUTER JOIN
               survival s2
          ON s1.tenure <= s2.tenure
          GROUP BY s1.tenure) ssum
    WHERE survival.tenure = ssum.tenure
```

Notice that this query uses a subquery with a self-join within the update statement. Some databases have extensions that make it possible to calculate the cumulative sum more directly. For instance, Oracle's implementation of window functions (which they call analytic functions) support the syntax SUM(popt) OVER (ORDER BY tenure ROWS UNBOUNDED PRECEDING) to do the calculation without a self-join.

### Step 4: Calculate the Hazard

The next step is to calculate the hazard probability and NUMDAYS:

```
UPDATE survival
    SET survival.hazard = stopt*1.0 / cumpopt,
        survival.numdays = endtenure - tenure + 1
```

### Step 5: Calculate the Survival

The survival calculation is another accumulation, but this time a product instead of a sum. What we are trying to do is to add survival as a column using logic such as the following:

```
SELECT s1.tenure, COALESCE(PRODUCT(1-s2.hazard), 1) as survival
FROM survival s1 LEFT OUTER JOIN
    survival s2
    ON s1.tenure > s2.tenure
    GROUP BY s1.tenure
```

The COALESCE() statement takes care of the case when the tenure is zero. In this case, there are no hazards, so the result would be NULL. COALESCE() returns the first non-NULL argument.

Unfortunately, SQL does not support PRODUCT() as an aggregation function. So, we have to go back to high school algebra, and remember how to use logarithms: raising $e$ to the power of the sum of the logarithms of numbers is the same as multiplying the numbers together. So, PRODUCT() is calculated as:

```
SELECT EXP(SUM(LOG(1-s2.hazard)))
```

This expression sums the logs of the incremental survivals and then undoes the log, a roundabout way to do the multiplication.

One way to express the update in Microsoft SQL is using a correlated subquery:

```
UPDATE survival
    SET survival =
        (CASE WHEN tenure = 0 THEN 1
            ELSE (SELECT EXP(SUM(LOG(1-hazard)))
                FROM survival s2
                WHERE s2.tenure < survival.tenure
                )
        END)
```

This differs from the method used in Excel. In this query, survival is calculated as the products of all the previous incremental survivals, rather than using a recursive calculation. The reason is that rows can be updated in any order. There is no guarantee that tenure zero be updated before tenure one. If tenure one is updated first, it would get the value of NULL using a recursive approach because survival at tenure zero is NULL before it is updated. Doing the full product calculates the correct value.

### Step 6: Fix ENDTENURE and NUMDAYS in Last Row

The last row of the table has a NULL value for ENDTENURE. The following code fixes this:

```
UPDATE survival
    SET endtenure = tenure+100000-1, numdays = 100000
    WHERE endtenure IS NULL
```

Extending the final survival for a long time makes it possible to look up survival values in the table, even for tenures that go beyond the range of data. Extrapolating beyond the range of data is not recommended, but it is sometimes necessary.

### Generalizing the SQL

Doing the survival calculations in SQL rather than Excel has an advantage, because Excel's limit on the number of rows limits the number of tenures. This is particularly important when including grouping parameters, such as market and rate plan and channel, in the query. The combination of all these exceeds the capacity of Excel.

Modifying the preceding queries to support such groups is not difficult. First, the groups need to be included in the survival table, and Step 2 needs to be modified to have the GROUP BY clause. Then, the queries in Steps 3 and 5 need to be modified so the tenure comparison only occurs within the same group. For a single group, the syntax would look like:

```
WHERE survival.tenure <= s2.tenure AND
      survival.group1 = s2.group1)
```

This structure readily generalizes to any number of columns used to define the groups. However, as the number of groups grows, the size of each group decreases, meaning that there is less data for the survival calculation.

## A Simple Customer Retention Calculation

Survival is one method of understanding how long customers stay around. Customer retention is an alternative approach. The purpose in presenting it here is to better understand survival by comparing it to another sensible measure. A typical customer retention question is: *Of customers who started xxx days ago, how many are still active?* This question can be answered directly in SQL:

```
SELECT DATEDIFF(day, start_date, '2006-12-28') as days_ago,
       COUNT(*) as numstarts,
       SUM(CASE WHEN stop_type IS NULL THEN 1 ELSE 0 END
           ) as numactives,
       AVG(CASE WHEN stop_type IS NULL THEN 1.0 ELSE 0 END
           ) retention
FROM subs
WHERE start_date >= '2004-01-01' AND tenure >= 0
GROUP BY DATEDIFF(day, start_date, '2006-12-28')
ORDER BY 1
```

This query counts the customers who started on a certain day, calculating the proportion that are still active.

The result has three columns of data. The first column is the number of days ago that customers started, relative to the cutoff date of the data. Other time units, such as weeks or months, might be more appropriate. The second column is the number of starts that occurred on that day. And the third column specifies how many of those customers are currently active. Figure 6-6 shows a plot of the results as a retention curve, which is the proportion of customers who are active as of the cutoff date.

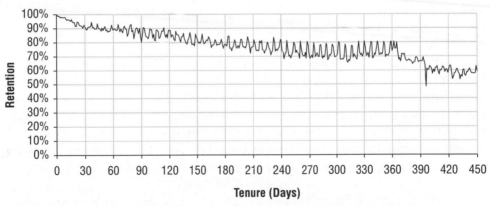

**Figure 6-6:** This is an example of a retention curve for the subscription data.

Like the survival curve, the retention curve always starts at 100%, because customers who just started are still active. Second, it generally declines. However, this decline can be jagged, with the curve going up in some places rather than down. For instance, of customers who started 90 days ago, 80.1% are still active on the cutoff date. Of customers who started 324 days ago, 80.4% are still active. Looked at in another way, this says that 19.9% of customers stopped in the first 90 days. But, only 19.6% of customers stopped in the first 324 days. Intuitively, this does not make sense. It is almost as if customers were reincarnating between the two days. In practice it probably means that particularly good customers were acquired 324 days ago and particularly bad customers were acquired 90 days ago. Jaggedness in retention is counterintuitive, because fewer older customers ought to be around than newer customers.

## Comparison between Retention and Survival

Figure 6-7 shows retention and survival on the same chart. This chart combines the curves in Figures 6-5 and 6-6.

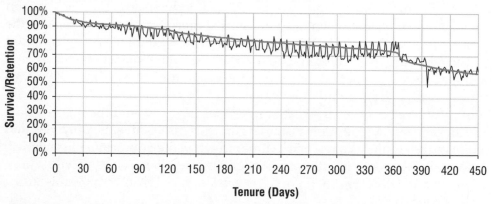

**Figure 6-7:** Retention and survival plots are shown for the same dataset.

Both curves start at 100% and decline. However, the survival curve has no jaggedness because it is always flat or declining. Mathematically, this property is called *monotonically non-increasing*, and it is always true for survival curves. Survival curves are smooth; they do not exhibit the jaggedness of retention curves.

One way of eliminating the jaggedness on retention curves is to smooth the curve using moving averages. The problem is that this smoothes away useful information. Also, the points no longer have a clear meaning, because they are averages of several different times, each of which has a different group of starts. A much better solution is to calculate the corresponding survival curve.

## Simple Example of Hazard and Survival

This section explores the simplest example of survival, the constant hazard, in order to better understand the concepts underlying survival. Although such simplicity does not occur with customers, it does readily apply to a very different domain, radioactivity. A radioactive isotope is one that decays at a constant rate; by emitting subatomic particles, it transmutes into other elements. The rate of decay is usually described in terms of the half-life. For instance, the most common isotope of uranium, U-238, has a half-life of about 4.5 billion years, meaning that half the U-238 in a sample decays in this time. On the other hand, another isotope called U-239 has a half-life of about 23 minutes. The longer the half-life, the slower the rate of decay, and the more stable the element.

There are several reasons for using radioactivity as an example. Because the decay rates are constant (at least according to modern theories of the physics), radioactivity provides simple examples outside the realm of human behavior. Also, constant hazards are a good baseline for understanding more complex hazards. We can always ask what constant survival rate would have resulted in the survival observed at a given tenure.

Constant hazards are also a good tool for understanding a phenomenon called *unobserved heterogeneity*. This phenomenon is quite important in the world of survival analysis. However, as its name suggests, it is not observed directly, making it a bit challenging to recognize and understand.

## Constant Hazard

A constant hazard is exactly what its name suggests, a constant. Excel can handle all the calculations for a constant hazard. Assuming a constant hazard, the half-life and hazard probability are interchangeable. If cell A1 contains the half-life, then the following formula in cell B1 translates this into a hazard probability:

```
=1-0.5^(1/A1)
```

Conversely, if B2 contains the hazard probability, then the following formula in cell C1 calculates the half-life:

```
-1/LOG(1-B1, 2)
```

Consider two radioactive isotopes of radium, RA-223 and RA-224. The first has a half-life of 11.43 days and the second a half-life of 3.63 days, which correspond respectively to daily hazard (decay) probabilities of 5.9% and 17.4%. This means that after one day, about 95.1% of RA-223 remains, and about 82.6% of RA-224 remains. Figure 6-8 shows the survival curves for these two elements.

The shape of the survival curve follows an exponential curve, which is always the case when the hazard is constant. These survival curves show that within a few weeks, almost all the RA-224 has disappeared. On the other hand, some of the RA-223 remains, because it decays more slowly.

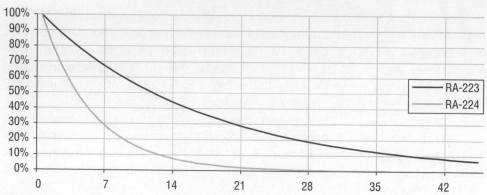

**Figure 6-8:** Survival curves for RA-223 and RA-224 show the proportion of the elements remaining after a given number of days.

## What Happens to a Mixture

Assume that a sample of radium contains 100 grams of RA-223 and 100 grams of RA-224. How does this mixture behave? Table 6-3 shows the amount of each isotope that remains after a given amount of time. (The actual mass of the sample remains pretty close to 200 grams, because the radium just changes into other elements, primarily radon, and very little mass is lost in the process.)

**Table 6-3**: Amount of Radium Left, Assuming 100 Grams of RA-223 and RA-224 at Beginning

| DAYS | RA-223 (GRAMS) | RA-224 (GRAMS) | TOTAL (GRAMS) | RA-223 % |
|------|----------------|----------------|---------------|----------|
| 0 | 100.0 | 100.0 | 200.0 | 50.0% |
| 1 | 94.1 | 82.6 | 176.7 | 53.3% |
| 2 | 88.6 | 68.3 | 156.8 | 56.5% |
| 3 | 83.4 | 56.4 | 139.8 | 59.7% |
| 4 | 78.5 | 46.6 | 125.1 | 62.7% |
| 5 | 73.8 | 38.5 | 112.3 | 65.7% |
| 6 | 69.5 | 31.8 | 101.3 | 68.6% |
| 7 | 65.4 | 26.3 | 91.7 | 71.3% |
| 8 | 61.6 | 21.7 | 83.3 | 73.9% |
| 9 | 57.9 | 17.9 | 75.9 | 76.4% |
| 10 | 54.5 | 14.8 | 69.3 | 78.6% |

The amount of radium remaining is the sum of the amount of RA-223 and RA-224. The proportion of the original radium remaining is this sum divided by 200 grams, a formula remarkably similar to taking the average of the survival curves. Actually, it is the weighted average times the original sample size in grams. Because the original sample started out with the same amount of the two isotopes, the weights are equal.

Given this proportion, what are the hazard probabilities that correspond to the overall radium mixture? One guess would be the average of the two hazard probabilities, or a constant hazard of about 11.6%. Although inspired, this guess is wrong. A mixture of two things with different constant hazards does not have a constant hazard.

The hazard can be calculated from the survival values. The hazard at a given time $t$ is the proportion of the population at risk that stops before time $t+1$ (or decays in the case of radioactivity). The hazard is one minus the ratio of the survival at $t+1$ divided by the survival at $t$.

Figure 6-9 shows the resulting hazards, along with the constant hazards for the two isotopes. The hazard of the mixture is not constant at all. In fact, it starts at the average value and declines to be more like RA-223's hazard as the mixture of radium becomes more and more RA-223. The RA-224 has decayed into something else. The proportion of the sample that is RA-223 increases over time, which is also shown in Table 6-3.

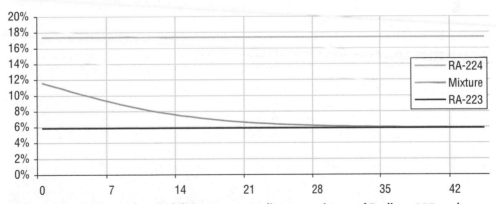

**Figure 6-9:** The hazard probabilities corresponding to a mixture of Radium 223 and Radium 224 are not constant, even though the two components have constant hazards.

The purpose of this example is to show what happens when a population consists of groups that behave differently. If we are given a sample of radium and measure the hazard probabilities and they follow the pattern in Figure 6-9, we might assume that the hazards are not constant. In fact, what is happening is that there are two groups with constant hazards mixed together. This phenomenon is called *unobserved heterogeneity*. Unobserved heterogeneity means that there are things that affect the survival that are not being taken into account.

The same phenomenon applies to customers. If there are two ways of acquiring customers, one that attracts lots of short-term customers ("bad") and one that attracts some long-term customers ("good"), which is better in the long term? Say 1,000 "bad" customers and 100 "good" customers start at the same time. After a year, 20 "bad" customers might remain compared to 60 "good" customers. Even though "good" customers were acquired at a rate one-tenth that of the bad customers, after a year, three times as many remain.

### Constant Hazard Corresponding to Survival

For each point on a survival curve, there is a constant hazard that would produce that survival value at that tenure. To calculate the corresponding constant hazard, assume that cell A1 contains the number of days and cell B1 contains the survival proportion at that day. The following formula in cell C1 calculates the corresponding daily hazard probability:

```
=1-B1^(1/A1)
```

For different tenures, this value changes, because in the real world, hazards are not constant. The "effective constant" hazard formally is fitting an exponential survival function to each point on the survival curve.

The comparison of this "effective constant" hazard to the actual hazard can be interesting, as shown in Figure 6-10 for the subscriber data. In a sense, the constant hazard is spreading the hazard risk equally over all tenures, so it provides an expected value for the hazard. So, when the actual hazard is less than the constant one, customers are leaving more slowly at that particular tenure than the long-term average would suggest. Similarly, when the average hazard is greater than the constant one, customers are leaving more quickly.

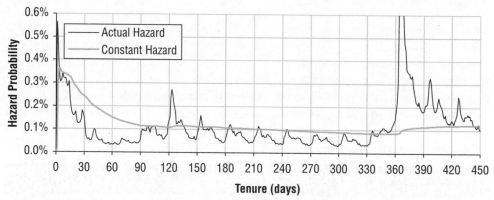

**Figure 6-10:** Comparison of the effective constant hazard to the actual hazard for the subscription data.

A survival curve (or retention plot) paints a pretty picture. Survival is not only for creating pretty pictures. It can also be used to measure different groups of customers, as discussed in the next section.

# Comparing Different Groups of Customers

Survival analysis facilitates comparing different groups of customers. This section walks through an example on the subscriber data using things that are known about customers when they start. These things are called time-zero covariates, because they are known at the start time (tenure 0). The next chapter investigates approaches for working with time-dependent covariates, things that happen during customers' lifetimes.

## Summarizing the Markets

The subscriber data contains three different markets, Gotham, Metropolis, and Smallville. A good way to start the analysis is by looking at the proportion of customers in each market who are active as of the cutoff date. Table 6-4 shows some information about the markets, such as the total number of customers, the average tenure of customers in the market, and the proportion of customers who are active. This table was generated by the following SQL query:

```
SELECT market, COUNT(*) as customers, AVG(tenure) as avg_tenure,
       SUM(CASE WHEN stop_type IS NULL THEN 1 ELSE 0 END) as actives,
       AVG(CASE WHEN stop_type IS NULL THEN 1.0 ELSE 0 END
          ) as actives_rate
FROM subs
WHERE start_date >= '2004-01-01' AND tenure >= 0
GROUP BY market
```

There are two pieces of evidence in this table that suggest that Gotham is the worst market and Smallville the best, in terms of customer retention. First, the average tenure of customers in Gotham is about 81 days shorter than the average tenure of customers in Smallville. Second, of all the customers that ever started in Gotham since 2004, only about 46% are still active. For Smallville, the proportion is close to 70%.

**Table 6-4**: Comparison of Customers and Active Customers by Market

| MARKET | CUSTOMERS | AVERAGE TENURE | ACTIVES | PROPORTION ACTIVE |
|---|---|---|---|---|
| Gotham | 1,499,396 | 383.5 | 685,176 | 45.7% |
| Metropolis | 995,572 | 415.3 | 519,709 | 52.2% |
| Smallville | 566,751 | 464.3 | 390,414 | 68.9% |

Combined, these two pieces of evidence are quite convincing that Smallville is inhabited by better customers. However, care must be taken when interpreting such evidence. For instance, imagine that there is another town, Shangri-La, where customers start and they never stop. We would expect Shangri-La to have a very high average tenure. However, what if our company only managed to break into the market three months ago? In that case, everyone would have started in the last three months and the average tenure would probably be about 45 days, much less than the other markets. Stratifying survival curves is a better way to compare markets.

## Stratifying by Market

To calculate survival for one market, a WHERE clause can be used:

```
SELECT tenure, COUNT(*) as popt,
       SUM(CASE WHEN stop_type IS NOT NULL THEN 1 ELSE 0 END) as stopt
FROM subs
WHERE start_date >= '2004-01-01' AND tenure >= 0 AND
      market = 'Gotham'
GROUP BY tenure
ORDER BY 1
```

However, it is cumbersome to do this for each market.

A better approach is to pivot the data so the columns contain the information about each market. The desired results would have the tenure, then the population for each market (in three columns), and then the number of stops in each market (in three more columns). The SQL to do this is:

```
SELECT tenure,
       SUM(CASE WHEN market = 'Gotham' THEN 1 ELSE 0 END) as popg,
       SUM(CASE WHEN market = 'Metropolis' THEN 1 ELSE 0 END) as popm,
       SUM(CASE WHEN market = 'Smallville' THEN 1 ELSE 0 END) as pops,
       SUM(CASE WHEN stop_type IS NOT NULL AND market = 'Gotham'
               THEN 1 ELSE 0 END) as stopg,
       SUM(CASE WHEN stop_type IS NOT NULL AND market = 'Metropolis'
               THEN 1 ELSE 0 END) as stopm,
       SUM(CASE WHEN stop_type IS NOT NULL AND market = 'Smallville'
               THEN 1 ELSE 0 END) as stops
FROM subs
WHERE start_date >= '2004-01-01' AND tenure >= 0
GROUP BY tenure
ORDER BY 1
```

**WARNING** Don't use the "LIKE" function when a direct comparison suffices, because "LIKE" is typically much less efficient. For instance, use "`market = 'Gotham'`" rather than "`market LIKE 'G%'`".

An alternative way to write the SQL is using indicator variables. That is, to create a separate variable for each market that takes on the values of 0 or 1. The performance of the two queries should be quite similar. The version with the indicator variables has the advantage that each comparison is defined only once, which reduces the possibility of error (such as misspelling the market name):

```
SELECT tenure,
       SUM(isg) as popg, SUM(ism) as popm, SUM(iss) as pops,
       SUM(isg*isstopped) as stopg, SUM(ism*isstopped) as stopm,
       SUM(iss*isstopped) as stopg
FROM (SELECT s.*,
             (CASE WHEN market = 'Gotham' THEN 1 ELSE 0 END) as isg,
             (CASE WHEN market = 'Metropolis' THEN 1 ELSE 0 END) as ism,
             (CASE WHEN market = 'Smallville' THEN 1 ELSE 0 END) as iss,
             (CASE WHEN stop_type IS NOT NULL THEN 1 ELSE 0 END
             ) as isstopped
      FROM subs s) s
WHERE start_date >= '2004-01-01' AND tenure >= 0
GROUP BY tenure
ORDER BY 1
```

Figure 6-11 shows the first few rows of the resulting table (the columns for Metropolis and Smallville are hidden). It also shows the formulas used for the calculation. Notice that the columns are in groups, with the population columns coming first and then the stop columns. This is on purpose, so the hazard and survival formulas can be entered once and then copied to adjacent cells — to the right as well as downward. Copying formulas is surely easier than typing them over and over.

These formulas have some minor differences from the earlier survival calculations:

- The formula for cumulative population is POPT plus the cumulative population at the next tenure.

- The hazard calculation takes into account the possibility that the population is 0. In this case, it returns the value #NA, because #NA works best in charts.

- The survival calculation refers to the tenure column with a column-fixed reference $C1117, instead of C1117. This makes it easier to copy the formula across multiple columns.

- The column headers include the population in parentheses.

The resulting survival curves are in Figure 6-12. Notice that the legend has the population in parentheses after the market name. The population was appended onto the market name for just this reason.

These curves confirm the earlier observation that survival in Gotham seems worse than survival in the other two markets. All three markets show the drop in survival at one year, which corresponds to the contract expiration date. At 450 days — safely after the contract expiration — only 50.1% of Gotham's customers remain, compared to 59.2% for Metropolis and 74.8% for Smallville.

| | C | D | E | F | G | H | I | J | K | N | Q |
|---|---|---|---|---|---|---|---|---|---|---|---|
| 37 | | | FROM SQL | | | | | | CALCULATED IN EXCEL | | |
| 38 | | Gotham | Metropolis | Smallville | | | | | POP | h | s |
| 39 | tenure | popg | popm | pops | stopg | stopm | stops | | Gotham (1,499,396) | Gotham (1,499,396) | Gotham (1,499,396) |
| 40 | 0 | 966 | 986 | 431 | 52 | 409 | 47 | | 1,499,396 | 0.00% | 100.0% |
| 41 | 1 | 8,951 | 6,155 | 3,248 | 8,588 | 5,770 | 2,948 | | 1,498,430 | 0.57% | 100.0% |
| 42 | 2 | 9,463 | 4,858 | 2,409 | 8,697 | 4,334 | 2,060 | | 1,489,479 | 0.58% | 99.4% |
| 43 | 3 | 6,830 | 4,361 | 2,092 | 6,039 | 3,667 | 1,640 | | 1,480,016 | 0.41% | 98.8% |
| 44 | 4 | 5,243 | 3,032 | 1,269 | 5,213 | 3,024 | 1,263 | | 1,473,186 | 0.35% | 98.4% |
| 45 | 5 | 6,301 | 3,696 | 1,749 | 5,218 | 2,771 | 1,163 | | 1,467,943 | 0.36% | 98.1% |
| 46 | 6 | 6,798 | 4,069 | 1,782 | 5,403 | 2,938 | 1,068 | | 1,461,642 | 0.37% | 97.7% |
| 47 | 7 | 7,057 | 4,297 | 2,112 | 5,695 | 3,307 | 1,296 | | 1,454,844 | 0.39% | 97.4% |
| 48 | 8 | 5,805 | 4,252 | 1,805 | 5,118 | 3,296 | 1,146 | | 1,447,787 | 0.35% | 97.0% |
| 49 | 9 | 6,208 | 4,342 | 1,715 | 5,065 | 3,345 | 1,039 | | 1,441,982 | 0.35% | 96.7% |
| 50 | 10 | 6,125 | 4,185 | 1,707 | 5,090 | 3,320 | 1,067 | | 1,435,774 | 0.35% | 96.3% |
| 51 | 11 | 5,694 | 3,954 | 1,456 | 4,807 | 3,257 | 977 | | 1,429,649 | 0.34% | 96.0% |
| 52 | 12 | 5,414 | 3,633 | 1,394 | 4,467 | 2,914 | 905 | | 1,423,955 | 0.31% | 95.7% |

| | C | D | E | F | G | H | I | J | K | N | Q |
|---|---|---|---|---|---|---|---|---|---|---|---|
| 37 | | | FROM SQL | | | | | | CALCULATED IN EXCEL | | |
| 38 | | Gotha | Metro | Small | | | | | POP | h | s |
| 39 | tenure | popg | popm | pops | stopg | stopm | stops | | =D38&" ("&TEXT(K40, "0,0")&")" | =K39 | =N39 |
| 40 | 0 | 966 | 986 | 431 | 52 | 409 | 47 | | =K41+D40 | =IF(K40=0, NA(), G40/K40) | =IF($C40=0, 1, Q39*(1-N39)) |
| 41 | 1 | 8951 | 6155 | 3248 | 8588 | 5770 | 2948 | | =K42+D41 | =IF(K41=0, NA(), G41/K41) | =IF($C41=0, 1, Q40*(1-N40)) |
| 42 | 2 | 9463 | 4858 | 2409 | 8697 | 4334 | 2060 | | =K43+D42 | =IF(K42=0, NA(), G42/K42) | =IF($C42=0, 1, Q41*(1-N41)) |
| 43 | 3 | 6830 | 4361 | 2092 | 6039 | 3667 | 1640 | | =K44+D43 | =IF(K43=0, NA(), G43/K43) | =IF($C43=0, 1, Q42*(1-N42)) |
| 44 | 4 | 5243 | 3032 | 1269 | 5213 | 3024 | 1263 | | =K45+D44 | =IF(K44=0, NA(), G44/K44) | =IF($C44=0, 1, Q43*(1-N43)) |
| 45 | 5 | 6301 | 3696 | 1749 | 5218 | 2771 | 1163 | | =K46+D45 | =IF(K45=0, NA(), G45/K45) | =IF($C45=0, 1, Q44*(1-N44)) |
| 46 | 6 | 6798 | 4069 | 1782 | 5403 | 2938 | 1068 | | =K47+D46 | =IF(K46=0, NA(), G46/K46) | =IF($C46=0, 1, Q45*(1-N45)) |
| 47 | 7 | 7057 | 4297 | 2112 | 5695 | 3307 | 1296 | | =K48+D47 | =IF(K47=0, NA(), G47/K47) | =IF($C47=0, 1, Q46*(1-N46)) |
| 48 | 8 | 5805 | 4252 | 1805 | 5118 | 3296 | 1146 | | =K49+D48 | =IF(K48=0, NA(), G48/K48) | =IF($C48=0, 1, Q47*(1-N47)) |
| 49 | 9 | 6208 | 4342 | 1715 | 5065 | 3345 | 1039 | | =K50+D49 | =IF(K49=0, NA(), G49/K49) | =IF($C49=0, 1, Q48*(1-N48)) |
| 50 | 10 | 6125 | 4185 | 1707 | 5090 | 3320 | 1067 | | =K51+D50 | =IF(K50=0, NA(), G50/K50) | =IF($C50=0, 1, Q49*(1-N49)) |
| 51 | 11 | 5694 | 3954 | 1456 | 4807 | 3257 | 977 | | =K52+D51 | =IF(K51=0, NA(), G51/K51) | =IF($C51=0, 1, Q50*(1-N50)) |
| 52 | 12 | 5414 | 3633 | 1394 | 4467 | 2914 | 905 | | =K53+D52 | =IF(K52=0, NA(), G52/K52) | =IF($C52=0, 1, Q51*(1-N51)) |

**Figure 6-11:** These screen shots show the data and Excel formulas for calculating survival by market (only Gotham is shown; the columns for Metropolis and Smallville are hidden).

**TIP** In Excel, it is possible to label a single point on a series. To do so, click the series to select it. Then click again to select the point. Then right click and choose "Format Data Point." Under the "Data Labels" tab, choose the Y Value. You can then double-click the text to format it. A good idea is to make the text the same color as the series itself.

## Survival Ratio

The ratio between survival curves is a good way of comparing different groups, because it captures long-term trends in survival. This ratio is simply dividing the survival for one market by the survival for another. Let's use the best survival as the standard, which is Smallville. Figure 6-13 shows the ratio of survival for the three markets to customers in Smallville. Smallville's survival ratio is uninteresting, because it is always one.

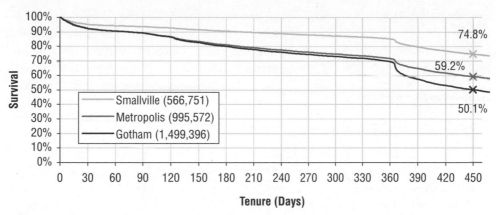

**Figure 6-12:** Survival by market for the subscription data shows that Smallville has the best survival and Gotham the worst.

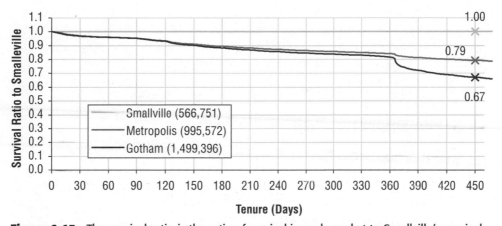

**Figure 6-13:** The survival ratio is the ratio of survival in each market to Smallville's survival.

The survival ratio chart shows that Gotham's survival is uniformly worse than Smallville's at all points in time. Survival in Metropolis is as bad as Gotham in the first year, but then it improves. Although the chart does not specify what is happening, the timing is suggestive. For instance, some customers start with one-year contracts, some with two-year contracts, and some with no contracts at all. Further, customers on one-year contracts are more likely to cancel at one year than during the first year. So, perhaps the difference between Metropolis and Gotham is due to the proportion of customers on one-year contracts. Whatever the cause, the survival ratio changes for different tenures. There is not a uniform proportionality between the curves.

Sometimes the ratio between survival curves can provide somewhat misleading results. For instance, if one market has very poor coverage in outlying areas, then customers from these areas would sign up for the service and quickly stop — their cell phone is not working. Say, 5% of the customers stop in the first couple of months due to bad coverage. This 5% lingers in the survival curves. So, even if the two markets are identical — except for the outlying coverage issue that only affects recent starts — the ratio will always show that the first market is worse because the ratio accumulates the differences in survival.

## Conditional Survival

The survival ratio suggests another question about survival. Two markets have essentially the same survival characteristics for the first year, but then their survival diverges after the contract expiration period. What about customers who make it beyond the contract expiration? Do customers start to look more similar or more different?

Conditional survival answers the question: *"What is the survival of customers given that they have survived a certain amount of time?"* Contract expiration typically occurs after one year. However, some customers procrastinate, so a period a bit longer than one year is useful, such as thirteen months (390 days).

There are two ways to calculate conditional survival. One way is to re-run the survival calculation, only on customers who survive at least 390 days. The following WHERE clause could be added onto the query:

```
WHERE tenure >= 390
```

This approach requires recalculating all the survival values.

There is a simpler approach. The conditional survival can also be calculated with the following two rules:

- For tenures <= 390, the conditional survival is 100% (because of the assumption that all customers survive to 390 days.
- For tenures > 390, the conditional survival is the survival at time *t* divided by the survival at time 390.

Excel's VLOOKUP() function makes it easy to find the survival at time 390. The conditional survival is then just the ratio of the survival to this value.

Figure 6-14 shows the survival and the conditional survival at time 390 for the three markets. The same pattern holds after thirteen months, with Smallville being the best and Gotham the worst for survival after thirteen months.

## Comparing Survival over Time

There are three years of complete starts in the subscription data. The analyses so far have mixed all the data together. One interesting question is whether the hazards have changed over time. This section presents three ways to approach this problem. The first looks at whether a particular hazard has changed over time. The second looks at customers by the year in which they started, answering the question: *What is the survival of customers who started in a given year?* The third takes snapshots of the hazards at the end of each year, answering the question: *What did the hazards look like at the end of each year?* All these ways of approaching this question use the same data. They simply require cleverness to calculate the hazards.

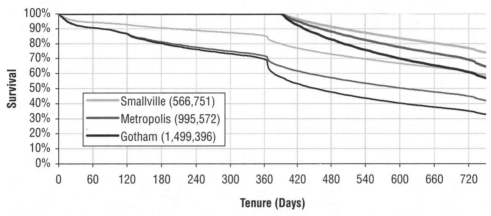

**Figure 6-14:** Conditional survival after thirteen months shows that Smallville is still the best market and Gotham the worst.

The next chapter presents yet another way to look at this problem. It answers the question: *What did the hazards look like based on the stops in each year?* Answering this question requires a different approach to the hazard calculation.

## How Has a Particular Hazard Changed over Time?

The calculation of the hazard is really the average of a particular hazard probability during a period of time. So far, this average has been over the three years of data starting in 2004. Trends in hazards, particularly in hazards relevant to the business, can provide important information.

Figure 6-15 shows the trend in the 365-day hazard over the course of 2005 and 2006 (there are not 365 days worth of data for 2004 since we are using only starts during these three years). This hazard is interesting because it is associated with anniversary churn; that is, customers leaving on the one-year anniversary after they start. As the chart shows, anniversary churn increased in 2005, hitting a peak at the end of the year, and then stabilized through 2006. The 28-day moving average removes much of the variability, helping to see the long-term pattern.

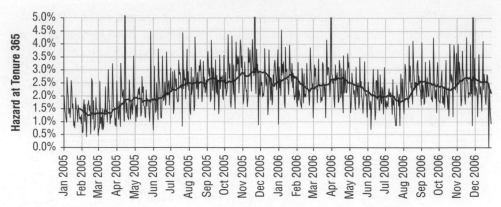

**Figure 6-15:** The hazard at 365 days changes throughout 2005 and 2006.

Calculating the hazard requires thinking carefully about the population at risk at each point in time. At any given tenure, the population at risk for the 365-day hazard probability is all customers whose tenure is exactly 365. Calculating this population for any given date, such as Feb 14, 2006, is easy:

```
SELECT COUNT(*) as pop365,
       SUM(CASE WHEN stop_date = '2006-02-14' THEN 1 ELSE 0 END) as s365,
       AVG(CASE WHEN stop_date = '2006-02-14' THEN 1.0 ELSE 0 END) as h365
FROM subs
WHERE start_date >= '2004-01-01' AND tenure >= 0 AND
      (stop_date >= '2006-02-14' OR stop_date IS NULL) AND
       DATEDIFF(dd, start_date, '2006-02-14') = 365
```

Almost all the work in this calculation is in the WHERE clause. The first two conditions are the standard conditions for filtering the data because of left truncation (these conditions are actually redundant in this case). The next condition says that only customers who were active on Feb 14, 2006, are being considered. And the final condition selects only customers whose tenure is exactly 365 on that date.

Extending this idea to all tenures is actually fairly easy. Customers are at risk for the 365-day hazard on exactly the day 365 days after they start. The following SQL extends the calculation to all dates in 2005 and 2006:

```
SELECT date365, COUNT(*) as pop365,
       SUM(CASE WHEN stop_date = date365 AND
                     stop_type IS NOT NULL THEN 1 ELSE 0 END) as stop365,
       AVG(CASE WHEN stop_date = date365 AND
                     stop_type IS NOT NULL THEN 1.0 ELSE 0 END) as h365
FROM (SELECT s.*, DATEADD(dd, 365, start_date) as date365 FROM subs s) s
WHERE start_date >= '2004-01-01' AND tenure >= 365
GROUP BY date365
ORDER BY 1
```

In this query, most of the work is being done in the GROUP BY and SELECT clauses. The date of interest is 365 days after the start. All customers who are active 365 days after they start are in the population at risk on exactly that date. Of these, some customers stop, as captured by the stop date being 365 days after the start date. Because no accumulations are necessary, the hazard can be readily calculated.

It is important to note that one particular hazard — even one as large as anniversary churn — has a very small impact on overall survival. However, trends in particular hazards can be useful for tracking particular aspects of the business. The next two subsections discuss changes in overall survival from one year to the next.

## What Is Customer Survival by Year of Start?

Filtering customers by their start date is an acceptable way of calculating hazards; that is, filters by start date do not bias the hazard estimates. So, calculating hazards by year of start is similar to calculating hazards by market. The only difference is that the groups are based on the year of the start:

```
SELECT tenure,
       SUM(is2004) as p2004, SUM(is2005) as p2005, SUM(is2006) as p2006,
       SUM(is2004*isstop) as s2004, SUM(is2005*isstop) as s2005,
       SUM(is2006*isstop) as s2006
FROM (SELECT s.*,
             (CASE WHEN YEAR(start_date) = 2004 THEN 1 ELSE 0 END
             ) as is2004,
             (CASE WHEN YEAR(start_date) = 2005 THEN 1 ELSE 0 END
             ) as is2005,
             (CASE WHEN YEAR(start_date) = 2006 THEN 1 ELSE 0 END
             ) as is2006,
             (CASE WHEN stop_type IS NOT NULL THEN 1 ELSE 0 END
             ) as isstop
      FROM subs s) s
WHERE start_date >= '2004-01-01' AND tenure >= 0
GROUP BY tenure
ORDER BY 1
```

Figure 6-16 shows the resulting survival curves for starts in each year. One thing apparent in the chart is that the length of the curves varies by year. Because the cutoff date is in 2006, the starts in 2006 only have survival for about one year. The starts in 2005 have survival values for two years, and 2004 starts have three years of survival.

## What Did Survival Look Like in the Past?

This question is more challenging than the previous one, because shifting the cutoff date to an earlier date potentially changes both the tenure and stop flag for customers. Figure 6-17 illustrates what happens. Customers who are now stopped, such as customers 3, 6, and 7, are active as of the earlier cutoff date.

Similarly, the tenure for most customers has also changed. Technically, the process of shifting the cutoff date is forcing the right censorship date to be at an earlier date than the cutoff date for the data. This discussion uses "cutoff date" to mean the latest date in the database, and "right censorship date" to be the earlier date. Up to now, these two dates have been the same.

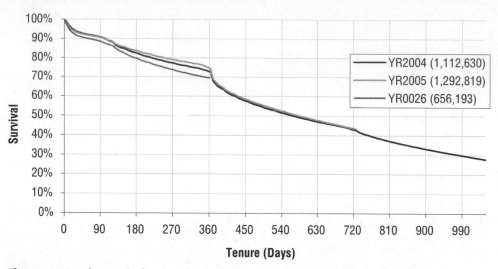

**Figure 6-16:** The survival curves here are based on starts in each of the years.

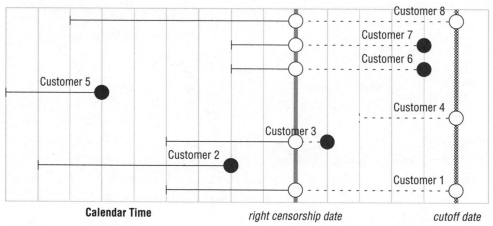

**Figure 6-17:** Shifting the right censorship date into the past changes the tenure, the stop flag, and the group of customers included in the survival calculation.

Consider a customer who started on 1 Jan 2004 and stopped on 1 Jan 2006. In the database, this customer has a tenure of two years and the stop flag is 1, indicating that the customer is no longer active. What does the customer look like at the end of 2004, though? The customer is active on that date, so the current stop flag is incorrect. And, the customer's tenure is one year, rather than two years. So, the tenure is also incorrect. Both the tenure and the stop flag need to be recalculated. Similarly, customers who start after the right censorship date should not be included.

Recalculating tenure and the stop flag as of some right censorship date, such as 2004-12-31, uses the following rules:

- Only customers who started on or before the right censorship date are included in the calculation.

- For customers who are currently active, the stop flag is 0, indicating that they were active as of the right censorship date.

- For customers who are currently stopped and whose stop date is after the right censorship date, the stop flag is 0. Otherwise the stop flag is 1.

The tenure on the right censorship date has a similar logic, incorporating the following rules:

- For customers whose stop date is on or before the right censorship date, the tenure is the stop date minus the start date.

- For the rest of the customers, the tenure is the right censorship date minus the stop date.

The following SQL uses two levels of subqueries to define the new stop flag and tenure columns:

```
SELECT tenure2004, COUNT(*) as pop2004, SUM(isstop2004) as stop2004
FROM (SELECT s.*,
             (CASE WHEN stop_type IS NULL THEN 0
                   WHEN stop_date > censordate THEN 0
                   ELSE 1 END) as isstop2004,
             (CASE WHEN stop_type IS NOT NULL AND
                        stop_date <= censordate THEN tenure
                   ELSE DATEDIFF(dd, start_date, censordate) END
             ) as tenure2004
      FROM (SELECT CAST('2004-12-31' as DATETIME) as censordate, s.*
            FROM subs s) s
      WHERE start_date <= censordate AND
            start_date >= '2004-01-01' AND tenure >= 0
     ) s
GROUP BY tenure2004
ORDER BY 1
```

Note that this query uses a subquery to define CENSORDATE as the right censorship date. The purpose is to define CENSORDATE only once, reducing the possibility of errors in the query.

Figure 6-18 shows the survival curves as of the end of the three years. These curves vary in length, with the 2004 curve only having one year of survival data, 2005 having two years, and 2006 having three years. Also, the 2004 curve is the survival for only 2004 starts. 2005 has both 2004 and 2005, and 2006 has starts from all three years. The survival curves as of the end of 2005 and 2006 are very similar to each other, because there is a big overlap in the customers used for the calculations.

## Important Measures Derived from Survival

Survival and hazard curves provide nice pictures of customers over time, and make it possible to compare different groups of customers visually. Graphics are great for conveying information, but survival analysis can also provide informative metrics. This section discusses three particular measures: the point estimate of survival, the median customer lifetime, and the average remaining customer lifetime. It ends with a discussion of confidence in the hazard values.

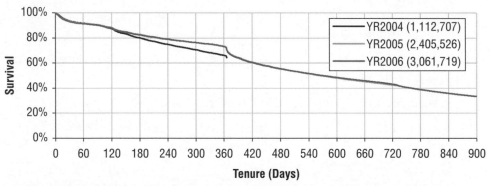

**Figure 6-18:** Shifting the right censorship date back to the end of each year makes it possible to reconstruct the survival curves as of the end of 2004, 2005, and 2006.

## Point Estimate of Survival

The point estimate of survival is the survival value at a particular tenure. For instance, earlier the point estimate at 450 days was used to compare survival in the three markets. This calculation looks up the survival value at a particular point tenure value. The point estimate answers the simple question: *How many customers do we expect to survive up to a given point in time?*

There are some situations where the point estimate is the best measure to use. For instance, many companies invest in customer acquisition, so customers must stay around long enough to recoup this investment. This is true when telephone companies give away handsets, when insurance companies pay commissions to agents, and so on. For a given acquisition effort, an important question is how many customers "graduate" to the profitable stage of the customer relationship?

Of course, answering such a question in detail might require understanding the cash flows that each customer generates and range of predictive models to handle expected tenure and expected revenues and expected costs. And all of that is difficult enough for existing customers, and harder still for prospects. A simpler approach is to see which customers survive to a particular tenure, which is usually a good enough approximation:

- Perhaps when the customer has passed the initial promo period and is paying the full bill;
- Perhaps when revenues from the customer have paid for initial outlays, such as commissions to agents or the cost of handsets; or,
- Perhaps a seemingly arbitrary period, such as one year.

The point estimate of the survival function is then a good measure for the effectiveness of such campaigns.

As an example, a major newspaper publisher used survival analysis for understanding its home delivery customers. Many things happen during the initial period when customers sign up for home delivery. For instance:

- The customer may never get a paper delivered because they live in a non-routable area.
- The customer may not pay their first bill.
- The customer may have only signed up for the initial promotional discount.

Each of these affects the survival during the first few months. After analyzing the customers, though, it became clear that four months was an important milestone, and quite predictive of longer-term survival. One advantage of four months over one year (the previous measure) is that four-month survival is available eight months sooner for new customers. That is, it became possible to measure the retention effectiveness of acquisition campaigns — using four-month survival — within a few months after the campaign starts.

## Median Customer Tenure

Another measure of survival is the *median customer tenure* or *customer half-life*. This is the tenure where exactly half the customers have left. The median customer tenure is easy to calculate. It is simply the place where the survival curve crosses the horizontal 50% line, as shown in Figure 6-19.

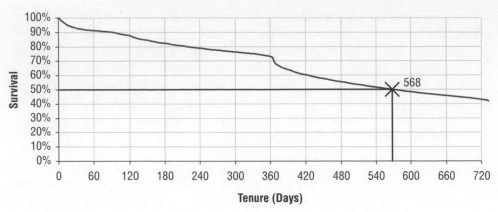

**Figure 6-19:** The median lifetime is the tenure where the survival curve passes the 50% line.

The median customer tenure suffers from the same problem that all medians do. It tells us about exactly one customer, the one in the middle. Consider three different scenarios.

1. Scenario 1: all customers survive for exactly one year and then all customers stop.

2. Scenario 2: customers stop at a uniform pace for the first two years, so half the customers have left after one year and the remaining half in the second year.

3. Scenario 3: half the customers minus one stop on the first day, then one customer stops after a year, and the remaining customers stay around indefinitely.

All of these scenarios have exactly the same median customer tenure, one year, because that is when half the customers have left. However, in the first scenario, all the customers survived for all of the first year, whereas in the third, almost half were gone immediately. The first scenario has no one surviving beyond one year; the second has no one surviving beyond two years, and in the third, they survive indefinitely. These examples illustrate that the median tenure does not provide information about what happens to customers before and after the median tenure. It simply says that the customer in the middle survived to that point in time.

The median tenure also illustrates one of the disadvantages of the retention curve, versus the survival curve. Because it is jagged, the retention curve might cross the 50% line several times. Which is the correct value for median retention? The right answer is to use survival instead of retention.

## Average Customer Lifetime

The median customer lifetime provides information about exactly one customer, the one in the middle. Averages are more useful, because they can be included in financial calculations. So if a customer generates $200 in revenue per year, and the average customer stays for two years, then the average customer generates $400 in revenue.

The *average truncated tenure* is the average tenure for a given period of time after customers start, answering a question such as: "What is the average number of days that customers are expected to survive in the first year after they start?" Limiting the span to one year is helpful for both business reasons and technical reasons. On the business side, it means that the results can be validated after one year. On the technical side, average truncated tenures are easier to calculate, because they are for a finite time period.

Calculating the average truncated tenure from the survival curve turns out to be quite easy. To illustrate the process, start with the simplest case, the average one-day tenure. That is, what is the average tenure of customers in the one day after they start? The number of customers who survived to day one is the number who started times day-one survival. The average divides by the number who started, so the average is just the survival on day one. If 99% of customers survive for one day, then the average customer survives for 0.99 days in the first day after they start.

What is the average two-day tenure? This is the average number of days that customers are active in the two days after they start. The total number of days that customers survive is the sum of those who were around on days one and two. So, the total number of days is day-one survival times the number of customers who started plus day-two survival times the number of customers who started. The average divides out the number of customers. The average two-day tenure is survival on day one plus survival on day two.

This generalizes to any tenure. The average tenure for any given time after a customer starts is the sum of the survival values up to that tenure.

Another way of looking at the calculation leads to the observation that the area under the survival curve is the average truncated tenure. Figure 6-20 shows how to calculate the area, by placing rectangles around each survival value. The area of each rectangle is the base times the height. The base is one time unit. The height is the survival value. Voila. The area under the curve is the sum of the survival values, which as we just saw, is the average truncated tenure.

> **TIP**  The area under the survival curve is the average customer lifetime for the period of time covered by the curve. For instance, for a survival curve that has two years of data, the area under the curve up to day 730 is the two-year average tenure.

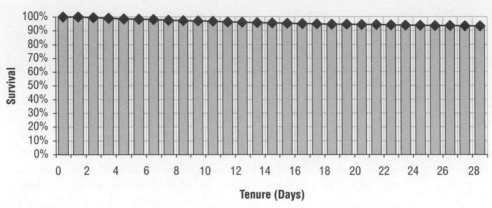

**Figure 6-20:** The average customer lifetime is the area under the survival curve.


## Confidence in the Hazards

An important question about the hazards is the confidence in how accurate they are. The way a statistician would pose the question is something like: How close are the observed hazard probabilities to the true hazards in the population? To the non-statistician, such a question can be a bit hard to understand. After all, aren't the calculations producing the true hazards?

So, let's phrase the question a bit differently. Say that there is one year of customer data that has been used to calculate one year of hazards. How does calculation compare to using two years of customer data instead of one? There is an intuitive sense that the results based on two years should be more stable, because there is more data supporting them. On the other hand, the one year data may be closer to what's happening now, because it is more recent.

Chapter 3 discussed confidence intervals in general and the standard error of a proportion in particular. Table 6-5 applies the standard error of a proportion to various hazard probabilities, based on calculations using one and two years of starts.

The most important thing to note is that the standard error is quite small. For this reason, it is safe to ignore it. Second, there are theoretical reasons why the standard error of a proportion overstates the error for hazards. It is worth noting that as the tenure gets larger, the population at risk declines, so the standard error gets bigger. This is particularly true for the one-year calculation in month 12. When the population at risk has one million customers, the standard error is so small that it can be ignored. However, when there are only one hundred customers, the standard error is quite large.

**Table 6-5**: Standard Error for Hazard Calculations Using One Year vs Two Years of Starts

| | ONE YEAR | | | TWO YEAR | | |
|---|---|---|---|---|---|---|
| TENURE | CUMULATIVE POPULATION | H | STANDARD ERROR | CUMULATIVE POPULATION | H | STANDARD ERROR |
| 0 | 656,193 | 0.016% | 0.002% | 1,949,012 | 0.016% | 0.001% |
| 30 | 544,196 | 0.158% | 0.005% | 1,747,837 | 0.151% | 0.003% |
| 60 | 492,669 | 0.042% | 0.003% | 1,676,349 | 0.035% | 0.001% |
| 90 | 446,981 | 0.070% | 0.004% | 1,616,928 | 0.059% | 0.002% |
| 120 | 397,010 | 0.110% | 0.005% | 1,539,639 | 0.145% | 0.003% |
| 150 | 339,308 | 0.097% | 0.005% | 1,445,250 | 0.073% | 0.002% |
| 180 | 290,931 | 0.076% | 0.005% | 1,372,105 | 0.052% | 0.002% |
| 210 | 246,560 | 0.073% | 0.005% | 1,305,919 | 0.051% | 0.002% |
| 240 | 205,392 | 0.049% | 0.005% | 1,245,427 | 0.038% | 0.002% |
| 270 | 159,290 | 0.058% | 0.006% | 1,182,404 | 0.037% | 0.002% |
| 300 | 108,339 | 0.051% | 0.007% | 1,116,510 | 0.032% | 0.002% |
| 330 | 59,571 | 0.045% | 0.009% | 1,053,415 | 0.033% | 0.002% |
| 360 | 4,272 | 0.094% | 0.047% | 969,757 | 0.173% | 0.004% |

The query used to generate the data for this is:

```
SELECT tenure,
       SUM(CASE WHEN start_date >= '2006-01-01' THEN 1 ELSE 0 END
           ) as oneyear,
       SUM(CASE WHEN start_date >= '2005-01-01' THEN 1 ELSE 0 END
           ) as twoyear,
       SUM(CASE WHEN start_date >= '2004-01-01' THEN 1 ELSE 0 END
           ) as threeyear,
       SUM(CASE WHEN start_date >= '2006-01-01' THEN isstop
               ELSE 0 END) as oneyears,
       SUM(CASE WHEN start_date >= '2005-01-01' THEN isstop
               ELSE 0 END) as twoyears,
       SUM(CASE WHEN start_date >= '2004-01-01' THEN isstop
               ELSE 0 END) as threeyears
FROM (SELECT s.*,
             (CASE WHEN stop_type IS NOT NULL THEN 1 ELSE 0 END) as isstop
      FROM subs s) s
WHERE start_date >= '2004-01-01' AND tenure >= 0
GROUP BY tenure
ORDER BY 1
```

This query is quite similar to earlier queries that calculated hazards.

**WARNING** Survival values and hazards are accurate when lots of data are used for the calculation. As the number of data points in the calculations decreases (even down to the few hundreds), the values have a much larger margin of error.

## Using Survival for Customer Value Calculations

The customer value calculation is theoretically quite simple. The value of a customer is estimated future revenue times the estimated future duration of the customer relationship. This just has one little challenge, knowing the future. We can make informed guesses using historical data.

How far in the future? One possibility is "forever"; however, a finite amount of time — typically, one, two, or five years — is usually sufficient. The future revenue stream is a guesstimation process. Remember, the goal is to understand customers. It is not a full financial profitability model, with all the checks and balances of corporate accounting.

The choice of revenue instead of profit or net revenue is quite intentional. In general, customers have some control over the revenue flow they generate because revenue is related to product usage patterns. Plus, because customers are actually paying the money, customers pay much more attention to the revenue they generate than to the costs.

Often, customers have little control over costs, which might be subject to internal allocation formulas. An actual profitability calculation would necessarily be making many assumptions about the future, and these assumptions might turn out to have a greater impact on customer value than customer behavior. So, although such profitability analyses are interesting and perhaps necessary for financial modeling, they do not necessarily benefit from being done at the granularity of individual customers.

Consider a magazine as a good example. Subscription customers receive the magazine, hopefully paying for copies that in turn generate revenue for the company. Customers continue their subscription while they see value in the relationship. However, profitability depends on all sources of revenue and costs, including the amount of advertising, the cost of paper, and the cost of postage. These cost factors are beyond customer control; on the other hand, revenue is based on when customers start and stop and is under their control.

This section discusses customer value, with particular emphasis on using survival analysis for estimating the customer duration. It starts with a method of estimating revenue, which is then applied to estimating the value of future starts. Then, the method is applied to existing customers. The purpose of customer value is generally to compare different groups of customers or prospects over time. Customer value is a tool to help enable companies to make more informed decisions about their customers.

## Estimated Revenue

The estimated revenue is assumed to be a stream of money that arrives at a given rate, such as $50/month. This rate may be calculated based on the history of a particular customer or group of customers. It might also be estimated for a group of prospects based on the products they will use after they start. Note that for a real financial calculation, future revenue might be discounted. However, because customer value calculations are for insight rather than accounting, discounts are usually a distraction.

The subscription data does not have a separate revenue history, so this section uses the initial monthly fee as a good estimate for the revenue stream. Actual billing data or payment data would be preferable, but it is not available.

Assume that number of future customers is forecast by market and channel. *What revenue should be used for prospective customers?* The monthly fee is already a revenue rate, so the question becomes: *What is the average monthly fee for recent starts by market and channel?* The following query answers this question for the most recent year of customers:

```
SELECT market, channel, COUNT(*) as numsubs,
       AVG(monthly_fee) as avgmonthly,
       AVG(monthly_fee)/30.4 as avgdaily
FROM subs
WHERE start_date >= '2006-01-01' AND tenure >= 0
GROUP BY market, channel
```

With three markets and four channels, there are twelve groups. Table 6-6 shows the average fee for each of the twelve groups, both per month and per day. Notice that the variation in rates is not that great, between $36.10 per month to $39.61. However, the "Chain" channel seems to have the lowest revenue, regardless of market. And Metropolis's revenue is higher than the other two markets.

**Table 6-6:** Average Monthly and Daily Revenue for Customer by Market and Channel

| MARKET | CHANNEL | NUMBER OF SUBSCRIBERS | $$ AVERAGE MONTHLY | $$ AVERAGE DAILY |
|---|---|---|---|---|
| Gotham | Chain | 9,032 | $36.10 | $1.19 |
| Gotham | Dealer | 202,924 | $39.05 | $1.28 |
| Gotham | Mail | 66,353 | $37.97 | $1.25 |
| Gotham | Store | 28,669 | $36.80 | $1.21 |
| Metropolis | Chain | 37,884 | $36.86 | $1.21 |
| Metropolis | Dealer | 65,626 | $38.97 | $1.28 |

*Continued on next page*

**Table 6-6**   *(continued)*

| MARKET | CHANNEL | NUMBER OF SUBSCRIBERS | $$ AVERAGE MONTHLY | $$ AVERAGE DAILY |
|---|---|---|---|---|
| Metropolis | Mail | 53,082 | $39.61 | $1.30 |
| Metropolis | Store | 65,582 | $38.19 | $1.26 |
| Smallville | Chain | 15,423 | $37.48 | $1.23 |
| Smallville | Dealer | 44,108 | $37.82 | $1.24 |
| Smallville | Mail | 24,871 | $38.43 | $1.26 |
| Smallville | Store | 42,640 | $37.36 | $1.23 |

## Estimating Future Revenue for One Future Start

Survival provides the estimated duration for new starts. The key is to generate separate survival curves for each market and channel combination and then to multiply each day of revenue by the average daily revenue from the previous section.

Table 6-7 shows an example; assume that 100 customers start tomorrow in Gotham from the Dealer channel. On the first day, there are 100 customers, and then the number decreases according to the survival curve. The revenue on any particular day is the product of the survival times the daily revenue times the number of customers. The total revenue for the first year after they start is the sum of the daily contributions.

This calculation can also be performed in SQL. The next two sections show two different methods.

**Table 6-7**: First Few Days of Survival Calculation for Market = Gotham and Channel = Dealer

| DAYS | SURVIVAL | NUMBER OF CUSTOMERS | DAILY REVENUE | CUMULATIVE REVENUE |
|---|---|---|---|---|
| 0 | 100.00% | 100.0 | $128.46 | $128.46 |
| 1 | 100.00% | 100.0 | $128.46 | $256.92 |
| 2 | 99.51% | 99.5 | $127.84 | $384.76 |
| 3 | 99.12% | 99.1 | $127.34 | $512.10 |
| 4 | 98.80% | 98.8 | $126.92 | $639.02 |
| 5 | 98.50% | 98.5 | $126.54 | $765.56 |

## SQL Day-by-Day Approach

Assume that there are two tables, Survivalmc and Revenue. Survivalmc has the following columns:

- Market;
- Channel;
- Tenure in days; and,
- Survival.

This table could be created using the process described earlier for calculating survival in SQL, breaking the results into groups based on market and channel. The Revenue table has:

- Market;
- Channel; and,
- Daily revenue.

This table could be created from the query used to generate Table 6-7.

With these two tables, it is possible to calculate the estimated revenue for the first 365 days after a customer starts:

```
SELECT s.market, s.channel,
       SUM(s.survival*r.avgdaily*numdays365) as yearrevenue
FROM (SELECT s.*,
             (CASE WHEN endtenure > 365 THEN 365 - tenure
                   ELSE numdays END) as numdays365
      FROM survivalmc s) s LEFT OUTER JOIN
     revenue r
     ON s.market = r.market AND
        s.channel = r.channel
WHERE tenure < 365
GROUP BY market, channel
```

The approach is to join Survivalmc to Revenue and then multiply the values together to get expected revenue per day. The first 365 days are then summed for each channel and market. The complication in the query comes from the possibility that some tenure values are missing in the survival table.

The calculation for revenue uses NUMDAYS, because some tenure values might be skipped in Survivalmc. For instance, if days 101 and 102 are missing, the row for tenure 100 would have NUMDAYS set to three. This means that the survival remains the same for three days. The next row in the table would be for tenure 103. These missing tenure values need to be included in the revenue calculation.

The need for NUMDAYS365 occurs when the missing tenures are at the end of the first year. For instance, if tenure 364 had NUMDAYS set to 10, its survival would be counted ten times instead of one. The use of NUMDAYS365 fixes this boundary-effect problem.

## SQL Summary Approach

An alternative approach calculates the sum of the survival values first, and then multiplies by the revenue. This is possible because the revenue is constant for each day, so it can, in essence, be factored out. The SQL looks like:

```
SELECT ssum.market, ssum.channel,
       (ssum.survdays*r.avgdaily) as yearrevenue
FROM (SELECT market, channel, SUM(s.survival*numdays365) as survdays
      FROM (SELECT s.*,
                   (CASE WHEN endtenure >= 365 THEN 365 - tenure
                         ELSE numdays END) as numdays365
            FROM survivalmc s) as s
      WHERE tenure < 365
      GROUP BY market, channel) ssum LEFT OUTER JOIN
     revenue r
     ON ssum.market = r.market AND
        ssum.channel = r.channel
```

The first approach multiplied survival by the revenue and then aggregated the result. This approach aggregates the survival first and then multiplies by revenue. The two are equivalent mathematically. In terms of processing, though, the second approach results in a smaller table being joined, perhaps having an impact on the efficiency of the query.

Table 6-8 shows the total first year revenue for each of the twelve groups. The table shows that per customer, Gotham Chain generates the least revenue and Smallville Dealer generates the most. These one-year revenue values can then be compared to the cost of acquisition to determine how much an additional $1000 in spending buys in terms of first year revenue.

**Table 6-8**: First Year Revenue for Market/Channel Combination

| MARKET | FIRST YEAR REVENUE BY CHANNEL | | | |
| | CHAIN | DEALER | MAIL | STORE |
|---|---|---|---|---|
| Gotham | $283.78 | $392.53 | $331.31 | $385.13 |
| Metropolis | $349.10 | $399.52 | $349.64 | $408.33 |
| Smallville | $402.90 | $420.56 | $387.89 | $417.33 |

## Estimated Revenue for a Simple Group of Existing Customers

Existing customers pose a different challenge from new starts. Obtaining historical revenue is simply a matter of adding up the revenue that existing customers have paid. For future revenue, there is a hitch. Existing customers are not starting at tenure zero, because these customers are active now and have a particular tenure. So, direct application of survival values is not the right approach. The solution is to use conditional survival, that is, survival conditioned on the fact that customers have already survived up to their current tenure.

### Estimated Second Year Revenue for a Homogenous Group

To illustrate this process, let's start with a simple group consisting of customers who started exactly one year prior to the cutoff date. What is the second year of revenue for these customers? The first year is already known, because that is before the cutoff date.

Because this group of customers has already survived for one year, the conditional survival for one year is needed. Remember the one-year conditional survival at tenure $t$ is simply the survival at tenure $t$ divided by the survival at 365 days. The following query calculates the conditional survival:

```
SELECT s.survival/s365.survival as survival365, s.*
FROM survivalmc s LEFT OUTER JOIN
     (SELECT market, channel, s.survival
      FROM survivalmc s
      WHERE 365 BETWEEN tenure AND endtenure
     ) s365
     ON s.market = s365.market AND
        s.channel = s365.channel
WHERE s.tenure >= 365
```

Applying the conditional survival to the group of existing customers uses a join. Each customer is joined to the conditional survival for days 365 through 730.

- The group of customers needs to be defined. This consists of customers who are active and who started exactly 365 days before the cutoff date. There are 1,928 of them.

- The conditional survival needs to be calculated. This uses the survival divided by the survival at day 365, and only applies to tenures greater than or equal to 365.

- Each customer is joined to the survival table, for all tenures between 365 and 729 (these are the tenures these customers have in the forecast year).

- This table is then aggregated by the market and channel dimensions.

The query that does this is:

```
SELECT ssum.market, ssum.channel, oneyear.numsubs, oneyear.numactives,
       oneyear.numactives*ssum.survdays*r.avgdaily as year2revenue
FROM (SELECT market, channel, COUNT(*) as numsubs,
             SUM(CASE WHEN stop_type IS NULL THEN 1 ELSE 0 END
                ) as numactives
      FROM subs
      WHERE start_date = '2005-12-28'
      GROUP BY market, channel
     ) oneyear LEFT OUTER JOIN
     (SELECT s.market, s.channel,
             SUM(numdays730*s.survival/s365.survival) as survdays
      FROM (SELECT s.*,
                   (CASE WHEN endtenure >= 730 THEN 730 - tenure
                         ELSE numdays END) as numdays730
            FROM survivalmc s) as s LEFT OUTER JOIN
           (SELECT s.market, s.channel, s.survival
            FROM survivalmc s
            WHERE 365 BETWEEN tenure AND endtenure
           ) s365
           ON s.market = s365.market AND
              s.channel = s365.channel
      WHERE s.tenure BETWEEN 365 AND 729
      GROUP BY s.market, s.channel) ssum
     ON oneyear.market = ssum.market AND
        oneyear.channel = ssum.channel LEFT OUTER JOIN
     revenue r
     ON ssum.market = r.market AND
        ssum.channel = r.channel
```

Table 6-9 shows the second year revenue for the group that started exactly one year previously. Notice that there are two ways of calculating revenue per customer. The "Year 2 Revenue Per Start" column is based on the original number of starts; the "Year 2 Revenue Per Year 1 Active" is based on the customers who survived the first year. Comparing this table to Table 6.8, we see that the second year revenue per start is always lower than the first year. That is because some customers leave during the first year. Some groups, such as Smallville/Store, have very high retention, so their second year revenue is almost as high as the first year revenue.

## Pre-calculating Yearly Revenue by Tenure

The preceding query is not only complicated, it is also starting to push the limits of SQL in terms of performance. The Subs table contains over one million rows (although most are filtered out), and it is being joined to 365 rows of Survivalmc. The intermediate result is, conceptually, a table with hundreds of millions of rows. Expanding the forecast period and increasing the numbers of customers causes this to grow quite quickly.

**Table 6-9**: Second Year Revenue per Customer by Market/Channel Combination

| | | NUMBER OF SUBSCRIBERS | | YEAR 2 REVENUE | | |
| MARKET | CHANNEL | STARTS | YEAR 1 ACTIVES | TOTAL | PER START | PER YEAR 1 ACTIVE |
|---|---|---|---|---|---|---|
| Gotham | Chain | 29 | 23 | $7,179.80 | $247.58 | $312.17 |
| Gotham | Dealer | 1,091 | 883 | $252,336.63 | $231.29 | $285.77 |
| Gotham | Mail | 15 | 9 | $3,314.24 | $220.95 | $368.25 |
| Gotham | Store | 55 | 44 | $16,269.76 | $295.81 | $369.77 |
| Metropolis | Chain | 348 | 239 | $79,047.43 | $227.15 | $330.74 |
| Metropolis | Dealer | 192 | 148 | $46,307.53 | $241.19 | $312.89 |
| Metropolis | Mail | 19 | 7 | $2,702.21 | $142.22 | $386.03 |
| Metropolis | Store | 169 | 148 | $57,627.20 | $340.99 | $389.37 |
| Smallville | Chain | 161 | 144 | $56,244.24 | $349.34 | $390.59 |
| Smallville | Dealer | 210 | 179 | $62,097.47 | $295.70 | $346.91 |
| Smallville | Mail | 13 | 6 | $2,403.04 | $184.85 | $400.51 |
| Smallville | Store | 107 | 95 | $38,043.21 | $355.54 | $400.45 |

The solution to the potential performance problem is to ask the question: *What is the yearly revenue for a single customer in the next year, for any given start tenure?* This query is answered by adding up the conditional survival value for days 365 through 729 for each market/channel combination. The result is then multiplied by the revenue, and then multiplied by the number of subs in each group. The following query returns the same values as the previous one, but the aggregations are done before the joins:

```
SELECT ssum.market, ssum.channel, oneyear.numsubs,
       oneyear.numsubs*ssum.survdays*r.avgdaily as year2revenue
FROM (SELECT market, channel, COUNT(*) as numsubs
      FROM subs WHERE tenure = 365 AND stop_type IS NULL
      GROUP BY market, channel
      ) oneyear LEFT OUTER JOIN
     (SELECT s.market, s.channel,
             SUM(numdays730*s.survival/s365.survival) as survdays
```

*(continued)*

```
     FROM (SELECT s.*,
                  (CASE WHEN endtenure >= 730 THEN 730 - tenure
                        ELSE numdays END) as numdays730
           FROM survivalmc s) as s LEFT OUTER JOIN
          (SELECT s.market, s.channel, s.survival
           FROM survivalmc s
           WHERE 365 BETWEEN tenure AND endtenure
          ) s365
          ON s.market = s365.market AND
             s.channel = s365.channel
        WHERE s.tenure BETWEEN 365 AND 729
        GROUP BY s.market, s.channel) ssum
     ON oneyear.market = ssum.market AND
        oneyear.channel = ssum.channel LEFT OUTER JOIN
     revenue r
     ON ssum.market = r.market AND
        ssum.channel = r.channel
```

Notice that the outermost query here does not do an aggregation. This is because each of the subqueries is aggregated by market and channel. The first subquery calculates the number of subscribers in each market/channel group among those who started 365 days before the cutoff date. The second calculates the sum of the conditional survival for days 365 through 729. These are joined to the revenue table, which is already at the level of market/channel.

**TIP** When combining multiple tables and doing an aggregation, it is often more efficient to aggregate first and then do the joins, if this is possible.

## Estimated Future Revenue for All Customers

Estimating the next year of revenue for all existing customers adds another level of complexity. Pre-calculating as much as possible helps. What is needed is a survival table with the following columns:

- Market;
- Channel;
- Tenure in days; and,
- Sum of conditional survival for the next 365 days.

One big problem is what happens to the oldest customers. The largest tenure is 1091 days. There is no data beyond this point. There are several approaches:

- Assume that everyone stops. This is not reasonable because these are good customers.

- Assume that no one stops. This is the approach we take, although it overestimates revenue for long-term customers, because it assumes they do not stop.

- Calculate a longer-term rate of decline, perhaps using a constant hazard. Add rows to the survival table incorporating this information.

The third approach is the simplest, because it uses the table of survival values directly.

The following query calculates the sum of the conditional survival values for the next 365 days. It uses a self-join for the calculation:

```
SELECT s.market, s.channel, s.tenure, s.numdays,
       SUM((s1year.survival/s.survival) *
           (CASE WHEN s1year.endtenure - s.tenure >= 365
                 THEN 365 - (s1year.tenure - s.tenure)
                 ELSE s1year.numdays END)) as sumsurvival1year
FROM survivalmc s LEFT OUTER JOIN
     survivalmc s1year
     ON s.market = s1year.market AND
        s.channel = s1year.channel AND
        s1year.tenure BETWEEN s.tenure AND s.tenure+364
GROUP BY s.market, s.channel, s.tenure, s.numdays
ORDER BY 1, 2, 3
```

The next step is to join this to the revenue table and to the original data. For convenience, the original data is aggregated by market, channel, and tenure.

```
SELECT subs.market, subs.channel, SUM(subs.numsubs) as numsubs,
       SUM(numactives) as numactives,
       SUM(subs.numactives*ssum.sumsurvival1year*r.avgdaily) as revenue
FROM (SELECT market, channel, tenure, COUNT(*) as numsubs,
             SUM(CASE WHEN stop_type IS NULL THEN 1 ELSE 0 END
                 ) as numactives
      FROM subs
      WHERE start_date >= '2004-01-01' AND tenure >= 0
      GROUP BY market, channel, tenure
     ) subs LEFT OUTER JOIN
     (SELECT s.market, s.channel, s.tenure, s.numdays,
             SUM((s1year.survival/s.survival) *
                 (CASE WHEN s1year.endtenure - s.tenure >= 365
                       THEN 365 - (s1year.tenure - s.tenure)
                       ELSE s1year.numdays END)) as sumsurvival1year
      FROM survivalmc s LEFT OUTER JOIN
           survivalmc s1year
           ON s.market = s1year.market AND
              s.channel = s1year.channel AND
              s1year.tenure BETWEEN s.tenure AND s.tenure+365
```

```
        GROUP BY s.market, s.channel, s.tenure, s.numdays
    ) ssum
    ON subs.market = ssum.market AND
        subs.channel = ssum.channel AND
        subs.tenure = ssum.tenure LEFT OUTER JOIN
    revenue r
    ON subs.market = r.market AND
        subs.channel = r.channel
GROUP BY subs.market, subs.channel
```

Table 6-10 shows the next year revenue for each of the groups based on starts since 2004. This table also shows the revenue per start and the revenue per active customer. There are three factors that affect the next year revenue. The first is the average revenue for the group. The second is the estimated survival over the next year. And the third is when the starts occurred. For example, a group might in general have poor survival. However, if lots and lots of starts came in two years ago and a significant number survived, then the next year revenue is probably pretty good because it is based on the conditional survival. However, the revenue per start will be much lower than the revenue per active, as is the case with customers from Gotham chains.

**Table 6-10**: Next Year Revenue for Existing Customers

| | | # SUBSCRIBERS | | REVENUE | | |
| | | | | | PER | PER |
| MARKET | CHANNEL | STARTS | ACTIVES | TOTAL | START | ACTIVE |
|---|---|---|---|---|---|---|
| Gotham | Chain | 67,054 | 18,457 | $6,354,927 | $94.77 | $344.31 |
| Gotham | Dealer | 1,089,445 | 480,811 | $170,636,341 | $156.63 | $354.89 |
| Gotham | Mail | 236,886 | 117,230 | $44,200,098 | $186.59 | $377.04 |
| Gotham | Store | 106,011 | 68,678 | $26,109,568 | $246.29 | $380.17 |
| Metropolis | Chain | 226,968 | 103,091 | $36,711,583 | $161.75 | $356.11 |
| Metropolis | Dealer | 301,656 | 140,632 | $51,799,400 | $171.72 | $368.33 |
| Metropolis | Mail | 204,862 | 102,085 | $40,388,696 | $197.15 | $395.64 |
| Metropolis | Store | 262,086 | 173,901 | $69,210,279 | $264.07 | $397.99 |
| Smallville | Chain | 68,448 | 49,903 | $20,025,906 | $292.57 | $401.30 |
| Smallville | Dealer | 240,753 | 152,602 | $57,849,788 | $240.29 | $379.09 |
| Smallville | Mail | 100,028 | 65,007 | $26,655,777 | $266.48 | $410.04 |
| Smallville | Store | 157,522 | 122,902 | $50,139,040 | $318.30 | $407.96 |
| TOTAL | | 3,061,719 | 1,595,299 | $600,081,404 | $195.99 | $376.16 |

Such a table often suggests more questions than it answers: What difference does the mix of rate plans make to the revenue? What is the revenue for starts by year in each of the groups? What other factors affect revenue?

## Lessons Learned

This chapter introduced survival analysis for understanding customers. The earliest origins of survival analysis were for understanding mortality rates to calculate the value of financial products. This was pretty sophisticated stuff for 1693. Since then, the technique has been used in many areas, from manufacturing to medical outcomes studies to understanding convicts released from prison.

Two key concepts in survival analysis are the hazard probability, which is the probability that someone will succumb to a risk at a given tenure, and survival, which is the proportion of people who have not succumbed to the risk. For customer-based survival, these two values are calculated for all tenures. The resulting hazard and survival charts can be quite informative and help us better understand customers.

Survival can also be quantified. The median customer tenure (or customer half-life) is the time it takes for half the customers to stop. The point estimate of survival, such as the one year survival, is the proportion of customers who make it to one year. The average truncated tenure is the average tenure of a customer during a period of time.

One powerful way that survival analysis can be used is to estimate customer value by estimating future customer revenue. This works for both new and existing customers. Although the calculations are a bit complicated, the ideas are fairly simple — just multiplying the average expected survival by the revenue.

The next chapter dives into survival analysis in more detail, introducing the concepts of time windows (to handle left truncation) and competing risks.

# Factors Affecting Survival: The What and Why of Customer Tenure

The previous chapter demonstrated the value of survival analysis for understanding customers and their stop behaviors. It introduced a powerful method for calculating hazards, called the *empirical hazards* method, where separate hazard probabilities are calculated for all tenures. And, it included several examples and extensions showing how to apply survival analysis to some business problems, including forecasting the number of active customers in the future.

This chapter builds on this foundation, by introducing three extensions of basic survival analysis. These extensions solve some common problems faced when applying survival analysis in the real world. They also make it possible to understand the effects of other factors besides tenure on survival.

The first extension focuses on the factors that are most important for determining who survives and who does not. A big complication here is that the effect of these factors depends on tenure. For instance, consider the effect of market on survival. Customers in Gotham and Metropolis have about the same survival for the first year. Around the one-year anniversary, Gotham customers start leaving at a much faster rate. In other words, the effect of market on survival varies by tenure.

The most prominent statistical technique in this area, Cox proportional hazards regression, assumes that such effects do not change over time. Although this method is outside the scope of this book, it does inspire us to look at the changing effects of each factor at different tenures. This chapter explains several different approaches for understanding how and when such factors affect survival.

The second extension is the calculation of hazards based on time windows. This chapter introduces time windows as a way to solve a problem that exists in many data sources, including the subscription data: starts come from a longer time period than stops — the left truncation problem. However, time windows do much more than just solve this problem. They are a powerful tool for estimating unbiased hazard probabilities based on a time window of stops, rather than on a time window of starts.

The third extension goes in a different direction. The factors that affect survival occur at the beginning of or during the customer life cycle. At the end of the life cycle, customers stop and they stop for some reason. This reason may be voluntary (the customer switches to a competitor); or the reason may be forced (the customer stops paying their bills); or the customer might migrate to a different product. Competing risks is a method for incorporating these different outcomes into survival analysis.

Competing risks is used to answer the question: "What happens next for all the customers?" That is, at a given point in the future, what proportion of customers have stopped for each of the competing risks? This question follows from the forecasting introduced in the previous chapter. Forecasts can include not only the numbers of remaining customers, but also of what happens to the stopped customers. Before diving into what happens next, let's start at the beginning; that is, with what we know at the beginning of the customer relationship and how these factors affect survival.

## What Factors Are Important and When

Survival probabilities can be used to compare different groups of customers by calculating separate probabilities for each group. This process is called *stratification*, and makes it possible to see the effect of market, or rate plan, or channel, or a combination of them on survival.

This section discusses quantifying the effects for factors at different tenures. For numeric variables, the comparison uses averages of the variable at different tenures for customers who stop and do not stop. For categorical variables, the comparison uses the ratio of hazards at different tenures. The key idea is that the effect of such variables may be stronger during some parts of the customer tenure and weaker during others. Being able to see the effects at different tenures sheds light on the effect of the variables on the duration of the customer relationship.

## Explanation of the Approach

Figure 7-1 shows a group of customers on the tenure timeline. The chart is similar to the charts in the previous chapter, which were used to illustrate the calculation of hazard probabilities. Here, though, we are going to look at the chart a bit differently. The chart shows eight customers. At tenure three, exactly one of them stops, and the rest remain active. This suggests the following question: *What differentiates the customer(s) who stop and the customers who remain active?*

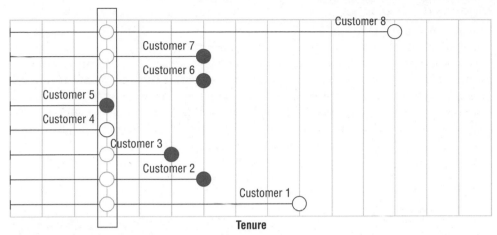

**Figure 7-1:** At any given tenure, what differentiates customers who stop and those who remain active?

Part of the answer is obvious: what differentiates them is that one group stopped and the other did not. A better way to phrase the question is to ask what differentiates the two groups by other variables. The goal is to estimate, understand, and visualize the effect of other variables on survival at any given tenure.

For tenures when no one stops, there is no answer because the group of stopped customers is empty. As mentioned earlier, the factors differentiating between the stopped customers and active customers are different for different tenures. For instance, during some tenure periods, initial promotions end. During others, customers are stopped because they do not pay their first bill. There is no reason to expect the groups of stopped customers at these tenures to be similar.

The comparison between the customers who stop at a particular tenure and those who remain active was first investigated by Sir David Cox. A statement such as "Every cigarette a person smokes reduces his or her life by 11 minutes" is an example of a result using this technique. Although it is outside the scope of this book, the aside "Proportional Hazards Regression" introduces the basic ideas.

The next two sections show reasonable ways to make the comparison for variables in customer data. In one sense, these techniques are more powerful than proportional hazards regression, because they eliminate the assumption of proportionality. They are also better suited for understanding and visualizing the effects. On the other hand, the proportional hazards regression is better for reducing the effects down to a single number, to a *coefficient* in the language of statistics.

## PROPORTIONAL HAZARDS REGRESSION

In 1972, Prof. David Cox at the University of Cambridge in England published a paper with the entertaining title, *"Regression Models and Life Tables (with discussion)."* This paper is purportedly one of the ten most cited scientific papers, because his techniques are widely used in medical research studies. Because of his contributions to statistics, Prof. Cox was knighted and is now known as Sir David Cox.

Why is this paper so important? Sir Cox devised a method of determining the effect of variables on survival without actually calculating the hazards. His method is quite clever and it is worthwhile understanding how it works. Although it is available in almost all statistics tools, it is not feasible to replicate the method directly in SQL and Excel. This is actually okay, because the method relies on an assumption that is generally not true in customer data. The *proportionality assumption* asserts that the effect of a variable is the same for all tenures. For the subscription data, it fails for market, channel, rate plan, and monthly fee. In general, the assumption is important for technical reasons and, unfortunately, not true for most customer data.

Nevertheless, proportional hazards regression is important for two reasons. Even when the proportionality assumption is not true, the results are often qualitatively correct. That is, the method can tell us which variables are more important than others. Also, the method inspires us to look at the effects of factors over time, the methods discussed in the text.

The basic idea behind Cox proportional hazards regression is quite simple. It asks the question: *What is the likelihood that exactly the customers who stopped at tenure* t *are those customers who actually did stop?* By assuming that each customer has his or her own hazard function, this likelihood can be expressed as a big equation consisting of products of expressions, such as $(1-h(t))$ for the customers who remain active at tenure *t* and $h(t)$ for customers who stop at that tenure. So, if there are four customers and the third stopped at tenure 5, then the likelihood equation for tenure 5 looks like: $(1-h_1(5))*(1-h_2(5))*h_3(5)*(1-h_4(5))$. Each of the customer hazard functions is then expressed as a function of the variables describing the customers.

Cox's clever idea was to ask this question for all tenures, and go further: *What values of the variables maximize the likelihood that exactly the set of customers who stopped are those who did stop?* The assumption of proportionality makes it possible to answer this question without referring to the hazard probabilities themselves. They simply cancel out. It does, however, rely on a technique called maximum likelihood estimation (MLE), a sophisticated statistical method used to answer such questions.

The result is a measure of the importance of each variable on survival. This measure is useful as an overall measure, but because the proportionality assumption is not necessarily reasonable on customer data, we need to do additional investigations anyway, investigations such as the methods discussed in the text.

## Using Averages to Compare Numeric Variables

A good way to see the effects of a numeric variable on survival is to compare the average value for stopped customers and for active customers at any given tenure. A chart then shows the two averages for all tenures. Such a chart displays the effect of the variable at different tenures.

There is one numeric variable in the subscription data, MONTHLY_FEE. The question is: *What is the difference in the average value of the monthly fee for customers who stop versus customers who remain active for all tenures?*

### The Answer

Figure 7-2 shows the chart for the monthly fee. This chart has two series; one shows the average monthly fee of the stopped customers, the other has the average monthly fee of active customers by tenure.

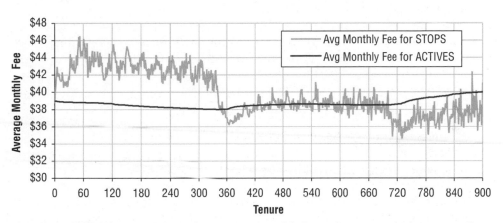

**Figure 7-2:** This chart compares the average monthly fees of customers who stop and who remain active at each tenure.

During the first year, customers who stop have higher monthly fees than those who remain active. This may be due to price sensitive customers who are paying too much when they sign up. Almost all customers start on a one- or two-year contract, with a penalty for breaking the contract. The purpose of the penalty is to prevent customers from stopping during the contract period. However, customers with higher monthly fees have more to gain by stopping than those with lower monthly fees, so it is not surprising that the contract penalty has less effect on customers who have higher fees.

Around the first year anniversary, the curves for the active and stopped customers intersect. The stopped customers initially have a higher monthly fee; after the one year mark, the order is inverted. In the second year stopped customers have a lower monthly fee. Presumably, the customers on less expensive plans who do not stop during the first year do stop around the anniversary date. This washes out after a month or two, and the averages for the two groups are essentially the same for the second year. After the second year, they reverse yet again, although by the third year, the data is becoming sparser because only three years of starts are used for the analysis.

Notice also that the average for the active customers is smooth and the average for the stopped customers jumps around. The average for the active customers is smooth because millions of customers are active for many of the tenures. In addition, the customers active for two tenures significantly overlap — because all customers active for the longer tenure are active for the shorter one. The average for the stopped customers jumps around because there are many fewer stopped customers (just a few hundred or thousand for any given tenure) and the stopped customers at two tenures do not overlap at all with each other.

## Answering the Question in SQL

Creating such a chart requires two values for each tenure: the average value for stopped customers at each tenure, and the average value for active customers at each tenure. The first of these quantities is quite easy to calculate, because each stopped customer is included in the average only at the tenure when the customer stops. The following SQL does this calculation:

```
SELECT tenure, AVG(monthly_fee) as avg_stop_monthly_fee
FROM subs
WHERE stop_type IS NOT NULL AND start_date >= '2004-01-01' AND tenure > 0
GROUP BY tenure
ORDER BY tenure
```

The calculation for active customers is more complicated and similar to the hazard probability calculation, although it needs to carry the monthly fee information as well as the population count. The key idea is as follows. The population at risk at each tenure is calculated just as for the hazards. It is then divided into two groups, those who remain active and those who stop. The total sum of the monthly fees is calculated for each tenure using the same summation method as for the population at risk. This total is divided into two groups, one for the customers who remain active and one for the customers who stop. The total monthly fees for the active and stopped customers are then divided by the total populations of the two groups, to get the average monthly fee for the active and stopped customers. This is best illustrated by walking through the calculation.

This calculation relies on five variables for each tenure:

- The tenure;
- The number of customers at each tenure;

- The number of customers who stop at each tenure;
- The sum of the initial monthly fees of all customers at each tenure; and,
- The sum of the initial monthly fees of stopped customers at each tenure.

These values are generated in SQL by simply summing and counting various values:

```
SELECT tenure, COUNT(*) as pop, SUM(isstop) as numstops,
       SUM(monthly_fee) as mfsumall, SUM(monthly_fee*isstop) as mfsumstop
FROM (SELECT s.*,
           (CASE WHEN stop_type IS NOT NULL THEN 1 ELSE 0 END) as isstop
       FROM subs s) s
WHERE start_date >= '2004-01-01' AND tenure >= 0
GROUP BY tenure
ORDER BY 1
```

The population at risk for each tenure is the sum of the customers with tenures as large as or larger than each tenure. The population at risk is split into two groups, one being the customers who stop at that tenure (which is one of the five variables returned by the query) and the other being everyone else.

Similarly, the total initial monthly fees of everyone at a given tenure is split into two groups. The first is the sum of the initial monthly fees of all customers who stop at exactly that tenure. The second is the sum of the initial monthly fees of customers who are active at that tenure. These calculated values provide the information to calculate the average for each group. Figure 7-3 shows an Excel spreadsheet that does this calculation.

| | C | D | E | F | G | I | J | K | L | M | N |
|---|---|---|---|---|---|---|---|---|---|---|---|
| 12 | | | **FROM SQL** | | | | | | **CALCULATED IN EXCEL** | | |
| 13 | tenure | pop | numstops | mfsumall | mfsumstop | Pop at Risk | Actives | STOPS | SUM MF | Actives MF | Stops MF |
| 14 | 0 | 2383 | 508 | 89712 | 19687 | =I15+D14 | =I14-E14 | =E14 | =SUM(F14:F$1107)-G14 | =L14/J14 | =G14/E14 |
| 15 | 1 | 18354 | 17306 | 728195 | 690405 | =I16+D15 | =I15-E15 | =E15 | =SUM(F15:F$1107)-G15 | =L15/J15 | =G15/E15 |
| 16 | 2 | 16730 | 15091 | 673535 | 614020 | =I17+D16 | =I16-E16 | =E16 | =SUM(F16:F$1107)-G16 | =L16/J16 | =G16/E16 |
| 17 | 3 | 13283 | 11346 | 541877 | 470617 | =I18+D17 | =I17-E17 | =E17 | =SUM(F17:F$1107)-G17 | =L17/J17 | =G17/E17 |
| 18 | 4 | 9544 | 9500 | 403210 | 401630 | =I19+D18 | =I18-E18 | =E18 | =SUM(F18:F$1107)-G18 | =L18/J18 | =G18/E18 |
| 19 | 5 | 11746 | 9152 | 487490 | 393325 | =I20+D19 | =I19-E19 | =E19 | =SUM(F19:F$1107)-G19 | =L19/J19 | =G19/E19 |
| 20 | 6 | 12649 | 9409 | 515355 | 399055 | =I21+D20 | =I20-E20 | =E20 | =SUM(F20:F$1107)-G20 | =L20/J20 | =G20/E20 |
| 21 | 7 | 13466 | 10298 | 544440 | 430485 | =I22+D21 | =I21-E21 | =E21 | =SUM(F21:F$1107)-G21 | =L21/J21 | =G21/E21 |
| 22 | 8 | 11862 | 9560 | 485685 | 402820 | =I23+D22 | =I22-E22 | =E22 | =SUM(F22:F$1107)-G22 | =L22/J22 | =G22/E22 |
| 23 | 9 | 12265 | 9449 | 499307 | 398427 | =I24+D23 | =I23-E23 | =E23 | =SUM(F23:F$1107)-G23 | =L23/J23 | =G23/E23 |
| 24 | 10 | 12017 | 9477 | 486785 | 394740 | =I25+D24 | =I24-E24 | =E24 | =SUM(F24:F$1107)-G24 | =L24/J24 | =G24/E24 |
| 25 | 11 | 11104 | 9041 | 450800 | 375620 | =I26+D25 | =I25-E25 | =E25 | =SUM(F25:F$1107)-G25 | =L25/J25 | =G25/E25 |
| 26 | 12 | 10441 | 8286 | 420944 | 342559 | =I27+D26 | =I26-E26 | =E26 | =SUM(F26:F$1107)-G26 | =L26/J26 | =G26/E26 |
| 27 | 13 | 10703 | 8419 | 431335 | 347815 | =I28+D27 | =I27-E27 | =E27 | =SUM(F27:F$1107)-G27 | =L27/J27 | =G27/E27 |
| 28 | 14 | 11037 | 8887 | 446100 | 367165 | =I29+D28 | =I28-E28 | =E28 | =SUM(F28:F$1107)-G28 | =L28/J28 | =G28/E28 |

**Figure 7-3:** This Excel spreadsheet calculates the average monthly fee for active customers and for stopped customers.

## Extension to Include Confidence Bounds

This process of taking the average initial monthly fee at each tenure for stopped and active customers is an example of taking a sample average. As discussed in Chapter 3, such averages have confidence intervals based on the standard error, so a reasonable enhancement is to include the standard error or confidence bounds in the chart.

Figure 7-4 shows the previous chart with 95% confidence bounds for the stopped customers. The confidence bounds for the active customers are so small as to be negligible, so they are not shown on the chart. Because the confidence bounds depend on the number of points at each point, the data is summarized at the weekly level rather than the daily level to narrow the confidence intervals for the stopped customers.

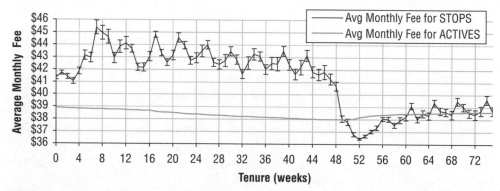

**Figure 7-4:** The comparison of averages can include error bars that show a confidence interval for either average. In this case, the 95% confidence bound is shown for the monthly fee average for stops.

This chart clearly illustrates that during the first year, stopped customers have an average monthly fee that is significantly higher than that of active customers. After a year and a few months, the averages become quite similar.

It is worth noting that even if the two curves had overlapping standard errors during the first year, there would probably still be a statistically significant difference between them because the trends are so apparent. Overlapping confidence intervals would normally suggest that at any given tenure, two points might be in either order due to random variation. However, a consistent trend undercuts this observation. If the difference between two groups with overlapping confidence were due to chance, there would not be long series where one is greater than the other.

**WARNING** When looking at confidence bounds on series, it is important to look at trends as well as overlapping confidence intervals.

The confidence bound uses the statistical formula for the standard error of a sample. The bound is 1.96 times the standard error. Recall from Chapter 3 that the standard error for a sample average is the standard deviation divided by the square root of the size of the sample. The standard deviation is calculated as follows:

- Take the sum of the squares of the monthly fees;
- Subtract the average monthly fee squared divided by the number of values;
- Divide the difference by one less than the number of values;
- Then the square root is an estimate of the standard deviation.

This calculation requires several aggregated values in addition to the values used for the average initial monthly fee averages. The following query does the necessary work:

```
SELECT FLOOR(tenure/7) as tenureweeks, COUNT(*) as pop,
       SUM(isstop) as numstops, SUM(monthly_fee) as mfsumall,
       SUM(monthly_fee*isstop) as mfsumstop,
       SUM(monthly_fee*monthly_fee) as sum2all,
       SUM(monthly_fee*monthly_fee*isstop) as mfsum2stop
FROM (SELECT s.*,
             (CASE WHEN stop_type IS NOT NULL THEN 1 ELSE 0 END) as isstop
       FROM subs s) s
WHERE start_date >= '2004-01-01' AND tenure >= 0
GROUP BY FLOOR(tenure/7)
ORDER BY 1
```

This query adds several aggregations to the SELECT clause of the query used in the previous section; this version includes the sum of the squares of the monthly fee for all customers and for stopped customers. The query also uses an indicator variable, ISSTOP, for the stop calculations, rather than a CASE statement. The two methods are equivalent.

The sum of squares values are accumulated for each tenure, and split into two groups for the actives and the stopped customers; this is the same process used for the monthly fee average calculation. The sum provides the missing information for the standard deviation calculation, which subtracts the number of values times the sum of squares of the averages from this value and divides the difference by one less than the number of values. The standard error is then the standard deviation divided by the square root of the number of stops. And, the 95% confidence bound is 1.96 times the standard error.

Showing the result as confidence bounds in the chart makes use of positive and negative Y-error bars. These are placed in the chart by selecting the series, right-clicking to bring up the "Format Data Series" dialog box, and going to the "Y Error Bars" tab. On this tab, choose the "Both" option choosing the

"Custom" option on the bottom. Place the cell range with the confidence bounds in the "+" and "−" boxes. The same range is used for both.

## Hazard Ratios

Averages work for numeric variables, but they do not work for categorical variables: The "average" value of something that takes on distinct values, such as Gotham, Smallville, and Metropolis does not make sense. Yet, there is still the question: *What is the effect of a categorical variable (such as market or rate plan) on survival for different tenures?* Because averages as discussed in the previous section do not work, an alternative approach is needed; this approach uses the ratio of hazard probabilities.

### *Interpreting Hazard Ratios*

Figure 7-5 shows two hazard ratio charts. The top chart shows the ratio of the hazards by market, so the curves are for the Smallville to Gotham ratio and Metropolis to Gotham ratio. The Gotham to Gotham ratio is not included in the chart, because it is uniformly one.

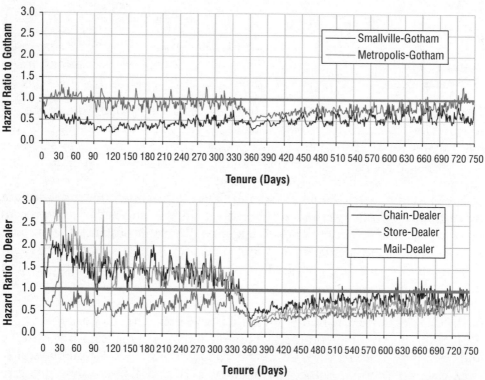

**Figure 7-5:** The top chart shows hazard ratios for market, compared to Gotham, and the bottom shows hazard ratios for channel, compared to Dealer.

Smallville's survival is better than Gotham's, so as expected, the ratio of Smallville's hazards to Gotham's hazards is uniformly less than one. However, this effect is strongest during the first year, with the ratio climbing up a bit in the second year. The first year average hazard ratio is 0.44, which rises to 0.55 in the second year. Although they are much better customers, Smallville's customers are becoming less good, relative to Gotham's, at longer tenures.

The situation with Metropolis is the opposite. During the first year, the hazard ratio is close to one, so Metropolis's customers are almost as bad as Gotham's in the first year. In the second year, the hazard ratio drops from 0.96 to 0.75. So, Metropolis's customers are getting better while Smallville's are getting worse. After two years, though, Smallville's customers are still stopping at a lower rate than Metropolis's.

The lower chart in Figure 7-5 shows the hazard ratios by channel for Chain, Store, and Mail compared to Dealer. The hazards for the Store channel are almost uniformly lower than for Dealer, implying that survival of customers from Store is better than customers from Dealer. This makes sense, because the Store channel consists of own-branded stores, where the personnel are actually employees of the cell phone company. It is not surprising that these stores attract and retain the best customers, and in particular, better than the independently owned dealers.

The Mail and Chain hazard ratios are interesting, because these ratios are greater than one during the first year and then lower during the second year. One possibility is that the Dealers are intentionally churning their customers in the second year. That is, the independently owned dealers switch customers who have been around a year to another carrier, because they then get an acquisition bonus from another carrier. Customers who were acquired through national chains and customers who come in by calling or through the Internet would not be subject to such a ploy.

## Calculating Hazard Ratios

Calculating the hazard ratios is basically the same as calculating the hazard probabilities. SQL is used to start the hazard calculation, which is finished in Excel, and then the ratio is calculated in Excel. The query to calculate the hazards by market and channel is:

```
SELECT tenure,
       SUM(CASE WHEN market = 'Small' THEN 1 ELSE 0 END) as small,
       . . .
       SUM(CASE WHEN channel = 'Chain' THEN 1 ELSE 0 END) as chain,
       . . .
       SUM(CASE WHEN market = 'Smallville' THEN isstop ELSE 0 END
          ) as stopsmall,
       . . .
       SUM(CASE WHEN channel = 'Chain' THEN isstop ELSE 0 END
```

*(continued)*

```
          ) as stopchain,
     . . .
FROM (SELECT s.*,
            (CASE WHEN stop_type IS NOT NULL THEN 1 ELSE 0 END) as isstop
      FROM subs s) s
WHERE start_date >= '2004-01-01' AND tenure >= 0
GROUP BY tenure
ORDER BY 1
```

The results are copied into Excel to calculate the hazards. For the ratios, Gotham and Dealer were chosen arbitrarily. The one with the best survival (Smallville) or worst survival (Gotham) are good choices. In other circumstances, it might be useful to compare each group to the population as a whole. This would be particularly true if the groups were rather small, because the overall group would have non-zero hazards even when some of the other groups occasionally have zero hazards.

One caution about the hazard ratio is that it does not work when there are no stops in the comparison group at a given tenure. However, for the comparison by market, the sizes of the various subgroups are large enough so this does not happen. In other cases, it might be desirable to use a larger time period, such as seven days (one week) or 30 days (approximately one month).

**TIP** When using hazard ratios, adjust the time period used for the tenure calculations to ensure that there are enough stops during each time period, for instance, by summarizing at the weekly level rather than the daily level.

## Why the Hazard Ratio

A question may be occurring to some readers: Why the hazard ratio and not the survival ratio? First, it is important to note that the survival ratio can also be informative. After all, the ratio of survival provides information about how much better one group is than another. It can even be used as a rough estimate of the difference in customer half-life. That is, if one group has a survival ratio half that of another group, the customer half-life for the first group should be about twice as long as the customer half-life for the second.

The hazard ratio has two advantages, one theoretical and one practical. The theoretical advantage is that there is a relationship between the hazard ratio and the methods used for Cox proportional hazards regression. Both techniques look at what happens at a particular tenure and determine who is stopping. This relationship is theoretically appealing.

The more practical reason is that the hazard ratio gives independent information for each tenure as opposed to survival, which accumulates information. In the charts, there was often a cutoff at one year, where the ratios flipped. This phenomenon would show up much more slowly in the survival ratio, because the information has to accumulate over many tenures. In fact, the hazard ratio shows that the hazard probabilities for Smallville are getting worse while the hazard probabilities for Metropolis are getting better. However, even after two years, Smallville still has better survival than Metropolis, because of what happens during the first year. The survival ratio does not show this phenomenon clearly at all.

One drawback of the hazard ratio is that there might be only a small amount of data at each tenure. This can be fixed by using longer tenure periods, such as weeks or multiples of weeks, instead of days.

# Left Truncation

Understanding variables improves our understanding of survival and hazards. This section moves to another topic, which is the accurate calculation of hazard probabilities. As noted in the previous chapter, the customers in the Subs table data have an unusual property: customers who stopped before 2004-01-01 are excluded from the table. This phenomenon, where customers are excluded based on their stop date, is called *left truncation*. In the previous chapter, the problem of left truncation was handled by ignoring customers who started before 2004-01-01. This section presents another method, based on an idea called time windows.

Left truncation is a problem, because hazard estimates on left truncated data are simply incorrect. The solution to left truncation uses stop time windows, a powerful enhancement to survival analysis that has other applications. Before discussing time windows in general, though, let's look at the left truncation problem that they solve.

## Recognizing Left Truncation

Left truncation is identified by looking at a histogram of starts and stops by date on the same chart. The chart itself is similar to other histograms, except two curves need to be shown on the same chart. One way to do this is to generate the data for each histogram separately, and then combine them in Excel. However, doing the combining in SQL simplifies the Excel work. The following query returns the number of starts and stops by month:

```
SELECT YEAR(thedate) as year, MONTH(thedate) as month,
       SUM(numstarts) as numstarts, SUM(numstops) as numstops
FROM ((SELECT start_date as thedate, COUNT(*) as numstarts, 0 as numstops
      FROM subs
      GROUP BY start_date)
     UNION ALL
```

*(continued)*

```
    (SELECT stop_date as thedate, 0 as numstarts, COUNT(*) as numstops
     FROM subs
     GROUP BY stop_date)) a
WHERE thedate IS NOT NULL
GROUP BY YEAR(thedate), MONTH(thedate)
ORDER BY 1, 2
```

Figure 7-6 shows the resulting histogram. This chart suggests that starts are coming from a much longer time period than stops. One way to confirm this is to ask the question: *How many years (or months or days) have both starts and stops and how many have one without the other?* The following query characterizes years according to whether or not the year has any starts and whether or not the year has any stops:

```
SELECT (CASE WHEN numstarts = 0 THEN 'NONE' ELSE 'SOME' END) as starts,
       (CASE WHEN numstops = 0 THEN 'NONE' ELSE 'SOME' END) as stops,
       COUNT(DISTINCT theyear) as numyears,
       MIN(theyear) as minyear, MAX(theyear) as maxyear
FROM (SELECT theyear, SUM(numstarts) as numstarts,
             SUM(numstops) as numstops
      FROM ((SELECT YEAR(start_date) as theyear, COUNT(*) as numstarts,
             0 as numstops
             FROM subs
             GROUP BY YEAR(start_date) )
           UNION ALL
           (SELECT YEAR(stop_date) as theyear, 0 as numstarts,
                   COUNT(*) as numstops
            FROM subs
            GROUP BY YEAR(stop_date) )) a
      GROUP BY theyear) b
GROUP BY (CASE WHEN numstarts = 0 THEN 'NONE' ELSE 'SOME' END),
         (CASE WHEN numstops = 0 THEN 'NONE' ELSE 'SOME' END)
ORDER BY 1, 2
```

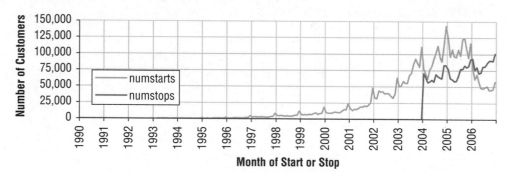

**Figure 7-6:** This histogram of start and stop counts by month suggests that prior to 2004, starts are recorded in the database but not stops.

Table 7-1 has the results from this query, which confirms what we already know. Prior to 2004, starts were recorded in the database but not stops. Chapter 6 got around this problem by filtering the starts to include only those since 2004. The resulting hazard calculation uses customers for whom full start and stop information is available.

**Table 7-1:** Number of Years, Characterized by Presence of Starts and Stops

| STARTS | STOPS | NUMBER OF YEARS | MINIMUM YEAR | MAXIMUM YEAR |
| --- | --- | --- | --- | --- |
| SOME | NONE | 17 | 1958 | 2003 |
| SOME | SOME | 3 | 2004 | 2006 |

The subscribers table has a particularly egregious form of left truncation, because *all* stopped customers were excluded. Often, left truncation is not quite so blatant. For instance, some stops might make it into the database, perhaps because they were pending on the cutoff date. Or, the left truncation may be within a single market or customer subgroup. Perhaps a small company was acquired, and only their active customers were included in the database. Fortunately, the techniques that deal with left truncation can be enhanced to deal a separate left truncation date for each customer.

## Effect of Left Truncation

Left truncation, in general, biases hazard probabilities by making them smaller. This is because customers are included in the population at risk, when these customers really are not at risk. For instance, a customer that started in 2001 is included in the population at risk for tenure one. If this customer had stopped at tenure one, she would not be in the data. Her stop date, if any, must be after the left truncation date. Yet, it is easy to include her in the population at risk for tenure one.

As a consequence, the denominator of the hazard probability ratio is too large, thereby making the hazard probability too small, which in turn makes the survival estimates too big. Figure 7-7 compares survival curves generated from all the customers and from only those who started after the left truncation date. The result from overestimating survival is that the survival values are too optimistic. Optimism is good. Ungrounded optimism bordering on fantasy might lead to incorrect decisions and assumptions. It is much preferable to calculate unbiased estimates.

Although left truncated data usually underestimates hazard probabilities, the resulting hazard probabilities could actually be either larger or smaller than the unbiased estimate. Consider the hazard probability at 730 days. It can be set to almost any value by making up data before the left truncation date. So, consider the customers who start on 1 Jan 2001. If all these customers stop at exactly 730 days, then they all stop before the left truncation date (1 Jan 2003 is before 1 Jan 2004), and they are not in the data. However, their stops would increase the 730-day hazard relative to the observed value. If, instead, these customers all stop at exactly 731 days of tenure, then they have survived 730 days without stopping, thereby decreasing the 730-day hazard. Because these customers are not in the data, we don't know which, if either, of these scenarios occurred.

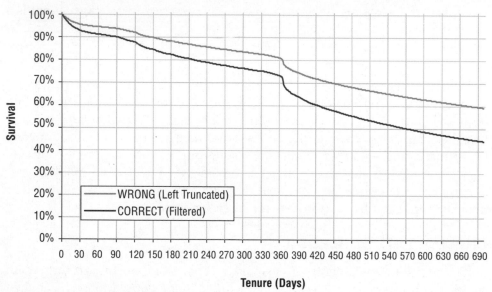

**Figure 7-7:** Calculations on left truncated data overestimate the survival. Filtering is one way to get unbiased estimates.

However, when doing survival analysis, we assume that the hazard probabilities do not change radically over time. This assumption of similarity over time has a name, the *homogeneity assumption*. The scenarios described in the previous paragraph severely violate the homogeneity assumption. Figure 6-15 did show that the 365-day hazard probability does change over time. However, the change is gradual, so this hazard does not severely violate homogeneity. With this assumption, the hazards calculated from left truncated data underestimate the hazard and hence overestimate the survival.

**TIP** The homogeneity assumption asserts that the hazard probabilities do not change radically or suddenly over time. This is usually a reasonable assumption for customer databases, although it is worth validating.

## How to Fix Left Truncation, Conceptually

Figure 7-8 shows several customers throughout time, on the calendar time line. Two dates are highlighted; the earlier is the left truncation date and the later is the cutoff date. Only customers who are active after the left truncation date are in the database.

Customer #5 started and stopped before the left truncation date. This customer is simply missing from the data. We do not even know to look for the customer, because the customer is not there. Customer #2 started at about the same time yet appears in the data, because this customer survived to the left truncation date. The fact that one customer is present and another absent is a property of the data, as opposed to a property of any particular record.

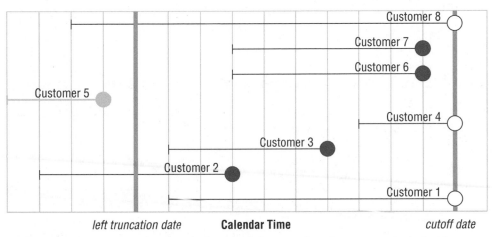

left truncation date     **Calendar Time**     cutoff date

**Figure 7-8:** Customers who stop before the left truncation date are not included in the database.

*How can the hazard probabilities be calculated without the biases introduced by missing data?* Answering this question requires a detailed look at the hazard calculation itself. Remember, the hazard probability at a particular tenure is the number of customers who have an observed stop at that tenure divided by the number of customers who are at risk of stopping. The population at risk is everyone who was active at that tenure who could have stopped, regardless of whether they stopped.

Left truncation adds a twist. Consider the at-risk population for customers at tenure zero in left truncated data. If a customer started before the left truncation date, the customer is not in the at-risk pool for tenure zero. Customers who started before the left truncation date and would have a tenure of zero are simply not available in the data. So, the at-risk population at tenure zero consists only of customers who started since the left truncation date.

Consider the at-risk population for customers at tenure one. These customers have to be at risk of stopping at tenure one and the stop needs to occur after the left truncation date. So, tenure one needs to occur on or after the left truncation date. In other words, the customer must start between one day before the left truncation date and one day before the cutoff date.

The general rule is that a customer is in the population at risk at tenure $t$ when that tenure occurs on or after the left truncation date and before the cutoff date. The following two rules for membership in the population at risk encapsulate this observation:

- Customers start in the time period from the left truncation date minus $t$ to the cutoff date minus $t$; and,

- Customers are active at tenure $t$.

Together, these two rules imply that the customer is active at that tenure in the period after the left truncation date.

## Estimating Hazard Probability for One Tenure

The preceding rules readily translate into SQL for a given tenure For instance, the hazard probability for tenure 100 is calculated as:

```
SELECT MIN(thetenure) as thetenure, COUNT(*) as poprisk_t,
       SUM(CASE WHEN tenure = thetenure THEN isstop ELSE 0 END
           ) as numstops,
       AVG(CASE WHEN tenure = thetenure THEN isstop*1.0 ELSE 0 END
           ) as haz_t
FROM (SELECT s.*, 100 as thetenure,
             (CASE WHEN stop_type IS NOT NULL THEN 1 ELSE 0 END) as isstop
      FROM subs s) s
WHERE tenure >= thetenure AND
      DATEADD(dd, thetenure, start_date) BETWEEN '2004-01-01' AND
                                                 '2006-12-31'
```

The result is 0.088%. Notice that this query sets the THETENURE variable in the subquery as a convenience for the overall calculation. Changing THETENURE results in estimates for other tenures. For instance, changing it to 1460 gives the tenure at four years (1460=365*4). That value is 0.07%.

Wow. Calculating the hazard for such a large tenure is quite remarkable. Up to this point, hazard probabilities have been limited to tenures less than three years, because starts before 1 Jan 2004 were filtered out. However, by using a time window for the stops, hazard probabilities can be calculated for any tenure.

## Estimating Hazard Probabilities for All Tenures

The method used to estimate hazard probabilities for a single tenure does not readily scale to all tenures. Doing the calculation efficiently for all tenures requires a bit more cleverness based on some observations about the population at risk. These observations look at the calculation from a different perspective, the relationship between the population at risk at one tenure and the population at risk for the previous tenure.

The observations are:

- The population at risk for a given tenure $t$ is the population at risk for $t–1$, plus
- Customers who enter the time window with tenure $t$ (that is, those who have tenure $t$ on the left truncation date), minus
- Customers who leave the time window with tenure $t–1$ (that is, those who are stopped or censored at the previous tenure).

These observations use the number of customers who enter and leave the time window defined by the left truncation date and the cutoff date. The number of customers who enter at a given tenure is easily calculated. If the customer started on or after the left truncation date, then the customer entered at tenure zero. Customers who start before the left truncation date enter the time window on their tenure as of the left truncation date. Only customers who have entered the time window are counted in the population at risk for a given tenure.

The number of customers who leave the time window at a given tenure is even easier. This is simply the number of customers with a given tenure, regardless of whether or not they stop. Any customers who stop before the left truncation date need to be excluded from both the "enters" and "leaves" calculations. This condition is a bit redundant, because customers who stop before the left truncation date are not in the data at all, which is why we are going through this effort to calculate unbiased hazards.

The following SQL calculates the columns NUMENTERS, NUMLEAVES, and NUMSTOPS for all tenures less than 1000 by placing all longer tenure customers into one group (this is just a convenience for the calculation and not necessary for handling left truncation):

```
SELECT (CASE WHEN thetenure < 1000 THEN thetenure ELSE 1000
        END) as tenure, SUM(enters) as numenters,
       SUM(leaves) as numleaves, SUM(isstop) as numstops
FROM ((SELECT (CASE WHEN start_date >= '2004-01-01' THEN 0
                   ELSE DATEDIFF(dd, start_date, '2004-01-01') END
              ) as thetenure,
              1 as enters, 0 as leaves, 0 as isstop, s.*
       FROM subs s) UNION ALL
      (SELECT tenure as thetenure, 0 as enters, 1 as leaves,
             (CASE WHEN stop_type IS NOT NULL THEN 1 ELSE 0 END
             ) as isstop, s.*
       FROM subs s) ) a
WHERE start_date IS NOT NULL AND tenure >= 0
GROUP BY (CASE WHEN thetenure < 1000 THEN thetenure ELSE 1000 END)
ORDER BY 1
```

The number of customers who enter and leave the time window are calculated in two subqueries, one for entering and one for leaving, connected with a UNION ALL. The second of these subqueries also keeps track of the customers who stop, because the tenure at the stop is the same as the tenure when the customer leaves the time window.

These columns provide the fodder for the Excel calculation, which follows the logic described in the preceding observations. Figure 7-9 shows an Excel spreadsheet that does the calculations. The population at risk for a given tenure is the previous population at risk plus the new customers that enter minus the ones that leave at the previous tenure. The hazard probabilities are then calculated by dividing the number of stops by the population at risk. When doing the calculation for all tenures, it is worth validating the result for one or two tenures, using the single tenure estimate in the previous section.

|  | C | D | E | F | G | H | I | J |
|---|---|---|---|---|---|---|---|---|
| 19 |  | FROM SQL | | | | | CALCULATED IN EXCEL | |
| 20 | thetenure | numenters | numleaves | numstops | | POP | h | S |
| 21 | 0 | 3061719 | 2383 | 508 | | =SUM(D$21:D21) | =F21/H21 | =IF($C21=0, 1, J20*(1-I20)) |
| 22 | 1 | 1789 | 18358 | 17310 | | =SUM(D$21:D22) | =F22/H22 | =IF($C22=0, 1, J21*(1-I21)) |
| 23 | 2 | 2319 | 16742 | 15103 | | =SUM(D$21:D23) | =F23/H23 | =IF($C23=0, 1, J22*(1-I22)) |
| 24 | 3 | 4315 | 13298 | 11361 | | =SUM(D$21:D24) | =F24/H24 | =IF($C24=0, 1, J23*(1-I23)) |
| 25 | 4 | 3847 | 9566 | 9522 | | =SUM(D$21:D25) | =F25/H25 | =IF($C25=0, 1, J24*(1-I24)) |
| 26 | 5 | 3750 | 11766 | 9172 | | =SUM(D$21:D26) | =F26/H26 | =IF($C26=0, 1, J25*(1-I25)) |
| 27 | 6 | 3925 | 12689 | 9449 | | =SUM(D$21:D27) | =F27/H27 | =IF($C27=0, 1, J26*(1-I26)) |
| 28 | 7 | 102 | 13504 | 10336 | | =SUM(D$21:D28) | =F28/H28 | =IF($C28=0, 1, J27*(1-I27)) |
| 29 | 8 | 3273 | 11898 | 9596 | | =SUM(D$21:D29) | =F29/H29 | =IF($C29=0, 1, J28*(1-I28)) |
| 30 | 9 | 5727 | 12296 | 9480 | | =SUM(D$21:D30) | =F30/H30 | =IF($C30=0, 1, J29*(1-I29)) |
| 31 | 10 | 5933 | 12068 | 9528 | | =SUM(D$21:D31) | =F31/H31 | =IF($C31=0, 1, J30*(1-I30)) |

**Figure 7-9:** The Excel calculation for handling left truncation is not much more difficult than the calculation for empirical hazards.

Notice that the number of customers who enter the time window at tenure zero is in the millions, but for the other tenures, the count is, at most, in the thousands. This is because all customers who start on or after the left truncation date enter the time window at tenure zero. So, the tenure zero number includes three years worth of starts. On the other hand, the customers who enter at larger tenures started that number of days before the left truncation date.

# Time Windowing

Time windows are more than just the solution to left truncation. They are a powerful technique for other purposes. This section investigates time windows in general and some ways that they can be used.

## A Business Problem

Once upon a time, a company was developing a forecasting application using survival analysis. This type of application was discussed in the previous chapter, and forecasting can be a powerful application of survival analysis. A large amount of data for tens of millions of customers was provided early in May for a proof-of-concept. The schedule called for the proof-of-concept to be reviewed in the summer, steadily improved upon, and then the final forecasting project would begin at the end of the year. So, using the historical data, the proof-of-concept began.

During that May, a shrewd person in finance decided to change one of the company's policies, just a little tweak actually. The old policy was to disconnect a customer on the date that the customer requested the stop. The new policy was to disconnect customers at the end of their billing cycle, unless the customer very loudly objected.

The merits of the new policy were multifold and manifest. The new policy meant that almost no monies needed to be refunded to customers, for instance, because accounts were paid up through the end of the billing period. Such refunds were generally small amounts of money, and the overhead for each refund was a significant proportion of the amount refunded. In addition, the new policy kept customers active for a longer period of time. In fact, assuming that customers call randomly during their billing periods to stop, it would add half a billing period — or two weeks — onto each customer's tenure.

Hmmm, would the new policy have an effect on customers' tenures? Could it conceivably be possible that adding an extra two weeks of tenure to every customer who stops would have an effect on the proof-of-concept project? No suspense here; the answer is "yes." The more important question is how to deal with the situation.

Filtering customers who started after the date the new policy went into effect would not work, because the population would consist of customers having only very short tenures — about one month for the proof-of-concept and less than one year for the larger project. A better solution would be to calculate unbiased hazard probabilities using only stops after the new policy went into effect. In other words, forcing the left truncation date to be a recent date would only use stops that have the new policy. Voila! The hazard estimates would reflect the new policy, while still having hazard estimates for all tenures.

Forcing left truncation solves the problem. Once this is recognized as a possibility other situations are amenable to the solution. Another company changed its initial non-payment policy. Previously, customers were cancelled after 63 days, if they did not pay their initial bill. This was changed to 77 days. And, yes, this has an impact on the forecast customer numbers. Eventually, the policy was made more complicated, varying from 56 days to 84 days for different groups of customers. By using left truncation to estimate hazards using stops only since the new policies went into effect, it was possible to get accurate survival estimates for a customer forecast application.

## Time Windows = Left Truncation + Right Censoring

The examples discussed in the previous section use forced left truncation to handle a business problem. However, a more general way to think about time windows is that they calculate unbiased estimates of hazard probabilities using a time window of stops. The beginning of the time window is the left truncation date and the end of the time window is the cutoff date (technically called the *right censor date* for the data).

Figure 7-10 illustrates a general time window for a small number of customers. As this example shows, a given time window is a combination of left truncation and forcing an earlier right censorship date (which we saw in the previous chapter in Figure 6-17). With these two ideas, it is possible to generate unbiased hazards using almost any time window where stops occur.

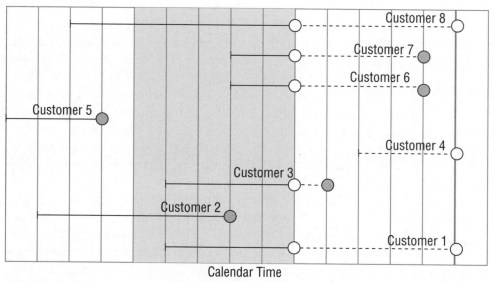

**Figure 7-10:** Time windows make it possible to estimate unbiased hazard probabilities for stops during a particular period of time (the shaded area).

### *Calculating One Hazard Probability Using a Time Window*

Consider the following question: *What are the hazard probabilities at tenure 100 based on stops in 2004, in 2005, and in 2006?* This is a question about changes in a hazard probability over time. The following SQL statement does the calculation based on stops in 2004:

```
SELECT MAX(thetenure) as tenure, COUNT(*) as poprisk_t,
       SUM(CASE WHEN tenure = thetenure THEN isstop ELSE 0 END
           ) as numstops,
       AVG(CASE WHEN tenure = thetenure THEN isstop*1.0 ELSE 0 END
           ) as haz_t
FROM (SELECT s.*, 100 as thetenure,
             (CASE WHEN stop_type IS NOT NULL AND
                        stop_date <= '2004-12-31'
              THEN 1 ELSE 0 END) as isstop
          FROM subs s) s
WHERE tenure >= thetenure  AND
      ADDDATE(dd, thetenure, start_date, thetenure)
          BETWEEN '2004-01-01' AND '2004-12-31'
```

This SQL statement combines left truncation and forced censoring. Left truncation is implemented in the WHERE clause, by restricting the customers only to those whose 100th day of tenure is during 2004. The forced censoring is as of the end of 2004, so the definition of ISSTOP is as of that date.

The queries for 2005 and 2006 are similar. Table 7-2 shows the hazard probability for tenure 100 for stops during each of the three years. The probability itself is quite low. It is interesting that the hazard is lowest during 2005, which also had the most starts.

**Table 7-2:** Hazard Probability for Tenure 100 Based on Stops in 2004, 2005, and 2006

| YEAR | TENURE | POPULATION AT RISK | STOPS | HAZARD PROBABILITY |
|------|--------|--------------------|-------|--------------------|
| 2004 | 100 | 956,937 | 957 | 0.10% |
| 2005 | 100 | 1,174,610 | 777 | 0.07% |
| 2006 | 100 | 750,064 | 808 | 0.11% |

### All Hazard Probabilities for a Time Window

Calculating a hazard probability for a single tenure is a good illustration of time windows. More interesting, though, is calculating hazard probabilities for all tenures. This calculation follows the same form as the left truncation calculation, where STOPS, ENTERS, and LEAVES variables are calculated for all tenures. These are then combined in Excel. The next section provides an example of this calculation.

## Comparison of Hazards by Stops in Year

The previous chapter showed two ways of comparing changes in survival probabilities over time. The first method was to use starts in a given year, which provides information about acquisition during the year, but not about all the customers who were active during that time. The second approach forces the right censorship date to be earlier, creating a snapshot of survival at the end of each year. Using starts, customers who start in 2006 have relatively lower survival than customers who start in 2004 or 2005. However, the snapshot method shows that 2006 survival looks better than survival at the end of 2004.

This section proposes another method, based on time windows. Using time windows, hazard probabilities are estimated based on the *stops* during each year, rather than the starts. Time windows make it possible to calculate hazard probabilities for all tenures.

The approach is to calculate the number of customers who enter, leave, and stop at a given tenure, taking into account the time window. The following query does the calculation for stops during 2006:

```
SELECT (CASE WHEN tenure < 1000 THEN tenure ELSE 1000 END) as tenure,
       SUM(enters) as numenters, SUM(leaves) as numleaves,
       SUM(isstop) as numstops
FROM ((SELECT (CASE WHEN start_date >= '2006-01-01' THEN 0
                    ELSE DATEDIFF(dd, start_date, '2006-01-01') END
             ) as tenure,
              1 as enters, 0 as leaves, 0 as isstop
       FROM subs s
       WHERE tenure >= 0 AND start_date <= '2006-12-31' AND
             (stop_date IS NULL OR stop_date >= '2006-01-01')
      ) UNION ALL
      (SELECT (CASE WHEN stop_date IS NULL OR stop_date >= '2006-12-31'
                    THEN DATEDIFF(dd, start_date, '2006-12-31')
                    ELSE tenure END) as tenure, 0 as enters, 1 as leaves,
              (CASE WHEN stop_type IS NOT NULL AND
                         stop_date <= '2006-12-31' THEN 1 ELSE 0 END
              ) as isstop
       FROM subs s
       WHERE tenure >= 0 AND start_date <= '2006-12-31' AND
             (stop_date IS NULL OR stop_date >= '2006-01-01') )
     ) a
GROUP BY (CASE WHEN tenure < 1000 THEN tenure ELSE 1000 END)
ORDER BY 1
```

This query calculates the variable ENTERS by determining the tenure when a customer enters the stop window — either the tenure on the left truncation date or zero for customers who start during the window. The variables LEAVES and STOPS are calculated based on the tenure on the right censorship date or the tenure when a customer stops.

Each subquery has the same WHERE clause in order to select only customers active during the time window—customers had to start before the end of the year and stop after the beginning of the year in order to be included. For good measure, each subquery also requires that TENURE be greater than zero, eliminating the row that has a spurious negative value.

Figure 7-11 shows the survival curves based on stops in each of the three years. These curves are comparable to Figure 6-16 and 6-18, which show the survival based on starts and the end-of-year snapshots, respectively. This chart has a more complete picture. By using time windows on stops, all three years have survival estimates for all tenures. None of the series are longer or shorter than the others.

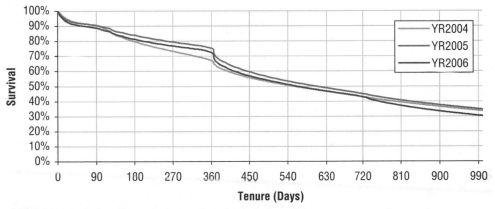

**Figure 7-11:** Using time windows, the stops during different years can be used to calculate hazard probabilities and survival.

The chart shows that the anniversary churn effect is much stronger in 2005 and 2006 versus 2004. Anniversary churn is the tendency of customers to stop on the one-year anniversary of their start, typically because their contracts expire. So, although customers in 2005 and 2006 survive better in the first year (compared to customers in 2004), as the tenures stretch out, the difference in survival disappears. Based on the stops, 2006 seems to be the worst of all possible worlds, with the worst short-term survival (in the first 90 days) and the worst long-term survival (over 720 days), although it does a bit better in between.

## Competing Risks

The opening lines to Leo Tolstoy's classic novel *Anna Karenina* is the insightful quote: "All happy families are alike; each unhappy family is unhappy in its own way." This book is not about literary criticism, but what Tolstoy wrote in the 19th century about families is also true of customers in the 21st century.

Happy customers who stay are all alike, because they remain customers. Unhappy customers stop, and they do so for a variety of reasons. Although perhaps not as compelling as the family tragedies in a Tolstoy novel, these different reasons are of analytic interest. Competing risks is the part of survival analysis that quantifies the effects of these different reasons.

## Examples of Competing Risks

One way to think of competing risks is to imagine a guardian angel "competing" with various devils of temptation for each customer. The guardian angel encourages the customer to remain a happy, loyal, paying customer. The various devils of temptation urge the customer to defect to a competitor, or to stop paying, or quit for some other reason. This competition goes on throughout the customer lifetime, with the guardian angel usually winning . . . but eventually a devil of temptation comes out ahead, and the customer stops.

This image of guardian angels and devils of temptation encapsulates the central notion of competing risks: at a given tenure, a customer not only has a risk of stopping, but of stopping for one of a variety of reasons. For instance, the subscription data has three types of customer unhappiness encoded in the STOP_TYPE column. So far, we have used the stop type to identify whether or not customers have stopped, lumping together all non-NULL values as stopped customers. The next three subsections explain these stop types in more detail.

> **TIP** When working with many different reasons for customers leaving, it is a good idea to classify them into a handful of different categories, say between two and five. These categories depend on the business needs.

### I=Involuntary Churn

Stop type "I" stands for "involuntary churn," which occurs when the company initiates the stop. In this dataset, involuntary churn is synonymous with customers not paying their bill. However, involuntary churn can arise in other situations. A company might close down its operations in a geographic area or sell a business unit to a competitor. These are examples of situations where customers cease being customers, but through no fault of their own.

Involuntary churn may not really be involuntary. Customers may communicate their desire to leave by not paying their bills. Once upon a time, a mobile telephone company believed that it had no involuntary churn at all; that is, the company performed credit checks and believed that all customers could pay their bills. What the company did have was poor customer service—the hold times in the call center were often measured in tens of minutes. Customers would call customer service, perhaps with a billing or coverage question, and very likely get angry over the long wait time. Instead of canceling by calling back—and waiting again—some customers simply stopped paying their bills. The data suggested this, because many customers who stopped paying had called customer service shortly before they stopped, even though they had high credit scores that indicated their ability to pay the bill.

### V=Voluntary Churn

Another form of churn is "V," which stands for "voluntary churn." This is a much more diverse array of reasons, because these are customer initiated. Customers may stop because the price is too high, or because the product does not meet expectations (such as coverage for a cell phone company), or because customer service has treated them poorly, or because they are moving, or because of a change in financial conditions, or to boycott the company's environmental policy, or because their astrologer recommended change. There are a myriad of reasons, and it is not uncommon for there to be dozens or hundreds of detailed stop codes. In the Subs table, all these reasons (and more) are grouped together into one group, "V."

Not all voluntary churn is necessarily truly voluntary. Often, customers cancel their accounts after late notices start appearing. They may stop voluntarily but they owe money. These customers were en route to involuntary churn, but took a detour by stopping on their own.

These borderline cases do not affect the applicability of competing risks. Instead, they suggest that under certain circumstances, additional data might be incorporated into the stop types. For instance, there might be a difference between customers who stop voluntarily with an outstanding balance (larger than a certain size or so many days past due) and other customers who stop voluntarily.

### M=Migration

The third type of churn in the subscription data is migration churn, indicated by "M." One example of migration churn is when a company introduces a new improved product and wants to move all customers to the new product. This occurred when companies introduced digital cell phone technologies, and moved customers from analog services.

The accounts in this dataset consist of customers on subscription accounts. These customers pay for service one month at a time as part of an ongoing service arrangement. Prepaid customers pay in advance for a block of time. The prepaid option is more appropriate for some customers, particularly those with limited financial means.

Migration from a subscription account to a prepaid account is a downgrade, because the prepay product is not as profitable as the subscription product. In other cases, migration might be an upgrade. For instance, in a credit card database, switching to a gold, platinum, titanium, or black card might close one credit card account but open another, more valuable account. In the pharmaceutical world, a patient might go from a 10 mg dose to a 40 mg dose.

From the holistic customer perspective, migration may not actually indicate a stop at all. After all, the customer remains a customer with the company. On the other hand, from the perspective of a particular product group, migrated customers no longer use that product. Whether or not migration indicates a stop is a business question whose answer varies depending on the particular analytic needs.

**TIP**  Whether or not a customer has stopped is sometimes a business question. For some analyses (more product-centric), customers who migrate to another product might be considered stopped. For other more customer-centric analyses, such customers would still be active.

### Other

Another type of churn is "expected" churn. For instance, customers may die or move outside the service area; in both cases, the cancellation is not because the customer does not want to be a customer; it is due to extraneous factors.

It would be possible to handle competing risks for all the dozens of types of churn specified by reason codes. However, it is usually better to work with a smaller number of reasons, classifying the reasons into a handful of important stop classes.

## Competing Risk "Hazard Probability"

The fundamental idea behind competing risks is that a customer who is still active has not succumbed to any of the risks. In the original imagery, this means that the guardian angel and the devils of temptation keep battling for the customer's fate. While a customer is active, the angel and the devils continue to compete for the customer.

Figure 7-12 illustrates a small group of customers. In this chart, open circles indicate that the customer is still active. The dark and light shadings indicate different ways that customers might leave. It is possible to calculate the hazard for each of the risks, by dividing the number of stops for that risk by the population at risk. Because the angel and the devils are all competing for the same customers, the population at risk is the same for all the risks. Actually, the population at risk might vary slightly for different risks, but this variation is a technical detail. For intuitive purposes, it is safe to assume that the populations are the same.

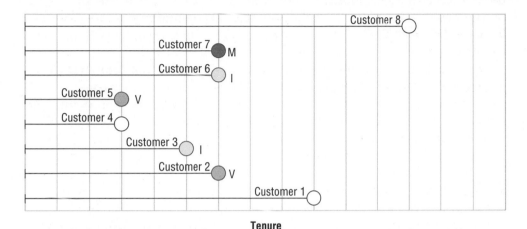

**Tenure**

**Figure 7-12:** Different customers stop for different reasons, such as voluntary and involuntary churn and migration.

The following query sets up the appropriate data in SQL:

```
SELECT tenure, COUNT(*) as pop,
       SUM(CASE WHEN stop_type = 'V' THEN 1 ELSE 0 END) as voluntary,
       SUM(CASE WHEN stop_type = 'I' THEN 1 ELSE 0 END) as involuntary,
       SUM(CASE WHEN stop_type = 'M' THEN 1 ELSE 0 END) as migration
FROM subs
WHERE start_date IS NOT NULL AND tenure >= 0 AND
      start_date >= '2004-01-01'
GROUP BY tenure
ORDER BY 1
```

This SQL simply divides the stops into three groups, the "V," the "I," and the "M" groups. Competing risk hazards are then calculated separately for each of these groups, using the same population at risk.

There is a theoretical reason for slightly tweaking the population at risk, by making a small adjustment for the customers who stop. Even though all stopped during the same discrete time interval, we can imagine that they stopped in some order. Once a customer has stopped for any reason, that customer is no longer in the population at risk for the other risks. On average, all the customers who stopped for a particular risk stopped halfway through the time interval. These customers are not at risk for stopping again. For this reason, a reasonable adjustment on the population at risk for a particular risk is to subtract half the stops of the other types of risk.

This adjustment generally has a negligible impact on the resulting hazard probabilities, because the number of stops at any given time is much smaller than the population at risk. When the number of stops and the population at risk are closer together, the adjustment is more important. However, this happens when the population at risk is small, so the confidence interval around the hazard probability is large. Incidentally, this same adjustment can be made for the overall hazard calculation.

What does the competing risk hazard mean? A good intuitive answer is that the hazard is the conditional probability of succumbing to a particular risk, given that the customer has not succumbed to any risk so far. Competing risk hazard probabilities are always smaller than or equal to the overall hazard probabilities at the same tenure. In fact, if all competing risks have been taken into account, the overall hazard probability is the sum of the competing risk hazard probabilities (or at least, very close to the sum if using the adjustment).

Is there an alternative approach? One idea might be to keep only the stops for one risk, filtering out all the others. This is a no-no. Previously, there was a warning that filtering or stratifying customers by anything that happens during or at the end of the customer relationship results in biased hazards. There is no exception for competing risks. The customers who stopped involuntarily were at risk of stopping voluntarily before their stop date. Removing them reduces the size of the population at risk, which, in turn, overestimates the hazards.

**WARNING** When using survival techniques, be sure that all stops are taken into account. Use competing risks to handle different stop reasons, rather than filtering the customers by stop reason.

## Competing Risk "Survival"

Given competing risk hazard probabilities, the next step is to calculate the competing risk survival, as shown in Figure 7-13. The survival values for one competing risk are always larger than the overall survival. For the data with large numbers of customers and relatively few stops at any given tenure, the product of all the competing risk survival values at a given tenure is a good approximation of the overall survival. This formula is not exact, but it is a good approximation.

Competing risk survival curves do not have an easy interpretation. They are conditional on a customer not stopping for other reasons. So, the "V" curve is answering the question: *What is the probability of surviving to a given tenure assuming that the customer does not stop for any reason other than "V"?* This question is rather arcane; customers do stop for other reasons.

Competing risk survival curves do not have the nice analytic properties of overall survival curves. In particular, the median value and the area under the curve do not have easily understood interpretations.

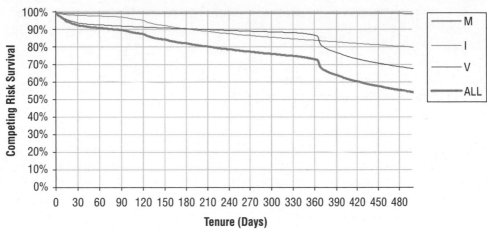

**Figure 7-13:** Competing risk survival is always larger than overall survival.

On the other hand, the curves are quite useful qualitatively. For instance, the chart shows that voluntary churn is the cause of anniversary churn. On the other hand, involuntary churn predominates at a few months after a customer starts, and becomes less significant after that. Migration is never a big cause of churn. This ability to see the importance of different cancellation types makes competing risk survival charts useful, though more qualitatively than quantitatively.

## What Happens to Customers over Time

Survival curves have a nice property. At any given tenure, the survival curve estimates the proportion of customers who are active; and hence the number who have stopped. Or, if the risk is something other than stopping, the curve tells us the proportion of customers who have succumbed to the risk and the proportion who have not. Competing risks extends this by refining the stopped population by risk type.

### Example

Figure 7-14 shows a graph of the subscribers by tenure, divided into four parts. The lowest region is the customers who are active. The next is the customers who stopped voluntarily and the next region is the customers who stopped involuntarily. At the very top is a thin line for customers who have migrated, but it is invisible because there are so few. For instance, at 730 days, 42.3% are still active, 37.1% have stopped voluntarily, 20.2% have stopped involuntarily, and 0.4% have migrated. At every point, all customers are accounted for, so the sum of the three curves is always 100%.

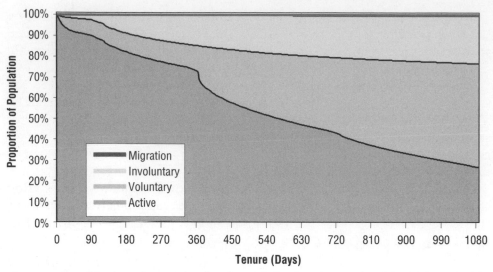

**Figure 7-14:** This chart shows what happens after subscribers start, by breaking the stops into different groups based on the stop type.

These curves show what happens *next* after customers start. The only possibilities are remaining active, or stopping, either voluntarily, involuntarily, or by migrating. However, some customers who stop may restart and become active again. Customers who migrate away may also migrate back. These curves do not take these more complex scenarios into account, because they only show the next thing that happens.

The boundary between the active customers and the voluntary customers is the overall survival curve. The other three regions are calculated from the hazards, but not in exactly the same way as the survival curves. There are two approaches for creating a "what-happens-next" chart. The first is a brute-force, cohort-based approach. The second uses survival analysis.

## A Cohort-Based Approach

One way to create a chart of what happens next is by doing a cohort-based calculation. This focuses on the outcomes of a group of customers who all start around the same time. For instance, the following SQL keeps track of the cohort of customers who start on 1 January 2004:

```
SELECT tenure, COUNT(*) as pop,
       SUM(CASE WHEN stop_type = 'V' THEN 1 ELSE 0 END) as voluntary,
       SUM(CASE WHEN stop_type = 'I' THEN 1 ELSE 0 END) as involuntary,
       SUM(CASE WHEN stop_type = 'M' THEN 1 ELSE 0 END) as migration
FROM subs
WHERE start_date = '2004-01-01'
GROUP BY tenure
ORDER BY 1
```

This query is quite similar to the previous query. The only difference is that the query restricts the population to one day of starts. The idea is to use this data to calculate the cumulative number of starts and stops for each tenure, directly from the data.

Calculating the cumulative numbers for all tenures relies on two rules. The number of active customers at a given tenure is the sum of all customers with longer tenures plus the number at that tenure who are active. For the other three groups, the rule is simply a cumulative sum. So, the number of voluntary stops is the sum of the number of voluntary stops for all tenures less than or equal to the given tenure.

Excel readily supports these calculations. Figure 7-15 shows the resulting chart, with the population of each group on a separate line. This chart is not stacked, so it is not obvious that the sum at any given tenure is the same value, the 349 customers who started on 1 January 2004.

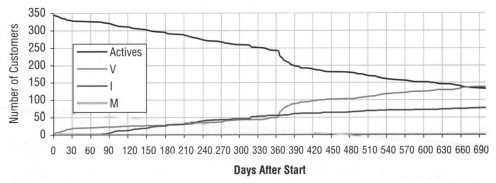

**Figure 7-15:** This chart shows what happens to customers who started on 1 Jan 2004, by showing the size of the groups that are active, voluntary stoppers, involuntary stoppers, and migrators.

The cohort approach is very useful for seeing what happens to a group of customers. With additional information, customers could be placed into different groups, such as:

- Active, with no overdue amount;
- Active, with overdue amount;
- Stopped voluntarily, no money owed;
- Stopped voluntarily, with an outstanding balance;
- Stopped involuntarily, outstanding balance written off;
- Stopped involuntarily, eventually paid outstanding balance;
- Migrated, still active on migration product;
- Migrated, stopped; and
- Migrated, but returned to subscription product.

These groups combine different types of information, such as the outstanding balance and whether a customer who migrated returned to the original product.

The cohort approach does have a downside. The wider the time period when customers start, the more difficult it is to use. The problem occurs because different groups of customers are eligible for different tenures. That is, customers who started in January 2004 can be tracked for thirty-six months. However, customers who started in January 2006 can only be tracked for twelve months; their data cannot be used for months thirteen through thirty-six.

It is possible to try to keep track of how many customers are eligible for each tenure, as well as the numbers who are in the various groups. Such attempts often result in a "big triangle" in Excel, with starts from each month being tracked for the month after the customers start. So one row in Excel is devoted to customers who start in January with separate columns describing what happens to them in February and March and April and so on. The next row then has the data for February. This gets complicated, both for generating the data and for managing it in Excel. It feels as though the cohort approach is reaching its limits. Fortunately, there is an alternative, using survival analysis and competing risks.

## The Survival Analysis Approach

This section explains how to use competing risk hazards to quantify the number of customers in each group for all tenures. The place to start is with the overall survival, which splits the customer base into the customers who are active and the customers who have stopped. There are two questions. The first is: *What proportion of customers stop at each tenure?* The second is: *Of the customers who stop at each tenure, what proportion stopped for each of the competing reasons?*

Answering the first question is easy. The proportion of customers who stop is the difference between overall survival at time $t$ and overall survival at time $t+1$. The answer to the second question is almost as easy. The solution is to divide the customers who stop proportionally among the competing risks. So, assume that 10, 20, and 70 customers stop for each of three risks at a given tenure. The proportion of customers who stop at that tenure is split into three groups, one with 10% of the stops, one with 20%, and one with 70%.

Earlier, we saw the query for calculating the competing risk hazards. Figure 7-16 shows a screen shot of the Excel spreadsheet that completes the calculation. This calculation determines the proportion of customers who stop at the tenure, by taking the survival at that tenure and subtracting the survival at the next tenure. The difference is then divided proportionately among the competing risks; their cumulative sum is the proportion of customers who have succumbed to a particular risk at a particular tenure.

This method of calculation has an advantage over the cohort approach, because it readily combines data from many start dates. It can also be extended to define additional groups, by introducing more competing risks. For instance, the risk for voluntary churn could be split into two risks, one where the outstanding balance is zero and the other where the customer owes money.

| | C | D | E | F | G | H | I | J | K | L | M | |
|---|---|---|---|---|---|---|---|---|---|---|---|---|
| 13 | tenu | pop | V | I | M | | pop | h | Active | Stops | Voluntary | Involu |
| 14 | 0 | 2383 | 77 | 1 | 430 | | =I15+D14 | =SUM(E14:G14)/I14 | 1 | =K14-K15 | 0 | 0 |
| 15 | 1 | 18354 | 14979 | 1888 | 439 | | =I16+D15 | =SUM(E15:G15)/I15 | =K14*(1-J14) | =K15-K16 | =M14+$L14*(E14/SUM($E14:$G14)) | =N14 |
| 16 | 2 | 16730 | 11130 | 3760 | 201 | | =I17+D16 | =SUM(E16:G16)/I16 | =K15*(1-J15) | =K16-K17 | =M15+$L15*(E15/SUM($E15:$G15)) | =N15 |
| 17 | 3 | 13283 | 8922 | 2255 | 169 | | =I18+D17 | =SUM(E17:G17)/I17 | =K16*(1-J16) | =K17-K18 | =M16+$L16*(E16/SUM($E16:$G16)) | =N16 |
| 18 | 4 | 9544 | 7404 | 1978 | 118 | | =I19+D18 | =SUM(E18:G18)/I18 | =K17*(1-J17) | =K18-K19 | =M17+$L17*(E17/SUM($E17:$G17)) | =N17 |
| 19 | 5 | 11746 | 6985 | 2047 | 120 | | =I20+D19 | =SUM(E19:G19)/I19 | =K18*(1-J18) | =K19-K20 | =M18+$L18*(E18/SUM($E18:$G18)) | =N18 |
| 20 | 6 | 12649 | 7249 | 2067 | 93 | | =I21+D20 | =SUM(E20:G20)/I20 | =K19*(1-J19) | =K20-K21 | =M19+$L19*(E19/SUM($E19:$G19)) | =N19 |
| 21 | 7 | 13466 | 8135 | 2091 | 72 | | =I22+D21 | =SUM(E21:G21)/I21 | =K20*(1-J20) | =K21-K22 | =M20+$L20*(E20/SUM($E20:$G20)) | =N20 |
| 22 | 8 | 11862 | 7471 | 2027 | 62 | | =I23+D22 | =SUM(E22:G22)/I22 | =K21*(1-J21) | =K22-K23 | =M21+$L21*(E21/SUM($E21:$G21)) | =N21 |
| 23 | 9 | 12265 | 7464 | 1905 | 80 | | =I24+D23 | =SUM(E23:G23)/I23 | =K22*(1-J22) | =K23-K24 | =M22+$L22*(E22/SUM($E22:$G22)) | =N22 |
| 24 | 10 | 12017 | 7637 | 1787 | 53 | | =I25+D24 | =SUM(E24:G24)/I24 | =K23*(1-J23) | =K24-K25 | =M23+$L23*(E23/SUM($E23:$G23)) | =N23 |
| 25 | 11 | 11104 | 7240 | 1755 | 46 | | =I26+D25 | =SUM(E25:G25)/I25 | =K24*(1-J24) | =K25-K26 | =M24+$L24*(E24/SUM($E24:$G24)) | =N24 |
| 26 | 12 | 10441 | 6707 | 1537 | 42 | | =I27+D26 | =SUM(E26:G26)/I26 | =K25*(1-J25) | =K26-K27 | =M25+$L25*(E25/SUM($E25:$G25)) | =N25 |

**Figure 7-16:** In Excel, it is possible to calculate what happens next using competing risk survival.

Competing risks makes it possible to understand what happens to customers over time. However, there is an interesting paradox involving competing risk hazard probabilities and survival values, discussed in the aside "A Competing Risks Conundrum."

## A COMPETING RISKS CONUNDRUM

Competing risks survival suggests two approximations that seem intuitive (or at least very reasonable). The first is that the product of the competing risk survival values equals the overall survival. The second approximation is that the sum of the competing risk hazard probabilities at a particular tenure equals the overall hazard probability.

Fortunately, these approximations are very good for customer data. In particular, both these statements are very close to being true when there are a large number of overall customers and few stops at each tenure. In extreme cases, though, the discrepancies are blatant and it is worth explaining this to help better understand competing risks in general.

The first approximation about the survival runs into a problem when all customers stop. Take the case where there are three customers at risk at a given tenure and all three stop, for three different reasons. The overall hazard is 100%, and the hazard probabilities for each competing risk are 33.3%. The survival at the next time period is 0%. However, the survival for each competing risk is 66.7%, so the product is 29.6%, quite different from 0%. A bit of reflection suggests that almost no matter how we handle the competing risk hazard probabilities, they are always going to be equal and less than 100%. The product of the resulting survival is never going to be 0%.

This problem arises because there is a singularity in the survival probabilities. The survival drops to zero when all customers stop. Fortunately, when working with large numbers of customers, this does not happen.

*Continued on next page*

**A COMPETING RISKS CONUNDRUM (CONTINUED)**

What about the sum of the competing risk hazards being the overall hazard? In this case, the explanation is a bit different. Imagine the same situation as before, with three customers each of who stops for a different reason. What is the "real" competing risk hazard when we look at this under a microscope? What would happen to the hazard probabilities if we assumed that the stops do not occur at exactly the same time, but in some sequence?

Well, the first customer who stops, say for competing risk A, has a hazard of 1/3, about 33.3%. An instant later, when the second customer stops for competing risk B, the population at risk now has only two members, B and C (because the first customer has stopped). So, the competing risk hazard is 1/2 or 50%. And for the third one, the hazard comes to 1/1 or 100%. These look quite different from the hazards as calculated over the whole population.

The problem is, we don't know the exact order that the customers stopped in. It could be A then B then C, or B then C then A, or A then C then B, and so on. One solution is to guesstimate the average by taking the average hazard probability for the three cases. This comes to 11/18 (61.1%).

An alternative approach is to say that for any given risk, the population at risk needs to be reduced by half the customers who stop for other reasons. That is, the customers who stop for reasons B and C cannot stop for reason A. And, on average, those customers stop for reasons B and C halfway through the time period. This yields a hazard probability of 50% for each of the risks.

All of this discussion is academic, because the number of customers who stop is much, much smaller than the population at risk for problems involving customers. Each competing risk hazard estimate can be made a bit more accurate when reducing the population at risk by half the number of customers who stop for other risks. In practice, though, this adjustment has a very small effect on the hazards. And, this effect is much less than the effect of other biases, such as left truncation.

# Before and After

The first topic in this chapter explained how to understand factors that are known about customers when they start, using stratification and hazard ratios. The previous section explained how to understand factors that occur at the end of the customer relationship, by using competing risks. The final topic in this chapter is about events that happen during customers' life cycles, technically known as *time-varying covariates*. In particular, this section talks about survival measures before and after an event occurs during the customer lifetime.

Understanding time-varying covariates starts to push the limits of what can be accomplished with SQL and Excel; statistical methods such as Cox proportional hazard regression continue the analysis beyond what we can accomplish. However, there are still interesting analyses that are possible.

This section discusses three techniques for understanding these types of factors. The first is to compare forecasts. The second is a brute-force approach using cohorts. And the third is to directly calculate survival curves for before the event and after the event. Before explaining the techniques, the section starts with three scenarios that illustrate these types of problems.

## Three Scenarios

This section discusses three business problems that involve time-varying events. These are only intended as examples. The scenarios are intended to show the challenges in approaching these problems.

### *A Billing Mistake*

Oops! An insurance company makes a little billing boo-boo. During one bill cycle, some long-standing customers who paid their premiums are accidentally sent dunning notices, accusing them of not paying their bill; worse, the notices continue even after the customers complain. Of course, this might anger a few customers, and angry customers are more likely to cancel their policies. *What is the cost of this mistake, in terms of lost customer revenue?*

Figure 7-17 shows this situation on both the calendar time line and the tenure time line. The "X"s indicate when the billing mistake occurred. It affects everyone at the same time on the calendar time line; however, this is at a different tenure for each customer on the tenure time line. From a business perspective, we expect the effect of such a one-time billing mistake to pass quickly. During the period when the error occurs, stops spike up and hazards go up. However, this effect should pass quickly, as the company recovers from the mistake. It is possible, of course, to test this assumption, by comparing hazards before and after the event using time windows to see if there are any long-term effects.

### *A Loyalty Program*

Not all events are negative. Consider customers in a subscription-based business who enroll in a loyalty program. *How can the company measure the effectiveness of the loyalty program in terms of increased customer tenure?*

In this case, customers enroll in the program at different points on both the calendar and tenure time lines. Of course, some enrollment tenures may be more common than others; this would be the case if customers were only eligible for their program after their first year, resulting in an enrollment spike at one year. Similarly, some calendar times may be more common than other times, particularly when there are marketing campaigns encouraging customers to enroll in the program. It is worth pointing out that with a loyalty program, we know everyone who is enrolled, which may not be the case for customers who stop due to a billing error.

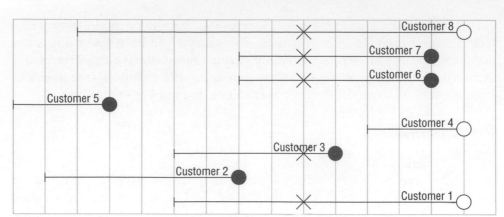

**Calendar Time**

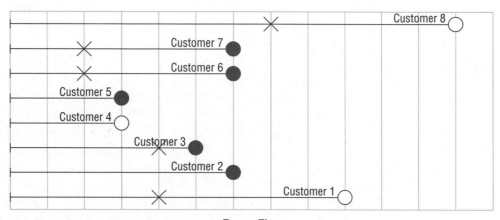

**Tenure Time**

**Figure 7-17:** These two diagrams show the effect of a billing mistake on the calendar time line and on the tenure time line.

When customers enroll during their lifetimes is interesting. In fact, the time of enrollment is another problem amenable to survival analysis. Perhaps more interesting is translating enrollment into increased tenure, and increased tenure into dollars and cents. Measuring an increase in tenure for the customers in the loyalty program does not illustrate that the program is causing the increase. An alternative explanation is that better customers join the program in the first place. This is an example of the difference between causation and correlation. Increased tenure is a correlation, but it does not imply that the program caused the increase.

**WARNING** Historical data can show correlation between different events. However, we have to reach outside mere data analysis to justify causation, either through formal testing or by suggesting how one thing causes the other.

Unlike the billing error, though, we expect the loyalty program to continue having an effect even after customers are enrolled. There is not some short period where the event (enrollment) affects customers' survival; there is a point in each customer's tenure where the customer changes state from unenrolled to enrolled, and we expect the enrolled customers to have better survival.

### Raising Prices

The third scenario is a price increase on a subscription product. An increase in prices can have two effects. Existing customers might leave in response to the price increase. This would occur around the period when the increase goes into effect. The second is that new customers may leave at a faster rate. Some of the customers who stop are identified; presumably, they complained about the price increase when they stopped. However, not all such customers give price as the reason. A customer might say "customer service is awful," when the customer really means "for the price I'm paying, customer service is awful." There is typically only one stop reason recorded, although customers may be unhappy for more than one reason.

Measuring the impact of the price increase requires looking at survival both when the event occurs and after the event occurs. There are several interesting questions:

- Who likely stopped during the period of the price increase and what impact did this have? This is a question about excess stops during a particular period.

- Did existing customers who survived the initial shake-out period have a degradation in survival after the price increase?

- Did new customers who started after the increase have a degradation in survival?

These questions are all related to the financial impact of the price increase on existing customers. Of course, the customers who stay are paying more money, so that often offsets the loss in customers who leave.

The remainder of this section discusses different ways of quantifying the effects of events during customer lifetimes, starting with an approach based on forecasting.

## Using Survival Forecasts

Forecasts, which were introduced in the previous chapter, are a powerful tool for measuring the impact of events on customers. Remember that a forecast takes a base of customers and applies a set of hazards to them, producing an estimate of the number of customers on any day in the future. Forecasts based on existing customers show declines over time, because new customers are not included. By adding up the forecast values over a period of time, the forecast turns into customer-days, which in turn can be turned into a financial value, based on the monetary value that a customer contributes on each day. There are two basic approaches for using forecasts to understand the effect of an event. The two differ, depending on whether the specific customers who stop can be identified.

### Forecasting Identified Customers Who Stopped

When the customers who stop are known, forecasting can be applied just to these customers. This is the most direct method of using survival forecasting to measure the impact of an event. The method is to apply the forecast hazards only to the subset of customers identified as leaving due to the event. The result of the forecast is the number of customer-days we would have expected from those customers but lost because they stopped prematurely. The difference between these expected days and the actual days observed is the lost customer-days, which can in turn be used to calculate a financial loss. For this to work, the stopped customers need to be clearly identified. Another challenge is getting the right set of hazards.

A good set of hazards would be based on stops from some period before the event occurred, such as the month or year before the event, using a stop time window to calculate unbiased hazards. This has the advantage of a clean set of comparison data.

Another approach for estimating the hazards is to use competing risks. Remove the customers who stopped for the particular reason, and calculate the hazards using the remaining customers and remaining stops. The previous section warned against using competing risks this way, because it underestimates the hazards. However, when the group of customers who leave is small relative to all stops, the error may be small enough to be ignored.

### Estimating Excess Stops

In some cases, the customers who leave for a specific reason are not clearly identified. In the case of the loyalty program, all the customers in the program are identified, but the customers of interest are those who do not even stop. In this case, the approach is to estimate an excess (or deficiency) of stops indirectly rather than directly.

The approach here is the difference between two forecasts. One is the forecast of what would have happened if the event had not occurred and the other is the forecast of what actually did happen. Because the customer base is the same — consisting of the customers who are active just when the event happens — the difference between the two forecasts is in the hazard probabilities.

The hazard probabilities for what actually did happen are easy to calculate using a time window of stops after the event. Similarly, the hazard probabilities ignoring the event can be calculated by taking a time period from before the event. The difference between the two is the lost customer-days.

The problem is slightly more complicated when the event occurs relative to the customer lifetime, such as joining a loyalty program that takes place at a different tenure for each customer. In this case, there is no overall "before" date. Instead, customers are right censored on the date that they join the program, if ever. Prior to joining the loyalty program, customers contribute to both the population at risk and the stops. Once they join, they no longer contribute to either one.

## Before and After Comparison

The before and after calculation of hazards is quite simple, using the time window technique for estimating hazards. These hazards are used to generate survival curves, and the area between the survival curves quantifies the effect in customer-days.

Because the effect starts at tenure zero, this is most readily applied to new customers. Figure 7-18 illustrates an example. Remember that the area between the curves is easy to calculate; it is simply the sum of the differences in the survival values during a particular period of time.

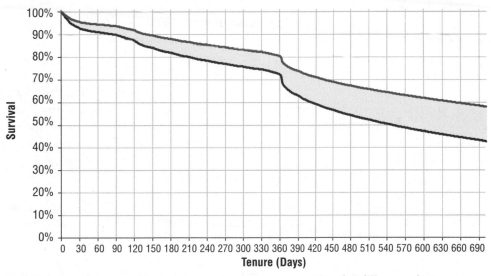

**Figure 7-18:** The area between two survival curves quantifies the difference between them in customer-days.

## Cohort-Based Approach

There is a cohort-based approach to calculating the remaining customer tenure after an event. It is appropriate when the event does not affect all customers at the same time, such as enrollment in a loyalty program. This approach is very computationally intensive. This section describes how to do the calculation, even though the calculation may not be feasible on even largish sets of data.

Figure 7-19 shows the basic idea behind the approach. This chart shows a customer who has an event that occurs at some point in the customer's lifetime. Also shown are a group of other customers who are candidates for this customer's cohort. To be in the cohort, the candidate customers must meet the following conditions:

- The cohort customers start at about the same time as the customer;
- The cohort customers have similar initial start characteristics to the customer;
- The cohort customers are active at the tenure when the event occurred to the customer; and,
- The cohort customers do not experience the event.

The cohort is a comparison group that can be used to understand survival after the event. The same customer can appear in multiple cohorts, so long as the customer meets the criteria for each one.

First, the survival for all customers who have the event is calculated after the event date. That is, the event date becomes time zero. Then, the survival of each cohort is calculated, after the event date that defines the cohort. These survivals are combined into a single survival curve, and compared to the survival of customers who experience the event.

For the customers that succumb to the event, it is easy to calculate the survival after the event assuming there is a column named something like EVENT_DATE. Although such a column is not available in the subscription data, the following examples will assume that it is. The survival after the event is the survival calculation, where the start date is fast-forwarded to the event date, and the tenure is measured only after the event:

```
SELECT tenure_after_event, COUNT(*) as pop, SUM(isstop) as stopped
FROM (SELECT DATEDIFF(dd, start_date, event_date) as tenure_after_event,
             (CASE WHEN stop_type IS NOT NULL THEN 1 ELSE 0 END) as isstop
      FROM subs
      WHERE event_date IS NOT NULL) s
GROUP BY tenure_after_event
ORDER BY 1
```

This generates the data needed to calculate the survival after the event for the group of customers who succumb to the event. The challenge is to get the survival for a cohort of customers, similar to the original customer. For any given customer, the cohort survival could be defined by:

```
SELECT cohort.tenure - tenure_at_event,
       COUNT(*) as pop,
       SUM(CASE WHEN cohort.stop_type IS NOT NULL THEN 1 ELSE 0
           END) as isstop
FROM (SELECT s.*,
             DATEDIFF(dd, start_date, event_date) as tenure_at_event
      FROM subs
      WHERE customer_id = <event cust id>) ev JOIN
     (SELECT *
      FROM subs
      WHERE event_date IS NULL) cohort
     ON cohort.start_date = ev.start_date AND
        cohort.market = ev.market AND
        cohort.channel = ev.channel AND
        cohort.tenure >= ev.tenure_at_event
GROUP BY tenure_after_event
ORDER BY 1
```

In this case, the cohort is defined as customers who started on the same date, in the same market, and did not have the event. The actual survival values can then be calculated in Excel.

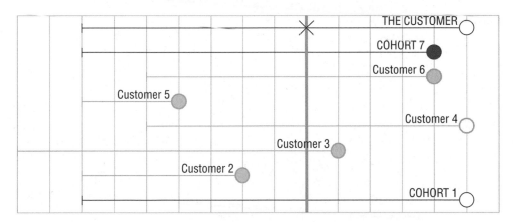

**Calendar Time**

**Figure 7-19:** A customer has a cohort defined by initial characteristics and when the event occurred. In this chart, THE CUSTOMER experiences an event at some time. Customers 1 and 7 are in the cohort, because they started at the same time and survived to the event time. The other customers fail one or both of these conditions.

The challenge is doing this for all cohorts and averaging the curves. It is tempting to modify the preceding query so the first subquery looks like:

```
FROM (SELECT s.*,
             DATEDIFF(dd, start_date, event_date) as tenure_at_event
      FROM subs
      WHERE event_date IS NOT NULL) s
```

However, this is not correct, because it combines all members of all cohorts into one big pool of customers, and then calculates the survival of the pool. The problem is that cohorts have different sizes, and the larger cohorts would dominate this calculation. We want one customer's cohort to have a weight of one, regardless of the size of the cohort.

The solution is to determine the size of the cohort in order to weight everything appropriately. Once the weight is determined, the counts POP and ISSTOP are just multiplied by the weight. The following query includes the weight:

```
SELECT cohort.tenure - ev.tenure_at_event,
       SUM(weight) as pop,
       SUM(CASE WHEN cohort.stop_type IS NOT NULL THEN weight ELSE 0 END
           ) as isstop
FROM (SELECT ev.customer_id, tenure_at_event,
             COUNT(*) as cohort_size, 1.0/COUNT(*) as weight
      FROM (SELECT s.*,
                   DATEDIFF(dd, start_date, event_date) as tenure_at_event
            FROM subs s
            WHERE event_date IS NOT NULL) ev JOIN
           (SELECT s.*
            FROM subs s
            WHERE event_date IS NULL) cohort
           ON cohort.start_date = ev.start_date AND
              cohort.market = ev.market AND
              cohort.channel = ev.channel AND
              cohort.tenure >= ev.tenure_at_event
      GROUP BY ev.customer_id, ev.tenure_at_event
     ) ev JOIN
     (SELECT s.*
      FROM subs s
      WHERE event_date IS NULL) cohort
     ON cohort.start_date = ev.start_date AND
        cohort.market = ev.market AND
        cohort.channel = ev.channel AND
        cohort.tenure >= ev.tenure_at_event
GROUP BY tenure_after_event
ORDER BY 1
```

These weighted estimates can then be brought into Excel and used the same way as unweighted counts. The only difference is that the population counts and stop counts are now decimal numbers rather than integers.

This approach is possible, but perhaps not feasible. This query can be very slow, because it is a non-equijoin on a large table. Although the join looks like an equijoin, it isn't because the join keys are not unique in the table. There are some alternatives to making this run faster. If the size of the group that experiences the event is rather small, the calculation could be done in Excel. Of course, if this is true, the SQL might be slow, but it will finish. Another alternative is to calculate the size of the cohort using SQL window functions, which are explained in Chapter 8.

However, it is possible to estimate the effect of a time-varying covariate without resorting to cohorts or to sophisticated statistical software. The next section explains how to calculate separate survival curves for before and after the event.

## Direct Estimation of Event Effect

This section explains stratifying survival based on whether or not a time-varying event has occurred. This method generates two separate survival curves; one for survival without the event and the other for survival with the event. These curves can be used to qualitatively describe what happens to customers before and after the event; or they can be used to quantitatively measure the difference between the two groups.

### Approach to the Calculation

To illustrate this, let's assume that something happens on June 1, 2005, such as a price increase. This is an arbitrary date that is being used just as an example; the technique works even when there is a different date for each customer. Customers who start before this date are in the "before" group until they reach June 1, 2005. Customers who start after this date are in the "after" group for their entire tenure. *What are the survival values for the "before" and "after" groups?*

The key to answering this question is determining how to calculate unbiased hazards for customers in the before and after groups. The stops for each group are easy, because we know whether customers stopped before or after the event date. The challenge is calculating the population at risk, because customers switch from one group to another. Other than the details on calculating the population at risk, the survival calculation follows the same methodology as in other examples.

Customers who start and stop before the event date are only in the "before" population at risk. Other customers who start before the event remain in the "before" population at risk until the event date. For larger tenures, they contribute to the "after" population at risk. And customers who start after the event date only contribute to the "after" population at risk.

The population at risk for the "after" group has two parts. One group consists of customers who start on or after the event date. They enter the population at risk from tenure zero; they leave the population at risk when they are censored or stop. The number of such customers at a given tenure is simply the population of such customers whose tenure is greater than or equal to the given tenure.

The second group consists of the customers who start before the event date and then remain active on the event date. This group starts being at risk in the "after" group on their tenure as of the event date and they remain at risk until they stop or are censored. The size of this group is determined by the following rules:

- The population at risk at tenure $t$ is the population at risk at tenure $t-1$,

- Plus the customers who started before the event date who passed the event date at tenure $t$,

- Minus the customers who started before the event date, who passed the event date, and who stopped or were censored at tenure $t$.

The population at risk here is calculated using a forward summation, rather than a backward summation.

### Time-Varying Covariate Survival Using SQL and Excel

To answer this question in SQL requires the following variables:

- Before Pop at Each Tenure: Count of all customers by the tenure of customers who started before the event date as of the event date.

- Before Stops at Each Tenure: Count of stopped customers who started and stopped before the event date.

- After Starts at Each Tenure: Count of all customers who start after the event date by tenure.

- After Stops at Each Tenure: Count of stopped customers who start and stop after the event date by tenure.

- Before Enters at Each Tenure: Count of customers who start before the event date by their tenure at the event date.

- Before Leaves at Each Tenure: Count of customers who start before the event date by their tenure when they stop or are censored.

- Before/After Stop at Each Tenure: Count of stopped customers who start before the event date and stop after the event date, by tenure.

The first two of these variables are used to calculate the population at risk and stops for customers who start before the event date. The next two do the same calculation for customers who start after the event date. The final three are for the population at risk and stops for customers who experience the event date. These three groups can be treated as three different groups for comparison purposes, which is useful for questions such as: *Did experiencing the billing error affect survival?* Or, the last two groups can be combined into one group, for questions such as: *What impact did the price increase have on survival?*

The following SQL uses two subqueries to answer these questions. The first subquery is for customers who started before the event date; it groups everything by the tenure as of the event date. The second subquery is for what happens after the event date; it aggregates by the full tenure:

```
SELECT tenure, SUM(bef) as bef, SUM(aft) as aft,
       SUM(stop_before) as stop_before, SUM(to_after) as to_after,
       SUM(stop_after) as stop_aft, SUM(before_stop_after) as bef_stop_aft
FROM ((SELECT (CASE WHEN stop_date < '2005-06-01' AND
                         stop_date IS NOT NULL THEN tenure
                    ELSE DATEDIFF(dd, start_date, '2005-06-01') END
              ) as tenure,
              1 as bef, 0 as aft,
              (CASE WHEN stop_date < '2005-06-01' AND
                         stop_date IS NOT NULL THEN 1 ELSE 0 END
              ) as stop_before,
              (CASE WHEN stop_date >= '2005-06-01' OR
                         stop_date IS NULL THEN 1 ELSE 0 END) as to_after,
              0 as stop_after, 0 as before_stop_after
       FROM subs s
       WHERE (start_date >= '2004-01-01') AND (tenure >= 0) AND
             start_date < '2005-06-01')
      UNION ALL
      (SELECT tenure, 0 as bef,
              (CASE WHEN start_date >= '2005-06-01' THEN 1 ELSE 0 END
              ) as aft,
              0 as stop_before, 0 as to_after,
              (CASE WHEN stop_date IS NOT NULL THEN 1 ELSE 0 END
              ) as stop_after,
              (CASE WHEN start_date < '2005-06-01' THEN 1 ELSE 0 END
              ) as before_stop_after
       FROM subs s
       WHERE (start_date >= '2004-01-01') AND (tenure >= 0) AND
             (stop_date IS NULL OR stop_date >= '2005-06-01') )
     ) a
GROUP BY tenure
ORDER BY 1
```

Figure 7-20 shows a screen shot of the Excel spreadsheet that implements the calculations. This figure shows the population at risk calculations for each of the three groups. Calculating the hazards is just a matter of dividing the population at risk by the appropriate stops; the survival is then calculated from the hazards.

This approach to handling an event date combines two ideas already discussed. The survival for the "before" group uses forced censoring, which was introduced in the previous chapter for historical snapshots of hazards. The censor date is the event date, and only stops before the event date are counted.

| | | FROM SQL | | | | | | | | | | CALCULATED IN EXCE | |
|---|---|---|---|---|---|---|---|---|---|---|---|---|---|
| | C | D | E | F | G | H | I | J | K | L | M | N | O |
| 21 | | FROM SQL | | | | | | | | | | | CALCULATED IN EXCE |
| 22 | tenure | bef | aft | stop_b | stop_a | to_aft | befstop | | Before Cum | After Cum | ToAfterCum | After Pop | h-before | h-afte |
| 23 | 0 | 292 | 2091 | 292 | 216 | 0 | 0 | | =K24+D23 | =L24+E23 | =IF($C23=0, 0, M22)+H23-I23 | =M23+L23 | =IF(K23=0,NA(),F23/K23) | =IF(N |
| 24 | 1 | 10016 | 10783 | 7559 | 9747 | 2457 | 12 | | =K25+D24 | =L25+E24 | =IF($C24=0, 0, M23)+H24-I24 | =M24+L24 | =IF(K24=0,NA(),F24/K24) | =IF(N |
| 25 | 2 | 9677 | 10830 | 5878 | 9213 | 3799 | 22 | | =K26+D25 | =L26+E25 | =IF($C25=0, 0, M24)+H25-I25 | =M25+L25 | =IF(K25=0,NA(),F25/K25) | =IF(N |
| 26 | 3 | 8461 | 8138 | 5113 | 6233 | 3348 | 32 | | =K27+D26 | =L27+E26 | =IF($C26=0, 0, M25)+H26-I26 | =M26+L26 | =IF(K26=0,NA(),F26/K26) | =IF(N |
| 27 | 4 | 7834 | 5143 | 4340 | 5160 | 3494 | 61 | | =K28+D27 | =L28+E27 | =IF($C27=0, 0, M26)+H27-I27 | =M27+L27 | =IF(K27=0,NA(),F27/K27) | =IF(N |
| 28 | 5 | 8010 | 7252 | 4387 | 4765 | 3623 | 107 | | =K29+D28 | =L29+E28 | =IF($C28=0, 0, M27)+H28-I28 | =M28+L28 | =IF(K28=0,NA(),F28/K28) | =IF(N |
| 29 | 6 | 7180 | 7717 | 4837 | 4572 | 2343 | 95 | | =K30+D29 | =L30+E29 | =IF($C29=0, 0, M28)+H29-I29 | =M29+L29 | =IF(K29=0,NA(),F29/K29) | =IF(N |
| 30 | 7 | 7352 | 7896 | 5486 | 4812 | 1866 | 84 | | =K31+D30 | =L31+E30 | =IF($C30=0, 0, M29)+H30-I30 | =M30+L30 | =IF(K30=0,NA(),F30/K30) | =IF(N |
| 31 | 8 | 7777 | 6620 | 5175 | 4385 | 2602 | 67 | | =K32+D31 | =L32+E31 | =IF($C31=0, 0, M30)+H31-I31 | =M31+L31 | =IF(K31=0,NA(),F31/K31) | =IF(N |
| 32 | 9 | 8370 | 6934 | 5228 | 4221 | 3142 | 103 | | =K33+D32 | =L33+E32 | =IF($C32=0, 0, M31)+H32-I32 | =M32+L32 | =IF(K32=0,NA(),F32/K32) | =IF(N |
| 33 | 10 | 8509 | 6816 | 5082 | 4395 | 3427 | 119 | | =K34+D33 | =L34+E33 | =IF($C33=0, 0, M32)+H33-I33 | =M33+L33 | =IF(K33=0,NA(),F33/K33) | =IF(N |
| 34 | 11 | 8113 | 6220 | 4767 | 4274 | 3346 | 117 | | =K35+D34 | =L35+E34 | =IF($C34=0, 0, M33)+H34-I34 | =M34+L34 | =IF(K34=0,NA(),F34/K34) | =IF(N |
| 35 | 12 | 7793 | 5878 | 4438 | 3848 | 3355 | 125 | | =K36+D35 | =L36+E35 | =IF($C35=0, 0, M34)+H35-I35 | =M35+L35 | =IF(K35=0,NA(),F35/K35) | =IF(N |
| 36 | 13 | 7670 | 6280 | 4272 | 4147 | 3398 | 151 | | =K37+D36 | =L37+E36 | =IF($C36=0, 0, M35)+H36-I36 | =M36+L36 | =IF(K36=0,NA(),F36/K36) | =IF(N |
| 37 | 14 | 6819 | 6227 | 4643 | 4244 | 2176 | 167 | | =K38+D37 | =L38+E37 | =IF($C37=0, 0, M36)+H37-I37 | =M37+L37 | =IF(K37=0,NA(),F37/K37) | =IF(N |
| 38 | 15 | 6030 | 4518 | 3430 | 3184 | 2600 | 114 | | =K39+D38 | =L39+E38 | =IF($C38=0, 0, M37)+H38-I38 | =M38+L38 | =IF(K38=0,NA(),F38/K38) | =IF(N |

**Figure 7-20:** This spreadsheet calculates the survival curves based on whether an event occurred or did not occur during the customer lifetime.

The "after" group (combining both the customers who start before and survive to the event date and those who start after) uses time windows to define the values. In this case, the event date becomes the left truncation date for the group.

This example uses a single calendar date as the event date. This is by no means a requirement. Instead of a constant date, the data could be defined on a customer-by-customer basis, requiring only minor modifications to the queries.

## Lessons Learned

The previous chapter introduced survival analysis and how to calculate hazard probabilities and survival probabilities using SQL and Excel. This chapter extends these ideas, showing ways to calculate survival in other situations and to determine which factors influence survival.

The chapter starts by showing how to understand the effects of initial value variables on survival. These effects might change over time, even though the variables remain constant during each customer's lifetime. Hazard ratios capture the changes over time for categorical variables, by taking the ratio of the hazards for different values. For numeric variables, the right measure is the average of a numeric variable at different points in the survival curve for active and stopped customers.

One of the biggest challenges in using survival analysis is calculating unbiased hazard estimates. This is particularly challenging when the data is left truncated — that is, when customers who stopped before some date are not included in the database. The solution to left truncation is the use of time windows. However, time windows are more versatile than just the solution to left truncation. They make it possible to calculate unbiased hazard probabilities based on stops during a particular period of time.

The chapter continues by looking at what happens at the end of the customer lifetime using competing risks. The survival analysis discussion assumes that all customers who leave are equal. However, the way that customers leave can also be quite important. This section calculates what happens to customers at a given point in time, by showing how many customers are still active, and how many have left due to voluntary churn, involuntary churn, and migration.

The chapter's final topic is estimating the hazards when an event occurs during the customer life cycle. The method for doing this combines forced right censoring (discussed in the previous chapter) with time windows.

The next chapter moves to a related topic, the subject of recurrent events. Unlike survival analysis so far, though, recurrent events happen more than once, a twist that we haven't yet considered.

# Customer Purchases and Other Repeated Events

Subscription-type customer relationships have well-defined starts and stops. This chapter moves from these types of relationships to those defined by multiple events that take place over time, such as purchases and web site visits, donations and clicks. Such relationships do not necessarily have a definite end because any particular event could be the customer's last, or it could be just another in a long chain of events.

The biggest challenge with repeated events is correctly assigning events to the same customer. Sometimes we are lucky and customers identify themselves using an account. Even in this case, identification can be challenging or confusing. Consider the example of Amazon.com and a family account. The purchase behavior — and resulting recommendations — might combine a teenage daughter's music preferences with her mother's technical purchases with a pre-teen son's choice of games.

Disambiguating customers within one account is a challenge; identifying the same customer over time is another. When there is no associated account, fancy algorithms match customers to transactions using name matching and address matching (and sometimes other information). This chapter looks at how SQL can help facilitate building and evaluating such techniques.

Sometimes, the events occur so frequently that they actually represent subscription-like behaviors. For instance, prescription data consists of drug purchases. Tracking patients who are taking a particular drug requires combining the purchases over time into one patient view. Web sites, such as

Yahoo! and eBay, have a similar conundrum. Users typically visit often; however, they do not signal the end of their relationship by politely closing their accounts. They stop visiting, emailing, bidding, or offering. At the other extreme are rare events. Automobile manufacturers trying to understand long-term customer relationships must deal with purchase intervals that stretch into multiple years.

This chapter focuses on retail purchase patterns that are in-between — not too frequent and not too rare. In addition to being a common example of repeated events, these purchases provide a good foundation for understanding the opportunities with such data. Because of this focus on retail data, the examples in this chapter use the purchases dataset exclusively.

The traditional method for understanding retail purchasing behaviors over time uses a technique which is called RFM analysis, which is explained later in this chaper. This is a good background for understanding customers and some of their behaviors over time. Unfortunately, RFM focuses on three specific dimensions of the customer relationship, leaving out many others.

Customer behaviors change over time, and tracking and measuring these changes is important. There are several approaches, such as comparing the most recent behavior to the earliest behaviors and fitting a trend line to each customer's interactions. Survival analysis is yet another alternative for addressing the question: how long until the next interaction? The answer in turn depends on the particular customer and what has happened in the past. If too much time has elapsed, perhaps it is time to start worrying about how to get the customer back. The place to begin, however, is the identification of customers on different transactions.

# Identifying Customers

Identifying different transactions as belonging to the same customer is challenging, both for retail customers (individuals and households) and for business customers. Even when customers have an ongoing relationship, such as a loyalty card, there is the question of whether they always use their identification number. This section discusses the definition of customer and how it is represented in the data. The next section looks at other types of data, such as addresses, that are not in this database.

## Who Is the Customer?

The transactions in the purchases dataset are the orders. The database has several ways to tie transactions together over time. Each contains an

ORDERID, which leads to a CUSTOMERID, and a HOUSEHOLDID. The following query provides the counts of orders, customers, and households:

```
SELECT COUNT(*) as numorders, COUNT(DISTINCT c.customerid) as numcusts,
       COUNT(DISTINCT householdid) as numhh
FROM orders o LEFT OUTER JOIN customer c ON o.customerid = c.customerid
```

This query shows that the data contains 192,983 orders for 189,559 customers comprising 156,258 households. So, there are about 1.02 orders per customer and about 1.2 customers per household. This data has some examples of repeating customers, but not very many.

There is a slightly different way to answer the same question, by directly counting the number of households, customers, and orders in subqueries:

```
SELECT numorders, numcusts, numhh
FROM (SELECT COUNT(*) as numorders FROM orders) o CROSS JOIN
     (SELECT COUNT(*) as numcusts, COUNT(DISTINCT householdid) as numhh
      FROM customer) c
```

Note that this query uses the CROSS JOIN operator, which creates all combinations of rows from two tables (or subqueries). The CROSS JOIN is sometimes useful when working with very small tables, such as the two one-row subqueries in this example.

The two approaches could yield different results. The first counts CUSTOMERIDs and HOUSEHOLDIDs that have orders. The second counts all of the ones that are in the database, even those that have no orders.

> **TIP** Even a seemingly simple question such as "how many customers are there" can have different answers depending on specifics: "how many customers have placed an order" and "how many households are in the database" may have very different answers.

The purchases data already has the customer and household columns assigned. The database intentionally does not contain identifying information (such as last name, address, telephone number, or email address), but it does contain gender and first name.

## How Many?

*How many customers are in a household?* This is a simple histogram question on the Customer table:

```
SELECT numinhousehold, COUNT(*) as numhh,
       MIN(householdid), MAX(householdid)
FROM (SELECT householdid, COUNT(*) as numinhousehold
      FROM customer c
```

*(continued)*

```
        GROUP BY householdid
    ) h
GROUP BY numinhousehold
ORDER BY 1
```

Table 8-1 shows the results, which emphasize that most households have only one customer. At the other extreme, two have over 100 customers each. Such large households suggest an anomaly in the householding algorithm. In fact, in this dataset, business customers from the same business are grouped into a single household. Whether or not this is correct depends on how the data is used.

**Table 8-1:** Histogram of Household Sizes

| ACCOUNTS IN HOUSEHOLD | NUMBER OF HOUSEHOLDS | CUMULATIVE NUMBER | CUMULATIVE PERCENT |
| --- | --- | --- | --- |
| 1 | 134,293 | 134,293 | 85.9% |
| 2 | 16,039 | 150,332 | 96.2% |
| 3 | 3,677 | 154,009 | 98.6% |
| 4 | 1,221 | 155,230 | 99.3% |
| 5 | 523 | 155,753 | 99.7% |
| 6 | 244 | 155,997 | 99.8% |
| 7 | 110 | 156,107 | 99.9% |
| 8 | 63 | 156,170 | 99.9% |
| 9 | 28 | 156,198 | 100.0% |
| 10 | 18 | 156,216 | 100.0% |
| 11 | 9 | 156,225 | 100.0% |
| 12 | 14 | 156,239 | 100.0% |
| 13 | 4 | 156,243 | 100.0% |
| 14 | 4 | 156,247 | 100.0% |
| 16 | 2 | 156,249 | 100.0% |
| 17 | 2 | 156,251 | 100.0% |
| 21 | 2 | 156,253 | 100.0% |
| 24 | 1 | 156,254 | 100.0% |
| 28 | 1 | 156,255 | 100.0% |
| 38 | 1 | 156,256 | 100.0% |
| 169 | 1 | 156,257 | 100.0% |
| 746 | 1 | 156,258 | 100.0% |

### How Many Genders in a Household

We might expect there to be only two genders assigned to customers, but one never knows what the values are until one looks at the data. Table 8-2 shows the results of the following simple histogram query:

```
SELECT gender, COUNT(*) as numcusts, MIN(customerid), MAX(customerid)
FROM customer
GROUP BY gender
ORDER BY 2 DESC
```

**TIP** Looking at the data is the only way to see what values really are in a column; the answer is a histogram created using GROUP BY.

**Table 8-2:** Genders and Their Frequencies

| GENDER | FREQUENCY | PROPORTION |
|--------|-----------|------------|
| M | 96,481 | 50.9% |
| F | 76,874 | 40.6% |
|  | 16,204 | 8.5% |

These results have the two expected genders, male and female. However, the field contains a third value that looks blank. Blanks in output are ambiguous. The column value could be NULL (some databases return NULL values as blank, although Microsoft SQL uses the string "NULL"), blank, or, perhaps, a string containing a space, or some other unorthodox value. The following variation on the query provides more clarity:

```
SELECT (CASE WHEN gender IS NULL THEN 'NULL' WHEN gender = '' THEN 'EMPTY'
             WHEN gender = ' ' THEN 'SPACE'
             ELSE gender END) as gender, COUNT(*) as numcusts
FROM customer
GROUP BY gender
ORDER BY 2 DESC
```

For further refinement, the function ASCII() returns the actual numeric value of any character. The results show that the third gender is actually the empty string ('') as opposed to the other possibilities. This query has an interesting feature; the GROUP BY expression differs from the SELECT expression.

This is worth a bit of discussion. SQL does allow the GROUP BY expression to differ from the corresponding SELECT expression, although this capability is rarely used. Consider the following query, which classifies the genders as

"GOOD" and "BAD." In the first version, the GROUP BY clause and the SELECT use the same expression:

```
SELECT (CASE WHEN gender IN ('M', 'F') THEN 'GOOD' ELSE 'BAD' END) as g,
       COUNT(*) as numcusts
FROM customer
GROUP BY (CASE WHEN gender IN ('M', 'F') THEN 'GOOD' ELSE 'BAD' END)
```

A slight variation uses only the GENDER variable in the GROUP BY clause:

```
SELECT (CASE WHEN gender IN ('M', 'F') THEN 'GOOD' ELSE 'BAD' END) as g,
       COUNT(*) as numcusts
FROM customer
GROUP BY gender
```

The first version returns two rows, one for "GOOD" and one for "BAD." The second returns three rows, two "GOOD" and one "BAD"; the two "GOOD" rows are for males and females. Figure 8-1 shows the dataflow diagrams that describe each of these cases. The difference is whether the CASE statement is calculated before or after the aggregation.

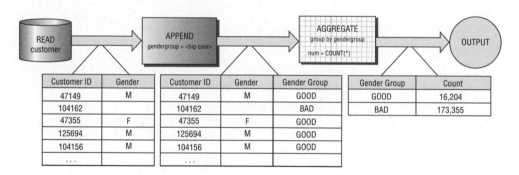

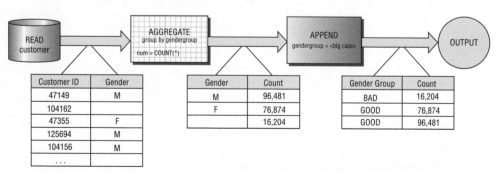

**Figure 8-1:** These dataflow diagrams show the difference in processing between aggregating first and then calculating an expression versus aggregating on the calculated value.

For this example, the only difference is two or three rows in the result set. However, in some situations there can be a big difference. For instance, the SELECT statement might assign values into ranges. If the corresponding GROUP BY does not have the same expression, the aggregation might not reduce the number of rows.

**WARNING** When using an expression in the SELECT statement of an aggregation query, be careful to think about whether the GROUP BY should contain the full expression or just the variable. In most cases, the full expression is the correct approach.

The relationship between genders and households leads to the next question: *How many households have one gender, two genders, and three genders?* This question does not require knowing the specific genders, just how many are in the household. Answering this question is fairly easy, but one question often leads to another. Because a household with only one member has only one gender, there is a relationship between household size and the number of genders. A related question is more interesting: *For each household size (by number of customers), how many households have one gender, two genders, and three genders?* The following SQL answers this question:

```
SELECT numcustomers, COUNT(*) as numhh,
       SUM(CASE WHEN numgenders = 1 THEN 1 ELSE 0 END) as gen1,
       SUM(CASE WHEN numgenders = 2 THEN 1 ELSE 0 END) as gen2,
       SUM(CASE WHEN numgenders = 3 THEN 1 ELSE 0 END) as gen3
FROM (SELECT householdid, COUNT(*) as numcustomers,
             COUNT(DISTINCT gender) as numgenders
      FROM customer c
      GROUP BY householdid) hh
GROUP BY numcustomers
ORDER BY 1
```

The results in Table 8-3 look suspicious. One would not expect 94.1% of households with two people to have only one gender. Further, in almost all these cases, the households consist of people with the same first name. The logical conclusion is that the identification of individuals does not work well. One customer gets assigned multiple values of CUSTOMERID. For this reason, and for others discussed later in this chapter, the HOUSEHOLDID is preferable for identifying customers over time.

**Table 8-3:** Count of Households by Number of Customers and Genders

| CUSTOMERS IN HOUSEHOLD | NUMBER OF HOUSEHOLDS | 1 GENDER | 2 GENDERS | 3 GENDERS |
|:---:|:---:|:---:|:---:|:---:|
| 1 | 134,293 | 134,293 | 0 | 0 |
| 2 | 16,039 | 15,087 | 952 | 0 |
| 3 | 3,677 | 3,305 | 370 | 2 |
| 4 | 1,221 | 1,102 | 118 | 1 |
| 5 | 523 | 478 | 43 | 2 |
| 6 | 244 | 209 | 35 | 0 |
| 7 | 110 | 99 | 11 | 0 |
| 8 | 63 | 57 | 6 | 0 |
| 9 | 28 | 24 | 4 | 0 |
| 10 | 18 | 16 | 2 | 0 |
| 11 | 9 | 8 | 1 | 0 |
| 12 | 14 | 13 | 1 | 0 |
| 13 | 4 | 3 | 1 | 0 |
| 14 | 4 | 4 | 0 | 0 |
| 16 | 2 | 2 | 0 | 0 |
| 17 | 2 | 2 | 0 | 0 |
| 21 | 2 | 2 | 0 | 0 |
| 24 | 1 | 1 | 0 | 0 |
| 28 | 1 | 1 | 0 | 0 |
| 38 | 1 | 0 | 0 | 1 |
| 169 | 1 | 1 | 0 | 0 |
| 746 | 1 | 0 | 0 | 1 |

## Investigating First Names

Something is awry when households consist of multiple customers having the same first name. These households probably have one individual being assigned multiple CUSTOMERIDs. To investigate this, let's ask the question: *How many households consist of "different" customers that have the same first name and the same gender?*

Two approaches to answering this question are presented here. One way is to enumerate the number of values of GENDER and of FIRSTNAME in each household and then count the number of households that have one of each:

```
SELECT COUNT(*) as numhh,
       SUM(CASE WHEN numgenders = 1 AND numfirstnames = 1 THEN 1 ELSE 0
           END) as allsame
FROM (SELECT householdid, COUNT(*) as numcustomers,
             COUNT(DISTINCT gender) as numgenders,
             COUNT(DISTINCT firstname) as numfirstnames
      FROM customer c
      GROUP BY householdid) hh
WHERE numcustomers > 1
```

The second approach is to compare the minimum and maximum values of the two columns. When these are the same, there is only one value in the household:

```
SELECT COUNT(*) as numhh,
       SUM(CASE WHEN minfname = maxfname AND mingender = maxgender
                THEN 1 ELSE 0 END) as allsame
FROM (SELECT householdid, COUNT (*) as cnt,
             MIN(firstname) as minfname, MAX(firstname) as maxfname,
             MIN(gender) as mingender, MAX(gender) as maxgender
      FROM customer
      GROUP BY householdid) hh
WHERE numcustomers > 1
```

Table 8-4 shows the results broken out by the number of customers in the household (by adding NUMCUSTOMERS to the SELECT clause and replacing the WHERE clause with GROUP BY numcustomers). It suggests that many households with multiple customers seem to consist of one individual who is assigned multiple customer IDs.

These queries may not be doing exactly what we expect when there are NULL values in the columns. If FIRSTNAME only contains NULL values for a given household, COUNT DISTINCT returns a value of zero, rather than one. So, in the first query, that household does not get counted as having all values identical. The second query produces the same result, but for a different reason. In this case, the minimum and maximum values are both NULL and these fail the equality test.

**Table 8-4:** Customers with Same Identifying Information in Household

| NUMBER OF CUSTOMERS | NUMBER OF HOUSEHOLDS | SAME GENDER AND FIRST NAME |
|---|---|---|
| 1 | 134,293 | 134,293 |
| 2 | 16,039 | 14,908 |
| 3 | 3,677 | 3,239 |
| 4 | 1,221 | 1,078 |
| 5 | 523 | 463 |
| 6 | 244 | 202 |
| 7 | 110 | 97 |
| 8 | 63 | 52 |
| 9 | 28 | 24 |
| 10 | 18 | 14 |
| 11 | 9 | 8 |
| 12 | 14 | 13 |
| 13 | 4 | 3 |
| 14 | 4 | 4 |
| 16 | 2 | 2 |
| 17 | 2 | 2 |
| 21 | 2 | 2 |
| 24 | 1 | 1 |
| 28 | 1 | 1 |
| 38 | 1 | 0 |
| 169 | 1 | 0 |
| 746 | 1 | 0 |

Similarly, if a household consists of customers with a mixture of NULL and one non-NULL value, the household gets counted as having only one customer. This is because COUNT DISTINCT counts the non-NULL values, and MIN() and MAX() ignore NULL values. To count NULL values separately, use the COALESCE() function to assign another value:

```
COALESCE(firstname, '<NULL>')
```

This conversion then treats NULL as any other value; be careful that the second argument to COALESCE() is not a valid value.

**WARNING** Using standard SQL, NULL values tend not to be counted when looking at the number of values a column takes on. Use an expression such as COALESCE(<column>, '<NULL>') to count all values including NULLs.

Counts of first names are interesting, but examples of first names are even better. *What are some examples of first names from each household where all members have the same genders?* The following query does a good job of getting examples:

```
SELECT householdid, MIN(firstname), MAX(firstname)
FROM customer
GROUP BY householdid
HAVING MIN(firstname) <> MAX(firstname) AND MIN(gender) = MAX(gender)
```

This query selects households that have multiple names all of the same gender. By using the HAVING clause, no subqueries or joins are needed. The MIN() and MAX() functions provide the examples of values in the column.

As with the previous query, households with NULL first names are not included in the results. To include them, the HAVING clause would be modified using the COALESCE() function:

```
HAVING (MIN(COALESCE(firstname, '<NULL>')) <>
        MAX(COALESCE(firstname, '<NULL>'))) AND . . .
```

This query returns 301 rows; the following are examples of customer names that appear in the same household:

- "T." and "THOMAS"
- "ELIAZBETH" and "ELIZABETH"
- "JEFF" and "JEFFREY"
- "MARGARET" and "MEG"

These four examples are probably referring to the same individual, but with variations on the name caused by:

- Use of an initial rather than the full name;
- Shortened version of a name;
- Misspellings; and,
- Nicknames.

Such are examples of the complications in matching customers using names.

There are some ways to mitigate this problem. When a household contains a name that is an initial of another name, ignore the initial. Or, when the first part of one name exactly matches another name, ignore the shorter one. These are reasonable rules for identifying what look like the same names on different records.

The rules are easy to express. However, implementing them in SQL is perhaps more challenging than one might think. The idea behind the SQL implementation is to introduce a new column for each name, called ALTFIRSTNAME, which is the full form of the name gleaned from other names on the household. Calculating ALTFIRSTNAME requires a self-join on the HOUSEHOLDID, because every name in a household has to be compared to every other name in the household:

```
SELECT c1.householdid, c1.customerid, c1.firstname, c1.gender,
       MAX(CASE WHEN LEN(c1.firstname) >= LEN(c2.firstname) THEN NULL
               WHEN LEFT(c1.firstname, 1) = LEFT(c2.firstname, 1) AND
                    SUBSTRING(c1.firstname, 2, 1) = '.' AND
                    LEN(c1.firstname) = 2
            THEN c2.firstname
            WHEN LEFT(c2.firstname, LEN(c1.firstname)) = c1.firstname
            THEN c2.firstname
            ELSE NULL END) as altfirstname
FROM customer c1 JOIN customer c2 ON c1.householdid = c2.householdid
GROUP BY c1.householdid, c1.customerid, c1.firstname, c1.gender
```

This query implements the first two rules, the ones for the initial and for the shortened version of names. Adding rules for misspellings and nicknames is more difficult because these need a lookup table to rectify the spellings.

These rules highlight issues about working with names and other short text data. Values are often subject to misspellings and interpretations (such as whether "T." is for "Thomas" or "Theodore" or "Tiffany") making it more challenging to extract information from the columns. SQL string and text processing functions are quite rudimentary. However, combined with SQL's data processing capability and the CASE statement, it is possible to use SQL to make some sense out of such data.

## Other Customer Information

A database with identified customers would normally also have full name, address, and possibly telephone numbers, email addresses, and social security numbers. None of these are ideal for matching customers over time, because customers move and change names. In the United States, even social security numbers may not be unique due to issues such as employment fraud. This section discusses these types of data.

### First and Last Names

Some names, such as James and Gordon, George and John, Kim and Kelly and Lindsey, are common as both first and last names. Other names, though, almost always fall in one or the other categories. When the FIRSTNAME column contains values such as "ABRAHAMSOM," "ALVAREZ," "ROOSEVELT," and

"SILVERMAN," it is suspicious that the first and last names are being interchanged on some records. This might either be a customer input error or a data processing error.

When both first name and last name columns are available, it is worth checking to see if they are being swapped. In practice, it is cumbersome to look at thousands of names and impossible to look at millions of them. A big help is to look at every record with a first and last name and calculate the suspicion that the names might be swapped. A convenient definition of this suspicion is the following:

```
suspicion = firstname as lastname rate + lastname as firstname rate
```

That is, a name is suspicious based on how suspicious the value in the FIRSTNAME column is and how suspicious the value in the LASTNAME column is.

The following query calculates the first name suspicion value, assuming the existence of a LASTNAME column, and outputs the results in order by highest suspicion:

```
SELECT c.householdid, c.firstname, susp.lastrate as firstnamesuspicion
FROM customer c JOIN
     (SELECT name,
             SUM(lastname) / (SUM(firstname)+SUM(lastname)) as lastrate,
             SUM(firstname) / (SUM(firstname)+SUM(lastname)) as firstrate
      FROM ((SELECT firstname as name, 1 as firstname, 0.0 as lastname
             FROM customer c)
            UNION ALL
            (SELECT lastname as name, 0 as firstname, 1.0 as lastname
             FROM customer c)) a
      GROUP BY name) susp
     ON c.firstname = susp.name
ORDER BY 3 DESC
```

The key to this query is calculating LASTRATE, which is the proportion of times that a particular name is used as a last name among all occurrences of the name. So, "Smith" might occur 99% of the time in the last name column. If we see "Smith" in the first name column, it has a suspicion value of 99%.

The subquery that gathers the occurrences of a name in both the first and last name columns needs to include all occurrences of a name; this suggests using the UNION ALL operator, as opposed to a join. The results are then aggregated by the new column NAME, which counts all occurrences as both a first name and as a last name. The first name suspicion is the proportion of times that the name occurs as a last name. If the name is always a first name, the suspicion is zero. If the name is almost always a last name, the suspicion is close to one.

Calculating the suspicion for the last name is the same process, and doing both together in the same query requires joining in another Susp subquery joined on the last name rather than the first name. The overall row suspicion is then the sum of the two values, all calculated using SQL. The best way to look at the results is by sorting suspicion in reverse order.

As an alternative to using proportions, it is also possible to calculate the chi-square value associated with a name. The calculation is a bit more cumbersome, but following the guidelines in Chapter 3, it is possible to use this measure as well.

## Addresses

Address matching is a cumbersome process that often uses specialized software or outside data vendors. There are many ways of expressing an address. The White House is located at "1600 Pennsylvania Avenue, NW." Is this the same as "1600 Pennsylvania Ave. NW"? "Sixteen Hundred Pennsylvania Avenue, Northwest"? The friendly Post Office recognizes all these as the same physical location, even though the addresses have subtle and not-so-subtle differences.

Address standardization transforms addresses by replacing elements such as "Street," "Boulevard," and "Avenue" with abbreviations ("ST," "BLVD," and "AVE"). Street names that are spelled out ("Second Avenue" or "First Street") are usually changed to their numeric form ("2 AVE" and "1 ST"). The United States Post Office has a standard address format (http://pe.usps.gov/cpim/ftp/pubs/Pub28/pub28.pdf).

Standardization only solves part of the problem. Addresses in apartment buildings, for instance, should include apartment numbers. Determining whether an address should have an apartment number requires comparing addresses to a master list that knows whether or not the building is multi-unit.

Fully disambiguating addresses is difficult. However, even an approximate solution can be helpful to answer questions such as:

- Are external householding algorithms capturing all individuals in the same household?

- How much duplicate mail is being sent out to the same household?

- Approximately how many households have made a purchase this year?

- Did prospects who received a marketing message respond through other channels?

- About how many new customers are returning customers?

These questions can help in evaluating assignments of household ids. They can also provide a very rudimentary way to understand which addresses belong in the same household when no household ids are available.

Using clever rules, rudimentary householding with names and addresses is possible. The following are simple rules that together identify many individuals in the one household:

- The last names are the same.
- The zip codes are the same.
- The first five characters in the address are the same.

The following SQL creates household keys using these rules:

```
SELECT lastname+ ': '+zip+': '+LEFT(address, 5) as tempkey, c.*
FROM customer c
```

This is not perfect and has some obvious failings (married couples with different last names, neighborhoods with high proportions of people with similar names, and so on). This is not a complete solution. The idea is to find individuals that look similar so they can be verified manually.

## Other Identifying Information

Other types of identifying information such as telephone numbers, email addresses, and credit card numbers are also useful for providing hints to identify that the same customer made multiple transactions. For instance, a customer might make two online purchases, one at work and one at home. The accounts could be different, with goods being sent to the work address during one purchase transaction and being sent to the home address during another. However, if the customer uses the same credit card, the credit card number can be used to tie the transactions together.

**WARNING** Do not store clear-text credit card numbers in an analysis database. Keep the first six digits to identify the type of credit card, and store the number using an id or hash code so the real value is hidden.

Of course, each type of identifying information has its own peculiarities. Telephone numbers might change through no fault of the customer, simply because the area code changes. Email addresses might change through no fault of the customer simply because one company purchases another and the domain changes. Credit cards expire and the replacement card may have a different number.

These challenges are aggravated by the fact that households themselves change over time. Individuals get married, and couples divorce. Children grow up, and move out. And sometimes, older children and elderly relatives move in. Although identifying the economic unit is a useful idea, there are many challenges, including the fact that such economic units shift over time as individuals combine into households and split apart.

## How Many New Customers Appear Each Year?

Regardless of the method used to identify customers, a basic question is: *How many new customers appear each year?* This section discusses this question and related questions about customers and purchase intervals.

### Counting Customers

The basic question is almost a trick question, easy if we think about it the right way, difficult if we think about it the wrong way. It is tempting to answer the question by determining all the customers who place an order in a given year and then filtering out those who made any purchase in previous years. Implementing such a query requires a complicated self-join on the Orders table. This is not unreasonable. But, there is a simpler line of reasoning.

From the perspective of the customer and not the date, every customer makes an initial purchase, which is determined by MIN(ORDERDATE). The year of the minimum of the order date is the year that the new customer appears, an observation that results in a simple query:

```
SELECT firstyear, COUNT(*) as numcusts,
       SUM(CASE WHEN numyears = 1 THEN 1 ELSE 0 END) as year1,
       SUM(CASE WHEN numyears = 2 THEN 1 ELSE 0 END) as year2
FROM (SELECT customerid, MIN(YEAR(orderdate)) as firstyear,
             COUNT(DISTINCT YEAR(orderdate)) as numyears
      FROM orders o
      GROUP BY customerid) a
GROUP BY firstyear
ORDER BY 1
```

This query also calculates the number of years when a customer id placed an order. It turns out that all customer ids are valid only during one year, shedding some light on why households are a better level for tracking customers.

Revising the query for households requires joining in the Customer table to get the HOUSEHOLDID:

```
SELECT firstyear, COUNT(*) as numcusts,
       SUM(CASE WHEN numyears = 1 THEN 1 ELSE 0 END) as year1,
       SUM(CASE WHEN numyears = 2 THEN 1 ELSE 0 END) as year2,
       MIN(householdid), MAX(householdid)
FROM (SELECT householdid, MIN(YEAR(orderdate)) as firstyear,
             COUNT(DISTINCT YEAR(orderdate)) as numyears
      FROM orders o JOIN customer c ON o.customerid = c.customerid
      GROUP BY householdid) a
GROUP BY firstyear
ORDER BY 1
```

Figure 8-2 shows a significant variation in attracting new customers/households from year to year.

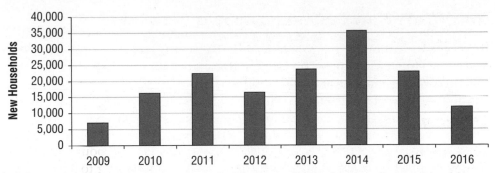

**Figure 8-2:** The number of new households that make purchases varies considerably from one year to another.

The next variation on the question is more difficult: *What proportion of customers who place orders in each year are new customers?* This question is more difficult because all transactions in the year need to be taken into account, not just the ones with new customers. There is a shortcut, because the number of new customers and the number of total customers can be calculated in separate subqueries:

```
SELECT theyear, SUM(numnew) as numnew, SUM(numall) as numall,
       SUM(numnew*1.0)/SUM(numall) as propnew
FROM ((SELECT firstyear as theyear, COUNT(*) as numnew, 0 as numall
       FROM (SELECT householdid, MIN(YEAR(orderdate)) as firstyear
             FROM orders o JOIN customer c ON o.customerid = c.customerid
             GROUP BY householdid) a
      GROUP BY firstyear)
     UNION ALL
     (SELECT YEAR(orderdate) as theyear, 0 as numnew,
             COUNT(DISTINCT householdid) as numall
      FROM orders o JOIN customer c ON o.customerid = c.customerid
      GROUP BY YEAR(orderdate))
     ) a
GROUP BY theyear
ORDER BY 1
```

The first subquery calculates the new households in the year. The second calculates the number of households that make a purchase each year, using COUNT DISTINCT. Perhaps the most interesting aspect of the query is the UNION ALL and subsequent GROUP BY at the outermost level. It is tempting to write this using a join:

```
SELECT theyear, n.numnew, a.numall
FROM (<first subquery>) n JOIN
     (<second subquery>) a
     ON n.firstyear = a.theyear
```

However, there might be years where one or the other groups have no data — years where there are no new customers, for instance. The join eliminates these years. Although this problem is unlikely with yearly summaries, the UNION ALL method is safer. This version does work with the FULL OUTER JOIN operator, rather than the JOIN.

The first row of the results in Table 8-5 shows that households that made purchases during the earliest year are all new households (as expected). After that, the proportion of new households tends to decrease from year to year, falling to less than 85%.

**Table 8-5:** New and All Customers by Year

| YEAR | NUMBER NEW CUSTOMERS | TOTAL NUMBER OF CUSTOMERS | % NEW |
|------|------|------|------|
| 2009 | 7,077 | 7,077 | 100.0% |
| 2010 | 16,291 | 17,082 | 95.4% |
| 2011 | 22,357 | 24,336 | 91.9% |
| 2012 | 16,488 | 18,693 | 88.2% |
| 2013 | 23,658 | 26,111 | 90.6% |
| 2014 | 35,592 | 39,814 | 89.4% |
| 2015 | 22,885 | 27,302 | 83.8% |
| 2016 | 11,910 | 14,087 | 84.5% |

### Span of Time Making Purchases

Households make multiple purchases over the course of several years. *During how many years do households make purchases?* This question is different from the total number of purchases a household makes, because it is asking about the number of years when a household is active. The following query answers the question:

```
SELECT numyears, COUNT(*), MIN(householdid), MAX(householdid)
FROM (SELECT householdid, COUNT(DISTINCT YEAR(orderdate)) as numyears
      FROM orders o JOIN customer c ON o.customerid = c.customerid
      GROUP BY householdid) a
GROUP BY numyears
ORDER BY 1
```

The number of years is calculated using COUNT DISTINCT in the subquery.

Table 8-6 shows that there are thousands of households that make purchases during more than one year. This is reassuring, because repeat business is usually important.

**Table 8-6:** Number of Years when Households Make Purchases

| NUMBER OF YEARS | COUNT |
|:---:|:---:|
| 1 | 142,111 |
| 2 | 11,247 |
| 3 | 2,053 |
| 4 | 575 |
| 5 | 209 |
| 6 | 50 |
| 7 | 11 |
| 8 | 2 |

The next question relates to the frequency of these purchases during the years that have purchases. Figure 8-3 shows several customers on the calendar time line. This chart, incidentally, is a scatter plot where the clip art for a shopping basket has been copied onto the points. To do this, adjust any picture to be the right size (which is usually quite small), select the series by clicking it, and type <control>-V to paste the image.

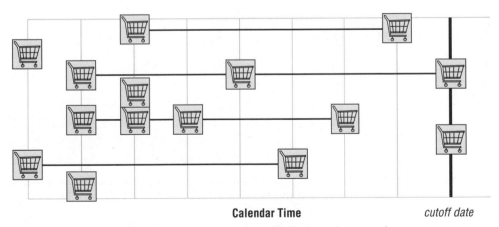

Calendar Time                    cutoff date

**Figure 8-3:** Customers make purchases at irregular frequencies over time.

Some households make purchases every year. Some make purchases occasionally. One way to measure the purchase frequency is to divide the total span of years by the number of years with purchases. So, a customer who makes three purchases over five years has a purchase frequency of 60%. The following query calculates the purchase frequency, broken out by the span in years from the first purchase to the last purchase and the number of purchases:

```
SELECT lastyear - firstyear + 1 as span, numyears, COUNT(*) as numhh,
       MIN(householdid), MAX(householdid)
FROM (SELECT householdid, MIN(YEAR(orderdate)) as firstyear,
             MAX(YEAR(orderdate)) as lastyear,
             COUNT(DISTINCT YEAR(orderdate)) as numyears
      FROM orders o JOIN customer c ON o.customerid = c.customerid
      GROUP BY householdid) a
GROUP BY lastyear - firstyear + 1, numyears
ORDER BY 1, 2
```

Figure 8-4 shows the results as a bubble chart, which shows that even customers who make purchases over large spans of time are often making purchases only during two particular years. A note about the bubble chart: Because there are many customers who make only one purchase and they have a span of one year, these are not included in the chart. Also, Excel eliminates the very smallest bubbles, because they are too small to see.

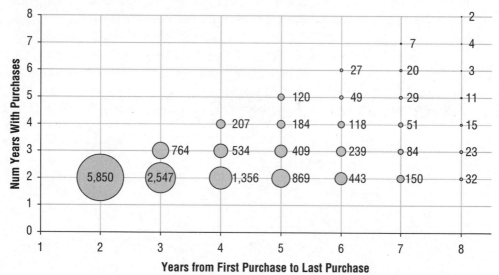

**Figure 8-4:** This bubble chart shows the number of years when customers make purchases versus the span of time from the earliest purchase to the latest purchase.

Households that made purchases long ago have had more opportunity to make a repeat purchase than households that started recently. This observation leads to another question: *What is the potential span for households?* The potential span is the potential number of years when a customer could have made a purchase. That is, it is the number of years from the first purchase to the last year in the data, 2016. The only change to the previous query is to change the definition of span to:

```
2016 - firstyear + 1 as potentialspan
```

This change affects both the SELECT clause and the GROUP BY clause. The results for the potential span are also heavily affected by the fact that most households only make a single purchase.

### Average Time between Orders

Closely related to the span of time covered by orders is the average time between orders, defined for those customers who have more than one order. The query uses the subquery in the previous examples:

```
SELECT FLOOR(DATEDIFF(dd, mindate, maxdate) / (numorders-1)),
       COUNT(*) as numhh
FROM (SELECT householdid, MIN(orderdate) as mindate,
             MAX(orderdate) as maxdate, COUNT(*) as numorders
      FROM orders o JOIN customer c ON o.customerid = c.customerid
      GROUP BY householdid
      HAVING COUNT(*) > 1) a
GROUP BY FLOOR(DATEDIFF(dd, mindate, maxdate) / (numorders-1))
ORDER BY 1
```

This query calculates the total span and then divides it by one less than the number of orders. The result is the average spacing of the orders. The query uses the HAVING clause to limit the results only to households with at least two orders, preventing a divide by zero error.

The cumulative proportion, which is the cumulative sum for the first *n* days divided by the total for all days, is calculated in Excel. This cumulative sum shows how fast customers are placing orders (on average). Figure 8-5 shows the average time to purchase for customers with two or more purchases, stratified by the number of purchases. This curve has some unexpected properties.

The curve for six purchases is very ragged because there are relatively few households with six purchases. This curve peaks at about 490 days, hitting 100%. That means that all customers with six purchases have an average time between purchase of 490 days or less. All the curves show an increase around the one-year mark, consisting of customers who make purchases once per year, probably during the holiday season.

At the 600-day mark, the curves are in the right order. The curve for six orders is at 100%, followed by five, four, three, and two. An interesting feature of the two-order households is the lack of marked increase around one year. This could be because customers who make two purchases one year apart are likely to make yet another purchase the following year.

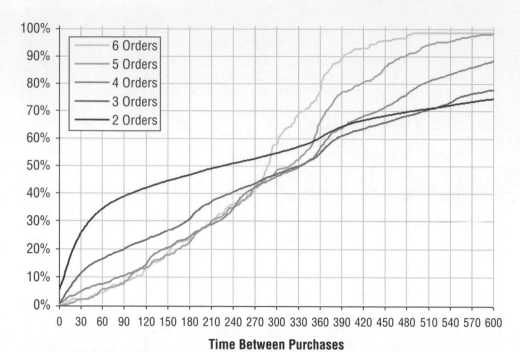

**Figure 8-5:** This chart shows the time to purchase (in days) stratified by the number of purchases a customer makes.

In addition, the curve for two-order households starts off very steep, indicating that many households with two orders make the purchases in rapid succession. So, 50% of the households with two purchases make the purchases within 136 days of each other. For households with more purchases, the median average time-to-purchase is closer to three hundreds days, or twice as long.

If the purchases were randomly distributed, the households with two orders would have a longer average purchase time than households with more than two. This is because the two-order households could make a purchase on the earliest date and on the latest date, in which case the span would be about seven years. If a household has three orders, one on the earliest date, one on the latest date, and one in-between, the average time between purchases is then about three and a half years.

One likely explanation for the speed of purchase results is marketing efforts directed at people who just made a purchase. A customer buys something and there is a coupon or offer that arrives with the purchase, spurring another purchase.

The average time between purchases is one way to measure *purchase velocity*. Later in this chapter, we'll use survival analysis to calculate time-to-next purchase, an alternative measure.

**TIP** Normally, we expect the average time between orders to be smaller for customers who have more orders.

## Purchase Intervals

Related to the average time between purchases is the average time from the first purchase to any other purchase. This shows cycles in customer purchasing patterns. For instance, Figure 8-6 shows the number of days from the first purchase in a household to any other purchase. If a household has several purchases, all of them are included.

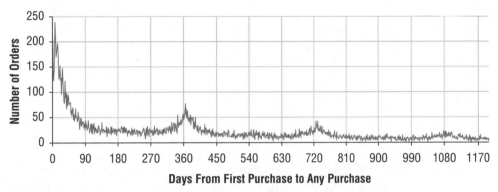

**Figure 8-6:** This chart shows the time from the first purchase to every other purchase; the wave pattern indicates customers who make a purchase at the same time every year.

This chart shows that there is a yearly cycle in the household purchasing behavior, as illustrated by peaks around 360 days and 720 days and even after that. These yearly peaks become smaller and smaller over time. One reason is because the data contains all customers. Some of them make their first purchase just one year before the cutoff; these customers do not have the opportunity to make repeated purchases at two years and three years and so on. On the other hand, customers who start in the beginning of the data have the opportunity for several years.

To calculate the data for the chart, subtract the first date of a household order from all other order dates:

```
SELECT DATEDIFF(dd, h1.mindate, ho.orderdate) as days,
       COUNT(*) as numorders
FROM (SELECT householdid, MIN(orderdate) as mindate
      FROM orders o JOIN customer c ON o.customerid = c.customerid
      GROUP BY householdid
      HAVING MIN(orderdate) < MAX(orderdate)) h1 JOIN
     (SELECT c.householdid, o.*
      FROM orders o JOIN customer c ON o.customerid = c.customerid) ho
     ON h1.householdid = ho.householdid
GROUP BY DATEDIFF(dd, h1.mindate, ho.orderdate)
ORDER BY 1
```

This query calculates the first order date in the first subquery for households that have orders on different dates. The second subquery contains all orders, and these in turn are aggregated by the difference between the order date and the first order date.

# RFM Analysis

RFM is a traditional approach to analyzing customer behavior in the retailing industry; the initials stand for *recency, frequency, monetary* analysis. This type of analysis divides customers into groups, based on how recently they have made a purchase, how frequently they make purchases, and how much money they have spent. RFM analysis has its roots in techniques going back to the 1960s and 1970s.

The purpose of discussing RFM analysis is not to encourage its use because there are often better ways of modeling customers for marketing efforts. RFM is worthwhile for other reasons. First, it is based on simple ideas that are applicable to many different industries and situations. Second, it is an opportunity to see how these ideas can be translated into useful technical measures that can be calculated using SQL and Excel. Finally, RFM introduces the idea of scoring customers by placing them in RFM cells; the idea of scoring customers is extended in the last three chapters.

The following observations explain why RFM is of interest to retailing businesses:

- Customers who have recently made a purchase are more likely to make another purchase soon.
- Customers who frequently make purchases are more likely to make more purchases.
- Customers who spend lots of money are more likely to spend more money.

Each of these observations corresponds to one of the RFM dimensions. This section discusses these three dimensions and how to calculate them in SQL and Excel.

## The Dimensions

RFM divides each of the three dimensions into equal sized chunks (which are formally called *quantiles*) and places customers in the corresponding chunk along each dimension. The examples here use five quantiles for each dimension (*quintiles*), although there is nothing magic about five. Figure 8-7 illustrates what is happening. The RFM cells form a large cube consisting of 125 subcubes. Each customer is assigned to a unique subcube based on his or her attributes along the three dimensions. This section discusses each of these dimensions and shows how to calculate the values as of a cutoff date, such as January 1, 2016.

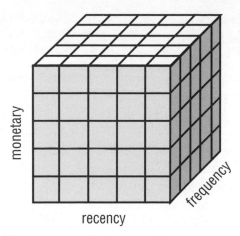

**Figure 8-7:** The RFM dimensions can be thought of as placing customers into small subcubes along the dimensions.

## Recency

Recency is the amount of time since the most recent purchase. Figure 8-8 shows a cumulative histogram of recency, as of the cutoff date of January 1, 2016 (orders after that date are ignored). This chart shows that 20% of the households have placed an order within the previous 380 days. The chart also has the four breakpoints that are used for defining the five recency quintiles.

Recency is calculated at the household level. The most recent purchase is the one with the maximum order date before the cutoff, as calculated by the following query:

```
SELECT DATEDIFF(dd, maxdate, '2016-01-01') as recency, COUNT(*)
FROM (SELECT householdid, MIN(orderdate) as mindate,
             MAX(orderdate) as maxdate, COUNT(*) as numorders
      FROM orders o JOIN customer c ON o.customerid = c.customerid
      WHERE orderdate < '2016-01-01'
      GROUP BY householdid) h
GROUP BY DATEDIFF(dd, maxdate, '2016-01-01')
ORDER BY 1
```

The cumulative histogram, calculated in Excel, makes it possible to identify the four breakpoints. The following SQL query then uses these breakpoints to assign a recency quintile to each household:

```
SELECT (CASE WHEN recency <= 380 THEN 1 WHEN recency <= 615 THEN 2
             WHEN recency <= 1067 THEN 3 WHEN recency <= 1686 THEN 4
             ELSE 5 END) as recbin, h.*
FROM (SELECT householdid,
             DATEDIFF(dd, MAX(orderdate) , '2016-01-01') as recency
```

*(continued)*

```
FROM orders o JOIN customer c ON o.customerid = c.customerid
WHERE orderdate < '2016-01-01'
GROUP BY householdid) h
```

The breakpoints are explicitly used in the CASE statement in the SELECT clause.

Finding the breakpoints using SQL and Excel is cumbersome. Fortunately, there are functions in SQL that make it possible to do all the work within the database, as discussed in the aside "SQL Ranking Functions."

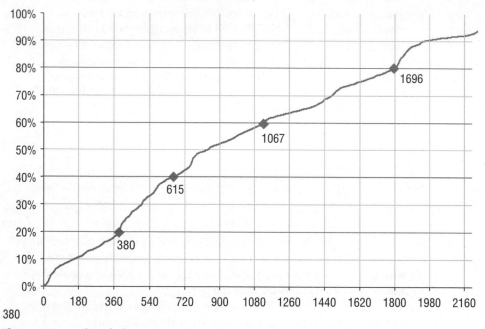

**Figure 8-8:** To break the recency into five equal sized buckets, look at the cumulative histogram and break it into five groups. The resulting four breakpoints are shown on the chart.

---

## SQL RANKING FUNCTIONS

**ANSI SQL has a special function, NTILE(), supported by SQL Server and Oracle, that assigns quantiles to values in a column. Because these are part of standard SQL and useful, other databases should eventually also include them.**

**NTILE() does exactly what we need it to do for finding quintiles. It divides the recency values into five equal sized groups and assigns them the values one through five. We might expect the syntax for NTILE() to look something like:**

```
NTILE(recency, 5)
```

**Alas, it is not that simple.**

**SQL RANKING FUNCTIONS (CONTINUED)**

`NTILE()` **is an example of a special class of functions called window functions. These functions combine information from multiple rows and use the information to do the calculation. The particular group of rows is the** *window* **being used. For recency, the correct syntax is:**

```
NTILE(5) OVER (ORDER BY recency)
```

**The argument "5" to** `NTILE()` **is a number that specifies the number of bins. The window specification says to include all values in all rows. The** `ORDER BY` **clause specifies the variable (or variables) that define the bins, and the ordering (whether 1 is high or low). Although this syntax may seem cumbersome, it is actually quite powerful for expressing many different transformations. Examples later in this chapter apply window functions to very different problems.**

**Putting this together into a query looks like:**

```
SELECT h.*, NTILE(5) OVER (ORDER BY recency)
FROM (SELECT householdid,
             DATEDIFF(dd, MAX(orderdate) , '2016-01-01') as recency
      FROM orders o JOIN customer c ON o.customerid = c.customerid
      WHERE orderdate < '2016-01-01'
      GROUP BY householdid) h
```

**This syntax is definitely much simpler than the other alternatives. The subquery is necessary, because window functions do not interact gracefully with** `GROUP BY`**s. Using window functions and aggregations together results in a syntax error. Fortunately, subqueries are an easy work-around.**

**It is also worth noting that window functions can be used multiple times in the same statement. So, we can produce bins for multiple variables in the same** `SELECT` **statement.**

**In addition to** `NTILE()`**, there are three other ranking functions:**

```
ROW_NUMBER() OVER (ORDER BY recency)
RANK() OVER (ORDER BY recency)
DENSE_RANK() OVER (ORDER BY recency)
```

**The first of these simply enumerates the rows by order of recency, assigning numbers starting at one. The other two differ from** `ROW_NUMBER()` **when two or more rows have the same value. In this case,** `RANK()` **gives all rows with the same value the same ranking and then skips the subsequent values. So, the ranking values might look like 1, 1, 1, 4, 5, 6, . . . if there are three ties for first place.** `DENSE_RANK()` **does almost the same thing, but without skipping intermediate values. It would produce the values 1, 1, 1, 2, 3, 4 in this case.**

**In the preceding example, the smallest value of recency gets the value of 1. To reverse this so the largest value gets a recency of one simply requires using the** `DESC` **modifier in the** `ORDER BY` **clause, to sort things in the opposite order.**

## Frequency

Frequency is the rate at which customers make purchases, calculated as the length of time since the earliest purchase divided by the number of purchases (sometimes it is calculated as the total number of purchases over all time). The breakpoints are determined the same way as for recency, and are shown in Table 8-7.

**Table 8-7:** Breakpoint Values for Recency, Frequency, and Monetary Bins

| BREAK POINT | RECENCY | FREQUENCY | MONETARY |
| --- | --- | --- | --- |
| 20% | 380 | 372 | 13 |
| 40% | 615 | 594 | 20 |
| 60% | 1067 | 974 | 28 |
| 80% | 1696 | 1628 | 59 |

The frequency itself is calculated in a way very similar to the span-of-time queries:

```
SELECT FLOOR(DATEDIFF(dd, mindate, '2016-01-01')/numorders) as frequency,
       COUNT(*)
FROM (SELECT householdid, MIN(orderdate) as mindate, COUNT(*) as numorders
      FROM orders o JOIN customer c ON o.customerid = c.customerid
      WHERE orderdate < '2016-01-01'
      GROUP BY householdid) h
GROUP BY FLOOR(DATEDIFF(dd, mindate, '2016-01-01')/numorders)
ORDER BY 1
```

This query calculates the total span of time between the cutoff date and the earliest purchase, and then divides by the number of purchases. Note that low values for frequency and recency are both associated with good customers, whereas high values are associated with poor customers.

## Monetary

The last RFM variable is the monetary variable. Traditionally, this is the total amount of money spent by households. However, this definition is usually highly correlated with frequency, because customers who make more purchases have larger total amounts. A better variable is the average amount of each order:

```
SELECT FLOOR(money) as dollars, COUNT(*)
FROM (SELECT householdid, AVG(totalprice) as money
      FROM orders o JOIN customer c ON o.customerid = c.customerid
```

```
        WHERE orderdate < '2016-01-01'
        GROUP BY householdid) h
GROUP BY FLOOR(money)
ORDER BY 1
```

The difference between using the average or the total is simply changing the definition of MONEY from AVG(totalprice) to SUM(totalprice). Excel can then be used to find the four breakpoints that divide the values into five equal sized bins, which are shown in Table 8-7. Note that unlike recency and frequency, low values for monetary are associated with worse customers.

## Calculating the RFM Cell

The RFM cell combines the bins used for recency, frequency, and monetary. The cell has a tag that looks like a number, so 155 corresponds to the cell with the highest recency value and the lowest frequency and monetary values. The tag is just a label; it is not sensible to ask whether bin 155 is greater than or less than another bin, say 244.

Although the customers are divided into equal sized chunks along each dimension, the 125 RFM cells are not equal sized. In fact, some of them are empty, such as cell 155. Others are quite large, such as cell 522, the largest, which has 5.6% of the customers. This cell consists of customers who have not made a purchase in a long time (worst recency). The household is highly infrequent, so the household probably made only one purchase. And, the purchase was on the high end of the monetary scale.

Cell sizes differ because the three measures are not independent. Good customers make frequent purchases that are higher in value, corresponding to one set of RFM values. One-time customers make few purchases (one) that might not be recent and are smaller in value.

Attempting to visualize the RFM cells is challenging using Excel chart capabilities. What we really want is a three-dimensional bubble chart, where each axis corresponds to one of the RFM dimensions. The size of the bubbles would be the number of households in that cell. Unfortunately, Excel does not offer a three-dimensional bubble plot capability.

Figure 8-9 shows a compromise using a two-dimensional bubble plot. The vertical axis has the recency bin and the horizontal axis has a combination of the frequency and monetary bins. The largest bubbles are along the diagonal, which shows that recency and frequency are highly correlated. This is especially true for customers who have made only one purchase. A one-time, recent purchase implies that the frequency is quite high. If the purchase was a long time ago, the frequency is quite low. In this data, most households have made only one purchase, so this effect is quite noticeable. By the way, when creating scatter plots and bubble plots using Excel, the axes need to be numbers rather than strings.

**WARNING** In Excel, bubble plots and scatter plots require that the axes be numbers rather than text values. Using text values results in all values being treated as zeros and sequential numbers placed on the axis.

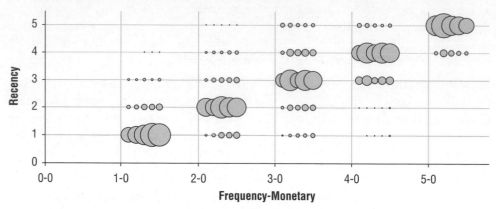

**Figure 8-9:** This chart shows the RFM cells, with the recency on the vertical axis and the frequency and monetary dimensions on the horizontal axis.

The following query calculates the sizes of the RFM bins for all customers:

```
SELECT recbin * 100 + freqbin * 10 + monbin as rfm, COUNT(*)
FROM (SELECT (CASE WHEN r <= 380 THEN 1 WHEN r <= 615 THEN 2
                WHEN r <= 1067 THEN 3 WHEN r <= 1686 THEN 4
                ELSE 5 END) as recbin,
             (CASE WHEN f <= 372 THEN 1 WHEN f <= 594 THEN 2
                WHEN f <= 974 THEN 3 WHEN f <= 1628 THEN 4
                ELSE 5 END) as freqbin,
             (CASE WHEN m <= 13 THEN 1 WHEN m <= 20 THEN 2
                WHEN m <= 28 THEN 3 WHEN m <= 59 THEN 4
                ELSE 5 END) as monbin
        FROM (SELECT householdid, MIN(orderdate) as mindate,
                DATEDIFF(dd, MAX(orderdate), '2016-01-01')as r,
                FLOOR(DATEDIFF(dd, MIN(orderdate), '2016-01-01')/
                    COUNT(*) ) as f,
                SUM(totalprice) / COUNT(*) as m
             FROM orders o JOIN customer c ON o.customerid = c.customerid
             WHERE orderdate < '2016-01-01'
             GROUP BY householdid) a ) b
GROUP BY recbin * 100 + freqbin * 10 + monbin
ORDER BY 1
```

The inner query assigns the RFM values, and the outer query then aggregates bins to count the values in each cell.

## Utility of RFM

RFM is a methodology that encourages the use of testing, and it encourages businesses to think about customers migrating from one cell to another. These two advantages of RFM are good ideas that are worth discussing in more detail.

### A Methodology for Marketing Experiments

The RFM methodology encourages a test-and-learn approach to marketing. Because marketing efforts incur some cost, companies do not want to contact every possible person; instead, they want to contact the customers or prospects who are most likely to respond. The RFM solution is to divide the customers into RFM cells and then to track the response of each cell. Once the process is up and running, the following happens:

- The customers in the RFM cells with the highest response rate in the previous campaign are included in the next campaign.
- A sample of customers in other RFM cells is included in the campaign, so there is information about all cells moving forward.

The first item is a no-brainer. The point of using a methodology such as RFM is to identify customers who are more likely to respond, so better responders can be included in the next campaign.

It is the second part that encompasses experimentation. Typically, the best-responding cells are the ones in the best bins, particularly recency. Other cells might not have the chance to prove themselves as having valuable customers. And, during the next iteration, these customers have not had encouragement to make a recent purchase, so they fall farther behind along the recency dimension and into even less valuable cells.

The solution is to include a sample of customers from all cells, even those cells that are not chosen for the marketing effort. This means that all cells can be tracked over time.

**TIP** For companies that have ongoing marketing campaigns, including test cells is highly beneficial and worth the effort in the long term. Even though such cells incur a cost in the short term, they provide the opportunity to learn about customers over the long term.

Including such a sample of customers does have a cost, literally. Some customers are being contacted even though their expected response rate is lower than the threshold. Of course, not all the customers are contacted, just a sample, but this is still a cost for any given campaign. The benefit is strategic: over time, the lessons learned apply to all customers rather than to the smaller number who would be chosen for each campaign.

## Customer Migration

The second advantage of RFM is that it encourages thinking about customers who migrate from one cell to another. Customers fall into particular RFM cells at the beginning of 2015 (which are based on different breakpoints). However, based on customer behavior, the cells may change during the course of the year. *What is the pattern of RFM cell migration from the beginning of 2015 to 2016?*

This question can be answered by a SQL query. One way to write the query would be to calculate the RFM bins for 2015 in one subquery and then calculate the RFM bins for 2016 and then join the results together. There is a more efficient way to do the calculation. The bins for the two years can be calculated in one subquery, although this requires judicious use of the CASE statement to select the right data for each year:

```sql
SELECT rfm.recbin2015*100+rfm.freqbin2015*10+rfm.monbin2015 as rfm2015,
       rfm.recbin2016*100+rfm.freqbin2016*10+rfm.monbin2016 as rfm2016,
       COUNT(*), MIN(rfm.householdid), MAX(rfm.householdid)
FROM (SELECT householdid,
             (CASE WHEN r2016 <= 380 THEN 1 WHEN r2016 <= 615 THEN 2
                   WHEN r2016 <= 1067 THEN 3 WHEN r2016 <= 1686 THEN 4
                   ELSE 5 END) as recbin2016,
             (CASE WHEN f2016 <= 372 THEN 1 WHEN f2016 <= 594 THEN 2
                   WHEN f2016 <= 974 THEN 3 WHEN f2016 <= 1628 THEN 4
                   ELSE 5 END) as freqbin2016,
             (CASE WHEN m2016 <= 13 THEN 1 WHEN m2016 <= 20 THEN 2
                   WHEN m2016 <= 28 THEN 3 WHEN m2016 <= 59 THEN 4
                   ELSE 5 END) as monbin2016,
             (CASE WHEN r2015 is null THEN null
                   WHEN r2015 <= 174 THEN 1 WHEN r2015 <= 420 THEN 2
                   WHEN r2015 <= 807 THEN 3 WHEN r2015 <= 1400 THEN 4
                   ELSE 5 END) as recbin2015,
             (CASE WHEN f2015 IS NULL THEN NULL
                   WHEN f2015 <= 192 THEN 1 WHEN f2015 <= 427 THEN 2
                   WHEN f2015 <= 807 THEN 3 WHEN f2015 <= 1400 THEN 4
                   ELSE 5 END) as freqbin2015,
             (CASE WHEN m2015 IS NULL THEN NULL
                   WHEN m2015 <= 13 THEN 1 WHEN m2015 <= 19 THEN 2
                   WHEN m2015 <= 28 THEN 3 WHEN m2015 <= 53 THEN 4
                   ELSE 5 END) as monbin2015
      from (SELECT householdid,
                   DATEDIFF(dd, MAX(CASE WHEN orderdate < '2015-01-01'
                                         THEN orderdate END),
                            '2015-01-01') as r2015,
                   FLOOR(DATEDIFF(dd,
                                  MIN(CASE WHEN orderdate < '2015-01-01'
                                           THEN orderdate END),
                                  '2015-01-01')/
                         SUM(CASE WHEN orderdate < '2015-01-01'
                                  THEN 1.0 END)) as f2015,
                   (SUM(CASE WHEN orderdate < '2015-01-01'
```

```
                       THEN totalprice END) /
            SUM(CASE WHEN orderdate < '2015-01-01' THEN 1.0 END
                 )) as m2015,
               DATEDIFF(dd, MAX(orderdate) , '2016-01-01') as r2016,
               FLOOR(DATEDIFF(dd, MIN(orderdate), '2016-01-01')/
                    COUNT(*)) as f2016, AVG(totalprice) as m2016
          FROM orders o JOIN customer c ON o.customerid = c.customerid
          WHERE orderdate < '2016-01-01'
          GROUP BY householdid) a
       ) rfm
GROUP BY rfm.recbin2015, rfm.freqbin2015, rfm.monbin2015,
         rfm.recbin2016, rfm.freqbin2016, rfm.monbin2016
ORDER BY COUNT(*) DESC
```

This query uses explicit thresholds to define the quintiles for the two years. This is for convenience. The thresholds could also be defined using RANK().

Households that first appear in 2016 have no previous RFM cell, so these are given the value NULL for 2015. The new households arrive in only five cells, as shown in Table 8-8.

**Table 8-8:** RFM Bins for New Customers in 2016

| 2016 RFM BIN | COUNT |
| --- | --- |
| 114 | 6,241 |
| 115 | 6,021 |
| 113 | 5,410 |
| 112 | 4,909 |
| 111 | 4,416 |

These five cells all have the highest values along the recency dimension for 2016, which is not surprising because these households have all made a recent purchase. They are also highest along the frequency dimension for the same reason. Only the monetary dimension is spread out, and it is skewed a bit toward higher monetary amounts. In fact, 53.4% are in the two highest monetary buckets, rather than the 40% that would be expected. So, new customers in 2016 seem to be at the higher end of purchase values.

The biggest interest is customers who change from the bad bins (high values along all dimensions) to good bins (low values along the dimensions). This brings up the question: *What campaigns in 2016 are converting long-term dormant customers into active customers?* This question could be answered by diving into the RFM bins. However, it is easier to rephrase the question by simply asking about customers who made no purchases in, say, the two years before January 1, 2015. This is easier than calculating all the RFM information, and probably just as accurate.

Figure 8-10 shows the channel of the first purchase made in 2016 as a 100% stacked, column chart. The purchases are split by the number of years since the household made a previous purchase. This chart suggests that email is a strong channel for bringing customers back. Unfortunately, the email channel is also extremely small, with only sixteen households making a first 2016 purchase in that channel, because email is used only for some small marketing tests.

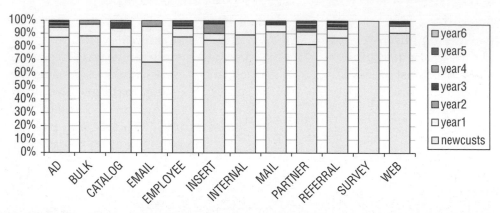

**Figure 8-10:** The channel of first purchases in 2016 shows that some channels are better at attracting new customers and others at bringing dormant customers back.

Of the significant channels, Partner seems to be the best in reactivating dormant customers. A total of 5.6% of the households that place an order in 2016 in the Partner channel are older than two years. By comparison, only 2.2% of the Web channel customers are older than two years.

## RFM Limits

RFM is an interesting methodology because it breaks customers into segments, promotes good experimental design (by requiring test cells in marketing), and encourages thinking about changes in customer behavior over time. However, the underlying methodology does have its limits.

One issue with RFM is that the dimensions are not independent. Customers who make frequent purchases have also, generally, made recent purchases. The example in this section uses five cells along each axis; of the 125 cells 15 have no customers at all. At the other extreme, the 12 most populated cells have over half the customers. In general, RFM does a good job of distinguishing the best customers from the worst. However, it does not do a good job of distinguishing among different groups of customers.

And, this is not surprising. Customer behavior is complex. The three dimensions of recency, frequency, and monetary value are important for understanding the customers' purchasing behaviors — which is why this section discusses them. However, RFM does not include the multitude of other behaviors that describe customers, such as geography and the products purchased. These other aspects of the customer relationship are also critical for understanding customers.

# Which Households Are Increasing Purchase Amounts Over Time?

This section discusses a common question: *Are purchase amounts increasing or decreasing over time for each household?* This question can be answered in several ways. The most sophisticated is to define a trend for each household, using the slope of the line that best fits that household's purchase patterns. Two other methods are also discussed. The first compares the earliest and latest spending values, using a ratio or difference for the comparison. The second uses the average of the earliest few purchases and compares them to the average amount of the last few purchases.

## Comparison of Earliest and Latest Values

The first and last purchase values for each household contain information about how customer purchase patterns change over time. There are two components to this analysis. The first is calculating the values themselves. The second is deciding how to compare them.

### Calculating the Earliest and Latest Values

*What is the order amount for the earliest and latest order in each household (that has more than one order)?* One approach to answering this question is the "find-the-transaction" method, which works with traditional SQL. Another approach uses clever aggregation, which is often more efficient and results in simpler SQL code. The third uses SQL window functions, which are not available in all databases.

#### "Find-the-Transaction" (Standard SQL Approach)

The standard SQL approach is to find the order that has the household's minimum (or maximum) ORDERDATE, as in the following query that looks for the order in a household having the smallest order date:

```
SELECT c.householdid, o.*
FROM orders o JOIN customer c ON o.customerid = c.customerid
WHERE o.orderdate IN
        (SELECT MIN(orderdate)
         FROM orders o1 JOIN customer c1
              ON o1.customerid = c1.customerid
         WHERE c1.householdid = c1.householdid)
```

This query uses a correlated subquery for the IN statement. Correlated subqueries can always be rewritten as joins (and we'll shortly see an example). This query is simple enough, but there is a catch. There might be more than one order on the minimum date.

The following query calculates the number of orders on the minimum date:

```
SELECT nummindateorders, COUNT(*) as numhh,
       MIN(householdid), MAX(householdid)
FROM (SELECT c.householdid, MIN(o.orderdate) as mindate,
             COUNT(*) as nummindateorders
      FROM orders o JOIN customer c ON o.customerid = c.customerid JOIN
           (SELECT householdid, MIN(orderdate) as mindate
            FROM orders o JOIN customer c ON o.customerid = c.customerid
            GROUP BY householdid) minhh
           ON c.householdid = minhh.householdid AND
              o.orderdate = minhh.mindate
      GROUP BY c.householdid) h
GROUP BY nummindateorders
ORDER BY 1 DESC
```

This calculation uses two subqueries. The first aggregates the order information by HOUSEHOLDID and ORDERDATE to get the number of orders on each date for each household. The second aggregates by HOUSEHOLDID to get the smallest ORDERDATE for each household. These are then joined together to get count on the minimum order date.

The counts are shown in Table 8-9. Although the vast majority of households do have only one order on their earliest order date, over one thousand have more than one. The strategy of looking for the one and only order on the minimum order date does not work correctly.

**Table 8-9:** Number of Orders on Household's First Order Date

| NUMBER OF PURCHASES ON FIRST DAY | NUMBER OF HOUSEHOLDS | PROPORTION |
|:---:|:---:|:---:|
| 1 | 155,016 | 99.21% |
| 2 | 1,184 | 0.76% |
| 3 | 45 | 0.03% |
| 4 | 9 | 0.01% |
| 5 | 1 | 0.00% |
| 6 | 2 | 0.00% |
| 8 | 1 | 0.00% |

Fixing this requires adding another level of subqueries. The innermost query finds the earliest order date for each household. The next level finds one ORDERID on that date for the household. The outermost then joins in the order information. Using JOINs instead of INs, the resulting query looks like:

```
SELECT c.householdid, o.*
FROM orders o JOIN customer c ON o.customerid = c.customerid JOIN
     (SELECT c.householdid, MIN(o.orderid) as minorderid
      FROM orders o JOIN customer c ON o.customerid = c.customerid JOIN
           (SELECT householdid, MIN(orderdate) as minorderdate
            FROM orders o JOIN customer c ON o.customerid = c.customerid
            GROUP BY householdid) ho
           ON ho.householdid = c.householdid AND
              ho.minorderdate = o.orderdate
      GROUP BY c.householdid) hhmin
     ON hhmin.householdid = c.householdid AND
        hhmin.minorderid = o.orderid
```

This is a rather complicated query for a rather simple question. Without an incredible SQL optimizer, it requires joining the Orders and Customer tables three times for what seems like a relatively direct question.

This query could be simplified if we assumed that the smallest ORDERID in a household occurred on the earliest ORDERDATE. This condition is definitely worth checking for, as done by the following query:

```
SELECT COUNT(*) as numhh,
       SUM(CASE WHEN o.orderdate = minodate THEN 1 ELSE 0 END) as numsame
FROM (SELECT householdid, MIN(orderdate) as minodate,
             MIN(orderid) as minorderid
      FROM orders o JOIN customer c ON o.customerid = c.customerid
      GROUP BY householdid
      HAVING COUNT(*) > 1) ho JOIN
     orders o
     ON ho.minorderid = o.orderid
ORDER BY 1
```

This query looks only at households that have more than one order. For those, it compares the minimum order date to the date of the order with the minimum order id.

This query finds 21,965 households with more than one order. Of these, 18,973 have the order date associated with the smallest id being the same as the earliest order date. There remain 2,992 households whose minimum order date differs from the order date on the minimum order id. Although it would simplify queries to assume that the minimum ORDERID occurred on the earliest ORDERDATE, this is simply not true.

## Clever Aggregation

The clever aggregation approach uses aggregations rather than complex subqueries. The specific aggregation function that we want might look something like:

```
MIN(orderid) WHERE (orderdate = MIN(orderdate))
```

Alas, this is fantasy SQL that simply does not exist. However, clever tricks with string values approximate the fantasy SQL. This method was first introduced in Chapter 3, but we'll review it here again.

The idea is to convert ORDERDATE to a string of the form YYYYMMDD (with or without hyphens). This string has the nice characteristic that it sorts alphabetically in the same order as the original date. So, the minimum value of these strings is the minimum value of the original date. The clever idea is to append something onto the end of the string. Now, the minimum value is dominated by the first part of the string, so it corresponds to the date. The basic expression looks like:

```
SUBSTRING(MIN(CAST(YEAR(orderdate)*10000+MONTH(orderdate)*100+
                DAY(orderdate) as CHAR)+(CAST(totalprice as CHAR))),
        9, 100)+0
```

The order date is first converted to a number, which is cast to a character value, and then TOTALPRICE is appended onto the end. The minimum value for this composite value is determined by the date which comes first, with the TOTALPRICE carried along. Extract the total price by taking the string from position nine onwards. The final "+0" converts the value back into a number.

The following SQL uses this technique:

```
SELECT ho.householdid, numorders,
       DATEDIFF(dd, mindate, maxdate) as daysdiff,
       (lasttotalprice - firsttotalprice) as pricediff
FROM (SELECT householdid, MIN(orderdate) as mindate,
            MAX(orderdate) as maxdate, COUNT(*) as numorders,
            CAST(SUBSTRING(MIN(CAST(YEAR(orderdate)*10000 +
                                MONTH(orderdate)*100 +
                                DAY(orderdate) as CHAR)+
                            CAST(totalprice as CHAR)), 9, 100
                   ) AS DECIMAL) as firsttotalprice,
            CAST(SUBSTRING(MAX(CAST(YEAR(orderdate)*10000 +
                                MONTH(orderdate)*100 +
                                DAY(orderdate) as CHAR)+
                            CAST(totalprice as CHAR)), 9, 100
                   ) AS DECIMAL) as lasttotalprice
      FROM orders o JOIN customer c ON o.customerid = c.customerid
      GROUP BY householdid
      HAVING MIN(orderdate) < MAX(orderdate) ) ho
```

Although it uses a complicated set of functions for getting the maximum and minimum TOTALPRICE, this query requires no extra joins or aggregations. The technical aside "SQL Window Functions" discusses the third method, which uses window functions to solve the problem.

### SQL WINDOW FUNCTIONS

The ranking functions discussed earlier in this chapter are examples of SQL window functions. SQL window functions are similar to aggregation functions in that they calculate summary values. However, instead of returning a smaller set of summary rows, the summary values are appended onto each row in the original data.

For example, the following statement appends the average order amount onto each order record:

```
SELECT AVG(totalprice) OVER (PARTITION BY NULL), o.*
FROM orders o
```

The syntax is similar to the syntax for the ranking functions. The OVER keyword indicates that this is a window aggregation function rather than a group by aggregation function. The part in parentheses describes the window of rows that the AVG() works on. In this case, there is no partition, so the statement takes the average of all rows.

The partitioning statement acts like a GROUP BY. So, the following calculates the average order amount for each household:

```
SELECT AVG(totalprice) OVER (PARTITION BY c.householdid), o.*
FROM orders o JOIN customer c ON o.customerid = c.customerid
```

Unlike grouping aggregation functions, though, the household average is appended onto every row.

Window aggregation functions are quite powerful and quite useful. The simplest way to get the first and last values would be to use the FIRST() and LAST() functions:

```
SELECT FIRST(totalprice) OVER (PARTITION BY c.householdid
                               ORDER BY orderdate) as pricefirst,
       LAST(totalprice) OVER (PARTITION BY c.householdid
                              ORDER BY orderdate) as pricelast,
       o.*
FROM orders o JOIN customer c ON o.customerid = c.customerid
```

Unfortunately, these functions are not available in SQL Server (although they are available in Oracle). Other functions such as MIN(), MAX(), and AVG() do not do what we want. They ignore the ORDER BY clause and return the minimum, maximum, or average value of the order amount.

*Continued on next page*

---

**SQL WINDOW FUNCTIONS (CONTINUED)**

There is a relatively simple work-around, using the `ROW_NUMBER()` **function to enumerate the orders in each household. This information can then be used to find the first and last values:**

```
SELECT householdid,
       MAX(CASE WHEN i = 1 THEN totalprice END) as pricefirst,
       MAX(CASE WHEN i = n THEN totalprice END) as pricelast
FROM (SELECT o.*, c.householdid,
             COUNT(*) OVER (PARTITION BY c.householdid) as n,
             ROW_NUMBER() OVER (PARTITION BY c.householdid
                                ORDER BY orderdate ASC) as i
      FROM orders o JOIN customer c ON o.customerid = c.customerid
     ) h
GROUP BY householdid
```

The window aggregation functions are very useful, but their functionality can usually be expressed using other SQL constructs (this is not true of the ranking window functions). They are equivalent to doing the following:

1. Doing a `GROUP BY` aggregation on the partition columns; and then,

2. Joining the resulting table back to the original on the partition columns.

However, window functions are a significant improvement over this process for two reasons. First, they allow values with different partitioning columns to be calculated in the same `SELECT` statement. Second, the ranking window functions introduce a new level of functionality that is much harder to replicate without the functions.

---

## Comparing the First and Last Values

Given the order amounts on the earliest and latest dates, what is the best way to compare these values? Four possibilities are:

- The difference between the earliest and latest purchase amounts. This is useful for determining the households whose spending is increasing (positive differences) and decreasing (negative differences).

- The ratio of the latest purchase amount to the earliest purchase amount. This is similar to the difference. Ratios between zero and one are decreasing and ratios over one are increasing.

- The difference divided by the time units. This makes it possible to say that the customer is increasing their purchase amounts by so many dollars every day (or week or month or year).

- The ratio raised to the power of one divided by the number of time units. This makes it possible to say that the customer is increasing their purchase amounts by some percentage every day (or week or month or year).

*What do the differences look like?* This is a reasonable question. There are only about twenty thousand households that have more than one order. This is a small enough number to include on an Excel scatter plot.

Figure 8-11 shows the distribution of the differences, because the differences provide more information. The cumulative percent crosses the $0 line at about 67%, showing that more households have decreasing order amounts than increasing order amounts. The summaries for the chart are done in Excel.

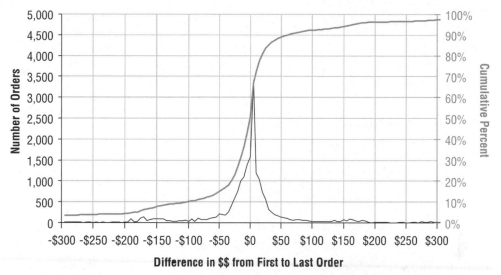

**Figure 8-11:** The distribution of the differences in total price between the first order and the last order shows that more households have decreases than increases in the order amounts.

## What Happens as Customer Span Increases

Figure 8-12 shows what happens to the difference as the span between the first and last purchases increases. There are two curves on the chart, one for the total number of households whose purchases have that span (in 30-day increments) and one for the average price difference.

For the shortest differences in time, the second purchase has a lower value than the first for a strong majority of households. However, after about six months, the breakdown is more even. As the time span between the first purchase and last purchase increases, the later purchase is more likely to be larger than the first. This count of purchases has a wave pattern that fades over time, corresponding to households that make purchases at the same time of the year.

The SQL for making this chart uses the subquery that finds the first and last total price amounts. The outer query does the aggregation:

```
SELECT FLOOR(daysdiff/30)*30 as daystopurchase,
       COUNT(*) as num, AVG(pricediff) as avgdiff
```

*(continued)*

```
FROM (<subquery>) ho
GROUP BY FLOOR(daysdiff/30)*30
ORDER BY 1
```

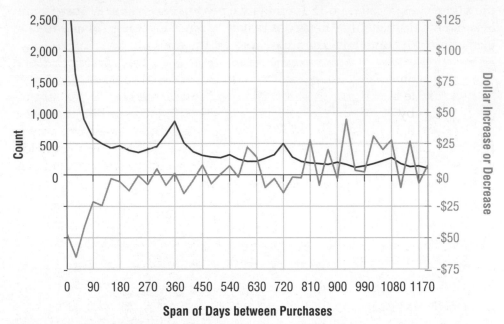

**Figure 8-12:** As the customer time span increases, the amount that customers increase their spending also increases.

The chart itself uses a trick to align the horizontal grid lines; this is challenging because the count on the left-hand axis has only positive values, and the dollar amount on the right-hand axis has both positive and negative values. The grid lines are lined up, by making the left-hand axis go from –1,500 to +2,500 and the right hand from –$75 to +$125. The left-hand axis spans 4,000 units, which is a multiple of the 200 spanned by the right-hand axis, making it easier to align the horizontal grid lines on both sides. The left-hand axis does not show negative values, because these make no sense for counts, by using a special number format, "#,##0;". This number format says "put commas in numbers greater than or equal to zero and don't put anything for negative numbers."

**TIP** When the left and right axes have different scales, make the horizontal grids line up. This is easiest if the range on one axis is a multiple of the range on the other axis.

## What Happens as Customer Order Amounts Vary

The alternative viewpoint is to summarize the data by the difference in TOTALPRICE between the later order and the earliest order. This summary works best when the difference is placed into bins. For this example, the bins are the first number of the difference following by a sufficient number of zeros, so the bins look like: $1, $2, $3, . . ., $8, $9, $10, $20, $30, . . . $90, $100, $200, and so on. Formally, these bins are powers of ten times the first digit of the difference. Other binning methods are possible, such as equal-sized bins. However, binning by the first digit makes the bins easy to read and easy to communicate what is happening.

The chart in Figure 8-13 shows the number of households in each bin and the average time between orders. The number of households is quite spiky, because of the binning process. Every power of ten, the size of the bin suddenly jumps by a factor of ten. The range of $90–$100 is in one bin. The next is not $100–$110, it is instead $100–$200, which is ten times larger. One way to eliminate the spikiness is to show the cumulative number of households, rather than the number in the bin itself. This eliminates the spikiness but may be less intuitive for people looking at the chart.

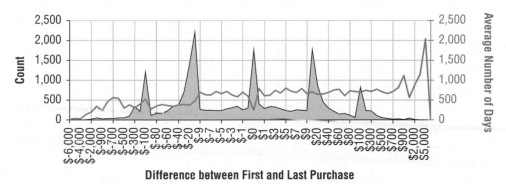

**Figure 8-13:** The span of time that customers make purchases is related to the average difference in dollar amounts between the first and last orders.

The average time span tends to increase as the difference increases. This suggests that the longer a customer is active, the more the customer is spending, on average. However, this effect is most pronounced for the most negative differences. Customers whose purchases decrease dramatically are making purchases during relatively short time spans.

The query that generates the data for this chart is similar to the previous query, except for the GROUP BY clause:

```
SELECT (CASE WHEN pricediff = 0 THEN '$0'
             WHEN pricediff BETWEEN -1 and 0 THEN '$-0'
             WHEN pricediff BETWEEN 0 AND 1 THEN '$+0'
             WHEN pricediff < 0
             THEN '$-'+LEFT(-pricediff, 1)+
```

*(continued)*

```
                    LEFT('000000000', FLOOR(LOG(-pricediff)/LOG(10)))
            ELSE '$'+LEFT(pricediff, 1)+
                    LEFT('000000000', FLOOR(LOG(pricediff)/LOG(10)))
        END) diffgroup,
        COUNT(*) as numhh, AVG(daysdiff) as avgdaysdiff
FROM (<subquery>) ho
GROUP BY (CASE WHEN pricediff = 0 THEN '$0'
                . . .
        END)
ORDER BY MIN(pricediff)
```

The two notable features in the query are the CASE statement for binning the difference in values and the ORDER BY statement. The bin definition uses the first digit of the difference and then turns the rest of the digits into zeros, so "123" and "169" go into the "100" bin. The first digit is extracted using the LEFT() function, which takes the first digit of a positive numeric argument. The remaining digits are set to zero, by calculating the number of digits using a particular mathematical expression. The number of zeros is the log in base 10 of the difference, and the log in base 10 is the log in any base divided by the log of 10 in that base (so the expression works even in databases where LOG() calculates the natural log). The process is the same for negative differences, except the absolute value is used and a negative sign prepended to the result.

The purpose of the ORDER BY clause is to order the bins numerically. An alphabetical order would order them as "$1," "$10," "$100," "$1000," and these would be followed by "$2." To get a numeric ordering, we extract one value from the bin, the minimum value, and order by this. Actually, any value would do, but the minimum is convenient.

## Comparison of First Year Values and Last Year Values

The previous section compared the first order amount value to the last order amount. This section makes a slightly different comparison: *How does the average household's purchase change from the first year they make a purchase to the most recent year?*

Table 8-10 contains the difference between the average order amount during the earliest year and during the latest year. When the purchases are on successive years, the difference is almost always negative. However, as the time span grows, the difference becomes positive indicating that the order sizes are growing, although this might be due to prices increasing during this time.

**Table 8-10:** Difference between Average First and Last Year Order Amounts

| YEAR | 2010 | 2011 | 2012 | 2013 | 2014 | 2015 | 2016 |
|------|------|------|------|------|------|------|------|
| 2009 | $7.54 | $2.29 | $22.49 | $34.83 | $29.31 | $47.24 | $46.38 |
| 2010 | -$17.44 | $1.76 | $24.59 | $10.07 | $17.08 | $30.22 | |
| 2011 | | -$0.02 | $16.42 | $12.63 | $7.49 | $27.44 | |
| 2012 | | $1.49 | -$1.66 | $9.54 | $45.75 | | |
| 2013 | | | -$21.26 | -$11.36 | $36.26 | | |
| 2014 | | | -$14.28 | -$7.05 | | | |
| 2015 | | | | -$41.56 | | | |

Figure 8-14 shows these results as a scatter plot, where the horizontal axis is the purchase amount on the earlier date and the vertical axis is the purchase amount on the later date. The diagonal line divides the chart into two regions. Below the line, purchases are decreasing over time and above the line, purchases are increasing over time. The lowest point in the chart shows the households whose earliest purchase was in 2009 and whose latest purchase was in 2011; the earlier purchase average was about $35 and the later was about $37. An interesting feature of the chart is that all the points below the line come from either one- or two-year spans. The longer the time span, the larger the later purchases.

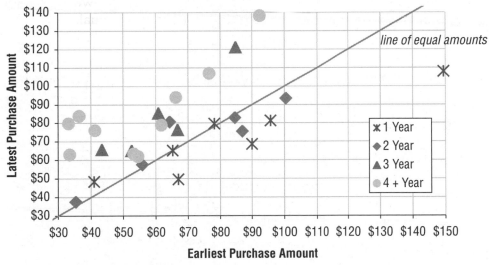

**Figure 8-14:** This scatter plot shows the average order amount for the earliest orders and latest orders for households. Households below the diagonal line have decreasing orders; those above have increasing orders.

The query calculates the average purchase size for pairs of years, the first and last years that households make purchases. Each row also contains the average size of the purchase during the first year and the average size during the second year:

```
SELECT minyear, maxyear, AVG (avgearliest) as avgearliest,
       AVG(avglatest) as avglatest, COUNT(*) as numhh
FROM (SELECT hy.householdid, minyear, maxyear,
             AVG(CASE WHEN hy.theyear = minyear THEN avgprice END
                 ) as avgearliest,
             AVG(CASE WHEN hy.theyear = maxyear THEN avgprice END
                 ) as avglatest
      FROM (SELECT householdid, MIN(YEAR(orderdate)) as minyear,
                   MAX(YEAR(orderdate)) as maxyear
            FROM orders o JOIN customer c ON o.customerid = c.customerid
            GROUP BY householdid
            HAVING MIN(YEAR(orderdate)) < MAX(YEAR(orderdate))
           ) hminmax JOIN
           (SELECT householdid, YEAR(orderdate) as theyear,
                   SUM(totalprice) as sumprice,
                   AVG(totalprice) as avgprice
            FROM orders o JOIN customer c ON o.customerid = c.customerid
            GROUP BY householdid, YEAR(orderdate) ) hy
           ON hy.householdid = hminmax.householdid AND
              (hy.theyear = hminmax.minyear OR
               hy.theyear = hminmax.maxyear)
      GROUP BY hy.householdid, minyear, maxyear) h
GROUP BY minyear, maxyear
```

This query aggregates the orders data in two subqueries, as shown in the dataflow diagram in Figure 8-15. The first is by HOUSEHOLDID to get the earliest and latest years with orders. The second is by HOUSEHOLDID and the year of the ORDERDATE to get the average order size in each year. These two subqueries are joined together to get the average order size in the first and last years, and this final result is again aggregated by the first and last year.

## Trend from the Best Fit Line

This section goes one step further by calculating the slope of the line that best fits the TOTALPRICE values. This calculation relies on some mathematical manipulation, essentially implementing the equation for the slope in SQL. The advantage to this approach is that it takes into account all the purchases over time, instead of just the first and last ones.

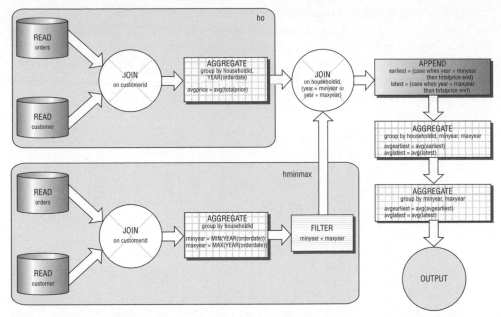

**Figure 8-15:** This dataflow diagram shows the processing necessary to get the average household purchases during the first and last year of purchases.

## Using the Slope

The purchases in this household have increased over time, although irregularly. Figure 8-16 shows the purchases for two households over several years. One household has seen their orders increase over time; the other has seen them decrease. The chart also shows the best fit line for each household. The household with increasing purchases has a line that goes up, so the slope is positive. The other line decreases, so its slope is negative. Chapter 11 discusses best fit lines in more detail.

The slope of the best fit line connecting the household with increasing purchases is 0.464, which means that for each day, the expected value of an order from the household increases by $0.46, or about $169 per year. The slope provides a simple summary of purchases over time. This summary can be useful for reporting purposes, although it works better when there are more data points. Slopes are better at summarizing data collected monthly, rather than at irregular, highly spaced transactions.

## Calculating the Slope

The formula for any straight line is written in terms of its slope and Y-intercept. If we knew the formula for the best fit line, the slope would fall out of it. Fortu-

nately, the best fit line is not difficult to calculate in SQL. Each data point —
each order — needs an X-coordinate and a Y-coordinate. The Y-coordinate is the
TOTALPRICE on the order at that point in time. The X-coordinate should be
the date. However, dates do not work particularly well in mathematical calculations, so instead we'll use the number of days since the beginning of 2000. The
idea is to use these X- and Y-coordinates to calculate the trend (slope) of the best
fit line.

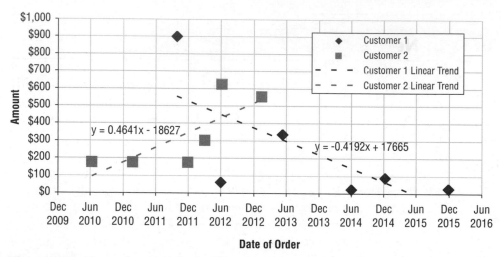

**Figure 8-16:** These customers have different purchase trends over time.

The formula requires five aggregation columns:

- N: the number of data points
- SUMX: the sum of the X-values of the data points
- SUMXY: the sum of the product of the X-value times the Y-value
- SUMY: sum of the Y-values
- SUMYY: sum of the squares of the Y-values

The slope is then the ratio between two numbers. The numerator is n*SUMXY
- SUMX*SUMY; the denominator is n*SUMXX - SUMX*SUMX. The following query
does this calculation:

```
SELECT h.*, (1.0*n*sumxy - sumx*sumy)/(n*sumxx - sumx*sumx) as slope
FROM (SELECT householdid, COUNT(*) as n,
             SUM(1.0*days) as sumx, SUM(1.0*days*days) as sumxx,
             SUM(totalprice) as sumy, SUM(days*totalprice) as sumxy
      FROM (SELECT o.*, DATEDIFF(dd, '2000-01-01', orderdate) as days
            FROM orders o
           ) o JOIN customer c ON o.customerid = c.customerid
      GROUP BY householdid
      HAVING MIN(orderdate) < MAX(orderdate) ) h
```

The innermost subquery defines DAYS, which is the difference between the order date and the beginning of 2000. Then the five variables are defined in another subquery, and finally SLOPE in the outermost:

The slope is defined only when a household has orders on more than one day. So, this query also limits the calculation to households where the span between the earliest date and the latest date is greater than zero. This eliminates households with only one purchase, as well as those with multiple purchases all on the same day.

# Time to Next Event

The final topic in this chapter combines the ideas from survival analysis with repeated events. This topic is quite deep, and this section introduces the ideas as they can be implemented in SQL and Excel. The question is: *How long until a customer places another order?*

## Idea behind the Calculation

To apply survival analysis to repeated events, we need the date of the next order in the household (if any) appended to every order. The order date and next order date provide the basic information needed for time-to-event survival analysis, although the definitions for survival analysis are inverted from the last two chapters:

- The "start" event is when a customer makes a purchase.
- The "end" event is either the next purchase date or the cutoff date.

This terminology is backwards. "Survival" ends up meaning the survival of the customer's "non-purchase" state. In fact, we are interested in the exact opposite of survival, 100%-Survival, which is the cumulative probability that customers have made a purchase up to some given point in time.

Figure 8-17 shows the overall time-to-next purchase curve for all households along with the daily "hazard" that a customer makes a purchase. The first thing to note is that after three years, only about 20% of customers have made another purchase. This is consistent with the fact that most households have only one order.

The hazards show an interesting story. There are clearly peaks after one year with echoes at two years and three years. These are customers making purchases once per year, most likely holiday shoppers. It suggests that there is a segment of such shoppers.

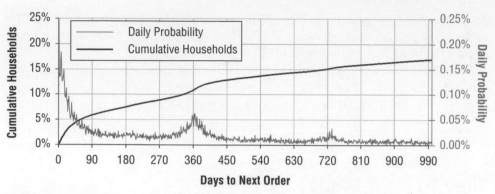

**Figure 8-17:** This chart shows the time to next order, both as a cumulative proportion of customers (1-Survival) and as a daily "risk" of making a purchase (hazard probability).

## Calculating Next Purchase Date Using SQL

The hardest part of answering the question is appending the date of the next order. Figure 8-18 shows a dataflow diagram of the logic for appending the next date. First, the Orders table and Customer table are joined together to append the HOUSEHOLDID to every order. This table is then joined to itself, so every order in a household is paired with every other one. The resulting self-joined table is aggregated by the original HOUSEHOLDID and ORDER-DATE. The next order is the minimum of the order date that occurs after the original ORDERDATE. The key idea here is to do a self-join and then aggregation to calculate the "next" date.

The following SQL accomplishes this:

```
SELECT o1.householdid, o1.orderdate as firstdate,
       MIN(CASE WHEN o2.orderdate > o1.orderdate THEN o2.orderdate END
           ) as nextdate,
       COUNT(*) as numords,
       MAX(CASE WHEN o2.orderdate > o1.orderdate THEN 1 ELSE 0 END
           ) as hasnext
FROM (SELECT c.householdid, o.*
      FROM orders o JOIN customer c ON o.customerid = c.customerid
     ) o1 LEFT OUTER JOIN
     (SELECT c.householdid, o.*
      FROM orders o JOIN customer c ON o.customerid = c.customerid) o2
     ON o1.householdid = o2.householdid
GROUP BY o1.householdid, o1.orderdate
```

This SQL follows the same logic as the dataflow, joining Orders and Customer, then doing a self-join, then the aggregation. This logic can be extended to do other things, such as calculating the total number of orders and the number of orders before the first one. The total number of orders is simply COUNT(*). The number of orders before the first one can also be calculated:

```
SUM(CASE WHEN o2.orderdate < o1.orderdate THEN 1
         ELSE 0 END) as numbef
```

Doing a self-join and aggregation is quite powerful, because it provides the means to calculate many different, interesting variables. However, it is probably not very efficient, and SQL extensions might be more efficient for the same calculation.

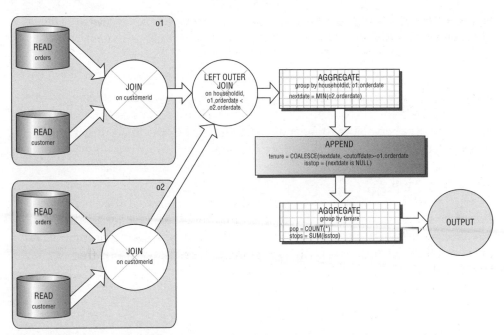

**Figure 8-18:** This dataflow diagram shows the processing needed to append the next order date to a specific order.

## From Next Purchase Date to Time-to-Event

The time to next purchase is calculated as follows:

- The days to next purchase is the next order date minus the order date.
- When the next purchase date is NULL, use the cutoff date of Sep 20, 2016.

This is the duration in days. In addition, a flag is needed to specify whether the event has occurred.

The following query aggregates by the days to the next purchase, summing the number of orders with that date and the number of times when another order occurs (as opposed to hitting the cutoff date):

```
SELECT DATEDIFF(dd, firstdate, ISNULL(nextdate, '2016-09-20')) as days,
       COUNT(*),
       SUM(CASE WHEN numbef = 1 THEN 1 ELSE 0 END) as ord1,
       . . .
       SUM(CASE WHEN numbef = 5 THEN 1 ELSE 0 END) as ord5,
       SUM(hasnext) as hasnext,
       SUM(CASE WHEN numbef = 1 THEN hasnext ELSE 0 END) as hasnext1,
       . . .
       SUM(CASE WHEN numbef = 5 THEN hasnext ELSE 0 END) as hasnext5
FROM (<subquery>) a
GROUP BY DATEDIFF(dd, firstdate, ISNULL(nextdate, '2016-09-20'))
ORDER BY 1
```

The calculation then proceeds by calculating the hazard, survival, and 1-S values for the data in the same way used in the previous two chapters. In addition to survival, the spreadsheet also calculates 1-S, because this is the more interesting number.

## Stratifying Time-to-Event

As with the survival calculation, the time-to-event can be stratified. For instance, Figure 8-19 shows the time-to-next-event stratified by the number of orders that the customer has already made. These curves follow the expected track: the more often that someone places orders, the sooner they make another order.

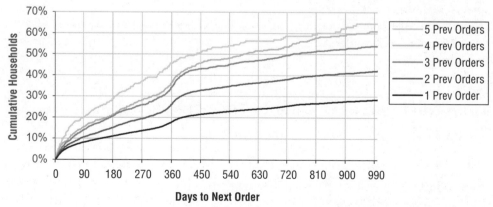

**Figure 8-19:** This chart shows the time to next purchase stratified by the number of previous purchases.

Of course, the number of previous orders is only one variable we might want to use. We can also stratify by anything that is known at the order time:

- Has the time-to-next order varied for orders placed in different years?
- Does the time-to-next order vary depending on the size of an order?
- Do customers make a repeat order sooner or later when a particular item is in their basket?

All of these are simple extensions of the idea of doing a self-join and then aggregating the data to get the next order date.

## Lessons Learned

This chapter introduces repeated events, using the purchases data. Repeated events are customer interactions that occur at irregular intervals.

The first challenge with repeated events is determining whether separate transactions belong to the same customer. In this chapter, we learned that the CUSTOMERID column is basically useless, because it is almost always unique. A better column for identifying transactions over time is HOUSEHOLDID.

Matching customers on transactions using names and addresses is challenging and often outsourced. Even so, it is useful to be able to use SQL to validate the results. Do the customers in the households make sense?

The classic way of analyzing repeated events is using RFM analysis, which stands for recency, frequency, monetary. This analysis is feasible using SQL and Excel, particularly when using the ranking functions in SQL. However, RFM is inherently limited, because it focuses on only three dimensions of customer relationships. It is a cell-based approach, where customers are placed into cells and then tracked over time.

An important topic in looking at repeated events is whether the sizes of purchases change over time. There are different ways of making the comparison, including simply looking at the first and last order to see whether the size is growing or shrinking. The most sophisticated way presented in this chapter is to calculate the slope of the best fit line connecting the orders. When the slope is positive, order sizes are increasing; when the slope is negative, order sizes are decreasing.

The final topic in the chapter applies survival analysis to repeated events, addressing the question of how long it takes a customer to make the next order. This application is quite similar to survival analysis for stopped customers, except that the important customers — the ones who make the purchase — are the ones who do not survive.

The next chapter continues analysis of repeated events, but from a perspective that is not covered in this chapter at all. It discusses the actual items purchased in each order and what this tells us about the items and the customers.

# What's in a Shopping Cart? Market Basket Analysis and Association Rules

The previous chapter discussed everything about customer behavior — when, where, how — with one notable exception: what customers purchase. This chapter dives into the detail, looking at the specific products being purchased, to learn both about the customers and the products they are buying. Market basket analysis is the general name for understanding product purchase patterns at the customer level.

Association rules form a big part of market basket analysis. An association rule specifies that certain products are purchased with other products. Historically, the classical example is beer and diapers. The story goes that these are purchased together as young families prepare for the weekend. Although this is a classic example of market basket analysis, association rules were not used to find this "unexpected" pattern, because retailers were already familiar with the purchase trends of the two products.

Association rules can reduce millions of transactions on thousands of items into easy-to-understand rules. This chapter introduces the techniques for discovering association rules using SQL. The processing is rather complex, so the queries in this chapter are advanced, sometimes making use of temporary tables to hold intermediate results.

Some data mining software includes algorithms for association rules. However, such software does not provide the flexibility available when using SQL directly. This chapter also improves on the basic algorithm by showing some interesting variations on association rules, including heterogeneous associations and sequential associations.

Market basket analysis is not only association rules. The chapter starts with exploratory analysis of purchases. Such analysis can help us understand which products are most associated with the customers who spend lots of money, which products are associated with one-time purchases, and similar questions.

# Exploratory Market Basket Analysis

This section explores the purchases database from the perspective of understanding the products in the orders.

## Scatter Plot of Products

There are about four thousand products in the Product table, which are classified into nine different product groups. Chapter 3 looked at product groups, and pointed out that the most popular group is BOOK.

Two of the most interesting features of products are price and popularity. Scatter plots are a good way to visualize this information, with different groups having different shapes and colors. The following query extracts the information for the scatter plot:

```
SELECT p.productid, p.productgroupname, p.fullprice, olp.numorders
FROM (SELECT ol.productid, COUNT(DISTINCT orderid) as numorders
      FROM orderline ol
      GROUP BY ol.productid) olp JOIN
     product p ON olp.productid = p.productid
ORDER BY p.productid
```

The scatter plot in Figure 9-1 shows relationships among these three features. Along the bottom of the chart are the few dozen products that have a price of $0. Most of these are, appropriately, in the FREEBIE category, along with a handful in the OTHER category. Although not obvious on the scatter plot, all FREEBIE products do, indeed, have a price of zero.

The upper left-hand portion of the chart consists almost entirely of products in the ARTWORK product group. These products are expensive and rarely purchased. There are a few products in the ARTWORK group that are quite popular (purchased by over one thousand customers) and some that are quite inexpensive (well under one hundred dollars), but these are exceptions within the category.

The most popular product group is BOOK, as seen by the abundance of triangles on the right part of the chart. Most are inexpensive, but one is among the most expensive products. This is, perhaps, an example of misclassification. The rest of the products tend to be in the middle, both in terms of pricing and popularity.

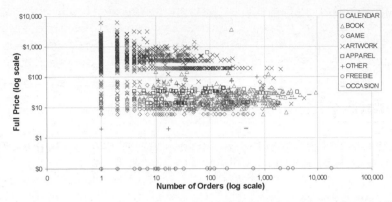

**Figure 9-1:** This scatter plot shows the relationship between product groups, price, and number of purchases.

This scatter plot is a log-log plot, meaning that both the horizontal and vertical axes are on a logarithmic scale where one unit on either axis increases by a factor of ten. Log scales are useful when all values are positive and there is a wide range of values.

Log-log plots are not able to plot zero (because the logarithm of zero is undefined), and yet the chart shows the "0" value. The trick is that zero is really 0.1, which, when formatted to have no decimal places, looks like "0" instead of "0.1." To make this work, the zeros in the data have to be replaced by the value 0.1, either using SQL:

```
(CASE WHEN <value> = 0 THEN 0.1 ELSE <value> END) as <whatever>
```

Or using Excel:

```
=IF(<cellref>>=0, 0.1, <cellref>)
```

The number format for the chart simply shows the value with no decimal places.

**TIP** Use the log scale on axes where the values have a wide range and are all positive. The log scale does not work when values are negative or zero; however, it is possible to show zero values by changing them to a small value and then using clever formatting.

## Duplicate Products in Orders

Sometimes, the same product occurs multiple times in the same order. This is an anomaly because such orders should be using the NUMUNITS column for multiple products rather than replicating order lines. What is happening?

Counting is a good place to start, as with the following query:

```
SELECT numinorder, COUNT(*) as cnt, COUNT(DISTINCT productid) as numprods
FROM (SELECT ol.orderid, ol.productid, COUNT(*) as numinorder
      FROM orderline ol
      GROUP BY ol.orderid, ol.productid) olp
GROUP BY numinorder
ORDER BY 1
```

The query counts the number of orders that have a product on more than one order line, and the number of different products that appear on those orders.

Table 9-1 shows that almost 98% of the time products appear on only one order line, as expected. However, there are clearly exceptions. One possible explanation is that some small group of products is to blame. Perhaps some products just have a tendency to appear on multiple order lines. The following query shows that there are, in fact, 1,343 such products:

```
SELECT COUNT(DISTINCT productid)
FROM (SELECT ol.orderid, ol.productid
      FROM orderline ol
      GROUP BY ol.orderid, ol.productid
      HAVING COUNT(*) > 1) olp
```

**Table 9-1:** Number of Order Lines within an Order Having the Same Product

| LINES IN ORDER WITH PRODUCT | NUMBER OF ORDERS | NUMBER OF PRODUCTS | % OF ORDERS |
| :---: | :---: | :---: | :---: |
| 1 | 272,824 | 3,684 | 97.9% |
| 2 | 5,009 | 1,143 | 1.8% |
| 3 | 686 | 344 | 0.2% |
| 4 | 155 | 101 | 0.1% |
| 5 | 51 | 40 | 0.0% |
| 6 | 20 | 14 | 0.0% |
| 7 | 1 | 1 | 0.0% |
| 8 | 4 | 3 | 0.0% |
| 9 | 1 | 1 | 0.0% |
| 11 | 2 | 2 | 0.0% |
| 12 | 1 | 1 | 0.0% |
| 40 | 1 | 1 | 0.0% |

Because about one-third of the products occur on multiple order lines within one order, the products do not seem to be the cause of order line duplication. A reasonable alternative hypothesis is that the duplicates come from a particular period of time. Perhaps there was a period of time when NUMUNITS was not used. Looking at the date of the first order containing each duplicate product sheds light on this:

```
SELECT YEAR(minshipdate) as year, COUNT(*) as cnt
FROM (SELECT ol.orderid, ol.productid, MIN(ol.shipdate) as minshipdate
      FROM orderline ol
      GROUP BY ol.orderid, ol.productid
      HAVING COUNT(*) > 1) olp
GROUP BY YEAR(minshipdate)
ORDER BY 1
```

The query uses SHIPDATE instead of ORDERDATE simply to avoid joining in the Orders table. The subquery finds orders with duplicate products by using the HAVING clause to choose only those ORDERID and PRODUCTID pairs that appear more than once.

Although some years have much higher occurrences of products on duplicate order lines, the phenomenon has occurred in all years for which there is data as shown in Table 9-2. The reason is not a short-term change in policy.

**Table 9-2**: Number of Orders with Duplicate Products by Year

| YEAR | NUMBER OF ORDERS WITH DUPLICATE PRODUCTS |
|------|------------------------------------------|
| 2009 | 66 |
| 2010 | 186 |
| 2011 | 392 |
| 2012 | 181 |
| 2013 | 152 |
| 2014 | 1,433 |
| 2015 | 2,570 |
| 2016 | 951 |

The duplicates seem to be due neither to products nor time. Perhaps in desperation, the next thing to consider is other data within the Orderline table. Two columns of interest are SHIPDATE and UNITPRICE. These columns suggest the question: *How often do multiple ship dates and unit prices occur for the same product within an order?*

The idea behind answering this question is to classify each occurrence of multiple lines into the following categories:

- "ONE" or "SOME" unit prices.
- "ONE" or "SOME" shipping dates.

Table 9-3 shows the results from such a classification. Having multiple values for SHIPDATE suggests an inventory issue. A customer orders multiple units of a particular item, but there is not enough in stock. Part of the order ships immediately, part ships at a later time.

**Table 9-3:** Classification of Duplicate Order Lines by Number of Shipping Dates and Prices within Order

| PRICES | SHIP DATES | NUMBER OF PRODUCTS | NUMBER OF ORDERS |
| --- | --- | --- | --- |
| ONE | ONE | 262 | 1,649 |
| ONE | SOME | 1,177 | 4,173 |
| SOME | ONE | 33 | 44 |
| SOME | SOME | 59 | 65 |

Having multiple values for UNITPRICE suggests that a customer may be getting a discount on some of the units, but the discount is not available on all of them. And, there are still over one thousand orders with duplicate products that have the same ship date and unit price on all of them. These might be errors. Or, they might be related to data that is unavailable such as orders going to multiple shipping addresses.

The following query was used to generate the table:

```
SELECT prices, ships, COUNT(DISTINCT productid) as numprods,
       COUNT(*) as numtimes
FROM (SELECT ol.orderid, ol.productid,
             (CASE WHEN COUNT(DISTINCT unitprice) = 1 THEN 'ONE'
                   ELSE 'SOME' END) as prices,
             (CASE WHEN COUNT(DISTINCT shipdate) = 1 THEN 'ONE'
                   ELSE 'SOME' END) as ships
      FROM orderline ol
      GROUP BY ol.orderid, ol.productid
      HAVING COUNT(*) > 1) olp
GROUP BY prices, ships
```

Figure 9-2 shows the dataflow diagram for this query. The order lines for each product are summarized, counting the number of different prices and ship dates on the lines. These are then classified as "ONE" or "SOME" and aggregated again. This query only uses GROUP BY to do the processing; it contains no joins at all.

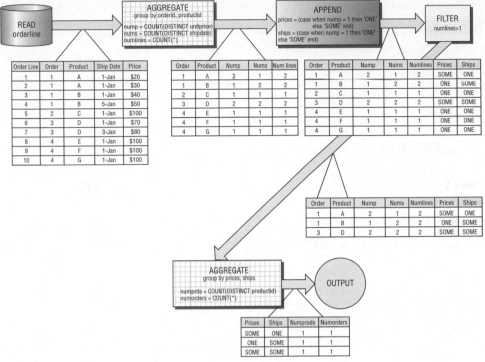

**Figure 9-2:** This dataflow diagram shows the processing for calculating the number of prices and of ship dates on order lines with the same product.

## Histogram of Number of Units

*What is the average number of units for products in a given order by product group?* It is tempting to answer this question using the following query:

```
SELECT productgroupname, AVG(numunits) as avgnumunits
FROM orderline ol JOIN product p ON ol.productid = p.productid
GROUP BY productgroupname
```

However, this query misses an important point: some products are split among multiple order lines in the data. Adding up NUMUNITS for each product in each order, and then taking the average solves this.

Both the correct average value and the incorrect value from the first query are in Table 9-4. The table shows that some products, such as ARTWORK, are less likely to have multiple units in the same order. Other products, such as those in the OCCASION product group, are more likely to be ordered in multiple quantities.

**Table 9-4:** Number of Units by Order and by Order Line

| PRODUCT GROUP | ORDER AVERAGE | ORDERLINE AVERAGE |
| --- | --- | --- |
| #N/A | 1.00 | 1.00 |
| APPAREL | 1.42 | 1.39 |
| ARTWORK | 1.26 | 1.20 |
| BOOK | 1.59 | 1.56 |
| CALENDAR | 1.67 | 1.64 |
| FREEBIE | 1.53 | 1.51 |
| GAME | 1.49 | 1.46 |
| OCCASION | 1.82 | 1.79 |
| OTHER | 2.44 | 2.30 |

For most of the product groups, the first method undercounts the number of units in an order by about 2%; this is consistent with the fact that about 2% of products in an order are on multiple lines. However, some categories are affected more than others. The undercounting for ARTWORK is over 5%, for instance.

The following query generated the data for the table:

```
SELECT productgroupname, AVG(ol.numunits) as orderaverage,
       SUM(ol.numunits) / SUM(ol.numlines) as orderlineaverage
FROM (SELECT ol.orderid, ol.productid, SUM(numunits)*1.0 as numunits,
             COUNT(*)*1.0 as numlines
      FROM orderline ol
      GROUP BY ol.orderid, ol.productid) ol JOIN
     product p ON ol.productid = p.productid
GROUP BY productgroupname
ORDER BY productgroupname
```

This query summarizes the Orderlines table, summing the NUMUNITS values for a given product in each order, and then taking the average. This is the real average of the number of products in an order. It is still possible to calculate the average number of products per order line by counting the total number of order lines for the product, and doing the division at the outer level. Both values can be calculated with a single query.

## Products Associated with One-Time Customers

Some products may be bad in the sense that customers purchase them and never purchase anything else. This suggests the question: *How many products are purchased exactly once by a household that never purchases anything else?* The following query returns the fact that 2,461 products have one-time purchasers:

```
SELECT COUNT(DISTINCT productid)
FROM (SELECT householdid, MIN(productid) as productid
      FROM customer c JOIN orders o ON c.customerid = o.customerid JOIN
           orderline ol ON o.orderid = ol.orderid
      GROUP BY householdid
      HAVING COUNT(DISTINCT ol.productid) = 1 AND
             COUNT(DISTINCT o.orderid) = 1) h
```

Much of the work in this query occurs in the HAVING clause. Of course, the Customer, Orders, and Orderline tables all need to be joined together. Then, the HAVING clause chooses only those households that have exactly one order and exactly one product. The HAVING clause counts the number of products by counting the number of distinct values of PRODUCTID and the number of orders by counting the number of distinct values of ORDERID.

**TIP** When bringing together data from different tables that have a one-to-many relationship, such as products, orders, and households, COUNT DISTINCT correctly counts the values at different levels. Use COUNT(DISTINCT orderid) rather than COUNT(orderid) to get the number of orders.

There are quite a few one-time products. More interesting are products that tend to be associated with one-time household purchasers: *Which products have a high proportion of their purchases associated with one-order households?* The answer to this question is the ratio of two numbers:

■ The number of households where the product is the only product the household ever buys.

■ The total number of households that purchase the product.

Both these numbers can be summarized from the data.

The following query performs the two calculations for each product:

```
SELECT p.productid, numhouseholds, COALESCE(numuniques, 0) as numuniques,
       COALESCE(numuniques*1.0, 0.0) / numhouseholds as prodratio
FROM (SELECT productid, COUNT(*) as numhouseholds
      FROM (SELECT c.householdid, ol.productid
            FROM customer c JOIN
                 orders o ON c.customerid = o.customerid JOIN
                 orderline ol ON o.orderid = ol.orderid
            GROUP BY c.householdid, ol.productid) hp
      GROUP BY productid) p LEFT OUTER JOIN
     (SELECT productid, COUNT(*) as numuniques
      FROM (SELECT householdid, MIN(productid) as productid
            FROM customer c JOIN
```

*(continued)*

```
              orders o ON c.customerid = o.customerid JOIN
              orderline ol ON o.orderid = ol.orderid
        GROUP BY householdid
        HAVING COUNT(DISTINCT ol.productid) = 1 AND
              COUNT(DISTINCT o.orderid) = 1) h
    GROUP BY productid) hp
  ON hp.productid = p.productid
ORDER BY 4 DESC
```

This query aggregates the product and household information two ways. The first subquery calculates the total number of households that purchase each product. The second subquery calculates the total number of households whose only order is a one-time purchase of the product.

The results are somewhat expected. The products that have the highest ratios are the products that have only one order. In fact, of the 419 products where every order is the only household order, only one has more than ten purchases. The results do highlight the fact that products have different behavior with respect to bringing in one-time households. The category of the product makes a difference. Of the 419 products that bring in exclusively one-time purchasers, 416 of them are in the ARTWORK category.

This suggests a follow-up question: *For the different product groups, what is the proportion of one-time purchasing households?* The following query answers this question:

```
SELECT productgroupname, COUNT(*) as numprods,
       SUM(numhouseholds) as numhh, SUM(numuniques) as numuniques,
       SUM(numuniques*1.0)/SUM(numhouseholds) as ratio
FROM   (<previous-query-without-order-by>) hp JOIN
       product p ON hp.productid = p.productid
GROUP BY productgroupname
ORDER BY 5 DESC
```

This query uses the previous query (without the ORDER BY clause) as a subquery and joins it to the Product table to get the product group:

Figure 9-3 shows number of households that have made a purchase and the proportion that are one-time-only within each category. By this measure, the worst product group is APPAREL, where over half the purchasers are one-time only. The best is FREEBIE, with less than 1%. That is presumably because the FREEBIE products are typically included in bundles with other products.

## Products Associated with the Best Customers

Once upon a time, in the 1990s, when bill paying services were very expensive (because banks actually had to write and send checks), Fidelity Investments considered canceling its bill paying service. Then someone in its special projects group noticed that customers who used the service had the largest balances and best retention. There is a similar story about a manager wanting to remove gourmet mustard from shelves in a food market to make room for other, faster moving items. Then further analysis showed that customers who purchase gourmet mustard do so in very large purchases. Without the mustard, the store feared losing the sales of everything else in those customers' carts.

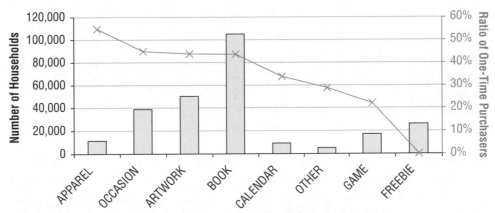

**Figure 9-3:** The proportion of households that purchase only one product varies considerably by product group. Some groups such as APPAREL are associated with such unique purchasers.

Such insights (as well as most people's personal experiences) illustrate that customers might make purchase decisions based on particular products. This leads to the question: *What products have the largest remaining average value in the orders where they appear?* Remaining value, also called *residual value*, is the value that remains in the order after said products are removed. An order containing only one product contributes no residual value for that product.

This section discusses an approach to residual value calculations, as well as certain biases in the calculation that are difficult to remove. The following query calculates the average residual value for each product; that is, it calculates the average remaining value in orders that contain the product:

```
SELECT op.productid, COUNT(*) as numorders, AVG(ototal) as avgorder,
       AVG(prodprice) as avgprod, AVG(ototal-prodprice) as avgresidual
FROM (SELECT orderid, SUM(ol.totalprice) as ototal
      FROM orderline ol
      GROUP BY orderid
      HAVING COUNT(DISTINCT productid) > 1) o JOIN
     (SELECT o.orderid, ol.productid, SUM(ol.totalprice) as prodprice
      FROM orderline ol JOIN orders o ON ol.orderid = o.orderid
      GROUP BY o.orderid, ol.productid
     ) op
     ON op.orderid = o.orderid
GROUP BY op.productid
ORDER BY AVG(o.ototal - prodprice) DESC
```

The innermost subquery summarizes orders with more than one product by product, thereby treating multiple order lines with the same product as a single product. The residual value for each product is the order total minus the amount for each product in the order (so an order contributes to the residual values of all products in it). The average of the residual is then calculated for each product.

Summarizing by product group uses the previous query as a subquery (without the ORDER BY clause):

```
SELECT p.productgroupname, COUNT(*) as numproducts,
       SUM(numorders) as numorders, AVG(avgresidual) as avgresidual
FROM (<previous-query-without-order-by>) o JOIN
     product p ON p.productid = o.productid
GROUP BY productgroupname
ORDER BY 1
```

This query calculates the average residual for each product and then returns the average for all products within a product group. This is different from calculating the average residual for a product group, which would require modifying the previous query to be at the product group level rather than the product level.

Table 9-5 shows the average residual value for a market basket as well as the average price of items. Not surprisingly, the most expensive products — ARTWORK — have, by far, the highest residual value. This suggests that customers are purchasing multiple expensive items at the same time, rather than mixing and matching less expensive items with more expensive ones.

**Table 9-5:** Average Residual Value by Product Group

| PRODUCT GROUP | NUMBER OF PRODUCTS | NUMBER OF ORDERS | AVERAGE ORDER RESIDUAL | AVERAGE HOUSEHOLD RESIDUAL |
|---|---|---|---|---|
| #N/A | 1 | 9 | $868.72 | $658.40 |
| APPAREL | 85 | 4,030 | $39.01 | $618.88 |
| ARTWORK | 2,576 | 21,456 | $1,032.24 | $1,212.27 |
| BOOK | 236 | 48,852 | $67.94 | $365.06 |
| CALENDAR | 31 | 3,211 | $37.01 | $387.74 |
| FREEBIE | 25 | 27,708 | $28.27 | $1,584.93 |
| GAME | 230 | 12,844 | $133.50 | $732.72 |
| OCCASION | 71 | 16,757 | $41.98 | $719.87 |
| OTHER | 53 | 3,100 | $36.49 | $1,123.14 |

Calculating the average residual at the household level requires joining in the household ID, using the Customer and Orders tables. The household average residual is larger than the residual at the order level, even though most households are one-time purchasers. The reason points to a challenge when working with market basket data.

There happen to be a few households with very many orders. These households have very large residual values for any product they purchase, and, they have purchased products from all product groups. In short, the problem is that large households dominate the residual value calculation for households. One way to remove the bias is to limit the calculations to households with only two purchases. Another way is to randomly choose one pair of products in each household, but such a technique is outside the scope of this book. The effect exists at the order level, but because there are many fewer humongous orders, the bias is smaller.

**WARNING** When analyzing market basket data, the size of orders (or of households) can introduce unexpected biases in results.

## Changes in Price

Some products have different prices within an order. More products have different prices throughout the historical data. *What is the number of different prices that products have?* Actually, this question is interesting, but it is more feasible to ask a slightly simpler question: *What proportion of products in each product group has more than one price?* The following query answers this question:

```
SELECT productgroupname, COUNT(*) as allproducts,
       SUM(CASE WHEN numprices > 1 THEN 1 ELSE 0 END) as morethan1price,
       SUM(CASE WHEN numol > 1 THEN 1 ELSE 0 END) as morethan1orderline
FROM (SELECT ol.productid, productgroupname, COUNT(*) as numol,
             COUNT(DISTINCT unitprice) as numprices
      FROM orderline ol JOIN product p ON ol.productid = p.productid
      GROUP BY ol.productid, productgroupname) a
GROUP BY productgroupname
ORDER BY 1
```

Products must appear in more than one order line to have more than one price. Table 9-6 shows that 74.9% of products appearing more than once have multiple prices. In some product groups, such as APPAREL and CALENDARS, almost all the products have more than one price. Perhaps this is due to inventory control. Calendars, by their very nature, become outdated, so once the year covered by the calendar begins, the value decreases. APPAREL is also quite seasonal, with the same effect.

**Table 9-6:** Products by Product Groups That Have More Than One Price

| PRODUCT GROUP | PRODUCTS WITH 2 OR MORE ORDERS | PRODUCTS WITH 2 OR MORE PRICES | PROPORTION |
|---|---|---|---|
| #N/A | 0 | 1 | 0.0% |
| APPAREL | 79 | 84 | 94.0% |
| ARTWORK | 2,145 | 2,402 | 89.3% |
| BOOK | 230 | 236 | 97.5% |
| CALENDAR | 30 | 30 | 100.0% |
| FREEBIE | 0 | 23 | 0.0% |
| GAME | 176 | 211 | 83.4% |
| OCCASION | 53 | 70 | 75.7% |
| OTHER | 37 | 50 | 74.0% |
| **TOTAL** | **2,750** | **3,107** | **88.5%** |

Figure 9-4 shows the average price by month for CALENDARs compared to BOOKs, for products costing less than $100 (expensive products appear for short periods confusing the results). For most years, the average unit price for calendars increases in the late summer, and then decreases over the next few months. By contrast, books tend to have their lowest price of the year in January, presumably during after-holiday sales. Such charts suggest questions about price elasticity (whether changes in price for a product affects demand), which we'll investigate in Chapter 11.

The query used to create this is:

```
SELECT YEAR(orderdate) as yr, MONTH(orderdate) as mon,
       AVG(CASE WHEN productgroupname = 'CALENDAR' AND fullprice < 100
               THEN unitprice END) as avgcallt100,
       AVG(CASE WHEN productgroupname = 'BOOK' AND fullprice < 100
               THEN unitprice END) as avgbooklt100
FROM orders o JOIN orderline ol ON o.orderid = ol.orderid JOIN
     product p ON ol.productid = p.productid
WHERE productgroupname IN ('CALENDAR', 'BOOK')
GROUP BY YEAR(orderdate), MONTH(orderdate)
ORDER BY 1, 2
```

This query selects appropriate product groups and then does the conditional aggregation using a CASE statement. The CASE statement does not have an ELSE clause, intentionally. Non-matching rows get NULL values, so they do not affect the average.

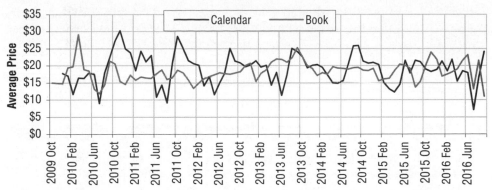

**Figure 9-4:** The average prices of calendars and books sold change during the year by month.

# Combinations (Item Sets)

Combinations, also called *item sets*, are groups of products that appear together within an order. This section looks at two-way combinations, showing how to use SQL to generate all such combinations. It then moves to some interesting variations, especially combinations of products at the household level rather than the order level. The next sections apply these ideas to generating association rules. Because the queries are starting to get more complicated, it can be useful to think about query performance, as discussed in the aside "Some SQL Efficiency Tips."

## Combinations of Two Products

Combinations of one product are not particularly interesting, so this section starts by looking at combinations of two products. A combination is of a set of items. The combination consisting of products A and B is the same as B and A. This section counts the number of product pairs in orders and shows how to use SQL to generate them.

### Number of Two-Way Combinations

If an order contains one product, how many two-way combinations of products does it have? The answer is easy. There are none, because there is only one product. If there are two products, then there is one, because A and B is the same as B and A.

And three-way combinations? The answer happens to be three, but the situation is starting to get more complicated. There is, however, an easy formula. Understanding it starts with the observation that the number of pairs of products is the number of products squared. Because pairs where the same product occurs twice are not interesting, subtract out the pairs that consist of identical products. And, because pairs are being counted twice this way (A and B as well as B and A), the difference needs to be divided in two. The number of two-way combinations in an order is half the difference between the number of products in the order and that number squared.

---

**SOME SQL EFFICIENCY TIPS**

Many of the queries involving item sets and association rules are complicated. The purpose of a database engine is to run queries accurately and quickly. Sometimes, we can help the engine do a better job.

One important thing is ensuring that columns being joined together have the same types. So, the ORDERID should always be an INTEGER (or whatever) regardless of the table where it appears.

Creating appropriate indexes is also important for enhancing performance. In a database that has lots of updating, indexes slow things down. However, in a database that is primarily query-only, indexes usually speed things up. Here are three tips for creating indexes:

1. Create an index on the primary keys of tables that are often used for joins, such as PRODUCT.PRODUCTID. Some databases do this automatically, if the column is declared as a primary key when the table is created.

2. Create an index on columns often used in COUNT(DISTINCT) expressions. These are often primary keys, so are covered by (1).

3. Create more than one index on a table if appropriate. Also, create indexes with multi-part keys if appropriate.

The normal syntax for creating an index is:

```
CREATE INDEX <name> ON <table>.<column>
```

And more than one column can be added for composite index keys.

The way the database engine runs a query is called a *query plan*. Sometimes, indexes confuse the database and there are circumstances where removing an index makes queries run faster. Alas, resolving these situations requires detailed knowledge of the particular database and particular query; when such situations arise, it is usually because the database engine needs to read all the rows in a table anyway and using the index to read all the rows slows it down.

Another trick is using intermediate tables. These result in simpler queries, which are easier to optimize. They also provide an opportunity to add indexes that may help to improve performance. On the other hand, intermediate tables can make SQL less readable and less maintainable, so they should not be overused and when used, should be given clear, understandable names.

One final comment is: do not to be afraid to try different things to see which combinations work best.

The following query calculates the number of two-way combinations among all orders in Orderline:

```
SELECT SUM(numprods * (numprods - 1)/2) as numcombo2
FROM (SELECT orderid, COUNT(DISTINCT productid) as numprods
      FROM orderline ol
      GROUP BY orderid) o
```

Notice that this query counts distinct products rather than order lines, so orders with the same product on multiple lines do not affect the count.

The number of two-way combinations is 185,791. This is useful because the number of combinations pretty much determines how quickly the query generating them runs. A single order with a large number of products can seriously degrade performance. For instance, if one order contains a thousand products, there would be about five hundred thousand two-way combinations in just that one order — versus 185,791 in all the orders data. As the number of products in the largest order increases, the number of combinations increases much faster.

**WARNING** Large orders that contain many items can seriously slow down queries for combinations and association rules. A particularly dangerous situation is when there is a "default" order id, such as 0 or NULL, that corresponds to many purchases.

## Generating All Two-Way Combinations

The approach for calculating the combinations is to do a self-join on the Orderline table, with duplicate product pairs removed. The goal is to get all pairs of products, subject to the conditions:

- The two products in the pair are different.

- No two combinations have the same two products.

The first condition is easily met by filtering out any pairs where the two products are equal. The second condition is also easily met, by requiring that the first product id be smaller than the second product id. The following query generates all the combinations in a subquery and counts the number of orders containing each one:

```
SELECT p1, p2, COUNT(*) as numorders
FROM (SELECT op1.orderid, op1.productid as p1, op2.productid as p2
      FROM (SELECT DISTINCT orderid, productid FROM orderline) op1 JOIN
           (SELECT DISTINCT orderid, productid FROM orderline) op2
          ON op1.orderid - op2.orderid AND
             op1.productid < op2.productid
     ) combinations
GROUP BY p1, p2
```

Figure 9-5 shows the data flow for this query. The innermost subqueries, OP1 and OP2, are joined together (actually this is a self-join) to generate all pairs of products within each order. The JOIN condition restricts these pairs to those having different products, with the first smaller than the second. The outer query aggregates each pair of products, counting the number of orders along the way.

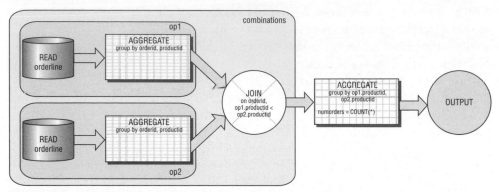

**Figure 9-5:** This dataflow generates all the two-way combinations of products in the Orders table.

Sometimes, we do not want to include all orders. The most common reason is to limit the combinations to reasonable market baskets, such as those with between two and ten products. Other reasons are to use orders from a particular source, or a particular geographic region, or a particular time frame. Because the preceding query works directly on the Orderline table, it is difficult to filter by conditions on the orders. The solution is to join in another subquery that selects the desired orders:

```
SELECT p1, p2, COUNT(*) as numorders
FROM (SELECT op1.orderid, op1.productid as p1, op2.productid as p2
      FROM (SELECT orderid FROM orderline GROUP BY orderid
            HAVING COUNT(DISTINCT productid) BETWEEN 2 and 10
           ) filter JOIN
           (SELECT DISTINCT orderid, productid FROM orderline) op1
           ON filter.orderid = op1.orderid JOIN
           (SELECT DISTINCT orderid, productid FROM orderline) op2
           ON op1.orderid = op2.orderid AND
              op1.productid < op2.productid
     ) combinations
GROUP BY p1, p2
```

The additional subquery chooses orders that have between two and ten orders. Here the subquery is really just an aggregation of the Orderline table, but it could also be choosing orders based on characteristics in the Orders table, or even other tables such as Customer or Campaign.

## Examples of Combinations

Generating thousands of combinations is interesting. Looking at a few examples is informative. The following query fetches the top ten pairs of products in orders with two to ten products, along with the associated product groups:

```
SELECT top 10 *, p1.productgroupname, p2.productgroupname
FROM (<combos-subquery>) combos JOIN
     product p1 ON combos.p1 = p1.productid JOIN
     product p2 ON combos.p2 = p2.productid
ORDER BY numorders DESC
```

This query uses the previous query as a subquery. Notice that SQL does not care that the alias for the Product table (P1 and P2) is the same as the name of a column in the Combos subquery. Although SQL does not care, people reading the query might get confused, and this is not an example of a best practice.

The ten most common product pairs are in Table 9-7. Of the ten, seven include FREEBIE products, which are usually part of promotions associated with one particular product. Sometimes there is more than one FREEBIE included in the promotion.

**Table 9-7:** Pairs of Products Appearing Together in the Most Orders

| PRODUCT 1 | PRODUCT 2 | NUMBER OF ORDERS | PRODUCT GROUP 1 | PRODUCT GROUP 2 |
|---|---|---|---|---|
| 12820 | 13190 | 2,580 | FREEBIE | FREEBIE |
| 12819 | 12820 | 1,839 | FREEBIE | FREEBIE |
| 11048 | 11196 | 1,822 | ARTWORK | BOOK |
| 10956 | 12139 | 1,481 | FREEBIE | OCCASION |
| 12139 | 12820 | 1,239 | OCCASION | FREEBIE |
| 12820 | 12851 | 1,084 | FREEBIE | OCCASION |
| 11196 | 11197 | 667 | BOOK | BOOK |
| 12820 | 13254 | 592 | FREEBIE | OCCASION |
| 12820 | 12826 | 589 | FREEBIE | ARTWORK |
| 11053 | 11088 | 584 | ARTWORK | OCCASION |

The three combinations that do not have a FREEBIE in them have ARTWORK and BOOK, BOOK and BOOK, and ARTWORK and OCCASION. These may be examples of product bundles, two or more products that are marketed together. The product-level combinations have reconstructed the bundles. In fact, this is something that commonly happens when looking at combinations of products.

## Variations on Combinations

This section looks at two useful variations on the idea of combinations. The first uses the product hierarchy to look at combinations of product groups. The second looks at adding more items into the combinations, moving beyond two-way combinations.

### *Combinations of Product Groups*

This example shows combinations of product groups, rather than products, to illustrate extending market basket analysis beyond products to product features. The idea is to treat each order as a collection of product groups, rather than a collection of products. An order with three books on three order lines becomes an order with one product group, BOOK. An order that has a CALENDAR and a BOOK has two product groups.

Because there are many fewer product groups than products, there are not going to be as many combinations, just a few dozen. The following query generates the two-way product group combinations, as well as the number of orders having the combination:

```
SELECT pg1, pg2, COUNT(*) as cnt
FROM (SELECT op1.orderid, op1.productgroupname as pg1,
             op2.productgroupname as pg2
      FROM (SELECT orderid, productgroupname FROM orderline ol JOIN
                   product p ON ol.productid = p.productid
            GROUP BY orderid, productgroupname) op1 JOIN
           (SELECT orderid, productgroupname FROM orderline ol JOIN
                   product p ON ol.productid = p.productid
            GROUP BY orderid, productgroupname) op2
           ON op1.orderid = op2.orderid AND
              op1.productgroupname < op2.productgroupname
     ) combinations
GROUP BY pg1, pg2
```

This query is very similar to the query for products. The difference is that the innermost subqueries look up the product group name, aggregating by that instead of the product id.

Figure 9-6 shows a bubble chart of the results. The two most common product group pairs are FREEBIE with BOOK and FREEBIE with OCCASION. This is not surprising, because FREEBIE products are used as marketing incentives.

The two axes in the bubble chart are the two types of product groups in an order. Creating this bubble chart is challenging, because Excel charting does not allow the axes of scatter plots and bubble charts to be names. The technical aside "Bubble Charts and Scatter Plots with Non-Numeric Axes" explains how to get around this limitation.

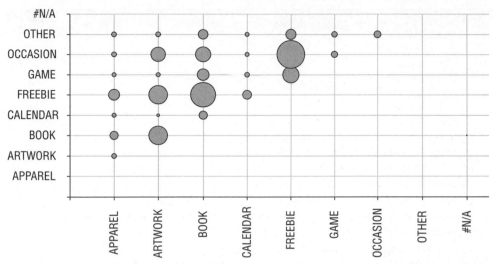

**Figure 9-6:** This bubble chart shows the most common product pairs. One product is along each dimension, with the bubble showing the number of orders containing the product.

## BUBBLE CHARTS AND SCATTER PLOTS WITH NON-NUMERIC AXES

Unfortunately, bubble charts and scatter plots only allow numbers for the X- and Y-coordinates. Fortunately, using the XY-labeler introduced in Chapter 4, we can make scatter plots and bubble plots with non-numeric dimensions, such as product group names. As a reminder, the XY chart labeler is not part of Excel. It uses an add-in, written by Rob Bovey, and available for download at http://www.appspro.com/Utilities/ChartLabeler.htm.

The idea is to transform the data to make the dimensions numbers. Then, two additional series are added to the chart along each dimension. These are given labels using the XY-labeler, which are the labels on the axes.

Assume that the data is in three columns, the first two are the X- and Y-values, the third is the bubble size, and the first two are names, rather than numbers. The example in Figure 9-6 has product group names in these columns. The bubble chart is created using the following steps:

1. Create a lookup table for the values in each dimension to map each value to a sequence of integers, the new dimension.

2. Look up the new dimensions for these two new columns.

3. Insert the chart, using the new dimensions rather than the names.

4. Insert two new series, for use as the X-labels and the Y-labels.

5. Format the new series so they are invisible.

6. Use the XY-labeler to label the points with strings.

7. Format the chart as you wish.

*Continued on next page*

**BUBBLE CHARTS AND SCATTER PLOTS WITH NON-NUMERIC AXES (CONTINUED)**

This process starts by creating the lookup table. An alternative to manually typing it in is to take all the distinct values in the columns, sort them, and create the new dimension value in an adjacent column using the formula `"=<prev cell>+1"`. To get the distinct values, copy both columns of product group names into one column, below the data. Filter out duplicates using the **Data ⇨ Filter ⇨ Advanced** menu option, and choose "Unique Records Only." Highlight the values using the mouse. To select only the visible values, use the **Edit⇨Goto** menu option, and click "Special" and then "Visible Cells Only" (toward the bottom in the left column). Now copy the values in the cells (`<control>-C`) and paste them into another column (`<control>-V`). Remember to go the **Data ⇨ Filter ⇨ Show All** menu selection to undo the filtering, so you can see all the distinct values.

The next step is to lookup the values in the desired X- and Y-columns to get their lookup dimensions. Use `VLOOKUP()` to look up the appropriate values:

```
VLOOKUP(<column cell>, <lookup table>, 2, 0)
```

This provides the number data accepted by the bubble chart. Labeling the axes requires more information, so add two more columns to the lookup table, the first with values set to zero and the second with values set to 1000. The first is the coordinate position of the labels; the second is the width of the bubbles.

The axis labels are attached to two new series. Add the series by right-clicking in the chart and choosing "Source Data." Then choose "Add" and give it the name "X-labels." The X-values for this are the second column in the lookup table, the Y-values are the third column (which is all zeros), and the sizes are the fourth column (all 1000). Repeat for the Y-values, reversing the X- and Y-coordinates. To make the series invisible, left-click each one and select "None" for both the "Border" and "Area" on the "Patterns" tab.

Now, choose the menu option **Tools ⇨ XY Chart Labels ⇨ Add Chart Labels**. The "X-labels" are the data series and the label range is the first column of the lookup table. Place the X-labels "Below" the data bubbles. Repeat for the "Y-labels," placing them to the "Left." The labels appear in the chart and can be formatted to any font or rotated by clicking them. It is also a good idea to adjust the scale of the axes to go from 0 to 9 in this case.

## Multi-Way Combinations

Although two-way combinations are often sufficient, multi-way combinations are also useful. Generating larger combinations in SQL requires adding additional JOINs for each item in the combination. To keep the combinations distinct (that is, to avoid listing A, B, C and A, C, B as two different combinations), an additional less than condition needs to be added for each product. The following query is an example for three items:

```
SELECT p1, p2, p3, COUNT(*) as cnt
FROM (SELECT op1.orderid, op1.productid as p1,
             op2.productid as p2, op3.productid as p3
      FROM (SELECT orderid, COUNT(DISTINCT productid) as numprods
            FROM orderline GROUP BY orderid
            HAVING COUNT(DISTINCT productid) > 2) o JOIN
           (SELECT DISTINCT orderid, productid FROM orderline) op1
           ON o.orderid = op1.orderid JOIN
           (SELECT DISTINCT orderid, productid FROM orderline) op2
           ON op1.orderid = op2.orderid AND
              op1.productid < op2.productid JOIN
           (SELECT DISTINCT orderid, productid FROM orderline) op3
           ON op2.orderid = op3.orderid AND
              op2.productid < op3.productid
     ) combinations
GROUP BY p1, p2, p3
```

This query has three subqueries that provide, respectively, the first, second, and third products in the combination. These subqueries use the DISTINCT keyword instead of a GROUP BY to eliminate duplicates; the two methods are equivalent. Because there can be a very large number of combinations, the first subquery limits the orders to those having at least three products.

Table 9-8 shows the top ten combinations of three products. The three-way combinations have lower counts than the two-way combinations. For instance, the top two-way combinations appeared in over two thousand orders. The top three-way combinations occur in fewer than four hundred. This is typical, because the more products in the order, the fewer the customers who have ordered all of them at once.

**Table 9-8:** Top Ten Combinations of Three Products

| PRODUCT 1 | PRODUCT 2 | PRODUCT 3 | COUNT | GROUP 1 | GROUP 2 | GROUP 3 |
|---|---|---|---|---|---|---|
| 12506 | 12820 | 12830 | 399 | FREEBIE | FREEBIE | GAME |
| 12820 | 13144 | 13190 | 329 | FREEBIE | APPAREL | FREEBIE |
| 11052 | 11196 | 11197 | 275 | ARTWORK | BOOK | BOOK |
| 12139 | 12819 | 12820 | 253 | OCCASION | FREEBIE | FREEBIE |
| 12820 | 12823 | 12951 | 194 | FREEBIE | OTHER | FREEBIE |
| 10939 | 10940 | 10943 | 170 | BOOK | BOOK | BOOK |
| 12820 | 12851 | 13190 | 154 | FREEBIE | OCCASION | FREEBIE |

*Continued on next page*

**Table 9-8** *(continued)*

| PROD-<br>UCT 1 | PROD-<br>UCT 2 | PROD-<br>UCT 3 | COUNT | GROUP 1 | GROUP 2 | GROUP·3 |
|---|---|---|---|---|---|---|
| 11093 | 12820 | 13190 | 142 | OCCASION | FREEBIE | FREEBIE |
| 12819 | 12820 | 12851 | 137 | FREEBIE | FREEBIE | OCCASION |
| 12005 | 12820 | 13190 | 125 | BOOK | FREEBIE | FREEBIE |

## Households Not Orders

There is no reason to look at combinations only in orders. Another possibility is to look at products within households. One application is particularly interesting, looking at combinations that occur within a household but not within a particular order.

### Combinations within a Household

The following query extends two-way combinations to products in the same household:

```
SELECT p1, p2, COUNT(*) as cnt
FROM (SELECT op1.householdid, op1.productid as p1, op2.productid as p2
      FROM (SELECT householdid, COUNT(DISTINCT productid) as numprods
            FROM orderline ol JOIN orders o ON o.orderid = ol.orderid JOIN
                 customer c ON o.customerid = c.customerid
            GROUP BY householdid) o JOIN
            (SELECT DISTINCT householdid, productid
            FROM orderline ol JOIN orders o ON o.orderid = ol.orderid JOIN
                 customer c ON o.customerid = c.customerid) op1
          ON o.householdid = op1.householdid AND
             o.numprods BETWEEN 2 AND 10 JOIN
            (SELECT DISTINCT householdid, productid
            FROM orderline ol JOIN orders o ON o.orderid = ol.orderid JOIN
                 customer c ON o.customerid = c.customerid) op2
          ON op1.householdid = op2.householdid AND
             op1.productid < op2.productid
     ) combinations
GROUP BY p1, p2
```

This query looks more complicated than the earlier two-way combination query, because the two subqueries look up each order's HOUSEHOLDID. The structure of the query remains the same, with the only difference being the innermost subqueries.

Because few households have repeated purchases, the results within a household are quite similar to the results within orders.

### Investigating Products within Households but Not within Orders

At this point, we can ask a more complicated question that illustrates the power of doing this work in SQL: *What pairs of products occur frequently among household purchases but do not appear in the same purchase?* Such a question can provide very valuable information on potential cross-selling opportunities, because such product pairs indicate affinities among products at different times.

Answering this question requires some minor modifications to the household query. This query had the following conditions:

- The household has two to ten products.
- Both products appear within the household.
- The first product in the pair has a lower product id than the second product.

One more condition is needed:

- The products are in the same household but not in the same order.

The following query adds this condition:

```
SELECT p1, p2, COUNT(*) as cnt
FROM (SELECT op1.householdid, op1.productid as p1, op2.productid as p2
      FROM (SELECT householdid, COUNT(DISTINCT productid) as numprods
            FROM orderline ol JOIN orders o ON o.orderid = ol.orderid JOIN
                 customer c ON o.customerid = c.customerid
            GROUP BY householdid) o JOIN
           (SELECT DISTINCT householdid, o.orderid, productid
            FROM orderline ol JOIN orders o ON o.orderid = ol.orderid JOIN
                 customer c ON o.customerid = c.customerid) op1
           ON o.householdid = op1.householdid AND
              o.numprods BETWEEN 2 AND 10 JOIN
           (SELECT DISTINCT householdid, o.orderid, productid
            FROM orderline ol JOIN orders o ON o.orderid = ol.orderid JOIN
                 customer c ON o.customerid = c.customerid) op2
           ON op1.householdid = op2.householdid AND
              op1.orderid <> op2.orderid AND
              op1.productid < op2.productid
      GROUP BY op1.householdid, op1.productid, op2.productid
     ) o
GROUP BY p1, p2
```

Now, the innermost queries obtain triples of order id, product id, and date. There is a slight complication. Previously, the aggregation ensured that a product only occurs once in each household. This condition is no longer true when a household purchases the same product on multiple occasions. To remove potential duplicates, there is an additional aggregation at the ORDERID, PRODUCTID1, PRODUCTID2 level.

Table 9-9 shows the top ten results from this query. These results differ from the products within an order because the FREEBIE product group is much less common. Some of the combinations are not particularly surprising. For instance, customers who purchase calendars one year are probably likely to purchase calendars in another year. This combination occurs three times in the top ten products.

**Table 9-9:** Top Ten Pairs of Products Purchased by Households in Different Orders

| PRODUCT1 | PRODUCT2 | COUNT | PRODUCT | PRODUCT |
| --- | --- | --- | --- | --- |
| 11196 | 11197 | 462 | BOOK | BOOK |
| 11111 | 11196 | 313 | BOOK | BOOK |
| 12139 | 12820 | 312 | OCCASION | FREEBIE |
| 12015 | 12176 | 299 | CALENDAR | CALENDAR |
| 11048 | 11196 | 294 | ARTWORK | BOOK |
| 12176 | 13298 | 279 | CALENDAR | CALENDAR |
| 10863 | 12015 | 255 | CALENDAR | CALENDAR |
| 11048 | 11052 | 253 | ARTWORK | ARTWORK |
| 11111 | 11197 | 246 | BOOK | BOOK |
| 11048 | 11197 | 232 | ARTWORK | BOOK |

## Multiple Purchases of the Same Product

The previous example suggests another interesting question, although one that is not directly related to product combinations: *How often does a household purchase the same product in multiple orders?* The following query answers this question:

```
SELECT numprodinhh, COUNT(*) as numhouseholds
FROM (SELECT householdid, productid,
             COUNT(DISTINCT o.orderid) as numprodinhh
      FROM customer c JOIN orders o ON c.customerid = o.customerid JOIN
           orderline ol ON o.orderid = ol.orderid
      GROUP BY householdid, productid
     ) h
GROUP BY numprodinhh
ORDER BY 1
```

The subquery aggregates the order lines by household id and product, using COUNT(DISTINCT) to count the number of orders containing the product within a household. The outer query then creates a histogram of the counts.

Over eight thousand households have purchased the same product more than once. The most frequent ones purchase the same product over fifty times. These very frequent purchases are anomalous, due to businesses purchasing the same product multiple times.

This question leads to another. *What are the top products appearing in these orders?* The following query answers a related question about product groups:

```
SELECT p.productgroupname, COUNT(*) as numhouseholds
FROM (SELECT householdid, productid,
             COUNT(DISTINCT o.orderid) as numorders
      FROM customer c JOIN orders o ON c.customerid = o.customerid JOIN
           orderline ol ON o.orderid = ol.orderid
      GROUP BY householdid, productid
     ) h JOIN
     product p ON h.productid = p.productid
WHERE numorders > 1
GROUP BY p.productgroupname
ORDER BY 2 DESC
```

This query is quite similar to the previous query, except the product information is being joined in, and then the outer query is aggregating by PRODUCT-GROUPNAME.

Table 9-10 shows that the top three product groups are BOOK, ARTWORK, and OCCASION. This differs from the common combinations, which always include FREEBIE products. In fact, one FREEBIE product, whose id is 12820, is the top product that appears in multiple orders within a household. Without this product, the FREEBIE category would have only 210 occurrences of the same product appearing in multiple orders, and would fall to the bottom of the table. This product, the 12820 product, is a catalog included in all shipments during a period of time. Customers who place multiple orders during this period of time received the catalog with each purchase.

**Table 9-10:** Products that Appear in More Than One Order, by Product Group

| PRODUCT GROUP | NUMBER OF HOUSEHOLDS |
|:---:|:---|
| BOOK | 2,709 |
| ARTWORK | 2,101 |
| OCCASION | 1,212 |
| FREEBIE | 935 |
| GAME | 384 |
| CALENDAR | 353 |
| APPAREL | 309 |
| OTHER | 210 |

# The Simplest Association Rules

This section starts the discussion of association rules by calculating the proportion of orders that have a given product. These are the simplest, most basic type of association rule, one where the "if" clause is empty and the "then" clause contains one product: given no information, what is the probability that a given product is an order? This idea of "zero-way" association rules is useful for two reasons. First, it provides a simple introduction to the ideas and terminology. Second, this overall probability is important for assessing more complex rules.

## Associations and Rules

An *association* is a group of products that appear together in one or more orders. The word "association" implies that the products have a relationship with each other based on the fact that they are found together in an order. An *association rule* has the form:

- ▪ <left-hand side> ⇨ <right-hand side>

The arrow in the rule means "implies," so this is read as "the presence of the products on the left-hand side implies the presence of the products on the right-hand side in the same order." Of course, a rule is not always true, so there is a probability associated with it. There can be any number of products on either side, although the right-hand side typically consists of one product. In more formal terminology, the left-and right-hand sides are *item sets*. The term *item* is a more general idea than product; and later in this chapter we'll see the power of such generalization.

The automatic generation of association rules demonstrates the power of using detailed data. It must be admitted that the resulting rules are not always necessarily interesting. One early example, published in the 1990s, comes from Sears after the company had invested millions of dollars in a data warehousing system. They learned that customers who buy large appliance warranties are very likely to buy large appliances. Maybe there is an affinity, because warranties are almost always added onto large appliance purchases.

**WARNING** Association rules are not necessarily interesting. They are sometimes *trivial*, telling us something we should already know.

Such a rule is *trivial*, because we should have known. Although trivial rules are not useful from a business perspective, they are resounding successes for the computer — because the pattern is undeniably in the data. An interesting use of trivial rules is to look at the exceptions, which might point to data quality or operational issues.

## Zero-Way Association Rules

The zero-way association is the probability that an order contains a given product. It is the probability that the following rule is true:

- <nothing> ⇨ <product id>

It is "zero" way because the left-hand side has no products. The probability, in turn, is the number of orders containing a product divided by the total number of orders:

```
SELECT productid, COUNT(*)/MAX(numorders) as p
FROM (SELECT DISTINCT orderid, productid FROM orderline) op CROSS JOIN
     (SELECT COUNT(*)*1.0 as numorders FROM orders o) o
GROUP BY productid
ORDER BY 2 DESC
```

This query counts up the number of orders having a product and removes duplicate order lines using SELECT DISTINCT (although this could also be accomplished with a GROUP BY, the SELECT DISTINCT is more succinct). The number of orders with the product is then divided by the total number of orders. A subquery, joined in using CROSS JOIN, calculates the total number, which is converted to a real number by multiplying by 1.0.

The result is each product with the proportion of orders containing the product. For instance, the most popular product is product id 12820, which is a FREEBIE product that occurs in about 9.6% of the orders.

## What Is the Distribution of Probabilities?

There are over 4,000 products so looking at all the probabilities individually is cumbersome. What do these probabilities look like? The following query provides some information about the values:

```
SELECT COUNT(*) as numprods, MIN(p) as minp, MAX(p) as maxp,
       AVG(p) as avgp, COUNT(DISTINCT p) as nump
FROM (SELECT ol.productid,
             (COUNT(DISTINCT orderid)*1.0/
              (SELECT COUNT(DISTINCT orderid) FROM orderline) ) as p
      FROM orderline ol
      GROUP BY ol.productid) op
```

Notice that this query calculates the total number of orders using an in-line query, rather than the CROSS JOIN. Both methods work equally well, but the CROSS JOIN makes it possible to add several variables at once and give them informative names.

These probabilities have the following characteristics:

- The minimum value is 0.0005%.
- The maximum value is 9.6%.
- The average value is 0.036%.
- There are 385 different values.

Why are there only a few hundred distinct values when there are thousands of products? The probabilities are ratios between two numbers, the number of times that a product appears, and the number of orders. For all products, the number of orders is the same, so the number of different probabilities is the number of different frequencies of products. There is much overlap, especially because over one thousand products appear only once.

With just a few hundred values, plotting them individually is possible as in Figure 9-7, which has both the histogram and the cumulative histogram. The histogram is on the left-hand axis. However, this histogram is visually misleading, because the points are not equally spaced.

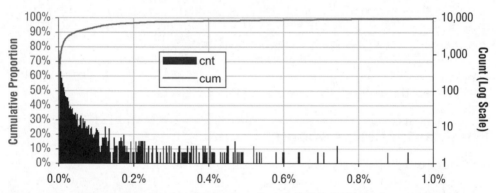

**Figure 9-7:** This chart shows the distribution of probabilities of an order containing a product.

The cumulative distribution is the other curve on the chart, and it provides more information. For instance, it says that half the products have a probability of less than about 0.0015%, so many products are quite rare indeed. Only half a percent of the products (23) occur in more than one percent of the orders.

## What Do Zero-Way Associations Tell Us?

Zero-way association rules provide basic information about products. Given no other information about purchases, such rules give the probability of a given product being in an order. For instance, the top product, with id 12820, occurs in about 9.6% of the orders. This is a FREEBIE product, which is not so interesting.

The second product is a book that occurs in 4.9% of orders; its product id is 11168. An association rule predicting it has the form:

- <LHS> ⇨ <product 11168>

If this rule is accurate 50% of the time, then it is useful. If it is accurate 10% of the time, then it is useful. However, if it is accurate 4.8% of the time, the rule does worse than a random guess. Such a rule is not useful. The overall probability is a minimum level required for a rule to be useful. This comparison is an important measure for the effectiveness of association rules.

# One-Way Association Rules

This section moves from combinations of products to rules suggesting that the presence of one product implies the presence of another. For many purposes, finding combinations of products that occur together is quite useful. However, these are still combinations, not rules.

This section starts with simple association rules, where both sides consist of a single product. Calculating such one-way rules is possible using a single query. However, the next section, which covers building more complex rules, needs to use intermediate tables to store information.

## Example of One-Way Association Rules

The two most common products have product ids 12820 and 13190, suggesting the rule:

- Product 12820 ⇨ Product 13190

This section looks at the traditional ways of evaluating such a rule. The place to begin is by gathering the following information:

- The total number of orders;
- The number of orders that contain the left-hand side of the rule;
- The number of orders that contain the right-hand side of the rule; and,
- The number of orders that contain both the left- and right-hand sides.

The following query calculates these values:

```
SELECT COUNT(*) as numorders, SUM(lhs) as numlhs, SUM(rhs) as numrhs,
       SUM(lhs*rhs) as numlhsrhs
FROM (SELECT orderid,
             MAX(CASE WHEN productid = 12820 THEN 1 ELSE 0 END) as lhs,
             MAX(CASE WHEN productid = 13190 THEN 1 ELSE 0 END) as rhs
      FROM orderline ol
      GROUP BY orderid) o
```

Notice that this query calculates the presence of the left-hand-side and right-hand-side products using MAX(CASE WHEN . . .). Because the maximum function is used, the calculation only counts the presence of these products, ignoring NUMUNITS as well as the number of order lines containing the products.

*Support* is the first measure in Table 9-11 for evaluating the rule. This is the proportion of orders where the rule is true. In other words, support is the number of orders that have both the left side and right side divided by the total number of orders. For this rule, the support is 1.3% = 2,588 / 192,983. Rules with higher support are more useful because they apply to more orders.

**Table 9-11:** Measures for the Rule Product 12820 ⇨ Product 13190

| MEASURE | VALUE |
| --- | --- |
| Number of Orders | 192,983 |
| Number of Orders with Left-Hand Side | 18,441 |
| Number of Orders with Right-Hand Side | 3,404 |
| Number of Orders with Both Sides | 2,588 |
| Support | 1.3% |
| Confidence | 14.0% |
| Lift | 8.0 |

A second measure is *confidence*, which is how often the rule is true, given that the left-hand side is true. For this rule, it is the ratio of orders that have both products to those that have product 12820. The confidence is 14.0% = 2,588/18,441.

The third important measure is *lift*, which tells us how much better the rule does rather than just guessing. Without the rule, 1.8% of the orders have product 13190 (this is the zero-way association rule for the product). With the rule, 14.0% have it. The rule does about eight times better than just guessing, so the rule has a high lift.

The following query calculates these values for this rule:

```
SELECT numlhsrhs/numorders as support, numlhsrhs/numlhs as confidence,
       (numlhsrhs/numlhs)/(numrhs/numorders) as lift
FROM (SELECT 1.0*COUNT(*) as numorders, 1.0*SUM(lhs) as numlhs,
             1.0*SUM(rhs) as numrhs, 1.0*SUM(lhs*rhs) as numlhsrhs
      FROM (SELECT orderid,
                   MAX(CASE WHEN productid = 12820 THEN 1 END) as lhs,
                   MAX(CASE WHEN productid = 13190 THEN 1 END) as rhs
            FROM orderline ol
            GROUP BY orderid) o
     ) a
```

This query does the calculation for only one rule. The challenge in this section is to calculate these values for all possible rules.

Before looking at all rules, let's look at just one other, the inverse rule:

- Product 13190 ⇨ Product 12820

The support for the inverse rule is exactly the same as the support for the original rule, because the two rules have the same combination of products. Perhaps more surprising, the lift for the two rules is the same as well. This is not a coincidence; it comes from the definition of lift. The formula simplifies to:

```
(numlhsrsh * numorders) / (numlhs * numrhs)
```

Both the rule and its inverse have the same values of NUMLHSRHS and NUMORDERS, so the numerator is the same. The values of NUMLHS and NUMRHS are swapped, but the product remains the same. As a result the lift is the same for any rule and its inverse.

The confidence values for a rule and its inverse are different. However, there is a simple relationship between them. The product of the confidence values is the same as the product of the support and the lift. So, given the confidence, support, and lift for one rule, it is simple to calculate the confidence for the inverse rule.

## Generating All One-Way Rules

The query to generate one-way association rules is similar to the query to calculate combinations, in that both involve self-joins on Orderline. The query starts by enumerating all the possible rule combinations:

```
SELECT (CAST(lhs as VARCHAR)+' --> '+ CAST(rhs as VARCHAR)) as therule,
       lhs, rhs, COUNT(*) as numlhsrhs
FROM (SELECT item_lhs.orderid, item_lhs.lhs, item_rhs.rhs
      FROM (SELECT orderid, productid as lhs FROM orderline
            GROUP BY orderid, productid) item_lhs JOIN
           (SELECT orderid, productid as rhs FROM orderline
            GROUP BY orderid, productid) item_rhs
           ON item_lhs.orderid = item_rhs.orderid AND
              item_lhs.lhs <> item_rhs.rhs
     ) rules
GROUP BY lhs, rhs
```

The order lines are aggregated to remove duplicates. This query carefully names the innermost subqueries, as Item_LHS and Item_RHS, with columns LHS and RHS. These names emphasize the roles of the subqueries and columns. Throughout this chapter, the association rule queries use these naming conventions.

Another difference from the combination query is that all pairs of products are being considered, rather than only unique pairs, because A ⇨ B and B ⇨ A are two different rules. The join condition uses `item_lhs.lhs <> item_rhs.rhs` rather than `item_lhs.lhs < item_rhs.rhs`. The subquery Rules generates all candidate rules in the Orders tables

This query returns the products in the rule as separate columns. In addition, it creates a text representation of the rule, by converting the product ids to characters and putting an arrow between the two sides.

This form of the query does not restrict the orders, say, to orders that have between two and ten products. This condition can be added using the filter subquery used for the same purpose in the combination query.

## One-Way Rules with Evaluation Information

The previous query generates all the possible one-way rules. This section discusses methods of evaluating them, by calculating support, confidence, and lift. The idea is similar to the calculation for an individual rule, but the details are quite different.

Figure 9-8 shows the dataflow diagram for the computation. The query starts by generating all the possible rules using the Rules subquery, which also calculates NUMLHSRHS. The challenge is to calculate NUMLHS, NUMRHS, and NUMORDERS for each rule. NUMLHS is the number of times that the left-hand side appears in an order. This is simply the number of orders containing the product in the left-hand side. The query that calculates this is:

```
SELECT productid, COUNT(DISTINCT orderid) as numlhs
FROM orderline
GROUP BY productid
```

Similar logic works for NUMRHS and NUMLHSRHS.

Combining these into a single query requires four subqueries:

```
SELECT lhsrhs.*, numorders, numlhs, numrhs,
       numlhsrhs*1.0/numorders as support,
       numlhsrhs*1.0/numlhs as confidence,
       numlhsrhs * numorders * 1.0/(numlhs * numrhs) as lift
FROM (SELECT lhs, rhs, COUNT(*) as numlhsrhs
      FROM (<rules>) rules GROUP BY lhs, rhs) lhsrhs JOIN
     (SELECT productid as lhs, COUNT(DISTINCT orderid) as numlhs
      FROM orderline GROUP BY productid) sumlhs
     ON lhsrhs.lhs = sumlhs.lhs JOIN
     (SELECT productid as rhs, COUNT(DISTINCT orderid) as numrhs
      FROM orderline GROUP BY productid) sumrhs
     ON lhsrhs.rhs = sumrhs.rhs CROSS JOIN
     (SELECT COUNT(DISTINCT orderid) as numorders FROM orderline) a
```

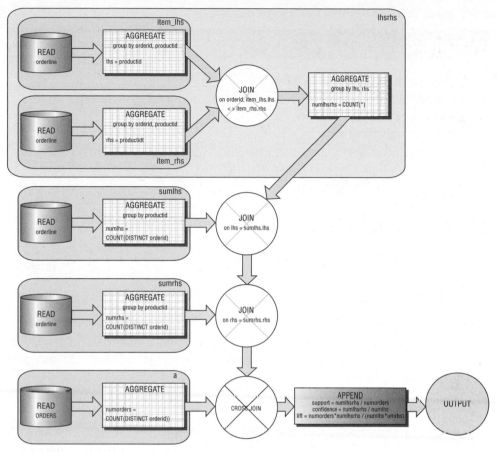

**Figure 9-8:** This dataflow generates all possible one-way rules with evaluation information.

There is one subquery for each item in the rules. The outer query calculates the support, confidence, and lift for each rule. The additional columns for NUMLHS, NUMRHS, and NUMORDERS are added by joining in summary queries. With these columns, the outer query calculates values for support, confidence, and lift.

Table 9-12 shows the top few rules with the highest lift. These are interesting though useless. The highest lift rules are the ones where two products appear together and the two products never appear without the other. This tends to occur somewhat randomly for the least common products.

**Table 9-12:** Top One-Way Rules with Highest Lift

| RULE | LHS-RHS | LHS | RHS | # ORDERS | SUP-PORT | CONFI-DENCE | LIFT |
|---|---|---|---|---|---|---|---|
| 10874 ⇨ 10879 | 1 | 1 | 1 | 192,983 | 0.0% | 100% | 192,983 |
| 12665 ⇨ 10705 | 1 | 1 | 1 | 192,983 | 0.0% | 100% | 192,983 |
| 12935 ⇨ 12190 | 1 | 1 | 1 | 192,983 | 0.0% | 100% | 192,983 |
| 13224 ⇨ 13859 | 1 | 1 | 1 | 192,983 | 0.0% | 100% | 192,983 |
| 13779 ⇨ 13232 | 1 | 1 | 1 | 192,983 | 0.0% | 100% | 192,983 |
| 10878 ⇨ 10892 | 1 | 1 | 1 | 192,983 | 0.0% | 100% | 192,983 |
| 13495 ⇨ 12353 | 1 | 1 | 1 | 192,983 | 0.0% | 100% | 192,983 |
| 12717 ⇨ 11786 | 1 | 1 | 1 | 192,983 | 0.0% | 100% | 192,983 |
| 13238 ⇨ 13752 | 1 | 1 | 1 | 192,983 | 0.0% | 100% | 192,983 |
| 11902 ⇨ 11915 | 1 | 1 | 1 | 192,983 | 0.0% | 100% | 192,983 |

One way to fix this is by putting in a threshold value for support. For instance, to consider only rules that are valid in at least 0.1% of the orders, use a WHERE clause:

```
WHERE numlhsrhs * 1.0/numorders >= 0.001
```

There are 126 rules that meet this restriction. Almost all of them have a lift greater than one, but there are a small number that have a lift less than one. There is no reason to expect generated rules with high support to have good lift as well.

## One-Way Rules on Product Groups

As another example of one-way association rules, let's consider rules about product groups. This requires changing the inner query used to calculate NUMLHSRHS to:

```
SELECT item_lhs.orderid, item_lhs.lhs, item_rhs.rhs
FROM (SELECT orderid, productgroupname as lhs
      FROM orderline ol JOIN product p ON ol.productid = p.productid
      GROUP BY orderid, productgroupname) item_lhs JOIN
     (SELECT orderid, productgroupname as rhs
      FROM orderline ol JOIN product p ON ol.productid = p.productid
      GROUP BY orderid, productgroupname) item_rhs
     ON item_lhs.orderid = item_rhs.orderid AND
        item_lhs.lhs <> item_rhs.rhs
```

In addition, the subqueries for NUMLHS and NUMRHS need to be modified to extract information about product groups, rather than products:

```
SELECT lhsrhs.*, numlhs, numrhs, numorders,
       numlhsrhs * 1.0/numorders as support,
       numlhsrhs * 1.0/numlhs as confidence,
       numlhsrhs * numorders * 1.0/(1.0*numlhs * numrhs) as lift
FROM (SELECT lhs, rhs, COUNT(*) as numlhsrhs
      FROM (<previous-query>) rules
      GROUP BY) lhsrhs JOIN
     (SELECT productgroupname as lhs, COUNT(DISTINCT orderid) as numlhs
      FROM orderline ol JOIN product p ON ol.productid = p.productid
      GROUP BY productgroupname) sumlhs
     ON lhsrhs.lhs = sumlhs.lhs JOIN
     (SELECT productgroupname as rhs, COUNT(DISTINCT orderid) as numrhs
      FROM orderline ol JOIN product p ON ol.productid = p.productid
      GROUP BY productgroupname) sumrhs
     ON lhsrhs.rhs = sumrhs.rhs CROSS JOIN
     (SELECT COUNT(DISTINCT orderid) as numorders FROM orderline) a
ORDER BY 9 DESC
```

Otherwise, this query follows the same form as the query for products.

Figure 9-9 shows the results as a bubble plot. The bubble plot contains two series. One consists of pretty good rules where the lift is greater than 1. The rest are grouped into not-good rules. This bubble chart uses the same tricks for labeling the axes that were discussed earlier.

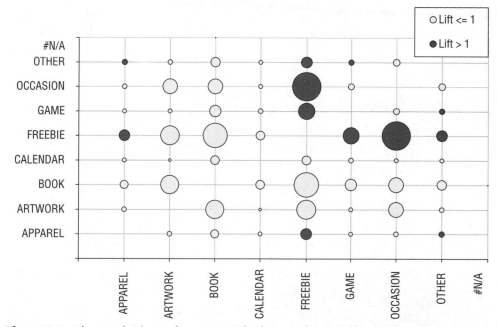

**Figure 9-9:** The good rules and not-so-good rules are shown in this bubble plot.

Not many of these rules have a good lift. One reason is that most orders have only one product and hence only one product group. These orders inflate the values of NUMLHS and NUMRHS, without contributing to the value of NUMLHSRHS.

Naively modifying the query to use only orders that have more than one product is complicated, because all four subqueries have to be modified. Such an approach is not only complicated, but making the same change in four places makes the resulting query more prone to error. The next two sections discuss two other approaches, one that uses an intermediate table and one that uses the window functions (introduced in Chapter 8).

### Calculating Product Group Rules Using an Intermediate Table

The product group rules are essentially finding all the LHS and RHS combinations, and then calculating the following values NUMLHSRHS, NUMLHS, NUMRHS, and NUMORDERS. The previous query does this calculation using four separate queries for each value. However, these could all be calculated from a single table that contains all the generated rules. The following query creates the Assoc_Rules_PG2PG table with products only from orders that have more than one product group in them:

```
SELECT item_lhs.orderid, item_lhs.lhs, item_rhs.rhs
INTO assoc_rules_pg2pg
FROM (SELECT orderid
      FROM orderline ol JOIN product p ON ol.productid = p.productid
      GROUP BY orderid
      HAVING COUNT(DISTINCT productgroupname) > 1) filter JOIN
     (SELECT orderid, productgroupname as lhs
      FROM orderline ol JOIN product p ON ol.productid = p.productid
      GROUP BY orderid, productgroupname) item_lhs
    ON filter.orderid = item_lhs.orderid JOIN
     (SELECT orderid, productgroupname as rhs
      FROM orderline ol JOIN product p ON ol.productid = p.productid
      GROUP BY orderid, productgroupname) item_rhs
    ON item_lhs.orderid = item_rhs.orderid AND
       item_lhs.lhs <> item_rhs.rhs
```

(The specific syntax for creating an intermediate table differs from database to database, although CREATE TABLE AS and SELECT INTO are common methods.) This query is similar to the Rules subquery used earlier. However, it has an additional join that selects the orders with more than one product group. Because all potential rules are in this table for every order where they appear, the table is rather large, having 80,148 rows. This type of query generates all the candidate rules for two-way association rules.

The rules in the intermediate table can now be used to calculate the remaining variables. The key is to count distinct order ids for the different items. So,

NUMORDERS is the number of distinct order ids in this table. NUMLHS is the number of distinct order ids among the left-hand products, and NUMRHS is the number of distinct orders among the right-hand products. The following query calculates these numbers along with support, confidence, and lift:

```
SELECT lhsrhs.*, numorders, numlhs, numrhs,
       numlhsrhs*1.0/numorders as support,
       numlhsrhs*1.0/numlhs as confidence,
       numorders*numlhsrhs*1.0/(1.0*numlhs*numrhs) as lift
FROM (SELECT lhs, rhs, COUNT(*) as numlhsrhs
      FROM assoc_rules_pg2pg GROUP BY lhs, rhs) lhsrhs JOIN
     (SELECT lhs, COUNT(DISTINCT orderid) as numlhs
      FROM assoc_rules_pg2pg GROUP BY lhs) sumlhs
     ON lhsrhs.lhs = sumlhs.lhs JOIN
     (SELECT rhs, COUNT(DISTINCT orderid) as numrhs
      FROM assoc_rules_pg2pg GROUP BY rhs) sumrhs
     ON lhsrhs.rhs = sumrhs.rhs CROSS JOIN
     (SELECT COUNT(DISTINCT orderid) as numorders
      FROM assoc_rules_pg2pg) a
ORDER BY lift DESC
```

The advantage of this approach is that the four values are guaranteed to be based on the same set of orders; eliminating one source of error — repeated complex subqueries.

The same basic intermediate table works in general. The idea is that the table contains all instances of rules, rather than a summary of the rules. Generating association rules at the household level is a simple modification:

```
SELECT item_lhs.householdid, item_lhs.lhs, item_rhs.rhs
INTO assoc_rules_h_pg2pg
FROM (SELECT householdid
      FROM orderline ol JOIN
           product p ON ol.productid = p.productid JOIN
           orders o ON ol.orderid = o.orderid JOIN
           customer c ON o.customerid = c.customerid
      GROUP BY householdid
      HAVING COUNT(DISTINCT productgroupname) > 1) filter JOIN
     (SELECT DISTINCT householdid, productgroupname as lhs
      FROM orderline ol JOIN
           product p ON ol.productid = p.productid JOIN
           orders o ON ol.orderid = o.orderid JOIN
           customer c ON o.customerid = c.customerid) item_lhs
     ON filter.householdid = item_lhs.householdid JOIN
     (SELECT DISTINCT householdid, productgroupname as rhs
      FROM orderline ol JOIN
           product p ON ol.productid = p.productid JOIN
           orders o ON ol.orderid = o.orderid JOIN
           customer c ON o.customerid = c.customerid) item_rhs
     ON item_lhs.householdid = item_rhs.householdid AND
        item_lhs.lhs <> item_rhs.rhs
```

This query is a bit more complicated only because it needs additional joins to the Orders and Customer tables to get the HOUSEHOLDID. However, it has the same structure as the earlier one, and the query that calculates the rule measures is almost the same as shown earlier; the only difference is that COUNT(DISTINCT orderid) becomes COUNT(DISTINCT householdid).

### Calculating Product Group Rules Using Window Functions

A second possible approach for calculating the product group rules is to use window functions. These make it possible to do all the aggregations conveniently in one query, without creating an intermediate table. Of course, this is only possible in databases that support this functionality.

The window functions approach is like using an intermediate table and putting all the calculations in one query. In fact, it can be illustrated on the intermediate table. Instead of using four subqueries to calculate the four values, these can all be calculated in a single query:

```
SELECT lhsrhs.*, numlhsrhs * 1.0/numorders as support,
       numlhsrhs * 1.0/numlhs as confidence,
       numlhsrhs * numorders * 1.0/(1.0*numlhs * numrhs) as lift
FROM (SELECT lhs, rhs, MIN(numlhsrhs) as numlhsrhs, MIN(numlhs) as numlhs,
            MIN(numorders) as numorders, MIN(numrhs) as numrhs
      FROM (SELECT orderid, lhs, rhs,
                   COUNT(DISTINCT orderid) OVER
                      (PARTITION BY lhs, rhs) as numlhsrhs,
                   COUNT(DISTINCT orderid) OVER
                      (PARTITION BY lhs) as numlhs,
                   COUNT(DISTINCT orderid) OVER
                      (PARTITION BY rhs) as numrhs,
                   COUNT(DISTINCT orderid) OVER
                      (PARTITION BY NULL) as numorders
            FROM assoc_rules_pg2pg
           ) o
      GROUP BY lhs, rhs
     ) lhsrhs
ORDER BY 9 DESC
```

This query follows very similar logic to the query that uses the intermediate table. The calculation of NUMLHSRHS, NUMLHS, NUMRHS, and NUMORDERS takes place in one subquery and then the aggregation on these values takes place in another, because window functions and aggregations do not mix. Replacing the table Assoc_Rules_PG2PG with the query that generates the data would put the whole result in one query.

The query has just one flaw, which is perchance fatal. SQL Server does not support COUNT(DISTINCT) as a window aggregation function. So this form of the query generates a syntax error in SQL Server, although it does work in Oracle.

**WARNING** SQL Server does not support COUNT(DISTINCT) **as a window function. Unfortunately, if you need this functionality, you have to use an intermediate table or subquery.**

# Two-Way Associations

The calculation for two-way association rules follows the same logic as for the one-way rules. This section looks at the SQL for generating such rules, as well as some interesting extensions by widening the idea of item.

## Calculating Two-Way Associations

The basic query for calculating two-way associations is quite similar to the query for one-way associations. The difference is that there are now two products on the left-hand side rather than one. Because the following two rules are equivalent:

- A and B ⇨ C
- B and A ⇨ C

the products on the left-hand side do not need to be repeated. This query includes the requirement that the first product id be smaller than the second on the left-hand side, as a way to eliminate duplicate equivalent rules.

The query that generates all two-way association rules looks like:

```
SELECT item_lhs1.orderid,
       (CAST(item_lhs1.lhs as VARCHAR)+', '+
        CAST(item_lhs2.lhs as VARCHAR)) as lhs, item_rhs.rhs
INTO assoc_rules_pp2p
FROM (SELECT orderid FROM orderline GROUP BY orderid
      HAVING COUNT(DISTINCT productid) > 2) filter JOIN
     (SELECT orderid, productid as lhs FROM orderline
      GROUP BY orderid, productid) item_lhs1
      ON filter.orderid = item_lhs1.orderid JOIN
     (SELECT orderid, productid as lhs FROM orderline
      GROUP BY orderid, productid) item_lhs2
     ON item_lhs1.orderid = item_lhs2.orderid AND
        item_lhs1.lhs < item_lhs2.lhs JOIN
     (SELECT orderid, productid as rhs FROM orderline
      GROUP BY orderid, productid) item_rhs
     ON item_lhs1.orderid = item_rhs.orderid AND
        item_rhs.rhs NOT IN (item_lhs1.lhs, item_lhs2.lhs)
```

This query has an extra join to capture the additional product on the left-hand side. Because two-way association rules contain three different products (two on the left and one on the right), the query only needs to consider orders that have at least three products.

The calculation of support, confidence, and lift follows a similar pattern to the one-way association method. The following query does this work:

```
SELECT lhsrhs.*, numlhs, numrhs, numorders,
       numlhsrhs * 1.0/numorders as support,
       numlhsrhs * 1.0/numlhs as confidence,
       numlhsrhs * numorders * 1.0/(numlhs * numrhs) as lift
FROM (SELECT lhs, rhs, COUNT(*) as numlhsrhs
      FROM assoc_rules_pp2p GROUP BY lhs, rhs) lhsrhs JOIN
     (SELECT lhs, COUNT(DISTINCT orderid) as numlhs
      FROM assoc_rules_pp2p GROUP BY lhs) sumlhs
     ON lhsrhs.lhs = sumlhs.lhs JOIN
     (SELECT rhs, COUNT(DISTINCT orderid) as numrhs
      FROM assoc_rules_pp2p GROUP BY rhs) sumrhs
     ON lhsrhs.rhs = sumrhs.rhs CROSS JOIN
     (SELECT COUNT(DISTINCT orderid) as numorders FROM assoc_rules_pp2p) a
ORDER BY 9 DESC
```

With the exception of the name of the intermediate table, this query is exactly the same as the query for one-way association rules. This is very useful. The query to evaluate different types of rules can be the same, by using well-thought-out naming conventions.

**TIP** By using careful naming conventions in the intermediate table, the same query can calculate support, confidence, and lift for one-way association rules and two-way association rules.

The results from this query are also rather similar to the results for the one-way associations. The rules with the highest lift are ones with three products that are extremely rare. By the measure of lift, the best rules seem to be those that have products that only occur together and never separately.

## Using Chi-Square to Find the Best Rules

Lift provides one measure of "best," but perhaps it is not the most practical because it seems to choose the least common products. The typical way to get around this is by requiring a certain level of support for the rule. However, the rules with the highest lift are often still the ones with the rarest products that meet the support criterion. This section discusses an alternative measure, the chi-square measure, because it produces a better subjective ordering of the rules.

### Applying Chi-Square to Rules

The chi-square measure was introduced in Chapter 3 as a way of measuring whether particular splits in data across multiple dimensions are due to chance.

The higher the chi-square value for a particular set of splits, the less likely that observed data is happening due to chance. The measure can be used directly or it can be converted to a p-value using the chi-square distribution.

Chi-square can also be applied to rules, and it provides a single value that determines whether or not the rule is reasonable. Lift, confidence, and support all measure how good a rule is, but they are three different measures. One warning, though. Chi-square does not work unless all cells have a minimum count; typically at least five.

To apply chi-square to rules, start by considering a general rule:

- LHS ⇨ RHS

This rule divides all the orders into four discrete groups:

- LHS is TRUE and RHS is TRUE
- LHS is TRUE and RHS is FALSE
- LHS is FALSE and RHS is TRUE
- LHS is FALSE and RHS is FALSE

Table 9-13 shows the counts of orders that fall into each of these groups for the rule 12820 ⇨ 13190. The rows indicate whether the orders contain the left-hand side of the rule. The columns are whether they contain the right-hand side. The upper-left cell, for instance, contains all orders where the rule is true.

**Table 9-13:** Counts of Orders for Chi-Square Calculation for Rule 12820 ⇨ 13190

|  | RHS TRUE | RHS FALSE |
| --- | --- | --- |
| **LHS TRUE** | 816 | 15,853 |
| **LHS FALSE** | 2,588 | 173,726 |

This matrix is the chi-square matrix discussed in Chapter 3. Calculating the chi-square values is not difficult in Excel. Sum the rows and columns and then create an expected value matrix using these sums. The expected value is the product of the row sum times the column sum divided by the total number of orders. The observed value minus the expected value is the variance. The chi-square value is the sum of the variances squared divided by the expected values.

Chi-square has some nice properties compared to lift. It provides a measure of how unexpected the rule is in the data, rather than the improvement from using it. In one measure, it takes into account how large the rule is as well as how good it is. The standard measures of support and lift address these issues separately.

## Applying Chi-Square to Rules in SQL

For one rule, the chi-square calculation is quite feasible in Excel. However, for thousands or millions of rules, Excel is not sufficiently powerful. As shown in Chapter 3, it is possible to do the chi-square calculation in SQL.

There have been four counts used for calculating support, confidence, and lift:

- NUMLHSRHS is the number of orders where the entire rule is true.
- NUMLHS is the number of orders where the left-hand side is true.
- NUMRHS is the number of orders where the right-hand side is true.
- NUMORDERS is the total number of orders.

The chi-square calculation, on the other hand, uses four slightly different values, based on the values in the chi-square matrix. The chi-square values are related to these counts:

- LHS true, RHS true: NUMLHSRHS
- LHS true, RHS false: NUMLHS – NUMLHSRHS
- LHS false, RHS true: NUMRHS – NUMLHSRHS
- LHS false, RHS false: NUMORDERS – NUMLHS – NUMRHS + NUMLHSRHS

With these values, the chi-square calculation is just a bunch of arithmetic in a couple of nested subqueries, as shown for the two-way rules in Assoc_PP2P:

```
SELECT (SQUARE(explhsrhs - numlhsrhs)/explhsrhs +
        SQUARE(explhsnorhs - numlhsnorhs)/explhsnorhs +
        SQUARE(expnolhsrhs - numnolhsrhs)/expnolhsrhs +
        SQUARE(expnolhsnorhs - numnolhsnorhs)/expnolhsnorhs
       ) as chisquare, b.*
FROM (SELECT lhsrhs.*, numlhs, numrhs, numorders,
             numlhs - numlhsrhs as numlhsnorhs,
             numrhs - numlhsrhs as numnolhsrhs,
             numorders - numlhs - numrhs + numlhsrhs as numnolhsnorhs,
             numlhs*numrhs*1.0/numorders as explhsrhs,
             numlhs*(1.*numorders-numrhs)*1.0/numorders as explhsnorhs,
             (1.0*numorders-numlhs)*numrhs*1.0/numorders as expnolhsrhs,
             ((1.0*numorders-numlhs)*(1.0*numorders-numrhs)/numorders
             ) as expnolhsnorhs,
             numlhsrhs*1.0/numorders as support,
             numlhsrhs*1.0/numlhs as confidence,
             numlhsrhs*numorders*1.0/(numlhs*numrhs) as lift
      FROM (SELECT lhs, rhs, COUNT(DISTINCT orderid) as numlhsrhs
            FROM assoc_rules_pp2p GROUP BY lhs, rhs) lhsrhs JOIN
           (SELECT lhs, COUNT(DISTINCT orderid) as numlhs
            FROM assoc_rules_pp2p GROUP BY lhs) sumlhs
          ON lhsrhs.lhs = sumlhs.lhs JOIN
           (SELECT rhs, COUNT(DISTINCT orderid) as numrhs
```

```
            FROM assoc_rules_pp2p GROUP BY rhs) sumrhs
        ON lhsrhs.rhs = sumrhs.rhs CROSS JOIN
        (SELECT COUNT(DISTINCT orderid) as numorders
         FROM assoc_rules_pp2p) a
    ) b
```

The innermost subqueries calculate the counts for the various components of each rule. The next level calculates the intermediate values needed for the chi-square calculation. And the outermost query combines these values into the chi-square value.

### Comparing Chi-Square Rules to Lift

At first glance, the rules with the highest chi-square values are the same as the rules with the highest lift. These are the rules consisting of products that appear in only one order. However, one of the conditions of the chi-square calculation is that every cell should have at least five orders. This condition is expressed as a WHERE condition:

```
numlhsrhs > 4 AND numlhs - numlhsrhs > 4 AND numrhs - numlhsrhs > 4
```

As a performance note, adding this WHERE clause is an example where SQL Server might fail to optimize the query correctly; with the WHERE clause, the query plan might be much less efficient. To get around this, create a summary table with the results and use a query to select rules from the summary table.

Table 9-14 shows the top ten rules with the highest chi-square values and the highest lift values. The first thing to notice is that there is no overlap between the two sets. The rules with the highest lift are quite different from the rules with the best chi-square.

**Table 9-14:** Top Rules by Lift and by Chi-Square Measures

| BEST CHI-SQUARE | SUPPORT | CHI-SQUARE | LIFT |
| --- | --- | --- | --- |
| 12820 + 12830 ⇨ 12506 | 2.09% | 14,044.9 | 35.5 |
| 12506 + 12820 ⇨ 12830 | 2.09% | 12,842.8 | 32.5 |
| 11070 + 11072 ⇨ 11074 | 0.38% | 10,812.5 | 148.6 |
| 11052 + 11197 ⇨ 11196 | 1.44% | 9,745.7 | 36.0 |
| 11072 + 11074 ⇨ 11070 | 0.38% | 9,144.6 | 125.9 |
| 11070 + 11074 ⇨ 11072 | 0.38% | 9,088.0 | 125.1 |
| 11196 + 11197 ⇨ 11052 | 1.44% | 8,880.6 | 32.9 |

*Continued on next page*

**Table 9-14** *(continued)*

| BEST CHI-SQUARE | SUPPORT | CHI-SQUARE | LIFT |
|---|---|---|---|
| 11157 + 11158 ⇨ 11156 | 0.29% | 8,260.1 | 148.2 |
| 11985 + 11988 ⇨ 11987 | 0.52% | 8,222.0 | 82.8 |
| 12810 + 12820 ⇨ 13017 | 0.52% | 8,146.7 | 83.0 |
| **BEST LIFT** | | | |
| 13947 + 13949 ⇨ 13948 | 0.04% | 6,476.5 | 926.0 |
| 13944 + 13947 ⇨ 13945 | 0.04% | 7,208.0 | 901.8 |
| 10969 + 10971 ⇨ 11086 | 0.03% | 4,324.3 | 865.9 |
| 13945 + 13950 ⇨ 13948 | 0.03% | 5,189.7 | 865.9 |
| 13946 + 13997 ⇨ 13948 | 0.04% | 5,977.5 | 854.8 |
| 13947 + 13949 ⇨ 13945 | 0.04% | 5,977.5 | 854.8 |
| 13944 + 13947 ⇨ 13948 | 0.04% | 5,977.5 | 854.8 |
| 13948 + 13950 ⇨ 13945 | 0.03% | 4,789.8 | 799.3 |
| 10069 + 10082 ⇨ 10078 | 0.03% | 3,963.3 | 793.8 |
| 13946 + 13997 ⇨ 13945 | 0.04% | 5,516.9 | 789.1 |

The rules with the highest lift are all similar. They all have low support and the products in the rules are quite rare. These rules do have reasonable confidence levels. What makes them good, though, is that the products are rare, so seeing them together in an order is very, very unlikely. Most of the top rules by lift are about ARTWORK, which has lots of expensive products with very low sales volumes.

The rules with the highest chi-square values look much more sensible. The top rule here has a support of over 2%. The smallest of the top ten rules has a support of 0.3%, about eight times the support of any of the lift rules. The support is much better, and the confidence is also much larger. Many of these rules involve FREEBIE products, which makes intuitive sense, because FREEBIE products are included in so many orders.

**TIP** The chi-square measure is better than support, confidence, or lift for choosing a good set of association rules.

The chi-square values and lift values are not totally independent. Figure 9-10 shows a bubble plot comparing decile values of chi-square with decile values of lift. The large bubbles along the axis show that there is a lot of overlap between the values; overall, they put the rules in a similar order. However, there are many examples of smaller bubbles, indicating that chi-square and lift are disagreeing on how good some rules are.

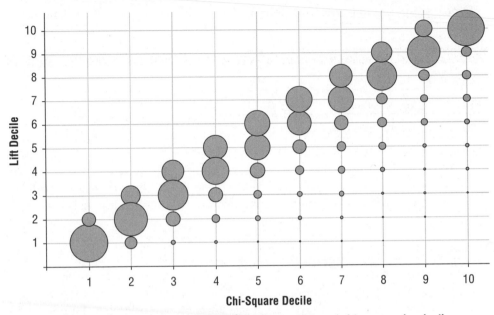

**Figure 9-10:** This bubble plot compares the values of lift and chi-square, by decile.

Calculating the deciles for the lift and chi-square uses the window functions:

```
SELECT chisquaredecile, liftdecile, COUNT(*), AVG(chisquare), AVG(lift)
FROM (SELECT NTILE(10) OVER (ORDER BY chisquare) as chisquaredecile,
             NTILE(10) OVER (ORDER BY lift) as liftdecile, a.*
      FROM (<previous-query>) a
      WHERE numlhsrhs >= 5 and numlhsnorhs >= 5 and numnolhsrhs >= 5) a
GROUP BY chisquaredecile, liftdecile
```

Notice that this query requires a subquery because windows functions cannot be mixed with aggregation functions. The results are plotted as a bubble chart in Excel.

## Chi-Square for Negative Rules

The chi-square value measures how unexpected the rule is. However, a rule can be unexpected in two ways. It could be unexpected because the right-hand side occurs much more often when the left-hand side appears. Or, it could be unexpected because the right-hand side occurs much less often.

In the previous example, all the rules with the highest chi-square values have a lift greater than one (as seen in Table 9.14). In this case, the lift is saying that the right hand size occurs more frequently than expected. For these rules, the chi-square value is indeed saying that the rule is a good rule.

What happens when the lift is less than one? There are no examples in Table 9.14. However, this situation can occur. In this case, we need to consider the negative rule:

- LHS ⇨ NOT RHS

The chi-square value for this rule is the same as the chi-square value for the original rule. On the other hand, the lift changes so the lift for this rule is greater than one when the lift for the original rule is less than one (and vice versa).

The chi-square value and lift can be used together. When the chi-square is high and the lift greater than one, then the resulting rule is the positive rule. When the chi-square value is high and the lift less than one, then the resulting rule is the negative rule. Using these values together makes it possible to look for both types of rules at the same time.

## Heterogeneous Associations

All the rules so far have either been about the products or the product groups, with the same items on both the left-hand and right-hand sides. This is traditional association rule analysis. Because we are building the rules ourselves, it is possible and feasible to extend the rules to include additional types of items.

The idea is to add other features about the order, or customer, or household as items into the rules. This section discusses two ways of doing this. The first is a "hard" approach, which generates rules where the left-hand side consists of two specific types of items in specific positions. The second is a "soft" approach, where the definition of item mixes different things together, allowing any item anywhere in the rule. The steps for calculating the measures, such as chi-square, are the same regardless of what is in the item sets.

### Rules of the Form "State Plus Product"

The first approach is to form rules with two different types of items on the left-hand side, such as an attribute of the order or customer followed by a product. The right-hand side is still a product. A typical rule is:

- NY + productid 11197 ⇨ productid 11196

The rules generated by this method are always of the form:

- state plus product ⇨ product

These types of rules require only a slight modification to the rule generation query. In this case, the first item is the STATE column from Orders, rather than PRODUCTID from Orderline. The following query generates the candidate rules:

```
SELECT item_lhs1.orderid,
       (item_lhs1.lhs+', '+CAST(item_lhs2.lhs as VARCHAR)) as lhs,
       item_rhs.rhs
INTO assoc_rules_sp2p
FROM (SELECT orderid FROM orderline GROUP BY orderid
             HAVING COUNT(DISTINCT productid) > 2) filter JOIN
     (SELECT orderid, state as lhs FROM orders o1) item_lhs1
     ON filter.orderid = item_lhs1.orderid JOIN
     (SELECT DISTINCT orderid, productid as lhs
      FROM orderline o1) item_lhs2
     ON item_lhs1.orderid = item_lhs2.orderid JOIN
     (SELECT DISTINCT orderid, productid as rhs
      FROM orderline o1) item_rhs
     ON item_lhs1.orderid = item_rhs.orderid AND
        item_lhs2.lhs <> item_rhs.rhs
```

This query has a couple tweaks. The two items on the left-hand side are never the same, because one is a state and the other a product id. There is no need to eliminate duplicates by insisting that the first be alphabetically before the second. Similarly, the right-hand side cannot be equal to the state (the first item), so that condition has been removed.

The resulting table has the same format as the earlier rule tables, so the same chi-square query can be used for choosing rules. Table 9-15 shows the top ten rules.

**Table 9-15:** Top Ten Rules with State and Product on Left-Hand Side

| RULE | RULE COUNTS | | | CHI-SQUARE | LIFT |
|------|-----|-----|--------|------------|------|
|      | LHS | RHS | LHSRHS |            |      |
| NY + 11197 ⇨ 11196 | 232 | 499 | 184 | 5,415.3 | 30.3 |
| NY + 11196 ⇨ 11197 | 248 | 480 | 184 | 5,255.3 | 29.4 |
| NY + 11076 ⇨ 11090 | 10 | 10 | 5 | 4,757.5 | 952.5 |
| NY + 11051 ⇨ 11050 | 16 | 31 | 11 | 4,636.7 | 422.5 |
| NY + 11197 ⇨ 11052 | 232 | 436 | 155 | 4,372.0 | 29.2 |
| NY + 11052 ⇨ 11197 | 211 | 480 | 155 | 4,371.6 | 29.2 |
| NY + 10970 ⇨ 11086 | 10 | 11 | 5 | 4,324.3 | 865.9 |
| NY + 10968 ⇨ 11086 | 10 | 11 | 5 | 4,324.3 | 865.9 |
| NY + 11072 ⇨ 11074 | 55 | 120 | 38 | 4,130.1 | 109.7 |
| NY + 11074 ⇨ 11072 | 48 | 139 | 38 | 4,087.3 | 108.5 |

## Rules Mixing Different Types of Products

Another method for adding different types of items is to expand the notion of item. By adding the state into the products, any of the following rules are possible:

- product plus product ⇨ product
- product plus product ⇨ state
- product plus state ⇨ product
- state plus product ⇨ product

In addition, the following rules are conceivable, but not possible, because there is only one state associated with each order:

- state plus state ⇨ state
- state plus state ⇨ product
- state plus product ⇨ state
- product plus state ⇨ state

This method would produce rules such as these if there were more than one state.

Creating such rules is a simple matter of modifying the item subqueries to include the state item, using the UNION ALL operator. The only tricky part is handling the data types, because PRODUCTID is an integer and the state a string, so PRODUCTID needs to be cast to a character:

```
SELECT item_lhs1.orderid, item_lhs1.lhs+', '+item_lhs2.lhs as lhs, rhs
INTO assoc_rules_spsp2p
FROM (SELECT orderid FROM orderline GROUP BY orderid
             HAVING COUNT(DISTINCT productid) > 2) filter JOIN
     (SELECT orderid, CAST(productid as VARCHAR) as lhs
      FROM orderline ol GROUP BY orderid, productid UNION ALL
      SELECT orderid, state as productid FROM orders) item_lhs1
    ON filter.orderid = item_lhs1.orderid JOIN
     (SELECT orderid, CAST(productid as VARCHAR) as lhs
      FROM orderline ol GROUP BY orderid, productid UNION ALL
      SELECT orderid, state as lhs FROM orders) item_lhs2
    ON item_lhs1.orderid = item_lhs2.orderid AND
       item_lhs1.lhs < item_lhs2.lhs JOIN
     (SELECT orderid, CAST(productid as VARCHAR) as rhs
      FROM orderline ol GROUP BY orderid, productid UNION ALL
      SELECT orderid, state as product FROM orders) item_rhs
    ON item_lhs1.orderid = item_rhs.orderid AND
       item_rhs.rhs NOT IN (item_lhs1.lhs, item_lhs2.lhs)
```

The best rules have no states, so they are the same as the ones in Table 9-14.

# Extending Association Rules

The association rule methods can be extended in several different ways. The most obvious extension is adding additional items on the left-hand side. Another extension is to have entirely different sets of items on the left-hand side and the right-hand side. And, perhaps the most interesting extension is the creation of sequential association rules, which look for patterns of items purchased in a particular order.

## Multi-Way Associations

Association rule queries handle more than two items on the left-hand side. The mechanism is to continue adding in joins for every possible item, similar to the method for going from one item on the left-hand side to two items. However, as the number of items grows, the size of the intermediate table storing the candidate rules can get unmanageably large and take a long, long time to create. The way to handle this is by adding restrictions so fewer candidate rules are considered.

> **TIP** As the number of items in association rules gets larger, query performance can get much and much worse. Be sure to use a filter table to limit the orders you are working on.

One obvious restriction is to consider only orders having at least as many items as are in the rule. Several examples in this chapter have used this restriction. A second restriction is to require a minimum support for the rule. This is used to filter out products that have less than the minimum support. A rule having a given level of support implies that each product in the rule have at least that level of support as well.

The third restriction is to remove the largest orders, because large orders have many products, which results in very large numbers of combinations. These orders typically add very little information, because there are few of them. However, they contribute to the vast bulk of processing time.

The following query combines these together for three-way combinations, with a minimum support of twenty and using orders with no more than ten products:

```
SELECT item_lhs1.orderid,
       (CAST(item_lhs1.lhs as VARCHAR)+','+
        CAST(item_lhs2.lhs as VARCHAR)+','+
        CAST(item_lhs3.lhs as VARCHAR)) as lhs, item_rhs.rhs
INTO assoc_rules_ppp2p
FROM (SELECT orderid FROM orderline GROUP BY orderid
      HAVING COUNT(DISTINCT productid) BETWEEN 4 AND 10) filter JOIN
```

*(continued)*

```
      (SELECT DISTINCT orderid, productid as lhs FROM orderline ol
       WHERE productid IN
            (SELECT productid FROM orderline GROUP BY productid
             HAVING COUNT(DISTINCT orderid) >= 20) ) item_lhs1
  ON filter.orderid = item_lhs1.orderid JOIN
      (SELECT DISTINCT orderid, productid as lhs FROM orderline ol
       WHERE productid IN
            (SELECT productid FROM orderline GROUP BY productid
             HAVING COUNT(DISTINCT orderid) >= 20) ) item_lhs2
  ON item_lhs1.orderid = item_lhs2.orderid AND
       item_lhs1.lhs < item_lhs2.lhs JOIN
      (SELECT DISTINCT orderid, productid as lhs FROM orderline ol
       WHERE productid IN
            (SELECT productid FROM orderline GROUP BY productid
             HAVING COUNT(DISTINCT orderid) >= 20) ) item_lhs3
  ON item_lhs1.orderid = item_lhs3.orderid AND
       item_lhs2.lhs < item_lhs3.lhs JOIN
      (SELECT DISTINCT orderid, productid as rhs FROM orderline ol
       WHERE productid IN
            (SELECT productid FROM orderline GROUP BY productid
             HAVING COUNT(DISTINCT orderid) >= 20) ) item_rhs
  ON item_lhs1.orderid = item_rhs.orderid AND
       item_rhs.rhs NOT IN (item_lhs1.lhs, item_lhs2.lhs, item_lhs3.lhs)
```

The different restrictions appear in different places. The limit on the number of products in an order is placed in the first subquery, which chooses the orders being processed. The restriction on products is placed in each of the item subqueries. The particular limit is using only products that appear in at least 20 orders. Multi-way associations are feasible, but it is important to pay attention to query performance.

## Rules Using Attributes of Products

So far, all the rules have been based on products or one attribute of products, the product group. Products could have different attributes assigned to them, such as:

- Whether the product is being discounted in the order;
- The manufacturer of the product;
- The "subject" of the product, such as whether art is photography or painting, whether books are fiction or non-fiction; and,
- The target of the product (kids, adults, left-handers).

The idea is that products could have one or more categories that can be used in rules. Adjusting the SQL to handle this is not difficult. It simply requires joining in the table containing the categories when generating the item sets.

There is another problem, though. Each product probably has the same set of categories, wherever it appears. So, categories are going to co-occur with each order, simply because they describe the same product, and occurring together may simply mean that a particular product is present. This is not what we want, because we don't want rules on categories to tell us what we already know.

Earlier, the section on combinations discussed a particular method for finding products that households purchase in different orders. The same idea can be used for categories. The approach is to find categories that are in the same order, but not in the same product, in order to find the strength of affinities among categories.

## Rules with Different Left- and Right-Hand Sides

Another variation on association rules is to include different types of items on different sides of the rule. A small example of this was having the state included as a product on the left-hand side, but not included on the right-hand side. The implementation in SQL is a simple modification to the association rule query to generate the right item set for items on the left-hand side and the right-hand side.

Why would this be a good idea? One application is when customers are doing a variety of different things. For instance, customers may be visiting web pages and then clicking advertisements; or they may be visiting web pages and then making a purchase, or they may be receiving multiple marketing messages through different channels and then responding. In these cases, the left-hand side of the rule could be the advertising pages exposed, the web pages visited, or the campaigns sent out. The right-hand side could be the clicks or purchases or responses. The rules then describe what combinations of actions are associated with the desired action.

This idea has other applications as well. When customizing banner ads or catalogs for particular types of products, the question might arise: *What items have customers purchased that suggest they are interested in these products?* Using association rules with purchases or visits on the left-hand side and banner clicks on the right-hand side is one possible way of approaching this question.

Such heterogeneous rules do bring up one technical issue. The question is whether to include customers that have no events on the right-hand side. Consider the situation where the left-hand side has pages on a web site and the right-hand side has products purchased by customers. The purpose of the rules is to find which web pages lead to the purchase of particular products. Should the data used to generate these rules include customers who have never made a purchase?

This is an interesting question, and there is no right answer. Using only customers who make purchases reduces the size of the data (since, presumably, many people do not make purchases). Perhaps the first step in approaching the problem is to ask which web pages lead to any purchase at all. The second step is to then find the product affinity based on the web pages.

## Before and After: Sequential Associations

Sequential associations are quite similar to simple product associations. The difference is that the rule enforces that purchases be in a particular order. So, a typical rule is:

- ▪ Product 12175 implies that Product 13297 will later be purchased

Such sequences can prove interesting, particularly when many customers have purchase histories. However, sequential rules cannot be found within a single order, because all the products within an order are purchased at the same time. Instead, sequential rules need to consider all orders of products within a household.

The basic structure for association rules applies to sequential rules. The difference is to include the condition on time when creating the candidate rules, as in the following:

```
SELECT item_lhs.householdid, item_lhs.lhs, item_rhs.rhs
INTO assocs_seqrules_p2p
FROM (SELECT householdid
      FROM orderline ol JOIN orders o ON ol.orderid = o.orderid JOIN
           customer c on c.customerid = o.customerid
      GROUP BY householdid
      HAVING COUNT(DISTINCT productid) > 1) filter JOIN
     (SELECT householdid, orderdate as lhsdate, productid as lhs
      FROM orderline ol JOIN orders o ON ol.orderid = o.orderid JOIN
           customer c on c.customerid = o.customerid
      GROUP BY householdid, orderdate, productid) item_lhs
     ON filter.householdid = item_lhs.householdid JOIN
     (SELECT householdid, orderdate as rhsdate, productid as rhs
      FROM orderline ol JOIN orders o ON ol.orderid = o.orderid JOIN
           customer c on c.customerid = o.customerid
      GROUP BY householdid, orderdate, productid) item_rhs
     ON item_lhs.householdid = item_rhs.householdid AND
        item_lhs.lhsdate < item_rhs.rhsdate AND
        item_rhs.rhs <> item_lhs.lhs
```

This query is similar to the one that generates combinations of products within a household but not within an order. The subqueries get the household id and then aggregate by the household id, product id, and order date. The date is needed to enforce the sequencing. For customers who purchase the same product at different times, candidate rules include each purchase. If this frequently happens, using the minimum order date for the left-hand side and the maximum for the right-hand side also works.

Table 9-16 shows the resulting sequential association rules. These are blissfully interesting, because they are intuitively obvious. Nine of the ten top rules (by the chi-square measure) are for calendars. That is, customers who purchase calendars at one point in time are likely to purchase calendars later in time, probably about a year later.

**Table 9-16:** Top Ten Sequential Association Rules

| RULE | PRODUCT GROUPS | SUPPORT | LIFT | CHI-SQUARE |
|---|---|---|---|---|
| 12175 ⇨ 13297 | CALENDAR ⇨ CALENDAR | 0.54% | 126.3 | 12,721.7 |
| 12176 ⇨ 13298 | CALENDAR ⇨ CALENDAR | 1.62% | 41.4 | 12,391.3 |
| 12014 ⇨ 12175 | CALENDAR ⇨ CALENDAR | 0.52% | 126.4 | 12,096.9 |
| 12015 ⇨ 12176 | CALENDAR ⇨ CALENDAR | 1.76% | 34.8 | 11,262.5 |
| 10003 ⇨ 12014 | CALENDAR ⇨ CALENDAR | 0.36% | 146.6 | 9,785.0 |
| 10863 ⇨ 12015 | CALENDAR ⇨ CALENDAR | 1.47% | 34.8 | 9,385.7 |
| 10862 ⇨ 10863 | CALENDAR ⇨ CALENDAR | 1.22% | 41.0 | 9,125.2 |
| 10002 ⇨ 10003 | CALENDAR ⇨ CALENDAR | 0.28% | 163.0 | 8,440.8 |
| 12014 ⇨ 13297 | CALENDAR ⇨ CALENDAR | 0.45% | 88.8 | 7,311.9 |
| 12488 ⇨ 13628 | BOOK ⇨ BOOK | 0.30% | 127.9 | 6,991.3 |

## Lessons Learned

This chapter looks at what customers purchase, rather than when or how they purchase. The contents of market baskets can be very interesting, providing information about both customers and products.

The chapter starts with exploratory analysis of products in purchases. A good way to look at products is by using scatter plots and bubble charts to visualize relationships. There is a useful Excel trick that makes it possible to see products along the X- and Y-axes for bubble charts and scatter plots.

Investigating products includes finding the products associated with the best customers, and finding the ones associated with the worst customers (those who only make one purchase). It is also interesting to explore other facets of products, such as the number of times a product changes price, the number of units in each order, the number of times products are repeated within an order, and how often customers purchase the same product again.

Simple association rules specify that when a customer purchases one product (the left-hand side), then the customer is likely to purchase another product (the right-hand side) in the same order. The traditional way of measuring the goodness of these rules is with support, confidence, and lift. Support measures the proportion of orders where the rule is true. Confidence measures how confident the rule is when it applies. And lift specifies how much better the rule works rather than just guessing.

A better measure for association rules, however, is based on the chi-square value discussed in Chapter 3. This gives an indication of how likely it is that the rule is based on something significant, as opposed to random chance.

Association rules are very powerful and extensible. Using SQL, the simple one-way associations can be extended to two-ways and beyond. Non-product items, such as the state where the customer resides and other customer attributes, can be incorporated into the rules. With a relatively simple modification, the same mechanism can generate sequential rules, where products occur in a specific order.

With association rules we have dived into the finest details of customer interactions. The next chapter moves back to the customer level, by using SQL to build basic models on customers.

# Data Mining Models in SQL

Data mining is the process of finding meaningful patterns in large quantities of data. Traditionally, the subject is introduced through statistics and statistical modeling. This chapter takes an alternative approach that introduces data mining concepts using databases. This perspective presents the important concepts, sidestepping the rigor of theoretical statistics to focus instead on the most important practical aspect: data.

The next two chapters extend the discussion begun in this chapter. Chapter 11 explains linear regression, a more traditional starting point for modeling, from the perspective of data mining. The final chapter focuses on data preparation. Whether the modeling techniques are within a database or in another tool, data preparation is often the most challenging part of a data mining endeavor.

Although earlier chapters have already shown the powerful techniques that are possible using SQL, snobs may feel that data mining is more advanced than mere querying of databases. Such a sentiment downplays the importance of data manipulation, which lies at the heart of even the most advanced techniques. Some powerful techniques adapt well to databases, and learning how they work — both in terms of their application to business problems and their implementation on real data — provides a good foundation for understanding modeling. Some techniques do not adapt as well to databases, so they require more specialized software. However, the fundamental ideas on using models and evaluating the results remain the same regardless of the sophistication of the modeling technique.

Earlier chapters contain examples of models, without describing them as such. The RFM methodology introduced in Chapter 8 assigns an RFM bin to each customer; the estimated response rate of the RFM bin is a model score that estimates response. The expected remaining lifetime from a survival model is a model score. Even the expected value from the chi-square test is an example of a model score, produced by a basic statistics formula. What these have in common is that they all find patterns in data that can be applied back to the original data or to new data, producing a meaningful result.

The first type of model in this chapter is the look-alike model, which takes an example — typically of something particularly good or bad — and finds other rows that are similar to the example. Look-alike models use a definition of similarity. Nearest neighbor techniques are an extension of look-alike models that estimate a value by combining information from neighbors where the value is already known.

The next type of model in the chapter is the lookup model, which summarizes data along various dimensions to create a lookup table. These models are quite powerful and fit naturally in any discussion of data mining and databases. However, they are limited to at most a few dimensions. Lookup models lead to naïve Bayesian models, a powerful technique that combines information along any number of dimensions, using some interesting ideas from the area of probability.

Before talking about these techniques, the chapter introduces important data mining concepts and the processes of building and using models. There is an interesting analogy between these processes and SQL. Building models is analogous to aggregation, because both are about bringing data together to identify patterns. Scoring models is like joining tables — applying the patterns to new rows of data.

## Introduction to Directed Data Mining

Directed data mining is the most common type of data mining. "Directed" means that target values are known in the historical data, so the data mining techniques have examples to learn from. Directed data mining makes the assumption that the patterns in historical data are applicable in the future.

Another type of data mining is undirected data mining, which uses sophisticated techniques to find groups in the data seemingly unrelated to each other. Undirected data mining does not have a target, so the groups may or may not be meaningful. Association rules are one example of undirected data mining. Other undirected techniques are typically more specialized, so this chapter and the next two focus on directed techniques.

**TIP** The purpose of a directed model may be to apply model scores to new data or to gain better understanding of customers and what's happening in the data.

## Directed Models

A directed model finds patterns in historical data using examples where the answer is known. The process of finding the patterns is called *training* or *building* the model. The most common way to use the model is by *scoring* data to append a model score.

Sometimes, understanding gleaned from a model is more important than the model scores. The models discussed in this book lend themselves to understanding, so they can contribute to exploratory data analysis as well as directed modeling. Other types of models, such as neural networks, are so complicated that they cannot explain how they arrive at their results. Such "black-box" models might do a good job of estimating values, but people cannot peek in and understand how they work or use them to learn about the data.

> **TIP** If it is important to know how a model is working (which variables it is choosing, which variables are more important, and so on), then use a technique that produces understandable models. The techniques discussed in this book fall in this category.

The models themselves take the form of formulas and auxiliary tables that can be used to generate scores. The process of training the model generates the information needed for scoring. This section explains important facets of modeling, in the areas of data and evaluation.

As a note, the word "model" has another sense in databases. As discussed in Chapter 1, a data model describes the contents of a database, the way that the data is structured. A data mining model, on the other hand, is a process that analyzes data and produces useful information about the business. Both types of model are about patterns, one about the structure of the database and the other about patterns in the content of the data.

## The Data in Modeling

Data is central to the data mining process. Data is used to build models. Data is used to assess models, and data is used for scoring models. This section discusses the different uses of data in modeling.

### Model Set

The *model set*, which is sometimes also called the *training set*, consists of historical data with known outcomes. It has the form of a table, with rows for each example. Typically, each row is the granularity of what is being modeled, such as a customer.

The *target* is what we are looking for; this is typically a value in a column. The target is known for all the rows in the model set. Most of the remaining columns consist of input columns. Figure 10-1 illustrates data in a possible model set.

This column is an id field that identifies the rows.

These columns are input columns.

This column is the target, what we want to predict.

| | | | | | | | |
|---|---|---|---|---|---|---|---|
| 2610000101 | 010377 | 14 | | A | 19.1 | 4 Spring . . . | TRUE |
| 2610000102 | 103188 | 7 | | A | 19.1 | NULL | TRUE |
| 2610000105 | 041598 | 1 | | B | 21.2 | 71 W. 19 St. | FALSE |
| 2610000171 | 040296 | 1 | | S | 38.3 | 3562 Oak. . . | FALSE |
| 2610000182 | 051990 | 22 | | C | 56.1 | 9672 W. 142 | FALSE |
| 2610000183 | 111191 | 45 | | C | 56.1 | NULL | TRUE |
| | | | | | | | |
| | | | | | | | |
| | | | | | | | |
| 2620000107 | 080891 | 6 | | A | 19.1 | P.O. Box 11 | FALSE |
| 2620000108 | 120398 | 3 | | D | 10.0 | 560 Robson | TRUE |
| 2620000220 | 022797 | 2 | | S | 38.3 | 222 E. 11th | FALSE |
| 2620000221 | 021797 | 3 | | A | 19.1 | 10122 SW 9 | FALSE |
| 2620000230 | 060899 | 1 | | S | 38.3 | NULL | TRUE |
| 2620000231 | 062099 | 10 | | S | 38.3 | RR 1729 | TRUE |
| 2620000300 | 032894 | 7 | | B | 21.2 | 1920 S. 14th | FALSE |

These rows have invalid customer ids, so they are ignored.

The data types in some columns are not suitable for the modeling techniques discussed in this chapter.

**Figure 10-1:** A model set consists of records with data where the outcome is already known. The process of training a model assigns a score or educated guess, estimating the target.

The goal of modeling is to intelligently and automatically "guess" the values in the target column using the values in the input columns. The specific techniques used for this depend on the nature of the data in the input and target columns, and the data mining algorithm. From the perspective of modeling, each column contains values that are one of a handful of types.

*Binary* columns (also called *flags*) contain one of two values. These typically describe specific aspects about a customer or a product. For instance, the subscription data consists of customers who are active (on the cutoff date) or stopped. This would lend itself naturally to a binary column.

*Category* columns contain one of multiple, known values. The subscription data, for instance, has several examples, including market, channel, and rate plan.

*Numeric* columns contain numbers, such as dollar amounts or tenures. Traditional statistical techniques work best on such columns.

*Date-time* columns contain dates and times stamps. These are often the most challenging type of data to work with. They are often converted to tenures and durations for data mining purposes.

*Text* columns (and other complex data types) contain important information. However, these are not used directly in the process of modeling. Instead, features of one of the other types are extracted, such as extracting the zip code from an address column.

Most of the techniques discussed in this chapter can handle missing values (represented as NULL). However, not all statistical and data mining techniques are able to handle missing values.

### Score Set

After a model is built, it can be applied to a *score set*, which has the same input columns as the model set, but does not necessarily have the target column. When the model is applied to the score set, the model processes the inputs to calculate the value of the target column, using formulas and auxiliary tables.

If the score set also has a target column, it is possible to determine how well the model is performing. So, the model set itself can be used as a score set. However, models almost always perform better on the data used to build them than on unseen data.

**WARNING** A model almost always works best on the model set. Do not expect the performance on this data to match performance on other data.

### Prediction Model Sets versus Profiling Model Sets

One very important distinction in data mining is the difference between profiling and prediction. This is a subtle concept, because the process of building models is the same for the two. The difference is in the data.

Each column describing a customer has a time frame associated with it, which is the "as-of" date when the data becomes known. For some columns, such as market and channel in the subscription data, the "as-of" date is when the customer starts. For other columns, such as the stop date and stop type columns, the "as-of" date is when the customer stops. For other data, such as the total amount spent, the "as-of" date may be some cutoff date. Unfortunately, the "as-of" date is not stored in the database, although it can usually be imputed from knowledge about how data is loaded into the database.

In a profiling model set, the input and target columns come from the same time period. That is, the target has an as-of date similar to some of the inputs. For a prediction model set, the input columns have an as-of date earlier than the target. The input columns are a "before" view of the customer and the target is the "after" view.

The upper part of Figure 10-2 shows a model set for prediction, because the inputs come from an earlier time period than the target. The target might consist of customers who stopped during July or who purchased a particular product in July. The lower part of the chart shows a model set for profiling, because the inputs and target all come from the same time period. The customers stopped during the same time period that the data comes from.

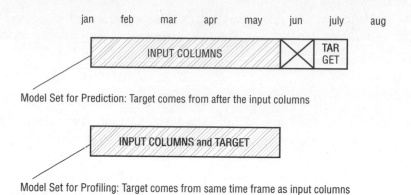

Model Set for Prediction: Target comes from after the input columns

Model Set for Profiling: Target comes from same time frame as input columns

**Figure 10-2:** In a model set used for prediction, the target column represents data from a time frame strictly after the input columns. For a model set used for profiling, the target comes from the same time frame.

Building a model set for profiling, rather than for prediction, is usually easier because profiling does not care about the as-of date. However, because of the "before" and "after" structure of the data, models built on prediction model sets do a better job of finding patterns related to actual causes rather than spurious correlations. One easy way to make prediction models is to limit the input columns to what is known when customers start, although such inputs are not as descriptive as customer behavior variables that use information after customers start.

To illustrate the distinction between profiling and prediction, consider the case of a bank that was building a model to estimate the probability of customers responding to an offer to open an investment account. The bank summarized customers in a table with various input columns describing the banking relationship — the balances in accounts of different types, dates when the accounts were opened, and so on. The bank also had a target column specifying which customers had an investment account.

The data contains at least one very strong pattern regarding investment accounts. Customers with investment accounts almost always have low savings account balances. On reflection, this is not so surprising. Such customers usually prefer to put their money in the higher yielding accounts. However, the reverse is not true. Targeting customers with low savings account balances to open investment accounts is a bad idea. Most such customers have few financial resources.

The problem is that the values in the input columns came from the same period of time as the target, so the model was a profiling model. It would have been better to take a snapshot of the customers *before* they opened an investment account, and to use this snapshot for the input columns. The target would then be customers who opened an investment account *after* the cutoff date. The better approach uses a prediction model set, rather than a profiling model set.

## Examples of Modeling Tasks

This section discusses several types of tasks that models might be used for.

### Similarity Models

Sometimes, the problem is to find more instances similar to a given target instance. In this case, an entire row is the target, and the score represents the similarity between any given row and the target instance.

The target may be a made up ideal, or it might be an actual example. For instance, the highest penetration zip code for the purchase data is 10007, a wealthy zip code in Manhattan. A similarity model might use census demographics to find similar zip codes from the perspective of the census data. The assumption is that what works in one wealthy zip code might work well in another, so marketing efforts can be focused on similar areas.

### Yes-or-No Models (Binary Response Classification)

Perhaps the most common type of modeling situation is assigning a "yes" or "no." The historical data contains both "yes" and "no" examples. This might be used to determine:

- Who is likely to respond to a particular marketing promotion;
- Who is likely to leave in the next three months;
- Who is likely to purchase a particular product;
- Who is likely to go bankrupt in the next year; or,
- Which transactions are likely to be fraud.

Each of these scenarios involves placing customers into one of two categories. Such a model can be used for:

- Saving money by contacting customers likely to respond to an offer;
- Saving customers by offering an incentive to those likely to stop;

- Optimizing campaigns by sending marketing messages to those likely to purchase a particular product;

- Reducing risk by lowering the credit limit for those likely to go bankrupt; or,

- Reducing loses by investigating transactions likely to be fraud.

Yes-or-no models are also called *binary response models*, because they are often used for determining the customers who are more likely to respond to a particular campaign.

### Yes-or-No Models with Propensity Scores

A very useful variation on yes-or-no models assigns a propensity to each customer, rather than a specific classification. Everyone gets a "yes" score that varies, say, from zero (definitely "no") to one (definitely "yes"). One reason why a propensity score is more useful is that any particular number of customers can be chosen for a campaign, by adjusting the threshold value. Values on one side of the threshold are "no" and values on the other side are "yes." The model can choose the top one percent, or the top forty percent, by choosing an appropriate threshold.

Often, the propensity score is actually a probability estimate. This is even more useful, because the probability can be combined with financial information to calculate an expected dollar amount. With such information, a campaign can be optimized to achieve particular financial and business results.

Consider a company that is sending customers an offer in the mail for a new product. From previous experience, the company knows that the product should generate an additional $200 in revenue during the first year. Each item of direct mail costs $1 to print, mail out, and process. How can the company use modeling to optimize its business?

Let's assume that the company wants to invest in expanding its customer relationships, but not lose money during the first year. The campaign then needs to meet the following conditions:

- Every customer contacted costs $1.

- Every customer who responds is worth $200 during the first year.

- The company wants to break even during the first year.

One responsive customer generates an excess of $199 in the first year, which is enough money to contact an additional 199 customers. So, if one out of two hundred customers (0.5%) respond, the campaign breaks even. To do this, the company looks at previous, similar campaigns and builds a model estimating the probability of response. The goal is to contact the customers whose expected response exceeds the break-even point of 0.5%.

### Multiple Categories

Sometimes, two categories ("yes" and "no") are not enough. For instance, consider the next offer to make to each customer. Should this offer be in books or apparel or calendars or something else?

When there are a handful of categories, building a separate propensity model for each category is a good way to handle this. For each customer, the product with the highest propensity among the models can then be assigned as the one with the highest affinity. Another approach is to multiply the propensity probabilities by the value of the product, and choose the product that has the highest expected value.

When there are many values in the category, association rules are probably a better place to start. Some of the most interesting information may be the products that are purchased together.

### Estimating Numeric Values

The final category is the traditional statistical problem of estimating numeric values. This might be a number at an aggregated level, such as the penetration within a particular area. Another example is the expected value of a customer over the next year. And yet another is tenure related, such as the number of days we expect a customer to be active over the next year.

There are many different methods to estimate real values, including regression and survival analysis.

## Model Evaluation

Model evaluation is the process of measuring how well a model works. The best way to do this is to compare the results of the model to actual results. How this comparison is made depends on the type of model. Later in this chapter, we will see three different methods, one for models that predict categories, one for models that estimate numbers, and one for yes-or-no models.

When evaluating models, the choice of data used for the evaluation is very important. Models almost always perform better on the model set, the data used to build the model in the first place. So, it is misleading to assume that performance on the model set generalizes to other data. It is better to use a hold-out sample, called a *test set*, for model evaluation. For models built on prediction model sets, the best test set is an out-of-time sample; that is, data that is a bit more recent than the model set. However, such an out-of-time sample is often not available.

> **TIP** Evaluating models on the data used to build the model is cheating. Use a hold-out sample for evaluation purposes.

## Look-Alike Models

The first modeling technique is look-alike models, which are used to measure similarity to known good or bad instances.

### What Is the Model?

The look-alike model produces a similarity score. The model itself is a formula that describes the similarity, and this formula can be applied to new data. Typically, the purpose of a look-alike model is to choose some groups of customers or zip codes for further analysis or for a marketing effort.

The similarity measure cannot really be validated quantitatively. However, we can qualitatively evaluate the model by seeing if the rankings look reasonable.

### What Is the Best Zip Code?

This example starts with the question: *Which zip codes have the highest penetration of orders and what are some of their demographic characteristics?* For practical purposes, the zip codes are limited to those with one thousand or more households. The following query answers this question:

```
SELECT TOP 10 o.zipcode, zco.state, zco.poname,
       COUNT(DISTINCT householdid) / MAX(zc.hh*1.0) as penetration,
       MAX(zc.hh) as hh, MAX(hhmedincome) as hhmedincome,
       MAX(popedubach + popedumast + popeduprofdoct) as collegep
FROM orders o JOIN customer c ON o.customerid = c.customerid JOIN
     zipcensus zc ON o.zipcode = zc.zipcode JOIN
     zipcounty zco ON zc.zipcode = zco.zipcode
WHERE zc.hh >= 1000
GROUP BY o.zipcode, zco.state, zco.poname
ORDER BY 4 DESC
```

Penetration is defined at the household level, by counting distinct values of HOUSEHOLDID within a zip code. The proportion of college graduates is the sum of three of the education variables.

The top ten zip codes by penetration are all well-educated and wealthy (see Table 10-1). *Which zip codes are similar to the zip code with the highest penetration?* This question suggests a look-alike model.

**Table 10-1:** Ten Zip Codes with Highest Penetration

| ZIP CODE | PO NAME AND STATE | PENE-TRATION | HOUSE-HOLDS | HOUSEHOLD MEDIAN INCOME | COLLEGE % |
|---|---|---|---|---|---|
| 10007 | New York, NY | 5.9% | 1,283 | $112,947 | 56.9% |
| 10504 | Armonk, NY | 5.2% | 2,315 | $130,789 | 60.7% |
| 10514 | Chappaqua, NY | 5.1% | 3,820 | $173,368 | 79.4% |
| 07078 | Short Hills, NJ | 5.0% | 4,279 | $185,466 | 79.2% |
| 10576 | Pound Ridge, NY | 4.9% | 1,648 | $152,863 | 70.5% |
| 10018 | New York, NY | 4.9% | 2,205 | $48,705 | 51.3% |
| 10510 | Briarcliff Manor, NY | 4.9% | 3,227 | $131,402 | 70.8% |
| 07043 | Montclair, NJ | 4.8% | 4,255 | $115,498 | 73.6% |
| 10538 | Larchmont, NY | 4.7% | 6,375 | $111,492 | 71.0% |
| 90067 | Los Angeles, CA | 4.7% | 1,553 | $74,830 | 46.4% |

The first decision with a look-alike model is to decide on the dimensions used for the comparison. For the statistically inclined, one interesting method might be to use something called principal components. However, using the raw data has an advantage, because the distance can be understood by humans.

Instead, the approach described in this section uses only two attributes of the zip codes, the median household income and the proportion of the population with a college education. The limit to two is for didactic reasons. Two dimensions can be plotted on a scatter plot. In practice, using more attributes is a good idea.

Figure 10-3 shows a scatter plot of the almost ten thousand largish zip codes that have orders. There are three symbols on the scatter plot. The diamonds are the zip codes with the highest number of orders, the squares are in the middle, and the triangles have the fewest orders. This scatter plot confirms that the highest penetration zip codes also have high median household incomes and are well educated.

Alas, this scatter plot is potentially misleading, because the three groups seem to differ in size. Many of the zip codes are in the big blob on the lower left-hand side of the chart — median income between $20,000 and $70,000 and college proportion between 20% and 50%. The three groups overlap significantly in this region. Because Excel draws one series at a time, a later series may hide the points on an earlier series, even when the symbols are hollow. The order of the series can affect the look of the chart. To change the order, select any of the series, right-click, and bring up the "Format Data Series" dialog box. The order can be changed under the "Series Order Tab."

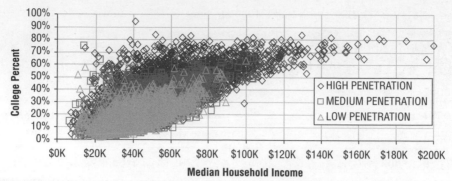

**Figure 10-3:** This scatter plot shows that the zip codes with the highest penetration do seem to have a higher median household income and higher education levels.

**WARNING** When plotting multiple series on a scatter plot, one series may overlap another, hiding some or many points. Use the "Series Order" option to rearrange the series and see the hidden points. Of course, changing the order may cause other points to be hidden.

## A Basic Look-Alike Model

Zip code 10007 has the highest penetration and the following characteristics:

- Median household income is $112,947; and,
- College rate is 56.7%.

The first attempt at a look-alike model simply calculates the distance from each zip code to these values using the Euclidean distance formula:

```
SQRT(SQUARE(hhmedincome - 112947)+SQUARE(collegep - 0.567))
```

This formula is the model. And, this model can be used to assign a similarity measure to all zip codes, as in the following query:

```
SELECT TOP 10 oz.*,
       SQRT(SQUARE(hhmedincome - 112947.)+
            SQUARE(collegep - 0.5689)) as dist
FROM (SELECT o.zipcode, MAX(hhmedincome) as hhmedincome,
             MAX(popedubach + popedumast + popeduprofdoct) as collegep
       FROM orders o JOIN customer c ON o.customerid = c.customerid JOIN
            zipcensus zc ON o.zipcode = zc.zipcode
       WHERE zc.hh >= 1000
       GROUP BY o.zipcode) oz
ORDER BY 1 ASC
```

This query hardwires the values for zip code 10007 directly into the SELECT statement.

Table 10-2 shows the ten closest zip codes by this measure. The median income for all these is right on the money, being very close to the value for 10007. On the other hand, the education levels vary rather widely. This is because the median income is measured in units of dollars with values going into the hundreds of thousands. The proportion college educated is always less than one. The median household income dominates the calculation.

**Table 10-2:** Ten Zip Codes Most Similar to 10007 (First Similarity Measure)

| DISTANCE | ZIP CODE | PENE-TRATION | HOUSE-HOLDS | HOUSEHOLD MEDIAN INCOME | COLLEGE % |
|---|---|---|---|---|---|
| 0.0 | 10007 | 5.9% | 1,283 | $112,947 | 56.9% |
| 29.0 | 06490 | 2.1% | 1,597 | $112,976 | 61.7% |
| 51.0 | 92679 | 0.1% | 9,966 | $112,998 | 52.5% |
| 138.0 | 48374 | 0.1% | 3,576 | $112,809 | 59.0% |
| 265.0 | 01921 | 0.2% | 2,560 | $113,212 | 62.8% |
| 375.0 | 90210 | 1.8% | 8,690 | $112,572 | 55.5% |
| 579.0 | 21029 | 0.2% | 2,323 | $113,526 | 64.2% |
| 647.0 | 46814 | 0.2% | 2,512 | $112,300 | 56.5% |
| 692.0 | 08836 | 1.0% | 1,348 | $113,639 | 55.6% |
| 841.0 | 20817 | 1.3% | 13,252 | $113,788 | 77.4% |

There are several ways to fix this. One way is to *normalize* values by subtracting the minimum from each value and dividing by the range (the difference between the maximum and the minimum). A better approach borrows an idea from Chapter 3.

## Look-Alike Using Z-Scores

Z-scores replace numeric values that have wildly different ranges with values on the same scale. The z-score is the number of standard deviations that a value differs from the average value.

The following query calculates the standard deviation and average value for the household median income and the proportion of college graduates:

```
SELECT AVG(hhmedincome) as avghhmedinc, STDEV(hhmedincome) as stdhhmedinc,
       AVG(collegep) as avgcollegep, STDEV(collegep) as stdcollegep
```

*(continued)*

```
FROM (SELECT o.zipcode, MAX(hhmedincome) as hhmedincome,
             MAX(popedubach + popedumast + popeduprofdoct) as collegep
      FROM orders o JOIN customer c ON o.customerid = c.customerid JOIN
           zipcensus zc ON o.zipcode = zc.zipcode
      WHERE zc.hh >= 1000
      GROUP BY o.zipcode) oz
```

Because the model is restricted to zip codes that have at least one thousand households, the z-scores are restricted to this group of zip codes, resulting in the following values:

- HH median income: average is $48,672; standard deviation is $19,273.

- Proportion College Grads: average is 27.8%; standard deviation is 15.6%.

A scatter plot using the z-scores instead of the original values would look almost exactly the same as the scatter plot already seen in Figure 10-3; the only difference is that the X- and Y-axes would have different scales on them. Instead of going from $0 to $200,000, the range for median household income would go from about –3 to +8. For the proportion of college graduates, the z-scores would go from about –1.8 to 4.7, rather than from 0% to 100%.

In order to apply the z-score to a look-alike model, the comparison values need to be transformed into z-score values as well as the values in the score set. Figure 10-4 shows the dataflow diagram for this processing. The following query uses this same logic to calculate the similarity score:

```
SELECT SQRT(POWER((hhmedincome-hhmedincome10007)/stdhhmedincome, 2) +
            POWER((collegep-collegep10007)/stdcollegep, 2)) as dist, oz.*
FROM (SELECT o.zipcode, MAX(hhmedincome) as hhmedincome,
             MAX(popedubach + popedumast + popeduprofdoct) as collegep
      FROM orders o JOIN customer c ON o.customerid = c.customerid JOIN
           zipcensus zc ON o.zipcode = zc.zipcode
      WHERE zc.hh >= 1000
      GROUP BY o.zipcode) oz CROSS JOIN
     (SELECT AVG(hhmedincome) as avghhmedincome,
             STDEV(hhmedincome) as stdhhmedincome,
             AVG(popedubach + popedumast + popeduprofdoct) as avgcollegep,
             STDEV(popedubach + popedumast + popeduprofdoct
                   ) as stdcollegep,
             MAX(CASE WHEN o.zipcode = '10007' THEN hhmedincome END
                 ) as hhmedincome10007,
             MAX(CASE WHEN o.zipcode = '10007'
                      THEN popedubach + popedumast + popeduprofdoct
                 END) as collegep10007
      FROM (SELECT DISTINCT zipcode
            FROM orders o JOIN customer c
            ON o.customerid = c.customerid) o JOIN
           zipcensus zc ON o.zipcode = zc.zipcode
      WHERE zc.hh >= 1000) vals
ORDER BY 1 ASC
```

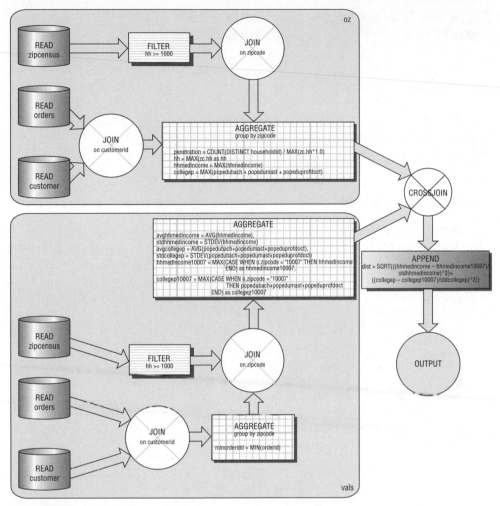

**Figure 10-4:** This dataflow calculation scores a look-alike model using z-scores rather than the original values.

There are several things to point out about this query. First, the subqueries, Oz and Vals, use a very similar set of joins to ensure that the z-score calculation uses the same set of rows for both the target instance and the score set. The difference between the two queries arises because zip codes can have multiple orders, so the join between Orders and Zipcensus results in duplicate zip codes. These duplicates do not affect Oz, because duplicates do not affect the value of the MAX() function.

On the other hand, Vals uses AVG() and STDEV(), which duplicates do affect. Vals only needs the zip codes that have orders. For this purpose, it uses the DISTINCT keyword in the innermost subquery to remove duplicate zip codes.

> **TIP** When calculating summary statistics on tables connected by complex sets of joins, be sure that none of the joins inadvertently change the number of rows.

The second subquery calculates the statistics for all zip codes. It also calculates the values for 10007, using a trick: the CASE statement converts all the values in non-10007 zip codes values to NULL, so the maximum returns the value for 10007.

The outermost SELECT calculates the difference of two z-scores, using the fact that the following two operations are equivalent:

■ Taking the difference of two z-scores.

■ Taking the difference of two values and converting the difference to a z-score, using the average and standard deviation of the original values.

The query uses the second approach, because it results in a simpler expression.

By the way, window functions can be used instead of analytic functions, as in the following version:

```
SELECT TOP 10
       SQRT(SQUARE((hhmedincome-hhmedincome10007)/stdhhmedinc) +
           SQUARE((collegep-collegep10007)/stdcollegep)) as dist, oz.*
FROM (SELECT oz.*,
             STDEV(hhmedincome) OVER () as stdhhmedinc,
             STDEV(collegep) OVER () as stdcollegep,
             MAX(CASE WHEN zipcode = '10007' THEN hhmedincome END) OVER
                 () as hhmedincome10007,
             MAX(CASE WHEN zipcode = '10007' THEN collegep END) OVER
                 () as collegep10007
      FROM (SELECT o.zipcode,
                   COUNT(DISTINCT householdid)/MAX(zc.hh*1.0) as penetrat,
                   MAX(zc.hh) as hh,
                   MAX(hhmedincome) as hhmedincome,
                   MAX(popedubach+popedumast+popeduprofdoct) as collegep
            FROM orders o JOIN customer c
                 ON o.customerid = c.customerid JOIN
                 zipcensus zc ON o.zipcode = zc.zipcode
            WHERE zc.hh >= 1000
            GROUP BY o.zipcode) oz
     ) oz
ORDER BY 1 ASC
```

This version of the query is simpler is several respects. First, COLLEGEP is calculated only once, eliminating problems caused by code duplication. Second, the average and standard deviations needed for the z-scores are calculated after the aggregation by zip code, so there are no duplicates. Using the window functions also ensures that the same rows are used for all calculations. Notice that the window functions have an empty OVER clause, which means to do the calculation over all rows. An equivalent formulation would be OVER (PARTITION BY NULL).

**TIP** When calculating statistics on a set of rows (such as the average and standard deviation for calculating z-scores), the window functions have an advantage because they reduce the amount of duplicated code in the query.

Table 10-3 shows the ten closest zip codes. All the zip codes in this table have similar median incomes and proportions of college graduates. The college proportion now varies from 55.5% to 59.1%, rather than from 52.5% to 77.4%. The household median incomes still cluster around the value for 10007.

**Table 10-3:** Ten Zip Codes Most Similar to 10007 (Z-Score Measure)

| DISTANCE | ZIP | PENE-TRATION | HOUSE-HOLDS | HOUSEHOLD MEDIAN INCOME | COLLEGE % |
|---|---|---|---|---|---|
| 0.000 | 10007 | 5.9% | 1,283 | $112,947 | 56.9% |
| 0.042 | 46814 | 0.2% | 2,512 | $112,300 | 56.5% |
| 0.089 | 08836 | 1.0% | 1,348 | $113,639 | 55.6% |
| 0.094 | 90210 | 1.8% | 8,690 | $112,572 | 55.5% |
| 0.131 | 07733 | 1.7% | 4,832 | $114,985 | 55.7% |
| 0.133 | 48374 | 0.1% | 3,576 | $112,809 | 59.0% |
| 0.181 | 94526 | 0.3% | 12,116 | $109,771 | 58.1% |
| 0.191 | 60010 | 0.4% | 14,102 | $110,470 | 59.1% |
| 0.199 | 92861 | 0.1% | 1,925 | $116,658 | 57.7% |
| 0.204 | 10536 | 2.8% | 3,441 | $109,542 | 58.5% |

The look-alike model now finds the zip codes that look like 10007 along both these dimensions, so the results are much more reasonable. However, the penetrations for similar zip codes vary from 0.1% to 2.8%. All these values are on the high side for household penetration. However, the wide range suggests that look-alike zip codes may not be similar in terms of penetration. On the other hand, perhaps the look-alike zip codes should be similar, and these other zip codes represent lost opportunity.

## Example of Nearest Neighbor Model

Nearest neighbor models are a variation on look-alike models. They use the measure of similarity to define a neighborhood of similar cases, and then summarize the cases to assign an estimated value.

As an example, the following query estimates the penetration for zip code 10007, using the similarity measure by median income and college proportion:

```
SELECT AVG(pen) as estpenetration
FROM (SELECT TOP 5
             SQRT(SQUARE((collegep - collegep10007)/stdcollp) +
                  SQUARE((hhmi - hhmi10007)/stdhhmi)) as dist, oz.*
      FROM (SELECT oz.*, AVG(hhmi) OVER () as avghhmi,
                   STDEV(hhmi) OVER () as stdhhmi,
                   AVG(collegep) OVER () as avgcollegep,
                   STDEV(collegep) OVER () as stdcollp,
                   MAX(CASE WHEN zipcode = '10007' THEN hhmi END
                       ) OVER () as hhmi10007,
                   MAX(CASE WHEN zipcode = '10007' THEN collegep END
                       ) OVER () as collegep10007
            FROM (SELECT o.zipcode, MAX(hhmedincome) as hhmi,
                         MAX(popedubach + popedumast + popeduprofdoct
                             ) as collegep,
                         COUNT(DISTINCT householdid)/MAX(hh*1.0) as pen
                  FROM orders o JOIN customer c
                       ON o.customerid = c.customerid JOIN
                       zipcensus zc ON o.zipcode = zc.zipcode
                  WHERE zc.hh >= 1000
                  GROUP BY o.zipcode) oz
           ) oz
      WHERE zipcode <> '10007'
      ORDER BY 1) score
```

This query uses a scoring subquery that is quite similar to the one used for the look-alike model. There are a handful of differences:

- The subquery excludes zip code 10007, because it is being scored.
- The subquery chooses the top five neighbors.
- The subquery defines the penetration variable, PEN.

The outermost query simply takes the average of PEN from the five most similar zip codes and uses this as the estimate for penetration in 10007.

This is only an example of using the nearest neighbor technique. In this case, the actual penetration in zip code 10007 is already known. However, the technique itself can be used in other situations for scoring new, unknown examples.

The model itself is the table of known instances along with the formula for calculating distance. It is reasonably efficient for scoring one row at a time. However, for scoring large numbers of rows, every row in the score set has to be compared to every row in the training set, which can result in long-running queries.

# Lookup Model for Most Popular Product

A lookup model partitions the data into non-overlapping groups, and then assigns a constant value within each group. Lookup models do not look like fancy statistical models, because they pre-calculate all the possible scores, rather than estimating coefficients for a complicated equation. Nevertheless, the language of statistics has a name for them, *contingency tables*.

The first example of a lookup model finds the most popular product group in a zip code using the purchases data. This model provides a good example of profiling.

## Most Popular Product

The most popular product group in a zip code is easy to calculate and to use. The model itself is a lookup table with two columns: a zip code and a product group. Using the model simply requires looking up the appropriate value in the table, using the customer's zip code.

Once upon a time, a company was customizing its email offers. One of the things known about prospects was their zip codes. The marketing idea was to customize each email by including information about products that would be of interest. Lacking other information, the geographic information proved useful. Prospects were indeed more interested in the most popular product in their neighborhood (as defined by zip code) than in random products.

## Calculating Most Popular Product Group

An earlier chapter noted that BOOKS is the most popular product group. The following query is one way to determine this information:

```
SELECT productgroupname
FROM (SELECT productgroupname, cnt, MAX(cnt) OVER () as maxcnt
      FROM (SELECT productgroupname, COUNT(*) as cnt
            FROM orders o JOIN orderline ol ON o.orderid = ol.orderid JOIN
                 product p
                 ON ol.productid = p.productid and
                    p.productgroupname <> 'FREEBIE'
            GROUP BY productgroupname
           ) pg
     ) a
WHERE cnt = maxcnt
```

This query has two levels of subqueries. The innermost calculates the order frequency for product groups. This subquery does not include FREEBIE products, because they are not interesting for cross-selling purposes. The next level then calculates the maximum of the frequency (the second subquery is needed because window functions cannot be used with GROUP BY). The outermost then chooses the product group whose count is the maximum. Instead of window functions, the query could also use another subquery to calculate the maximum.

The most popular product is, in itself, a very simple model. However, we want to refine the model by zip code, resulting in the rather similar query:

```
SELECT zipcode, productgroupname
FROM (SELECT zipcode, productgroupname, cnt,
             MAX(cnt) OVER (PARTITION BY zipcode) as maxcnt
      FROM (SELECT zipcode, productgroupname, COUNT(*) as cnt
            FROM orders o JOIN orderline ol ON o.orderid = ol.orderid JOIN
                 product p
                 ON ol.productid = p.productid and
                    p.productgroupname <> 'FREEBIE'
            GROUP BY zipcode, productgroupname
            ) pg
     ) a
WHERE cnt = maxcnt
```

Notice that the only thing that changes between the two queries is the PARTITION BY clause. In this version, it partitions by the zip code, to return the maximum count within the zip code. The query then returns the product groups whose counts match the maximum.

**TIP** When finding rows containing the minimum and maximum values in a table, always consider that there might be more than one matching row.

There is a slight problem with this approach. Some zip codes might have multiple product groups all having the maximum frequency. Where there are ties, the query needs to choose one product group (any will do), or else the results will have duplicate zip codes. One way to choose is by calculating the minimum product group name that has a given count in each zip code, as in the following variation:

```
SELECT zipcode, productgroupname
FROM (SELECT zipcode, productgroupname, cnt,
             MAX(cnt) OVER (PARTITION BY zipcode) as maxcnt,
             MIN(productgroupname) OVER (PARTITION BY zipcode, cnt
                 ) as minpg
      FROM (SELECT zipcode, productgroupname, COUNT(*) as cnt
            FROM orders o JOIN orderline ol ON o.orderid = ol.orderid JOIN
                 product p
                 ON ol.productid = p.productid and
                    p.productgroupname <> 'FREEBIE'
            GROUP BY zipcode, productgroupname
            ) pg
     ) a
WHERE cnt = maxcnt AND
      productgroupname = minpg
```

This query uses the window functions to break ties by choosing the first product group name alphabetically.

The result contains two columns: the zip code and the most popular product group. This is the lookup model by zip code for the most popular product group. This model is a profiling model because the zip code and product group come from the same time frame. There is no "before" and "after." Here the most popular product group has been defined as the one with the most orders. Other definitions are possible, such as the one with the most households purchasing it or the largest dollar amount per household.

Table 10-4 shows each product group and the number of zip codes where that group is the most popular. Not surprisingly, BOOKS win in over half the zip codes, as shown by the following query:

```
SELECT productgroupname, COUNT(*) as numzips
FROM (<zipcode-productgroupname-subquery>) subquery
GROUP BY productgroupname
ORDER BY 2 DESC
```

This query uses the previous query as a subquery. It then aggregates by product group name and counts the number of zip codes where that product group is the most popular.

**Table 10-4:** Number of Zip Codes Where Product Groups Are Most Popular

| PRODUCT GROUP | NUMBER OF ZIPS | % OF ALL ZIPS |
| --- | --- | --- |
| BOOK | 8,402 | 53.9% |
| ARTWORK | 2,917 | 18.7% |
| OCCASION | 2,064 | 13.2% |
| GAME | 899 | 5.8% |
| APPAREL | 771 | 4.9% |
| CALENDAR | 403 | 2.6% |
| OTHER | 123 | 0.8% |

## Evaluating the Lookup Model

This model uses all the zip codes for determining the most popular product. There is no data left over to quantify how good it is.

One idea for testing it would be to partition the data into two parts, one for determining the most popular product and the other for testing it. This strategy of testing a model on a separate set of data is a good idea and important to data mining. However, the next section describes an alternative approach that is often more useful.

## Using a Profiling Lookup Model for Prediction

This model is a profiling model because the target (the most popular product group) comes from the same time frame as the input (the zip code). This is the nature of the model and the model set used to create it. However, it is possible to use a profiling model for prediction by making a small assumption.

The assumption is that the most popular product group prior to 2016 is the most popular after 2016. This assumption also requires building the model — still a profile model because of the dataset — using data prior to 2016. The only modification to the query is to add the following WHERE clause to the innermost subquery:

```
WHERE order_date < '2016-01-01'
```

The model now finds the most popular product group prior to the cutoff date.

A *classification matrix* is used to evaluate a model that classifies customers. It is simply a table where the modeled values are on the rows and the correct values are across the columns (or vice versa). Each cell in the table consists of the count (or proportion) of rows in the score set that have that particular combination of model prediction and actual result.

Table 10-5 shows a classification matrix, where the rows contain the predicted product group (the most popular group prior to 2016) and the columns contain the actual product group (the most popular after 2016). Each cell contains the number of zip codes with that particular combination of predicted and actual product groups. All the zip codes in the table have orders in the model set (prior to 2016) and the score set (after 2016). There are 1,406 zip codes where BOOK is predicted to be the most popular product and it is actually BOOK. However, there are an additional 1,941 zip codes (483+938+303+149+30+38) where BOOK is predicted to be the most popular and it is not.

| | H | I | J | K | L | M | N | O | P |
|---|---|---|---|---|---|---|---|---|---|
| 56 | | | | | | ACTUAL | | | |
| 57 | | | BOOK | OCCASION | ARTWORK | GAME | APPAREL | CALENDAR | OTHER |
| 58 | | BOOK | 1,406 | 483 | 938 | 303 | 149 | 30 | 38 |
| 59 | P R E D I C T E D | OCCASION | 138 | 89 | 84 | 35 | 16 | 6 | 5 |
| 60 | | ARTWORK | 225 | 114 | 227 | 64 | 20 | 2 | 8 |
| 61 | | GAME | 56 | 25 | 30 | 25 | 12 | 2 | 1 |
| 62 | | APPAREL | 46 | 15 | 30 | 6 | 16 | 1 | 2 |
| 63 | | CALENDAR | 26 | 11 | 10 | 4 | 4 | 4 | 3 |
| 64 | | OTHER | 6 | 4 | 4 | 1 | 1 | 1 | 1 |

**Figure 10-5:** This classification matrix shows the number of zip codes by the predicted and actual most popular product group in 2016. The highlighted cells are where the prediction is correct.

The cells in the table where the row and the column have the same value are shaded using Excel's conditional formatting capability. This is explained in the aside "Conditional Formatting in Excel."

Although BOOK is still the most popular product group in 2016, its popularity is waning. If we totaled the values across the rows, BOOK consists of about 70% of the predicted values. However, if we total the rows across the columns, BOOK accounts for only about 40% of the actual values.

*How well is the model doing?* In this case, not so well. The model does well when its prediction agrees with what actually happens. So, there are 1,406 + 89 + 227 + 25 + 16 + 4 + 1 = 1,768 zip codes where the prediction matches what actually happened. This comes to 37.4% of the zip codes. This is much better than randomly guessing one out of seven categories. However, it is doing worse than just guessing that BOOK is going to be the most popular.

### CONDITIONAL FORMATTING IN EXCEL

Excel has the ability to format cells individually based on the values in the cells. That is, the border, color, and font in the cell can be controlled by the contents of the cell or even by a formula that refers to other cells. This *conditional formatting* can be used to highlight cells as shown in Table 10-5.

Conditional formatting comes in two flavors, formatting by the value in the cell or by a formula. For both flavors, the "Conditional Formatting" dialog box is accessed using the Format ⇨ Conditional Formatting menu option (or using the key sequence <alt>-O<alt>-D).

Use formatting by a value to highlight cells with particular values. For instance, in a table showing chi-square values, the cells with a chi-square value exceeding a threshold can be given a different color. To do this, bring up the "Conditional Formatting" dialog box, choose the "Cell Value Is" option, and set the condition. Click the "Format" button to define the desired format.

Using a formula provides even more power. A formula can describe whether the formatting gets applied, which occurs when the formula evaluates to TRUE. For instance, the shaded format in Table 10-5 is when the name of the row and the name of the header have the same value. The formula for this is:

```
=($I42=J$41)
```

Where row 41 has the column names and column "I" has the row names. The formula uses "$" to ensure that the formula is correct when copied. When copied, cell references in a conditional formatting formula change the same way that cell references for a regular formula do.

Conditional formatting can be used for many things. For instance, to color every other row, use:

```
=MOD(ROW(), 2) = 0
```

*Continued on next page*

---

**CONDITIONAL FORMATTING IN EXCEL** *(CONTINUED)*

**To color every other column, use:**

```
=MOD(COLUMN(), 2) = 0
```

**To create a checkerboard pattern, use:**

```
=MOD(ROW()+COLUMN(), 2) = 0
```

**These formulas use the** ROW() **and** COLUMN() **functions, which return the current row and current column of the cell.**

**Conditional formatting can also be used to put borders around regions in a table. Say column C has a key in a table that takes on repeated values and then changes. To put a line between blocks of similar values, use the following condition in the cells on row 10:**

```
=($C10<>$C11)
```

**This says to apply the formatting when cell C11 has a different value from C10. Make the formatting the bottom border. When this formatting is copied to the rest of the table, horizontal lines appear between the different groups.**

**Using the paintbrush copies the conditional formatting as well as the overall formatting, so it is easy to copy formats from one cell to a group of cells.**

---

## Using Binary Classification Instead

BOOK is so popular that we might tweak the model a bit, to look just for BOOK or NOT-BOOK as the most popular category, grouping all the non-book products together into a single group. To do this in SQL, replace the innermost references to product group with the following CASE statement:

```
(CASE WHEN productgroupname = 'BOOK' THEN 'BOOK'
      ELSE 'NOT-BOOK' END) as productgroupname
```

This model performs better than the categorical model, as shown in the classification matrix in Table 10-5. Now, there are 805+1,812 zip codes where the model is correct (55.4% versus 37.4%). In particular, the model is working better on predicting NOT-BOOK, where it is correct 63.4% of the time versus only 43.1% when it predicts BOOK.

**Table 10-5:** Classification Matrix for BOOK or NOT-BOOK

|  | BOOK | NOT-BOOK |
| --- | --- | --- |
| BOOK | 805 | 1,048 |
| NOT-BOOK | 1,062 | 1,812 |

Notice that the number of zip codes where BOOK is the most popular before and after has dropped from 1,406 to 805. These 805 zip codes are where the majority of orders are in BOOK. The rest are where BOOK has the most orders, but not over 50%.

This example shows a modeling challenge. When working with two categories of about the same size, binary models do a good job of distinguishing between them. When working with multiple categories, a single model often works less well.

Another challenge in building a model is the fact that BOOK is becoming less popular as a category over time, relative to the other categories. There is a big word to describe this situation, *nonstationarity*, which means that patterns in the data change over time. Nonstationarity is the bane of modeling, but is, alas, quite common in the real world.

**TIP** When building models, we are assuming that the data used to build the model is representative of the data used when scoring the model. This is not always the case, due to changes in the market, in the customer base, in the economy, and so on.

## Lookup Model for Order Size

The previous model was a lookup model for classification, both for multiple classification and binary classification. The lookup itself was along a single dimension. This section uses lookup models for estimating a real number. It starts with the very simplest case, no dimensions, and builds the model up from there.

### Most Basic Example: No Dimensions

Another basic example of a lookup model is assigning an overall average value. For instance, we might ask the question: *Based on purchases in 2015, what do we expect the average order size to be in 2016?* The following query answers this question, by using the average of all purchases in 2015:

```
SELECT YEAR(o.orderdate) as year, AVG(totalprice) as avgsize
FROM orders o
WHERE YEAR(o.orderdate) in (2015, 2016)
GROUP BY YEAR(o.orderdate)
ORDER BY 1
```

This query gives the estimate of $85.51. This is a reasonable estimate, but it is a bit off the mark, because the actual average in 2016 is $112.64.

This example is a predictive model. The average from 2015 is being used to estimate the value in 2016. This is a big assumption, but not unreasonable.

## Adding One Dimension

The next step is to add a dimension, as in the following query that calculates the average by state:

```
SELECT state,
       AVG(CASE WHEN YEAR(orderdate)=2015 THEN totalprice END) as avg2015,
       AVG(CASE WHEN YEAR(orderdate)=2016 THEN totalprice END) as avg2016
FROM orders o
WHERE YEAR(o.orderdate) in (2015, 2016)
GROUP BY state
```

This query calculates the average order sizes in 2015 and 2016 using the AVG() function with a CASE statement that quite intentionally does not have an ELSE clause. Rows that do not match the year are given a NULL value rather than the TOTALPRICE. The NULL values are ignored when SQL takes the average. Of course, we could get the same effect by including ELSE NULL in the statement. The results from this query are a lookup table.

Evaluating the results requires applying the model to data that was not used to create it. A good score set is orders in 2016. Applying the model means joining the score set to the lookup table by state. One caveat is that some customers may be in states that did not place orders in 2015. These customers need a default value, and a suitable value is the overall average order size in 2015.

The following query attaches the estimated order size for 2016 onto each row in the score set:

```
SELECT o.*, COALESCE(statelu.avgamount, defaultlu.avgamount) as predamount
FROM (SELECT o.*
      FROM orders o
      WHERE YEAR(o.orderdate) = 2016) o LEFT OUTER JOIN
     (SELECT state, AVG(totalprice) as avgamount
      FROM orders o
      GROUP BY state) statelu
     ON o.state = statelu.state CROSS JOIN
     (SELECT AVG(totalprice) as avgamount
      FROM orders o
      WHERE YEAR(o.orderdate) = 2015) defaultlu
```

Figure 10-6 shows the dataflow diagram for this query. There are three subqueries. The first is for the score set that chooses orders from 2016. The second two are the lookup tables, one for state and one for the default value (when no state matches). These lookup tables use the orders from 2015 to calculate values.

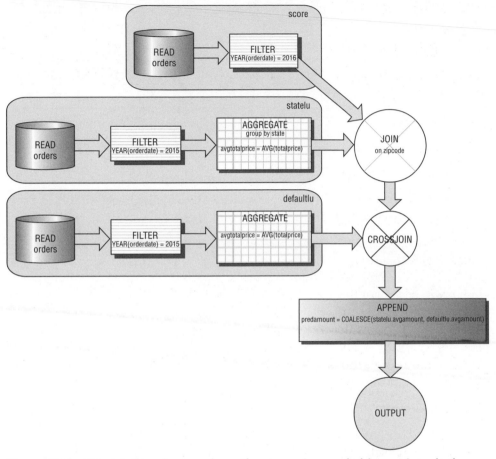

**Figure 10-6:** This dataflow diagram shows the processing needed for scoring a lookup model with one dimension.

Comparing the average predicted amount to the average actual amount is an overall measure of how good the model is doing:

```
SELECT AVG(predamount) as avgpred, AVG(totalprice) as avgactual
FROM (<lookup-score-subquery>) subquery
```

This query uses the previous lookup score query as a subquery.

This model actually produces basically the same overall results as before. However, this structure makes it easy to evaluate different dimensions by replacing state with another column name. Table 10-6 shows the average amounts for various different dimensions, including channel, zip code, payment type, and month of order.

**Table 10-6:** Performance of Various One-Dimensional Lookup Models

| DIMENSION | PREDICTED 2016 | ACTUAL 2016 |
|---|---|---|
| State | $85.33 | $112.64 |
| Zip Code | $87.65 | $112.64 |
| Channel | $85.92 | $112.64 |
| Month | $87.50 | $112.64 |
| Payment Type | $85.42 | $112.64 |

## Adding More Dimensions

Adding more dimensions is a simple modification to the basic query. The following query uses month and zip code as the dimensions:

```
SELECT AVG(predamount) as avgpred, AVG(totalprice) as avgactual
FROM (SELECT o.*,
             COALESCE(dim1lu.avgamount, defaultlu.avgamount) as predamount
      FROM (SELECT o.*, c.channel, MONTH(orderdate) as mon
            FROM orders o JOIN campaign c on o.campaignid = c.campaignid
            WHERE YEAR(o.orderdate) = 2016) o LEFT OUTER JOIN
           (SELECT MONTH(orderdate) as mon, zipcode,
                   AVG(totalprice) as avgamount
            FROM orders o JOIN campaign c on o.campaignid = c.campaignid
            WHERE YEAR(o.orderdate) = 2015
            GROUP BY MONTH(orderdate), zipcode) dim1lu
           ON o.mon = dim1lu.mon AND
              o.zipcode = dim1lu.zipcode CROSS JOIN
           (SELECT AVG(totalprice) as avgamount
            FROM orders o
            WHERE YEAR(o.orderdate) = 2015) defaultlu) a
```

The structure of the query is the same as the query for one dimension. The only difference is the additional column in the Dim1lu subquery and the join.

With the lookup table, the average rises to a bit over $90. The two-dimensional lookup table is doing a better job, but the average is still off from the actual value.

## Examining Nonstationarity

As shown in Table 10-7, the average order size is increasing from year to year. Without taking into account this yearly increase, estimates based on the past are not going to work so well. This is another example of nonstationarity.

**Table 10-7:** Average Order Size Varies Over Time

| YEAR | AVERAGE ORDER SIZE | CHANGE YEAR OVER YEAR |
|------|--------------------|-----------------------|
| 2009 | $33.63 | |
| 2010 | $51.90 | 54.3% |
| 2011 | $50.98 | -1.8% |
| 2012 | $67.94 | 33.3% |
| 2013 | $74.50 | 9.7% |
| 2014 | $70.08 | -5.9% |
| 2015 | $85.51 | 22.0% |
| 2016 | $112.64 | 31.7% |

What is causing this change is perhaps a mystery. Perhaps prices increase from year to year. Perhaps the product mix changes from year to year. Perhaps customers' initial orders are smaller than repeat orders, and the number of repeat orders (as a proportion of the total) increases from year to year. There are many possible reasons for orders increasing in size.

We could make an adjustment. For instance, note that the average purchase size increased by 22% from 2014 to 2015. If we increased the 2015 estimate by the same amount, the result would be much closer to the actual value.

Of course, to choose the appropriate increase it helps to understand what is happening. This requires additional understanding of the data and of the business.

## Evaluating the Model Using an Average Value Chart

An average value chart is used to visualize model performance for a model with a numeric target. The average value chart breaks customers into equal sized groups, by ordering them by the customers' predicted values. For instance, it might break the customers into ten equal sized groups called deciles, with the first decile consisting of customers with the highest predicted order amounts, and the next highest in the second decile, and so on. The chart then shows the average of the predicted value and the average of the actual value for each decile.

Figure 10-7 shows an example for the lookup model using month and zip code as dimensions. The dotted line is the predicted average amount in each decile. It starts high and then decreases, although the values for deciles two through seven are flat.

The actual values look quite different. They are basically a horizontal line, meaning that there is no relationship between the predicted amount and the actual amount. The model is doing a poor job.

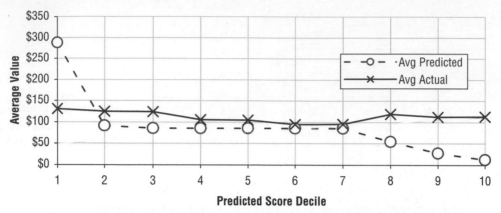

**Figure 10-7:** This average value chart is for a model that does not work for predicting the size of 2016 orders. This is apparent because the actual values are a horizontal line.

The goal in the average value chart is for the actual values to correspond to the predicted values. Figure 10-8 shows a better model, which uses channel, payment type, and customer gender. In this case, the actual values are higher when the predicted values are higher and lower when the predicted values are lower. There are some anomalies, such as the third decile doing better than the second, but overall, this model is doing a better job than the previous one.

One observation about both models is that the actual values are almost always higher than the predicted values. This is a result of the fact that order sizes in 2016 are larger than in 2015.

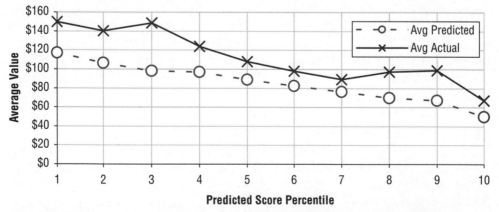

**Figure 10-8:** This average value chart uses channel, payment type, and customer gender. Here the model is working better, because the actual values are decreasing as the predicted values decrease.

Creating an average value chart starts by assigning a decile to customers in the score set, based on the predicted amount. For each decile, the averages of the predicted value and of the actual value are calculated, as in the following query:

```
SELECT decile, AVG(predamount) as avgpred, AVG(totalprice) as avgactual
FROM (SELECT lss.*, NTILE(10) OVER (ORDER BY predamount DESC) as decile
      FROM (<lookup-score-subquery>) lss
     ) b
GROUP BY decile
ORDER BY 1
```

This query uses the scoring subquery to get the predicted amount. The middle level uses the NTILE() window function to divide the scores into ten equal sized groups. The outermost level calculates the average for the predicted amount and average amount for each of the groups.

## Lookup Model for Probability of Response

This section looks at a different sort of problem, related to the subscription data. *What is the probability that a customer who starts in 2005 is going to last for one year?* This question uses the subscription data to address the question, building a model using the 2004 starts and testing it using the 2005 starts.

### The Overall Probability as a Model

The way to start thinking about this problem is to consider all customers who start in 2004 and ask how many of them survive for exactly one year. Using one year of starts dampens seasonal effects occurring within a year. Also, the subscription table has no stops prior to 2004, limiting how far back in time we can go.

Chapter 8 addressed several different methods for looking at survival and retention. This section looks only at the point estimate after one year, as calculated by the following query:

```
SELECT AVG(CASE WHEN tenure < 365 AND stop_type IS NOT NULL
                THEN 1.0 ELSE 0 END) as stoprate
FROM subs
WHERE YEAR(start_date) = 2004
```

Customers who stop within one year have tenures less than one year and a non-NULL stop type. Strictly speaking, the test for stop type is unnecessary, because all customers who start in 2004 and have tenures less than 365 are stopped.

This query uses AVG() to calculate the proportion of customers who stop. The argument to the average is 1.0, rather than 1, because some databases return the average of an integer as an integer rather than as a real number. In such databases, the integer average would always be zero except when all customers stop within their first year.

Of the customers who start in 2004, 28.0% stop during the first year after they start. Given a new customer who starts in 2005, the best guess for that customer's stop rate during the first year is 28.0%. Of course, this assumes that the conditions affecting stops remain the same from one year to the next.

The actual stop rate for 2005 starts is 27.2%, which is quite similar to the rate in 2004. This supports using the 2004 data to develop a model for 2005.

## Exploring Different Dimensions

There are five dimensions in the subscription data that are known when customers start:

- Channel;
- Market;
- Rate Plan;
- Initial Monthly Fee; and,
- Date of Start.

These are good candidates for modeling dimensions. Although the monthly fee is numeric, it only takes on a handful of values.

The following query calculates the stop rate by channel:

```
SELECT channel,
       AVG(CASE WHEN tenure < 365 AND stop_type IS NOT NULL
               THEN 1.0 ELSE 0 END) as stoprate
FROM subs
WHERE YEAR(start_date) = 2004
GROUP BY channel
```

The result is a lookup table that has the expected stop rate for different channels.

Applying this lookup table as a model requires joining it back to a score set. The following query calculates the probability that a customer who starts in 2005 is going to leave, using the channel for the lookup:

```
SELECT score.*, COALESCE(lookup.stoprate, def.stoprate) as predrate
FROM (SELECT s.*,
             (CASE WHEN tenure < 365 AND stop_type IS NOT NULL
                  THEN 1 ELSE 0 END) as is1yrstop
     FROM subs s
     WHERE YEAR(start_date) = 2005) score LEFT OUTER JOIN
     (SELECT channel,
```

```
             AVG(CASE WHEN tenure < 365 AND stop_type IS NOT NULL
                     THEN 1.0 ELSE 0 END) as stoprate
      FROM subs
      WHERE YEAR(start_date) = 2004
      GROUP BY channel) lookup
 ON score.channel = lookup.channel CROSS JOIN
 (SELECT AVG(CASE WHEN tenure < 365 AND stop_type IS NOT NULL
                     THEN 1.0 ELSE 0 END) as stoprate
      FROM subs
      WHERE YEAR(start_date) = 2004) def
```

This query takes into account the fact that there might be no matching channel. The query has three subqueries. The Def subquery calculates the default value for the one-year stop rate. The Lookup subquery calculates the one-year stop rate by channel. And the Score subquery finds the set of customers who started in 2005. The logic for scoring is to take the stop rate from Lookup, if available, and otherwise take the stop rate from Def using the COALESCE() function. In this particular case, the Def subquery is superfluous, because all channels are represented in both years.

The following query calculates the overall stop rate and the predicted stop rate, using the previous query as a subquery:

```
SELECT AVG(predrate) as predrate, AVG(1.0*is1yrstop) as actrate
FROM (<scoring-subquery>) subquery
```

This query compares the average of the predicted rate, over all the rows, to the actual stop rate.

The model works very well overall. In fact, the query predicts an overall stop rate of 27.2%, which is exactly what is observed. However, Table 10-8 shows that the model does not work so well within each channel.

**WARNING** Just because a model works well overall does not mean that the model works well on all subgroups of customers.

**Table 10-8:** Actual and Predicted Stop Rates by Channel for 2005 Starts, Based on 2004 Starts

| CHANNEL | PREDICTED | ACTUAL | DIFFERENCE |
|---------|-----------|--------|------------|
| Chain   | 41.0%     | 24.7%  | 16.4%      |
| Dealer  | 25.0%     | 27.6%  | -2.6%      |
| Mail    | 36.8%     | 35.2%  | 1.5%       |
| Store   | 16.3%     | 18.1%  | -1.8%      |

## How Accurate Are the Models?

Table 10-9 compares the overall predicted stop rates and actual stop rates of one-dimensional lookup models, using each of five different dimensions. All the models do a reasonable job of estimating the overall stop rate. Notice that the accuracy of the models does not improve as the number of values in the dimension increases.

For all the models, the overall predicted stop rate is close to the actual stop rate. However, the business goal could be to identify a group of customers that has a much greater chance of stopping than other customers, probably to offer them an incentive to remain. Such incentives cost money, suggesting the question: *How many customers who actually stop are captured by the model in the top ten percent of model scores?*

The answer to this question is a *cumulative gains chart*, which is used to visualize model performance for models with binary targets. The horizontal axis is a percentage of customers chosen based on the model score, ranging from 0% to 100%, with the highest scoring customers chosen first. The vertical axis measures the proportion of the desired target found in that group of customers, ranging from 0% — none of the desired target — to 100% — all of the desired target. The curves start at the lower left at 0% on both axes and rise to the upper right to 100% on both axes. If customers are chosen randomly, the cumulative gains chart is a line.

Figure 10-9 shows a cumulative gains chart for the channel lookup model for stops. The horizontal axis is the percentage of customers with the highest scores. So, 10% means the top decile of all customers. The vertical axis is the percentage of stoppers captured by that segment of customers.

**Table 10-9:** Actual and Predicted Stop Rates by Modeling Dimension for 2005 Starts, Based on 2004 Starts

| DIMENSION | NUMBER OF VALUES | PREDICTED | ACTUAL | DIFFERENCE |
|-----------|------------------|-----------|--------|------------|
| Channel | 4 | 27.2% | 27.2% | 0.00% |
| Market | 3 | 27.1% | 27.2% | -0.04% |
| Rate Plan | 3 | 27.8% | 27.2% | 0.69% |
| Monthly Fee | 24 | 23.1% | 27.2% | -4.04% |
| Month | 12 | 29.0% | 27.2% | 1.82% |

There are three curves on the chart. The highest one is the best one, and this is the performance of the model on the model set used to build it. Models generally perform best on the data used to create them. The middle curve is for the test set using 2005 starts, and the straight line is a reference assuming no model. For instance, the point at the 25% mark on the 2005 curve says that the top 25% of customers with the highest model score captures 28.6% of the customers who stop. *Lift* is one way to measure how well the model is working. At the 25% mark the lift is 28.6%/25%= 14.4%. Note that lift always declines to one as the percentage moves toward 100%.

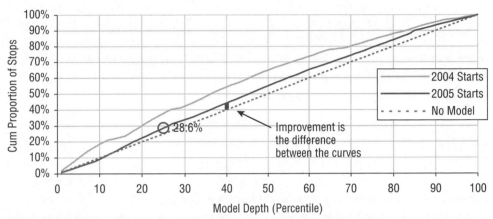

**Figure 10-9:** This cumulative gains chart shows the performance of the channel model on both the model set (2004 starts) and on the score set (2005 starts).

The cumulative gains chart is a good way to compare models. Figure 10-10 shows the chart for several lookup models on the test set of 2005 starts. The cumulative gains chart can also be used to select how many customers are needed to get a certain number of customers expected to have the target value.

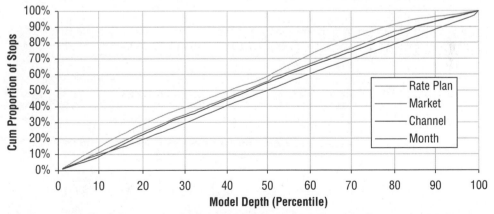

**Figure 10-10:** Cumulative gains charts for five models using 2005 charts are a good way to compare the performance of different models.

The cumulative gains charts are based on a summary of the data, shown in Table 10-10, having the following information:

- The decile, which divides the customers into ten equal sized groups (the charts in the text divide the customers into percentiles);
- The predicted stop rate for the decile (the average model score);
- The predicted number of stops (the average model score times the number of customers);
- The predicted and actual stop rate for the decile;
- The cumulative number of actual stops up to and including the decile and the cumulative stop rate; and
- The lift of actual stops compared to no model.

Only the first and last of these are used for the cumulative gains chart. However, the other information is quite informative for understanding model performances and to create other informative charts.

**Table 10-10:** Summary Information for Cumulative Gains Chart

| DECILE | NUMBER OF STOPS PRED-ICTED | ACT-UAL | STOP RATE PRED-ICTED | ACT-UAL | CUMULATIVE STOPS # | RATE | PROP | LIFT |
|---|---|---|---|---|---|---|---|---|
| 1 | 42,670 | 41,294 | 33.0% | 31.9% | 41,294 | 31.9% | 11.8% | 1.18 |
| 2 | 42,670 | 42,540 | 33.0% | 32.9% | 83,834 | 32.4% | 23.9% | 1.19 |
| 3 | 42,667 | 39,345 | 33.0% | 30.4% | 123,179 | 31.8% | 35.1% | 1.17 |
| 4 | 42,667 | 35,949 | 33.0% | 27.8% | 159,128 | 30.8% | 45.3% | 1.13 |
| 5 | 42,667 | 36,964 | 33.0% | 28.6% | 196,092 | 30.3% | 55.9% | 1.12 |
| 6 | 37,938 | 37,532 | 29.3% | 29.0% | 233,624 | 30.1% | 66.5% | 1.11 |
| 7 | 37,430 | 35,185 | 29.0% | 27.2% | 268,809 | 29.7% | 76.6% | 1.09 |
| 8 | 35,839 | 36,729 | 27.7% | 28.4% | 305,538 | 29.5% | 87.0% | 1.09 |
| 9 | 12,997 | 22,139 | 10.1% | 17.1% | 327,677 | 28.2% | 93.3% | 1.04 |
| 10 | 12,997 | 23,418 | 10.1% | 18.1% | 351,095 | 27.2% | 100.0% | 1.00 |

The following steps are used to calculate the information in the table:

1. Apply the model to the score set to obtain the predicted stop rate.
2. Divide the scored customers into ten (or whatever) equal sized groups.
3. Calculate the summary information for each group.

The following query follows these steps:

```
SELECT decile, COUNT(*) as numcustomers, SUM(is1yrstop) as numactualstops,
       SUM(predstoprate) as predactualstops,
       AVG(is1yrstop*1.0) as actualstop, AVG(predstoprate) as predstoprate
FROM (SELECT customer_id, predrate, is1yrstop,
             NTILE(10) OVER (PARTITION BY NULL ORDER BY predrate DESC
                            ) as decile
      FROM (<scoring-subquery>) score
GROUP BY decile
ORDER BY 1
```

This query uses the score query as a subquery. Calculating the percentile uses the window ranking function NTILE() to divide the customers into equal sized buckets based on their predicted stop rates. Within each bucket, the query counts the number of customers who do actually stop and estimates the number of predicted stops by taking the average predicted stop rate and multiplying it by the number of customers in the decile. The cumulative number of stops is calculated in Excel.

## Adding More Dimensions

Using more than one dimension for the lookup model is feasible. Up to a point, increasing the number of dimensions can improve the model. Figure 10-11 shows the cumulative gains chart for the model using three dimensions. This model does better than the model with one dimension.

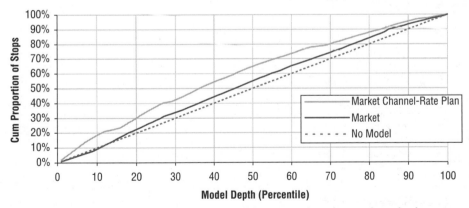

**Figure 10-11:** The lookup model with three dimensions does better than the best model with one dimension.

Generating such a model is simply a matter of replacing the Lookup subquery with a more refined lookup table, resulting in a scoring query such as:

```
SELECT score.*, COALESCE(lookup.stoprate, def.stoprate) as predstoprate
FROM (SELECT subs.*,
```

*(continued)*

```
                        (CASE WHEN tenure < 365 AND stop_type IS NOT NULL THEN 1
                              ELSE 0 END) as is1yrstop
           FROM subs
           WHERE YEAR(start_date) = 2005) score LEFT OUTER JOIN
        (SELECT market, channel, rate_plan,
                  AVG(CASE WHEN tenure < 365 AND stop_type IS NOT NULL THEN 1.0
                            ELSE 0 END) as stoprate
           FROM subs
           WHERE YEAR(start_date) = 2004
           GROUP BY market, channel, rate_plan ) lookup
        ON score.market = lookup.market AND
            score.channel = lookup.channel AND
            score.rate_plan = lookup.rate_plan CROSS JOIN
        (SELECT AVG(CASE WHEN tenure < 365 AND stop_type IS NOT NULL THEN 1.0
                            ELSE 0 END) as stoprate
           FROM subs
           WHERE YEAR(start_date) = 2004) def
```

This creates the lookup table using three dimensions rather than one.

Adding more dimensions is beneficial, because the lookup model captures more features of the customers, and more interactions among those features. However, as the number of dimensions increases, each cell in the lookup table has fewer and fewer customers. In fact, using MONTHLY_FEE instead of RATE_PLAN for the third dimension, some of the combinations have no customers at all and more than one in six cells have fewer than ten customers, as shown in the histogram of cell sizes in Figure 10-12. The largest cell (for the market Gotham, the channel Dealer, and a monthly fee of $40) accounts for 15% of all customers.

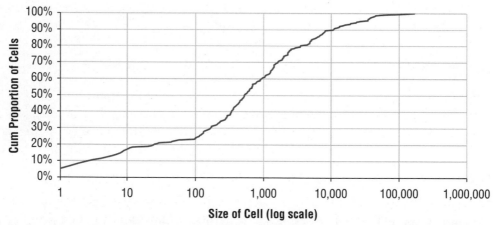

**Figure 10-12:** This histogram chart shows the cumulative number of cells that have up to each number of customers for the market, dealer, monthly fee lookup model. Note that the horizontal axis uses a log scale, because the range of cell sizes is very large.

Having large numbers of cells has another effect as well. The resulting estimate for the stop rate has a confidence interval, as discussed in Chapter 3. The fewer customers contributing to the proportion, the wider the confidence interval.

For this reason, cells in the lookup table should have some minimum size, such as having at least 500 customers. This is accomplished by including a HAVING clause in the Lookup subquery:

```
HAVING COUNT(*) >= 500
```

Combinations of market, channel, and monthly fee that are not in the lookup table but are in the score set are then given the default value.

The next section presents another method for bringing together data from many dimensions, a method that borrows ideas from probability.

# Naïve Bayesian Models (Evidence Models)

Naïve Bayesian models extend the idea of lookup models for probabilities to the extreme. It is possible to have any number of dimensions and still use the information along each dimension to get sensible results, even when the corresponding lookup model would have an empty cell for that combination of values. Instead of creating ever smaller cells, naïve Bayesian models combine the information from each dimension.

The "naïve" part of the name is the assumption that the dimensions are independent of each other. This makes it possible to combine information along the dimensions into a single score. The Bayesian part of the name refers to a simple idea from probability. Understanding this idea is a good way to get started.

## Some Ideas in Probability

One way of looking at the chi-square value is as a model score for estimating counts that combines information along various dimensions. In practice, this is taken one step further by measuring how different the expected value is from the actual value. However, the expected value is itself an estimate of the actual value.

In a similar way, a naïve Bayesian model produces an expected value for a probability based on summaries of the probabilities along the dimensions. The model itself is just some complicated arithmetic. However, to get a feel for what it is doing requires some language from probability.

## Probabilities

Figure 10-13 shows four distinct groups of customers. The light gray shaded ones are customers who stop in the first year. The striped customers are from a particular market. Everyone is in exactly one of the groups:

- 38 customers stopped and are not in the market (gray, unstriped area);
- 2 customers stopped and are in the market (gray striped area);
- 8 customers are in the market and not stopped (not gray, striped); and,
- 52 customers are not in the market and not stopped (not gray, not striped).

The purpose of the chart is to illustrate some ideas and vocabulary about probability. The chart itself is a Venn diagram, showing overlapping sets in the data.

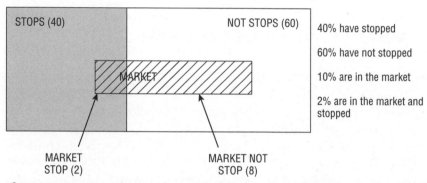

**Figure 10-13:** Four groups of customers here are represented as a Venn diagram, showing the overlaps between the customers in one market and the stopped and not stopped customers.

What is the probability that someone stops? (Strictly speaking, the question should be "if we choose one of these customers at random, what is the probability of choosing a customer who stops?") This is the number of customers who stop divided by the total number of customers. There are forty customers who stop (38+2) out of one hundred customers (38+2+8+52), so the probability is 40%. Similarly, the probability of someone being in the market shown in the chart is 10%.

It is worth pondering how informative this situation is. If told that there are one hundred customers, and 40% stop and 10% are in a given market, what does this tell us about the relationship between stops and the market? The answer is: very little. All the customers in the market could be stopped. All the customers in the market could be not stopped. Or, anything in between.

However, once the probability of stops within the market is known, then the various counts are all determined. This probability of stopping within the market is an example of a *conditional probability*. It is the number of customers in the market who stop divided by the number of customers in the market, or 20% (2/10).

When the conditional probability is the same as the overall probability, the two phenomena are said to be *independent*. Being independent simply means that knowing the market provides no additional information about stopping and vice versa. In this case, the probability of stopping is 40% and the probability of stopping for customers in the market is 20%, so the two are not independent.

## Odds

Another important concept from probability is *odds*. These are familiar to anyone who has ever used the expression "50-50" to mean an equal chance. The odds for something are the number of times something happens for every time it does not happen.

Overall, 40% of customers stop and 60% do not, so the odds are forty-to-sixty. This is often simplified, so two-to-three and 0.667 (the "to one" being implicit) are equivalent ways of saying the same thing. When the probability is 50%, the odds are one.

There is a simple relationship between odds and probabilities and back again:

```
odds = probability / (1 - probability) =  -1 + 1/(1 - probability)
probability = 1 - (1/(1 + odds))
```

Odds and probability are two ways of describing the same thing. Given the probability it is easy to calculate the odds, and vice versa.

## Likelihood

Likelihood has a specific meaning in probability theory. The likelihood of someone in a market stopping is the ratio between two conditional probabilities: the probability of someone being in the market given that they stopped and the probability of someone being in the market given that they did not stop.

Figure 10-14 illustrates what this means as a picture. The probability of someone being in the market given they stopped is two divided by forty. The probability of someone being in the market given they did not stop is eight divided by sixty. The ratio is 3/8. This means that someone in the market has a 3/8 chance of stopping compared to not stopping.

An alternative way of expressing the likelihood is as the ratio of two odds. The first is the odds of stopping in the market and the second is the overall odds of stopping. The odds of stopping in the market are 2/8; the overall odds are 4/6. The ratio produces the same value: (2/8)/(4/6)=(2*6)/(4*8)=3/8.

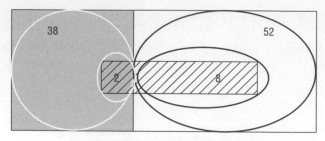

Likelihood is ratio of 8/(8+52) and 2/(2+38)

**Figure 10-14:** A likelihood is the ratio of two conditional probabilities.

## Calculating the Naïve Bayesian Model

This section moves from the simple ideas in probability to an intriguing observation by Thomas Bayes and then naïve Bayesian models. Although Bayes himself probably did not realize it, the observation also has philosophical implications, and is the foundation of a branch of statistics called Bayesian statistics (which has little relationship to naïve Bayesian modeling). The aside "Bayes and Bayesian Statistics" discusses the man and the statistics.

> ### BAYES AND BAYESIAN STATISTICS
>
> Rev. Thomas Bayes was born at the beginning of the 18th century to a family of Nonconformists. According to English law at the time, members of non-Anglican churches were officially classified as "nonconformist"; eventually, he took a ministering position in a Presbyterian church.
>
> Bayes was quite interested in mathematics, yet he lived up to his religious affiliation in one striking way. His ideas in probability theory were published in 1763, three years after his death — distinctly nonconformist.
>
> The paper, *An Essay Towards Solving a Problem in the Doctrine of Chances*, appeared in the *Philosophical Transactions of the Royal Society of London* (the paper is available at `http://www.stat.ucla.edu/history/essay.pdf`). For several decades the paper languished, until found and expounded upon by a French mathematician Pierre-Simon Laplace.
>
> By the mid-20th century, statistics had two competing perspectives, the Frequentists and the Bayesians. To outsiders (and many insiders), this competition often looks like a religious debate, so it is perhaps fitting that Bayes himself was a religiously ordained Nonconformist.
>
> The primary difference between the two groups is how to deal with subjective information in probability theory. Both Bayesians and Frequentists would agree that the probability of a coin about to be flipped landing heads side up is 50% (because this is not a trick question).

**BAYES AND BAYESIAN STATISTICS *(CONTINUED)***

Consider a slightly different scenario, though. Someone has flipped the coin, hidden it from view, and looked at whether the coin is heads or tails. Now, is the probability still 50% even though you cannot see the coin? Frequentists would say that probability does not apply, because the event has occurred. The coin either is or is not heads, so the "probability" is either 0% or 100%. Bayesians are more comfortable saying that the probability is 50%. Which is true? There is no right answer. This is a question as much about philosophy as about probability.

Chapter 3 introduced the concept of the confidence interval and the p-value as a confidence. These are Frequentist notions. The Bayesian perspective has similar ideas, called "credible intervals" and Bayesians often treat p-values as actual probabilities. Thankfully, the mathematics is the same for basic statistical measures.

The Bayesian perspective makes it possible to incorporate prior beliefs when analyzing data. This can be quite powerful and can make it possible to solve some very difficult problems, often using lots of computer power. Frequentists counter that any given outcome can be generated, just by choosing the appropriate prior beliefs.

Of course, there is an old saying that "statistics don't lie but statisticians do." Even without resorting to complex mathematical modeling, it is possible to mislead with statistics. Responsible analysts and statisticians — whether Bayesian or Frequentist — are not trying to mislead. They are trying to analyze data to increase understanding and provide useful results.

There is a lesson to be learned from this history. When analyzing data, the only responsible thing to do is to be explicit about assumptions being made. This is particularly important when working with databases, where business processes can result in unusual behavior. Be explicit about assumptions, so the results rest on a solid and credible foundation.

## An Intriguing Observation

Thomas Bayes made a key observation in the realm of statistics. It connects the following two probabilities:

- What is the probability of stopping for a customer in the particular market?
- What is the probability of being in the market for a customer who stops?

These are two ways of understanding the relationship between markets and stops, one focusing on what happens in the market and the other focusing on the customers who stop. It turns out that these probabilities are related to each other by a simple formula.

The two probabilities themselves are conditional probabilities. The first is the probability of stopping, given that a customer is in a market. The second is the probability of being in a market, given that a customer stops. In the example data, the first is 20% because two out of ten customers in the market stop. The second is 5%, because two out of forty stopped customers are in the market.

Simple enough. The ratio between these numbers is four (20%/5% = 4). Remarkably, this is also the ratio between the overall stop rate (40%) and the overall proportion of customers in the given market (10%).

This observation is true in general. The ratio between two conditional probabilities that are the inverses of each other is the ratio between the two probabilities with no conditions. In a sense, the conditional parts of the probabilities cancel out. This is Bayes' formula.

### Bayesian Model of One Variable

The Bayesian model of one variable applies the formula in the following way: the odds of stopping given that a customer is in the market are the product of two numbers. The first is the overall odds of stopping; the second is the likelihood of the customer in the market stopping.

Let's work this out for the example. The probability of stopping given that a customer is in the market is 20%. Hence, the odds of a customer stopping are 20%/(1–20%) = 1/4. Is this the same as the product of the overall odds and the likelihood?

As observed earlier, the overall odds of stopping are 2/3. The likelihood of the customer stopping was also calculated as 3/8. Well, in this case, the result holds: 1/4 = (2/3)*(3/8).

The case with one dimension is trivially correct. Recall the alternative way of expressing the likelihood is the ratio of the odds of a customer stopping divided by the overall odds. The Bayesian model becomes the product of the overall odds times this ratio, and the overall odds cancel out. The result is just the odds of the customer stopping given the market — which is what we were looking for to begin with.

### Bayesian Model of One Variable in SQL

The goal of the Bayesian model is to calculate the conditional probability of a customer stopping. For the simple example in one dimension, the formula is not necessary. The following query calculates the odds by market:

```
SELECT market,
       AVG(CASE WHEN tenure < 365 AND stop_type IS NOT NULL
               THEN 1.0 ELSE 0 END) as stoprate,
       (-1+1/(1-AVG(CASE WHEN tenure < 365 AND stop_type IS NOT NULL
                   THEN 1.0 ELSE 0 END))) as stopodds,
```

```
        SUM(CASE WHEN tenure < 365 AND stop_type IS NOT NULL
               THEN 1 ELSE 0 END) as numstops,
        SUM(CASE WHEN tenure < 365 AND stop_type IS NOT NULL
               THEN 0 ELSE 1 END) as numnotstops
FROM subs
WHERE YEAR(start_date) = 2004
GROUP BY market
```

The results are shown in Table 10-11. Although the direct calculation is easy, it is instructive to show the alternative approach using the odds times likelihood approach. For this alternative approach, the following is needed:

- The overall odds; and,
- The likelihood of a customer stopping given that the customer is in the market.

The odds given the market are then the overall odds times the likelihood of stopping in the market. These odds can easily be converted to a probability.

**Table 10-11:** Results by Market for Bayesian Model of One Variable

| MARKET | STOP RATE | STOP ODDS | NUMBER OF STOPS | NUMBER OF NOT STOPS |
|--------|-----------|-----------|-----------------|---------------------|
| Gotham | 33.0% | 0.49 | 176,065 | 357,411 |
| Metropolis | 29.0% | 0.41 | 117,695 | 288,809 |
| Smallville | 10.1% | 0.11 | 17,365 | 155,362 |

Both of these values can readily be calculated in SQL, because they are both based on counting and dividing:

```
SELECT market, (1-(1/(1+overall_odds*likelihood))) as p,
       overall_odds*likelihood as odds, overall_odds, likelihood,
       numstop, numnotstop, overall_numstop, overall_numnotstop
FROM (SELECT dim1.market,
             overall.numstop / overall.numnotstop as overall_odds,
             ((dim1.numstop / overall.numstop)/
              (dim1.numnotstop / overall.numnotstop)) as likelihood,
             dim1.numstop, dim1.numnotstop,
             overall.numstop as overall_numstop,
             overall.numnotstop as overall_numnotstop
      FROM (SELECT market,
                   SUM(CASE WHEN tenure < 365 AND stop_type IS NOT NULL
                           THEN 1.0 ELSE 0 END) as numstop,
                   SUM(CASE WHEN tenure < 365 AND stop_type IS NOT NULL
                           THEN 0.0 ELSE 1 END) as numnotstop
            FROM subs
```

*(continued)*

```
            WHERE YEAR(start_date) = 2004
            GROUP BY market) dim1 CROSS JOIN
     (SELECT SUM(CASE WHEN tenure < 365 THEN 1.0 ELSE 0
                  END) as numstop,
                SUM(CASE WHEN tenure < 365 AND stop_type IS NOT NULL
                      THEN 0.0 ELSE 1 END) as numnotstop
        FROM subs
        WHERE YEAR(start_date) = 2004
      ) overall
   ) a
```

The first subquery, Dim1, calculates the number of customers who do and do not stop in each market. The second, Overall, calculates the same values overall. The middle query then calculates the likelihood and overall odds, which are brought together in the outermost query.

Using the alternative formulation for odds just changes the definition of likelihood to the arithmetically equivalent:

```
(dim1.numstop/dim1.numnotstop)/(overall.numstop/overall.numnotstop)
```

This formulation is easier to calculate in SQL.

These results in Table 10-12 are exactly the same as the results calculated directly. This is not a coincidence. With one variable, the Bayesian model is exact.

**Table 10-12:** Results for the Naïve Bayesian Approach, with Intermediate Results

| MARKET | P | ODDS | OVERALL ODDS | LIKELIHOOD |
|---|---|---|---|---|
| Gotham | 33.0% | 0.493 | 0.388 | 1.269 |
| Metropolis | 29.0% | 0.408 | 0.388 | 1.050 |
| Smallville | 10.1% | 0.112 | 0.388 | 0.288 |

## The "Naïve" Generalization

The "naïve" part of naïve Bayesian means "independent," in the sense of probability. This implies that each variable can be treated separately in the model. With this assumption, the formula for one dimension generalizes to any number of dimensions: the odds of stopping given several attributes in several dimensions are the overall odds of stopping times the product of the likelihoods for each attribute. What makes this powerful is the ease of calculating the overall odds and the individual likelihoods.

**TIP** Naïve Bayesian models can be applied to any number of inputs (dimensions). There are examples with hundreds of input dimensions.

Table 10-13 shows the actual probability and the estimated probability by channel and market for stopping in the first year. The estimates from the model are pretty close to the actual values. In particular, the ordering is quite similar. Unlike the one-attribute case, the estimate for two attributes is an approximation, because the attributes are not strictly independent. This is okay; we should not expect modeled values to exactly match actual values.

**Table 10-13:** Results from Naïve Bayesian Model, Using Channel and Market for First Year Stops

| | | PROBABILITY | | | RANK | |
| MARKET | CHANNEL | PRED-ICTED | ACT-UAL | DIFFER-ENCE | PRED-ICTED | ACT-UAL |
| --- | --- | --- | --- | --- | --- | --- |
| Gotham | Chain | 46.9% | 58.7% | -11.8% | 1 | 1 |
| Gotham | Dealer | 29.7% | 28.9% | 0.8% | 5 | 5 |
| Gotham | Mail | 42.5% | 41.9% | 0.6% | 2 | 2 |
| Gotham | Store | 19.8% | 21.3% | -1.5% | 7 | 7 |
| Metropolis | Chain | 42.2% | 38.2% | 4.1% | 3 | 4 |
| Metropolis | Dealer | 25.9% | 23.1% | 2.7% | 6 | 6 |
| Metropolis | Mail | 37.9% | 41.1% | -3.2% | 4 | 3 |
| Metropolis | Store | 17.0% | 17.9% | -0.9% | 8 | 8 |
| Smallville | Chain | 16.7% | 9.1% | 7.6% | 9 | 11 |
| Smallville | Dealer | 8.7% | 9.7% | -1.0% | 11 | 10 |
| Smallville | Mail | 14.4% | 13.9% | 0.4% | 10 | 9 |
| Smallville | Store | 5.3% | 8.5% | -3.2% | 12 | 12 |

The following query calculates the values in this table:

```
SELECT market, channel,
       1-1/(1+pred_odds) as predp, 1-1/(1+actual_odds) as actp,
       1-1/(1+market_odds) as marketp, 1-1/(1+channel_odds) as channelp,
       pred_odds, actual_odds, market_odds, channel_odds
FROM (SELECT dim1.market, dim2.channel, actual.odds as actual_odds,
             (overall.odds*(dim1.odds/overall.odds)*
             (dim2.odds/overall.odds)) as pred_odds,
          dim1.odds as market_odds, dim2.odds as channel_odds
      FROM (SELECT market,
                  -1+1/(1-(AVG(CASE WHEN tenure < 365 AND
                                    stop_type IS NOT NULL
                              THEN 1.0 ELSE 0 END))) as odds
```

*(continued)*

```
                    FROM subs
                    WHERE YEAR(start_date) = 2004
                    GROUP BY market) dim1 CROSS JOIN
                  (SELECT channel,
                          -1+1/(1-(AVG(CASE WHEN tenure < 365 AND
                                              stop_type IS NOT NULL
                                    THEN 1.0 ELSE 0 END))) as odds
                    FROM subs
                    WHERE YEAR(start_date) = 2004
                    GROUP BY channel) dim2 CROSS JOIN
                  (SELECT -1+1/(1-(AVG(CASE WHEN tenure < 365 AND
                                              stop_type IS NOT NULL
                                    THEN 1.0 ELSE 0 END))) as odds
                    FROM subs
                    WHERE YEAR(start_date) = 2004
                  ) overall JOIN
                  (SELECT market, channel,
                          -1+1/(1-(AVG(CASE WHEN tenure < 365 AND
                                              stop_type IS NOT NULL
                                    THEN 1.0 ELSE 0 END))) as odds
                    FROM subs
                    WHERE YEAR(start_date) = 2004
                    GROUP BY market, channel) actual
                  ON dim1.market = actual.market AND
                     dim2.channel = actual.channel
          ) a
    ORDER BY 1, 2
```

This query has four subqueries. The first two calculate the odds for the market and channel separately. The third calculates the odds for the overall data. And the fourth calculates the actual odds, which are used only for comparison purposes. The middle subquery combines these into predicted odds, and the outermost query brings together the data needed for the table.

The expression to estimate the odds multiplies the overall odds by several odds ratios. This can be simplified by combining the overall odds into one expression:

```
POWER(overall.odds, -1)*dim1.odds*dim2.odds as pred_odds
```

The simpler expression is helpful as the model incorporates more attributes.

## Naïve Bayesian Model: Scoring and Lift

This section generates scores for the naïve Bayesian model, using the estimates from 2004 to apply to 2005.

### Scoring with More Attributes

Adding more dimensions to the naïve Bayesian model is relatively simple. For the most part, it is just a matter of adding in more dimensions in the inner query and updating the expression for predicted odds:

```
POWER(overall.odds, 1-<N>)*dim1.odds* . . . *dimN.odds as pred_odds
```

That is, the overall odds are raised to the power of one minus the number of dimensions and these are then multiplied by the odds along each dimension.

The one complication occurs when the score set has values that have no corresponding odds. This can occur for two reasons. One is that new values appear, from one year to the next. The second is restricting the model to a minimum number of instances for calculating the odds, so some values are missing from the dimensional tables. The naïve Bayesian approach handles missing values in the dimension quite well, theoretically. If a value is not available along a dimension, the likelihood value for the dimension is simply not used. However, as with many things, the practice is a bit more detailed than the theory.

The missing dimension shows up in two places:

▪ The likelihood value will be NULL.

▪ The exponent used for the POWER() function needs to be decreased by one for each missing dimension.

Neither of these are insurmountable; they just require arithmetic and cleverly setting up the subqueries.

The first thing is to use LEFT OUTER JOIN rather than JOIN for combining the dimensions tables with the score set. The second is to default the missing odds to one (rather than NULL or zero), so they do not affect the multiplication. The third is to count the number of dimensions that match.

The first is trivial. The second uses the COALESCE() function. The third could use a gargantuan, ugly nested CASE statement. But there is an alternative. Within each dimension subquery, a variable called *N* is given the value 1. The following expression calculates the number of matching dimensions:

```
COALESCE(dim1.n, 0) + COALESCE(dim2.n, 0) + . . . + COALESCE(dimn.n, 0)
```

Missing values are replaced by zeros, so the sum is the number of matching dimensions.

> **TIP** In a query that has several outer joins, it is possible to count the number that succeed by adding a dummy variable in each subquery (let's call it N) and giving it a value of 1. Then, the expression COALESCE(q1.N, 0) + . . . + COALESCE(qn.N, 0) **counts the number of successful joins.**

The following query calculates the naïve Bayesian predicted score for two dimensions, channel and market:

```
SELECT customer_id, score.channel, score.market, is1yrstop,
       (POWER(overall.odds,
              1-(COALESCE(market.n, 0) + COALESCE(channel.n,0))) *
        COALESCE(channel.odds,0)*COALESCE(market.odds, 0)) as predodds
FROM (SELECT s.*,
             (CASE WHEN tenure < 365 AND stop_type IS NOT NULL THEN 1.0
                   ELSE 0 END) as is1yrstop, MONTH(start_date) as mon
      FROM subs s
      WHERE YEAR(start_date) = 2005) score CROSS JOIN
     (SELECT -1+1/(1-(AVG(CASE WHEN tenure < 365 AND stop_type IS NOT NULL
                               THEN 1.0 ELSE 0 END))) as odds
      FROM subs
      WHERE YEAR(start_date) = 2004) overall LEFT OUTER JOIN
     (SELECT channel, 1 as n,
             -1+1/(1-(AVG(CASE WHEN tenure < 365 AND stop_type IS NOT NULL
                               THEN 1.0 ELSE 0 END))) as odds
      FROM subs
      WHERE YEAR(start_date) = 2004
      GROUP BY channel) channel
    ON score.channel = channel.channel LEFT OUTER JOIN
     (SELECT market, 1 as n,
             -1+1/(1-(AVG(CASE WHEN tenure < 365 AND stop_type IS NOT NULL
                               THEN 1.0 ELSE 0 END))) as odds
      FROM subs
      WHERE YEAR(start_date) = 2004
      GROUP BY market) market
    ON score.market = market.market
```

This query has a separate subquery for each dimension, using the ideas just described. In addition, the odds for each dimension are then combined using COALESCE(), so the query can handle values that don't match the dimension tables.

## Creating a Cumulative Gains Chart

Creating a cumulative gains chart uses the preceding query as a subquery, calculating the percentile based on the predicted odds. For this purpose, the predicted odds and predicted probability are interchangeable, because they have the same ordering. The resulting query is basically the same query used earlier for creating these charts:

```
SELECT percentile, COUNT(*) as numcustomers,
       SUM(is1yrstop) as numactualstops,
       AVG(is1yrstop*1.0) as actualstop,
       AVG(1-(1/(1+predodds))) as avgpredp
FROM (SELECT score_subquery.*,
```

```
                   1-(1/(1+predodds)) as predp,
              NTILE(100) OVER (ORDER BY 1-(1/(1+predodds))) as percentile
      FROM (<score-subquery>) score_subquery
      ) a
GROUP BY percentile
ORDER BY 1
```

This query calculates the percentile based on the predicted score and counts the number of actual stops in each percentile.

The cumulative gains chart in Figure 10-15 shows the cumulative proportion of stops for two score sets. As expected, the better one is for the scores on the model set. The data from 2005 is a more reasonable score set. It demonstrates that the model does still work on data a year later, although it is not quite as powerful.

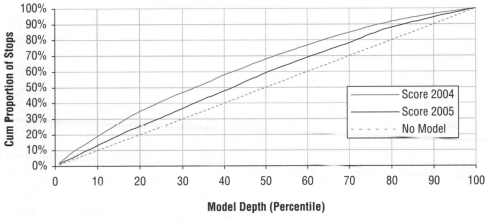

**Figure 10-15:** This chart shows cumulative gains charts for the naïve Bayesian model on the training set (2004 starts) and on the score set (2005 starts).

## Comparison of Naïve Bayesian and Lookup Models

Both naïve Bayesian models and lookup models estimate probabilities based on values along dimensions. The two modeling techniques produce exactly the same results when there is only one dimension; the results differ when there are more dimensions.

It is worthwhile to think about the two different approaches. The lookup approach is a brute force approach that breaks the data into smaller and smaller cells. As there become more cells — either because there are more dimensions or because each dimension has more possible values — the cells become smaller and smaller. The data is literally divided among the cells. This means that the number of cells needs to be limited in some way, probably by using few dimensions that take on few values (as in the subscription data).

By contrast, naïve Bayesian models use all the data to estimate values for each dimension. The data is not divided and subdivided over and over. Instead, the approach uses probability theory and a reasonable assumption to combine the values along the dimensions into an estimated prediction. The assumption works well in practice, despite the fact that dimensions are almost never independent.

Of course, both approaches are making another, unstated assumption. The models use data from 2004. The assumption is that the past tells us about the future. As we saw in the cumulative gains charts that compare the two values, the models do work, but they do not work as well on the data being scored as they do on the data used to build the model.

## Lessons Learned

A data mining model takes inputs and produces an output, which is typically a prediction or estimation of some value. There are two major processes involved with models. The first is training or building the model. The second is applying the model to new data.

SQL provides a good basis for learning the basics about data mining. Although this may seem surprising, some powerful techniques are really more about manipulating data than about fancy statistical techniques. The GROUP BY operation in SQL is analogous to creating a model (both summarize data). The JOIN operation is analogous to scoring a model.

This chapter discusses several different types of models. The first is a look-alike model, where the model score indicates how close one example is to another. For instance, the model score might indicate how similar zip codes are to the zip code that has highest market penetration.

Lookup models are another type. These create a lookup table, so the process of scoring the model is the process of looking up values. The values might be the most popular product, or the probability of someone stopping, or something else. Although any number of dimensions could be used to create the lookup table, the data gets partitioned into smaller and smaller pieces, meaning that the values in the table become more uncertain or even empty when there are more dimensions.

Naïve Bayesian models address this shortcoming. They use some basic probability theory along with Bayes' formula, an important formula in probability proven almost three hundred years ago. This approach to modeling makes it possible to calculate lookup tables along each dimension separately, and then to combine the values together. The big advantage to the naïve Bayesian approach is the ability to handle many, many dimensions.

The naïve Bayesian models also make an assumption about the data. This assumption is that the different dimensions are independent (in the probabilistic sense). Although this assumption is not true when working with business data, the results from the model are often still useful. In a sense, naïve Bayesian models produce an expected value for a probability, similar to the way that the chi-square approach calculates an expected value.

Evaluating models is as important as creating them. A cumulative gains chart shows how well a binary response model is performing. An average value chart shows the performance of a model estimating a number. And a classification chart shows the performance of classification models.

This chapter has introduced modeling in the context of SQL and working with large databases. The traditional way of introducing modeling is through linear regression, which is discussed in the next chapter.

# The Best-Fit Line: Linear Regression Models

The previous chapter introduced data mining ideas using various types of models well suited to databases, such as look-alike models, lookup tables, and naïve Bayesian models. This chapter extends these ideas to the realm of more traditional statistical techniques: linear regression and best-fit lines.

Unlike the techniques in the previous chapter, linear regression requires that the input and target variables all be numeric; the results are coefficients in a mathematical formula. A formal treatment of linear regression involves lots of mathematics and proofs. However, this chapter steers away from an overly theoretical approach.

In addition to providing a basis for statistical modeling, linear regression has many applications. To understand relationships between different numeric quantities, regressions — especially best-fit lines — are the place to start. The examples in this chapter include estimating potential product penetration in zip codes, studying price elasticity (investigating the relationship between product prices and sales volumes), and quantifying the effect of monthly fee on yearly stop rates.

The simplest linear regression models are best-fit lines that have one input and one target. Because the data can be plotted using a scatter plot, such models are readily understood visually. In fact, Excel builds linear regression models into charts using the best-fit trend line, one of six built-in types of trend lines.

Excel can calculate best-fit lines in several ways. For the simplest case with one input and one target, there are several methods. The general function introduces a new class of Excel functions, because it needs to return values in several cells. Array functions, introduced in Chapter 4, solve this dilemma; an array function can return values in more than one cell.

Apart from the built-in functions, there are two other ways to calculate the linear regression formulas in Excel. These methods are more powerful than the built-in functions. One is a direct method, using somewhat complicated formulas for the parameters in the model. The other uses the Solver capability to calculate the parameters. Solver is a general-purpose tool included with Excel that finds optimal solutions to problems. Its ability to build linear regression models is just one example of its power.

Measuring how well the best-fit line fits the data introduces the idea of correlation. Correlation is easy to calculate. As with many statistical measures, it does what it does well, but it comes with some warnings. It is easy to overinterpret correlation values.

Multiple regression extends the "best-fit line" regression by using more than one input variable. Fortunately, multiple regression is quite feasible in Excel. Unfortunately, it does not produce pretty scatter plots, because there are too many dimensions.

SQL can also be used to build basic linear regression models, when there are one or two input variables. Unfortunately, standard SQL does not have built-in functions to do this, so the equations have to be entered explicitly. These equations become more complicated as more variables are added, as we'll see with the two-variable example at the end of this chapter. The chapter begins not with complicated SQL statements, but rather with the best-fit line, which enables us to visualize linear regression.

# The Best-Fit Line

The simplest case of the linear regression has one input variable and one target variable. This case is best illustrated with scatter plots, making it readily understandable visually and giving rise to the name "best-fit line."

## Tenure and Amount Paid

The first example of a best-fit line is for a set of customers in a subscription-based business. This example compares the relationship between the tenure of customers and the total amount the customers paid. In a subscription business, there is an evident relationship between these. The longer customers remain active, the more they pay.

Figure 11-1 shows best-fit line for these customers, with the tenure on the X-axis and the amount paid on the Y-axis. The chart clearly shows the relationship; both the points and the best-fit line start low and slope upward to the right.

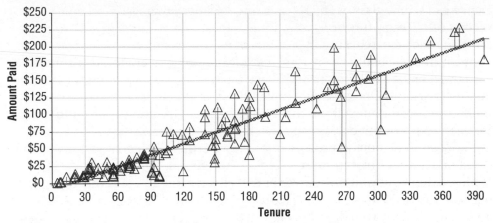

**Figure 11-1:** This chart shows the best-fit line for a set of data points showing the relationship between customers' tenures and the amount they have paid.

One way to use the best-fit line is to estimate how much customers would pay if they survived to a given tenure. A typical customer with tenure of 240 days should pay about $125. Such an estimate could be used to estimate the amount to spend on customer acquisition. For instance, a typical customer seems to be worth $192.30 in the first year (which is the value for 365 days on the chart); this amount might direct acquisition budgets.

This simple example shows that the best-fit line is a good way to visualize data and summarize the relationship between two variables. It can also be useful for estimating values.

> **TIP** The best-fit line can be seen in a chart by selecting a series, right-clicking, and adding a trend line. The linear best-fit line makes it possible to see trends in the data.

## Properties of the Best-fit Line

There are many different possible lines that go near the data points. Of all these possible lines, the best-fit line is a very specific one. Figure 11-1 shows the vertical line segments, connecting each observed data point to the point on the line directly above or beneath it. The best-fit line is the one where the vertical distances between the observed point and the line are as small as possible — for some definition of "small."

### What Does Best-Fit Mean?

The specific definition is that the best-fit line minimizes the sum of the squares of the distances between the observed data points and the line, along the vertical dimension. In fact, one name for linear regression is *ordinary least squares* (OLS) regression.

The sum of squares measures results in relatively simple calculations. Being simpler, these calculations were feasible before the era of computers, as explained in the aside "Ceres and Least Squares Regression." This fact leads to another reason the method works well in practice: after centuries of use, the models are well understood. There are a plethora of measures to understand them and to determine when and whether they are working.

The definition of the best-fit line is along the Y-dimension (all the line segments are vertical instead of being horizontal, for instance). Why the Y-dimension? The simple answer is that the Y-value is the thing we are trying to estimate.

## CERES AND LEAST SQUARES REGRESSION

An asteroid and linear regression may not seem to have much to do with each other. However, the method of least squares regression was invented by Carl Friederich Gauss, and first applied to the problem of finding this celestial body.

In January 1801, the Italian astronomer Joseph Piazzi discovered the asteroid Ceres and observed it until mid-February when it disappeared behind the sun. Based on his observations, astronomers rushed to figure out the full orbit of Ceres, so they could continue observations when Ceres reappeared.

Of course, in those days, the telescopes were using mirrors ground by hand and the positions were recorded on paper, so the observations themselves were rather inexact. Gauss recognized several key aspects of the problem, some involving astronomy, but the most innovative part was dealing with the inaccuracy in the measurements.

Based on only three of the observed positions, Gauss estimated the orbit and accurately predicted where Ceres would reappear from behind the sun. By the fall of 1801, Ceres did reappear, very close to where Gauss predicted and quite far from where other astronomers expected it to be. This reinforced the strength of Gauss's methods.

This history is interesting for several reasons. First, Gauss is considered by some to be the greatest mathematician ever, for his contributions to a wide range of subjects, including statistics.

It is also interesting because the first problem was not a linear regression problem as explained in the text. Gauss was trying to estimate an ellipse rather than a line.

The third reason is practical. Ordinary least squares regression uses the sum of the distances from the line, rather than the distances themselves. Perhaps this is because the distance is the square root of some quantity, so it is easier to calculate the distance squared than the distance itself. In a world where all the calculations have to be done by hand, Gauss may have preferred the simpler calculation that ignores taking the final square root.

Although the best-fit line is unique and well-understood, it is worth pointing out that slight variations in the definition would result in different lines. If another distance were used, such as the horizontal distance, the resulting "best-fit" line would be different. If the lengths of the line segments were combined in a way other than by taking the sum of the squares, say by taking the sum of the distances instead, the resulting line would also be different. However, the best-fit line is quite useful because it is so well understood and does capture important features of data.

### Formula for Line

The best-fit line is a line that is defined by a formula that readers may recall from high school math:

```
Y = m*X + b
```

In this equation, m is the slope of the line and b is the Y-intercept, because this is where the line crosses the Y-axis. When the slope is positive, the values of Y increase as the values of X increase (positive correlation); when the slope is negative, the line goes down instead (negative correlation). When the slope is zero, the line is horizontal. The goal of linear regression is to find the values of m and b that minimize the sum of the squares of vertical distance between the line and the observed points.

The best-fit line in Figure 11-1 has a formula:

```
<amount paid> = $0.5512 * <tenure> - $8.8558
```

This line defines a simple relationship between the two variables (tenure and amount paid). They are positively correlated. One easy way to calculate the values m and b is using the SLOPE() and INTERCEPT() functions in Excel.

There is nothing special about calling the slope m and the intercept b. In fact, statisticians have different names for them. They use the Greek letter beta for the coefficients, calling the Y-intercept $\beta_0$ and the slope $\beta_1$. This notation has the advantage of being readily extensible to more coefficients.

Renaming the coefficients (albeit for a good reason) is not the only oddity in standard statistical terminology. From that perspective, the Xs and Ys are constants, the betas are variables, and lines do not have to be straight. The aside "Some Strange Statistical Terminology" explains this in more detail.

### Expected Value

For a given value of X, the equation for the line can be used to calculate a value of Y. This *expected value* represents what the model "knows" about the relationship between X and Y, applied to a particular value of X.

## SOME STRANGE STATISTICAL TERMINOLOGY

In the equation for the line, the "X"s and "Y"s are normally thought of as being variables and the coefficients as being constants. That is because we are thinking of using the line to estimate a Y-value given an X-value. In data analysis, though, the problem is estimating the values of the coefficients.

The language of statistical modeling turns this terminology upside down. The Xs and Ys are constants, because they refer to known data points. There may be two data points or two million, but for all of them the X- and Y-values are known. On the other hand, the challenge in statistical modeling is to find the line, by finding coefficients that minimize the sum of the squares of the distances between the points and the line. The coefficients are the variables that need to be solved for.

This inverse terminology actually explains why the following are also examples of "linear" models although the formulas do not look like the formula for a line:

$$Y = \beta_1 * X^2 + \beta_0$$
$$\ln(Y) = \beta_1 * X + \beta_0$$
$$\ln(Y) = \beta_1 * X^2 + \beta_0$$

These are linear because they are linear in the coefficients. The fact that there are funky functions of Xs and Ys involved does not make a difference. The coefficients are what's important. We know the values of X and Y; the coefficients are unknown.

A good way to think about this is that all the observed data could be transformed. For example, in the first example, the X-value could be squared and called Z:

$$Z = X^2$$

In terms of Y and Z, the first equation becomes:

$$Y = \beta_1 * Z + \beta_0$$

This is a linear relationship between Y and Z. And Z is known as X is, because it is just the square of the X value.

For example, Table 11-1 shows the expected values for various tenure values for the data in Figure 11-1. The expected values can be higher or lower than the actual values. They can also be out-of-range, in the sense that it makes no sense for the amount paid to be negative (and the expected values for small tenures are negative). On the other hand, all values of tenure have expected values, making it possible to estimate the value of a customer after one year. In this case, it is $192.30.

**Table 11-1:** Some Expected Values for Best-fit Line in Figure 11-1

| TENURE | EXPECTED $$ (0.55*TENURE - $8.86) | ACTUAL $$ | DIFFERENCE |
|--------|-----------------------------------|-----------|------------|
| 5 | -$6.10 | $1.65 | $7.75 |
| 8 | -$4.45 | $0.90 | $5.35 |
| 70 | $29.72 | $15.75 | -$13.97 |
| 140 | $68.30 | $91.78 | $23.48 |
| 210 | $106.88 | $71.45 | -$35.43 |
| 365 | $192.30 | None | N/A |

In Excel, the expected value can be calculated directly from two columns of X- and Y-values using the FORECAST() function. This function takes three arguments: the value to make the estimate for, the Y-values, and the X-values. It returns the expected value, using a linear regression formula. FORECAST() applies the model, without producing any other information to determine how good the model is or what the model looks like.

One rule of thumb when using best-fit lines is to use the line for interpolation rather than extrapolation. In English, this means calculating expected values only for values of X that are in the range of the data used to calculate the line.

## Error (Residuals)

Of course, the expected value generally differs from the actual value, because the line does not perfectly fit the data. The difference between the two is called the *error* or *residual*. For the best-fit line, the sum of the residuals is zero, because all the positive values cancel out all the negative ones. Although the best-fit line is not the only line with this property, it also has the property that the sum of the squares of the residuals is as small as possible.

There is a wealth of statistical theory about residuals. For instance, a model is considered a good fit on data when the residuals follow a normal distribution (which was discussed in Chapter 3). The residuals should not be related to the X-values.

Figure 11-2 plots the residuals from the data in Figure 11-1 against the X-values. As a general rule, the residuals should not exhibit any particular pattern. In particular, long sequences of positive or negative residuals indicate that the model is missing something. Also, the residuals should not get bigger as the X-values get bigger.

These residuals are pretty good, but not perfect. For instance, the initial residuals are almost all positive and relatively small. This is because the expected values are negative for small values of X, but the actual values are never negative. The model is not perfect, and this shouldn't be surprising because it is only taking tenure into account. Although tenure is important, other things also affect customers' total payments.

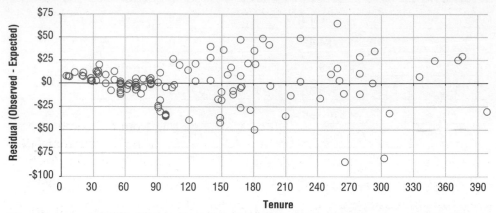

**Figure 11-2:** This chart shows the residuals for the data in Figure 11-1. Notice that the residuals tend to get larger as the X-values get larger.

> **TIP** Creating a scatter plot of the residuals and the X-values in the model is one way to see if the model is doing a good job. In general, the scatter plot should look random, with no long sequences of positive or negative values.

## Preserving the Averages

One very nice characteristic of best-fit lines (and linear regression models in general) is that they preserve averages. The average of the expected values of the original data is the same as the average of the observed values. Geometrically, this implies that all best-fit lines go through a particular point. This point is the average of the X-values and the average of the Y-values of the data used to build the model.

In practical terms, best-fit lines preserve some key characteristics of the data used to build them. Applying the model does not "move" the center of the data. So, taking the average of a large number of expected values (such as for all customers) is usually a fairly accurate estimate of the average of the actual values, even if the individual estimates are different.

## Inverse Model

Another very nice feature is the fact that the inverse can be readily constructed. That is, given a value of Y it is possible to calculate the corresponding value of X, using the following formula:

```
X = (Y - b) / m
```

Such a model can calculate the value of X for any given value of Y.

Note that the inverse model calculated this way is different from the inverse model calculated by reversing the roles of X and Y. For instance, for the best-fit line in Figure 11-1, the "mathematical" inverse is:

```
<tenure> = 1.8145 * <tenure> + 16.0687
```

However, reversing the roles of X and Y generates a different line:

```
<tenure> = 1.5029 * <tenure> + 35.6518
```

The fact that these two lines are different is interesting from a theoretical perspective. Reversing the roles of X and Y is equivalent to using the horizontal distance, rather than the vertical distance to calculate the best-fit line. For practical purposes, if we need the inverse relationship, then either works well enough.

**WARNING** The inverse relationship for a linear regression model is easy to calculate from the model equation. However, this is not the same as building another model by swapping the X-values and the Y-values.

## Beware of the Data

There are many ways of understanding how well a model fits a particular set of data. However, a model is only as good as the data used to build it. Alas, there are many fewer ways of determining whether the right data is being used for the model.

The data used for the scatter plot in Figure 11-1 is missing an important subset of customers; the data excludes customers who never paid. Hence, the relationship between payment and tenure is only for the customers who make a payment, not for everyone.

Almost half the customers in this sample never make a payment, because the customers come from the worst channel. When these freeloading customers are included, they have a small effect on the best-fit line, as shown in Figure 11-3. The non-payers are shown as the circles along the X-axis, and the best-fit line is the dashed line. The line has shifted a bit to the right and become a bit steeper.

Before diving into the contents of the chart, it is worth commenting on how this chart is created. Although only two series are visible, the chart actually has three series. One is for all customers and is used to generate the dotted best-fit line. Although the trend line for this series is visible, the points are not. Another series is for the paying customers, shown in Figure 11-1. The best-fit line for this dataset is the solid gray line. Then, the third series is the non-payers, and is used to show the customers who never paid. The best-fit lines are also given names, to make them clearer in the legend.

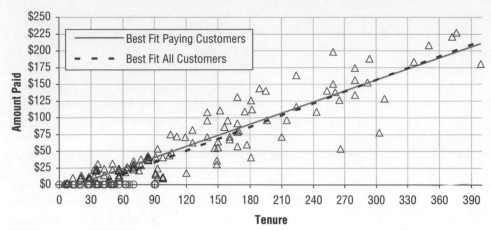

**Figure 11-3:** When non-paying customers are included, the best-fit line shifts a bit to the right and becomes a bit steeper.

There are 226 customers, of which 108 are non-payers (48%). Including the non-payers has an effect on the line. Consider the following question: What is the expected revenue for a new customer who survives for one year? For the original data, the answer was $192.30. When all customers are included, the value is $194.41.

The expected value has gone up by including customers who do not pay. This is counterintuitive. One could argue that linear regressions are not good for extrapolation. However, this example does not extrapolate beyond the end of the data, because there are data points beyond 365 days (although 365 days is among the higher tenure values). One could argue that the values are close and within some margin of error, which is undoubtedly true because there are just a couple hundred data points overall. The irony is, though, that we could add more and more non-paying customers to obtain almost any value at the one-year mark.

With a bit more thought, the issue goes from counterintuitive to absurd. Consider using the model to estimate revenue for customers who survive for one year. If one hundred customers start and are expected to stay for one year, what is their expected revenue during the first year? Including all customers, the estimate is $19,441. However, only including customers who pay reduces the estimate to $19,230. Although the difference is small, it raises the question: how does including non-paying customers increase the one-year estimated revenue? And, as noted earlier, additional non-paying customers in the data used to calculate the line could push the estimate up even more.

Something interesting is happening. A line is a rigid model. If a line goes down on one side, then either the whole line shifts downward (if the slope remains the same), or it goes up somewhere else. The freeloading customers all have low tenures, because non-payers stop (or are stopped) soon after starting.

Hence, the non-paying customers are all on the left of the scatter plot. These customers pull down the best-fit line, which in turn gets steeper. And steeper lines produce higher values for longer tenures.

One might ask which is the better estimate. The example shows that there are different factors at work, one for initial non-payment and one for the longer term trend. For paying customers, using the initial model makes more sense, because it is built using only paying customers. It is not distracted by the non-payers.

The purpose of this example is to stress the importance of choosing the right data for modeling. Be aware of the effects of data on the resulting model.

## Trend Lines in Charts

Best-fit lines are one of several types of trend lines supported in Excel's charts. The purpose of trend lines is to see patterns in charts that may not be apparent when looking at disparate points. They are only available when there is one input and one target variable. Nevertheless, the trend lines are useful for seeing patterns in data; and the best-fit line is useful for understanding linear regression.

### Best-fit Line in Scatter Plots

A powerful and simple way to calculate a linear regression is directly within a chart using the best-fit trend line, as already shown in Figures 11-1 and 11-3. The following steps add the best-fit trend line:

1. Left-click the series to select it.
2. Right-click again to bring up the "Format Trendline" dialog box.
3. Choose the "Linear" option on the upper left-hand side.

At this point, you can exit the dialog box, and the best-fit line appears between the first and the last X-values.

The line appears in the chart as a solid black line. Because the trend line is generally less important than the data, it is a good idea to change its format to a lighter color or dotted pattern. When there is more than one series on the chart, make the color of the trend line the same color as the data. As with any other series, just click the series to change its format.

**TIP** When placing a trend line in a scatter plot or a bubble plot, change its format to be lighter than the data points but similar in color, so the trend line is visible but does not dominate the chart.

There are several useful options under the "Options" tab of the "Format Trendline" dialog box:

- To give the trend line a name that appears in the chart legend, click by "Custom" and type in the name.

- By default, the trend line is only for the range of X-values in the data. To extend beyond this range, use the "Forecast" area and specify the number of units "Forward" after the last data point.

- To extend the range to values before the first data point, use the "Forecast" area and specify the number of units "Backward" before the first data point.

- To see the formula, choose "Display equation on chart." Once the equation appears, it is easy to modify the font and move it around.

- To see how well the model fits the data, choose "Display R-squared value on chart." The $R^2$ value is discussed later in this chapter.

If you forget to add options when the trend line is created, double-click the trend line and choose "Format Trendline" to bring up the dialog box. One nifty feature is that the trend line itself can be formatted to be invisible, so only the equation appears on the chart. Also note that when the data in the chart changes, the trend line and its equation change as well.

### Logarithmic, Power, and Exponential Trend Curves

Three types of trend curves are variations on the best-fit line, the difference being the shape used for the curve that fits the data is not a line:

- Logarithmic: $Y = \ln(\beta_1 * X + \beta_0)$
- Power: $Y = \beta_0 * X \hat{} \beta_1$
- Exponential: $Y = \exp(\beta_1 * X + \beta_0)$

Fitting these curves has the same spirit as linear regression, because all three formulas have two coefficients that are analogous to the slope and intercept values for a line. Each of these curves has its own particular properties. The first two, the logarithmic and power curves, require that the X-values be positive. The second two always produce Y-values that are positive (Excel does not allow $\beta_0$ to be negative for the power trend line).

The logarithmic curve decreases slowly, much more slowly than a line does. So, doubling the X-value only increases the Y-value by a constant. The left side of Figure 11-4 shows the logarithmic trend line for the payment data. Because the data has a linear relationship, the logarithmic curve is not a particularly good fit.

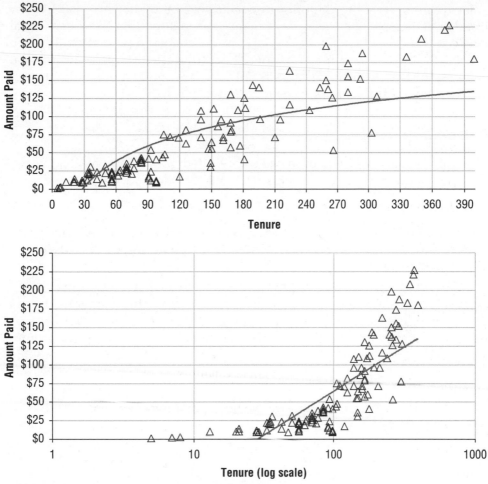

**Figure 11-4:** When the X-axis has a logarithmic scale, the logarithmic trend line looks like a line.

There is a relationship between the logarithmic trend line and the best-fit line. Changing the X-axis to be on a "logarithmic" scale (by clicking the "Logarithmic Scale" button on the "Scale" tab of the "Format axis" dialog box) makes the logarithmic curve look like a line. Figure 11-4 shows a side-by-side comparison of the same data, with one chart having the normal scale on the X-axis and the other, the logarithmic scale.

The exponential curve increases very rapidly, much more rapidly than a line. Its behavior is similar to the logarithmic trend line, but with respect to the Y-axis rather than the X-axis. That is, when the Y-axis has a logarithmic scale, the exponential curve looks like a line.

The power curve increases more slowly than the exponential. It looks like a line when both the X-axis and the Y-axis have a logarithmic scale. It also looks like a line under normal scaling when $ß_1$ is close to one.

One way of thinking about these trend lines is that they are best-fit lines, but the data is transformed. This is, in fact, the method that Excel uses to calculate the curves. As we'll see the later in the chapter, this method is useful practically, but it is an approximation. The results are a bit different from calculating the best-fit curves. Excel's trend curves are good, but not the theoretically correct best-fit curves.

## Polynomial Trend Curves

The polynomial curve is a bit more complicated because polynomial curves can have more than two coefficients. The form for these curves is:

▪ Polynomial: $Y = ß_n*X_n + \ldots + ß_2*X_2 + ß_1*X + ß_0$

The degree of the polynomial is the value of $n$ in the equation, which is input into the box labeled "Order" on the "Type" tab of the "Format Trendline" dialog box.

Polynomial fitting can be quite powerful. In fact, for any given set of points, there is a polynomial that fits them exactly. This polynomial has a degree one less than the number of points. Figure 11-5 shows an example with five data points and polynomials of degree one (a line) through four. Higher degree polynomials capture more of the specific features of the data points, rather than the general features. This is an example of *overfitting*, which is when a model memorizes the detail of the training data without finding larger patterns of interest. Also notice that the equations for the polynomials have nothing to do with each other. So, finding the best-fit polynomial of degree two is not a simple matter of adding a squared term to the equation for the best-fit line.

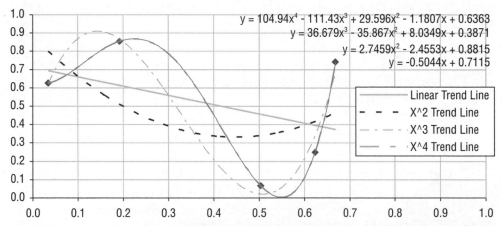

$$y = 104.94x^4 - 111.43x^3 + 29.596x^2 - 1.1807x + 0.6363$$
$$y = 36.679x^3 - 35.867x^2 + 8.0349x + 0.3871$$
$$y = 2.7459x^2 - 2.4553x + 0.8815$$
$$y = -0.5044x + 0.7115$$

Linear Trend Line
X^2 Trend Line
X^3 Trend Line
X^4 Trend Line

**Figure 11-5:** A polynomial of sufficiently high degree can fit any set of data exactly. This example shows five points and the best-fit polynomials of degrees one through four. The fourth degree polynomial goes through all five points.

When the order of the polynomial is odd, the curve starts high and goes low or starts low and goes high. The typical example of this is the line, which either slants upwards or downwards, but all odd degree polynomials have this property.

Polynomials of even degree either start and end high or start and end low. These have the property that there is either a minimum or maximum value, among the values. For some optimization applications, this is a very useful property.

**WARNING** When fitting polynomial trend curve to data points, be sure that the degree of the polynomial is much smaller than the number of data points. This reduces the likelihood of overfitting.

## Moving Average

After the best-fit line, probably the most useful type of trend line is the moving average. These are often used when the horizontal axis is time, because they can wash away variation within a week or within a month.

Figure 11-6 shows starts by day for the subscription data. There is a lot of variation within the week, because some days have more starts than others. Human eyes tend to follow the maximum and minimum values, which might obscure what's really happening. The trend line shows the 7-day moving average, which eliminates the within-week variation, making the longer term trend more visible.

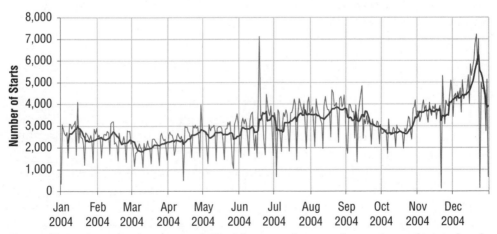

**Figure 11-6:** Starts by day are very jagged, because there are few starts on the weekend. The 7-day moving average does a better job of showing the trend during the year.

Sometimes moving averages can be used to spot very subtle patterns. This example looks at the relationship between the proportion of a zip code that has graduated from college and the proportion on public assistance, for zip codes in Minnesota. This data comes from the Zipcensus table, using the following query:

```
SELECT zipcode, (popedubach+popedumast+popeduprofdoct) as popcollege,
       hhpubassist
FROM zipcensus
WHERE state = 'MN'
ORDER BY 1
```

The scatter plot in Figure 11-7 does not show an obvious pattern, although it does seem that zip codes where most adults have a college degree have relatively few residents on public assistance.

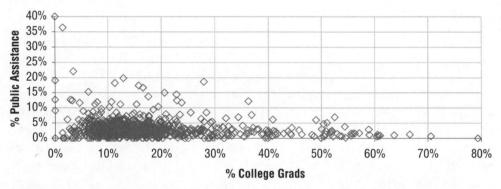

**Figure 11-7:** The relationship between the proportion of a zip code with a college education and the proportion on public assistance in the state of Minnesota is not obvious.

The top chart in Figure 11-8 shows one of the dangers when adding a moving average trend line. This chart applies the moving average directly to the data as pulled from the database, producing a zigzag line that bounces back and forth and makes no sense. The lower chart fixes this problem by sorting the data by the X-values. Here, a pattern is visible, although the relationship is not a line. As zip codes have more college graduates, they have fewer households on public assistance.

In general, when using moving averages, make sure that the data is sorted. Although this is always true for line charts, it may not be true for scatter plots and bubble charts. To sort the data in place, select the table to be sorted and use the Data ➪ Sort menu option (or type <alt>-D, <alt>-S) and choose the column or columns for sorting. The sort dialog box allows you to sort by up to three columns. If you need to sort by more columns, create an additional column in the table, using the concatenation function to append the column values together. Sorting is only needed for the moving average trend line; the other types are insensitive to the ordering of the data.

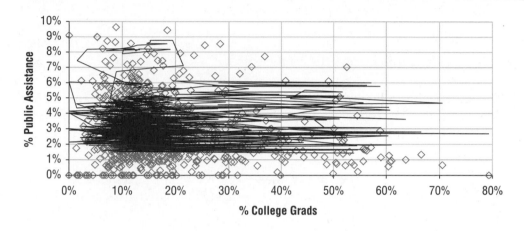

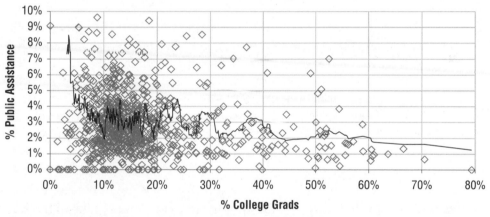

**Figure 11-8:** A moving average can find patterns in the data, as shown in the lower chart where the X-values are sorted. However, if the data is not sorted, the moving average is a meaningless scribble.

**TIP** When using the moving average trend line, be sure that the data is sorted by the X-values.

## Best-fit Using LINEST() Function

Trend lines are not the only way to do linear regression in Excel. The function called LINEST() provides the full functionality of linear regression, including calculating various statistics that describe the goodness of fit. It returns the following information:

- The $R^2$ value;
- The standard error for the coefficients;
- The standard error for the Y-estimate;
- The degrees of freedom;
- The sum of squares; and,
- The sum of the squares of the residuals.

This chapter discusses the first of these. The remaining are more advanced statistical measures, which are more appropriately discussed in a statistics book.

### Returning Values in Multiple Cells

Before moving to the statistics and the calculation of these values, there is the issue of how a single function in Excel can return more than one value. All the functions we have seen so far reside in only a single cell. In fact, the intuitive definition of function is something that returns one value assigned in a single cell.

The solution is array functions, as discussed in the aside "Excel Functions Returning More Than One Value." The call to an array function that returns multiple values is in many ways similar to any other function. The call to LINEST() looks like:

```
=LINEST(<y-values>, <x-values>, TRUE, TRUE)
```

The first argument is the target values (typically a column of values); the second argument is the input values (typically another column). The final two arguments are flags. The first flag says to do a normal linear regression (when FALSE, this would force the constant $\beta_0$ to have the value of zero, which is sometimes useful). The final flag says to calculate various statistics along with the coefficients.

Although this is an Excel formula, it is not entered in quite the same way as other Excel formulas. First, the formula is entered for a group of cells rather than just one. In this particular case, the function calculates values in ten cells, two across by five down. The function LINEST() always returns values in five rows when the last argument is TRUE. In addition, there is one column for each input variable. With one column of X-values, there are two coefficients.

Another difference is that array formulas are entered using <control>-<shift>-<enter> rather than <enter>. Excel shows the formula surrounded by curly braces ("{" and "}") to indicate that it is an array formula; however, these curly braces are not typed in when the formula is entered.

Once the formula is in place, it can only be modified by highlighting all the cells where it appears. Attempts to modify a single cell in the array cause an error: "You cannot change part of an array." Similarly, removing the formula requires selecting all the cells in the formula and hitting the <delete> key.

**WARNING** When you try to change one cell in an array of cells that has an array function, Excel returns an error. Select the whole array of cells to delete or modify the formula.

## EXCEL FUNCTIONS RETURNING MORE THAN ONE VALUE

Chapter 4 introduced array functions as a way of performing complicated arithmetic on columns of numbers. For instance, array functions can combine the functionality of IF() and SUM().

Array functions not only have the ability to accept arrays of cells as arguments, they can also return arrays of values. In fact, almost any Excel function can be used in this fashion.

Consider a simple situation, where columns A and B each contain 100 numbers and each cell in column C contains a formula that adds the values in the same row in columns A and B. Cells in column C have formulas that look like:

```
=A1+B1
=A2+B2
 . . .
=A100+B100
```

The formula is repeated on every row; typically, the first formula is typed on the first row and then copied down using <control>-D.

An alternative method of expressing this calculation is to use an array function. After selecting the first 100 rows in column C, the array function can be entered as:

```
=A1:A100+B1:B100
```

And then completed using <control>-<shift>-<enter>, rather than just <enter>. Excel recognizes this as an array function and puts curly braces around the formula to indicate this:

```
{=A1:A100+B1:B100}
```

*Continued on next page*

**EXCEL FUNCTIONS RETURNING MORE THAN ONE VALUE** *(CONTINUED)*

There is one function for all 100 rows.

Excel recognizes the array function and figures out that the range of 100 cells in the A column matches the 100 cells in the B column and this also matches the 100 cells in the C column containing the array formula. Because all these ranges match, Excel figures out to iterate over the values in the cell ranges. So the formula is equivalent to `C1` containing `A1+B1` and `C2` containing `A2+B2` and so on to `C100`.

This simple example of an array formula is not particularly useful, because in this case (and many similar cases), the appropriate formula can simply be copied down the column. One advantage of array formulas is that they take up less storage space, because an array formula is stored only once, rather than once for every cell. This can make a difference when there are thousands of rows in the array.

There are a handful of functions that are designed to work as array functions because they return values in arrays of cells. This chapter discusses `LINEST()`, which is one such function. A similar function, `LOGEST()`, is also an array function. It fits an exponential curve to data, rather than a line.

Excel also has functions that support matrix operations. Three of these are array functions that return values in a group of cells: `TRANSPOSE()`, `MINVERSE()`, and `MMULT()`.

## Calculating Expected Values

Although staring at the coefficients and statistics that describe a linear regression model may be interesting, probably the most important thing to do with a model is to apply it to new data. Because `LINEST()` produces coefficients for a line, it is simple enough to apply the model using the formula for a line:

```
=$D$2*A2+$D$3
```

Where `$D$2` and `$D$3` contain the coefficients calculated by `LINEST()`. Notice that the last coefficient is the constant.

Excel offers several different ways of calculating the coefficients. For instance, the formula produced in a chart for the best-fit line is the same as the one calculated by `LINEST()`. In addition, there are several other functions in Excel that can be used to calculate the expected value for a line that has one input variable:

```
=SLOPE(<y-values>, <x-values>)*A2+INTERCEPT(<y-values>, <x-values>)
=FORECAST(A2, <y-values>, <x-values>)
=TREND(<y-values>, <x-values>, A2, TRUE)
```

The first method calculates the slope and intercept separately, using the functions `SLOPE()` and `INTERCEPT()`. The second and third use two functions that are almost equivalent. The only difference is that TREND() takes a final argument specifying whether or not to force the Y-intercept to be zero. The advantage of using the formula explicitly with LINEST() is that it generalizes to more variables. The advantage to the other methods is that all the calculations are in one cell.

The difference between the actual value and the expected value is called the residual. Figure 11-2 showed a plot of the residuals by X-value. For a good model, the points should look random. When there is an evident pattern, such as the residuals getting bigger as the X-values getting bigger or many of the residuals being the same size, then the model is not as good as it could be.

### LINEST() for Logarithmic, Exponential, and Power Curves

The logarithmic, exponential, and power curves are the three types of trend lines that are related to the best-fit line, and these formulas can be approximated using LINEST() as well. The results are not exact, but they are useful.

The key is to transform the X-values, Y-values, or both using logs and exponential functions. To understand how this works, recall how logarithms and exponentiation work. These functions are inverses of each other, so EXP(LN(<any number>)) is the original number. A useful property of logarithms is that the sum of the logs of two numbers is the same as the log of the product of the numbers.

The first example shows how to calculate the coefficients for the logarithmic curve by transforming the variables. The idea is to calculate the best-fit line for the X-values and the exponentiation of the Y-values. The resulting equation is:

```
EXP(Y) = ß₁*X + ß₀
```

By taking the logarithm of both sides, this equation is equivalent to the following:

```
Y = LN(ß₁*X + ß₀)
```

This is the formula for the logarithmic trend line. The coefficients calculated with the transformed Y-values are the same as the coefficients calculated in the chart.

The transformation for the exponential is similar. Instead of using EXP(Y), use LN(Y), so the resulting best-fit equation is for:

```
LN(Y) = ß₁*X + ß₀
```

When "undoing" the log by taking the exponential, the formula becomes:

```
Y = EXP(ß₁*X + ß₀) = EXP(ß₀)*EXP(ß₁*X)
```

This is very similar to the formula for the exponential trend line. The only difference is that the $\beta_0$ coefficient produced this way is the log of the coefficient given in the chart.

Finally, the transformation for the power curve uses the log of both the X-values and the Y-values:

```
LN(Y) = ß₁*LN(X) + ß₀ = LN(EXP(ß₀)*X^ß₁)
```

Undoing the log on both sides produces:

```
Y = EXP(ß₀)*X^ß₁
```

The only difference between these coefficients and the ones in the chart is that the $\beta_0$ calculated using `LINEST()` is the logarithm of the value calculated in the chart.

There is an additional Excel function `LOGEST()` that fits the exponential curve. The coefficients are related to the coefficients in the charts. In this case, the $\beta_0$ is the same, but log of $\beta_1$ is the corresponding coefficient in the chart.

When calculated in any of these methods — in the charts, using `LOGEST()`, or by transforming the original data — the resulting coefficients are only approximations of the correct values. The problem is that transforming the Y-value also changes the distance metric. Hence, what is the "best-fit" for the transformed data may not quite be the "best-fit" on the original data, although the answers are usually similar. However, the transformation method does make it possible to fit these curves in a "quick and dirty" way. To obtain more exact answers in Excel, use the Solver method described later in this chapter.

**TIP** The exponential, logarithmic, and power curve trend lines, as well as `LOGEST()`, are approximately correct. The coefficients are not optimal, but they are close.

# Measuring Goodness of Fit Using $R^2$

How good is the best-fit line? Understanding this is as important as building the model in the first place. Scatter plots of some data looks a lot like a line; in such cases, the best-fit line fits the data quite well. In other cases, the data looks like a big blob, and the line is not very descriptive. Fortunately, there is a simple but somewhat flawed measure of how good the fit is. This is called the $R^2$ value.

## The $R^2$ Value

$R^2$ is a measure of how well the best-fit line fits the data. When the line does not fit the data at all, the value is zero. When the line is a perfect fit, the value is one.

The best way to understand this measure is to see it in action. Figure 11-9 shows four sets of data artificially created to illustrate different scenarios. The two on the top have an $R^2$ value of 0.9; the two on the bottom have an $R^2$ value of 0.1. The two on the left have positive correlation, and the two on the right have negative correlation.

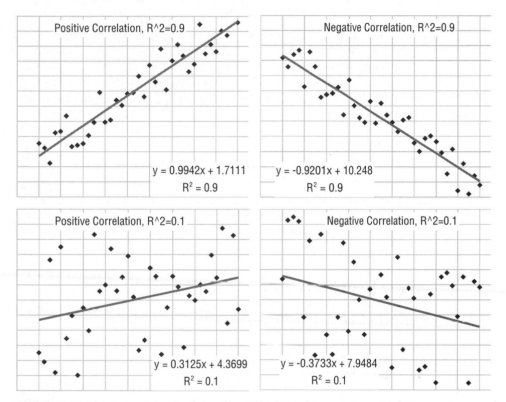

**Figure 11-9:** The four examples here show the different scenarios of positive and negative correlation among the data points, and examples with $R^2$ of 0.1 (loose fit) and 0.9 (tight fit).

Visually, when the $R^2$ value is close to one, the points are quite close to the best-fit line. They differ a little bit here and there, but the best-fit line is doing a good job of capturing the trend in the data. Another way to think about this is that moving or removing one or two points would not have a big impact on the resulting line. When the $R^2$ value is close to one, the model is stable in the sense that changing the values of a few points has a small effect on the best-fit line.

On the other hand, when the $R^2$ value is close to zero, the resulting line does not have much to do with the data. This is probably because the X-values do not contain enough information to estimate the Y-values very well, or because there is enough information, but the relationship is not linear. In this case, changing a few data points could have a big impact on the best-fit line.

So, the $R^2$ tells us how tightly the data points fit around the best-fit line. This information gives a good description of how well the line fits the data.

## Limitations of $R^2$

$R^2$ measures how good the best-fit line (or best-fit curve in other cases) describes the data. It does not tell us whether there is a relationship between the X- and Y-values. Conversely, there may be an obvious relationship, even when the $R^2$ value is zero.

Figure 11-10 shows two such cases. In the chart on the left, the data forms a U-shape. There is an obvious relationship, and yet the best-fit line has an $R^2$ value of zero. This is actually true for any symmetric pattern flipped around a vertical line. Although there is a pattern, it is not captured by the best-fit line.

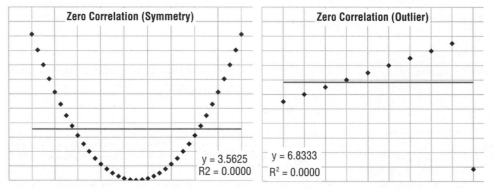

**Figure 11-10:** There may be an obvious relationship even when the $R^2$ value is zero. The relationship is not the best-fit line, however.

The chart on the right side of Figure 11-10 shows what can happen with outliers. For any given set of data, it is possible to add one data point that makes the $R^2$ value be zero. This occurs when the additional data point causes the best-fit line to be horizontal.

These examples are intended to show the limits of $R^2$. When the value is close to one, the regression line explains the data well. When the value is close to zero, the particular regression does not explain what is happening.

**TIP** When the $R^2$ value is close to one, the particular model explains the relationship between the input variables and the target. When the value is close to zero, the particular model does not explain the relationship, but there may be some other relationship between the variables.

## What $R^2$ Really Means

The $R^2$ value has a very specific meaning. It is the ratio of two values. The numerator is the total variation in the Y-values explained by the model. The denominator is the total variation the Y-values. The ratio describes how much of the total variation in the data is explained by the model.

Simple enough. Excel can calculate the value using the CORREL() function. This function calculates the Pearson correlation coefficient, which is called $r$. As its name implies, $R^2$ is the square of $r$.

The $R^2$ value can also be calculated directly from the data. The numerator is the sum of the squares of the differences between the expected Y-values and the average Y-value; that is, the numerator measures how far the expected values are from the overall average. The denominator is the sum of the squares of the differences between the observed Y-values and the average Y-value. The denominator measures how far the observed values are from the overall average.

Table 11-2 walks through the calculation for the example on the right of Figure 11-10 where the $R^2$ value is zero. Columns two and three have the observed Y-value and the expected Y-value. Columns four and six have the differences between these and the average. Columns five and seven have the squares. The $R^2$ value is then the ratio of the sums of these squared values.

**Table 11-2:** Example of an $R^2$ Calculation

| X | Y | YEXP | YEXP-YAVG | (YEXP-YAVG)² | Y-YAVG | (Y-YAVG)² |
|---|---|------|-----------|--------------|--------|-----------|
| 1.0 | 5.5 | 6.83 | 0.0 | 0.0 | -1.3 | 1.78 |
| 2.0 | 6.0 | 6.83 | 0.0 | 0.0 | -0.8 | 0.69 |
| 3.0 | 6.5 | 6.83 | 0.0 | 0.0 | -0.3 | 0.11 |
| 4.0 | 7.0 | 6.83 | 0.0 | 0.0 | 0.2 | 0.03 |
| 5.0 | 7.5 | 6.83 | 0.0 | 0.0 | 0.7 | 0.44 |
| 6.0 | 8.0 | 6.83 | 0.0 | 0.0 | 1.2 | 1.36 |
| 7.0 | 8.5 | 6.83 | 0.0 | 0.0 | 1.7 | 2.78 |
| 8.0 | 9.0 | 6.83 | 0.0 | 0.0 | 2.2 | 4.69 |
| 9.0 | 9.5 | 6.83 | 0.0 | 0.0 | 2.7 | 7.11 |
| 10.0 | 0.8 | 6.83 | 0.0 | 0.0 | -6.0 | 36.00 |
| **Sum** | | 0.0 | 55.00 | | | |
| **$R^2$** | | | 0.0 | | | |

This table explains what happens when the $R^2$ value is zero. The expected value is a constant, and this constant is the average of the Y-values (one of the properties of the best-fit line is that it goes through the point that is the average of the X-values and the average of the Y-values). The $R^2$ value can only be zero when the expected value is always constant. Similarly, when the $R^2$ value is small, the expected values do not vary very much.

Notice that the $R^2$ value can never be negative, because the sums of squares are never negative. However, the Pearson correlation ($r$) can be negative, with the sign indicating whether the relationship is positive correlation (as X gets bigger, Y gets bigger) or negative correlation (as X gets bigger, Y gets smaller).

The $R^2$ value only makes sense for the best-fit line. For an arbitrary line, the value can be greater than one, although this never happens for the best-fit line.

# Direct Calculation of Best-Fit Line Coefficients

This section delves into the arithmetic for calculating the coefficients of the best-fit line. There are two reasons for explaining the arithmetic. Directly calculating the coefficients makes it possible to do the calculation in SQL as well as Excel. More importantly, though, there is a bit of functionality missing from Excel, and this functionality is quite useful. This is the ability to do a weighted best-fit line.

## Doing the Calculation

Calculating the best-fit line means finding the values of the coefficients $ß_1$ and $ß_0$ in the equation for the line. The mathematics needed for the calculation is simple addition, multiplication, and division. There is nothing magical about the calculation itself, although the proof that it works is beyond the scope of this book.

The calculation uses the following easily calculated intermediate results:

- Sx is the sum of the X-values;
- Sy is the sum of the Y-values;
- Sxx is the sum of the squares of the X-values; and,
- Sxy is the sum of each X-value multiplied by the corresponding Y-value.

The first coefficient, $ß_1$, is calculated using the following formula:

```
ß₁ = (n*Sxy - Sx*Sy) / (n*Sxx - Sx*Sx)
```

The second coefficient has the following formula:

```
ß₀ = (Sy/n) - beta1*Sx/n
```

Table 11-3 shows the calculation for the data used in the $R^2$ example. The top portion of this table contains the data points, along with the squares and products needed. The sums and subsequent calculation are at the bottom of the table.

**Table 11-3:** Direct Calculation of the Coefficients

| | X | Y | X^2 | X*Y |
|---|---|---|---|---|
| | 1.0 | 5.5 | 1.00 | 5.5 |
| | 2.0 | 6.0 | 4.00 | 12.0 |
| | 3.0 | 6.5 | 9.00 | 19.5 |
| | 4.0 | 7.0 | 16.00 | 28.0 |
| | 5.0 | 7.5 | 25.00 | 37.5 |
| | 6.0 | 8.0 | 36.00 | 48.0 |
| | 7.0 | 8.5 | 49.00 | 59.5 |
| | 8.0 | 9.0 | 64.00 | 72.0 |
| | 9.0 | 9.5 | 81.00 | 85.5 |
| | 10.0 | 0.8 | 100.00 | 8.3 |
| **VARIABLE** | **SX** | **SY** | **SXX** | **SXY** |
| Sum | 55.0 | 68.3 | 385.0 | 375.8 |
| n*Sxy-Sx*Sy | 0.00 | | | |
| n*Sxx-Sx*Sx | 825.00 | | | |
| Beta1 | 0.0000 | | | |
| Beta0 | 6.8333 | | | |

## Calculating the Best-Fit Line in SQL

Unlike Excel, SQL does not have functions built-in to calculate the coefficients for a linear regression formula. The calculations can be done explicitly, using the preceding formulas. The following query does this for the Minnesota example in Figure 11-7:

```
SELECT (1.0*n*Sxy - Sx*Sy)/(n*Sxx - Sx*Sx) as beta1,
       (1.0*Sy - Sx*(1.0*n*Sxy - Sx*Sy)/(n*Sxx - Sx*Sx))/n as beta0,
       POWER(1.0*n*Sxy - Sx*Sy, 2)/((n*Sxx-Sx*Sx)*(n*Syy-Sy*Sy)) as r2,
       b.*
FROM (SELECT COUNT(*) as n,
             SUM(popcollege) as Sx,
             SUM(hhpubassist) as Sy,
```

*(continued)*

```
            SUM(popcollege*popcollege) as Sxx,
            SUM(popcollege*hhpubassist) as Sxy,
            SUM(hhpubassist*hhpubassist) as Syy
     FROM (SELECT (popedubach+popedumast+popeduprofdoct) as popcollege,
                  hhpubassist
           FROM zipcensus
           WHERE state = 'MN') a
     ) b
```

The innermost subquery calculates of the Sx, Sy, Sxx, Sxy, and Syy (the latter is needed for $R^2$). These are then combined in the next level into the coefficients. This query also calculates the $R^2$ value, using an alternative formula that does the calculation directly, rather than by first calculating expected values.

The values produced by this are in Table 11-4. Although the moving average suggests a relationship, the $R^2$ value suggests that the relationship is not a line.

**Table 11-4:** Coefficients for Relationship College Education and Public Assistance in Minnesota Zip Codes

| COEFFICIENT/STATISTIC | VALUE |
| --- | --- |
| N | 868 |
| Sx | 148.8791 |
| Sy | 27.9332 |
| Sxx | 36.8076 |
| Sxy | 4.2998 |
| Syy | 1.7657 |
| Beta1 | -0.0436 |
| Beta0 | 0.0397 |
| $R^2$ | 0.0247 |

## Price Elasticity

Price elasticity is the economic notion that product prices and product sales are inversely related to each other. As prices go up, sales go down, and vice versa. In practice, price elasticity provides information about the impact of raising or lowering prices. Although the economic relationship is approximate, and sometimes quite weak, price elasticity is useful for what-if analyses that investigate the effects of changing prices.

The subject of price elasticity opens up the subject of prices in general. Typically, a product has a full price. Customers may pay the full price, or they may pay a discounted price for a variety of reasons — the item may be on sale, the customer may have a loyalty relationship with an associated discount, the item may be bundled with other products, the customer may have a group discount, and so on.

This section starts by investigating prices, first by product group and then more specifically for books whose full price is $20. It then shows how basic regression analysis can be used to estimate elasticity effects. These effects are only approximate, because demand is based on more than pricing (what competitors are doing, marketing programs, and so on). Even so, regression analysis sheds some light on the subject.

### Price Frequency

Visualizing the relationship between sales volume and price is a good place to start. A price frequency chart shows how often products are sold at a given price. The horizontal axis is the price; the vertical axis is the frequency, so each point shows the number of products sold at a particular price. A pricing frequency chart might use the full price, the average price, or a bar showing the range of prices.

Figure 11-11 shows a full price frequency chart broken out by product groups. Because the range of values is so large and values are always positive, both axes use a logarithmic scale. The seven symbols represent the seven product groups of interest. Each point in the chart is an instance of products in the product group having a particular full price.

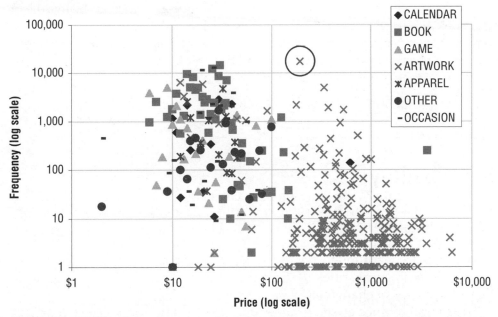

**Figure 11-11:** This pricing frequency chart shows the relationship between sales volume and full price by product group.

As a whole, the chart gives an idea of the relationship between full prices, product groups, and demand. The circled point at the top, for instance, indicates that there are 17,517 orders that contain ARTWORK products whose full price is $195. Although not shown on the chart, this point actually corresponds to 670 different products in the product table, all in the ARTWORK group and all having the same full price.

The pricing frequency chart has other interesting information. The most commonly sold items are ARTWORK products having a full price of $195 (the circled point is the highest point in the chart). Although relatively expensive, the ARTWORK products selling at this price are inexpensive relative to other ARTWORK products. The products in this category typically cost more, as seen by the fact that the ARTWORK products (labeled with "x"s) are to the right of the highlighted marker.

Almost all the expensive products are ARTWORK, with the exception of one BOOK and one CALENDAR (and these may be examples of misclassification). On the other hand, the BOOK group is quite well represented as having many products selling in more than one thousand orders — these are the solid squares on the upper left of the chart. Books are also generally moderately priced. The least expensive products are further to the left. These include many GAMES and CALENDARS. FREEBIES, which are by definition free, are not included in the chart.

The pricing frequency chart is a good way to visualize the relationship between pricing and sales. With respect to price elasticity, its use is limited. The best selling books, for instance, have a price point pretty much in the middle of the book prices. Books that are more expensive sell fewer copies. But also, books that are less expensive sell fewer copies. Clearly and unsurprisingly, something besides price is important for book sales.

The following query gathers the data for the chart:

```
SELECT productgroupname, fullprice, COUNT(*)
FROM orderline ol JOIN product p ON ol.productid = p.productid
WHERE fullprice > 0
GROUP BY productgroupname, fullprice
ORDER BY 3 DESC
```

This query uses the Orderline table to calculate the total number of orders and the Product table to get the FULLPRICE. This query counts the number of lines in orders, which is reasonable. Another possibility would be to count the number of units.

The results are broken out by product group, because this is a natural way to compare products. To create the chart, there is a separate column for each product group. The FULLPRICE is placed in the appropriate column for each row, with NA() going in the other columns. A scatter plot is created from the pivoted data.

## Price Frequency for $20 Books

Seeing the range of prices and sales volumes is interesting. For elasticity, though, it is better to look at a single product or group of similar products. This section investigates products in the BOOK category whose full price is $20. Even though the full price is $20, these are often discounted, using marketing techniques such as coupons, clearance offers, product bundles, and customer loyalty discounts.

Price elasticity suggests that when prices are lower, there should be more orders and when prices are higher, there should be fewer orders. Of course, this is economic theory, and a lot of things get in the way in the real world. Prices lower than the full price may indicate special promotions for the product that further increase demand, beyond the change in price. Or, low prices may indicate inventory clearance sales for the last few copies of otherwise popular books. In such a case, demand might be high, but there are few sales because there is insufficient inventory to fulfill all demand.

A good summary for this investigation is prices and sales by month:

- The average price of $20 full-price books sold in the month.
- The total units sold in the month for these products.

Just to be clear, the full price is $20, but customers may be getting a discount of one form or another. Also, a given book always has the same full price, which is in the Product table, not the Orders table. In the real world, products may have different full prices at different times. If this is the case, the Orders table should include the full price as well as the price the customer pays.

The following query does this summarization:

```
SELECT YEAR(orderdate) as year, MONTH(orderdate) as mon,
       COUNT(DISTINCT ol.productid) as numprods,
       AVG(unitprice) as avgprice, SUM(ol.numunits) as numunits
FROM orders o JOIN orderline ol ON o.orderid = ol.orderid JOIN
     (SELECT *
      FROM product
      WHERE productgroupname = 'BOOK' and fullprice = 20) p
     ON ol.productid = p.productid
GROUP BY YEAR(orderdate), MONTH(orderdate)
ORDER BY 1, 2
```

The scatter plot in Figure 11-12 shows the results, with the horizontal axis being the price in the month and the vertical axis being the total units sold. Each point in the scatter plot is the summary of one month of data for $20 books. The chart does not show which point corresponds to which month, because the purpose is to look at the relationship between average price and volume, not to see trends over time.

In most months, the books have an average price over $17, as seen by the prevalence of points on the lower right. During these months, the sales are often on the low side, particularly as the average increases toward $20. This does suggest a relationship between price and demand. During some months, the average price is absurdly low, less than $10, suggesting that many $20 books are sometimes sold at a hefty discount.

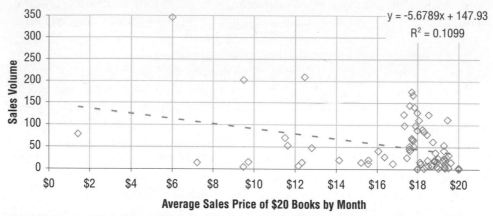

**Figure 11-12:** This scatter plot shows the actual prices of books whose full price is $20. Each point is the average price by month and the average sales by month.

The best-fit line is also shown in the chart. This line is not a particularly good fit, but it does suggest that as the price increases, demand decreases. The slope of the line is minus 5.7, which means that for every dollar increase in price, the demand decreases by 5.7 units per month.

There is no a priori reason to believe that the relationship is a simple line, which implies that more sophisticated models might be needed. On the other hand, a line produces a very handy number — minus 5.7 — that can be used to direct pricing and discounting efforts.

One complication is the fact that there are different numbers of products for sale at that price in any given month, and there are different amounts of inventory for those products. When inventory is an issue, demand may be represented by customers wanting to purchase the product, even if they cannot because there is insufficient inventory. The relationship between price and demand is interesting to investigate; it is also related to many other factors that can make it challenging to tease out a particular formula.

### Price Elasticity Model in SQL

The coefficients for the line can also be calculated in SQL. The following query performs the same analysis, finding the relationship between the price of $20 full-price books and the volume of sales on a monthly basis:

```
SELECT (1.0*n*Sxy - Sx*Sy)/(n*Sxx - Sx*Sx) as beta1,
       (1.0*Sy - Sx*(1.0*n*Sxy - Sx*Sy)/(n*Sxx - Sx*Sx))/n as beta0,
```

```
            POWER(1.0*n*Sxy - Sx*Sy, 2)/((n*Sxx-Sx*Sx)*(n*Syy-Sy*Sy)) as R2
FROM (SELECT COUNT(*) as n,
             SUM(x) as Sx,
             SUM(y) as Sy,
             SUM(x*x) as Sxx,
             SUM(x*y) as Sxy,
             SUM(y*y) as Syy
      FROM (SELECT YEAR(orderdate) as year, MONTH(orderdate) as mon,
                   1.0*SUM(ol.numunits) as y,
                   AVG(unitprice) as x
            FROM orders o JOIN orderline ol ON o.orderid = ol.orderid JOIN
                 (SELECT *
                  FROM product
                  WHERE productgroupname = 'BOOK' and fullprice = 20
                 ) p
                 ON ol.productid = p.productid
            GROUP BY YEAR(orderdate), MONTH(orderdate)
           ) a
     ) b
```

The innermost query summarizes the appropriate orders by month. Subquery A is basically the same query used for the scatter plot, with minor cosmetic differences. One is that the columns are named X and Y, which recognizes the roles that these columns play in the calculation of the coefficients. Also, the Y-value is multiplied by 1.0 so it is not treated as an integer in the calculation. Reassuringly, this SQL calculates the same coefficients as the best-fit line in Excel's charts.

## Price Elasticity Average Value Chart

Price elasticity models estimate the amount of demand at a given price point. As discussed in the previous chapter, the average value chart is a good way to evaluate a model whose target is numeric. This chart divides the expected number of sales into ten deciles, and then shows the actual number of sales and the expected number of sales in each group. Figure 11-13 shows the average value chart corresponding to the best-fit line for estimating demand based on price.

The average value chart shows that the model is not working well (which we already suspected because of the low $R^2$ value). The expected number of sales decreases as the deciles increase, with the expected number being rather flat after the first three deciles. However, the actual sales start high, dip, then go up again. The top two deciles also have much lower average prices than the rest of the deciles ($8.31 and $13.77 versus over $17 in the remaining months). This suggests that in months when the average prices are very low, something is going on besides just the change in price.

A big reason why the model has a low $R^2$ value is because of deciles 4 and 5, where the actual volume is much larger than the expected volume (or alternatively that demand for the first three deciles is much lower than it should be). Despite the low $R^2$ value, there does seem to be a relationship between price and volume, albeit with exceptions. The model results suggest that pricing discounts on the books are not the only factor driving sales. Some discounts are intended to drive sales of popular books even higher. Other discounts are intended to sell the last copies of books that happen to still be in stock. When it comes to estimating sales volume, price is only one factor affecting the volume of sales.

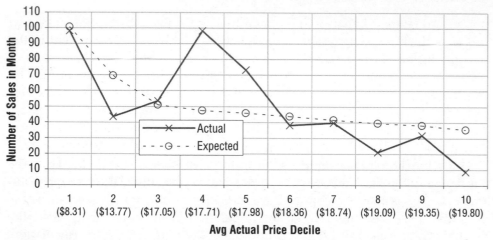

**Figure 11-13:** This average value chart shows the relationship between the expected number of sales and the actual number of sales by sales price for books whose full price is $20.

## Weighted Linear Regression

Bubble charts are a typical way to visualize summarized data. The data is located on the chart according to X- and Y-values, and the size of each bubble is the frequency count. Alas, when Excel calculates the best-fit line in a bubble chart, it does not take into account the sizes of bubbles. The resulting best-fit line does a poor job showing trends in the data.

> **WARNING** When Excel calculates best-fit lines in bubble charts, it does not take the size of the groups into account. This can significantly skew the resulting line. The desired line requires doing a weighted linear regression.

The way to solve this problem is by using a technique called weighted linear regression, which takes the sizes of the bubbles into account. Unfortunately, this capability is not built into Excel directly. There are two ways to do the calculation. One is to apply the formulas from the previous section, adjusting the various intermediate sums for the frequencies. The other uses special function-ality in Excel called Solver, which is a general-purpose tool that can be used for this specific need.

This section starts with a basic business problem where weighted linear regression is needed. It then discusses various ways to address the problem in Excel and SQL.

## Customer Stops during the First Year

Is there a relationship between the monthly fee (in the subscription data) and the stops during the first year? The hypothesis is that each increment in the monthly fee has an effect on the overall stop rate.

The bubble chart in Figure 11-14 shows the monthly fee on the horizontal axis and the proportion of customers who stop during the first year on the vertical axis. The size of each bubble is the number of customers in the group. Many bubbles are so small that they do not appear in the chart. For instance, there are two customers who started with a monthly fee of $3, and one of them stopped. However, they are not on the chart because a bubble for two cus-tomers is simply too small to see on a chart where the largest bubbles represent hundreds of thousands of customers.

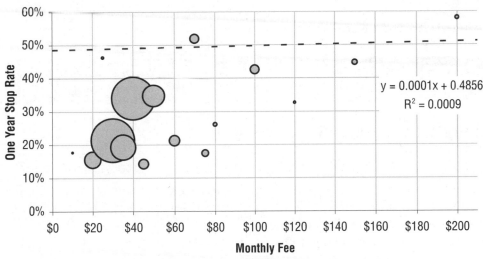

**Figure 11-14:** This bubble chart shows the relationship between the initial monthly fee (horizontal axis) and the stop rate during the first year for customers who started in 2004 and 2005. The size of the bubble is the number of customers.

The chart itself includes the best-fit line for the data, as produced in Excel. The best-fit line is almost horizontal, suggesting that there is almost no rela-tionship between the monthly fee and the stop rate. The lack of relationship is corroborated by the miniscule $R^2$ value, which suggests that any relationship that does exist is not linear.

The following query provides the data for the bubble chart:

```
SELECT monthly_fee,
       AVG(CASE WHEN tenure < 364 AND stop_type IS NOT NULL THEN 1.0
              ELSE 0 END) as stoprate,
       COUNT(*) as numsubs
FROM subs
WHERE start_date BETWEEN '2004-01-01' and '2005-12-31'
GROUP BY monthly_fee
ORDER BY 1
```

This query simply aggregates all the customers who started in 2004 and 2005, keeping track of those who stopped during the first year.

## Weighted Best Fit

Table 11-5 shows the data used to create the bubble chart. This table highlights the fact that most of the groups are quite small. Over half have fewer than three hundred customers, and these do not even show up on the chart. When Excel calculates the best-fit line, it does not take into account the size of the bubbles, so these invisible points are worth as much as the visible ones, which have 99.9% of the customers. This is true both for the best-fit line in the charts and for the LINEST() function.

**Table 11-5:** First Year Stop Rate and Count by Initial Monthly Fee

| MON-THLY FEE | STOP RATE | # SUB-SCRI-BERS | MON-THLY FEE | STOP RATE | # SUB-SCRI-BERS | MON-THLY FEE | STOP RATE | # SUB-SCRI-BERS |
|---|---|---|---|---|---|---|---|---|
| $0 | 100% | 1 | $25 | 46% | 2,901 | $80 | 26% | 7,903 |
| $7 | 0% | 1 | $27 | 57% | 7 | $90 | 32% | 79 |
| $10 | 18% | 1,296 | $30 | 21% | 803,481 | $100 | 43% | 34,510 |
| $12 | 100% | 1 | $35 | 19% | 276,166 | $117 | 0% | 1 |
| $13 | 50% | 2 | $37 | 100% | 1 | $120 | 33% | 3,106 |
| $15 | 89% | 38 | $40 | 34% | 797,629 | $130 | 81% | 26 |
| $16 | 100% | 1 | $45 | 14% | 39,930 | $150 | 45% | 11,557 |
| $18 | 50% | 2 | $50 | 35% | 193,917 | $160 | 100% | 4 |
| $19 | 100% | 3 | $60 | 21% | 48,266 | $200 | 58% | 6,117 |
| $20 | 15% | 120,785 | $70 | 52% | 35,379 | $300 | 10% | 241 |
| $22 | 67% | 9 | $75 | 17% | 22,160 | $360 | 100% | 6 |

This is a problem, because some bubbles are clearly more important than others. One approach is to filter the data, and choose only the bubbles that exceed a certain size. To do this, select the cells and turn on filtering using the Data ⇨ Filter ⇨ AutoFilter menu option (or the sequence of three keys, `<alt>-D <alt>-F <alt>-F`). When the filter appears, apply a "(Custom…)" filter in the NUMSUBS column to select the rows that have a count greater than, say, 1000. When the data is filtered, the chart automatically updates both the data and the best-fit line. The resulting $R^2$ value increases to 0.4088, suggesting that there is a relationship between monthly fee and surviving the first year.

**TIP** When filtering rows of data that have an associated chart on the same worksheet, be sure that the chart is either above or below the data. Otherwise, the filters might reduce the height of the chart, or cause it to disappear altogether.

Using filters is an ad hoc approach, because it depends on choosing an arbitrary threshold. A better approach is to use all the data to calculate a weighted best-fit line. Before diving into the calculations, the weighted best-fit is used when data is summarized, and the groups have different sizes. This is a common occurrence, particularly when summarizing data from large databases and analyzing the data in Excel.

The calculations for the weighted best-fit is quite similar to the calculations for the best-fit line. The only difference is that the formulas take the weights into account when calculating the various intermediate sums.

Table 11-6 shows the calculation of $\beta_1$, $\beta_0$, and $R^2$ for the best-fit line with and without weights. The calculation of N, the total number of points, shows the difference. In the unweighted case, there are 33 points, because there are 33 different values of monthly fee. These groups correspond to 2.4 million customers, which is the value of N using the weights. The 1,296 customers who initially paid $10 and have a stop rate of 17.6% are instead treated as 1,296 rows with the same information.

**Table 11-6:** Comparison of Calculations with and without Weights

| COEFFICIENT/STATISTIC | UNWEIGHTED | WEIGHTED |
| --- | --- | --- |
| N | 33.00 | 2,405,526.00 |
| Sx | 2,453.00 | 94,203,540.00 |
| Sy | 16.33 | 647,635.68 |
| Sxx | 404,799.00 | 4,394,117,810.00 |
| Sxy | 1,241.02 | 27,310,559.03 |
| Syy | 11.68 | 190,438.85 |

*Continued on next page*

**Table 11-6** *(continued)*

| COEFFICIENT/STATISTIC | UNWEIGHTED | WEIGHTED |
|:---:|:---:|:---:|
| Beta1 | 0.00 | 0.00 |
| Beta0 | 0.49 | 0.16 |
| $R^2$ | 0.0009 | 0.3349 |

The resulting best-fit line now has the following characteristics:

- slope = 0.0028
- intercept = 0.2665
- $R^2$ = 0.3349

The slope indicates that for each dollar that the monthly fee increases, the stop rate increases by 0.28%. Without the weighting, the increase was a negligible 0.01%. The $R^2$ value suggests that the pattern is of medium strength, not dominant, but potentially informative. Without the weights there was no discernible pattern.

So, based on this analysis, if the company were to raise the monthly fee by $10 for new customers, it would expect an additional 2.8% of them to leave during the first year. Whether this is financially viable depends on the business needs of the company.

## Weighted Best-Fit Line in a Chart

Being able to plot the weighted best-fit line in a chart is useful, even though Excel's charts do not support this functionality directly. We have to trick the software into doing what we want.

The idea is to insert another series in the chart corresponding to the best-fit line, add the line for the series, and make the new series invisible so only the line is visible:

1. For each monthly fee, apply the weighted best-fit formula to get the expected value.

2. Add a new data series to the chart with the monthly fee and the expected value. Because this is a bubble chart, be sure to include a size for the bubbles as well.

3. Add the trend line for the new monthly fee series.

4. Format the series so it is invisible, either making the pattern and area be transparent or by making the width of the bubbles equal to zero.

Figure 11-15 shows the original data with the two trend lines. Clearly, the sloping trend line that takes into account the sizes of the bubbles does a better job of capturing the information in the chart.

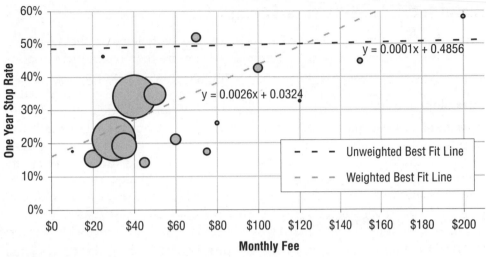

**Figure 11-15:** The weighted best-fit line does a much better job of capturing the patterns in the data points.

## Weighted Best-Fit in SQL

The following query uses the same ideas to calculate the coefficients and $R^2$ value directly in SQL for a weighted linear regression:

```sql
SELECT (1.0*n*Sxy - Sx*Sy)/(n*Sxx - Sx*Sx) as beta1,
       (1.0*Sy - Sx*(1.0*n*Sxy - Sx*Sy)/(n*Sxx - Sx*Sx))/n as beta0,
       (POWER(1.0*n*Sxy - Sx*Sy, 2)/((n*Sxx-Sx*Sx)*(n*Syy-Sy*Sy))
       )as Rsquare
FROM (SELECT SUM(cnt) as n,
             SUM(x*cnt) as Sx,
             SUM(y*cnt) as Sy,
             SUM(x*x*cnt) as Sxx,
             SUM(x*y*cnt) as Sxy,
             SUM(y*y*cnt) as Syy
      FROM (SELECT monthly_fee as x,
                   AVG(CASE WHEN tenure < 364 THEN 1.0 ELSE 0 END) as y,
                   COUNT(*) as cnt
            FROM subs
            WHERE start_date BETWEEN '2004-01-01' and '2005-12-31'
            GROUP BY monthly_fee) a
     ) b
```

The only difference between this query and the unweighted query is the calculation of the intermediate values in the middle subquery. This query returns the same results at the Excel calculation.

## Weighted Best-Fit Using Solver

Using the formulas is one way to calculate the coefficients of the weighted best-fit line. However, this does not work with more than one input variable, not to mention the fact that remembering the formulas is onerous.

This section discusses an alternative approach using an Excel add-in called Solver (this is included for free with Excel). The fundamental idea behind Solver is to set up a spreadsheet model, where certain cells are inputs and one cell is an output. Solver then finds the right set of inputs to obtain the desired output — very powerful functionality. The question is how to set up a spreadsheet model that does the weighted best-fit line.

### The Weighted Best-Fit Line

So far, this chapter has approached the problem of finding the coefficients for a best-fit line by applying complicated mathematical formulas. However, a spreadsheet could calculate the sum of the squares of the distances between the data points and any given line. The spreadsheet would have two input cells for the coefficients. The distance from each point to the line can be calculated, and the total error added up in another cell. By trying out different values for the coefficients, we could manually attempt to minimize the total error.

Such a spreadsheet is an example of a spreadsheet model. As with the models discussed in this chapter and the previous chapter, it takes inputs (the coefficients in the input cells) and calculates an output (the total error value). What happens in between depends on the data and calculations in the spreadsheet.

Setting up a spreadsheet model for the basic best-fit line is not useful, because there are built-in functions that do exactly what is needed. However, no such functions exist for the weighted version, making this a better example. Figure 11-16 shows a spreadsheet that contains the grouped data with frequency counts, various columns that do calculations, two cells for input (I3 and I4), and one that has the error (I5).

The first of the additional columns contains the expected value, which is calculated using the input cells:

```
=<beta1>*<monthly_fee>+<beta0>
```

The next column has the error, which is the absolute value of difference between the expected value and the actual value, and the column after that, the error squared. The final column calculates the square of the error times the count. The total error cell contains the sum of these squares, which is what the best-fit line minimizes.

| | G | H | I | J | K | L | M |
|---|---|---|---|---|---|---|---|
| 3 | INPUT | Beta1 | 0.002763607807 | | | | |
| 4 | INPUT | Beta0 | 0.161001811113 | | | | |
| 5 | OUTPUT | Sum Dist^2 | =SUM(M9:M41) | | | | |
| 6 | | | | | | | |
| 7 | | | FROM SQL | | | | |
| 8 | Monthly Fee | Stop Rate | Count | Expected | Error | Squared | Weighted |
| 9 | 0 | 1 | 1 | =G9*$I$3+$I$4 | =ABS(H9-J9) | =K9*K9 | =L9*I9 |
| 10 | 7 | 0 | 1 | =G10*$I$3+$I$4 | =ABS(H10-J10) | =K10*K10 | =L10*I10 |
| 11 | 10 | 0.175925 | 1296 | =G11*$I$3+$I$4 | =ABS(H11-J11) | =K11*K11 | =L11*I11 |
| 12 | 12 | 1 | 1 | =G12*$I$3+$I$4 | =ABS(H12-J12) | =K12*K12 | =L12*I12 |
| 13 | 13 | 0.5 | 2 | =G13*$I$3+$I$4 | =ABS(H13-J13) | =K13*K13 | =L13*I13 |
| 14 | 15 | 0.894736 | 38 | =G14*$I$3+$I$4 | =ABS(H14-J14) | =K14*K14 | =L14*I14 |
| 15 | 16 | 1 | 1 | =G15*$I$3+$I$4 | =ABS(H15-J15) | =K15*K15 | =L15*I15 |
| 16 | 18 | 0.5 | 2 | =G16*$I$3+$I$4 | =ABS(H16-J16) | =K16*K16 | =L16*I16 |
| 17 | 19 | 1 | 3 | =G17*$I$3+$I$4 | =ABS(H17-J17) | =K17*K17 | =L17*I17 |
| 18 | 20 | 0.153769 | 120785 | =G18*$I$3+$I$4 | =ABS(H18-J18) | =K18*K18 | =L18*I18 |
| 19 | 22 | 0.666666 | 9 | =G19*$I$3+$I$4 | =ABS(H19-J19) | =K19*K19 | =L19*I19 |

**Figure 11-16:** This is a spreadsheet model for calculating the error between a given line and the data points (taking the weight into account).

Modifying the values in cells I3 and I4 changes the error value. One way to minimize the error is to manually try different combinations of values. Because there are two values, this can be tricky. However, the spreadsheet recalculates very quickly and there are only two cells, so a person can get reasonably close to the minimum value.

### Solver Is Better Than Guessing

Solver uses the same spreadsheet model. However, instead of guessing the values of the coefficients that minimize the error, Solver finds the coefficients automatically. Although Solver comes with Excel, the functionality is not automatically available. To load Solver into Excel, use the menu item Tools ⇨ AddIns (<alt>-T <alt>-I), click "Solver," and then "OK." Once installed, Solver is available under the menu Tools ⇨ Solver or using the keys strokes <alt>-T then <alt>-V.

The "Solver Parameters" dialog box, shown in Figure 11-17, has several prompts for information. At the top is the entry "Set Target Cell" to specify the target cell. The goal can be to minimize, maximize, or to set it to a particular value.

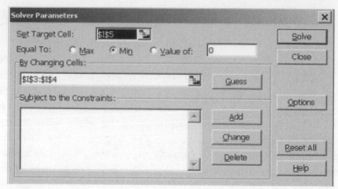

**Figure 11-17:** The "Solver Parameters" dialog box has areas for the cell to optimize, the type of optimization, the cells whose values can change, and any constraints on the problem.

The list of cells that Solver can change is in the area called "By Changing Cells." In addition, Solver allows you to set constraints on the cells, such as requiring that all values be positive or in some range. This is not functionality needed for finding the weighted best-fit line.

Clicking "Solve" causes Excel to try many different combinations of coefficients looking for the optimal value. In this case, the problem is not particularly complicated, and Solver finds the right solution quickly, placing the optimal coefficients in the input cells. Solver finds the best-fit line using the spreadsheet model. The aside "Discussion of Solver" discusses this add-in in a bit more detail.

## More Than One Input Variable

Linear regression has been introduced using the best-fit line, which has one input and one target variable. In practice, there is usually more than one possible input variable. This section touches on the topic. So-called *multiple regression* pushes the abilities of SQL. In general, such problems are better solved with statistics tools rather than Excel.

### Multiple Regression in Excel

The function LINEST() can take more than one input column, although the input columns do need to be adjacent. The function call is the same, except for the size of the array containing the returned values. The width of this array should be the number of different input variables plus one. The array should always have five rows.

## DISCUSSION OF SOLVER

Solver is an add-in developed by the company Frontline Systems (www.solver.com). A basic version of Solver has been bundled with Excel since 1991. More advanced versions are offered by Frontline Systems.

The idea of finding the optimal value is to find the coefficients that minimize or maximize some *objective function*. For our purposes, the objective function simply means the value in the target cell, such as the example in the text for the total error for the weighted best-fit line. The objective function can be quite complicated, because it can depend directly on the input cells or there could be many intermediate calculations, using other cells in the spreadsheet.

The weighted best-fit line is a particularly simple type of problem to solve, because it is in a class called convex conic quadratics. The simplest example of this, a parabola, has a single minimum value, and by analyzing information at any point along the curve, it is possible to determine whether the minimum is to the left or right of that point. Solver guesses the solution and then refines the guess, getting closer and closer each time.

Making even small changes to the spreadsheet model can change the structure of the problem. So, changing the objective function to something more complicated could have a big impact on the efficiency of the algorithm. A small change could result in Solver taking much more time to find the optimal solution.

The Solver software is quite powerful. It can detect when a problem is easy to solve and solve it using the appropriate methods. More complicated problems have more complicated methods, which can take longer to solve.

Finding the coefficients for a best-fit line is only a taste of what Solver can do. One interesting class of problems is resource allocation. This occurs when there are many constraints and the goal is to maximize profit. An example of this is dividing the marketing budget to bring in new customers in various channels. Different channels have different costs for acquiring customers. The customers who come in may behave differently, and different times of year may have better response or different mixes, and each channel has a maximum or minimum capacity. It is possible to set up a spreadsheet that, given a mix of customers, is able to calculate the profit. Then, the overall profit can be maximized using Solver. Of course, the result is only as good as the assumptions going into the worksheet model, and these assumptions are only estimates about what might happen in the future.

This type of resource allocation problem is called a linear programming problem (for technical reasons; it is not related to linear regression), and Solver knows how to solve such problems quite efficiently.

## Getting the Data

In the orders data, there is a relationship between the penetration of a zip code and the average household income, the proportion college educated, and the proportion of people on public assistance. Such relationships can be investigated further using multiple regression.

This example uses zip codes that have more than one thousand households and that have at least one order. The query calculates the variables needed for this example:

```
SELECT o.zipcode, numorders * 1.0/hh as pen,
       hhmedincome, hhpubassist, pcoll
FROM (SELECT zc.*, (popedubach + popedumast + popeduprofdoct) as pcoll
     FROM zipcensus zc) zc JOIN
     (SELECT zipcode, COUNT(*) as numorders
     FROM orders o
     GROUP BY zipcode) o
    ON zc.zipcode = o.zipcode
WHERE hh >= 1000
```

The returned data has 9,947 rows. The second column PEN is the Y-value. The last three columns are X-values.

## Investigating Each Variable Separately

A good first step is to investigate each of the variables one-by-one. The best-fit-line and $R^2$ values for each variable can be calculated using the functions SLOPE(), INTERCEPT(), and CORREL().

Table 11-7 shows this information. There are several things to note about these values. First, the best variable is the proportion of the zip code in college. This is the best because it has the highest $R^2$ value. This variable does a better job than the others in predicting product penetration.

**Table 11-7:** Relationship between Three Variables Individually and Product Penetration

|  | SLOPE | INTERCEPT | R-SQUARE |
|---|---|---|---|
| **HH Median Income** | 0.0000 | -0.00436 | 0.2406 |
| **% HH On Public Assistance** | -0.0324 | 0.00347 | 0.0325 |
| **College Percent** | 0.0186 | -0.00268 | 0.2751 |

The signs of the slope are interesting. Positive slope means that as the input value increases, the target value increases. So, penetration increases as median income goes up and as the proportion who graduated college goes up. On the other hand, penetration decreases as a greater proportion of the population is on public assistance.

It would seem that variables with larger slope (steeper lines) would have a bigger impact on the target. Unfortunately, the sizes of the slope do not provide any information about which variables are better or which have a bigger impact on the target. The reason is that the original variables have very different ranges. The median income is measured in thousands of dollars, so its coefficient is going to be very close to zero. The other two variables are proportions which vary between zero and one, so their coefficients are higher.

This is unfortunate, because it is useful to know which variable is having a greater effect on the target. Standardizing the inputs fixes this problem. As explained in Chapter 3, standardizing variables calculates the number of standard deviations that a value is from the average, and this is easily done in Excel, using a formula such as:

```
=(A1 - AVERAGE($A$1:$A9947)/STDEV($A$1:$A9947)
```

This formula is then copied down the column to get standardized value for all inputs.

**TIP** If you want to compare the effects of a variable on the target (in a linear regression), standardize the input value before calculating the coefficients.

Table 11-8 shows the results with the standardized values. The $R^2$ values remain the same, although the slopes and intercepts have changed. Standardizing the inputs has no impact on how good the resulting line is.

**Table 11-8:** Relationship between Standardized Values and Product Penetration

| | SLOPE | INTERCEPT | R-SQUARE |
|---|---|---|---|
| **HH Median Income** | 0.0025 | 0.0025 | 0.2406 |
| **% HH On Public Assistance** | -0.0010 | 0.0025 | 0.0325 |
| **College Percent** | 0.0029 | 0.0025 | 0.2751 |

The constant in the formula ($\beta_0$) is the same for all three formulas. This is not a coincidence. When doing the linear regression on standardized input values, the constant is always the average of the Y-values. The converse is not true, however. If the intercept happens to be the average, this does not mean that the X-values are standardized.

The bigger the slope (either positive or negative) on the standardized values, the bigger the impact on the predicted penetration.

## Building a Model with Three Input Variables

Building a model with all three input variables is as easy as building a model with one, except for one thing. The function LINEST() is an array function that returns values in an array of cells. The number of columns in this array is one more than the number of variables in the model. The number of rows is always five.

The call to LINEST() looks like:

```
=LINEST('T11-07'!D14:D9960, 'T11-07'!E14:G9960, TRUE, TRUE)
```

Remember, this is an array function. Because there are three input variables (in columns E, F, and G), the function needs to be entered into an array of four cells across and five cells down, as shown in the screen shot in Figure 11-18. All the cells in the array have the same formula, shown in the formula bar. The curly braces are not part of the formula; Excel includes them to indicate that the formula is an array formula.

| B3 | ▾ | *fx* {=LINEST('T11-07'!$D$14:$D$9960, 'T11-07'!$E$14:$G$9960, TRUE, TRUE)} | | | |
|---|---|---|---|---|---|
| | B | | C | D | E |
| 2 | CollegeP | | % Pub Assist | HH Med Inc | Intercept |
| 3 | =LINEST('T11-07'!$D$14:$D$9960, 'T11-07'!$E$14:$G$9960, TRUE, TRUE) | | =LINEST('T11- | =LINEST('T11 | =LINEST('T11 |
| 4 | =LINEST('T11-07'!$D$14:$D$9960, 'T11-07'!$E$14:$G$9960, TRUE, TRUE) | | =LINEST('T11- | =LINEST('T11 | =LINEST('T11 |
| 5 | =LINEST('T11-07'!$D$14:$D$9960, 'T11-07'!$E$14:$G$9960, TRUE, TRUE) | | =LINEST('T11- | =LINEST('T11 | =LINEST('T11 |
| 6 | =LINEST('T11-07'!$D$14:$D$9960, 'T11-07'!$E$14:$G$9960, TRUE, TRUE) | | =LINEST('T11- | =LINEST('T11 | =LINEST('T11 |
| 7 | =LINEST('T11-07'!$D$14:$D$9960, 'T11-07'!$E$14:$G$9960, TRUE, TRUE) | | =LINEST('T11- | =LINEST('T11 | =LINEST('T11 |

**Figure 11-18:** The call to LINEST() with three input columns requires entering the formula in an array four columns wide and five rows down.

How does this model compare to the models with a single variable? The $R^2$ value is in the middle cell in the first column. The value is higher, so by that measure the model is better. Of course, the $R^2$ value is only 0.32, which is not a big increase over the best single variable model, which had an $R^2$ value of 0.275. Adding new variables may produce a model that is only marginally better.

The coefficients for this model are all positive, which is interesting. When used in the model alone, the coefficient for the proportion of the population on public assistance is negative, meaning that it is negatively correlated with penetration. With other variables in the model, this variable becomes positively correlated. Whatever else, this illustrates that the coefficients can change dramatically as new variables are added into the regression. How and why does this happen?

This is an important question. The answer is at once simple and rather profound. The simple answer is that the other variables overcompensate for the proportion of the population on public assistance. That is, all the variables are trying to determine what makes a good zip code for penetration, and it seems to be wealthier, better educated zip codes. The other variables do a better job of finding these, so when they are included, the effect of the public assistance variable changes dramatically.

More formally, the mathematics of multiple regression assume that the variables are independent. This has a specific meaning. It means that the correlation coefficient — the CORREL() function in Excel — is zero (or very close to zero) for any two input variables. The correlation between the household median income and the proportion of the population on public assistance is −0.55. It is negative because as one goes up the other goes down (wealthier people tend to have fewer neighbors on public assistance). The correlation is rather strong, so the variables are somewhat redundant.

In fact, when doing linear regression, it is easy to forget the fact that the technique works best when the variables are independent. This is because, in practice, input variables are rarely independent unless we make them so. One way of doing that is by using a technique called *principal components*, which is beyond the scope of this book, although it is included in many statistics packages.

## Using Solver for Multiple Regression

Just as Solver was used for weighted regression, Solver can also be used for multiple regression. The coefficients are entered into one area of the spreadsheet. The spreadsheet calculates the expected values and total error. Solver can be used to minimize the total error to find the optimal coefficients.

There are several reasons why this is useful. First, it makes it easy to create more complicated expressions, such as ones using logarithms, or exponentials, or other fancy mathematical functions. Second, using Solver makes it possible to incorporate weights, which is just as useful for multiple regression as for the one-input variety.

The third reason is more esoteric but perhaps the most important. The methods that Excel uses to calculate the values returned by LINEST() are numerically unstable. This means that when intermediate values get very large, the results are prone to errors caused by the computer not being able to keep enough significant digits during the computation.

As an example, when the multiple regression is run on the standardized inputs rather than the non-standardized inputs, the coefficients are different from the results using Solver as shown in Table 11-9.

**Table 11-9:** Comparison of Coefficients Using Three Variables, by LINEST() and Solver

|  | SOLVER | LINEST() |
|---|---|---|
| **Intercept** | 0.002501 | 0.002501 |
| **Collegep** | 0.002076 | 0.000000 |
| **HHPubAssist** | 0.000871 | 0.000000 |
| **HHMedInc** | 0.001717 | 0.002076 |

The coefficients on the standardized data do not make sense, because two of the variables have coefficients of zero, so there is effectively only one variable in the equation. Yet, the coefficient for the variable is different (0.002076) from the coefficient when this is the only variable in the equation (0.002907). This is not reasonable. Solver calculates the correct value, which is also verified by looking at the total error for the model.

> **WARNING** The method that Excel uses to calculate the results for LINEST()
> is numerically unstable. When there are many rows of data, it is better to use
> Solver to find the coefficients.

## Choosing Input Variables One-By-One

One powerful way of using regression is to choose the variables one at a time, first the best variable, then the next best, and so on. This is called forward selection and is particularly useful when there are many potential variables, such as the many variables that describe zip codes.

Excel is not the optimal tool for doing forward selection, because the LINEST() function requires that the X-values all be in adjacent columns. This means that essentially every combination of variables needs to be placed into a separate set of adjacent columns.

Different pairs of variables can be tested manually. The idea is to build the regression on a set of adjacent columns, and then copy in the data from the original columns. However, instead of copying in the data, the OFFSET() function can be used with a column offset. Changing the value of the column offset changes the data in the column.

With this set up, it is easy to try different pairs of columns by changing the offset values and looking at the resulting $R^2$ value. It would be convenient to find the optimal offsets using Solver. Unfortunately, the version of Solver provided with Excel cannot handle this type of optimization. Frontline Systems does offer other versions that do.

## Multiple Regression in SQL

As more variables are added into the regression formula, it becomes more and more complicated. The problem is that solving the regression requires matrix algebra, in particular, inverting a matrix. When there is one input variable, the problem is a two-by-two matrix, which is pretty easy to solve. Two input variables require a three-by-three matrix, which is at the edge of solving explicitly, as this section demonstrates. And for larger numbers of variables, standard SQL is simply not the best tool.

Solving the equation for two input variables (X1 and X2) requires quite a bit more arithmetic than for one. In this case, there are three coefficients ($\beta_0$, $\beta_1$, and $\beta_2$), and more intermediate sums. The following combinations are needed to calculate the coefficients:

- Sx1, which is the sum of the X1-values;
- Sx2, which is the sum of the X2-values;
- Sx1x1, which is the sum of the squares of the X1-values;

- Sx2x2, which is the sum of the product of X1-values and X2-values;

- Sx2x2, which is the sum of the squares of X2 values;

- Sx1y, which is the sum of the products of the X1-values and Y-values;

- Sx2y, which is the sum of the products of X2-values and Y-values; and

- Sy, which is the sum of the Y-values.

And a few more similar variables are needed for $R^2$. These then need to be combined in very complicated ways.

The following example calculates the coefficients for penetration, using HHMEDINCOME and PCOLL as the two input variables. The purpose of this example is to demonstrate that such mathematical manipulations are possible in SQL. The innermost subquery renames these to Y, X1, and X2, so the arithmetic in the outer subqueries is generic.

```
SELECT beta0, beta1, beta2,
       (1-(Syy-2*(beta1*Sx1y+beta2*Sx2y+beta0*Sy) +
        beta1*beta1*Sx1x1+beta2*beta2*Sx2x2+beta0*beta0*n +
        2*(beta1*beta2*Sx1x2+beta1*beta0*Sx1+beta2*beta0*Sx2))/
       (Syy-Sy*Sy/n)) as rsquare
FROM (SELECT (a11*Sy+a12*Sx1y+a13*Sx2y)/det as beta0,
             (a21*Sy+a22*Sx1y+a23*Sx2y)/det as beta1,
             (a31*Sy+a32*Sx1y+a33*Sx2y)/det as beta2, c.*
      FROM (SELECT (n*(Sx1x1*Sx2x2-Sx1x2*Sx1x2) -
                    Sx1*(Sx1*Sx2x2-Sx1x2*Sx2) +
                    Sx2*(Sx1*Sx1x2-Sx1x1*Sx2)) as det,
                   (Sx1x1*Sx2x2-Sx1x2*Sx1x2) as a11,
                   (Sx2*Sx1x2-Sx1*Sx2x2) as a12,
                   (Sx1*Sx1x2-Sx2*Sx1x1) as a13,
                   (Sx1x2*Sx2-Sx1*Sx2x2) as a21,
                   (n*Sx2x2-Sx2*Sx2) as a22, (Sx2*Sx1-n*Sx1x2) as a23,
                   (Sx1*Sx1x2-Sx1x1*Sx2) as a31,
                   (Sx1*Sx2-n*Sx1x2) as a32,
                   (n*Sx1x1-Sx1*Sx1) as a33,
                   b.*
            FROM (SELECT COUNT(*) as n, SUM(x1) as Sx1, SUM(x2) as Sx2,
                         SUM(y) as Sy, SUM(x1*x1) as Sx1x1,
                         SUM(x1*x2) as Sx1x2, SUM(x2*x2) as Sx2x2,
                         SUM(x1*y) as Sx1y, SUM(x2*y) as Sx2y,
                         SUM(y*y) as Syy
                  FROM (SELECT o.zipcode, numorders * 1.0/hh as y,
                               hhmedincome as x1, pcoll as x2
                        FROM (SELECT zc.*,
                                     (popedubach + popedumast +
                                      popeduprofdoct) as pcoll
                              FROM zipcensus zc) zc JOIN
                             (SELECT zipcode, COUNT(*) as numorders
                              FROM orders o
```

*(continued)*

```
                        GROUP BY zipcode) o
            ON zc.zipcode = o.zipcode
            WHERE hh >= 1000) a
        ) b
      ) c
    ) d
```

Embedded within the query are aliases such as A11 and A12. These values represent cells in a matrix. In any case, after all the arithmetic, the results are in Table 11-10. These results match the results in Excel using the same two variables.

**Table 11-10:** Coefficients for Regression of HHMEDINCOME, PCOLL, to Predict Penetration, Calculated Using SQL

| COEFFICIENT/STATISTIC | VARIABLE | VALUE |
|---|---|---|
| beta0 | Intercept | -0.0043317186 |
| beta1 | HHMedInc | 0.0000000683 |
| beta2 | Pcoll | 0.0126225403 |
| $R^2$ | R-square | 0.3029921767 |

Understanding the particular arithmetic is not important. At this point, though, we have clearly pushed the limits of what can be accomplished with SQL, and adding more variables is not feasible. Doing more complicated regressions requires the use of statistics tools that support such functionality.

## Lessons Learned

This chapter introduces the ideas of linear regression (best-fit lines) from the perspective of SQL and Excel. Linear regression is an example of a statistical model and is similar to the models discussed in the previous chapter.

There are several ways to approach linear regressions using the combination of SQL and Excel. Excel has at least four ways to create such models for a given set of data. Excel charting has a very nice feature where a trend line can be added to a chart. One of the types of trend lines is the best-fit line, which can be included on a chart along with its equation and statistics describing the line. Other types of trend lines — polynomial fits, exponential curves, power curves, logarithmic curves, and moving averages — are also quite useful for capturing and visualizing patterns in data.

A second way to estimate coefficients for a linear regression is with the array function LINEST() and various other functions that return individual coefficients, such as SLOPE() and INTERCEPT(). LINEST() is more powerful than the best-fit line in charts, because it can support more than one X-variable. However, all these functions use numerically unstable methods that fail to produce accurate results when there is a large amount of data (although the methods work quite well for many problems).

The third way is to calculate the coefficients explicitly, using the formulas from mathematics. And, the fourth way is to set up the linear regression problem as a spreadsheet model. The coefficients are in input calls and the target cell has the sum of the squares of the differences between the expected values and the actual values. The coefficients that minimize the sum define the model. The optimization process is handled by an Excel add-in called Solver. The advantage to this approach is that it supports regressions on summarized data by doing weighted regressions. This is quite powerful, and not otherwise supported in Excel.

Regression has many variations. Besides weighted regression, there is multiple regression, which includes more than one input variable. A good way to choose variables is using forward selection. That is, selecting one variable at a time to maximize the $R^2$ value. The mathematics behind regression work when all input variables are statistically independent. However, that is rarely true in the real world.

For one or two input variables, the calculations can be set up in SQL as well as Excel. This has the advantage of overcoming the limits of the spreadsheet. However, the arithmetic quickly becomes too complicated to express in SQL, and most dialects do not have built-in support for multiple regression.

Although Excel is quite useful for getting started, the serious user will want to use statistical packages for this type of work. The next and final chapter of this book recognizes that SQL and Excel cannot solve all problems. Some problems require more powerful tools. Setting up the data for these tools — the topic in the next chapter — is an area that takes advantage of the power of SQL.

# Building Customer Signatures for Further Analysis

The combination of SQL and Excel is powerful for manipulating data, visualizing trends, exploring interesting features, and finding patterns. However, SQL is still a language designed for data access, and Excel is still a spreadsheet designed for investigating relatively small amounts of data. Although powerful, the combination has its limits.

The solution is to use more powerful data mining and statistical tools, provided by vendors such as SAS, SPSS, and Insightful (among others, including open source software). Because the data typically resides in a relational database, SQL can play an important role in transforming it into the format needed for further analysis.

Preparing the data for such applications is where customer signatures fit in. A customer signature summarizes the attributes of a customer, putting important information in one place. The model sets discussed in the previous two chapters are examples of customer signature tables. Signatures are useful beyond sophisticated modeling, having their roots in customer information files and marketing information files developed for reporting purposes.

Customer signatures are powerful because they summarize both customer behavior and customer demographics in one place. The term "customer" should not be taken too literally. In some businesses, for instance, prospecting is much more important than customers. So, the "customer" may be a prospect and "customer behavior" may be exposure to marketing campaigns.

The word "signature" comes from the notion that customers are unique in the specific behavior and demographic traces that each leaves behind in databases. This is an intriguing notion of human individuality. Unlike human signatures, though, uniquely identifying each individual is not our purpose. The purpose is descriptive, often to enhance marketing efforts to individuals and groups of individuals.

A customer signature is more than a summary of customer behavior. It is a summary designed for analytic purposes that takes special care with regards to the naming of columns, the time frame of the data going into the signature, and similar considerations.

Even though other tools offer more advanced analytics, SQL has an advantage for data preparation: databases exploit parallel processing. In simple terms, this means that database engines can keep multiple disks spinning, multiple processors active, and lots of memory filled while working on a single query.

Even for smaller amounts of data, SQL has an advantage. It is possible to do all the data processing for a customer signature in a single query, eliminating the need for intermediate tables.

Many of the ideas in this chapter have been discussed in earlier chapters. Here, the ideas are brought together around the concept of a customer signature, information that summarizes customers along multiple dimensions. This chapter starts by explaining customer signatures and time frames in more detail. It then discusses the technical operations for building signatures, and interesting attributes to include in them.

## What Is a Customer Signature?

A customer signature is a row in a table that satisfies certain conditions making it more useful for analysis. The table is important, but the process that creates it more so. There is not a single signature for a customer, but a family of signatures used for different purposes.

This section introduces customer signatures, how they are used, and why they are important. The process of building customer signatures should make it possible to reconstruct what customers look like at any point in time. This may be a snapshot on the same date for all customers, or a different date for each customer, such as one year after the customer starts, when the customer first complains, or when the customer enrolled in the loyalty program.

**TIP** The process for creating customer signatures should be customizable to take a snapshot of customers any point in time or relative to events during the customer tenure. The process for building a customer signature is as important as the table itself.

Another way to think about customer signatures is that they contain *longitudinal* information. Here, longitudinal does not mean the distance east or west of Greenwich, England. Longitudinal is a word borrowed from medical research where it describes keeping track of patients over time including all the treatments and things that happen to the patients. Almost everything is of interest to medical researchers, because they are often dealing with life and death issues. Although information about customers is not typically quite so detailed and personal, customer signatures serve a similar purpose in the business world.

## What Is a Customer?

The definition of customer permeates all the earlier chapters. Chapter 1 brought up the difficulties of identifying customers, and Chapter 8 discussed difficulties in tracking them over time, which is one of the critical capabilities needed for creating signatures. As we've seen, there are different answers to the question of "what is a customer?" Four typical answers are:

- An anonymous transaction;
- An account;
- An individual; and,
- A household.

From the perspective of identifying customers in the database, accounts and anonymous transactions are usually easy; individuals and households require more work.

The ability to define the customer is not merely theoretical. Information is often most useful when it can be tied back to customers. Different definitions have different strengths and weaknesses.

When "account" is the level used to define the customer, one quickly discovers that individuals and households can have multiple account relationships. Multiple accounts belonging to the same customer result in operational inefficiencies — multiple contacts to the same household, for instance. These multiple accounts can interfere with analysis. For instance, when trying to understand why customers stop, summaries at the account level may miss the fact that people are really remaining customers — on another account.

On the other hand, when using individuals and households to define customer, a lot of work goes into identifying the same customer across multiple transactions and accounts. This results in a dependence on the methods used for the identification.

In the case of households, this is a particularly acute problem, due to the fact that households change over time. These changes are important because households whose composition changes (due to marriage, divorce, children moving in, children moving out, and so on) often present marketing opportunities.

The purchases dataset contains a customer id table that provides lookups for the household for any account. These customer IDs tie disparate transactions together over time. In many cases, customer ids are assigned by matching names and addresses on the transactions. These are then grouped together into households, assigned by a third-party householding vendor. If more complete data were available, these household ids would have effective dates on them, identifying when the household information is active and when the information changes.

## Sources of Data for the Customer Signature

Data about customers is located in many different tables, some of which do not even know that they help describe customers. For instance, the Product table in the purchases dataset is intended to describe products, not customers. Yet, when combined with transaction information, this table can help answer questions such as:

- Which customers only purchase products at discounted prices?
- Does a customer have an affinity with a particular product group?
- Does this affinity change over time?

These questions highlight the interplay between different types of data.

Information about customers comes from diverse subject areas. Figure 12-1 shows conceptually different types of information collected about customers that go into a customer signature. This section discusses these types of information. One particularly important attribute is the time frame for each item of data. The time frame is when the data becomes known for analysis purposes.

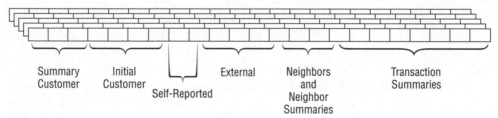

**Figure 12-1:** Customer signatures are records that describe customers, containing information from different subject areas.

### *Current Customer Snapshot*

There is often a table that describes the current customers (and perhaps former customers as well), containing information such as:

- Customer id;
- Customer name;

- Original start date or first purchase date;
- Current product or most recent purchase date;
- Total spending; and,
- Current contact information.

This information is a snapshot of what customers look like at the present time. Such a snapshot is a good starting point for a customer signature, because it has useful information and is at the right level of granularity. The most useful columns in it are the ones that do not change over time.

For instance, the customer id and original start date do not change. The contact information does change over time, although slowly, so the summary contains the current contact information. Total spending, most recent product, and most recent purchase date all change frequently. "Frequently," of course, depends on the business. Updates on automobile purchases might change over a period of years; updates on telephone usage, every month or even more frequently.

In a poorly designed data warehouse, snapshot information might contain data elements not otherwise available in transaction tables. In one such system, the customer snapshot contained a column called *dunning level*, which described customers as they became later and later in paying their bills. This information was only kept current in the snapshot information, with no historical transaction table. Although quite important for understanding customers and a driver of important behaviors, the dunning level could not be used for analysis, because the values could not be reconstructed in the past.

The solution was simple enough. On the analysis side, we could capture the dunning level periodically from the current snapshot, and create a dunning transaction table for analysis purposes.

## Initial Customer Information

Initial customer information remains constant for the duration of the customer relationship (except when households merge or split). This information includes:

- When the customer first becomes a customer;
- Initial products and spending amounts;
- Channel and marketing promotions that led to the initial relationship; and,
- Other relevant information (underwriting, credit scores, and so on).

For many businesses, the initial customer relationship is quite important, because it sets expectations about the ongoing relationship. Exceeding expectations can result in delighted customers who survive for long periods of time. On the other hand, unfulfilled expectations can lead to disappointed customers who were, perhaps, never in the target market in the first place, but were led to start by aggressive marketing tactics.

**TIP** Initial customer information, both demographic and behavioral, is quite valuable for understanding customers, because the initial interactions set customers' longer term expectations.

## Self-Reported Information

Customers explicitly provide some valuable data. Basic contact information, such as name, address, telephone number, and/or email address is provided when they start. Addresses used for billing and delivery lead to geocoding and associated geographic information. Email addresses contain domain information. Names suggest gender and ethnicity. Credit cards provide credit card types.

In addition, customers may complete application forms, provide information for credit checks, and respond to questionnaires and surveys. These are additional sources of self-reported information, although such data is often available only for a minority of customers. One challenge is to extend learnings from this subset to all customers. A survey might find an interesting subset of customers; the next problem is to find similar customers in the overall data. Similarity models described in Chapter 10 are one way to approach this.

Self-reported information has a time frame associated with it. Some is available at the beginning of the customer relationship, because such information is part of the application process. Some is only available sporadically after customers begin.

## External Data (Demographic and So On)

External data is typically purchased from outside bureaus that specialize in demographic data; another source of external data is business partners who share the information. Such information is usually a current snapshot of customers. Unfortunately, reconstructing what a customer used to look like is difficult.

Changes in such information can be quite informative. When a couple marries, the woman often legally changes her name. After a period of time, the newlyweds often unify their financial accounts into a single household account. This offers an opportunity to the wife's bank, because it receives notice of the name change (either from the customer or from an external source). However, more often than not, a name change gets recorded in a database as the current name, and the previous name is simply forgotten, or at least unavailable outside operational systems.

When a customer moves from one neighborhood to another, the neighborhood demographics change. The address is usually updated, and the old address forgotten (or at least not readily available for analysis). Without the ability to compare neighborhood demographics, it is not possible to know if the customer is moving up or moving down, into a good school district or into a retirement community.

Banks usually know when customers reach retirement age. Do the banks cease marketing to customers who are no longer eligible to contribute to individual retirement accounts (IRAs)? Customers are no longer eligible for these once they reach retirement age.

The time frame for demographic information usually represents a compromise, because the information is not maintained over time. Only the current snapshot of data is available for current customers, and the last snapshot is available for stopped customers.

## About Their Neighbors

Some information does not tell us directly about customers, but instead about the neighborhoods where they live. This information comes in two forms. Much information is available for free from the Census Bureau and other sources. Other "neighborhood" information consists of dynamic summaries of customer behavior, projected onto the neighborhood level. Although neighborhood does usually refer to geography, it could refer to similarity in other ways (such as all customers who arrived via a particular marketing campaign).

Using geographic data requires geocoding addresses to find the specific geographic areas — typically census block groups — where an individual lives. Zip codes are a poor man's geocoding, and they do not work as well as the census geographies for understanding customers.

Census blocks typically change every ten years, but not in between. Some data within the blocks may be updated between the decennial censuses; however, both the data and the geographic definitions are updated every ten years. If you are looking at customers over long periods of time, maintaining the history of the census variables can be useful for understanding how neighborhoods and customers are evolving.

Neighborhood information has a hybrid time frame. The information itself is typically static (updated every ten years). However, the geography may be the most recent geography for the customer, and customers may move several times between census refreshes.

Census information is also used for developing marketing clusters, of which the best known are probably Claritas's Prizm codes. These are descriptions of the people living in particular areas using catchy names such as "Young Digerati," "Kids & Cul-de-Sacs," "Shotguns and Pickups," and "Park Bench Seniors," that are based primarily on census data augmented with market research data (you can look up your zip code at `http://www.claritas.com/MyBestSegments/Default.jsp`.

## Transaction Summaries

Transactions are the most voluminous of the data sources, at least by number of rows of data. Transactions contain a wealth of information, because they describe customers' behaviors. However, the information is not readily apparent.

The key to effectively using transactional history is summarization. There are some basic methods of summarization, such as taking sums and averages and counts. Then there are more advanced types of summaries, where particular behaviors are identified and the presence, absence, or extent of these behaviors are recorded in the signature. These types of summaries can prove very useful.

Transaction history is quite amenable to the use of time frames, assuming that enough data is available. Shifting the time frame is simply a matter of taking transactions before a certain date and then summarizing them appropriately.

## Using Customer Signatures

Customer signatures summarize customer behavior and demographics. Such summaries have a variety of uses.

### Predictive and Profile Modeling

Customer signatures provide the inputs to models, including predictive models and profiling models. The signature can also be useful for clustering and segmentation. The signatures would typically be placed in a table accessed by more advanced analysis tools, or perhaps exported as a file and re-imported into those tools.

### Ad Hoc Analysis

Customer signatures provide a location where many types of information about customers are brought together in one place. Transactional summaries are available with demographics and so on. Reporting systems do a good job of slicing and dicing business information along important dimensions, such as geography, customer type, department, product, and so on. However, it is difficult to develop reporting systems for customer longitudinal data, because the volume of data is so large and the data is quite complex.

As a consequence, customer signatures are often used for ad hoc analysis on customers, typically using the most recent snapshot of customer behavior.

### Repository of Customer-Centric Business Metrics

Some of the columns in a customer signature may go beyond merely gathering data from other tables. Customer signatures are a place to put interesting metrics, particularly derived information that describes customer behaviors.

For instance, the history of marketing efforts might include attempted contacts by email, telephone, direct mail, and other channels. One of the attributes in the signature might be "email responsiveness." Customers who responded to email offers in the past would have high email responsiveness scores. Customers who have been contacted many times and never responded would have low email responsiveness scores.

This idea can extend beyond the channel preference, of course. The times when customers shop might be summarized to determine who is a "weekend" shopper, who is a "weekday" shopper, and who is an "after-work" shopper. The times when customers go to the web site might distinguish between "work browsers" and "home browsers." Customers who buy the newest products without a discount might be "leading edge" shoppers. Credit card customers might be classified as revolvers (keep a high balance and pay interest), transactors (pay off the bill every month), or convenience users (charge up for a vacation or furniture or something and then pay the balance over several months). And so on.

These types of business metrics and customer categories might be developed on an ad hoc basis. Once developed, placing them in a customer signature makes them available for other purposes.

**TIP** Customer signatures are a good place to incorporate important measures about customers that might otherwise go undocumented and be forgotten.

## Designing Customer Signatures

Before going into the details of the data manipulations, there are some key ideas in designing customer signatures. These ideas ensure that they work well for analytic purposes, and that they can be generated to be as-of arbitrary points in time.

## Column Roles

The columns in a customer signature have various roles, related to how the columns are used in modeling. From our perspective, the roles are important to consider because they affect how the columns are created. Of course, columns that are not useful for a particular purpose — such as customer IDs for predictive modeling — do not have to be used even though they are in the signature.

### Identification Columns

Some columns uniquely identify each customer. These *identification columns* are important, because they provide a link back to the actual customer information. There may be more than one such column. For instance, the customer id in the data warehouse is different from the customer id in the operational systems. Sometimes external vendors return match keys, which are different from the keys used internally.

What is important about an identification column is that it uniquely identifies each customer for the duration of the data in the customer signature. The identification column prevents customers from being confused with each other.

### Input Columns

Most columns in the customer signature are *input columns*. These are columns that describe customer characteristics and are intended for use as inputs in modeling. Input columns are all defined by a cutoff date. No information from after the cutoff date should be included in the inputs.

This date may be a single date for the entire customer signature. In this case, the customer signature is a snapshot of what customers look like on a particular date. Alternatively, the cutoff date could be defined individually for each customer. For instance, it could be one year after the customer starts, or when the customer adds a particular product, or the first time that the customer complains.

### Target Columns

When present, the target columns are the goals of the modeling effort, typically something related to interesting customer behaviors, such as response, cross-selling, managing risk, or stopping. In the subscription data, targets might be the customer tenure or the type of stop. In the purchases data, an appropriate target would be the time to the next purchase, the type of purchase, or whether the customer made a purchase during the most recent year. There can be more than one target in the data, because different aspects of the business have different needs.

Although the discussion of customer signatures is centered on modeling, target columns are actually optional. The signature might be used for reporting purposes. Or, the target columns might be provided through another data source not in the database. Or, the desired modeling may be *undirected*, meaning that the purpose is to find groups of similar customers without any particular goal in mind.

### Foreign Key Columns

Some columns are used to look up additional information. Usually, the additional information is simply added in by joining other tables or subqueries. The key used for the join might remain in the signature, although it is not usually as useful as the data brought in from other tables.

Some data sources may not be available in the database. In this case, the customer signature is not going to be complete and subsequent processing outside the database would add additional columns using a foreign key.

### Cutoff Date

The cutoff date should be included in each customer signature record. This date may be fixed for all customers, or it may vary. The purpose of including the cutoff date is to inform subsequent analysis. It should not be used as an input column for modeling. The cutoff date refers to the cutoff date for the input columns; target information may come from after the cutoff.

## Profiling versus Prediction

Chapter 10 introduced the distinction between a profiling model set and a prediction model set. In a profiling model set, the inputs and the targets come from the same time frame. In a prediction model set, the inputs come from a time frame strictly before the target. That is, the inputs are known before the target. The same ideas hold for customer signatures.

This chapter focuses on creating prediction model sets, because this is the more general situation. In a profiling model set, the target variables can simply be created in the same way as the input variables. In a prediction model set, the cutoff date is for the input variables, and the target comes from a time frame after the cutoff date.

## Time Frames

One of the key questions in designing customer signatures is: "What do we know and when did we know it?" All the inputs in the signature come from a time frame before the cutoff date. In addition, each column has a time frame associated with it, because each value in a database becomes known at some point in time and the value in the column may be replaced at a later point in time. Columns are only available for analysis when the cutoff date for the customer signature is during the time frame for the values in those columns.

> **TIP** "What do we know?" and "When do we know it?" are key questions about columns going into customer signatures.

The reason this is called a time frame and not simply "load time" is because data can have an end time as well as an available time; at some point, a new value may come along superseding the previous value. This can occur for many reasons. The most common is because the data values change. A customer's current address is only current until the customer moves. A column in the customer signature for the current address would have different values depending on the cutoff date for the signature. Other data columns may be purchased and only available for a specific period of time.

The goal of using time frames is to be able to create the customer signature with arbitrary cutoff dates. This goal has some consequences in terms of naming columns, handling dates and times, and incorporating seasonality.

### Naming of Columns

Column names need to respect the fact that the cutoff date for the customer signature may occur at any point in time. The process for creating the signature should take the cutoff date as an input. Column names should not be tied to particular dates or date ranges. Instead they should be relative. Good examples of columns are:

- Sales in the customer's first year;
- Average number of weekend visits to a web site; and,
- Most recent month billing invoice.

On the other hand, bad examples of columns specify particular dates (such as months and years) that would not be relevant in another time frame.

### Eliminating Seasonality

Columns that include data from explicit dates and times cause problems in customer signatures, because they interfere with generating the signatures for different time frames. Instead of including explicit dates, tenures and time spans are better:

- Instead of the start date, include the number of days before the cutoff date when the customer started.
- Instead of the date of the first purchase and the second purchase, include the number of days from one to the next.
- Instead of the date when a customer enrolled in a program, include the tenure of the customer at that time.
- Instead of the date of the most recent complaint, include the tenure of the customer on the first complaint and on the most recent complaint.

As a general rule, specific dates are less important relative to the calendar time line than relative to the customer life cycle time line. Dates on the calendar time line should be turned into numbers of days before the cutoff date for the signature.

This also eliminates many effects of seasonality. For instance, many cell phone customers sign up in the holiday season. Many pre-paid customers stop in May, which is four or five months after the phones are activated. These are customers who never replenish their phone account.

This peak in May is not really related to the month of May. Instead, it is related to the peak in starts during the preceding December and January and the business rules that define churn for pre-paid customers. On the customer time line, the same proportion stops after four or five months regardless of when they started. A peak in starts, though, does result in a peak of stops several months later.

Having the tenure of the customer in the customer signature rather than the dates themselves makes signature independent of such inadvertent seasonality effects.

## Adding Seasonality Back In

Of course, some seasonality is useful and informative. For instance, purchases in August are related to back-to-school events. As customers, students may behave differently from other customers. They may be more likely to change brands, more responsive to certain types of promotions, and have fewer financial resources.

Some of this information could be captured by including information in the customer signature, such as the season when a customer started. Customers who start during the back-to-school season may be different from customers who start at other times. In fact, in the subscription data, there is a slight difference in survival for customers who start in August and September versus December, as shown in Figure 12-2. The important point here is just that customers who start during different seasons may have different behaviors.

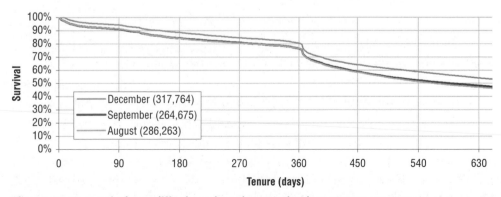

**Figure 12-2:** Survival can differ based on the month when customers start.

The following are some examples of seasonality variables that might be added in to capture particular characteristics that might be important to the business:

- Quarter of the year when a customer started;
- Proportion of transactions on the weekend;
- Web site visits during the traditional work day;
- Volume of purchases during the preceding holiday season; and,
- Day of the week of the start and stop.

The idea is to first wash seasonality out of the data, to get a better picture of what customers are doing independently of the calendar year. This makes it easier to focus on customers, rather than on extraneous events. Of course, seasonality can be quite important; seasonal effects should go into the customer signature intentionally rather than accidentally. For this reason, separate variables that capture seasonality information are more useful than having it mixed in with other data.

### Multiple Time Frames

For predictive modeling purposes, it is beneficial to have multiple time frames included in the customer signature. This prevents the models from "memorizing" one particular time frame. Figure 12-3 shows an example.

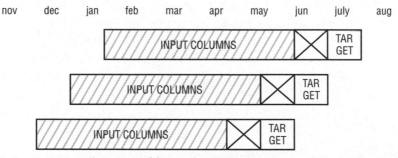

**Figure 12-3:** Customer signature tables can mix signatures from different time frames. Having multiple time frames is actually a best practice for prediction model sets.

Adding multiple time frames is not difficult. There are two methods. One is to build separate customer signatures for each time frame. These can then be merged to create a single customer signature table.

An alternative method is to assign different cutoff dates to different customers. This makes it possible to define the customer signature in a single step. However, the resulting SQL can be a bit more complicated.

When adding multiple time frames into a signature, the same customer can appear more than once. In general, this is not a big problem, although in general, it is better to not have too many duplicates in a table of customer signatures used for modeling.

## Operations to Build a Customer Signature

Building customer signatures is about bringing data together from disparate data sources. Figure 12-4 shows conceptually what needs to be done. Some data is already in the right format, and at the right granularity. This data merely needs to be copied. Some fields are keys into other tables, where information can be looked up. Other data is in the format of regular time series that can be pivoted. Irregular time series, such as transactions, need to be summarized. This section describes these operations in the context of building customer signatures.

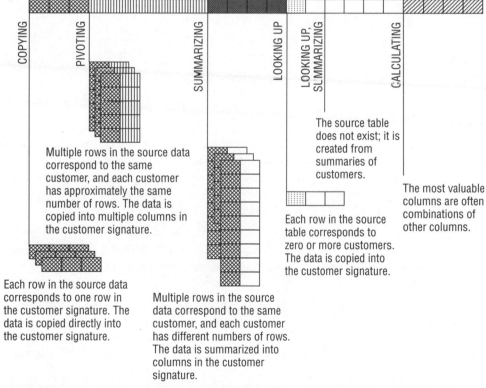

**Figure 12-4:** The data in customer signatures needs to be brought together using a variety of processing methods.

## Driving Table

The first step in building a customer signature is identifying the correct group of customers and the cutoff date for each one. A customer signature has a set of conditions that determine whether any given customer should be in the signature. The table that defines these customers is the *driving table*, which may be an actual table or a subquery.

If the customer signature is based on an event during the customer life cycle, the customer signature applies only to customers who have that event. Other customers, although interesting for other purposes, are not part of this signature.

The driving table maintains the information about the correct group of customers for the signature and additional date information. Each customer has a cutoff date, whether the signature is event-based or time-based.

In an ideal situation, all other subqueries would simply be joined into the driving table using LEFT OUTER JOINs. The overall query would schematically look like:

```
SELECT *
FROM (<driving table>) dt LEFT OUTER JOIN
     (SELECT customerid, <summary information>
      FROM <other table>
      GROUP BY customerid) t1
     ON dt.customerid = t1.customerid LEFT OUTER JOIN
     <ref table> rt
     ON rt.<key> = dt.<key>
```

That is, the driving table would be joined to summaries and reference tables to calculate the columns in the customer signature. This ensures that the correct set of customers remain in the customer signature.

However, the conditions that define the driving table, particularly the cutoff date, are needed for the summaries as well. For performance reasons, the driving table might be created and well-indexed on the customer id column, because this column gets used extensively. When all customers have the same cutoff date, then the cutoff date can be included in the subqueries, eliminating the need to join in the driving table.

### Using an Existing Table as the Driving Table

Often, the driving table is readily available, because there is a table with the right level of granularity. In such cases, not all the fields are necessarily appropriate for the table.

Consider the Subs table as an example. A first attempt only uses information about customers when they start, such as start date, channel, and market.

Information that occurs after the customer start date is not appropriate. The following query provides an example of a driving table using Subs:

```
SELECT customer_id, rate_plan as initial_rate_plan,
       monthly_fee as initial_monthly_fee,
       market as initial_market, channel as initial_channel,
       DATEDIFF(dd, start_date, cutoff_date) as days_ago_start,
       cutoff_date
FROM subs s CROSS JOIN
     (SELECT '2005-01-01' as cutoff_date) const
WHERE start_date < cutoff_date
```

This query has several interesting features. First, there is a cutoff date, which is joined in using a CROSS JOIN on a table containing constants. This can be a useful way to incorporate constants into queries (note that the syntax of the Const subquery varies among databases). Only customers who started before cutoff date are included in the driving table. Start dates are also transformed into tenures, as of the cutoff date. And, only columns whose value is known at the beginning of the customer relationship are included in the query.

> **TIP** The CROSS JOIN operation is a convenient way to incorporate constants into queries, by using a subquery that defines the constants and that returns one row.

Often, an existing table is really a snapshot of a customer at a given point in time. Some columns may still be usable for the driving table, assuming they are modified for different cutoff dates. For instance, the TENURE and STOP_TYPE columns could also be included, but they have to be modified to take the CUT-OFF_DATE into account. The following SELECT shows how this is handled:

```
SELECT customer_id, rate_plan as initial_rate_plan,
       monthly_fee as initial_monthly_fee,
       market as initial_market, channel as initial_channel,
       DATEDIFF(dd, start_date, cutoff_date) as days_ago_start,
       DATEDIFF(dd, start_date,
                (CASE WHEN stop_date IS NOT NULL AND
                           stop_date < cutoff_date
                      THEN stop_date ELSE cutoff_date END)) as tenure,
       (CASE WHEN stop_date IS NOT NULL AND stop_date < cutoff_date
             THEN stop_type ELSE '' END) as stop_type
FROM subs s CROSS JOIN
     (SELECT '2005-01-01' as cutoff_date) const
WHERE start_date < cutoff_date
```

The logic says that customers who stopped after the cutoff date are considered active as of the cutoff date, and customers who stopped before the cutoff date are considered stopped. For the customers who are stopped, the stop type does not change.

Some columns in a snapshot table simply cannot be used directly in the customer signature. These columns contain information that cannot be rolled back in time, such as total number of purchases, the date of the last complaint, and the customer's billing status. These have to be derived again from transaction tables.

### Derived Table as the Driving Table

Sometimes, the appropriate table is not available. In this case, the driving table needs to be derived. For example, the household level is a very reasonable level of granularity for customer signatures for the purchases dataset. However, there is no household table in the database. It needs to be derived from other tables.

The same ideas apply when using a summary for the driving table. No input columns from after the cutoff date can be used. The table only includes households known before the cutoff date. Care must also be taken to remove current snapshot columns.

The following query provides a basic summary of households, based on the Customer and Orders tables:

```
SELECT householdid, COUNT(DISTINCT c.customerid) as numcustomers,
       SUM(CASE WHEN gender = 'M' THEN 1 ELSE 0 END) as nummales,
       SUM(CASE WHEN gender = 'F' THEN 1 ELSE 0 END) as numfemales,
       MIN(first_orderdate) as first_orderdate,
       DATEDIFF(dd, MIN(first_orderdate),
               MIN(cutoff_date)) as days_since_first_order,
       MIN(cutoff_date) as cutoff_date
FROM customer c JOIN
     (SELECT customerid, MIN(orderdate) as first_orderdate
      FROM orders o
      GROUP BY customerid) o
    ON c.customerid = o.customerid CROSS JOIN
     (SELECT '2016-01-01' as cutoff_date) const
WHERE o.first_orderdate < const.cutoff_date
GROUP BY householdid
```

This query looks up the earliest order date for customers. Only customers with an order before the cutoff date are included in the driving table. Notice that the cutoff date is included as a constant date, using a CROSS JOIN and Const subquery.

## Looking Up Data

Looking up data uses the JOIN operation. There are actually two forms of lookup, one using a fixed table that describes features that do not change. The other type summarizes customers along various dimensions and incorporates this information back into the customer signature. Such historical summaries along business dimensions can be very valuable.

### Fixed Lookup Tables

Fixed lookup tables contain information that does not change over time. Therefore, these tables can be included without reference to the cutoff date. The classic example is census information and other reference tables in the database. The data from the 2000 Census is the data from the 2000 Census. Although this data does not change, the 2010 Census data will supersede it, just as the 2000 Census data replaced the 1990 data.

The following information from the census data would be useful in a customer signature for purchases:

- Household median income;
- Education variables; and,
- Number of households.

Using this information requires a zip code for each customer. Often, the zip code (and other geocoded information) would be a column in a household table and hence part of the driving table. This example uses the most recent zip code in each household, obtained from the following query:

```
SELECT householdid, RIGHT(datezip, 5) as firstzip
FROM (SELECT householdid, MAX(cal.iso+zipcode) as datezip
      FROM customer c JOIN orders o ON o.customerid = c.customerid JOIN
           calendar cal ON o.orderdate = cal.date CROSS JOIN
           (SELECT '2016-01-01' as cutoff_date) const
      WHERE SUBSTRING(zipcode, 1, 1) BETWEEN '0' AND '9' AND
            SUBSTRING(zipcode, 2, 1) BETWEEN '0' AND '9' AND
            SUBSTRING(zipcode, 3, 1) BETWEEN '0' AND '9' AND
            SUBSTRING(zipcode, 4, 1) BETWEEN '0' AND '9' AND
            SUBSTRING(zipcode, 5, 1) BETWEEN '0' AND '9' AND
            LEN(zipcode) = 5 AND
            orderdate < cutoff_date
      GROUP BY householdid) h
```

Notice that "most recent zip code" really means "most recent zip code before the cutoff date," so the cutoff date is needed. This query converts the order date to a string of the form "YYYYMMDD," using the Calendar table. It then appends the zip code to this value, and then takes the maximum value. The result is the most recent order date before the cutoff date with its zip code. The last five characters from this maximum value constitute the most recent zip code. This method was discussed in Chapter 2.

This query only considers zip codes that contain five digits, because some zip codes have invalid values. Some households do not have a corresponding zip code.

Note that the expression in the WHERE clause that chooses the appropriate zip codes is not:

```
zipcode BETWEEN '00000' AND '99999'
```

The problem is that poorly formed zip codes such as '1ABC9' would fall into this range. Each digit needs to be tested separately.

With the appropriate zip code, the lookup then takes the form:

```
SELECT householdid, zc.*
FROM (<hh first zip subquery>) hhzip LEFT OUTER JOIN
     zipcensus zc
     ON hhzip.firstzip = zc.zipcode
```

This query simply takes the zip code query, joins in `zipcensus`, and extracts the columns of interest.

## Customer Dimension Lookup Tables

Some very powerful lookup tables are summaries of customer behavior along various dimensions. For example, the following might be interesting for various applications:

- Penetration by zip code;
- Average transaction amount by channel;
- Average transaction amount in the state; and,
- Stop rate by channel, market, and monthly fee.

These are examples of summaries of customer behavior that are looked up along specific dimensions.

It is tempting to create the summaries using simple aggregations. Resist this temptation, because this is the wrong approach. All the data in the summaries have to be from a period before the cutoff date to meet the requirements of the input variables. A simple aggregation over all the data includes information from the same time frame as the target.

> **WARNING** When summarizing variables for customer signatures — such as historical churn rates by handset type or historical purchases by zip code — be sure that the data in the summary table comes from a time frame *before* the target variables'.

As an example, let's consider penetration by zip code, which is the number of households in a zip code that have an order divided by the number of households in the zip code. For the purpose of this discussion, only the number of households needs to be calculated, because the penetration is simply this number divided by the number of households in the zip code.

The following query is the basic query for this type of information when there is a constant cutoff date:

```
SELECT zipcode, COUNT(DISTINCT householdid) as numhhwithorder
FROM customer c JOIN orders o ON c.customerid = o.customerid
GROUP BY zipcode
```

This query simply counts the number of households in a zip code.

There are two problems with this summary, one obvious and one subtle. The obvious problem is that it does not use the cutoff date. This means that the resulting columns include information from the target time frame. The subtle problem is that as the cutoff date changes, different amounts of time are used to determine the penetration. As a result, customer signatures with more recent cutoff dates necessarily have larger penetrations than customer signatures with earlier cutoff dates. The penetration can only grow over time.

The following query solves both these problems:

```
SELECT zipcode, COUNT(DISTINCT householdid) as numhh
FROM customer c JOIN orders o ON c.customerid = o.customerid CROSS JOIN
     (SELECT '2016-01-01' as cutoffdate) const
WHERE DATEDIFF(dd, orderdate, cutoffdate) BETWEEN 1 AND 365
GROUP BY zipcode
```

This query calculates the number of households in each zip code that make a purchase in the year before the cutoff date. Using a fixed period of time before the cutoff date makes the variable more comparable for different cutoff dates.

The preceding approach works for a fixed cutoff date. When the cutoff date differs for each household, the driving table is needed to get the date:

```
SELECT zipcode, COUNT(DISTINCT dt.householdid) as numhh
FROM (<driving table>) dt LEFT OUTER JOIN
     (SELECT c.householdid, o.*
      FROM customer c JOIN orders o ON c.customerid = o.customerid) c
     ON c.householdid = dt.householdid AND
        DATEDIFF(dd, orderdate, cutoff_date) BETWEEN 1 AND 365
GROUP BY zipcode
```

This query is similar to the previous query. The difference is that the cutoff date is not constant. Instead, it comes from the driving table. Using the cutoff date ensures that future information is not accidentally incorporated into the signature.

## Initial Transaction

A lot of information about customers is available in the first transaction. This might include the sections of the web page on the first visit, the contents of the market basket on the first purchase, or the subject of the first complaint. This example brings in information from the first transaction into the Orders table.

### Without Window Functions

Unfortunately, SQL does not have direct support for joining in the first transaction. With the purchases data, it is possible to do something quite close, because the driving table includes the customer start date, which is also the first order date. This can be used to join in the orders data:

```
SELECT dt.householdid, firsto.*
FROM (<driving table>) dt LEFT OUTER JOIN
     (SELECT c.householdid, o.*
      FROM customer c JOIN orders o
           ON c.customerid = o.customerid) firsto
     ON firsto.householdid = dt.householdid AND
        firsto.orderdate = dt.first_orderdate
```

Although this looks like a good idea, the problem is that some customers have multiple orders on the first day. There are several approaches to solving the problem:

- Fix the orders data so the order date has a time stamp in addition to a date stamp.
- Treat all orders on the first day as a single order.
- Choose a single, reasonable first day transaction.

The first possibility is generally a non-starter. Data analysis projects often find situations where the source data could be better. Alas, fixing data problems is usually outside the scope of such projects.

The second approach requires combining multiple orders on the same day. The problem is that data such as the original channel and the original payment type need to be combined from more than one order. There is no obvious way to do this consistently.

The preferred solution is to choose a single, reasonable first day transaction. We have already encountered his problem of having multiple transactions on the same date in Chapter 8. To review, this is a cumbersome query that requires the following steps:

1. Find the earliest order date for each household;
2. Find the minimum order id for each household on that order date; and then,

3. Use the minimum order id to identify the correct order for the customer signature.

Figure 12-5 shows the dataflow diagram for the following query:

```
SELECT householdid, o.*
FROM (SELECT ho.householdid, MIN(o.orderid) as minorderid
      FROM (SELECT householdid, MIN(orderdate) as orderdate
            FROM customer c JOIN orders o ON o.customerid = c.customerid
            GROUP BY householdid) ho JOIN
            customer c
            ON ho.householdid = c.householdid JOIN
            orders o
            ON c.customerid = o.customerid AND
               o.orderdate = ho.orderdate
      GROUP BY ho.householdid) firstorder JOIN
      orders o
      ON o.orderid = firstorder.minorderid
```

This query follows the structure just described. The innermost query finds the first order date. The next subquery identifies the first order id on the first order date, which is then used to select the columns of interest from the first order.

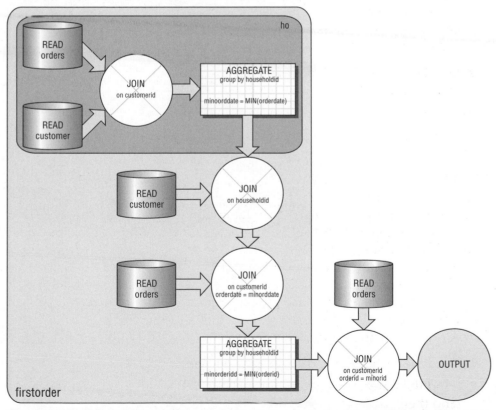

**Figure 12-5:** This dataflow diagram finds the first order for each household.

## With Window Functions

Window ranking functions greatly simplify finding the first transaction, because they make it easy to assign a sequence number to the orders based on the order date:

```
SELECT h.*
FROM (SELECT householdid, o.*,
             ROW_NUMBER() OVER (PARTITION BY householdid
                                ORDER BY orderdate, orderid) as seqnum
      FROM customer c JOIN orders o ON o.customerid = c.customerid) h
WHERE seqnum = 1
```

The subquery uses the ROW_NUMBER() window function to assign a sequence number to the orders. This function assigns numbers to orders within each household, starting with the first one (defined by the earliest ORDERDATE and smallest ORDERID). The first order is simply the one whose sequence number is one.

Sequence numbers can be quite convenient for analytic purposes. They make it easier to determine what happens first and next and right before something else. For this reason, it can be a good idea to include them when creating a data warehouse. If they are not there, then window functions can calculate them.

**TIP** Sequence numbers on transactions are useful for finding the first transaction (as well as the next and previous ones). They can be added easily using the ROW_NUMBER() window function.

## Pivoting

Pivoting is a common, special case of summarizing data. It is the process of taking customer transactions that follow a regular pattern and placing them into buckets along a specified dimension. Each pivot column corresponds to a particular value or group of values, such as transactions during a month or transactions containing a particular product. The columns themselves contain basic summaries, such as:

- Counts of orders;
- Sum of dollar amounts;
- Average of dollar amounts; or,
- Counts of some distinguishing feature (such as counts of distinct orders).

The examples in this section calculate the first of these.

The purchases dataset has several obvious pivots along purchase dimensions:

- Payment type pivot — summarizing the transactions by payment type.
- Campaign pivot — summarizing the transactions by campaign.
- Time pivot — summarizing the transactions by time period.
- Product pivot — summarizing the transactions by product information.

This section walks through the process of adding all these pivots to the customer signature.

---

## USING EXCEL TO GENERATE SQL CODE

Creating pivot columns requires repetitive code that can be quite cumbersome to type in. Chapter 2 contains examples of using SQL to generate code. Excel can also be used to generate SQL statements.

For example, the payment type pivot contains several SELECT statements similar to:

```
SUM(CASE WHEN paymenttype = 'VI' THEN 1 ELSE 0 END) as pt_vi,
```

Assume that the various payment type values are in one column (for instance, the column B) and the preceding statement in cell $A$1. To get the appropriate statement in column C, use the following formula:

```
=SUBSTITUTE($A$1, "VI", $B2)
```

And copy this down the appropriate rows in column C. These values can then be copied into the SQL expression. Notice that the resulting SQL expression includes the column name.

It is a good idea to include extra spaces before the SUM() for aesthetic reasons. Also, the final comma may need to be removed from the last expression to prevent a syntax error in the SQL.

The ability to generate code in Excel is useful for other purposes as well. For instance, sometimes character strings contain unrecognized characters and we might want to look at the actual numeric values (these are typically ASCII values on most modern computers). For this, the SELECT statement might look like:

```
SELECT ASCII(SUBSTRING(<str>, 1, 1)), SUBSTRING(<str>, 1, 1),
       ASCII(SUBSTRING(<str>, 2, 1)), SUBSTRING(<str>, 2, 1)
       . . .
```

Each expression extracts one character from the string and converts it to the ASCII code. The character itself is also included after the code.

Generating all these SELECT statements is cumbersome. Excel can make this much easier, using basically the same process explained previously. The only difference is that column B contains the numbers 1, 2, 3, and so on, rather than values from the database.

SQL does have a shortcoming when it comes to pivoting columns. There is no automatic pivot statement that creates multiple columns. Each column has to be created independently. Although this is a hassle, it only needs to be done once. When there are large numbers of columns, Excel can be used to automatically generate the code, as discussed in the aside "Using Excel to Generate SQL Code."

### Payment Type Pivot

The first example of a pivot is by payment type. This is the simplest, because it is simply an attribute of an order, independent of time. There are six different payment types, which are shown in Table 12-1.

**Table 12-1:** Payment Types in Orders Table

| PAYMENT TYPE | # ORDERS | DESCRIPTION |
| --- | --- | --- |
| ?? | 313 | Unknown |
| AE | 47,382 | American Express |
| DB | 12,739 | Debit Card |
| MC | 47,318 | MasterCard |
| OC | 8,214 | Other Credit Card |
| VI | 77,017 | Visa |

The two smallest groups, "OC" and "??," can be combined into a single group, indicating some other credit card. The following query does the pivot:

```
SELECT householdid,
       SUM(CASE WHEN paymenttype = 'VI' THEN 1 ELSE 0 END) as pt_vi,
       SUM(CASE WHEN paymenttype = 'MC' THEN 1 ELSE 0 END) as pt_mc,
       SUM(CASE WHEN paymenttype = 'AX' THEN 1 ELSE 0 END) as pt_ax,
       SUM(CASE WHEN paymenttype = 'DB' THEN 1 ELSE 0 END) as pt_db,
       SUM(CASE WHEN paymenttype IN ('??', 'OC') THEN 1 ELSE 0 END
          ) as pt_oc
FROM orders o JOIN customer c ON o.customerid = c.customerid CROSS JOIN
     (SELECT '2016-01-01' as cutoff_date) const
WHERE orderdate < cutoff_date
GROUP BY householdid
```

The pivoting aspect of the query simply uses the CASE statement to calculate columns based on the payment type and assigning them reasonable names. Because the results are for the customer signature, the aggregation is at the household level, which requires joining in the Customer table. The cutoff date is also needed to restrict orders to those before the cutoff date.

## Channel Pivot

The next step is to add in the channel pivot into the same query. This is only slightly more complicated, because the channel is in the Campaign table, so an additional join is needed. Table 12-2 shows the campaigns with the number of orders.

**Table 12-2:** Channels in Orders Table

| CHANNEL | COUNT |
| --- | --- |
| PARTNER | 84,518 |
| WEB | 53,362 |
| AD | 40,652 |
| INSERT | 7,333 |
| REFERRAL | 2,550 |
| MAIL | 1,755 |
| BULK | 1,295 |
| CATALOG | 710 |
| EMPLOYEE | 642 |
| EMAIL | 128 |
| INTERNAL | 34 |
| CONFERENCE | 3 |
| SURVEY | 1 |

As with many categorical columns, a small number are quite common and many are uncommon. There are pivot columns for the first three, with the remaining going into an "OTHER" column.

The channel pivot can be added right onto the query for the payment type pivot, as in the query:

```
SELECT householdid,
       SUM(CASE WHEN paymenttype = 'VI' THEN 1 ELSE 0 END) as pt_vi,
       . . .
       SUM(CASE WHEN channel = 'PARTNER' THEN 1 ELSE 0 END) as ca_partner,
       SUM(CASE WHEN channel = 'WEB' THEN 1 ELSE 0 END) as ca_web,
       SUM(CASE WHEN channel = 'AD' THEN 1 ELSE 0 END) as ca_ad,
       SUM(CASE WHEN channel NOT IN ('PARTNER', 'WEB', 'AD') THEN 1
              ELSE 0 END) as ca_other
FROM orders o JOIN campaign ca ON o.campaignid = ca.campaignid JOIN
```

*(continued)*

```
     customer c ON o.customerid = c.customerid CROSS JOIN
     (SELECT '2016-01-01' as cutoff_date) const
WHERE orderdate < cutoff_date
GROUP BY householdid
```

This query joins in the campaign table to get the channel code. It would be more fitting to use LEFT OUTER JOIN rather than a regular JOIN, because this explicitly preserves all the rows in the Orders table. However, in this case, the JOIN never has an unmatched value, because all campaign ids in the orders table are present in the lookup table.

### Year Pivot

The next example of pivoting is by time. The cutoff date used for the driving table is 2016-01-01. The idea is to summarize the number of orders placed in each year. A first attempt at doing this might have column names such as ORDERS2013, ORDERS2014, and ORDERS2015. This works when the cutoff date is in 2016, but not for other cutoff dates.

Instead, the column names should be relative to the cutoff date. The following query adds the appropriate SELECT clauses onto the payment type/ channel pivot:

```
SELECT householdid,
       . . .,
       SUM(CASE WHEN DATEDIFF(YY, orderdate, cutoff_date) = 0 THEN 1
               ELSE 0 END) as yr_1,
       SUM(CASE WHEN DATEDIFF(YY, orderdate, cutoff_date) = 1 THEN 1
               ELSE 0 END) as yr_2,
       SUM(CASE WHEN DATEDIFF(YY, orderdate, cutoff_date) = 2 THEN 1
               ELSE 0 END) as yr_3,
       SUM(CASE WHEN DATEDIFF(YY, orderdate, cutoff_date) = 3 THEN 1
               ELSE 0 END) as yr_4
FROM orders o JOIN campaign ca ON o.campaignid = ca.campaignid JOIN
     customer c ON o.customerid = c.customerid CROSS JOIN
     (SELECT '2016-01-01' as cutoff_date) const
WHERE orderdate < cutoff_date
GROUP BY householdid
```

This pivot calculates the number of years before the cutoff date using the DATEDIFF() function with the YY argument. Calculating the number of years between two dates is a bit complicated because of leap years. For instance, there is one year from Feb 28, 2001 to Feb 28, 2002. Is there one year from Feb 28, 2000 to Feb 27, 2001? There are the same number of days between both pairs of dates. This formulation leaves the business rules for dealing with leap years to the database.

**TIP** When possible, leave date calculations up to the database, for things like calculating the number of months or years between two dates.

## Order Line Information Pivot

The goal of the product pivot is to count the number of orders having a product in each of the eight product groups, which are summarized in Table 12-3. It is desirable to include the order line information in the same subquery as the order information, because order lines are logically related to orders. This also limits the number of places where the query needs to lookup HOUSEHOLDID and apply the date restriction.

**Table 12-3:** Product Group Information in Orders

| PRODUCT GROUP | NUMBER OF ORDER LINES | NUMBER OF ORDERS |
|---|---|---|
| BOOK | 113,210 | 86,564 |
| ARTWORK | 56,498 | 45,430 |
| OCCASION | 41,713 | 37,898 |
| FREEBIE | 28,073 | 22,261 |
| GAME | 18,469 | 11,972 |
| APPAREL | 12,348 | 10,976 |
| CALENDAR | 9,872 | 8,983 |
| OTHER | 5,825 | 5,002 |
| #N/A | 9 | 9 |

Ignoring the desire to include the product pivot in the ongoing pivot query, the following subquery summarizes the order line information:

```
SELECT householdid,
       SUM(CASE WHEN p.productgroupname = 'BOOK' THEN 1 ELSE 0 END
           ) as pg_book,
       SUM(CASE WHEN p.productgroupname = 'ARTWORK' THEN 1 ELSE 0 END
           ) as pg_artwork,
       SUM(CASE WHEN p.productgroupname = 'OCCASION' THEN 1 ELSE 0 END
           ) as pg_occasion,
       SUM(CASE WHEN p.productgroupname = 'FREEBIE' THEN 1 ELSE 0 END
           ) as pg_freebie,
       SUM(CASE WHEN p.productgroupname = 'GAME' THEN 1 ELSE 0 END
           ) as pg_game,
       SUM(CASE WHEN p.productgroupname = 'APPAREL' THEN 1 ELSE 0 END
           ) as pg_apparel,
       SUM(CASE WHEN p.productgroupname = 'CALENDAR' THEN 1 ELSE 0 END
           ) as pg_calendar,
       SUM(CASE WHEN p.productgroupname = 'OTHER' THEN 1 ELSE 0 END
           ) as pg_other
```

*(continued)*

```
FROM orderline ol JOIN product p ON ol.productid = p.productid JOIN
     orders o ON ol.orderid = o.orderid JOIN customer c
     ON c.customerid = o.customerid CROSS JOIN
     (SELECT '2016-01-01' as cutoff_date) const
WHERE orderdate < cutoff_date
GROUP BY c.householdid
```

This query works, but not as part of the pivot query we've been building. Just joining in the Orderline table causes problems, because there are multiple order lines in each order. In other words, the SUM(CASE . . .) statements end up counting order lines instead of orders, which is not the intention.

There are two ways to include the product group pivot in the pivoting query. One method is to include the Orderline and then change all the previous SUM(CASE . . .) expressions to COUNT(DISTINCT CASE . . . orderid). This counts all the distinct ORDERIDs and hence orders rather than order lines.

This is a clever solution, and it works for a handful of columns. However, changing the structure of the previous query is generally not a good idea, because such changes make queries less clear and less maintainable. In addition, counting distinct order ids is likely to be slower than simply adding up a bunch of ones and zeros.

A better approach is to summarize the order line data twice, once at the orders level and then again at the household level. The following query shows the summary at the order level:

```
SELECT orderid,
       MAX(CASE WHEN p.productgroupname = 'BOOK' THEN 1 ELSE 0 END
           ) as pg_book,
       MAX(CASE WHEN p.productgroupname = 'ARTWORK' THEN 1 ELSE 0 END
           ) as pg_artwork,
       MAX(CASE WHEN p.productgroupname = 'OCCASION' THEN 1 ELSE 0 END
           ) as pg_occasion,
       MAX(CASE WHEN p.productgroupname = 'FREEBIE' THEN 1 ELSE 0 END
           ) as pg_freebie,
       MAX(CASE WHEN p.productgroupname = 'GAME' THEN 1 ELSE 0 END
           ) as pg_game,
       MAX(CASE WHEN p.productgroupname = 'APPAREL' THEN 1 ELSE 0 END
           ) as pg_apparel,
       MAX(CASE WHEN p.productgroupname = 'CALENDAR' THEN 1 ELSE 0 END
           ) as pg_calendar,
       MAX(CASE WHEN p.productgroupname = 'OTHER' THEN 1 ELSE 0 END
           ) as pg_other
FROM orderline ol JOIN product p ON ol.productid = p.productid
GROUP BY orderid
```

This query uses MAX() to create an indicator of whether each order has a particular product group, rather than SUM(), which counts the order lines. This query does not join in the HOUSEHOLDID, nor does it apply the restriction on ORDERDATE. These restrictions can be applied at the next level, because a single order has the same household id and order date. On the other hand, the database is doing additional processing, summarizing the order lines for orders that are not part of the final result. So, in some circumstances, including the restrictions is useful.

Summarizing the order lines at the order level is only half the work. This order summary needs to be summarized again at the household level. The result is that the final summarization of the order information has the form:

```
SELECT householdid,
       . . .
       SUM(pg_book) as pg_book,
       SUM(pg_artwork) as pg_artwork,
       SUM(pg_occasion) as pg_occasion,
       SUM(pg_freebie) as pg_freebie,
       SUM(pg_game) as pg_game,
       SUM(pg_apparel) as pg_apparel,
       SUM(pg_calendar) as pg_calendar,
       SUM(pg_other) as pg_other
FROM orders o JOIN campaign ca
     ON o.campaignid = ca.campaignid LEFT OUTER JOIN
     (<order summary query>) olsum
     ON olsum.orderid = o.orderid JOIN
     customer c
     ON o.customerid = c.customerid CROSS JOIN
     (SELECT '2016-01-01' as cutoff_date) const
WHERE orderdate < cutoff_date
GROUP BY householdid
```

The order line subquery is joined in using a LEFT OUTER JOIN. This ensures that orders are not lost, even if those orders have no order lines. This is good practice, even though all orders do have order lines in this case.

By the way, the subquery that summarizes the order lines at the order level could use SUM() to count order lines rather than MAX() to create an indicator flag. The outer query would need to count orders using a slightly different expression:

```
SUM(CASE WHEN pg_book > 0 THEN 1 ELSE 0 END) as pg_book
```

These two forms are equivalent, but the first way has slightly simpler code. On the other hand, the second produces an intermediate result that could be used for other purposes.

Although this query looks complicated, it is actually composed of well-defined pieces, carefully sewn together. It is worth emphasizing again that this structure works for a couple of reasons. First, each subquery is created subject to the constraints of the customer signature. Also, each table and subquery is carefully joined in with consideration of how it affects the number of rows in the final result. Care is taken not to lose rows or to multiply rows inadvertently.

> **WARNING** When joining tables together for a customer signature, be very careful that there are no duplicate rows in the tables being joined into the driving table. Duplicate rows can inadvertently multiply the number of rows in the customer signature table.

## Summarizing

Pivoting data is one method of summarizing transactions, basically aggregating information along various dimensions. There are other ways to summarize data. Some fit directly into the pivoting query built in the previous section. Some are a bit more complicated and provide an opportunity to add in customer-centric business measures.

### Basic Summaries

Basic summaries of the orders data include information such as:

- Total number of orders;
- Total number of units ordered;
- Total dollar amount of orders; and,
- Average dollar amount.

These summaries can be calculated in the same way as the pivoted data. The only difference is the particular expressions used for calculating the values.

### More Complex Summaries

There are interesting indicators of customer behavior lurking inside customer transactions. For instance, one credit card company tracks how often a customer spends more than $100 at a restaurant more than 50 miles from the customer's home.

In the purchases data, the following are potentially interesting questions:

- How many of the customer's orders are over $200?
- What is the maximum number of different products in any one order?
- How many different products has the customer ordered over time?
- What is the longest duration between the order date and the ship date?
- How often has the ship date been more than one week after the order date?

These are posed as questions. However, they suggest customer attributes that might be useful for the customer signature.

The following query calculates answers to the questions:

```
SELECT householdid,
       COUNT(DISTINCT CASE WHEN o.totalprice > 200 THEN o.orderid END
            ) as numgt2000,
       COUNT(DISTINCT productid) as numhhprods,
       MAX(op.numproducts) as maxnumordprods,
       MAX(DATEDIFF(dd, o.orderdate, ol.shipdate)) as maxshipdelay,
       COUNT(DISTINCT CASE WHEN DATEDIFF(dd, o.orderdate, ol.shipdate) > 7
                        THEN o.orderid END)
FROM customer c JOIN orders o ON c.customerid = o.customerid JOIN
     orderline ol ON o.orderid = ol.orderid JOIN
     (SELECT o.orderid, COUNT(DISTINCT productid) as numproducts
      FROM orders o JOIN orderline ol ON o.orderid = ol.orderid
      GROUP BY o.orderid) op
     ON o.orderid = op.orderid
GROUP BY householdid
```

This version of the query has the same problem as some of the earlier queries. It does not take the cutoff date into account. Adding the Const subquery fixes this. In addition, the WHERE clause needs to take into account that both ORDER-DATE and SHIPDATE should be before the cutoff date:

```
SELECT householdid,
       COUNT(DISTINCT CASE WHEN o.totalprice > 200 THEN o.orderid END
             ) as numgt2000,
       COUNT(DISTINCT productid) as numhhprods,
       MAX(op.numproducts) as maxnumordprods,
       MAX(DATEDIFF(dd, o.orderdate, ol.shipdate)) as maxshipdelay,
       COUNT(DISTINCT CASE WHEN DATEDIFF(dd, o.orderdate, ol.shipdate) > 7
                        THEN o.orderid END)
FROM customer c JOIN orders o ON c.customerid = o.customerid JOIN
     orderline ol ON o.orderid = ol.orderid JOIN
     (SELECT o.orderid, COUNT(DISTINCT productid) as numproducts
      FROM orders o JOIN
           orderline ol
           ON o.orderid = ol.orderid
      GROUP BY o.orderid) op
     ON o.orderid = op.orderid CROSS JOIN
     (SELECT '2016-01-01' as cutoffdate) const
WHERE o.orderdate < cutoffdate AND
      ol.shipdate < cutoffdate
GROUP BY householdid
```

Instead of a constant cutoff date, the driving table could be joined in on the household id to get a cutoff date for each customer.

Clearly, only orders whose order date precedes the cutoff date should be included in the customer signature. However, it is not clear if the ship date should have this restriction. The decision depends on how the data is loaded into and updated in the database. To understand how to handle the ship date, it helps to understand how it is created. The following are possibilities:

- Only completed orders are in the data. An order is completed when the last item is shipped.
- All orders are in the data; order lines have ship dates that are updated as new information is available.
- All orders are in the data, but order lines are available only after they ship.

These different scenarios affect the relationship between the ship date and the cutoff date. If the first is true, then orders are only available after the last ship date, so the signature should only include orders whose last ship date is before the cutoff date. If the second scenario is true, then it is okay to ignore the ship date. Future ship dates are "intended ship dates." If the third is true, then very recent orders should be smaller than orders even a week old. In addition, some orders might have no order lines.

Understanding the relationship between dates in the database and when the data is loaded is important. We could imagine a scenario where order lines are only available after they ship, although the corresponding orders are already in the database. An analysis might "discover" that the most recent orders are smaller than expected. This fact would merely be an artifact of how the data is loaded into the database, because not all order lines have shipped for the most recent orders (in this scenario).

**WARNING** It is important to understand the process of loading the database. This process leaves artifacts in the data that might be discovered when analyzing the data.

## Extracting Features

In some data sources, the most interesting features are the descriptions of products and channels, markets and retailers. These descriptions include more complex data types, such as text and geographic position. The information in these columns can be quite informative. This section discusses some ideas about extracting information for geographic and character data types.

### Geographic Location Information

Geographic location information is represented as latitudes and longitudes. When mapped, this information is quite interesting. However, maps do not fit well into customer signatures nor are they well-suited for statistical and data mining algorithms.

Longitudes and latitudes are generated when addresses are geocoded. The most obvious address is the customer address. However, there are addresses for retailers, and ATM machines, and city centers, and phone lines, and Internet service provider points-of-presence, and so on. Such geocoding leads to questions such as:

- How far is a customer from the center of the nearest MSA (metropolitan statistical area)?
- How many purchases were made more than 100 miles from home?
- What proportion of ATM transactions is within 10 miles of home?
- What is the direction from the customer to the nearest MSA center?

These questions readily turn into customer attributes.

There are two basic types of information. The most common is distance, which was discussed in Chapter 4, along with formulas for calculating the distance between two geographic points.

The other type of information is directional. This is calculated using a basic trigonometric formula:

```
direction = ATAN(vertical distance/horizontal distance))*180/PI()
```

Calculating distances was discussed in Chapter 4.

## Date Time Columns

Customer behavior varies by time of day and day of week and season of the year. These behaviors can distinguish between customers. Some businesses classify their customers as "weekday lunch buyers" or "weekend shoppers" or "Monday complainers." These are examples of business classifications that can be captured in the customer signature.

> **TIP** The timing of customer behavior is a good example of a business metric to incorporate in the customer signature.

The customer signature can capture the raw information by pivoting date and time information. For instance, the following SELECT statement can be added to the pivot query to add up the number of orders made on different days of the week:

```
SELECT householdid,
       . . .
       SUM(CASE WHEN cal.dow = 'Mon' THEN 1 ELSE 0 END) as dw_mon,
       SUM(CASE WHEN cal.dow = 'Tue' THEN 1 ELSE 0 END) as dw_tue,
       SUM(CASE WHEN cal.dow = 'Wed' THEN 1 ELSE 0 END) as dw_wed,
       SUM(CASE WHEN cal.dow = 'Thu' THEN 1 ELSE 0 END) as dw_thu,
```

*(continued)*

```
       SUM(CASE WHEN cal.dow = 'Fri' THEN 1 ELSE 0 END) as dw_fri,
       SUM(CASE WHEN cal.dow = 'Sat' THEN 1 ELSE 0 END) as dw_sat,
       SUM(CASE WHEN cal.dow = 'Sun' THEN 1 ELSE 0 END) as dw_sun,
       . . .
FROM orders o JOIN campaign ca ON o.campaignid = ca.campaignid JOIN
     calendar cal ON o.orderdate = cal.date JOIN
     customer c ON o.customerid = c.customerid CROSS JOIN
     (SELECT '2016-01-01' as cutoff_date) const
WHERE orderdate < cutoff_date
GROUP BY householdid
```

This query uses the Calendar table to find the day of the week. An alternative is to use a database function, such as DATENAME(dw, <col>). Using the Calendar table makes further refinements possible, such as distinguishing holidays from non-holidays.

If ORDERDATE had a time component, the following SELECT statement would add up the number of orders during from midnight to 3:59:59.999 a.m.:

```
SELECT SUM(CASE WHEN DATEPART(hh, orderdate) BETWEEN 0 AND 3
               THEN 1 ELSE 0 END) as hh00_03
```

This is the same idea as the earlier pivot statements, but applied to times.

## Patterns in Strings

Character strings contain descriptions that often have interesting information embedded in them. SQL has only rudimentary string manipulation functions, but these are often sufficient for extracting interesting features. Although the LIKE operator can be useful, it is often quite inefficient and can be replaced with more efficient functions. This section contains some examples of feature extraction.

**TIP** Descriptions and names often contain very interesting information. However, this needs to be extracted feature by feature to be most useful for the customer signature.

### Email Addresses

An email address has the form "<user name>@<domain name>", where the domain name has an extension, such as ".com," ".uk," or ".gov." The domain name and domain name extension can be interesting features about users.

The following code extracts these features from an email address:

```
SELECT LEFT(emailaddress, CHARINDEX('@', emailaddress)-1) as username,
       SUBSTRING(emailaddress, CHARINDEX('@', emailaddress)+1, 1000
              ) as domain,
       RIGHT(emailaddress, CHARINDEX('.', REVERSE(emailaddress))
           ) as extension
```

The user name takes all characters up to the "@," and the domain is all characters after it. The domain extension is everything after the last period. This expression uses a trick to find the position of the last period by finding the position of the first period in the reversed string.

## Addresses

Addresses are complicated strings that are difficult to understand. Geocoding them provides one set of information. However, the address line itself might provide information about customers:

- Is the address is for an apartment?
- Is the address is for a PO Box?

The following code identifies whether there is an apartment number in an address or a post office box, assuming that there is a column called ADDRESS:

```
SELECT (CASE WHEN CHARINDEX('#', address) > 0 OR
             CHARINDEX('apt.', LOWER(address)) > 0 OR
             CHARINDEX(' apt ', LOWER(address)) > 0 OR
             CHARINDEX(' unit ', LOWER(address)) > 0 THEN 1
        ELSE 0 END) as hasapt,
     (CASE WHEN LEFT(REPLACE(UPPER(address), '.', ''), 6) = 'PO BOX'
```

To find an apartment indicator, the query looks for " apt." or "apt " (rather than "apt") to avoid matching street names such as "Sanibel-Captiva Road," "Captains Court," and "Baptist Camp Road." For post office boxes, the address should start with "PO BOX" or "P.O. Box."

## Product Descriptions

Product descriptions often contain information such as:

- Color;
- Flavor; and,
- Special attributes (such as organic, low calories, and so on).

Interesting attributes can be turned into flags, by determining whether the description contains a particular string. For instance:

```
(CASE WHEN CHARINDEX('diet', desc) > 0 THEN 1 ELSE 0 END) as is_diet,
(CASE WHEN CHARINDEX('red', desc) > 0 THEN 1 ELSE 0 END) as is_red,
(CASE WHEN CHARINDEX('organic', desc) > 0 THEN 1 ELSE 0 END) as is_org
```

These cases look for particular substrings in the description.

A product description might have a specific format. For instance, the first word may be the product group name. It can be extracted using:

```
SUBSTRING(desc, CHARINDEX(' ', desc), 1000) as productgroup
```

Or, the last word might be something interesting such as the price:

```
RIGHT(desc, CHARINDEX(' ', REVERSE(desc)), 1000) as price
```

Discovering what is interesting is a manual process that often involves reading through the descriptions and making judgments as to what is important for distinguishing among customers.

## Credit Card Numbers

Credit card numbers are useful for analysis in two ways. The first is by identifying the type of credit card. The second is by identifying whether the same card is used over time. The first few digits of a credit card indicate the type of card, as discussed in Chapter 2, which has both the table mapping credit card numbers to credit card types and a SQL query for transforming the information.

Comparing credit card numbers on different payment transactions is as easy as comparing two columns. However, storing credit card numbers in analytic databases poses a security risk, so it is not a good idea to store them explicitly.

An alternative is to convert the credit card number to something that is not recognizable as a credit card number. One way is to have a master table that contains credit card numbers, with no duplicates. The row number in this table is stored instead of the credit card number, and very few people have access to the master table.

Another approach uses *hashing*. There are many different hashing algorithms. One very simple algorithm that works well is something like the following:

1. Treat the credit card number as a number.
2. Multiply the number by a large prime number.
3. Add another prime number.
4. Divide by yet another and take the remainder.

This works because two different numbers very, very, very rarely get mapped to the same number. In addition, it is very difficult to extract the original credit card number unless you know the specific primes used in the formula.

For instance, the following is an example of a formula to encode credit card numbers:

```
(ccnum*367373 + 101) % 2147483647
```

All the constants used in this calculation are prime numbers.

# Summarizing Customer Behaviors

The customer signature has been presented as a place to put lots of data elements and basic summaries. It is also a place to put more complex summaries of customer behaviors that rise to being customer-centric business metrics.

This section discusses three examples. The first is calculating the slope, the beta value, for series of transactions. The second is identifying weekend shoppers, and the third is applying metrics to identify customers whose usage is decreasing.

## Calculating Slope for Time Series

Pivoting numeric values creates time series, such as the dollar amount of purchases in a series of months. Using the ideas from Chapter 11, we can calculate the slope for these numbers.

Most households in the purchases data have one order, which does not provide a good example for finding a trend. Instead, the example is a related summary at the zip code level: *Which zip codes have seen an increase in customers in the years before the cutoff date?* Notice that this question is still about what happens before the cutoff date, so the resulting measures can be included in the customer signature.

This section answers the question three different ways. The first is to use the pivoted values to calculate the slope. This is possible, but the SQL is messy. The second way is to summarize each year of data for the zip codes. The third method generalizes the second for any series of values.

### Calculating Slope from Pivoted Time Series

Pivoted data has a separate column for each period of time. The following query calculates the number of households who place an order in each year for each zip code.

```
SELECT zipcode, COUNT(*) as cnt,
       FLOOR(DATEDIFF(yy, '2009-01-01', MIN(cutoffdate))) as numyears,
       COUNT(DISTINCT (CASE WHEN DATEDIFF(yy, orderdate, cutoffdate) = 1
                            THEN householdid END)) as year1,
       COUNT(DISTINCT (CASE WHEN DATEDIFF(yy, orderdate, cutoffdate) = 2
                            THEN householdid END)) as year2,
       COUNT(DISTINCT (CASE WHEN DATEDIFF(yy, orderdate, cutoffdate) = 3
                            THEN householdid END)) as year3,
       COUNT(DISTINCT (CASE WHEN DATEDIFF(yy, orderdate, cutoffdate) = 4
                            THEN householdid END)) as year4,
       COUNT(DISTINCT (CASE WHEN DATEDIFF(yy, orderdate, cutoffdate) = 5
                            THEN householdid END)) as year5,
       COUNT(DISTINCT (CASE WHEN DATEDIFF(yy, orderdate, cutoffdate) = 6
```

*(continued)*

```
                               THEN householdid END)) as year6,
       COUNT(DISTINCT (CASE WHEN DATEDIFF(yy, orderdate, cutoffdate) = 7
                       THEN householdid END)) as year7
FROM orders o JOIN customer c ON o.customerid = c.customerid CROSS JOIN
     (SELECT '2016-01-01' as cutoffdate) const
GROUP BY zipcode
```

This query is carefully dependent on the cutoff date, so the results can be used in the customer signature. The number of years of data is contained in the column NUMYEARS. The remaining columns contain the summaries by year.

Chapter 11 provided the formula for the slope:

```
slope = (n*Sxy - Sx*Sy) / (n*Sxx - Sx*Sx)
```

In the case of pivoted data, there are no explicit X-values. However, the X-values can be assumed to be a sequence of numbers starting with one for the oldest value. The resulting slope can be interpreted as the average number of additional households that make a purchase in each succeeding year.

The following query calculates the intermediate values and then the slope:

```
SELECT (n*Sxy - Sx*Sy)/(n*Sxx - Sx*Sx), a.*
FROM (SELECT zipcode, cnt,
             numyears*1.0 as n,
             numyears*(numyears+1)/2 as Sx,
             numyears*(numyears+1)*(2*numyears+1)/6 as Sxx,
             (CASE WHEN numyears < 2 THEN NULL
                   WHEN numyears = 3 THEN year3 + year2 + year1
                   WHEN numyears = 4 THEN year4 + year3 + year2 + year1
                   WHEN numyears = 5 THEN year5 + year4 + year3 + year2 +
                                        year1
                   WHEN numyears = 6 THEN year6 + year5 + year4 + year3 +
                                        year2 + year1
                   ELSE year7 + year6 + year5 + year4 + year3 + year2 +
                        year1 END) as Sy,
             (CASE WHEN numyears < 2 THEN NULL
                   WHEN numyears = 3 THEN 1*year3 + 2*year2 + 3*year1
                   WHEN numyears = 4 THEN 1*year4 + 2*year3 + 3*year2 +
                                        4*year1
                   WHEN numyears = 5 THEN 1*year5 + 2*year4 + 3*year3 +
                                        4*year2 + 5*year1
                   WHEN numyears = 6 THEN 1*year6 + 2*year5 + 3*year4 +
                                        4*year3 + 5*year2 + 6*year1
                   ELSE 1*year7 + 2*year6 + 3*year5 + 4*year4 + 5*year3 +
                        6*year2 + 7*year1 END) as Sxy
      FROM (<zip summary query>) z) a
```

This follows the logic from Chapter 11. The slope represents the growth in terms of the number of additional customers who make purchases each year in a zip code.

Eliminating the intermediate sums makes the query even more cumbersome and prone to error:

```
SELECT (CASE WHEN numyears < 2 THEN NULL
             WHEN numyears = 3
             THEN numyears*(1*year3 + 2*year2 + 3*year1)-
                  (numyears*(numyears+1)/2)*(year3 + year2 + year1)
             WHEN numyears = 4
             THEN numyears*(1*year4 + 2*year3 + 3*year2 + 4*year1)-
                (numyears*(numyears+1)/2)*(year4 + year3 + year2 + year1)
             WHEN numyears = 5
             THEN numyears*(1*year5 + 2*year4 + 3*year3 + 4*year2 +
                    5*year1) - (numyears*(numyears+1)/2)*(year5 + year4 +
                    year3 + year2 + year1)
             WHEN numyears = 6
             THEN numyears*(1*year6 + 2*year5 + 3*year4 + 4*year3 +
                    5*year2 + 6*year1) -
                    (numyears*(numyears+1)/2)*(year6 + year5 + year4 +
                    year3 + year2 + year1)
             ELSE numyears*(1*year7 + 2*year6 + 3*year5 + 4*year4 +
                    5*year3 + 6*year2 + 7*year1) -
                    (numyears*(numyears+1)/2)*(year7 + year6 + year5 +
                    year4 + year3 + year2 + year1)
             END) / (1.0*numyears * numyears*(numyears+1)*(2*numyears+1)/6
             - ((numyears*(numyears+1)/2))*(numyears*(numyears+1)/2)
       ) as slope, z.*
FROM (<zip summary query>) z
```

Under these circumstances, keeping the intermediate sums is preferable, even though they are not useful for modeling. One simplification is to remove the complicated CASE statement by assuming that all the pivot columns have data, but this assumption may not be true.

## Calculating Slope for a Regular Time Series

An alternative approach that does not use the pivot columns is to change the summary used for the slope calculation, by creating a table with a separate row for each zip code and year:

```
SELECT zipcode, DATEDIFF(yy, orderdate, cutoffdate) as yearsago,
       DATEDIFF(yy, '2009-01-01', MIN(cutoffdate)) as numyears,
       (DATEDIFF(yy, '2009-01-01', MAX(cutoffdate)) -
        DATEDIFF(yy, orderdate, cutoffdate)) as x,
       COUNT(DISTINCT householdid) as y
FROM orders o JOIN customer c ON o.customerid = c.customerid CROSS JOIN
     (SELECT '2016-01-01' as cutoffdate) const
WHERE orderdate < cutoffdate
GROUP BY zipcode, DATEDIFF(yy, orderdate, cutoffdate)
```

When there are no sales, the data is simply missing from this summary. The slope calculated this way may be a bit different from the slope calculated on the pivoted data (for zip codes that have years with no customers).

The following query calculates the intermediate values and slope:

```
SELECT ((CASE WHEN n = 1 THEN 0
              ELSE (n*Sxy - Sx*Sy)/(n*Sxx - Sx*Sx) END) as slope, b.*
FROM (SELECT zipcode, MAX(numyears) as numyears, COUNT(*)*1.0 as n,
             SUM(x) as Sx,
             SUM(x*x) as Sxx,
             SUM(x*y) as Sxy,
             SUM(y) as Sy
      FROM (<zipcode-year subquery>) zy
      GROUP BY zipcode
     ) b
ORDER BY n DESC
```

This query is much simpler than the previous query. Instead of using the pivoted time series, it calculates the X-value implicitly from the years before the cutoff date. The CASE statement in the SELECT assigns a value for slope when there are purchases in only one year; otherwise, the query would result in a divide-by-zero error. Note that the results from this query are slightly different from the pivoted version, because the pivoted version treats years with no data as having zero sales, whereas this excludes such years from the calculation.

### Calculating Slope for an Irregular Time Series

The previous calculation can be extended to irregular time series as well as regular time series. An irregular time series is one where the spacing between the X-values is not constant. Purchases for customers are a typical example, and determining the trend can be quite useful.

The query for this is essentially the same as the query the previous example, except the X-values would represent some other value in the data.

## Weekend Shoppers

There may be certain behaviors that are of particular interest, such as weekend shoppers. Consider what a shopper who only makes purchases on weekends looks like. Such a "perfect" weekend shopper has the following characteristics:

- All of their shopping by number of orders is on Saturday or Sunday.
- All of their shopping by dollar value is on Saturday or Sunday.
- All of their shopping by number of units is on Saturday or Sunday.

For the perfect weekender, these are all equivalent, because all shopping on the weekends implies that all units, orders, and dollars are spent on the weekends. They also suggest defining a metric that defines how close a customer is to being a "perfect" weekender.

Table 12-4 shows some examples of customers with multiple orders: one is a perfect weekender, one a partial weekender, and one a never weekender.

**Table 12-4:** Examples of Transactions for Weekend and Non-Weekend Shoppers

| HOUSEHOLD ID | ORDER ID | ORDER DATE | DAY OF WEEK | DOLLARS | UNITS |
|---|---|---|---|---|---|
| 21159179 | 1102013 | 2013-08-17 | Sat | $40.00 | 3 |
| 21159179 | 1107588 | 2013-09-16 | Mon | $67.00 | 5 |
| 21159179 | 1143702 | 2014-08-03 | Sun | $90.00 | 6 |
| 36207142 | 1089881 | 2013-06-13 | Thu | $10.00 | 1 |
| 36207142 | 1092505 | 2013-11-27 | Wed | $8.00 | 1 |
| 36207142 | 1084048 | 2013-12-23 | Mon | $49.00 | 3 |
| 36207142 | 1186443 | 2014-12-05 | Fri | $5.00 | 2 |
| 36207142 | 1206093 | 2014-12-31 | Wed | $7.00 | 1 |
| 36528618 | 1013609 | 2011-01-29 | Sat | $182.00 | 2 |
| 36528618 | 1057400 | 2012-11-25 | Sun | $195.00 | 1 |
| 36528618 | 1059424 | 2012-11-25 | Sun | $195.00 | 1 |
| 36528618 | 1074857 | 2013-12-14 | Sat | $570.00 | 2 |

The following ratios help distinguish among these groups:

- Proportion of all orders that are on weekends;
- Proportion of all dollars spent on weekends; and,
- Proportion of all units on weekends.

These all vary from zero (no evidence of weekend shopping behavior) to one (always a weekend shopper). Table 12-5 shows the summaries with this information.

**Table 12-5:** Some Shoppers and Their Weekend Shopping Behavior

| HOUSEHOLD | # ORDERS | | DOLLARS | | # UNITS | |
|---|---|---|---|---|---|---|
| | ALL | WEEKEND | ALL | WEEKEND | ALL | WEEKEND |
| 21159179 | 3 | 66.7% | $197 | 66.0% | 14 | 64.3% |
| 36207142 | 5 | 0.0% | $79 | 0.0% | 8 | 0.0% |
| 36528618 | 4 | 100.0% | $1,142 | 100.0% | 6 | 100.0% |

Recalling some ideas from probability, these can be combined into a single likelihood measure. The following SQL query does this calculation:

```
SELECT h.*,
       (CASE WHEN weekend_orders = 1 OR weekend_units = 1 OR
                  weekend_dollars = 1 THEN 1
            ELSE (weekend_orders/(1-weekend_orders))*
                 (weekend_units/(1-weekend_units))*
                 (weekend_dollars/(1-weekend_dollars)) END) as weekendp
FROM (SELECT householdid,
             SUM(CASE WHEN cal.dow IN ('Sat', 'Sun') THEN 1.0
                     ELSE 0 END)/COUNT(*) as weekend_orders,
             SUM(CASE WHEN cal.dow IN ('Sat', 'Sun') THEN numunits*1.0
                     ELSE 0 END)/SUM(numunits) as weekend_units,
             SUM(CASE WHEN cal.dow IN ('Sat', 'Sun') THEN totalprice
                     ELSE 0 END)/SUM(totalprice) as weekend_dollars
      FROM orders o JOIN calendar cal ON o.orderdate = cal.date JOIN
           customer c ON o.customerid = c.customerid CROSS JOIN
           (SELECT '2016-01-01' as cutoff_date) const
      WHERE orderdate < cutoff_date AND
            numunits > 0 AND
            totalprice > 0
      GROUP BY householdid) h
```

This query calculates the "probabilities" of being a weekend shopper along the three dimensions of orders, units, and price. The likelihood of someone being a weekend shopper is one minus the product of one minus each of these proportions, a method of combining probabilities discussed in Chapter 10 in the context of naïve Bayesian models. Although these are not independent, the combination still gives an overall measure of being a weekend shopper.

This method for calculating the weekend shoppers has a problem when customers have very few purchases. The aside "Incorporating Prior Information" discusses a method for handling this.

## Declining Usage Behavior

Declining usage is often a precursor to customers stopping. However, there are many ways to specify declining usage. One way is to use the beta value (slope) of a usage measure — such as dollars spent per month or web visits per week.

---

**INCORPORATING PRIOR INFORMATION**

The definition of weekend shopper works well when there is a lot of data for each customer. However, it does not work well when there are only a few transactions. For instance, should the score of someone who has made one purchase that is on the weekend be the same as someone who has made one hundred purchases, all on the weekend?

## INCORPORATING PRIOR INFORMATION (CONTINUED)

Intuitively, the answer is "no," because there is much more evidence accumulated for the second customer. How can the weekend shopper score reflect this intuition?

There is a way to handle this situation. The idea is to assume that everyone has a score of being a weekend shopper that is between zero and one. Orders on the weekend take this score into account. Such an assumption is called a *prior*, and this is a central notion in Bayesian statistics.

For this discussion, let's consider using only the proportion of transactions as the indicator for a weekend shopper (rather than the combined likelihood value). What is an appropriate value for the prior? The appropriate prior is the overall proportion of weekend orders in the data, which is 21.6%. That means that given no other information, we are making the assumption that someone has a weekend shopper score of 21.6%, even before they make any purchases.

The next question is how to combine information from orders with the prior. The way to approach this is incrementally. What is the estimate for being a weekend shopper for someone who has exactly one purchase on the weekend? Remember, the method in the text gives this person a perfect 100% score, which seems a bit too high.

The idea is to combine the prior estimate with the new evidence, using a weighted average:

```
new estimate = ((prior*K) + 1)/(K+1)
```

The value K represents how much weight we put on the prior. If the value is zero, the result is the same as in the text. A reasonable value is one, which results in the score of 60.8% for the customer with one weekend purchase.

What happens for the next weekend purchase? The reasoning is the same, except the value of K is incremented by one, because there is an additional observation. Because the prior now includes one data point, it gets weighted more heavily.

The following table shows the scores for customers who make only weekend purchases and no weekend purchases:

| ONLY WEEKEND SHOPPER | | | NON-WEEKEND SHOPPER | | |
|---|---|---|---|---|---|
| # ORDERS | K | SCORE | # ORDERS | K | SCORE |
| 0 | 1 | 21.6% | 0 | 1 | 21.6% |
| 1 | 2 | 60.8% | 1 | 2 | 10.8% |
| 2 | 3 | 73.9% | 2 | 3 | 7.2% |
| 3 | 4 | 80.4% | 3 | 4 | 5.4% |
| 4 | 5 | 84.3% | 4 | 5 | 4.3% |
| 5 | 6 | 86.9% | 5 | 6 | 3.6% |

*Continued on next page*

> **INCORPORATING PRIOR INFORMATION (CONTINUED)**
>
> So, a customer who has made five weekend purchases has a score of 86.9%. A customer who has made five weekday purchases has a score of 3.6%. These seem reasonable.
>
> The previous formulas explain how the prior is used in the calculation. However, there is a simpler formula based on the number of observations and the average observed value:
>
> ```
> Est = (K*prior + number * average)/(K + number)
> ```
>
> Using this formula, we can calculate what happens to a customer who has 100 purchases all on the weekend. In this case, the number is 100 and the average is 1. Using the same values as before, the score is 99.2%.
>
> This method of incorporating priors requires both finding an appropriate prior estimate to use when there is no evidence, and a way of combining new evidence with the prior. The use of priors does not require complicated formulas. It does, however, produce more intuitive scores than directly using the proportion.

However, the beta value can be misleading, because it fits a long-term trend to the data. Often, customer behaviors are relatively steady (varying within a range) and then declining. Other measures of declining behavior include:

- Ratio of recent activity to historical activity, such as most recent month of usage divided by usage twelve months ago;
- Number of recent months where usage is less than the month before; and,
- Ratio of the most recent month to the average over the previous year.

These are all reasonable measures of declining usage.

These measures are all possible to implement in SQL. We'll investigate such measures by looking at the corresponding quantities for zip codes by year:

- Ratio of most recent number of customers to the year before;
- Ratio of the most recent number of customers to the average of preceding years (the index value); and,
- Number of recent years where the number of customers is declining.

The following query calculates these quantities from the pivoted zip code columns:

```
SELECT z.*,
       (CASE WHEN year2 > 0 THEN year1 / year2 END) as year1_2_growth,
       (CASE WHEN (COALESCE(year1, 0) + COALESCE(year2, 0) +
                   COALESCE(year3, 0) + COALESCE(year4, 0) +
                   COALESCE(year5, 0) + COALESCE(year6, 0) +
                   COALESCE(year7, 0)) = 0 THEN 1
```

```
                    ELSE year1 / ((COALESCE(year1, 0) + COALESCE(year2, 0) +
                           COALESCE(year3, 0) + COALESCE(year4, 0) +
                           COALESCE(year5, 0) + COALESCE(year6, 0) +
                           COALESCE(year7,0))/7.0) END) as year1_index,
          COALESCE(CASE WHEN numyears < 2 OR year1 >= year2 THEN 0 END,
                   CASE WHEN numyears < 3 OR year2 >= year3 THEN 1 END,
                   CASE WHEN numyears < 4 OR year3 >= year4 THEN 2 END,
                   CASE WHEN numyears < 5 OR year4 >= year5 THEN 3 END,
                   CASE WHEN numyears < 6 OR year5 >= year6 THEN 4 END,
                   CASE WHEN numyears < 7 OR year6 >= year7 THEN 5 END,
                   6) as years_of_declining_sales,
        z.*
FROM (<zip code summary query>) z
```

The calculation for growth is fairly obvious; it uses a CASE statement to prevent division by zero. If there were no customers the previous year, the growth is undefined.

The index calculation does a direct calculation of the average over the previous seven years. This is the explicit approach. A simpler approach would be to calculate the sum or average in the subquery. However, the preceding query uses the zip code summary subquery exactly as originally written.

The number of years of declining sales uses the COALESCE() function extensively. This function returns the first non-null value. So, the logic proceeds as follows:

1. If the *YEAR1 >= YEAR2* then the first value is zero and COALESCE() returns this value. Otherwise, the value is NULL and processing continues.

2. If *YEAR2 >= YEAR3* then the second value is one. This means that the previous condition was met, so there is one year of declining values. Otherwise, the value is NULL and processing continues.

3. And so on.

An alternative to the COALESCE() function is a more complicated CASE statement. These values can then be included in the customer signature as indicators of declining usage.

> **TIP** The COALESCE() **function can be very useful for calculating indexes, counts, and averages in sets of columns where some of the values may be** NULL.

## Lessons Learned

When analytic needs go beyond the capabilities of SQL and Excel, customer signatures can be used to summarize customer behavior and demographic information for use in other tools. SQL has an advantage for building customer signatures, because it has powerful data manipulation capabilities.

The customer signature should be based on a cutoff date, only incorporating input columns from before the date. For predictive modeling, the targets come from a time frame after the cutoff date. A customer signature consists of a set of columns coming from many different tables. Most columns are input columns. The customer signature might also include target columns, identification columns, and the cutoff date.

Creating customer signatures requires gathering information from many different sources. Some columns might be copied directly. Others might come from fixed lookup tables. Yet others might come from dynamic lookup tables that summarize customer behavior along customer dimensions. And others come from pivoting and summarizing the most voluminous part of the data, customer transactions. These operations can be combined to create very powerful features for data mining purposes.

Combining information from multiple columns makes it possible to add very powerful features. For instance, trends over time can be added by incorporating the slope of the best fit line, an idea discussed in the previous chapter.

The customer signature provides a structure for understanding customers and using many of the techniques described in earlier chapters. Much of the effort in data analysis is in bringing the data together and understanding the contents. The ability of SQL to express very complex data manipulations, and the ability to optimize the resulting queries on large hardware, makes it a natural choice for creating customer signatures.

As earlier chapters have shown, the combination of SQL and Excel is a powerful analysis tool itself for understanding customers. When the combination is not powerful enough, they provide the foundation for bringing the right data into even more sophisticated tools.

# Equivalent Constructs Among Databases

Relational databases support SQL in the same way that English is the language of the Great Britain, the United States, India, and Jamaica. Although there is much in common among the databases, each dialect has its own vocabulary and accents.

Throughout the book, the SQL examples have used Microsoft T-SQL as the dialect of choice. There are a number of things in SQL that varies from database to database. The purpose of the appendix is to show equivalent SQL constructs in different databases. The five database engines are:

- IBM UDB, version 7 and above;
- Microsoft, version 2005;
- mysql, version 5 and above;
- Oracle version 9 and above; and
- SAS proc sql.

The databases from IBM, Microsoft, and Oracle are commercial products, although single-user versions can often be downloaded for no cost. mysql is a free database engine. SAS proc sql is the SQL engine within the SAS language (the most popular commercial statistical software). When using SAS, proc sql can be used in two different modes. In one, it communicates directly to a database, and supports the language of the database. In the other, it runs within SAS and uses SAS's particular constructs.

This appendix is provided as is, without any guarantees that the software has not changed for whatever reason. The following documentation web sites are available for each of the databases:

- `http://download-east.oracle.com/docs/cd/B19306_01/server.102/b14200/toc.htm`
- `http://msdn2.microsoft.com/en-us/library/ms189826.aspx`
- `http://publib.boulder.ibm.com/infocenter/db2luw/v9`
- `http://dev.mysql.com/doc/refman/5.1/en/index.html`
- `http://support.sas.com/onlinedoc/913/docMainpage.jsp`

In some cases, additional navigation is required from the first documentation page, and for some sites, registration is required. Unfortunately, the ANSI standard for SQL is only available by purchasing it from the ISO organization.

This appendix is organized by the following topics:

- String Functions;
- Date/Time Functions;
- Mathematical Functions; and,
- Other Functions and Features.

Within each topic, specific functions are in subsections. Within each subsection, the structure for each database is shown.

# String Functions

This section includes functions that operate on string values.

## Searching for Position of One String within Another

What is the function that searches for one string inside another string? The arguments are:

- `<search string>` — the string to be searched
- `<pattern>` — the string to look for
- `<occurrence>` — which occurrence
- `<offset>` — where to start searching

### *IBM*

```
LOCATE(<pattern>, <search string>, <offset>)
```

The argument <offset> is optional and defaults to 1. The function returns the position in the search string where the pattern is found and 0 if the pattern is not found.

An alternative method:

```
POSSTR(<search string>, <pattern>)
```

The function returns the position in the search string where the pattern is found and 0 if the pattern is not found.

### Microsoft

```
CHARINDEX(<pattern>, <search string>, <offset>)
```

The argument <offset> is optional and defaults to 1. The function returns the position in the search string where the pattern is found and 0 if the pattern is not found.

### mysql

```
INSTR(<search string>, <pattern>)
```

The function returns the position in the search string where the pattern is found and 0 if the pattern is not found.

An alternative method:

```
LOCATE(<pattern>, <search string>, <offset>)
```

The argument <offset> is optional and defaults to 1. The function returns the position in the search string where the pattern is found and 0 if the pattern is not found.

### Oracle

```
INSTR(<search string>, <pattern>, <occurrence>)
```

The argument <occurrence> is optional and defaults to 1. The function returns the position in the search string where the pattern is found and 0 if the pattern is not found.

### SAS proc sql

```
FIND(<search string>, <pattern >)
```

The function returns the position in <search string> where the pattern is found, and 0 if the pattern is not found.

## String Concatenation

What is the function and operator that appends strings together?

### IBM

```
CONCAT(<string 1>, <string 2>)
```

Note that this function only takes two arguments, but the function can be nested. In addition, the operator "||" also concatenates strings.

### Microsoft

```
<string 1> + <string 2>
```

The concatenation operator is an overloaded "+" operator. When mixing character and numeric types, be sure to cast the numeric types to strings.

### mysql

```
CONCAT(<string 1>, <string 2>, . . .)
```

Note: this function can take two or more arguments.

### Oracle

```
CONCAT(<string 1>, <string 2>)
```

Note that this function only takes two arguments, but the function can be nested. In addition, the operator "||" also concatenates strings.

### SAS proc sql

```
CAT(<string 1>, <string 2>, . . .)
```

Note: this function can take two or more arguments.

## String Length Function

What is the function and operator that returns the length of a string?

### IBM

```
LENGTH(<string>)
```

### Microsoft

```
LEN(<string>)
```

### mysql

```
LENGTH(<string>)
```

### Oracle

```
LENGTH(<string>)
```

### SAS proc sql

```
LENGTH(<string>)
```

Note that this function ignores trailing blanks.

## Substring Function

What is the function and operator that returns a substring?

### IBM

```
SUBSTRING(<string>, <offset>, <len>)
```

The argument `<len>` is optional; when missing, the function returns the rest of the string. The argument `<offset>` must be non-negative.

### Microsoft

```
SUBSTRING (<string>, <offset>, <len>)
```

All arguments are required and the last two must be non-negative.

### mysql

```
substring(<string>, <offset>, <len>)
```

The argument `<len>` is optional; when missing, the function returns the rest of the string. If `<offset>` is negative, the function counts from the end of the string rather than the beginning.

### Oracle

```
SUBSTR(<string>, <offset>, <len>)
```

The argument <len> is optional; when missing, the function returns the rest of the string. If <offset> is negative, the function counts from the end of the string rather than the beginning.

### SAS proc sql

```
SUBSTRN(<string>, <offset>, <len>)
```

The argument <len> is optional; when missing, the function returns the rest of the string. Note: SUBSTRN() is preferable to SUBSTR() because it does not produce errors or warnings when <offset>+<len> extends beyond the length of <string>.

## Replace One Substring with Another

This function is the same across all databases, but differs in SAS.

### IBM

```
REPLACE(<string>, <from>, <to>)
```

### Microsoft

```
REPLACE(<string>, <from>, <to>)
```

### mysql

```
REPLACE(<string>, <from>, <to>)
```

### Oracle

```
REPLACE(<string>, <from>, <to>)
```

### SAS proc sql

```
RXCHANGE(RXPARSE('<from> to <to>'), 999, <string>))
```

## Remove Leading and Trailing Blanks

How can spaces at the beginning and end of a string be removed?

### IBM

```
LTRIM(RTRIM(<string>))
```

### Microsoft

```
LTRIM(RTRIM(<string>))
```

### mysql

```
TRIM(<string>)
```

### Oracle

```
TRIM(<string>)
```

Note: LTRIM() and RTRIM() also work.

### SAS proc sql

```
BTRIM(<string>)
```

## RIGHT Function

What is the function and operator that returns a substring of length <len> from the end of a string?

### IBM

```
RIGHT(<string>, <len>)
```

### Microsoft

```
RIGHT(<string>, <len>)
```

### mysql

```
RIGHT(<string>, <len>)
```

### Oracle

Function does not exist. Use:

```
SUBSTR(<string>, LENGTH(<string>) + 1 - <len>, <len>)
```

### SAS proc sql

Function does not exist. Use:

```
SUBSTR(<string>, LENGTH(<string> + 1 - <len>, <len>)
```

## LEFT Function

What is the function and operator that returns a substring from the beginning of a string with length <len>?

### IBM

```
LEFT(<string>, <len>)
```

### Microsoft

```
LEFT(<string>, <len>)
```

### mysql

```
LEFT(<string>, <len>)
```

### Oracle

Function does not exist. Use:

```
SUBSTR(<string>, 1, <len>)
```

### SAS proc sql

Function does not exist. Use:

```
SUBSTRN(<string>, 1, <len>)
```

## ASCII Function

What functions returns the ASCII value of a character?

### IBM

```
ASCII(<char>)
```

### Microsoft

```
ASCII(<char>)
```

### mysql

```
ASCII(<char>)
```

### Oracle

```
ASCII(<char>)
```

### SAS proc sql

```
RANK(<char>)
```

# Date Time Functions

This section has functions that deal with dates and times.

## Date Constant

How is a constant represented in the code?

### IBM

```
DATE('YYYY-MM-DD')
```

### Microsoft

```
CAST('YYYY-MM-DD' as SMALLDATETIME)
```

Microsoft also seems to recognize strings of the form "MM/DD/YYYY" and "MMMMM DD, YYYY".

### mysql

```
CAST('YYYY-MM-DD' as DATE)
```

mysql also recognizes strings of the form "YYYY-MM-DD" as dates.

### Oracle

```
DATE 'YYYY-MM-DD'
```

Oracle also seems to recognize strings of the form DD-MMM-YYYY as dates in an appropriate context.

### SAS proc sql

```
'ddMmmyyyy'd
```

## Current Date and Time

What is the current date and time?

### IBM

```
CURRENT DATE
```

Note: This is not a function.

### Microsoft

```
GETDATE()
```

### mysql

```
CURDATE()
```

### Oracle

```
SYSDATE()
```

### SAS proc sql

```
TODAY()
```

## Convert to YYYYMMDD String

How can a date be converted to the format YYYYMMDD?

### IBM

```
REPLACE(LEFT(CHAR(<date>, ISO), 10), '-', '')))
```

### Microsoft

```
CONVERT(<date>, VARCHAR, 8, 112)
```

### mysql

```
DATE_FORMAT(<date>, '%Y%m%d')
```

### Oracle

```
TO_CHAR(<date>, 'YYYYMMDD')
```

### SAS proc sql

```
PUT(<date>, YYMMDD10.)
```

This returns a string of the form YYYY-MM-DD. This format is usually sufficient, and removing the hyphens in SAS is cumbersome.

# Year, Month, and Day of Month

What functions extract the year, month, and day from a date as numbers?

### IBM

```
YEAR(date)
MONTH(date)
DAY(date)
```

### Microsoft

```
YEAR(date)
MONTH(date)
DAY(date)
```

The following also works:

```
DATEPART(yy, <date>)
DATEPART(m, <date>)
DATEPART(d <date>)
```

### mysql

```
EXTRACT(YEAR FROM <date>)
EXTRACT(MONTH FROM <date>)
EXTRACT(DAY FROM <date>)
```

The following also works:

```
YEAR(date)
MONTH(date)
DAY(date)
```

### Oracle

```
EXTRACT(YEAR FROM <date>)
EXTRACT(MONTH FROM <date>)
EXTRACT(DAY FROM <date>)
```

The following also works:

```
TO_CHAR(<date>, 'YYYY')+0
TO_CHAR(<date>, 'MM')+0
TO_CHAR(<date>, 'DD')+0
```

### SAS proc sql

```
YEAR(date)
MONTH(date)
DAY(date)
```

## Day of Week (Integer and String)

What functions extract the day of the week as a day number (starting with 1 for Sunday) and as a name?

### IBM

```
DAYOFWEEK(<date>)
DAYNAME(<date>)
```

### Microsoft

```
DATEPART(dw, <date>)
DATENAME(dw, <date>)
```

### mysql

```
DAYOFWEEK(<date>)
DAYNAME(<date>)
```

### Oracle

```
1 + MOD(<date> - DATE '1970-01-01'+4, 7)
TO_CHAR(<date>, 'DY')
```

### SAS proc sql

```
WEEKDAY(<date>)
PUT(<date>, weekdate3.)
```

## Adding (or Subtracting) Days from a Date

How are a given number of days added or subtracted from a date?

### IBM

```
<date> + <days> DAYS
```

### Microsoft

```
DATEADD(d, <days>, <date>)
```

### mysql

```
ADDDATE(<date>, <days>)
```

### Oracle

```
<date> + <days>
```

### SAS proc sql

```
<date> + <days>
```

## Adding (or Subtracting) Months from a Date

How are a given number of months added or subtracted from a date?

### IBM

Not supported, use the approximation:

```
<date> + <months> * 30.4
```

### Microsoft

```
DATEADD(m, <months>, <date>)
```

### mysql

```
<date> + INTERVAL <months> MONTH
```

### Oracle

```
ADD_MONTHS(<date>, <months>)
```

### SAS proc sql

```
INTNX('MONTH', <date>, <months>)
```

## Difference between Two Dates in Days

How is the difference between two dates in days calculated?

### IBM

```
DAYS(<datelater>) - DAYS(<dateearlier>)
```

### Microsoft

```
DATEDIFF(d, <dateearlier>, <datelater>)
```

### mysql

```
DATEDIFF(<datelater>, <dateearlier>)
```

### Oracle

```
<datelater> - <dateearlier>
```

### SAS proc sql

```
<datelater> - <dateearlier>
```

## Difference between Two Dates in Months

How is the difference between two dates in months calculated?

### IBM

Not directly supported in database, use:

```
(DAYS(<datelater>) - DAYS(<dateearlier>))/30.4
```

### Microsoft

```
DATEDIFF(m, <dateearlier>, <datelater>)
```

### mysql

Not directly supported in database, use:

```
DATEDIFF(<datelater>, <dateearlier>)/30.4
```

### Oracle

```
MONTHS_BETWEEN(<datelater>, <dateearlier>)
```

### SAS proc sql

```
INTCK('MONTH', <dateearlier>, <datelater>)
```

Note that this counts the number of month boundaries between two values, rather than the number of full months.

## Extracting Date from Date Time

How is a date extracted from a date time value, setting the time to zero?

### IBM

```
DATE(<date>)
```

### Microsoft

```
DATEADD('1900-01-01', DATEDIFF(dd, '1900-01-01', <date>))
```

### mysql

```
DATE(<date>)
```

### Oracle

```
TRUNC(<date>)
```

### SAS proc sql

```
DATEPART(<date>)
```

# Mathematical Functions

The functions operate on numeric values.

## Remainder/Modulo

What function returns the remainder when one number, <num>, is divided by another, <base>?

### IBM

```
MOD(<num>, <base>)
```

### Microsoft

```
<num> % <base>
```

### mysql

```
MOD(<num>, <base>)
<num> MOD <base>
<num> % <base>
```

### Oracle

```
MOD(<num>, <base>)
```

### SAS proc sql

```
MOD(<num>, <base>)
```

## Power

How do you raise one number, <base>, to another number, <exp>?

### IBM

```
POWER(<base>, <exp>)
```

### Microsoft

```
POWER(<base>, <exp>)
```

### mysql

```
POWER(<base>, <exp>)
```

### Oracle

```
POWER(<base>, <exp>)
```

### SAS proc SQL

```
<base>**<exp>
```

## Floor

What function removes the fractional part of a number?

### IBM

```
FLOOR(<number>)
```

### Microsoft

```
FLOOR(<number>)
```

### mysql

```
FLOOR(<number>)
```

### Oracle

```
FLOOR(<number>)
```

### SAS proc sql

```
FLOOR(<number>)
```

## "Random" Numbers

How can we get random numbers between 0 and 1? This is useful, for instance, for returning a randomized set of rows. For random number generators that accept a seed as an argument, the sequence is always the same for a given seed.

### IBM

```
RAND()
```

### Microsoft

```
RAND()
RAND(<seed>)
```

### mysql

```
RAND()
RAND(<seed>)
```

### Oracle

No built-in function; use a pseudo-random number generator such as:

```
(ROWNUM * prime1 + prime2 MOD prime3)/prime3
```

Example: `(ROWNUM * 83 + 19 MOD 101)/(101.0)`

### SAS proc sql

```
RAND('UNIFORM')
```

Note: SAS has a wide variety of random number generators that pull numbers from many different distributions.

## Left Padding an Integer with Zeros

How can an integer value be converted to a string of a fixed length and padded with zeros on the left?

### IBM

```
RIGHT(CONCAT(REPEAT('0', <len>), CAST(<num> as CHAR)), <len>)
```

### Microsoft

```
RIGHT(REPLICATE('0', <len>) + CAST(<num> as VARCHAR), <len>)
```

### mysql

```
RIGHT(CONCAT(REPEAT('0', <len>), CAST(<num> as CHAR)), <len>)
```

### Oracle

```
TO_CHAR(<num>, RPAD('0', '0', <len>))
```

### SAS proc sql

```
PUTN(<num>, Z<len>.)
```

## Conversion from Number to String

How is a number converted to a string?

### IBM

```
CAST(<arg> as CHAR)
```

### *Microsoft*

```
CAST(<arg> as VARCHAR)
```

### *mysql*

```
CAST(<arg> as CHAR)
```

Note that VARCHAR does not work.

### *Oracle*

```
TO_CHAR(<arg>)
```

### *SAS proc sql*

```
PUT(<arg>, BEST.)
```

The default puts the number into 12 characters. For a wider format, use BEST<width>. (such as BEST20.) for the format.

## Other Functions and Features

These are miscellaneous functions and features that do not fall into any of the previous categories.

### Least and Greatest

How do you get the smallest and largest values from a list?

### *IBM*

```
(CASE WHEN <arg1> < <arg2> THEN <arg1> ELSE <arg2> END)
(CASE WHEN <arg1> > <arg2> THEN <arg1> ELSE <arg2> END)
```

If you have to worry about NULL values:

```
(CASE WHEN <arg2> IS NULL OR <arg1> < <arg2> THEN <arg1>
      ELSE <arg2> END)
(CASE WHEN <arg2> IS NULL or <arg1> > <arg2> THEN <arg1>
      ELSE <arg2> END)
```

### Microsoft

```
(CASE WHEN <arg1> < <arg2> THEN <arg1> ELSE <arg2> END)
(CASE WHEN <arg1> > <arg2> THEN <arg1> ELSE <arg2> END)
```

If you have to worry about NULL values:

```
(CASE WHEN <arg2> IS NULL OR <arg1> < <arg2> THEN <arg1>
      ELSE <arg2> END)
(CASE WHEN <arg2> IS NULL or <arg1> > <arg2> THEN <arg1>
      ELSE <arg2> END)
```

### mysql

```
LEAST(<arg1>, <arg2>)
GREATEST(<arg1>, <arg2>)
```

### Oracle

```
LEAST(<arg1>, <arg2>)
GREATEST(<arg1>, <arg2>)
```

### SAS proc sql

```
(CASE WHEN <arg1> < <arg2> THEN <arg1> ELSE <arg2> END)
(CASE WHEN <arg1> > <arg2> THEN <arg1> ELSE <arg2> END)
```

If you have to worry about NULL values:

```
(CASE WHEN <arg2> IS NULL OR <arg1> < <arg2> THEN <arg1>
      ELSE <arg2> END)
(CASE WHEN <arg2> IS NULL or <arg1> > <arg2> THEN <arg1>
      ELSE <arg2> END)
```

## Return Result with One Row

How can a query return a value with only one row? This is useful for testing syntax and for incorporating subqueries for constants.

### IBM

```
SELECT <whatever>
FROM SYSIBM.SYSDUMMY1
```

### *Microsoft*

```
SELECT <whatever>
```

### *mysql*

```
SELECT <whatever>
```

### *Oracle*

```
SELECT <whatever>
FROM dual
```

### *SAS proc sql*

Does not seem to support this; can be implemented by creating a data set with one row.

## Return a Handful of Rows

How can a query return just a handful of rows? This is useful to see a few results without returning all of them.

### *IBM*

```
SELECT . . .
FROM . . .
FETCH FIRST <num> ROWS ONLY
```

### *Microsoft*

```
SELECT TOP <num> . . .
FROM . . .
```

### *mysql*

```
SELECT . . .
FROM . . .
LIMIT <num>
```

### Oracle

```
SELECT . . .
FROM . . .
WHERE ROWNUM < <num>
```

### SAS proc sql

```
proc sql outobs=2;
    SELECT . . .;
```

# Get List of Columns in a Table

How can a query return a list of columns in a table?

### IBM

```
SELECT colname
FROM syscat.columns
WHERE tabname = <tablename> AND
    tabschema = <tableschema>
```

### Microsoft

```
SELECT column_name
FROM information_schema.columns
WHERE table_name = <tablename> AND
    table_schema = <tableschema>
```

### mysql

```
SELECT column_name
FROM information_schema.columns
WHERE table_name = <tablename> AND
    table_schema = <tableschema>
```

### Oracle

```
SELECT column_name
FROM all_tab_columns
WHERE table_name = <tablename> AND
    owner = <owner>
```

### SAS proc sql

```
SELECT name
FROM dictionary.columns
WHERE upper(memname) = <tablename> AND
      upper(libname) = <tableschema>
```

## ORDER BY in Subqueries

Is the ORDER BY clause supported in subqueries?

### IBM

Apparently Supported

### Microsoft

Partially supported — supported only when TOP is used in the select.

### mysql

Supported

### Oracle

Not Supported

### SAS proc sql

Not Supported

## Window Functions

Does the database support window functions?

### IBM

Not Supported

### Microsoft

Supported

### mysql

Not Supported

### Oracle

Supported; called analytic functions.

### SAS proc sql

Not Supported

## Average of Integers

Is the average of a set of integers, using the AVG() function, an integer or a floating-point number?

### IBM

Integer

### Microsoft

Integer

### mysql

Floating point

### Oracle

Integer

### SAS proc sql

Floating point

# Index